THE NEW ULTIMATE
BOOK OF HOME PLANS

CREATIVE HOMEOWNER®, Upper Saddle River, New Jersey

VP/Editorial Director: Timothy O. Bakke
Production Manager: Kimberly H. Vivas

Home Plans Editor: Kenneth D. Stuts, CPBD
Home Plans Designer Liaison: Timothy Mulligan

Design and Layout: Arrowhead Direct (David Kroha, Cindy DiPierdomenico, Judith Kroha); Maureen Mulligan

Cover Design: David Geer

Current Printing (last digit)
10

Manufactured in the United States of America

The New Ultimate Book of Home Plans
Library of Congress Control Number: 2006934227
ISBN-10: 1-58011-336-2
ISBN-13: 978-1-58011-336-6

CREATIVE HOMEOWNER®
A Division of Federal Marketing Corp.
24 Park Way
Upper Saddle River, NJ 07458
www.creativehomeowner.com

Note: The homes as shown in the photographs and renderings in this book may differ from the actual blueprints. When studying the house of your choice, please check the floor plans carefully.

Front cover: *main plan* 161056, page 530; *left to right: plan* 161028, page 135; *plan* 161101, page 185; *plan* 161101, page 185; *plan* 401004, page 531 **page 1:** *plan* 391071, page 535 **page 3:** *top to bottom: plan* 391040, page 579; *plan* 391055, page 569; *plan* 391069, page 538 **page 4:** *plan* 391053, page 576 **page 5:** *plan* 391056, page 252 **page 6:** *top to bottom: plan* 271024, page 529; *plan* 271007, page 553 **page 7:** *plan* 391052, page 321 **pages 110–111:** *both* George Ross/CH **page 112:** *all* Christine Elasigue/CH **page 113:** *top right* George Ross/CH; *bottom all* Christine Elasigue/CH **page 114:** *left* George Ross/CH; *right all* Christine Elasigue/CH **pages 115–117:** *all* Christine Elasigue/CH **page 196:** Tria Giovan **page 197:** *both* Bob Greenspan, stylist: Susan Andrews **pages 198–202:** *all* www.davidduncanlivingston.com **page 203:** Mark Lohman, design: Kyser Interiors **pages 334–341:** illustrations by Warren Cutler, Tony Davis (site plans), Elizabeth Eaton, Biruta Hansen, Paul Mirocha, Gordon Morrison, Michael Rothman, Michael Wanke **page 370:** Robert Perron **page 371:** *top and bottom center* Home and Garden Editorial Services; *bottom right* courtesy of Hartco/Armstrong; *bottom left* courtesy of Mannington **pages 372–373:** *top center, right row and left* Home and Garden Editorial Services; *bottom center* Robert Perron **pages 374–375:** courtesy of Jasba **page 376:** Home and Garden Editorial Services **page 377:** *top right and left* Mark Samu; *bottom right* Carl Weese **pages 456–457:** www.davidduncanlivingston.com **page 458:** Mark Lohman, design: Kathryne Designs **page 459:** Mark Lohman, design: Roxanne Packham Design & Michele Hughes Design **page 460:** Mark Lohman, design: Barclay Butera **page 461:** Beth Singer, architect: Dominick Tringoli Associates, builder: Custom Homes by DeRocher, Inc. **pages 462–463:** *all* Mark Lohman, design: Harte Brownlee & Associates **page 597:** *plan* 161016, page 154 **page 601:** *top to bottom plan* 211011, page 133; *plan* 211007, page 529; *plan* 121153, page 261 **page 608:** *plan* 391066, page 547; *plan* 271001, page 495; *plan* 211071, page 528 **back cover:** *top plan* 561002, page 300, page 261; *left to right: plan* 211127, page 182; *plan* 161101, page 185; *plan* 211127, page 182

Contents

Getting Started

Maybe you can't wait to bang the first nail. Or you may be just as happy leaving town until the windows are cleaned. The extent of your involvement with the construction phase is up to you. Your time, interests, and abilities can help you decide how to get the project from lines on paper to reality. But building a house requires more than putting pieces together. Whoever is in charge of the process must competently manage people as well as supplies, materials, and construction. He or she will have to

- Make a project schedule to plan the orderly progress of the work. This can be a bar chart that shows the time period of activity by each trade.
- Establish a budget for each category of work, such as foundation, framing, and finish carpentry.
- Arrange for a source of construction financing.
- Get a building permit and post it conspicuously at the construction site.
- Line up supply sources and order materials.
- Find subcontractors and negotiate their contracts.
- Coordinate the work so that it progresses smoothly with the fewest conflicts.
- Notify inspectors at the appropriate milestones.
- Make payments to suppliers and subcontractors.

You as the Builder

You'll have to take care of every logistical detail yourself if you decide to act as your own builder or general contractor. But along with the responsibilities of managing the project, you gain the flexibility to do as much of your own work as you want and subcontract out the rest. Before taking this path, however, be sure you have the time and capabilities. Do you also have the

time and ability to schedule the work, hire and coordinate subs, order materials, and keep ahead of the accounting required to manage the project successfully? If you do, you stand to save the amount that a general contractor would charge to take on these responsibilities, normally 15 to 30 percent of the construction cost. If you take this responsibility on but mismanage the project, the potential savings will erode and may even cost you more than if you had hired a builder in the first place. A subcontractor might charge extra for hav-

Acting as the builder, above, requires the ability to hire and manage subcontractors.

Building a home, opposite, includes the need to schedule building inspections at the appropriate milestones.

ing to return to the site to complete work that was originally scheduled for an earlier date. Or perhaps because you didn't order the windows at the beginning, you now have to pay for a recent cost increase. (If you had hired a builder in the first place he or she would absorb the increase.)

Hiring a Builder to Handle Construction

A builder or general contractor will manage every aspect of the construction process. Your role after signing the construction contract will be to make regular progress payments and ensure that the work for which you are paying has been completed. You will also consult with the builder and agree to any changes that may have to be made along the way.

Leads for finding builders might come from friends or neighbors who have had contractors build, remodel, or add to their homes. Real-estate agents and bankers may have some names handy but are more likely familiar with the builder's ability to complete projects on time and budget than the quality of the work itself.

The next step is to narrow your list of candidates to three or four who you think can do a quality job and work harmoniously with you. Phone each builder to see whether he or she is interested in being considered for your project. If so, invite the builder to an interview at your home. The meeting will serve two purposes. You'll be able to ask the candidate about his or her experience, and you'll be able to see whether or not your personalities are compatible. Go over the plans with the builder to make certain that he or she understands the scope of the project. Ask if they have constructed similar houses. Get references, and check the builder's standing with the Better Business Bureau. Develop a short list of builders, say three, and ask them to submit bids for the project.

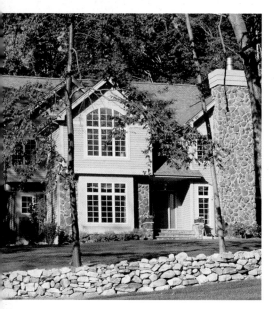

Contracts

Lump-Sum Contracts

A lump-sum, or fixed-fee, contract lets you know from the beginning just what the project will cost, barring any changes made because of your requests or unforeseen conditions. This form works well for projects that promise few surprises and are well defined from the outset by a complete set of contract documents. You can enter into a fixed-price contract by negotiating with a single builder on your short list or by obtaining bids from three or four builders. If you go the latter route, give each bidder a set of documents and allow at least two weeks for them to submit their bids. When you get the bids, decide who you want and call the others to thank them for their efforts. You don't have to accept the lowest bid, but it probably makes sense to do so since you have already honed the list to builders you trust. Inform this builder of your intentions to finalize a contract.

Cost-Plus-Fee Contracts

Under a cost-plus-fee contract, you agree to pay the builder for the costs of labor and materials, as verified by receipts, plus a fee that represents the builder's overhead and profit. This arrangement is sometimes referred to as "time and materials." The fee can range between 15 and 30 percent of the incurred costs. Because you ultimately pick up the tab—whatever the costs—the contractor is never at risk, as he is with a lump-sum contract. You won't know the final total cost of a cost-plus-fee contract until the project is built and paid for. If you can live with that uncertainty, there are offsetting advantages. First, this form allows you to accommodate unknown conditions much more easily than does a lump-sum contract. And rather than being tied down by the project documents, you will be free to make changes at any point along the way. This can be a trap, though. Watching the project take shape will spark the desire to add something or do something differently. Each change costs more, and the accumulation can easily exceed your budget. Because of the uncertainty of the final tab and the built-in advantage to the contractor, you should think twice before entering into this form of contract.

Contract Content

The conditions of your agreement should be spelled out thoroughly in writing and signed by both parties, whatever contractual arrangement you make with your builder. Your contract should include provisions for the following:

- The names and addresses of the owner and builder.
- A description of the work to be included ("As described in the plans and specifications dated . . .").
- The date that the work will be completed if time is of the essence.
- The contract price for lump-sum contracts and the builder's allowed profit and overhead costs for changes.
- The builder's fee for cost-plus-fee contracts and the method of accounting and requesting payment.
- The criteria for progress payments (monthly, by project milestones) and the conditions of final payment.
- A list of each drawing and specification section that is to be included as part of the contract.
- Requirements for guarantees. (One year is the standard period for which contractors guarantee the entire project, but you may require specific guarantees on

When submitting bids, all of the builders should base their estimates on the same specifications. Once the work begins, communicate with your builder to keep the work proceeding smoothly.

Inspect your newly built home, if possible, before the builder closes it up and finishes it.

certain parts of the project, such as a 20-year guarantee on the roofing.)
- Provisions for insurance.
- A description of how changes in the work orders will be handled.

The builder may have a standard contract that you can tailor to the specifics of your project. These contain complete specific conditions with blanks that you can fill in to fit your project and a set of "general conditions" that cover a host of issues from insurance to termination provisions. It's always a good idea to have an attorney review the draft of your completed contract before signing it.

Working with Your Builder

The construction phase officially begins when you have a signed copy of the contract and copies of any insurance required from the builder. It's not unheard of for a builder to request an initial payment of 10 to 20 percent of the total cost to cover mobilization costs, those costs associated with obtaining permits and getting set up to begin the actual construction. If you agree to this, keep a careful eye on the progress of the work to ensure that the total paid out at any one time doesn't get too far out of sync with the actual work completed.

What about changes? From here on, it's up to you and your builder to proceed in good faith and to keep the channels of communication open. Even so, changes of one sort or another beset every project, and they usually add to its cost.

Light at the End of the Tunnel.
The builder's request for a final inspection marks the end of the construction phase—almost. At the final inspection meeting, you and the builder will inspect the work, noting any defects or incomplete items on a "punch list." When the builder tidies up the punch list items, you should reinspect. Sometimes, builders go on to another job and take forever to clean up the last few details, so only after all items on the list have been completed satisfactorily should you release the final payment, which often accounts for the builder's profit.

Some Final Words

Having a positive attitude is important when undertaking a project as large as building a home. A positive attitude can help you ride out the rigors and stress of the construction process.

Stay Flexible. Expect problems, because they certainly will occur. Weather can upset the schedule you have established for subcontractors. A supplier may get behind on deliveries, which also affects the schedule. An unexpected pipe may surprise you during excavation. Just as certain, every problem that comes along has a solution if you are open to it.

Be Patient. The extra days it may take to resolve a construction problem will be forgotten once the project is completed.

Express Yourself. If what you see isn't exactly what you thought you were getting, don't be afraid to look into changing it. Or you may spot an unforeseen opportunity for an improvement. Changes usually cost more money, though, so don't make frivolous decisions.

Finally, watching your home go up is exciting, so stay upbeat. Get away from your project from time to time. Dine out. Take time to relax. A positive attitude will make for smoother relations with your builder. An optimistic outlook will yield better-quality work if you are doing your own construction. And though the project might seem endless while it is under way, keep in mind that all the planning and construction will fade to a faint memory at some time in the future, and you will be getting a lifetime of pleasure from a home that is just right for you.

Plan #131033

Dimensions: 84'10" W x 48' D
Levels: 1.5
Square Footage: 2,813
Main Level Sq. Ft.: 1,890
Upper Level Sq. Ft.: 923
Bedrooms: 5
Bathrooms: 3½
Foundation: Crawl space or slab; basement for fee
Materials List Available: Yes
Price Category: G

Contemporary styling, luxurious amenities, and the classics that make a house a home are all available here.

Features:

- **Family Room:** A sloped ceiling with skylight and a railed overlook to make this large space totally up to date.

- **Living Room:** Sunken for comfort and with a cathedral ceiling for style, this room features a fireplace flanked by windows and sliding glass doors.

- **Master Suite:** Unwind in this room, with its cathedral ceiling, with a skylight, walk-in closet, and private access to the den.

- **Upper Level:** A bridge overlooks the living room and foyer and leads through the family room to three bedrooms and a bath.

- **Optional Guest Suite:** 500 sq. ft. above the master suite and den provides total comfort.

Images provided by designer/architect.

Main Level Floor Plan

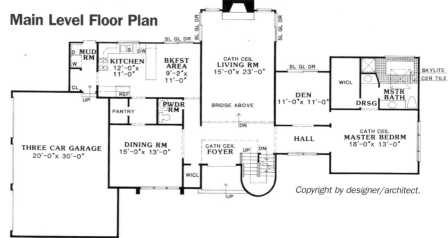

Copyright by designer/architect.

Upper Level Floor Plan

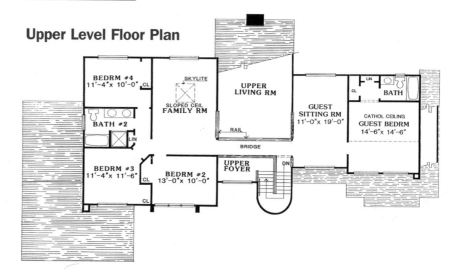

Living Room / Foyer

Entry

Living Room

Rear View

Plan #271016

Dimensions: 45'4" W x 49'6" D
Levels: 2
Square Footage: 2,170
Main Level Sq. Ft.: 1,169
Upper Level Sq. Ft.: 1,001
Bedrooms: 3
Bathrooms: 2½
Foundation: Basement
Materials List Available: Yes
Price Category: D

Images provided by designer/architect.

With plenty of living space, this attractive design is just right for a growing family.

Features:

- **Entry:** This two-story reception area welcomes guests with sincerity and style. A coat closet stands ready to take winter wraps.

- **Great Room:** This sunken and vaulted space hosts gatherings and formal meals of any size, and a handsome fireplace adds warmth and ambiance.

- **Kitchen:** A U-shaped counter keeps the family cook organized. A bayed breakfast nook overlooks a backyard deck.

- **Family Room:** The home's second fireplace adds a cozy touch to this casual area. Relax here with the family after playing in the snow!

- **Master Suite:** A vaulted ceiling presides over the master bedroom. The private bath hosts a separate tub and shower, a dual-sink vanity, and two walk-in closets.

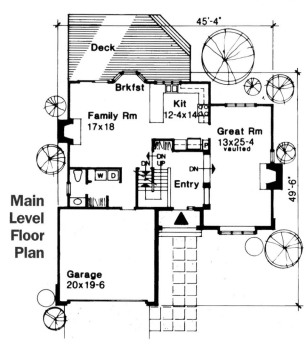

Main Level Floor Plan

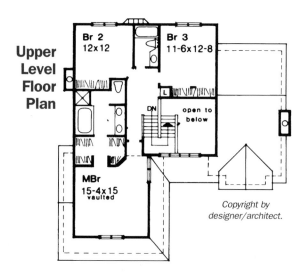

Upper Level Floor Plan

Copyright by designer/architect.

Plan #441029

Dimensions: 70' W x 71' D

Levels: 2

Square Footage: 3,217

Main Level Sq. Ft.: 2,292

Upper Level Sq. Ft.: 925

Bedrooms: 3

Bathrooms: 3½

Foundation: Crawl space; slab or basement available for fee

Material List Available: No

Price Category: G

Images provided by designer/architect.

Influenced by the Modernist movement, this California contemporary design is grand in façade and comfortable to live in.

Features:

- **Entry:** The two-story foyer opens to the formal dining room (also two-story) and the great room. Decorative columns help define these spaces. The curved wall of glass overlooking the rear patio brightens the great room.

- **Master Suite:** This suite, which has a salon with curved window wall, features a private bath with spa tub and walk-in closet.

- **Bedrooms:** The two family bedrooms share the upper level with the library, which has built-ins. Each upper-level bedroom has its own bathroom and walk-in closet.

- **Home Office:** The left wing of the main level contains this space, which features a curved window wall.

Main Level Floor Plan

◄ 70' ►

▲ 71' ▼

Upper Level Floor Plan

Copyright by designer/architect.

Rear View

Plan #161031

Dimensions: 99'8" W x 68'8" D
Levels: 2
Square Footage: 3,793
Opt. Lower Level Sq. Ft.: 1,588
Bedrooms: 3
Bathrooms: 2½
Foundation: Basement or walkout
Materials List Available: Yes
Price Category: F

This home, as shown in the photograph, may differ from the actual blueprints. For more detailed information, please check the floor plans carefully.

Images provided by designer/architect.

If you're looking for a compatible mixture of formal and informal areas in a home, look no further!

Features:

• Great Room: Columns at the entry to this room and the formal dining room set a gracious tone that is easy around which to decorate.

• Library: Set up an office or just a cozy reading area in this quiet room.

• Hearth Room: Spacious and inviting, this hearth room is positioned so that friends and family can flow from here to the breakfast area and kitchen.

• Master Suite: The luxury of this area is capped by the access it gives to the rear yard.

• Lower Level: Enjoy the 9-ft.-tall ceilings as you walk out to the rear yard from this area.

Entry

Rear View

Main Level Floor Plan

Deck

Bedroom
16'8" x 12'

Hearth Room
Breakfast
23' x 16' irr.

Master Bedroom
15'8" x 22"

Bath

Bath

Hall

Great Room
16' x 21'6"

tray ceiling

Bedroom
16'8" x 12'

Kitchen
17'7" x 14'8"

Sloped Ceiling

Sloped Ceiling

Laun.

Dressing

walk-in closet

Three Car
Garage
20' x 33'4"

Dining Room
13'6" x 15'3" irr.

Foyer

Porch

Library
12'4" x 16'2" irr.

walk-in closet

Main Level Floor Plan

Copyright by designer/architect.

Optional Lower Level Floor Plan

Bedroom
12' x 10'

Rec Room
44'1" x 31'2" Irreg.

Unfinished Basement

Bath

Bar

**Optional Lower Level
Floor Plan**

Dining Room

Rear Elevation

Left Elevation

Right Elevation

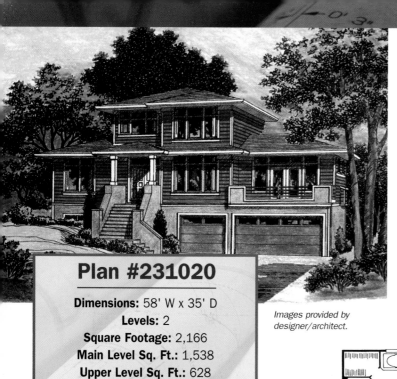

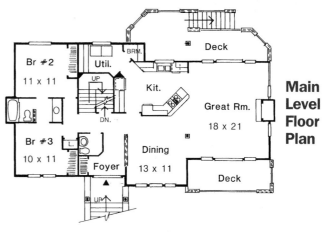

Main Level Floor Plan

Br #2
11 x 11

Util.

BRm.

Deck

Kit.

Great Rm.
18 x 21

UP

DN.

Br #3
10 x 11

L.

Foyer

Dining
13 x 11

Deck

UP

Plan #231020

Dimensions: 58' W x 35' D

Levels: 2

Square Footage: 2,166

Main Level Sq. Ft.: 1,538

Upper Level Sq. Ft.: 628

Bedrooms: 3

Bathrooms: 2½

Foundation: Slab, basement

Materials List Available: No

Price Category: D

Images provided by designer/architect.

Shop
13 x 13

UP

Garage
31 x 27

Unfin. Stor.
13 x 15

Unfin.Stor.
9-6 x 9

Upper Level Floor Plan

DN.

M.Br
13 x 20-6

OPEN TO FOYER

Garage Level Floor Plan

UP

Copyright by designer/architect.

Plan #321036

Dimensions: 78'4" W x 68'6" D

Levels: 1

Square Footage: 2,900

Bedrooms: 4

Bathrooms: 2½

Foundation: Basement

Materials List Available: No

Price Category: F

Images provided by designer/architect.

CAD FILE AVAILABLE

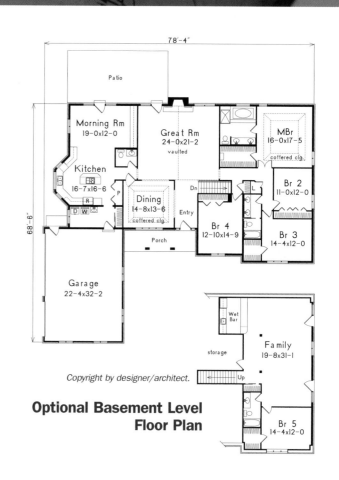

78'-4"

Patio

Morning Rm
19-0x12-0

Great Rm
24-0x21-2
vaulted

MBr
16-0x17-5
coffered clg.

Kitchen
16-7x16-6

Dining
14-8x13-6
coffered clg.

Dn

L

Br 2
11-0x12-0

68'-6"

D W

P

R

Entry

Br 4
12-10x14-9

Br 3
14-4x12-0

Garage
22-4x32-2

Porch

Optional Basement Level Floor Plan

Wet Bar

Family
19-8x31-1

storage

Up

Br 5
14-4x12-0

Copyright by designer/architect.

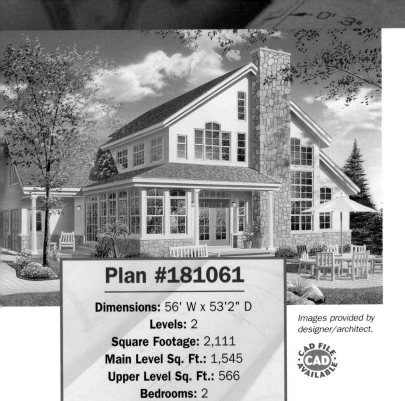

**Main Level
Floor Plan**

*Images provided by
designer/architect.*

Plan #181061

Dimensions: 56' W x 53'2" D

Levels: 2

Square Footage: 2,111

Main Level Sq. Ft.: 1,545

Upper Level Sq. Ft.: 566

Bedrooms: 2

Bathrooms: 2½

Foundation: Crawl space, basement

Materials List Available: Yes

Price Category: F

CAD FILE
CAD
AVAILABLE

**Upper Level
Floor Plan**

*Copyright by
designer/architect.*

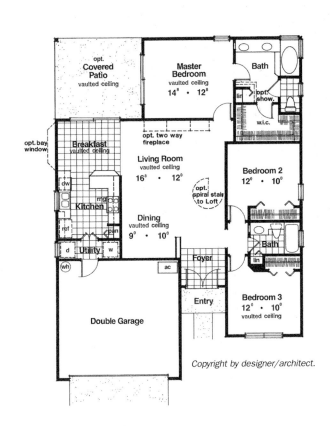

Plan #661033

Dimensions: 40' W x 55' D

Levels: 1

Square Footage: 2,036

Bedrooms: 3

Bathrooms: 2

Foundation: Slab

Materials List Available: No

Price Category: D

*Images provided by
designer/architect.*

CAD FILE
CAD
AVAILABLE

opt.
**Covered
Patio**
vaulted ceiling

**Master
Bedroom**
vaulted ceiling
14⁸ • 12⁸

Bath

opt.
show.

lin

w.i.c.

opt. bay
window

Breakfast
vaulted ceiling

opt. two way
fireplace

Living Room
vaulted ceiling
16⁸ • 12⁰

Bedroom 2
12⁰ • 10⁰

dw

Kitchen
rng

opt.
spiral stairs
to Loft

ref
pan

Dining
vaulted ceiling
9⁰ • 10⁰

Bath
lin

d **Utility** w

Foyer

wh
ac

Bedroom 3
12⁰ • 10⁰
vaulted ceiling

Double Garage

Entry

Copyright by designer/architect.

Plan #161027

Dimensions: 59'10" W x 37'4" D

Levels: 2

Square Footage: 2,388

Main Level Sq. Ft.: 1,207

Upper Level Sq. Ft.: 1,181

Bedrooms: 4

Bathrooms: 2½

Foundation: Basement

Materials List Available: No

Price Category: E

Double gables, wood trim, an arched window, and sidelights at the entry give elegance to this family-friendly home.

Features:

- Foyer: Friends and family will see the angled stairs, formal dining room, living room, and library from this foyer.

- Family Room: A fireplace makes this room cozy in the evenings on those chilly days, and multiple windows let natural light stream into it.

- Kitchen: You'll love the island and the ample counter space here as well as the butler's pantry. A breakfast nook makes a comfortable place to snack or just curl up and talk to the cook.

- Master Suite: Tucked away on the upper level, this master suite provides both privacy and luxury.

- Additional Bedrooms: These three additional bedrooms make this home ideal for any family.

Images provided by designer/architect.

Main Level Floor Plan

Deck

Breakfast
16'11" x 15'10"

Family Room
20'0" x 13'6"

Kitchen

Two-car Garage
21' x 22'2"

pantry

butler's pantry

Bath

Living Room /Library
11'6" x 15'4"

Laun.

stairs dn.

Dining Room
13'2" x 12'0"

Foyer

Porch

37'4"

59'10"

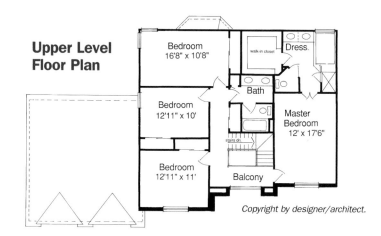

Upper Level Floor Plan

Bedroom
16'8" x 10'8"

walk-in closet

Dress.

Bedroom
12'11" x 10'

Bath

Master Bedroom
12' x 17'6"

stairs dn.

Bedroom
12'11" x 11'

Balcony

Copyright by designer/architect.

Plan #151495

Dimensions: 67'2" W x 64'8" D
Levels: 1
Square Footage: 2,121
Bedrooms: 3
Bathrooms: 2
Foundation: Slab; basement for fee
CompleteCost List Available: Yes
Price Category: D

Treasure the countless amenities that make this home ideal for family and welcoming guests.

Features:

- Great Room: This large gathering area, which is open to the kitchen, boasts a 10-ft.-high ceiling. The sliding glass doors allow natural light into the room and provide access to the rear lanai.

- Master Suite: A convenient private office with French door entry and built-ins is part of this extravagant master suite. The master bath pampers you with its whirlpool tub and separate toilet area.

- Secondary Bedrooms: Two additional bedrooms share the second bathroom. Bedroom 3 features a vaulted ceiling.

- Garage: This two-car front-loading garage includes a storage area and easy access to the kitchen through the laundry room.

Images provided by designer/architect.

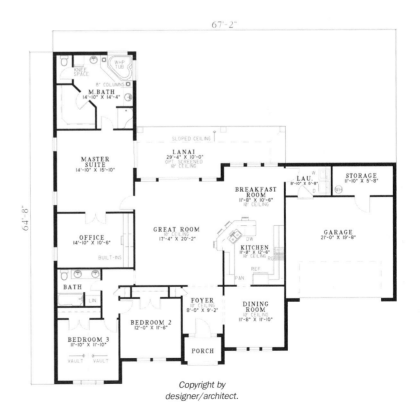

Copyright by designer/architect.

Plan #211009

Dimensions: 72' W x 60' D

Levels: 1

Square Footage: 2,396

Bedrooms: 4

Bathrooms: 2

Foundation: Slab

Materials List Available: Yes

Price Category: E

Images provided by designer/architect.

Beautiful arched windows lend a luxurious feeling to the exterior of this one-story home.

Features:

- Ceiling Height: 9 ft. unless otherwise noted.

- Entry: Guests will be greeted by a dramatic 12-ft. ceiling in this elegant foyer.

- Living Room: The 12-ft. ceiling continues through the foyer into this inviting living room. Everyone will feel welcomed by the crackling fire in the handsome fireplace.

- Covered Porch: When the weather is warm, invite guests to step out of the living room directly into this covered porch.

- Kitchen: This bright and cheery kitchen is designed for the way we live today. It includes a pantry and an angled eating bar that will see plenty of impromptu family meals.

- Energy-Efficient Walls: All the outside walls are framed with 2x6 lumber instead of 2x4. The extra thickness makes room for more insulation to lower your heating and cooling bills.

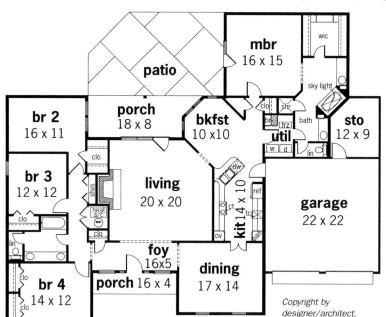

Copyright by designer/architect.

SMARTtip

Ornaments in a Garden

Placement is everything with ornaments in a garden. Some elements are best sitting by themselves. Others are better when they are part of a cohesive whole, perhaps placed in the greenery at a corner or flanking a structure.

Plan #271025

Dimensions: 61'4" W x 56'4" D

Levels: 2

Square Footage: 2,223

Main Level Sq. Ft.: 1,689

Upper Level Sq. Ft.: 534

Bedrooms: 3

Bathrooms: 2½

Foundation: Basement

Materials List Available: Yes

Price Category: E

This traditional home's unique design combines a dynamic, exciting exterior with a fantastic floor plan.

Features:

- **Living Room:** To the left of the column-lined, barrel-vaulted entry, this inviting space features a curved wall and corner windows.

- **Dining Room:** A tray ceiling enhances this formal meal room.

- **Kitchen:** This island-equipped kitchen includes a corner pantry and a built-in desk. Nearby, the sunny breakfast room opens onto a backyard deck via sliding glass doors.

- **Family Room:** A corner bank of windows provides a glassy backdrop for this room's handsome fireplace. Munchies may be served on the snack bar from the breakfast nook.

- **Master Suite:** This main-floor retreat is simply stunning, and includes a vaulted ceiling, access to a private courtyard, and of course, a sumptuous bath with every creature comfort.

Main Level Floor Plan

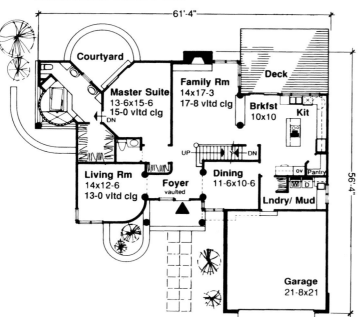

Upper Level Floor Plan

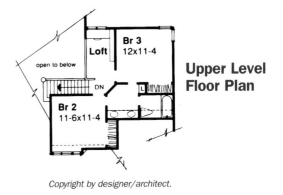

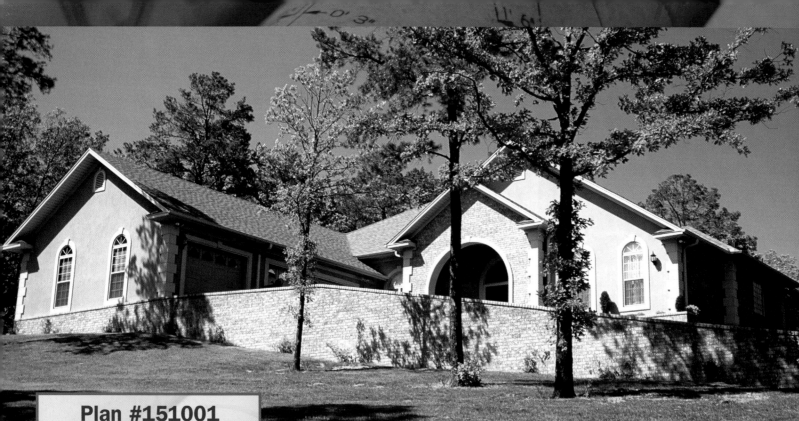

Plan #151001

Dimensions: 70' W x 88'2" D

Levels: 1

Square Footage: 3,124

Bedrooms: 4

Bathrooms: 3½

Foundation: Crawl space, slab

CompleteCost List Available: Yes

Price Category: G

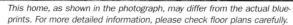

This home, as shown in the photograph, may differ from the actual blueprints. For more detailed information, please check floor plans carefully.

Images provided by designer/architect.

From the double front doors to sleek arches, columns, and a gallery with arched openings to the bedrooms, you'll love this elegant home.

Features:

• **Grand Room:** With a 13-ft. pan ceiling and column entry, this room opens to the rear covered porch as well as through French doors to the bay-windowed morning room that, in turn, leads to the gathering room.

• **Gathering Room:** A majestic fireplace, built-in entertainment center, and book shelves give comfort and ease.

• **Kitchen:** A double oven, built-in desk, and a work island add up to a design for efficiency.

• **Master Suite:** Enjoy the practicality of walk-in closets, the comfort of a private sitting area, and the convenience of an adjacent study or nursery. The bath features a step-up whirlpool tub and separate shower.

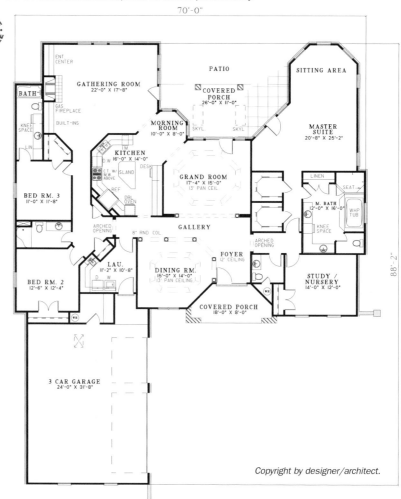

Copyright by designer/architect.

Plan #121009

Dimensions: 50' W x 58' D
Levels: 1
Square Footage: 1,422
Bedrooms: 3
Bathrooms: 2
Foundation: Basement
Materials List Available: Yes
Price Category: B

This amenity-filled home is perfect for the growing family or as a retirement retreat.

Features:

- Ceiling Height: 8 ft. unless otherwise noted.

- Great Room: This inviting space is the perfect place for gatherings of all sizes. It shares 12-ft. ceilings with the dining room and kitchen.

- Dining Room: In addition to the 12-ft. ceiling, arched openings, and built-in book cases make this an elegant place to dine.

- Private Porch: After dinner, step through a door in the dining room to enjoy a summer breeze in this inviting porch.

- Master Suite: The boxed ceiling lends drama to this suite and a walk-in closet adds convenience. Luxury comes from the whirlpool bath.

- Garage: You won't be short of parking and storage space in this two-bay garage. As a bonus there is space for a workbench.

SMARTtip

Window Cornices

You can transform plain rooms by making jogs in cornice molding that will hold shades, blinds, and other window treatments. You can create individual pockets over each window or continue the molding past narrow wall sections between windows to form a more expansive detail. Housings below the cornice can be painted or papered.

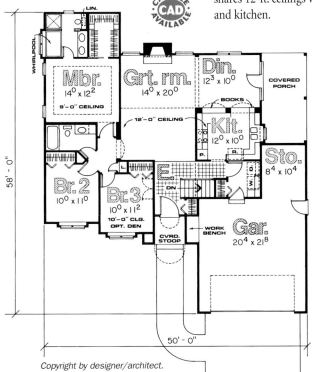

Copyright by designer/architect.

Plan #131045

Dimensions: 81'4" W x 68'3" D
Levels: 1
Square Footage: 2,347
Bedrooms: 4
Bathrooms: 2½
Foundation: Crawl space or slab; basement for fee
Materials List Available: Yes
Price Category: F

You'll love the character and flexibility in sitting that the angled design gives to this contemporary ranch-style home.

Features:

• Porch: A wraparound rear porch adds distinction to this lovely home.

• Great Room: Facing the rear of the house, this great room has a high, stepped ceiling, fireplace, and ample place for built-ins.

• Kitchen: This large room sits at an angle to the great room and is adjacent to both a laundry room and extra powder room.

• Office: Use the 4th bedroom as a home office, study, or living room, depending on your needs.

• Master Suite: This area is separated from the other bedrooms in the house to give it privacy. The beautiful bay window at the rear, two large walk-in closets, and luxurious bath make it an ideal retreat after a hectic day.

Great Room

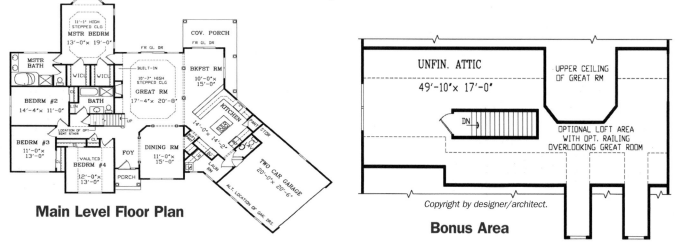

Main Level Floor Plan

Bonus Area

Plan #391013

Dimensions: 52' W x 41'4" D
Levels: 2
Square Footage: 1,894
Main Level Sq. Ft.: 1,108
Upper Level Sq. Ft.: 786
Bedrooms: 3
Bathrooms: 2½
Foundation: Crawl space, slab, or basement
Materials List Available: Yes
Price Category: D

Images provided by designer/architect.

This home hints at Tudor lineage, with its rising half-timber-effects and peaked roofline. Inside, it's a different, more contemporary story.

Features:

- Living Room. The foyer opens to this room, which basks in the light of a two-story arched window. Even the open dining room enjoys the brightness.

- Family Room: This room warms up with a fireplace, plus a built-in desk, wet bar, and entry to an outdoor deck.

Rear View

- Kitchen: The angular plan of this room, with a convenient pass-through to the dining area, features a picture window with built-in seat for taking time to meditate. Excellent shelving, storage, half-bath, and hall coat closet offer behind-the-scenes support.

- Bedrooms: Bedroom 2 looks over the front yard and shares a bath with bedroom 3, which oversees the backyard.

- Master Bedroom: The second level master bedroom overlooks the living room from a beautiful balcony. Double windows along one wall fill the area with natural light, and a windowed corner illuminates the master bath.

Copyright by designer/architect.

Second Floor Plan

Upper Level Floor Plan

Main Level Floor Plan

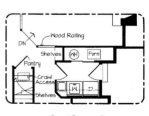

Optional Crawl Space/Slab Floor Plan

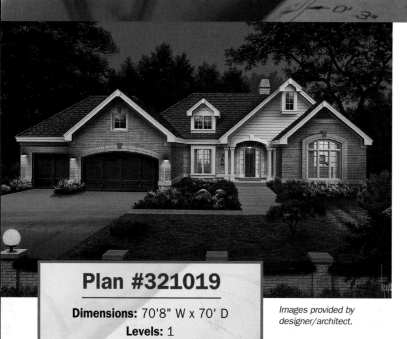

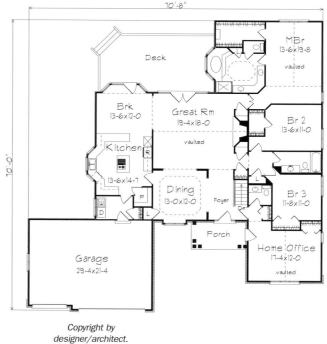

Plan #321019

Dimensions: 70'8" W x 70' D

Levels: 1

Square Footage: 2,452

Bedrooms: 4

Bathrooms: 2½

Foundation: Basement

Materials List Available: Yes

Price Category: E

Images provided by designer/architect.

CAD FILE CAD AVAILABLE

Copyright by designer/architect.

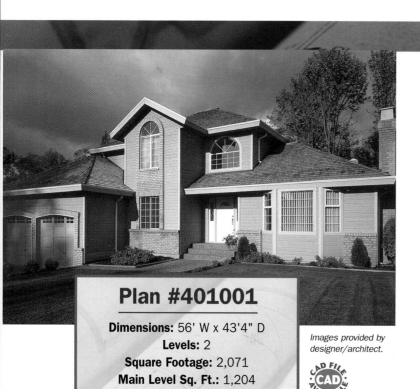

Plan #401001

Dimensions: 56' W x 43'4" D

Levels: 2

Square Footage: 2,071

Main Level Sq. Ft.: 1,204

Upper Level Sq. Ft.: 867

Bedrooms: 3

Bathrooms: 2½

Foundation: Basement

Materials List Available: Yes

Price Category: D

Images provided by designer/architect.

CAD FILE CAD AVAILABLE

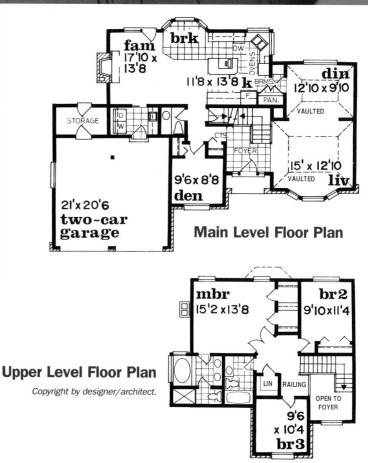

Main Level Floor Plan

Upper Level Floor Plan

Copyright by designer/architect.

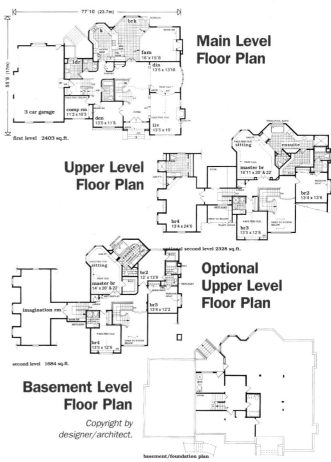

Main Level Floor Plan

first level 2403 sq.ft.

Upper Level Floor Plan

optional second level 2328 sq.ft.

Optional Upper Level Floor Plan

second level 1684 sq.ft.

Basement Level Floor Plan

basement/foundation plan

Copyright by designer/architect.

Plan #401049

Images provided by designer/architect.

Dimensions: 77'10" W x 55'8" D

Levels: 2

Square Footage: 4,087

Main Level Sq. Ft.: 2,403

Upper Level Sq. Ft.: 1,684

Bedrooms: 4

Bathrooms: 4½

Foundation: Basement

Materials List Available: Yes

Price Category: I

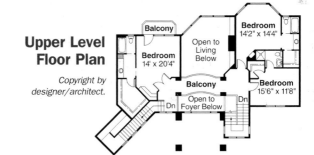

Upper Level Floor Plan

Copyright by designer/architect.

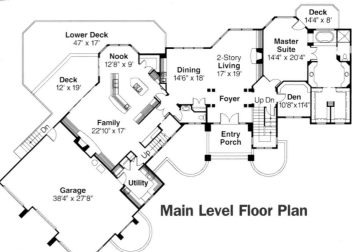

Main Level Floor Plan

Plan #361423

Images provided by designer/architect.

CAD FILE AVAILABLE

Dimensions: 115'6" W x 81'4" D

Levels: 2

Square Footage: 4,284

Main Level Sq. Ft.: 3,030

Upper Level Sq. Ft.: 1,254

Bedrooms: 4

Bathrooms: 4½

Foundation: Basement

Material List Available: No

Price Category: I

Plan #271086

Dimensions: 56'6" W x 67'6" D

Levels: 2

Square Footage: 1,910

Main Level Sq. Ft.: 1,324

Upper Level Sq. Ft.: 586

Bedrooms: 3

Bathrooms: 2

Foundation: Crawl space, daylight basement

Materials List Available: Yes

Price Category: D

Images provided by designer/architect.

A passive-solar sunroom is the highlight of this popular home and helps to minimize heating costs.

Features:

• **Living/Dining Area:** This expansive space is brightened by numerous windows and offers panoramic views of the outdoor scenery. A handsome woodstove gives the area a delightful ambiance, especially when the weather outside is frightful. Your dining table goes in the corner by the sun room.

• **Kitchen:** This room's efficient design keeps all of the chef's supplies at the ready. A snack bar could be used to help serve guests during parties.

• **Bedrooms:** With three bedrooms to choose from, all of your family members will be able to find secluded spots of their very own.

• **Lower Level:** This optional space includes a recreation room with a second woodstove. Let the kids gather here and make as much noise as they want.

Main Level Floor Plan

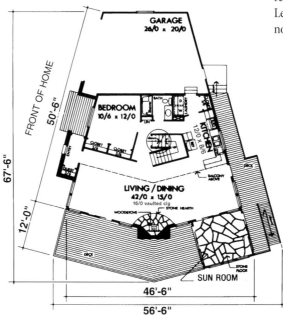

Optional Basement Level Floor Plan

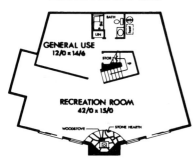

Upper Level Floor Plan

Plan #121017

Dimensions: 54' W x 50' D

Levels: 2

Square Footage: 2,353

Main Level Sq. Ft.: 1,653

Upper Level Sq. Ft.: 700

Bedrooms: 4

Bathrooms: 2½

Foundation: Basement; slab for fee

Materials List Available: Yes

Price Category: E

Images provided by designer/architect.

The dramatic two-story entry with bent staircase is the first sign that this is a gracious home.

Features:

- Ceiling Height: 8 ft. except as noted.

- Great Room: A row of transom-topped windows and a tall, beamed ceiling add a sense of spaciousness to this family gathering area.

- Formal Dining Room: The bayed window helps make this an inviting place to entertain.

- See-through Fireplace: This feature spreads warmth and coziness throughout the informal areas of the home.

- Breakfast Area: This sunny area shares a see-through fireplace with the great room. It's the perfect place to start the day.

- Master Suite: Here are all the features you expect to find in large luxury homes. Wake up to tall, sloped ceilings, and enjoy the corner whirlpool, separate shower, and vanity. A large walk-in closet provides plenty of wardrobe storage.

Main Level Floor Plan

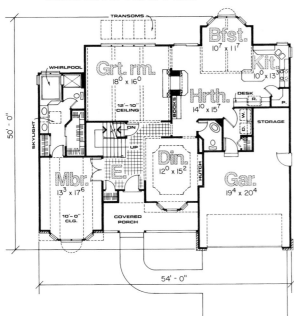

Upper Level Floor Plan

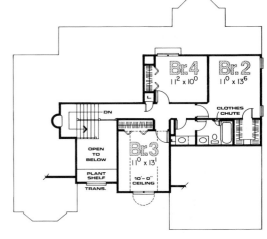

Copyright by designer/architect.

Plan #121025

Dimensions: 60' W x 59'4" D
Levels: 2
Square Footage: 2,562
Main Level Sq. Ft.: 1,875
Upper Level Square Footage: 687
Bedrooms: 4
Bathrooms: 2½
Foundation: Basement; crawl space or slab for fee
Materials List Available: Yes
Price Category: E

Images provided by designer/architect.

Dramatic arches are the reoccurring architectural theme in this distinctive home.

Features:

- Ceiling Height: 8 ft. unless otherwise noted.

- Foyer: This is a grand two-story entrance. Plants will thrive on the plant shelf thanks to light streaming through the arched window.

- Great Room: The foyer flows into the great room through dramatic 15-ft.-high arched openings.

- Kitchen: An island is the centerpiece of this highly functional kitchen that includes a separate breakfast area.

- Office: French doors open into this versatile office that features a 10-ft. ceiling and transom-topped windows.

- Master Suite: The master suite features a volume ceiling, built-in dresser, and two closets. You'll unwind in the beautiful corner whirlpool bath with its elegant window treatment.

Main Level Floor Plan

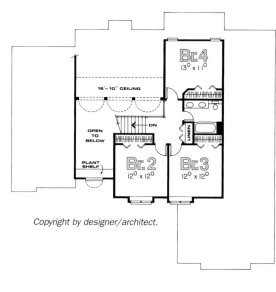

Upper Level Floor Plan

Copyright by designer/architect.

Plan #121029

Dimensions: 58'8" W x 54' D

Levels: 2

Square Footage: 2,576

Main Level Sq. Ft.: 1,735

Upper Level Sq. Ft.: 841

Bedrooms: 4

Bathrooms: 2½

Foundation: Basement

Materials List Available: Yes

Price Category: E

Images provided by designer/architect.

This gracious home is designed with the contemporary lifestyle in mind.

Features:

• Ceiling Height: 8 ft. unless otherwise noted.

• Great Room: This room features a fireplace and entertainment center. It's equally suited for family gatherings and formal entertaining.

• Breakfast Area: The fireplace is two-sided so it shares its warmth with this breakfast area—the perfect spot for informal family meals.

• Master Suite: Halfway up the staircase you'll find double-doors into this truly distinctive suite featuring a barrel-vault ceiling, built-in bookcases, and his and her walk-in closets. Unwind at the end of the day by stretching out in the oval whirlpool tub.

• Computer Loft: This loft overlooks the great room. It is designed as a home office with a built-in desk for your computer.

• Garage: Two bays provide plenty of storage in addition to parking space.

CAD FILE AVAILABLE

Main Level Floor Plan

Upper Level Floor Plan

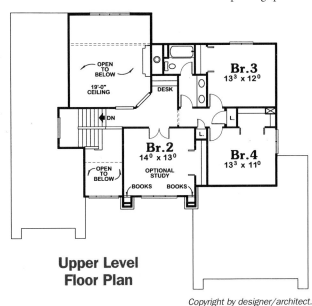

Copyright by designer/architect.

Plan #121031

Dimensions: 52' W x 51'4" D
Levels: 2
Square Footage: 1,772
Main Level Sq. Ft.: 1,314
Upper Level Sq. Ft.: 458
Bedrooms: 3
Bathrooms: 2½
Foundation: Basement; crawl space or slab for fee
Materials List Available: Yes
Price Category: C

Images provided by designer/architect.

This home features architectural details reminiscence of earlier fine homes.

Features:

• Ceiling Height: 8 ft. unless otherwise noted.

• Foyer: This grand entry soars two-stories high. The U-shaped staircase with window leads to a second-story balcony.

• Great Room: You'll be drawn to the impressive views through the triple-arch

windows at the front and rear of this room.

• Kitchen: Designed for maximum efficiency, this kitchen is a pleasure to be in. It features a center island, a full pantry, and a desk for added convenience.

• Breakfast Area: This area adjoins the kitchen. Both rooms are flooded with sunlight streaming from a shared bay window.

• Master Suite: The stylish bedroom includes a walk-in closet. Luxuriate in the whirlpool tub at the end of a long day.

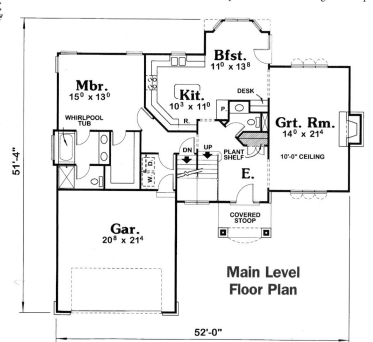

Main Level Floor Plan

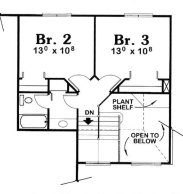

Copyright by designer/architect.

Upper Level Floor Plan

Plan #401029

Dimensions: 37'6" W x 48'4" D
Levels: 2
Square Footage: 2,163
Main Level Sq. Ft.: 832
Upper Level Sq. Ft.: 1,331
Bedrooms: 3
Bathrooms: 2½
Foundation: Basement
Materials List Available: Yes
Price Category: D

Images provided by designer/architect.

This two-level plan has a bonus--a roof deck with hot tub! A variety of additional outdoor spaces make this one wonderful plan.

Features:

• First Level: Family bedrooms, a full bath room, and a cozy den are on the first level, along with a two-car garage.

• Living Area: The living spaces are on the second floor and nclude a living/dining room combination with a deck and a fireplace. The dining room has buffet space.

• Family Room: Featuring a fireplace and a built-in entertainment center, the gathering area is open to the breakfast room and sky lighted kitchen.

• Master Bedroom: This room features a private bath with a whirlpool tub and two-person shower, a walk-in closet, and access to still another deck.

Master Bathroom

Rear Elevation

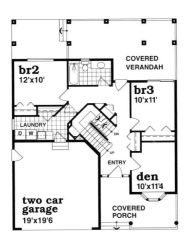

**Main Level
Floor Plan**

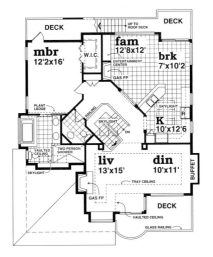

Upper Level Floor Plan

Copyright by designer/architect.

Plan #121015

Dimensions: 52' W x 47'4" D

Levels: 2

Square Footage: 1,999

Main Level Sq. Ft.: 1,421

Upper Level Sq. Ft.: 578

Bedrooms: 4

Bathrooms: 2½

Foundation: Basement

Materials List Available: Yes

Price Category: D

This home, as shown in the photograph, may differ from the actual blueprints. For more detailed information, please check the floor plans carefully.

Images provided by designer/architect.

Hipped roofs and a trio of gables bring distinction to this plan.

Features:

• Ceiling Height: 8 ft.

• Open Floor Plan: The rooms flow into each other and are flanked by an abundance of windows. The result is a light and airy space that seems much larger than it really is.

• Formal Dining Room: Here is the perfect room for elegant entertaining.

• Breakfast Nook: This bright, bayed nook is the perfect place to start the day. It's also great for intimate get-togethers.

• Great Room: The family will enjoy gathering in this spacious area.

• Bedrooms: This large master bedroom, along with three secondary bedrooms and an extra room, provides plenty of room for a growing family.

• Attached Garage: The garage provides two bays of parking plus plenty of storage space.

Main Level Floor Plan

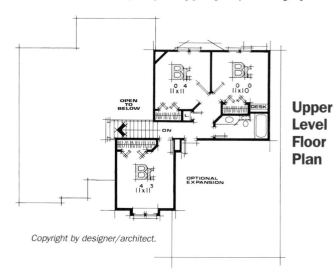

Upper Level Floor Plan

Copyright by designer/architect.

Plan #401048

Dimensions: 57'8" W x 103'6" D
Levels: 2
Square Footage: 5,159
Main Level Sq. Ft.: 2,473
Upper Level Sq. Ft.: 2,686
Bedrooms: 4
Bathrooms: 4½
Foundation: Basement
Materials List Available: Yes
Price Category: I

Images provided by designer/architect.

This unusual stucco-and-siding design opens with a grand portico to a foyer that extends to the living room with a fireplace.

Features:

• Dining Room: Step up a fw steps to this dining room, withi ts coffered ceiling and butler's pantry, which connects to the gourmet kitchen.

• Hearth Room: Attached to the kitchen, this hearth room has the requisite fireplace and three sets of french doors that lead to the covered porch.

• Family Room: This room features a coffered ceiling and a fireplace flanked by French doors.

• Master Suite: This area includes a tray ceiling, covered deck, and lavish bath.

• Bedrooms: All bedrooms are located on the second floor. Two full bathrooms serve the family bedrooms and a bonus room that might be used as an additional bedroom or hobby space.

Great Room

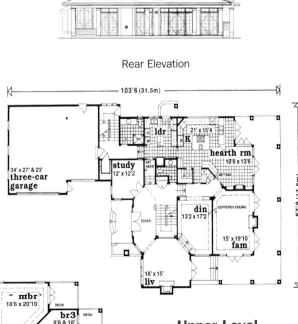

Rear Elevation

Upper Level Floor Plan

Copyright by designer/architect.

Main Level Floor Plan

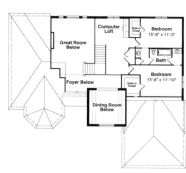

Main Level Floor Plan

Copyright by designer/architect.

Deck

Master Bath

Great Room 16'-5" x 17'-2"

Breakfast 12'-0" x 12'-6"

Hearth Room 19'-6" x 14'-10"

Kitchen 14'-6" x 15'-6"

Master Bedroom 14'-0" x 18'-1"

Bath

Foyer

Laun.

Sitting Area 11'-8" x 11'-8"

Porch

Dining Room 13'-8" x 13'-0"

Garage 21'-0" x 32'-10"

Images provided by designer/architect.

Upper Level Floor Plan

Great Room Below

Computer Loft

Walk-in Closet

Bedroom 15'-8" x 11'-3"

Bath

Foyer Below

Walk-in Closet

Bedroom 15'-8" x 11'-10"

Dining Room Below

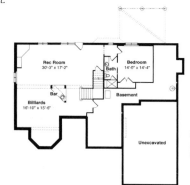

Rec Room 30'-3" x 17'-2"

Bath

Bedroom 14'-0" x 14'-4"

Bar

Basement

Billiards 16'-10" x 15'-6"

Unexcavated

Optional Lower Level Floor Plan

Plan #161097

Dimensions: 70' W x 56'10" D
Levels: 2
Square Footage: 3,144
Main Level Sq. Ft.: 2,237
Upper Level Sq. Ft.: 900
Optional Basement Level Sq. Ft.: 1,450
Bedrooms: 3
Bathrooms: 2½
Foundation: Walkout; basement for fee
Material List Available: No
Price Category: G

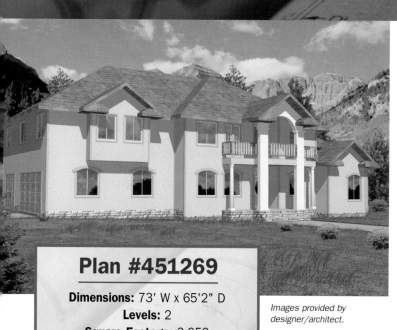

Main Level Floor Plan

COVERED AREA

DINING 12'⁸ x 13'⁰

GREAT ROOM 18'⁰ x 21'⁸

CONC. PATIO

KITCHEN 13'⁰ x 15'⁰

MASTER SUITE 15' x 17'⁵

3 CAR GARAGE 23'⁸ x 33'⁴

FOYER 9'⁴ x 8'⁰

MASTER BATH

WIC 9' x 9'

UTILITY

LIVING 10'⁸ x 13'

Upper Level Floor Plan

OPEN TO BELOW

BDRM. #3 13' x 14'

UNFINISHED ROOM 19'⁸ x 33'⁰

BDRM. #2 15' x 11'⁵

OFFICE 10'⁵ x 13'

Plan #451269

Dimensions: 73' W x 65'2" D
Levels: 2
Square Footage: 3,952
Main Level Sq. Ft.: 2,080
Upper Level Sq. Ft.: 1,872
Bedrooms: 3
Bathrooms: 3
Foundation: Crawl space
Material List Available: No
Price Category: H

Images provided by designer/architect.

CAD FILE AVAILABLE

Rear Elevation

Copyright by designer/architect.

Main Level Floor Plan

media
Breakfast
up
Pdr
opt. ref
dw
Kitchen
Great Room
29⁰ · 16⁴
Covered Patio
12⁴ · 8⁰
Master Bedroom
volume ceiling
15⁰ · 12⁰
pantry
w
d
ac
wh
Dining
Double Garage
Foyer
Entry
w.i.c.
plant shelf
Bath

Images provided by er/architect.

design-

Plan #661057

Dimensions: 50' W x 40' D
Levels: 2
Square Footage: 1,887
Main Level Sq. Ft.: 1,371
Upper Level Sq. Ft.: 516
Bedrooms: 3
Bathrooms: 2½
Foundation: Slab
Materials List Available: No
Price Category: D

Upper Level Floor Plan

Breakfast Below
down
Balcony
shelf
Great Room Below
Bath
linen
lin
w.i.c.
Bedroom 3
12⁰ · 10⁰
Bedroom 2
12⁰ · 10⁰

Copyright by designer/architect.

Main Level Floor Plan

12'-0" X 8'-4"
3,60 X 2,50
14'-0" X 12'-0"
4,20 X 3,60
38'-0"
11,4 m
18'-4" X 14'-0"
5,50 X 4,20
13'-4" X 20'-4"
4,00 X 6,10
7'-4" X 8'-0"
2,20 X 2,40

Copyright by designer/architect.

Images provided by designer/architect.

Plan #181162

Dimensions: 38' W x 38' D
Levels: 2
Square Footage: 1,867
Main Level Sq. Ft.: 911
Upper Level Sq. Ft.: 956
Bedrooms: 3
Bathrooms: 2½
Foundation: Basement
Materials List Available: Yes
Price Category: F

Upper Level Floor Plan

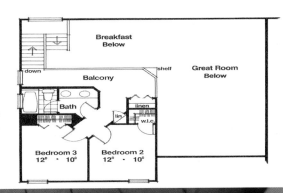

38'-0"
11,4 m
14'-8" X 12'-0"
4,40 X 3,60
10'-4" X 14'-0"
3,10 X 4,20
11'-8" X 14'-0"
3,50 X 4,20

Plan #151021

Dimensions: 75'2" W x 89'6" D
Levels: 2
Square Footage: 3,385
Main Level Sq. Ft.: 2,633
Upper Level Sq. Ft.: 752
Bedrooms: 4
Bathrooms: 4
Foundation: Crawl space, or slab
CompleteCost List Available: Yes
Price Category: F

From the fireplace in the master suite to the well-equipped game room, the amenities in this home will surprise and delight you.

Features:

• Great Room: A bank of windows on the far wall lets sunlight stream into this large room. The fireplace is located across the room and is flanked by the built-in media center and built-in bookshelves. Gracious brick arches create an entry into the breakfast area and kitchen.

• Breakfast Room: Move easily between this room with 10-foot ceiling either into the kitchen or onto the rear covered porch.

• Game Room: An icemaker and refrigerator make entertaining a snap in this room.

• Master Suite: A 10-ft. boxed ceiling, fireplace, and access to the rear porch give romance, while the built-ins in the closet, whirlpool tub with glass blocks, and glass shower give practicality.

Upper Level Floor Plan

Main Level Floor Plan

Copyright by designer/architect.

Plan #161113

Dimensions: 120'2" W x 60'4" D
Levels: 2
Square Footage: 4,365
Main Level Sq. Ft.: 3,298
Upper Level Sq. Ft.: 1,067
Optional Lower Level Sq. Ft.: 1,761
Bedrooms: 3
Bathrooms: 2½
Foundation: Basement, or walkout
Materials List Available: No
Price Category: I

Images provided by designer/architect.

A covered porch welcomes friends and family to this elegant home.

Features:

• Library: Just off the foyer is this library, which can be used as a home office. Notice the connecting door to the master bathroom.

• Kitchen: Release the chef inside of you into this gourmet kitchen, complete with seating at the island and open to the breakfast area. Step through the triple sliding door, and arrive on the rear porch.

• Master Suite: This luxurious master suite features a stepped ceiling in the sleeping area and private access to the rear patio. The master bath boasts an oversized stall shower, a whirlpool bath, dual vanities, and an enormous walk-in closet.

• Lower Level: For family fun times, this lower level is finished to provide a wet bar, billiard room, and media room. The area also includes two additional bedrooms and an exercise room.

• Garage: You'll have storage galore in this four-car garage, complete with an additional set of stairs to the unfinished part of the basement.

Optional Lower Level

Copyright by designer/architect.

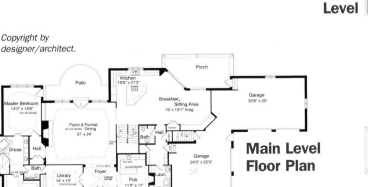

Main Level Floor Plan

Upper Level Floor Plan

Plan #271061

Dimensions: 68' W x 52' D
Levels: 1
Square Footage: 1,750
Bedrooms: 1
Bathrooms: 1½
Foundation: Walkout basement
Material List Available: No
Price Category: C

Stucco and a contemporary design give this home a simplistically elegant look.

CAD FILE AVAILABLE

Features:

- Entry: A small porch area welcomes guests out of the weather and into the warmth. Inside, this entryway provides an inviting introduction to the rest of the home.

- Kitchen: Opening to both the full dining room and a bayed dinette, this kitchen is both beautifully and efficiently designed. The space includes a walk-in pantry and plenty of work-space for the budding gourmet.

- Master Suite: This space is fit for the king (or queen) of the castle. Separated from the rest

of the house by a small entry, the suite includes its own full bath with dual sinks, bathtub, shower stall, and water closet.

- Basement: This area can be finished to include two bedrooms with wide closets, a full bathroom, a family room, and storage space.

- Garage: Whether you actually have three cars you need kept from the climate, you are a collector of things, or you prefer a hobby area, this three-bay garage has plenty of space to fit your needs.

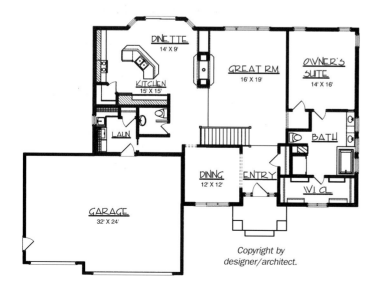

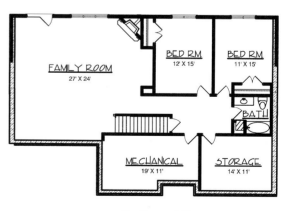

Optional Basement Level Floor Plan

Plan #271034

Dimensions: 45' W x 43' D
Levels: 2
Square Footage: 1,531
Main Level Sq. Ft.: 1,062
Upper Level Sq. Ft.: 469
Bedrooms: 4
Bathrooms: 2
Foundation: Basement
Materials List Available: Yes
Price Category: C

Images provided by designer/architect.

This versatile home design adapts to today's constantly changing and nontraditional families.

Features:

• Great Room: Both old and young are sure to enjoy this great room's warm and charming fireplace. The vaulted ceiling and high fixed windows add volume and light to the room.

• Family/Kitchen: This joined space is perfect for weekend get-togethers. On warm evenings, step through the sliding glass doors to the backyard deck.

• Den/Bedroom: The flexible den can serve as a nursery or as a guestroom for visiting family members of any age.

• Master Bedroom: When the golden years near, you'll appreciate its main-floor locale.

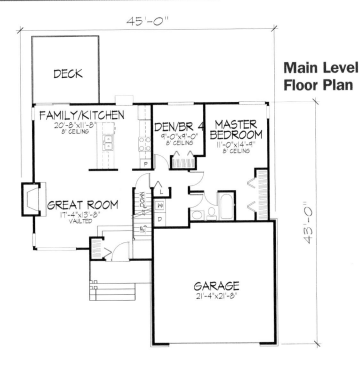

Main Level Floor Plan

Upper Level Floor Plan

Copyright by designer/architect.

Plan #451237

Dimensions: 66' W x 69'6" D

Levels: 1

Square Footage: 1,898

Bedrooms: 3

Bathrooms: 2½

Foundation: Slab

Material List Available: No

Price Category: D

Images provided by designer/architect.

CAD FILE AVAILABLE

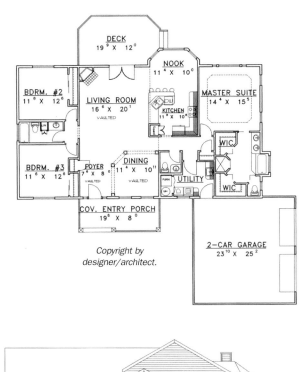

Copyright by designer/architect.

Side Elevation

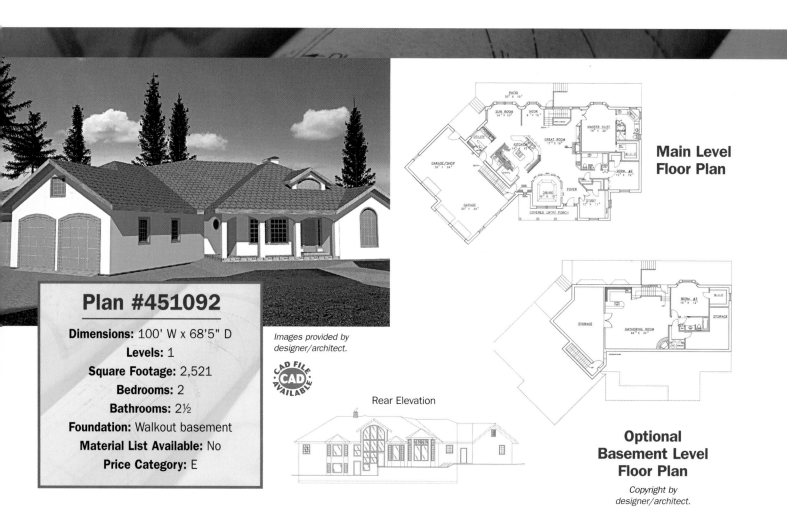

Plan #451092

Dimensions: 100' W x 68'5" D

Levels: 1

Square Footage: 2,521

Bedrooms: 2

Bathrooms: 2½

Foundation: Walkout basement

Material List Available: No

Price Category: E

Images provided by designer/architect.

CAD FILE AVAILABLE

Rear Elevation

Main Level Floor Plan

Optional Basement Level Floor Plan

Copyright by designer/architect.

Plan #361493

Dimensions: 73' W x 60'8" D

Levels: 1

Square Footage: 2,350

Bedrooms: 2

Bathrooms: 2½

Foundation: Crawl space

Material List Available: No

Price Category: E

Images provided by designer/architect.

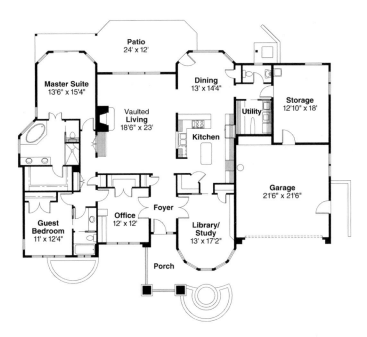

Copyright by designer/architect.

Plan #361435

Dimensions: 81' W x 64' D

Levels: 1

Square Footage: 2,507

Bedrooms: 5

Bathrooms: 3

Foundation: Crawl space or basement

Materials List Available: No

Price Category: E

Images provided by designer/architect.

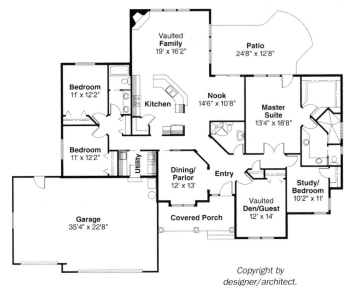

Copyright by designer/architect.

Plan #271036

Dimensions: 43'4" W x 50' D
Levels: 2
Square Footage: 1,602
Main Level Sq. Ft.: 1,112
Upper Level Sq. Ft.: 490
Bedrooms: 3
Bathrooms: 2½
Foundation: Basement
Materials List Available: No
Price Category: C

A country-styled home, like this one, is a perfect fit for any neighborhood.

CAD FILE AVAILABLE

Images provided by designer/architect.

Features:

- **Living Room:** Just off the entry you will find this large gathering area with a cozy fireplace. The front wall of windows will allow the area to be flooded with natural light.

- **Kitchen:** The chef in the family will love the layout of this efficiently designed kitchen. On nice days step out the glass doors onto the rear patio, and dine in the sunshine.

- **Master Bedroom:** This main-level retreat features an elegant double-door entry. The master bath offers efficiency in a compact design.

- **Secondary Bedrooms:** Located on the upper level, these two bedrooms offer adequate space for furniture and toys. The second full bathroom is located close by.

Upper Level Floor Plan

Copyright by designer/architect.

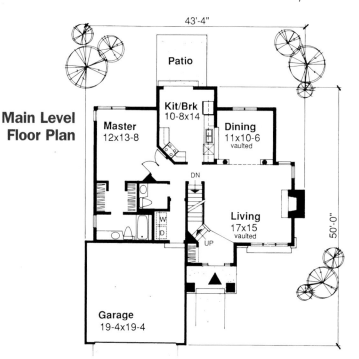

Main Level Floor Plan

Plan #321058

Dimensions: 39' W x 42'8" D
Levels: 2
Square Footage: 1,700
Main Level Sq. Ft.: 896
Upper Level Sq. Ft.: 804
Bedrooms: 4
Bathrooms: 2½
Foundation: Basement
Materials List Available: Yes
Price Category: C

Images provided by designer/architect.

Graceful architectural details, including unique window designs, create an exterior that mirrors the beauty and efficiency of the interior.

Features:

- Entry: This two-story entry is illuminated by a decorative oval window.

- Family Room: This large family room will be bathed in warm light no matter the time of day thanks to plenty of windows and a built-in fireplace.

- Kitchen: A built-in pantry and ample counter space make a great work area for the family cook and the aspiring chef alike. An open transition to the breakfast area simplifies

morning chaos, while a defined separation formalizes the dining room.

- Bedrooms: Having the bedrooms separated from the other living areas means a restful space for sleep and a quiet place for study or work. The master suite is spacious and features a walk-in closet and full bath. The three secondary bedrooms are all near a full bathroom, and all have generous closet storage. If three bedrooms are one too many, use one as an office, study, or entertainment space.

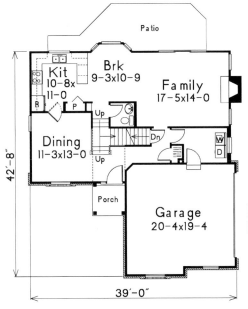

Main Level Floor Plan

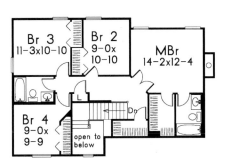

Upper Level Floor Plan

Copyright by designer/architect.

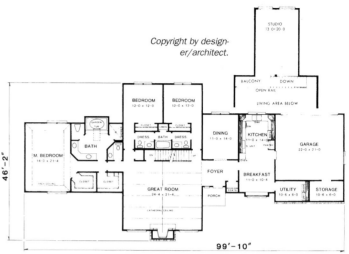

Plan #301001

Dimensions: 99'10" W x 46'2" D

Levels: 1

Square Footage: 2,720

Bedrooms: 3

Bathrooms: 2

Foundation: Crawl space or basement

Materials List Available: Yes

Price Category: F

Images provided by designer/architect.

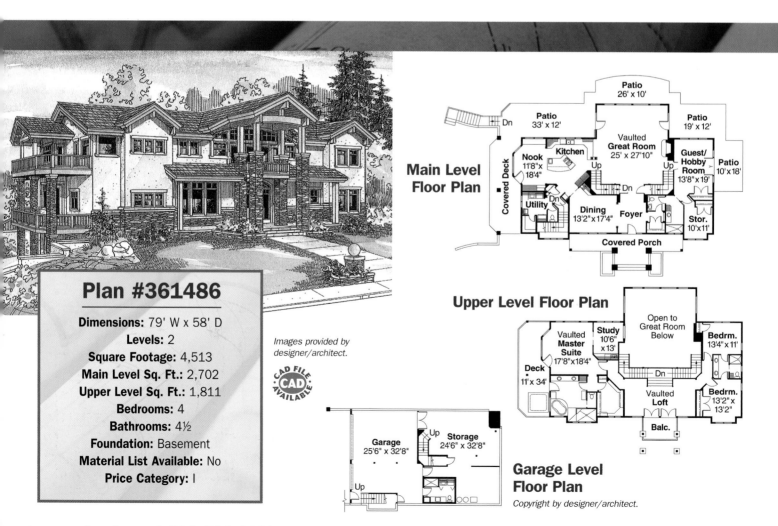

Plan #361486

Dimensions: 79' W x 58' D

Levels: 2

Square Footage: 4,513

Main Level Sq. Ft.: 2,702

Upper Level Sq. Ft.: 1,811

Bedrooms: 4

Bathrooms: 4½

Foundation: Basement

Material List Available: No

Price Category: I

Images provided by designer/architect.

Copyright by designer/architect.

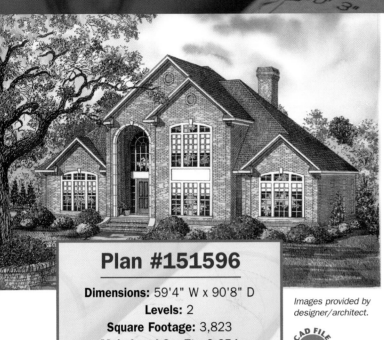

Plan #151596

Dimensions: 59'4" W x 90'8" D

Levels: 2

Square Footage: 3,823

Main Level Sq. Ft.: 2,654

Upper Level Sq. Ft.: 1,169

Bedrooms: 3

Bathrooms: 3½

Foundation: Crawl space, slab

CompleteCost List Available: Yes

Price Category: H

Images provided by designer/architect.

Main Level Floor Plan

Copyright by designer/architect.

Upper Level Floor Plan

Plan #321060

Dimensions: 36' W x 46'8" D

Levels: 2

Square Footage: 1,575

Main Level Sq. Ft.: 802

Upper Level Sq. Ft.: 773

Bedrooms: 3

Bathrooms: 2½

Foundation: Basement

Materials List Available: Yes

Price Category: C

Images provided by designer/architect.

Main Level Floor Plan

Upper Level Floor Plan

Copyright by designer/architect.

Plan #151384

Dimensions: 76'8" W x 77'7" D
Levels: 1.5
Square Footage: 2,742
Bedrooms: 3
Bathrooms: 2½
Foundation: Crawl space or slab
CompleteCost List Available: Yes
Price Category: F

With its fine detailing, this is a home created for the ages.

Features:

- Great Room: A fireplace nicely settled between built-ins punctuates this enormous room.

This home, as shown in the photograph, may differ from the actual blueprints. For more detailed information, please check the floor plans carefully.

Images provided by designer/architect.

- Hobby Room: This oversized room offers space galore for those do-it-yourself home projects.

- Master Suite: This elaborate suite presents an entire wall of built-ins, along with an angled private entrance to the porch.

- Bedrooms: The two secondary bedrooms are located on the opposite side of the home from the master suite and share the full bathroom adjacent to Bedroom 2.

Copyright by designer/architect.

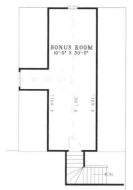

Bonus Area Floor Plan

Front View

Plan #121059

Dimensions: 52' W x 59'4" D
Levels: 1
Square Footage: 1,782
Bedrooms: 3
Bathrooms: 2
Foundation: Basement
Materials List Available: Yes
Price Category: C

Images provided by designer/architect.

This home is ideal for families looking for luxury and style mixed with convenience.

Features:

• Great Room: This large room is enhanced by the three-sided fireplace it shares with adjacent living areas.

• Hearth Room: Enjoy the fireplace here, too, and decorate to emphasize the bayed windows.

• Kitchen: This kitchen was designed for efficiency and is flooded with natural light.

• Breakfast Area: Picture-awing windows are the highlight in this area.

• Master Suite: A boxed ceiling and walk-in closet as well as a bath with a double-vanity, whirlpool tub, shower, and window with a plant ledge make this suite a true retreat.

• Bedrooms: These lovely bedrooms are served by a luxurious full bath.

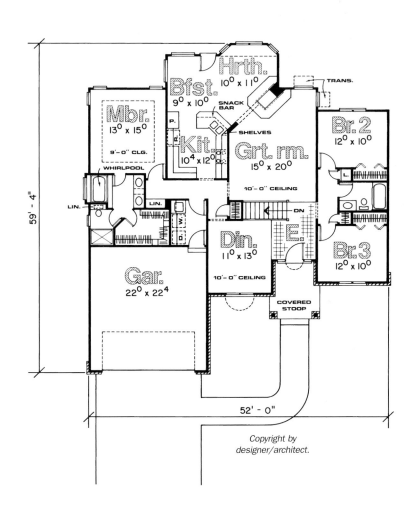

Copyright by designer/architect.

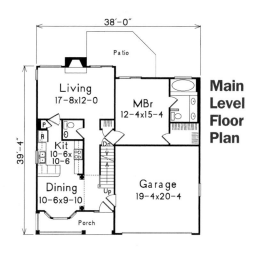

Main Level Floor Plan

38'-0"

39'-4"

Patio

Living
17-8x12-0

MBr
12-4x15-4

Kit
10-6x
10-6

Dn

Dining
10-6x9-10

Up

Garage
19-4x20-4

Porch

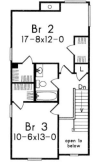

Upper Level Floor Plan

Br 2
17-8x12-0

L

Dn

Br 3
10-6x13-0

open to below

Copyright by designer/architect.

Plan #321057

Dimensions: 38' W x 39'4" D

Levels: 2

Square Footage: 1,524

Main Level Sq. Ft.: 951

Upper Level Sq. Ft.: 573

Bedrooms: 3

Bathrooms: 2½

Foundation: Basement

Materials List Available: Yes

Price Category: C

Images provided by designer/architect.

CAD FILE AVAILABLE

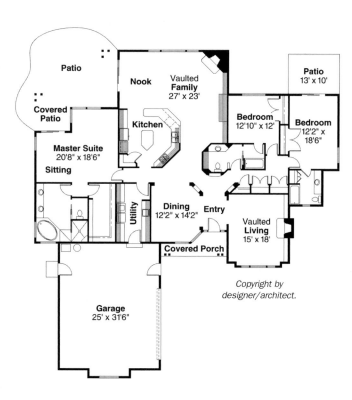

Patio

Nook

Vaulted Family
27' x 23'

Patio
13' x 10'

Covered Patio

Kitchen

Bedroom
12'10" x 12'

Bedroom
12'2" x 18'6"

Master Suite
20'8" x 18'6"

Sitting

Utility

Dining
12'2" x 14'2"

Entry

Vaulted Living
15' x 18'

Covered Porch

Garage
25' x 31'6"

Copyright by designer/architect.

Plan #361231

Dimensions: 77' W x 83' D

Levels: 1

Square Footage: 3,026

Bedrooms: 3

Bathrooms: 3

Foundation: Crawl space

Material List Available: No

Price Category: G

Images provided by designer/architect.

CAD FILE AVAILABLE

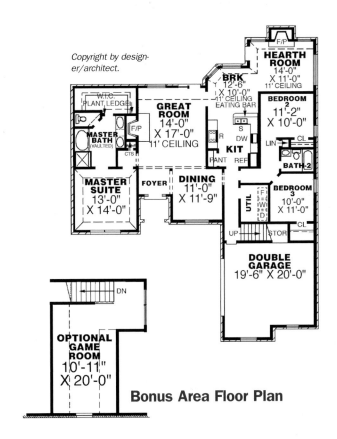

Copyright by design-
er/architect.

HEARTH ROOM 14'-0" X 11'-0" 11' CEILING

BRK 12'-6" X 10'-0" 11' CEILING EATING BAR

BEDROOM 2 11'-2" X 10'-0"

W.T.C. PLANT LEDGE

GREAT ROOM 14'-0" X 17'-0" 11' CEILING

MASTER BATH (VAULTED)

KIT

BATH-2

MASTER SUITE 13'-0" X 14'-0"

FOYER

DINING 11'-0" X 11'-9"

BEDROOM 3 10'-0" X 11'-0"

UTIL

UP

STOR

DOUBLE GARAGE 19'-6" X 20'-0"

DN

OPTIONAL GAME ROOM 10'-11" X 20'-0"

Bonus Area Floor Plan

Plan #241046

Dimensions: 53'4" W x 69'3" D

Levels: 1

Square Footage: 1,919

Bedrooms: 3

Bathrooms: 2

Foundation: Slab

Material List Available: No

Price Category: D

Images provided by designer/architect.

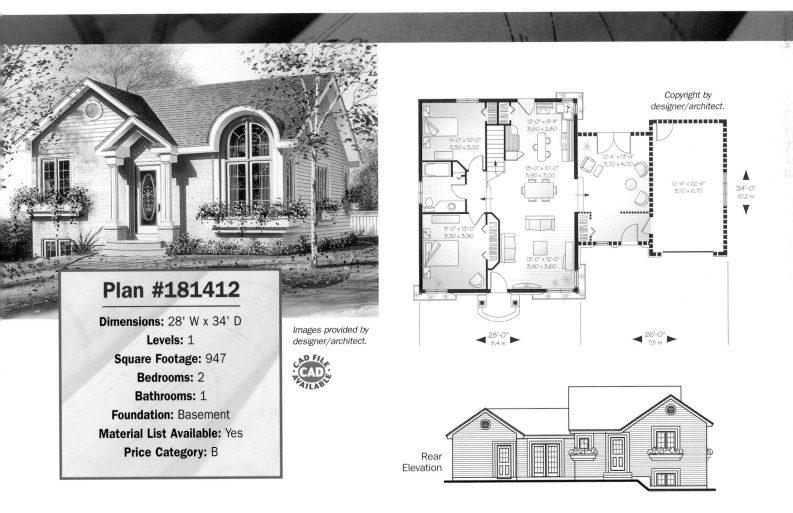

Copyright by designer/architect.

11'-0" x 10'-0" 3.30 x 3.00

12'-0" x 9'-4" 3.60 x 2.80

12'-4" x 13'-4" 3.70 x 4.00

12'-4" x 22'-4" 3.70 x 6.70

13'-0" x 10'-0" 3.90 x 3.00

11'-0" x 13'-0" 3.30 x 3.90

13'-0" x 12'-0" 3.90 x 3.60

34'-0" 10.2 m

28'-0" 8.4 m

26'-0" 7.8 m

Plan #181412

Dimensions: 28' W x 34' D

Levels: 1

Square Footage: 947

Bedrooms: 2

Bathrooms: 1

Foundation: Basement

Material List Available: Yes

Price Category: B

Images provided by designer/architect.

CAD FILE **CAD** AVAILABLE

Rear Elevation

Plan #161096

Dimensions: 67'6" W x 75'6" D
Levels: 2
Square Footage: 3,435
Main Level Sq. Ft.: 2,479
Upper Level Sq. Ft.: 956
Bedrooms: 4
Bathrooms: 3½
Foundation: Walkout basement;
basement for fee
Material List Available: No
Price Category: G

A stone-and-brick exterior is excellently coordinated to create a warm and charming showplace.

Features:

• **Great Room:** The spacious foyer leads directly into this room, which visually opens to the rear yard, providing natural light and outdoor charm.

• **Kitchen:** This fully equipped kitchen is located to provide the utmost convenience in serving the formal dining room and the breakfast area, which is surrounded by windows and has a double-soffit ceiling treatment. The combination of breakfast room, hearth room, and kitchen creatively forms a comfortable family gathering place.

• **Master Suite:** A tray ceiling tops this suite and its luxurious dressing area, which will pamper you after a hard day.

• Balcony: Wood rails decorate the stairs leading to this balcony, which offers a dramatic view of the great room and foyer below.

• Bedrooms: A secondary private bedroom suite with personal bath, plus two bedrooms that share a Jack-and-Jill bathroom, complete the exciting home.

Great Room

Main Level Floor Plan

Deck

Hearth Room
15'11" X 17'3"
Irregular

Breakfast
12'5" X 12'10"
Irregular

Great Room
18'6" X 22'3"

Dressing

WALK-IN CLOSET

Master Bedroom
13'8" X 17'0"
Tray Ceiling

Kitchen
13'6" X 16'11"
Irregular

STAIRS UP

Laun.

Foyer

Hall

Bath

Dining Room
12'4" X 13'10"
Double Soffit Ceiling

Porch

Library
12'4" X 12'3"
Irregular

Garage
21'2" X 33'10"
Irregular

Copyright by designer/architect.

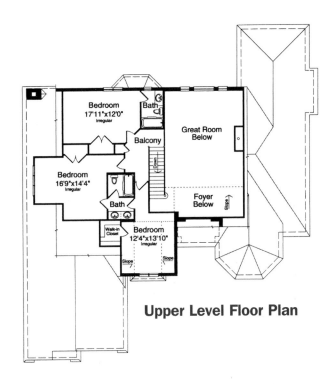

Upper Level Floor Plan

Bedroom
17'11"x12'0"
Irregular

Bath

Great Room Below

Balcony

Bedroom
16'9"x14'4"
Irregular

Down

Bath

Foyer Below

Slope

Walk-in Closet

Bedroom
12'4"x13'10"
Irregular

Slope

Slope

Hearth Room

Front View

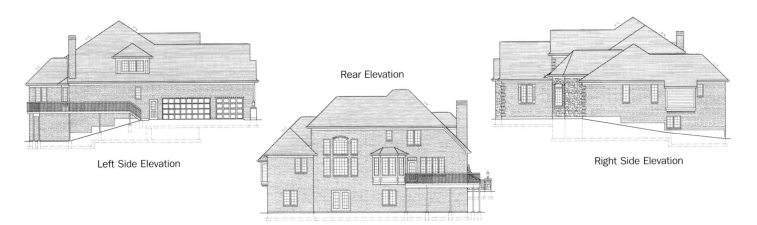

Left Side Elevation

Rear Elevation

Right Side Elevation

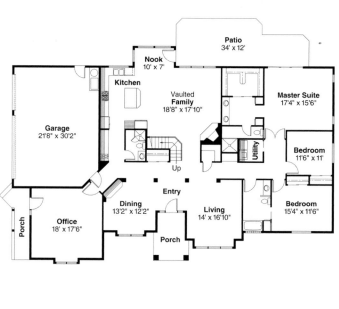

Plan #361096

Dimensions: 82' W x 55' D

Levels: 1

Square Footage: 2,950

Bedrooms: 3

Bathrooms: 3

Foundation: Crawl space

Material List Available: No

Price Category: F

Images provided by designer/architect.

CAD FILE AVAILABLE **CAD**

Bonus Area Floor Plan

Copyright by designer/architect.

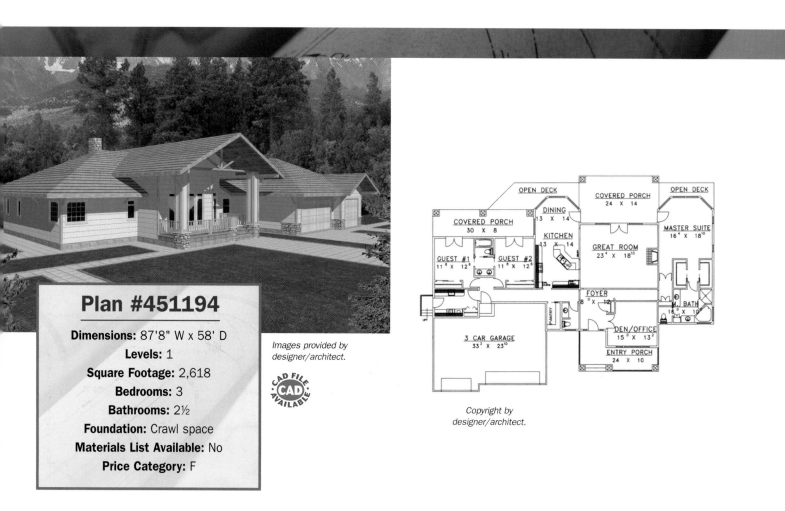

Plan #451194

Dimensions: 87'8" W x 58' D

Levels: 1

Square Footage: 2,618

Bedrooms: 3

Bathrooms: 2½

Foundation: Crawl space

Materials List Available: No

Price Category: F

Images provided by designer/architect.

CAD FILE AVAILABLE **CAD**

Copyright by designer/architect.

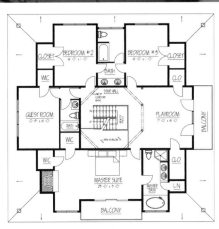

Plan #641007

Dimensions: 50' W x 50' D

Levels: 2

Square Footage: 3,650

Main Level Sq. Ft.: 1,686

Upper Level Sq. Ft.: 1,964

Bedrooms: 4

Bathrooms: 3½

Foundation: Crawl space; slab, basement or walkout for fee

Material List Available: Yes

Price Category: H

Images provided by designer/architect.

CAD FILE AVAILABLE CAD

Main Level
Floor Plan

Copyright by designer/architect.

Plan #661109

Dimensions: 70' W x 58'8" D

Levels: 1

Square Footage: 2,321

Bedrooms: 4

Bathrooms: 3

Foundation: Slab

Material List Available: No

Price Category: E

Images provided by designer/architect.

Copyright by designer/architect.

Plan #151383

Dimensions: 70'4" W x 57'2" D
Levels: 1
Square Footage: 2,534
Bedrooms: 3
Bathrooms: 2
Foundation: Crawl space or slab
CompleteCost List Available: Yes
Price Category: G

The arched entry of the covered porch welcomes you to this magnificent home.

Features:

- Foyer: Welcome your guests in this warm foyer before leading them into the impressive dining room with magnificent columns framing the entry.

- Great Room: After dinner, your guests will enjoy conversation in this spacious room, complete with fireplace and built-ins.

- Study: Beautiful French doors open into this quiet space, where you'll be able to concentrate on that work away from the office.

- Rear Porch: This relaxing spot may be reached from the breakfast room or your secluded master suite.

This home, as shown in the photograph, may differ from the actual blueprints. For more detailed information, please check the floor plans carefully.

Images provided by designer/architect.

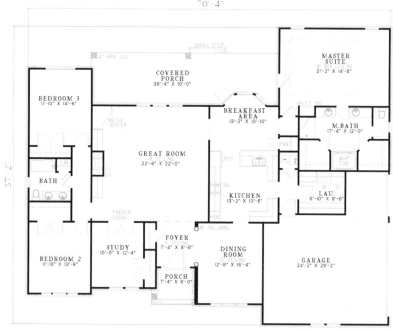

Copyright by designer/architect.

Front View

Plan #121111

Dimensions: 52' W x 45'4" D
Levels: 1.5
Square Footage: 1,685
Main Level Sq. Ft.: 1,297
Upper Level Sq. Ft.: 388
Bedrooms: 3
Bathrooms: 2½
Foundation: Basement;
crawl space for fee
Materials List Available: Yes
Price Category: C

Beauty meets practicality in this charming home. Lovely architectural details and an interior designed with daily living in mind create an ideal environment for the growing family.

This home, as shown in the photograph, may differ from the actual blueprints. For more detailed information, please check the floor plans carefully.

Images provided by designer/architect.

Features:

- Great Room: When the day is done and its time to relax, this is the place where the family will gather. The fireplace is a great start to creating an atmosphere tailored to your family's lifestyle.

- Kitchen: Great for the busy family, the kitchen has all the workspace and storage that the family chef needs, as well as a snack bar that acts as a transition to the large breakfast room.

- Dining Room: A triplet of windows projecting onto the covered front porch creates a warm atmosphere for formal dining.

- Master Bedroom: A romantic space, this master bedroom features a window seat facing the front elevation and a compartmentalized full master bath that includes his and her sinks, a walk-in closet, and a whirlpool tub with a skylight.

- Second Floor: In a quiet space of their own, the two secondary bedrooms both include ample closet space and access to the second full bathroom.

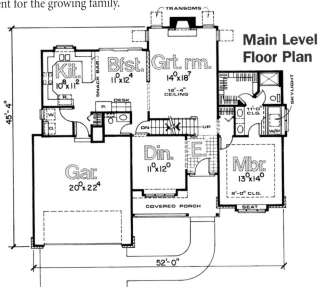

Main Level Floor Plan

Upper Level Floor Plan

Copyright by designer/architect.

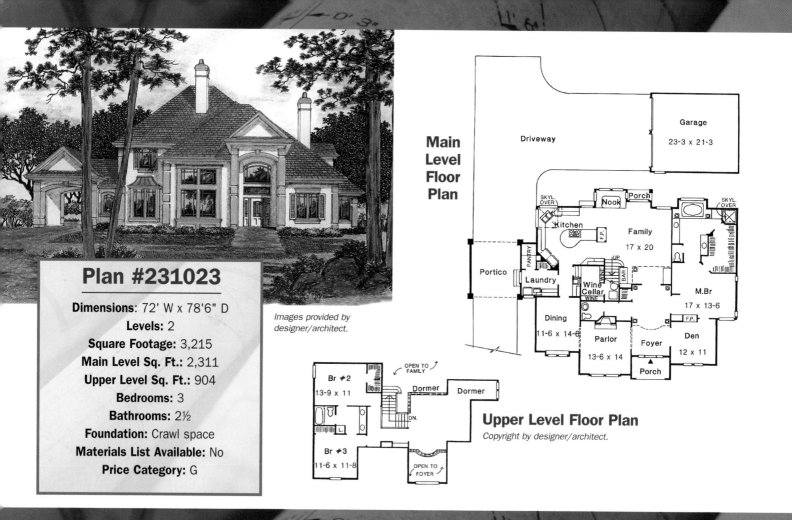

Images provided by
designer/architect.

Plan #231023

Dimensions: 72' W x 78'6" D

Levels: 2

Square Footage: 3,215

Main Level Sq. Ft.: 2,311

Upper Level Sq. Ft.: 904

Bedrooms: 3

Bathrooms: 2½

Foundation: Crawl space

Materials List Available: No

Price Category: G

Main Level Floor Plan

Garage
23-3 x 21-3

Driveway

SKYL. OVER

Nook   Porch

Kitchen

Family
17 x 20

SKYL. OVER

Portico

PANTRY

F.P.

M.Br
17 x 13-6

Laundry

Wine Cellar
WINE

UP
BAR

Dining
11-6 x 14-6

Parlor
13-6 x 14

Foyer

Den
12 x 11

F.P.

Porch

Upper Level Floor Plan

OPEN TO FAMILY

Br #2
13-9 x 11

Dormer   Dormer

DN.

L.

Br #3
11-6 x 11-8

OPEN TO FOYER

Copyright by designer/architect.

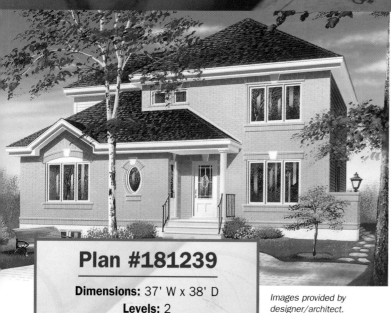

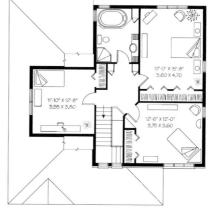

Upper Level Floor Plan

12'-0" X 15'-8"
3.60 X 4.70

11'-10" X 12'-8"
3.55 X 3.80

12'-6" X 12'-0"
3.75 X 3.60

Plan #181239

Dimensions: 37' W x 38' D

Levels: 2

Square Footage: 2,181

Main Level Sq. Ft.: 1,307

Upper Level Sq. Ft.: 874

Bedrooms: 4

Bathrooms: 2½

Foundation: Basement

Materials List Available: Yes

Price Category: F

Images provided by
designer/architect.

CAD FILE AVAILABLE

11'-11" X 12'-0"
3.58 X 3.60

13'-4" X 10'-6"
4.00 X 3.15

14'-3" X 13'-0"
4.28 X 3.90

12'-0" X 8'-10"
3.60 X 2.68

14'-3" X 11'-0"
4.28 X 3.30

5'-4" X 11'-0"
4.60 X 3.30

Main Level Floor Plan

Copyright by
designer/architect.

Plan #151240

Dimensions: 67' W x 59'2" D

Levels: 1

Square Footage: 2,007

Bedrooms: 4

Bathrooms: 2

Foundation: Crawl space or slab

CompleteCost List Available: Yes

Price Category: E

Images provided by designer/architect.

Copyright by designer/architect.

Plan #451259

Dimensions: 75'2" W x 55'6" D

Levels: 2

Square Footage: 3,798

Main Level Sq. Ft.: 2,485

Upper Level Sq. Ft.: 1,313

Bedrooms: 6

Bathrooms: 6½

Foundation: Walk-out basement

Materials List Available: No

Price Category: H

Images provided by designer/architect.

Copyright by designer/architect.

Main Level Floor Plan

Upper Level Floor Plan

Basement Level Floor Plan

Plan #271019

Dimensions: 40'4" W x 41'8" D

Levels: 2

Square Footage: 1,556

Main Level Sq. Ft.: 834

Upper Level Sq. Ft.: 722

Bedrooms: 3

Bathrooms: 2½

Foundation: Basement

Materials List Available: Yes

Price Category: C

This traditional home features a combination of stone and wood, lending it a distinctive old-world flavor.

Features:

- Kitchen: The centerpiece of the home, this country kitchen features ample work surfaces, a nice-sized eating area with built-in bookshelves, and access to a large backyard deck.

- Dining Room: This formal eating space is highlighted by a dramatic three-sided fireplace that is shared with the adjoining living room.

- Living Room: Enhanced by a dramatic vaulted ceiling, this living room also boasts corner windows that flood the area with natural light.

- Master Suite: Residing on the upper floor along with two other bedrooms, the master bedroom features a vaulted ceiling and a plant shelf that tops the entry to a private bath and walk-in closet.

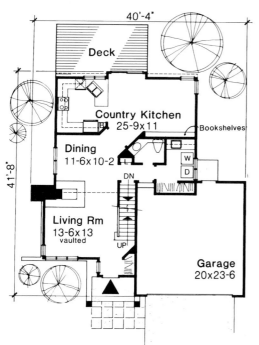

Main Level Floor Plan

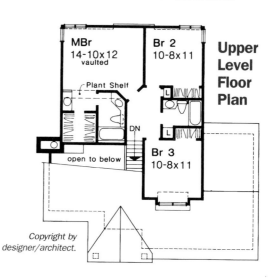

Upper Level Floor Plan

Copyright by designer/architect.

Plan #151711

Dimensions: 64' W x 60'2" D
Levels: 1
Square Footage: 2,554
Bedrooms: 4
Bathrooms: 2½
Foundation: Crawl space or slab
CompleteCost List Available: Yes
Price Category: E

Images provided by designer/architect.

An alluring arched entry welcomes guests into your home, giving them a taste of the lavishness they'll find once inside.

CAD FILE AVAILABLE

Features:

- **Kitchen:** Counter space on all sides and a center island provide ample space for the budding chef. This kitchen is located across the hall from the dining room and opens into the hearth room, providing easy transitions between preparing and serving. A snack bar acts as a shift between the kitchen and hearth room.

- **Hearth Room:** This spacious area is lined with windows on one side, shares a gas fire place with the great room, and opens onto the grilling porch, which makes it ideal for gatherings of all kinds and sizes.

- **Master Suite:** Larger than any space in the house, this room will truly make you feel like the master. The bedroom is a blank canvas waiting for your personal touch and has a door opening to the backyard. The compartmentalized master bath includes his and her walk-in closets and sinks, a glass shower stall, and a whirlpool bathtub.

- **Secondary Bedrooms:** If three bedrooms is one too many, the second bedroom can easily be used as a study with optional French doors opening from the foyer. Every additional bedroom has a large closet and access to the central full bathroom.

Front View

This home, as shown in the photograph, may differ from the actual blueprints. For more detailed information, please check the floor plans carefully.

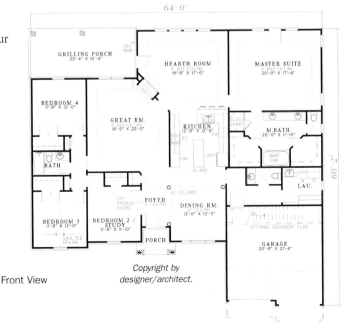

Copyright by designer/architect.

Plan #391036

Dimensions: 28' W x 32' D
Levels: 2
Square Footage: 1,710
Main Level Sq. Ft.: 728
Upper Level Sq. Ft.: 573
Lower Level Sq. Ft.: 409
Bedrooms: 3
Bathrooms: 2
Foundation: Basement
Materials List Available: Yes
Price Category: C

This home is a vacation haven, with views from every room, whether it is situated on a lake or a mountaintop.

Features:

• Main Floor: A fireplace splits the living and dining rooms in this area.

• Kitchen: This kitchen flows into the dining room and is gracefullly separated by a bar.

• Master Suite: A large walk-in closet, full bathroom, and deck make this private area special.

• Bedroom or Loft: The second floor has this bedroom or library loft, with clerestory windows, which opens above the living room.

• Lower Level: This lower floor has a large recreation room with a whirlpool tub, bar, laundry room, and garage.

Images provided by designer/architect.

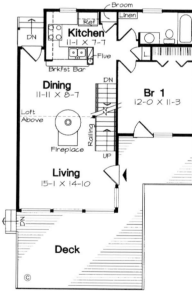
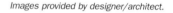

**Main Level
Floor Plan**

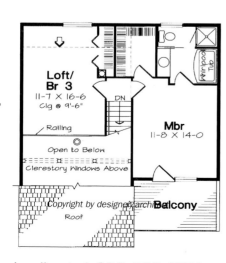

**Upper
Level
Floor
Plan**

**Lower
Level
Floor Plan**

order direct: 1-800-523-6789

Plan #271015

Dimensions: 48' W x 28' D
Levels: 2
Square Footage: 1,359
Main Level Sq. Ft.: 668
Upper Level Sq. Ft.: 691
Bedrooms: 3
Bathrooms: 2½
Foundation: Basement
Materials List Available: Yes
Price Category: B

Images provided by designer/architect.

Strong vertical lines and pairs of narrow windows give this compact home an airy feel. Its clever floor plan makes good use of every square foot of space.

Features:

• Living Room: Beyond the sidelighted front door, the living room enjoys a vaulted ceiling and a flood of light from a striking corner window arrangement.

• Kitchen/Dining: A central fireplace separates the living room from this kitchen/dining room, where a French door opens to a rear deck.

• Master Suite: Sacrifice no luxuries in this sweet, upper-floor retreat, where a boxed-out window catches morning rays or evening stars. Next to the roomy walk-in closet, the private split bath enjoys a window of its own.

• Secondary Bedrooms: A balcony overlooks the living room and leads to one bedroom and the flexible loft.

Main Level Floor Plan

Upper Level Floor Plan

Copyright by designer/architect.

Plan #151203

Dimensions: 46' W x 38'10" D

Levels: 1

Square Footage: 1,214

Bedrooms: 3

Bathrooms: 2

Foundation: Crawl space, slab; basement or walkout basement option for fee

CompleteCost List Available: Yes

Price Category: B

Images provided by designer/architect.

46'-0"

38'-10"

PATIO
8'-0" X 8'-0"

BEDROOM 3
11'-10" X 11'-8"

BEDROOM 2
10'-0" X 9'-0"

MASTER SUITE
13'-0" X 12'-6"

SITTING ROOM
7'-0" X 8'-0"

LAU.
6'-0" X 2'-10"

BATH
8'-2" X 5'-4"

M. BATH
8'-4" X 5'-4"

STORAGE
6'-8" X 4'-0"

GREAT ROOM
14'-4" X 17'-6"

KITCHEN
9'-10" X 8'-5"

GARAGE
20'-10" X 19'-8"

BREAKFAST ROOM
9'-6" X 9'-0"

COVERED PORCH
14'-8" X 4'-0"

VAULTED

Copyright by designer/architect.

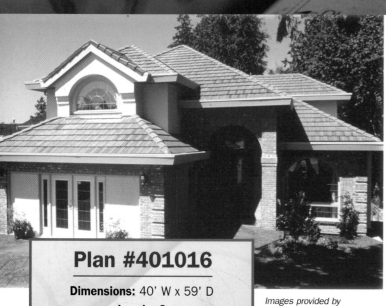

Plan #401016

Dimensions: 40' W x 59' D

Levels: 2

Square Footage: 2,539

Bedrooms: 4

Bathrooms: 3

Foundation: Basement

Material List Available: Yes

Price Category: E

Images provided by designer/architect.

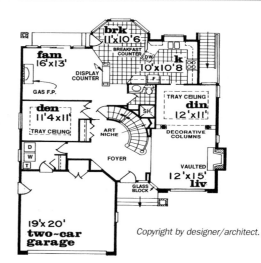

brk
11'x10'6

fam
16'x13'

BREAKFAST COUNTER

k
10'x10'8

GAS F.P.

DISPLAY COUNTER

den
11'4"x11'

TRAY CEILING

din
12'x11'

TRAY CEILING

SH.

ART NICHE

DECORATIVE COLUMNS

FOYER

VAULTED
12'x15'
liv

GLASS BLOCK

19'x20'
two~car garage

Main Level Floor Plan

Copyright by designer/architect.

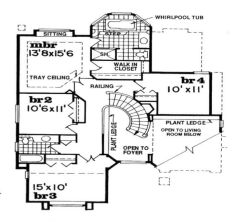

WHIRLPOOL TUB

SITTING

STEP

mbr
13'8x15'6

SH.

WALK IN CLOSET

TRAY CEILING

RAILING

br 4
10'x11'

br2
10'6x21'

PLANT LEDGE

PLANT LEDGE
OPEN TO LIVING ROOM BELOW

OPEN TO FOYER

15'x10'
br3

Upper Level Floor Plan

Copyright by designer/architect.

Main Level Floor Plan

Copyright by designer/architect.

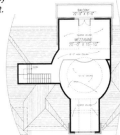

Images provided by designer/architect.

Plan #571036

Dimensions: 87'6" W x 51'3" D

Levels: 2

Square Footage: 6,175

Main Level Sq. Ft.: 2,628

Upper Level Sq. Ft.: 3,024

Bonus Area Sq. Ft.: 523

Bedrooms: 4

Bathrooms: 2½

Foundation: Basement

Material List Available: Yes

Price Category: K

Bonus Area Floor Plan

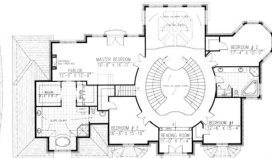

Upper Level Floor Plan

Plan #391168

Dimensions: 93'6" W x 48' D

Levels: 1

Square Footage: 2,352

Main Level Sq. Ft.: 2,352

Bedrooms: 3

Bathrooms: 2½

Foundation: Basement

CompleteCost List Available: No

Price Category: E

Images provided by designer/ architect.

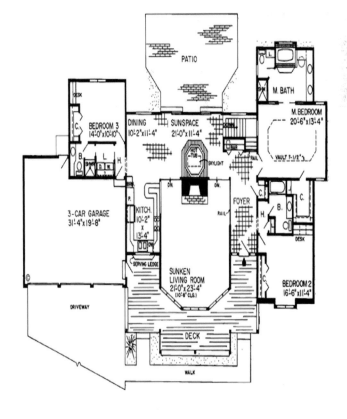

Plan #661191

Dimensions: 58'8" W x 68' D
Levels: 2
Square Footage: 2,998
Main Level Sq. Ft.: 2,227
Upper Level Sq. Ft.: 771
Bedrooms: 4
Bathrooms: 4
Foundation: Slab
Material List Available: No
Price Category: F

A soaring, two-story ceiling and dramatic staircase help create the "wow factor" in the grand entryway of this home.

This home, as shown in the photograph, may differ from the actual blueprints. For more detailed information, please check the floor plans carefully.

Images provided by designer/architect.

Features:

- **Family Room:** This open, airy space is wonderful for entertaining guests or enjoying a movie with the family. Close proximity to the kitchen makes getting a quick snack even easier.

- **Kitchen:** This gourmet kitchen offers easy access to everything the family cook requires. A large pantry and plentiful counter space are just two of the special amenities.

- **Rear Patio:** This versatile covered patio at the back of the house is great for entertaining guests or watching the kids play in the back-yard. It is conveniently accessed through the family room and kitchen, creating a wonderful flow during large get-togethers.

- **Master Suite:** You'll love to escape to this luxurious master suite, made complete with his and her sinks, walk-in closet, and large tub.

Main Level Floor Plan

Copyright by designer/architect.

Upper Level Floor Plan

Plan #131054

Dimensions: 107'4" W x 75'3" D
Levels: 1
Square Footage: 2,753
Bedrooms: 3
Full Bathrooms: 2 1/2
Foundation: Crawl space, slab, basement or walk-out
Materials List Available: Yes
Price Category: G

Images provided by designer/architect.

This beautifully designed interior area combined with plenty of outdoor living space create a striking and efficient home.

Features:

• Outdoor Living: Sit on the front porch and watch the world go by, enjoy a peaceful moment on the screened-in porch, or entertain on the wooden deck. If you enjoy the outdoors, this home is for you.

• Great Room: A vaulted ceiling, built-in fireplace, and flanking windows create a bright and comfortable space for entertaining or simply hanging out with the family.

• Kitchen: With plenty of workspace and storage, this kitchen suits all cooking styles. An exit onto the back deck and screened-in porch provide outdoor meal options for any kind of weather.

• Master Suite: Down a hallway of its own, this oasis inspires total relaxation. It features two walk-in closets, a desk, his and her vanities, extra large tub, and separate stall shower.

Main Level Floor Plan

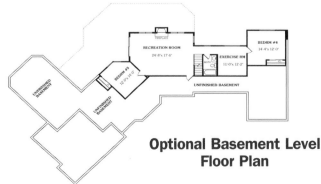

Optional Basement Level Floor Plan

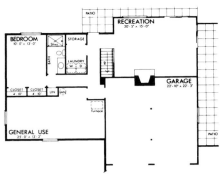

Copyright by designer/architect.

Plan #271084

Dimensions: 51'9" W x 38'9" D
Levels: 1
Square Footage: 1,602
Bedrooms: 3
Bathrooms: 1½
Foundation: Daylight
Materials List Available: Yes
Price Category: C

Images provided by designer/architect.

Optional Basement Level Floor Plan

Upper Level Floor Plan

Main Level Floor Plan

Copyright by designer/architect.

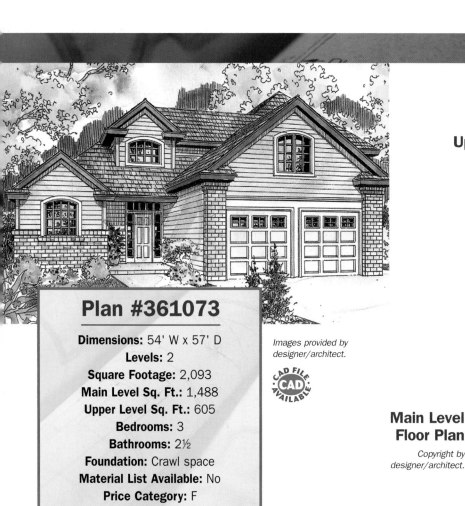

Plan #361073

Dimensions: 54' W x 57' D
Levels: 2
Square Footage: 2,093
Main Level Sq. Ft.: 1,488
Upper Level Sq. Ft.: 605
Bedrooms: 3
Bathrooms: 2½
Foundation: Crawl space
Material List Available: No
Price Category: F

Images provided by designer/architect.

CAD FILE AVAILABLE

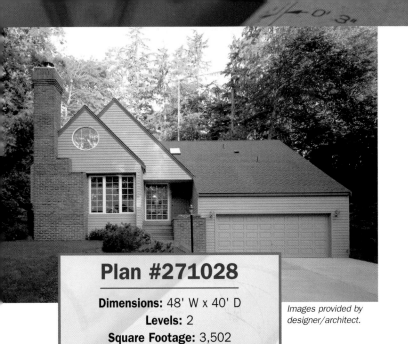

Plan #271028

Dimensions: 48' W x 40' D

Levels: 2

Square Footage: 3,502

Main Level Sq. Ft.: 1,168

Upper Level Sq. Ft.: 1,167

Lower Level Sq. Ft.: 1,167

Bedrooms: 3

Bathrooms: 3

Foundation: Basement, crawl space

Materials List Available: Yes

Price Category: E

Images provided by designer/architect.

Main Level Floor Plan

Upper Level Floor Plan

Copyright by designer/architect.

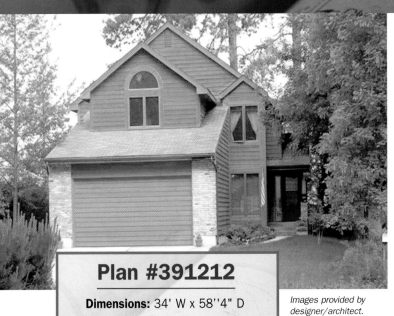

Plan #391212

Dimensions: 34' W x 58''4" D

Levels: 2

Square Footage: 1,701

Upper Level Sq. Ft. 928

Lower Level Sq. Ft.: 773

Bedrooms: 3

Bathrooms: 2 1/2

Foundation: Basement

Materials List Available: Yes

Price Category: B

Images provided by designer/architect.

CAD FILE AVAILABLE

Upper Level Floor Plan

Copyright by designer/architect.

Main Level Floor Plan

Plan #271011

Dimensions: 36' W x 40'8" D

Levels: 2

Square Footage: 1,296

Main Level Sq. Ft.: 891

Upper Level Sq. Ft.: 405

Bedrooms: 3

Bathrooms: 2

Foundation: Basement

Materials List Available: Yes

Price Category: B

Images provided by designer/architect.

Perfectly sized for a narrow lot, this charming modern cottage boasts space efficiency and affordability.

Features:

• Living Room: The inviting raised foyer steps down into this vaulted living room, with its bright windows and eye-catching fireplace.

• Dining Room: This vaulted formal eating space includes sliding-glass-door access to a backyard deck.

• Kitchen: Everything is here: U-shaped efficiency, handy pantry—even bright windows.

• Master Suite: Main-floor location ensures accessibility in later years, plus there's a walk-in closet and full bathroom.

• Secondary Bedrooms: On the upper floor, a bedroom and a loft reside near a full bath. The loft can be converted easily to a third bedroom, or use it as a study or play space.

Main Level Floor Plan

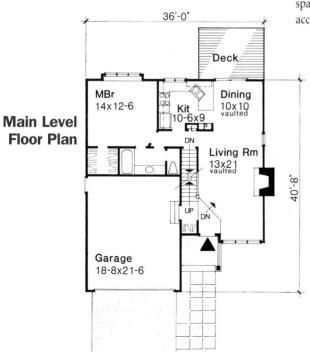

Upper Level Floor Plan

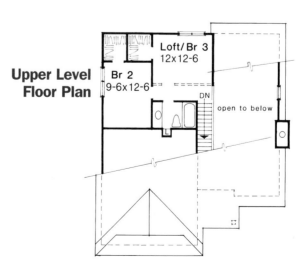

Plan #131067

Dimensions: 60'8" W x 29'4" D
Levels: 2
Square Footage: 1,909
Main Level Sq. Ft.: 1,159
Upper Level Sq. Ft.: 750
Bedrooms: 3
Bathrooms: 2½
Foundation: Crawl Space, Slab, or basement
Materials List Available: Yes
Price Category: E

Images provided by designer/architect.

This dramatic contemporary home features large dormers and windows.

Features:

• Foyer: This cathedral-ceiling entry welcomes you into this home. The open and airy feeling of the space makes you feel comfortable.

• Family Room: This sunken room is the comfortable space in which you and your family can relax after a busy day. The sliding glass doors lead out to the rear patio.

• Kitchen: This U-shaped kitchen is open to the adjacent breakfast area and only a few steps to the washer and dryer.

• Master Suite: Located on the upper level with two secondary bedrooms, this retreat offers two large closets. The master bath is an added plus.

Main Level Floor Plan

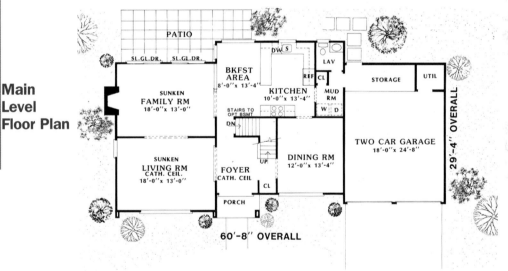

Upper Level Floor Plan

Copyright by designer/architect.

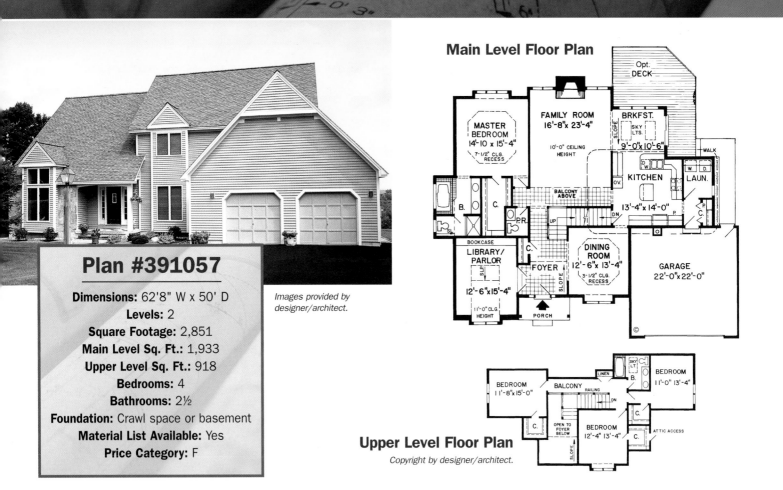

Main Level Floor Plan

MASTER BEDROOM
14'-10 x 15'-4"
7-1/2" CLG. RECESS

FAMILY ROOM
16'-8"x 23'-4"
10'-0" CEILING HEIGHT

Opt. DECK

BRKFST.
SKY LTS.
9'-0"x10'-6"

WALK

B.

C.

D.W
OV.

KITCHEN
13'-4" x 14'-0"

LAUN.

W. D.

BALCONY ABOVE

PR.

UP

DN

P

P

C.

LIBRARY/ PARLOR
12'-6"x15'-4"
11'-0" CLG. HEIGHT

BOOKCASE

C.

FOYER

DINING ROOM
12'-6"x 13'-4"
3-1/2" CLG. RECESS

GARAGE
22'-0"x 22'-0"

SLOPE

PORCH

Upper Level Floor Plan

Copyright by designer/architect.

BEDROOM
11'-8"x 15'-0"

BALCONY
RAILING

LINEN

SKY LT

B.

BEDROOM
11'-0" 13'-4"

C.

C.

C.

OPEN TO FOYER BELOW

BEDROOM
12'-4" 13'-4"

ATTIC ACCESS

SLOPE

Plan #391057

Dimensions: 62'8" W x 50' D

Levels: 2

Square Footage: 2,851

Main Level Sq. Ft.: 1,933

Upper Level Sq. Ft.: 918

Bedrooms: 4

Bathrooms: 2½

Foundation: Crawl space or basement

Material List Available: Yes

Price Category: F

Images provided by designer/architect.

OWNER'S SUITE
14' X 16'

SCREEN PORCH
15' X 14'

BATH

CLOSET

GREAT RM.
21' X 19'

DINING
14' X 12'

KITCHEN
14' X 13'

GARAGE
30' X 28'

Main Level Floor Plan

STUDY
14' X 9'

ENTRY

LAUN.

PORCH

Plan #271078

Dimensions: 83' W x 52' D

Levels: 1

Square Footage: 3,620

Main Level Sq. Ft.: 1,855

Lower Level Sq. Ft.: 1,765

Bedrooms: 2

Bathrooms: 2½

Foundation: Walk-out

Materials List Available: No

Price Category: H

Images provided by designer/architect.

CAD FILE AVAILABLE

BED RM
14' X 16'

BA.

EXERCISE ROOM
9' X 11'

LIVING ROOM
21' X 19'

SHOP
13' X 21'

MECHANICAL
18' X 9'

STORAGE
13' X 8'

STORAGE
13' X 13'

Lower Level Floor Plan

Copyright by designer/architect.

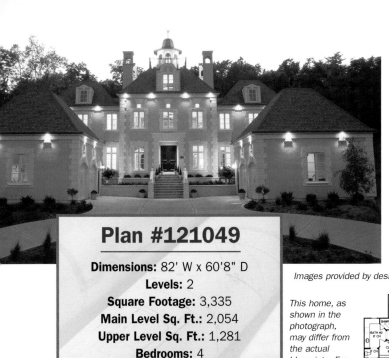

Plan #121049

Dimensions: 82' W x 60'8" D
Levels: 2
Square Footage: 3,335
Main Level Sq. Ft.: 2,054
Upper Level Sq. Ft.: 1,281
Bedrooms: 4
Bathrooms: 3½
Foundation: Slab; basement for fee
Materials List Available: Yes
Price Category: G

**Main Level
Floor Plan**

Images provided by designer/architect.

This home, as shown in the photograph, may differ from the actual blueprints. For more detailed information, please check the floor plans carefully.

**Upper Level
Floor Plan**

**Third Floor Bedroom
Floor Plan**

Copyright by designer/ architect.

Plan #151121

Dimensions: 66'8" W x 60'4" D
Levels: 2
Square Footage: 3,108
Main Level Sq. Ft.: 2,107
Upper Level Sq. Ft.: 1,001
Bedrooms: 3
Bathrooms: 2½
Foundation: Crawl space, slab; basement option for fee
CompleteCost List Available: Yes
Price Category: G

Images provided by designer/architect.

This home, as shown in the photograph, may differ from the actual blueprints. For more detailed information, please check the floor plans carefully.

**Upper Level
Floor Plan**

**Main Level
Floor Plan**

Copyright by designer/ architect.

Plan #151020

Dimensions: 96'10" W x 75'10" D
Levels: 2
Square Footage: 4,532
Main Level Sq. Ft.: 3,732
Upper Level Sq. Ft.: 800
Bedrooms: 3
Bathrooms: 3½
Foundation: Crawl space or slab;
basement available for fee
CompleteCost List Available: Yes
Price Category: I

From the arched entry to the lanai and exercise and game rooms, this elegant home is a delight.

CAD FILE AVAILABLE **CAD**

Images provided by designer/architect.

Features:

- Foyer: This spacious foyer with 12-ft. ceilings sets an open-air feeling for this home.

- Hearth Room: This cozy hearth room shares a 3-sided fireplace with the breakfast room. French doors open to the rear lanai.

- Dining Room: Entertain in this majestic dining room, with its arched entry and 12-ft. ceilings.

- Master Suite: This stunning suite includes a sitting room and access to the lanai. The bath

features two walk-in closets, a step-up whirlpool tub with 8-in. columns, and glass-block shower.

- Upper Level: You'll find an exercise room, a game room, and attic storage space upstairs.

Rear View

Main Level Floor Plan

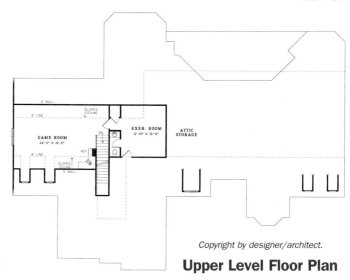

Copyright by designer/architect.

Upper Level Floor Plan

Plan #271002

Dimensions: 44'8" W x 50'8" D
Levels: 1
Square Footage: 1,252
Bedrooms: 3
Bathrooms: 2
Foundation: Basement
Materials List Available: Yes
Price Category: B

This traditional home combines a modest square footage with stylish extras.

Features:

• Living Room: Spacious and inviting, this gathering spot is brightened by a Palladian window arrangement, warmed by a fireplace, and topped by a vaulted ceiling.

• Dining Room: The vaulted ceiling also crowns this room, which shares the living room's fireplace. Sliding doors lead to a backyard deck.

• Kitchen: Smart design ensures a place for everything.

• Master Suite: The master bedroom boasts a vaulted ceiling, cheery windows, and a private bath.

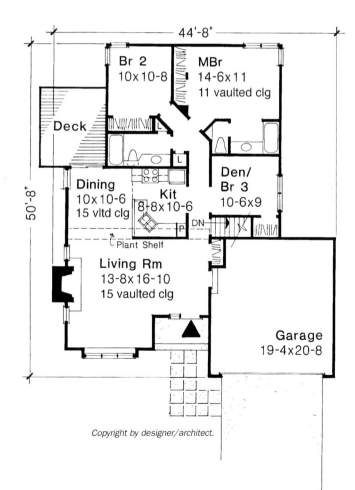

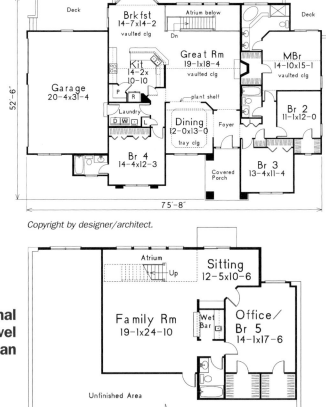

Copyright by designer/architect.

Images provided by designer/architect.

Plan #321034

Dimensions: 75'8" W x 52'6" D
Levels: 1
Square Footage: 3,508
Bedrooms: 4
Bathrooms: 3
Foundation: Basement, walkout
Material List Available: Yes
Price Category: H

Optional Basement Level Floor Plan

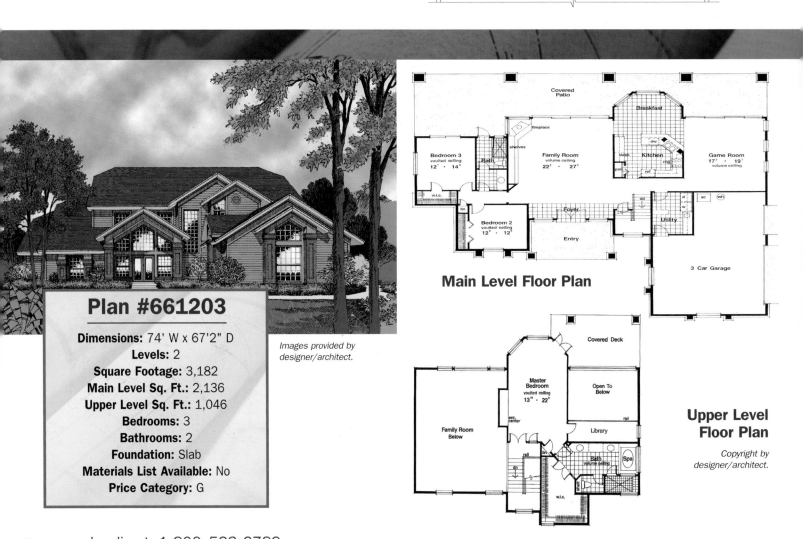

Plan #661203

Dimensions: 74' W x 67'2" D
Levels: 2
Square Footage: 3,182
Main Level Sq. Ft.: 2,136
Upper Level Sq. Ft.: 1,046
Bedrooms: 3
Bathrooms: 2
Foundation: Slab
Materials List Available: No
Price Category: G

Images provided by designer/architect.

Main Level Floor Plan

Upper Level Floor Plan

Copyright by designer/architect.

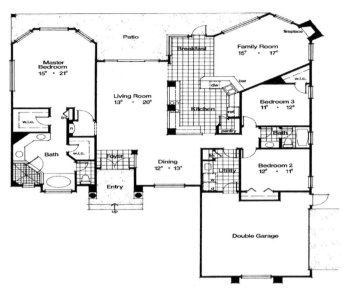

Images provided by designer/architect.

Plan #661102

Dimensions: 58' W x 71'8" D

Levels: 1

Square Footage: 2,278

Bedrooms: 3

Bathrooms: 2

Foundation: Slab

Materials List Available: No

Price Category: E

Copyright by designer/architect.

Images provided by designer/architect.

Plan #271042

Dimensions: 69'8" W x 71'4" D

Levels: 2

Square Footage: 3,469

Main Level Sq. Ft.: 2,132

Upper Level Sq. Ft.: 1,337

Bedrooms: 5

Bathrooms: 3½

Foundation: Basement

Materials List Available: No

Price Category: G

Upper Level Floor Plan

Main Level Floor Plan

Copyright by designer/architect.

Plan #121117

Dimensions: 76' W x 46' D
Levels: 1
Square Footage: 2,172
Bedrooms: 4
Bathrooms: 3
Foundation: Basement;
Crawl space for fee
Materials List Available: Yes
Price Category: D

Images provided by designer/architect.

Tall ceilings and an efficient design complement this home's stately exterior.

Features:

• Great Room: Whether welcoming guests in for an elegant evening or just spending time with the family, this great room provides plenty of space and is warmed by a built-in fireplace.

• Kitchen: This unique design includes a walk-in pantry, desk, and large square island, the kitchen drinks in the sunlight from the adjacent breakfast room, which provides a simple transition from meal preparation to dining.

• Master Suite: With windows flanking one wall of the bedroom and a skylight in the bathroom, natural light romanticizes this space, Other features include a large walk-in closet, a whirlpool tub with a view, and a separate stall shower.

• Secondary Bedrooms: Two equally sized bedrooms each have access to their own semi-private full bathrooms. A living area by the entry can serve as a third bedroom for a growing family or a guest bedroom for the occasional visitor.

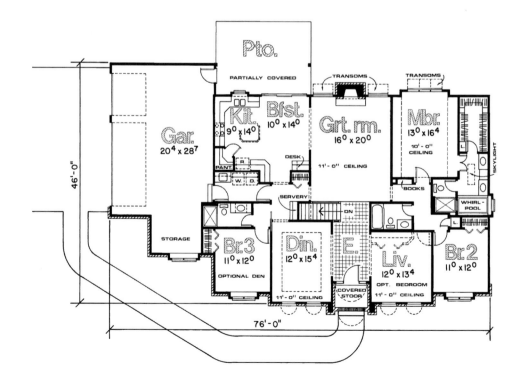

Plan #391030

Dimensions: 60' W x 82'6" D
Levels: 1
Square Footage: 3,903
Main Level Sq. Ft.: 2,376
Lower Level Sq. Ft.: 1,241
Bedrooms: 4
Bathrooms: 3
Foundation: Basement
Materials List Available: Yes
Price Category: H

This home as shown in the photograph, may differ from the actual blueprints. For more detailed infloration, please check the floor plans carefully.

Images provided by designer/architect.

All decked out with rich wood decking that sweeps around the family room to the dining and kitchen areas as well as to the main-floor family room, this home has the feel of living in harmony with nature.

Features:

• Dining Room: A greenhouse window adds exotic flair to this formal dining room.

• Master Suite: This master suite is lavish with amenities--skylight over the tub, double vanitysinks, separate shower, two walk-in closets, and a dressing room.

• Bedroom: Teenagers an appreciate the seond bedroom with built-in cabinet and private bath. Plus, its ideally situated near the kitchen for late night snacking, close to the laundry room for quick wardrobe freshening, and its only a quick jog to the garage.

• Dramatic Features: The house is outfitted with a massive family-room fireplace, built-in shelves, and a soaring loft with study.

Main Level Floor Plan

Lower Level Floor Plan

Copyright by designer/architect.

Plan #181063

Dimensions: 55' W x 41' D
Levels: 2
Square Footage: 2,037
Main Level Sq. Ft.: 1,347
Upper Level Sq. Ft.: 690
Bedrooms: 4
Bathrooms: 2
Foundation: Full basement
Materials List Available: Yes
Price Category: F

Quaint brick and stone, plus deeply pitched rooflines, create the storybook aura folks fall for when they see this home, but it's the serenely versatile interior layout that captures their hearts.

CAD FILE AVAILABLE

Features:

- Family Room: The floor plan is configured to bring a panoramic view to nearly every room,

beginning with this room, with its fireplace and towering cathedral ceiling.

- Kitchen: This kitchen, with its crowd-pleasing island, has an eye on the outdoors. It also has all the counter and storage space a cook would want, plus a lunch counter with comfy seats and multiple windows to bring in the breeze.

- Bedrooms: Downstairs, you'll find the master bedroom, with its adjoining master bath. Upstairs, three uniquely shaped bedrooms, styled with clever nooks and windows to dream by, easily share a large bathroom.

- Mezzanine: This sweeping mezzanine overlooks the open living and dining rooms.

Front View

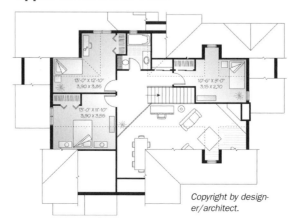

Upper Level Floor Plan

Main Level Floor Plan

Copyright by designer/architect.

Living Room

Master Bath

Plan #271005

Dimensions: 48'4" W x 48'4" D
Levels: 1
Square Footage: 1,368
Bedrooms: 3
Bathrooms: 2
Foundation: Basement
Materials List Available: Yes
Price Category: B

Images provided by designer/architect.

This traditional home boasts an open floor plan that is further expanded by soaring vaulted ceilings.

Features:

- Great Room: Front and center, this large multipurpose room features a gorgeous corner fireplace, an eye-catching boxed out window, and dedicated space for casual dining—all beneath a vaulted ceiling.

- Kitchen: A vaulted ceiling crowns this galley kitchen and its adjoining breakfast nook.

- Master Suite: This spacious master bedroom, brightened by a boxed-out window, features a vaulted ceiling in the sleeping chamber and the private bath.

Copyright by designer/architect.

SMARTtip

Design with Computers

Consider using a computer-aided design (CAD) program to plan your deck. Some programs let you see three-dimensional views of your design complete with railings, stairs, planters, hot tubs, and the surrounding landscaping.

Plan #281030

Dimensions: 50' W x 48'6" D

Levels: 2

Square Footage: 2,517

Main Level Sq. Ft.: 1,384

Upper Level Sq. Ft.: 1,133

Bedrooms: 4

Bathrooms: 3

Foundation: Basement

Materials List Available: Yes

Price Category: E

A tall covered entry welcomes you home.

Images provided by designer/architect.

Features:

- Entry: This spacious entry, accented by a regal curved stairway and a full two-story-high ceiling, sets the theme for this unique home.

- Living Room: This formal gathering area is just off of the foyer and is open into the formal dining room. The gas fireplace will add an elegant feel.

- Family Room: This large casual gathering area is open to the kitchen and the breakfast nook.

French doors open to the rear covered patio.

- Master Suite: Located on the upper level, this retreat features a private sitting area. The master bath boasts dual vanities, a whirlpool tub, and a stand-up shower.

- Garage: This side-loading two-car garage gives the front of the home a nice, clean look.

Main Level Floor Plan

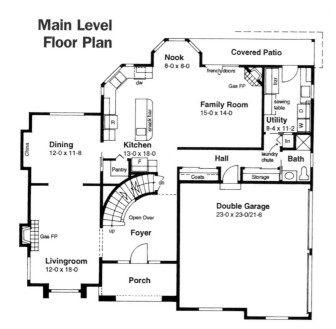

Upper Level Floor Plan

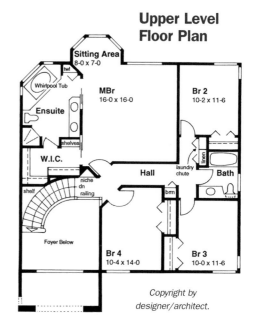

Copyright by designer/architect.

Plan #181329

Dimensions: 30' W x 45' D

Levels: 1

Square Footage: 1,116

Bedrooms: 2

Bathrooms: 1

Foundation: Basement

Materials List Available: Yes

Price Category: C

Round-top window and a large front porch make this home bright and airy.

Features:

- **Foyer:** This sunken entry, complete with a coat closet, introduces you to the wonderful home. Up two steps, and you are in the dining room.

- **Living Room:** Open to the dining room and the kitchen, this gathering area has plenty of room for friends and family. The large triple window will flood the area with natural light.

- **Kitchen:** A large open kitchen, complete with an island, is just what the family chef ordered. Sliding glass doors open to the front porch.

- **Bedrooms:** Two bedrooms share a the full bathroom and complete this floor plan. The larger bedroom has two closets.

Images provided by designer/architect.

Rear Elevation

11'-0" X 13'-0"
3,30 X 3,90

9'-0" X 13'-0"
2,70 X 3,90

45'-0"
13,5 m

12'-0" X 11'-0"
3,60 X 3,30

9'-0" X 13'-0"
2,70 X 3,90

13'-8" X 14'-0"
4,10 X 4,20

Copyright by designer/architect.

30'-0"
9,0 m

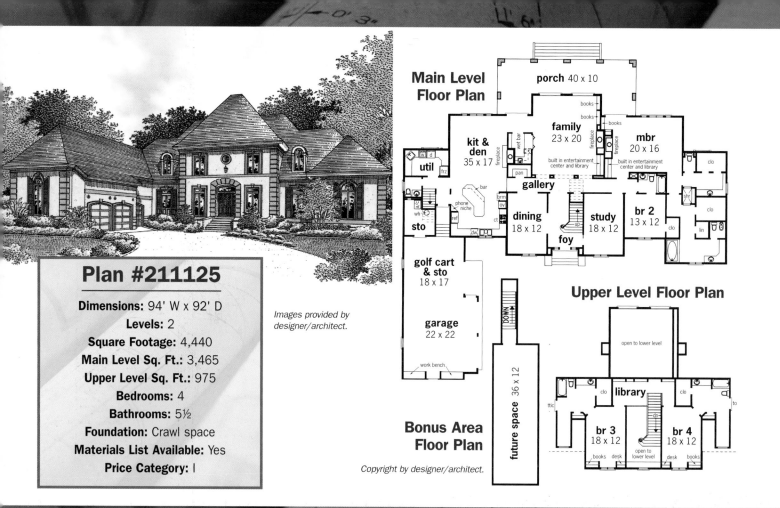

Plan #211125

Dimensions: 94' W x 92' D

Levels: 2

Square Footage: 4,440

Main Level Sq. Ft.: 3,465

Upper Level Sq. Ft.: 975

Bedrooms: 4

Bathrooms: 5½

Foundation: Crawl space

Materials List Available: Yes

Price Category: I

Images provided by designer/architect.

Main Level Floor Plan

porch 40 x 10

family 23 x 20

kit & den 35 x 17

util

mbr 20 x 16

built in entertainment center and library

built in entertainment center and library

gallery

sto

dining 18 x 12

study 18 x 12

br 2 13 x 12

foy

golf cart & sto 18 x 17

garage 22 x 22

work bench

Upper Level Floor Plan

open to lower level

library

br 3 18 x 12

br 4 18 x 12

open to lower level

Bonus Area Floor Plan

future space 36 x 12

Copyright by designer/architect.

Plan #571088

Dimensions: 38' W x 42' D

Levels: 1

Square Footage: 1,202

Bedrooms: 2

Bathrooms: 1

Foundation: Basement

Material List Available: Yes

Price Category: B

Images provided by designer/architect.

MASTER BEDROOM 12'-0" X 14'-0"

LIVING ROOM 12'-4" X 15'-4"

DINING ROOM 12'-0" X 11'-0"

KITCHEN 12'-0" X 9'-0"

PANTRY

BEDROOM #2 12'-6" X 13'-6"

GARAGE 12'-0" X 20'-0"

Copyright by designer/architect.

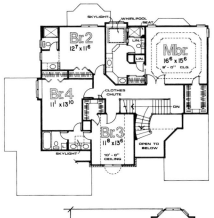

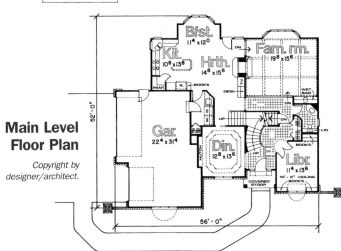

Upper Level Floor Plan

Main Level Floor Plan

Copyright by designer/architect.

Plan #121061

Dimensions: 56' W x 52' D

Levels: 2

Square Footage: 3,025

Main Level Sq. Ft.: 1,583

Upper Level Sq. Ft.: 1,442

Bedrooms: 4

Bathrooms: 3½

Foundation: Basement

Materials List Available: Yes

Price Category: G

Images provided by designer/architect.

CAD FILE AVAILABLE • CAD •

Upper Level Floor Plan

Copyright by designer/architect.

Main Level Floor Plan

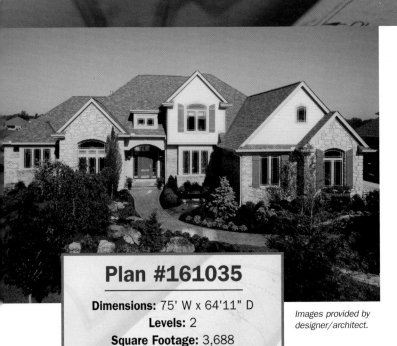

Plan #161035

Dimensions: 75' W x 64'11" D

Levels: 2

Square Footage: 3,688

Main Level Sq. Ft.: 2,702

Upper Level Sq. Ft.: 986

Bedrooms: 4

Bathrooms: 3½

Foundation: Basement

Materials List Available: No

Price Category: H

Images provided by designer/architect.

Plan #181228

Dimensions: 68' W x 36' D

Levels: 2

Square Footage: 2,393

Main Level Sq. Ft.: 1,279

Upper Level Sq. Ft.: 1,114

Bedrooms: 4

Bathrooms: 2

Foundation: Slab

Materials List Available: Yes

Price Category: G

Come home to this fine home, and relax on the front or rear porch.

Features:

• Living Room: This large, open entertaining area has a cozy fireplace and is flooded with natural light.

• Kitchen: This fully equipped kitchen has an abundance of cabinets and counter space. Access the rear porch is through a glass door.

• Laundry Room: Located on the main level, this laundry area also has space for storage.

• Upper Level: Climb the U-shaped staircase, and you'll find four large bedrooms that share a common bathroom.

Images provided by designer/architect.

**Main Level
Floor Plan**

Copyright by designer/architect.

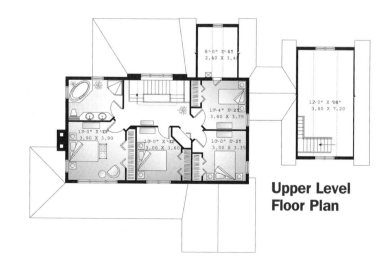

**Upper Level
Floor Plan**

Rear View

Dining Room

Living Room

Living Room

Kitchen

Master Bath

Plan #441007

Dimensions: 70' W x 64' D
Levels: 1
Square Footage: 2,197
Bedrooms: 4
Bathrooms: 2½
Foundation: Crawl space
Materials List Available: Yes
Price Category: D

Welcome to this roomy ranch, embellished with a brick facade, intriguing roof peaks, and decorative quoins on all the front corners.

CAD FILE AVAILABLE

Features:

• Great Room: There's a direct sightline from the front door through the trio of windows in this room. The rooms are defined by columns and changes in ceiling height rather than by walls, so light bounces from dining room to breakfast nook to kitchen.

• Kitchen: The primary workstation in this kitchen is a peninsula, which faces the fireplace. The peninsula is equipped with a sink, dishwasher, downdraft cooktop, and snack counter.

• Den/Home Office: Conveniently located off the foyer, this room would work well as a home office.

• Master Suite: The double doors provide an air of seclusion for this suite. The vaulted bedroom features sliding patio doors to the backyard and an arch-top window. The adjoining bath is equipped with a whirlpool tub, shower, double vanity, and walk-in closet.

• Secondary Bedrooms: The two additional bedrooms, each with direct access to the shared bathroom, occupy the left wing of the ranch.

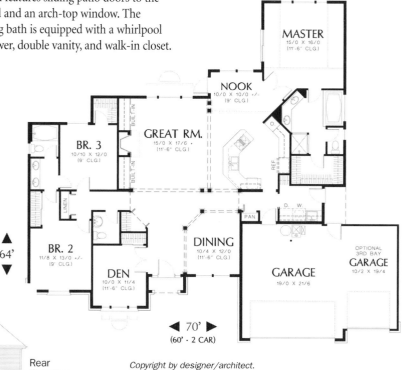

Rear Elevation

Copyright by designer/architect.

Plan #131040

Dimensions: 50' W x 37' D
Levels: 1
Square Footage: 1,630
Bedrooms: 3
Bathrooms: 2
Foundation: Crawl space, slab, or basement
Materials List Available: Yes
Price Category: D

Images provided by designer/architect.

The raised main level of this home makes this plan ideal for any site that has an expansive view, and you can finish the lower level as an office, library, or space for the kids to play.

Features:

• **Living Room:** This sunken living room with a prow-shaped front is sure to be a focal point where both guests and family gather in this lovely ranch home. A see-through fireplace separates this room from the dining room.

• **Dining Room:** A dramatic vaulted ceiling covers both this room and the adjacent living room, creating a spacious feeling.

• **Kitchen:** Designed for efficiency, you'll love the features and location of this convenient kitchen.

• **Master Suite:** Luxuriate in the privacy this suite affords and enjoy the two large closets, sumptuous private bath, and sliding glass doors that can open to the optional rear deck.

Rear Elevation

Main Level Floor Plan

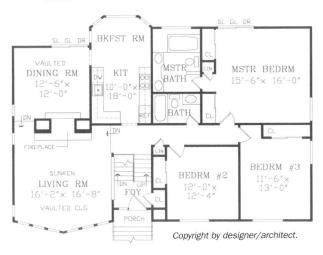

Copyright by designer/architect.

Lower Level Floor Plan

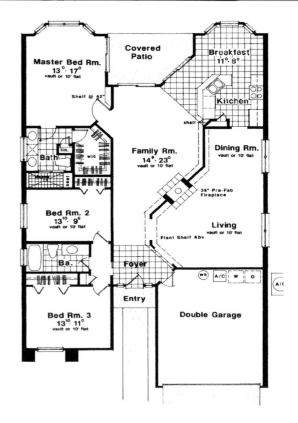

Plan #661055

Dimensions: 40' W x 66'8" D

Levels: 1

Square Footage: 1,872

Bedrooms: 3

Bathrooms: 2

Foundation: Slab

Materials List Available: No

Price Category: D

Images provided by designer/architect.

Copyright by designer/architect.

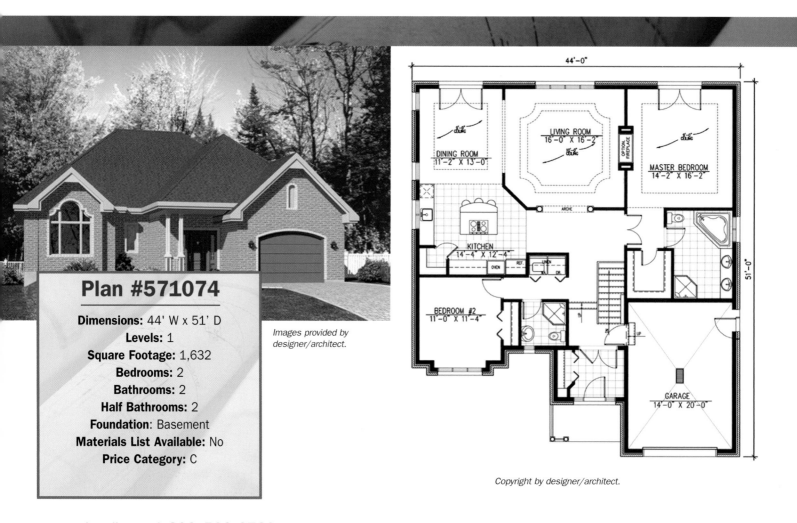

Plan #571074

Dimensions: 44' W x 51' D

Levels: 1

Square Footage: 1,632

Bedrooms: 2

Bathrooms: 2

Half Bathrooms: 2

Foundation: Basement

Materials List Available: No

Price Category: C

Images provided by designer/architect.

Copyright by designer/architect.

Main Level Floor Plan

MAIN FLOOR

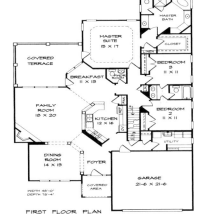

Lower Level Floor Plan

Copyright by designer/architect.

LOWER LEVEL

Plan #541038

Dimensions: 76'6" W x 69' D
Levels: 1
Square Footage: 4,823
Main Level Sq. Ft.: 2,583
Loweer Level Sq. Ft.: 2,240
Bedrooms: 7
Bathrooms: 3½
Foundation: Basement
Materials List Available: No
Price Category: I

Images provided by designer/architect.

CAD FILE AVAILABLE

Main Level Floor Plan

FIRST FLOOR PLAN

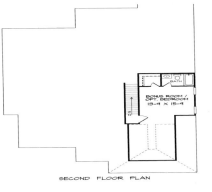

Upper Level Floor Plan

Copyright by designer/architect.

SECOND FLOOR PLAN

Plan #461202

Dimensions: 48' W x 78'4" D
Levels: 1
Square Footage: 2,215
Bedrooms: 3
Bathrooms: 2½
Foundation: Slab
Materials List Available: No
Price Category: E

Images provided by designer/architect.

Plan #371092

Dimensions: 71'6" W x 70'8" D
Levels: 2
Square Footage: 3,836
Main Level Sq. Ft.: 2,981
Upper Level Sq. Ft.: 855
Bedrooms: 5
Bathrooms: 4
Foundation: Slab, crawl space or basement for fee
Materials List Available: No
Price Category: H

Images provided by designer/architect.

Front View

This grand home has an arched covered entry and great styling that would make this home a focal point of the neighborhood.

CAD FILE AVAILABLE

Features:

- **Family Room:** This large gathering area boasts a fireplace flanked by a built-in media center. Large windows flood the room with natural light, and there is access to the rear porch.

- **Kitchen:** This large island kitchen has a raised bar and is open to the family room. Its walk-in pantry has plenty of room for supplies.

- **Master Suite:** This retreat features a stepped ceiling and a see-through fireplace to the master bath, which has a large walk-in closet, dual vanities, a glass shower, and a marble tub.

- **Secondary Bedrooms:** Bedrooms 2 and 3 are located on the main level and share a common bathroom. Bedrooms 4 and 5 are located on the upper level and share a Jack-and-Jill bathroom.

Copyright by designer/architect.

Main Level Floor Plan

Upper Level Floor Plan

Plan #101019

Dimensions: 58'4" W x 55'2" D

Levels: 2

Square Footage: 2,954

Main Level Sq. Ft. 2,093

Upper Level Sq. Ft. 861

Bedrooms: 4

Bathrooms: 3½

Foundation: Crawl space, slab, or basement

Materials List Available: No

Price Category: F

Images provided by designer/architect.

This luxurious home features a spectacular open floor plan and a brick exterior.

Features:

• Ceiling Height: 9 ft. unless otherwise noted.

• Foyer: This inviting two-story foyer, which vaults to 18 ft., will greet guests with an impressive "welcome."

• Dining Room: To the right of the foyer is this spacious dining room surrounded by decorative columns.

• Family Room: There's plenty of room for all kinds of family activities in this enormous room, with its soaring two-story ceiling.

• Master Suite: This sumptuous retreat boasts a tray ceiling. Optional pocket doors provide direct access to the study. The master bath features his and her vanities and a large walk-in closet.

• Breakfast Area: Perfect for informal family meals, this bayed breakfast area has real flair.

• Secondary Bedrooms: Upstairs are three large bedrooms with 8-ft. ceilings. One has a private bath.

CAD FILE AVAILABLE

Main Level Floor Plan

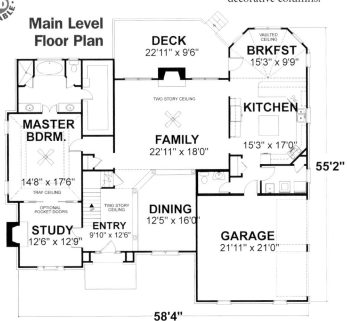

Upper Level Floor Plan

Copyright by designer/architect.

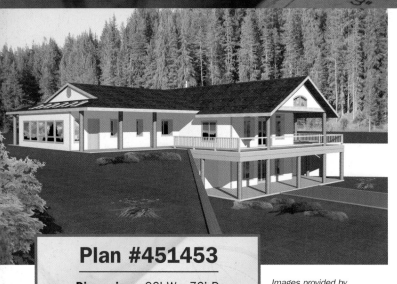

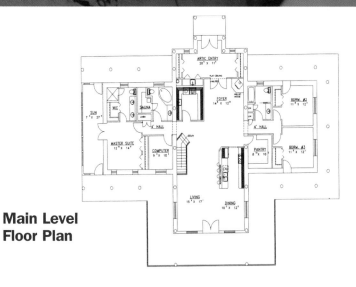

**Main Level
Floor Plan**

*Images provided by
designer/architect.*

Plan #451453

Dimensions: 96' W x 76' D
Levels: 1
Square Footage: 4,868
Main Level Sq. Ft.: 3,296
Lower Level Sq. Ft.: 1,572
Bedrooms: 3
Bathrooms: 3½
Foundation: Basement or Walk-out
Materials List Available: No
Price Category: I

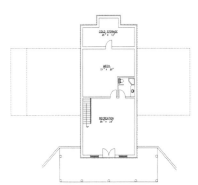

**Lower Level
Floor Plan**

Copyright by designer/architect.

**Main Level
Floor Plan**

*Images provided by
designer/architect.*

Plan #571037

Dimensions: 95' W x 84' D
Levels: 2
Square Footage: 6,440
Main Level Sq. Ft.: 4,409
Upper Level Sq. Ft.: 2,031
Bedrooms: 4
Bathrooms: 3½
Foundation: Basement
Material List Available: Yes
Price Category: K

**Upper Level
Floor Plan**

*Copyright by
designer/architect.*

Plan #321051

Dimensions: 69'8" W x 46' D
Levels: 2
Square Footage: 2,624
Main Level Sq. Ft.: 1,774
Upper Level Sq. Ft.: 850
Bedrooms: 4
Bathrooms: 2½
Foundation: Basement
Materials List Available: Yes
Price Category: F

This home, as shown in the photograph, may differ from the actual blueprints. For more detailed information, please check the floor plans carefully.   *Images provided by designer/architect.*

The dramatic exterior design allows natural light to flow into the spacious living area of this home.

Features:

- Entry: This two-story area opens into the dining room through a classic colonnade.

- Dining Room: A large bay window, stately columns, and doorway to the kitchen make this room both beautiful and convenient.

- Great Room: Enjoy light from the fireplace or the three Palladian windows in the 18-ft. ceiling.

- Kitchen: The step-saving design features a walk-in pantry as well as good counter space.

- Breakfast Room: You'll love the light that flows through the windows flanking the back door.

- Master Suite: The vaulted ceiling and bayed areas in both the bed and bath add elegance. You'll love the two walk-in closets and bath with a sunken tub, two vanities, and separate shower.

Main Level Floor Plan

MBr 17-0x17-8 (vaulted, plant shelf)
Garage 21-4x20-4
Great Rm 20-6x15-10
Brk 14-10x10-0
Kitchen 14-10x10-6
Dining 14-10x12-4
Foyer

Copyright by designer/architect.

Master Bath

Upper Level Floor Plan

Br 4 12-6x12-0
Br 2 11-8x10-4
Br 3 12-6x12-0
open to below

Plan #151055

Dimensions: 82'4" W x 81'6" D
Levels: 1
Square Footage: 3,183
Bedrooms: 4
Bathrooms: 2½
Foundation: Crawl space or slab; basement or walkout available for fee
CompleteCost List Available: Yes
Price Category: E

Images provided by designer/architect.

This stunning large ranch home has a well-designed floor plan that is perfect for today's family.

CAD FILE AVAILABLE

Features:

• Living Room: This large gathering area features a beautiful fireplace and a vaulted ceiling. On nice days, exit through the atrium doors and relax on the grilling porch.

• Kitchen: The raised bar in this island kitchen provides additional seating for informal

meals. The family will enjoy lazy weekend mornings in the adjoining breakfast room and intimate hearth room.

• Master Suite: This retreat, with its built-in media center and romantic fireplace in the sleeping area, features a boxed ceiling. The

master bath boasts a whirlpool tub, his and her vanities and lavatories, and a glass shower.

• Bedrooms: These three family bedrooms are located on the opposite side of the home from the master suite for privacy and share a common bathroom.

Copyright by designer/architect.

Front View

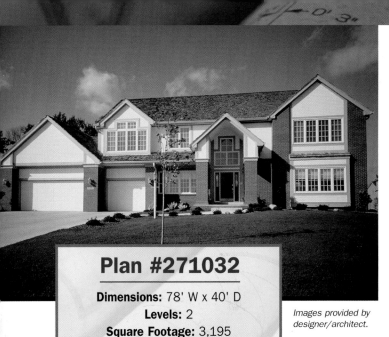

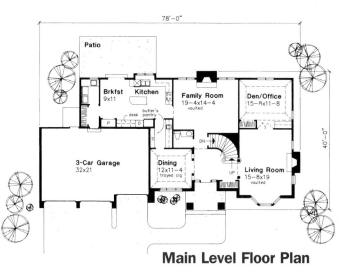

Main Level Floor Plan

78'-0"

Patio

Brkfst 9x11 | Kitchen

Family Room 19-4x14-4 vaulted

Den/Office 15-8x11-8

desk | butler's pantry

3-Car Garage 32x21

Dining 12x11-4 trayed clg

DN

UP

Living Room 15-8x19 vaulted

40'-0"

Plan #271032

Dimensions: 78' W x 40' D
Levels: 2
Square Footage: 3,195
Main Level Sq. Ft.: 1,758
Upper Level Sq. Ft.: 1,437
Bedrooms: 4
Bathrooms: 2½
Foundation: Basement
Materials List Available: No
Price Category: E

Images provided by designer/architect.

CAD FILE AVAILABLE

Upper Level Floor Plan

Copyright by designer/architect.

Br 3 15-8x11-6

M Suite 12-8x18-6 window seat

Br 4/ Sitting 11x10-6

DN

open to below

shelf

Br 2 15-8x13-4

Main Level Floor Plan

67'-0"

Deck

Family Rm 21x13-6

Brkfst 8x9

Kitchen 13-4x12-6

Dining 11-4x10-8 13 vaulted clg

Desk | P

Garage 32-6x21

Living Rm 14-6x16-6 15 vaulted clg

Foyer 17 vltd clg

UP

Porch

37'-0"

Plan #271018

Dimensions: 67' W x 37' D
Levels: 2
Square Footage: 2,445
Main Level Sq. Ft.: 1,290
Upper Level Sq. Ft.: 1,155
Bedrooms: 4
Bathrooms: 2½
Foundation: Basement; walkout for fee
Materials List Available: Yes
Price Category: E

Images provided by designer/architect.

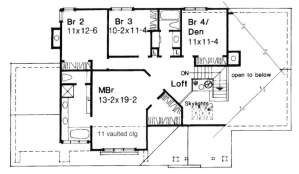

Upper Level Floor Plan

Copyright by designer/architect.

Br 2 11x12-6

Br 3 10-2x11-4

Br 4/ Den 11x11-4

DN

open to below

MBr 13-2x19-2

Loft

Skylights

11 vaulted clg

Plan #121026

Dimensions: 66'8" W x 76' D

Levels: 2

Square Footage: 3,926

Main Level Sq. Ft.: 2,351

Upper Level Sq. Ft.: 1,575

Bedrooms: 4

Bathrooms: 3 full, 2 half

Foundation: Basement; slab for fee

Materials List Available: Yes

Price Category: H

Images provided by designer/architect.

Plenty of space and architectural detail make this a comfortable and gracious home.

Features:

- Ceiling Height: 8 ft. unless otherwise noted.

- Great Room: A soaring cathedral ceiling makes this great room seem even more spacious than it is, while the fireplace framed by windows lends warmth and comfort.

- Eating Area: There's a dining room for more formal entertaining, but this informal eating area to the left of the great room will get plenty of daily use. It features a built-in desk for compiling shopping lists and recipes and access to the backyard.

- Kitchen: Next door to the eating area, this kitchen is designed to make food preparation a pleasure. It features a center cooktop, a recycling area, and a corner pantry.

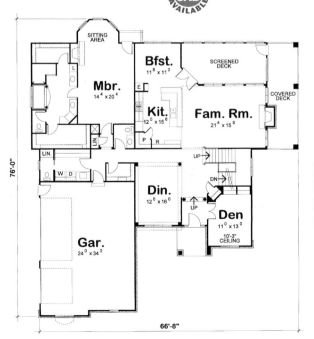

Main Level Floor Plan

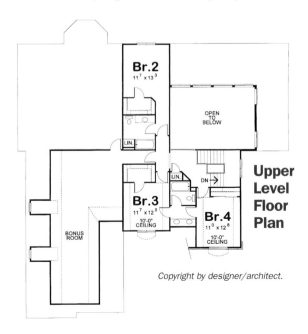

Upper Level Floor Plan

Copyright by designer/architect.

Plan #391009

Dimensions: 73'4" W x 60'4" D

Levels: 2

Square Footage: 3,440

Main Level Sq. Ft.: 2,486

Upper Level Sq. Ft.: 954

Bedrooms: 4

Bathrooms: 3½

Foundation: Basement, Crawl Space, Slab

Materials List Available: Yes

Price Category: G

This home, as shown in the photograph, may differ from the actual blueprints. For more detailed information, please check the floor plans carefully.

Images provided by designer/architect.

This home offers classic Victorian details combined with modern amenities.

Features:

• Ceiling Height: 9 ft. unless otherwise noted

• Porch: Enjoy summer breezes on this large wraparound porch, with its classic turret corner.

• Family Room: This room has a fireplace and two sets of French doors. One set of doors leads to the porch; the other leads to a rear sun deck.

• Living Room: This large room at the front of the house is designed for entertaining.

• Kitchen: This convenient kitchen features an island and a writing desk.

• Master Bedroom: Enjoy the cozy sitting area in the turret corner. The bedroom offers access to a second story balcony.

• Laundry: The second-floor laundry means that you won't have to haul clothing up and down stairs.

Main Level Floor Plan

Upper Level Floor Plan

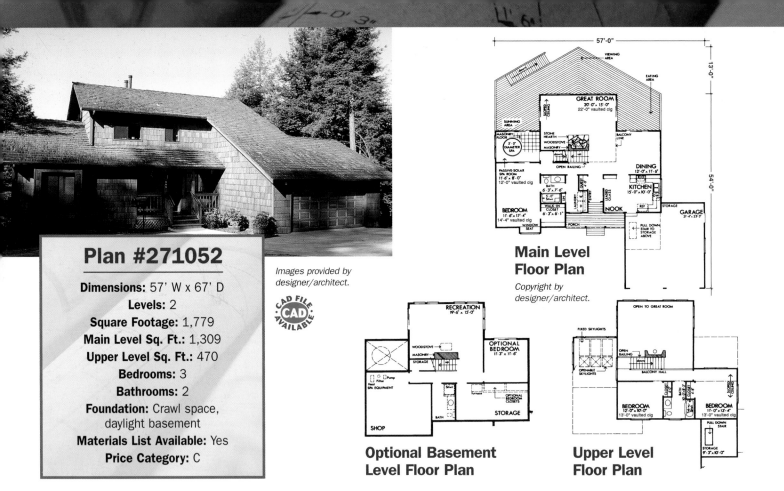

Plan #271052

Dimensions: 57' W x 67' D

Levels: 2

Square Footage: 1,779

Main Level Sq. Ft.: 1,309

Upper Level Sq. Ft.: 470

Bedrooms: 3

Bathrooms: 2

Foundation: Crawl space, daylight basement

Materials List Available: Yes

Price Category: C

Images provided by designer/architect.

CAD FILE AVAILABLE — CAD

Main Level Floor Plan

Copyright by designer/architect.

Optional Basement Level Floor Plan

Upper Level Floor Plan

Plan #181100

Dimensions: 74'6" W x 44' D

Levels: 2

Square Footage: 4,200

Main Level Sq. Ft.: 2,207

Upper Level Sq. Ft.: 1,993

Bedrooms: 4

Bathrooms: 3½

Foundation: Basement

Material List Available: Yes

Price Category: K

Images provided by designer/architect.

CAD FILE AVAILABLE — CAD

Main Level Floor Plan

Upper Level Floor Plan

Copyright by designer/architect.

Main Level Floor Plan

Images provided by designer/architect.

Plan #331005

Dimensions: 85'11" W x 55'7" D

Levels: 2

Square Footage: 3,585

Main Level Sq. Ft.: 2,691

Upper Level Sq. Ft.: 894

Bedrooms: 4

Bathrooms: 3½

Foundation: Crawl space, slab, or basement

Materials List Available: No

Price Category: H

Upper Level Floor Plan

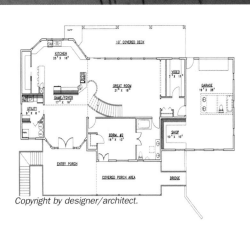

Rear View

Copyright by designer/architect.

Main Level Floor Plan

Copyright by designer/architect.

Plan #451448

Dimensions: 90' W x 39' D

Levels: 2

Square Footage: 2,717

Main Level Sq. Ft.: 2,064

Upper Level Sq. Ft.: 653

Bedrooms: 2

Bathrooms: 2

Foundation: Walk-out

Materials List Available: No

Price Category: F

Images provided by designer/architect.

CAD FILE AVAILABLE

Upper Level Floor Plan

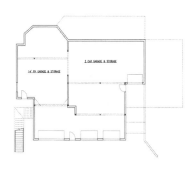

Lower Level Floor Plan

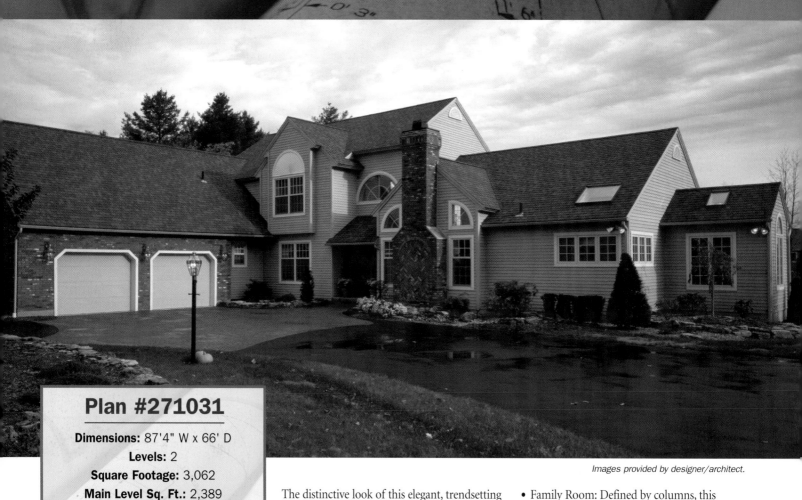

Plan #271031

Dimensions: 87'4" W x 66' D
Levels: 2
Square Footage: 3,062
Main Level Sq. Ft.: 2,389
Upper Level Sq. Ft.: 673
Bedrooms: 4
Bathrooms: 3½
Foundation: Basement
Materials List Available: Yes
Price Category: G

Images provided by designer/architect.

The distinctive look of this elegant, trendsetting estate reflects a refined sense of style and taste.

Features:

- Parlor/Dining: Off the vaulted foyer, this cozy sunken parlor boasts a vaulted ceiling and a warm fireplace. Opposite the parlor, this formal dining room is serviced by a stylish wet bar.

- Kitchen: This open room features an angled snack bar and serves a skylighted breakfast room.

- Family Room: Defined by columns, this skylighted, vaulted family room offers a handsome fireplace with a built-in log bin. Sliding glass doors open to a backyard deck.

- Master Suite: This deluxe getaway boasts a vaulted ceiling and unfolds to a skylighted sitting area and a private deck. The garden tub in the master bath basks under its own skylight.

- Library/Guest Room: This versatile room enjoys a high ceiling and a walk-in closet.

- Secondary Bedrooms: Two reside on the upper floor.

Main Level Floor Plan

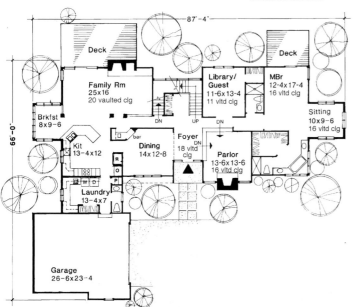

Upper Level Floor Plan

Copyright by designer/architect.

Plan #131031

Dimensions: 69'8" W x 48'4" D
Levels: 2
Square Footage: 4,027
Main Level Sq. Ft.: 2,198
Upper Level Sq. Ft.: 1,829
Bedrooms: 5
Bathrooms: 4½
Foundation: Slab; basement for fee
Materials List Available: Yes
Price Category: I

If you love dramatic lines and contemporary design, you'll be thrilled by this lovely home.

Features:

• Foyer: A gorgeous vaulted ceiling sets the stage for a curved staircase flanked by a formal living room and dining room.

• Living Room: The foyer ceiling continues in this room, giving it an unusual presence.

• Family Room: This sunken family room features a fireplace and a wall of windows that look out to the backyard. It's open to the living room, making it an ideal spot for entertaining.

• Kitchen: With a large island, this kitchen flows into the breakfast room.

• Master Suite: The luxurious bedroom has a dramatic tray ceiling and includes two walk-in closets. The dressing room is fitted with a sink, and the spa bath is sumptuous.

Images provided by designer/architect.

Main Level Floor Plan

Copyright by designer/architect.

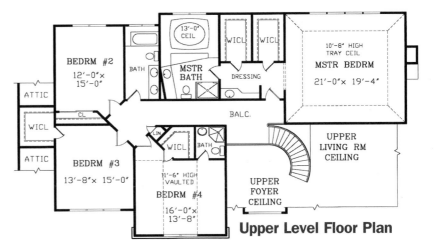

Upper Level Floor Plan

Plan #151030

Dimensions: 59' W x 73' D

Levels: 2

Square Footage: 2,802

Main Level Sq. Ft.: 2,058

Upper Level Sq. Ft.: 744

Bonus Room Sq. Ft.: 493

Bedrooms: 3

Bathrooms: 3½

Foundation: Crawl space, slab; basement for fee

CompleteCost List Available: Yes

Price Category: F

Images provided by designer/architect.

CAD FILE AVAILABLE

Main Level Floor Plan

Upper Level Floor Plan

Copyright by designer/architect.

Plan #151723

Dimensions: 49'10" W x 64'4" D

Levels: 1

Square Footage: 1,552

Bedrooms: 4

Bathrooms: 2

Foundation: Crawl space or slab; basement or walkout for fee

CompleteCost List Available: Yes

Price Category: C

Images provided by designer/architect.

Copyright by designer/architect.

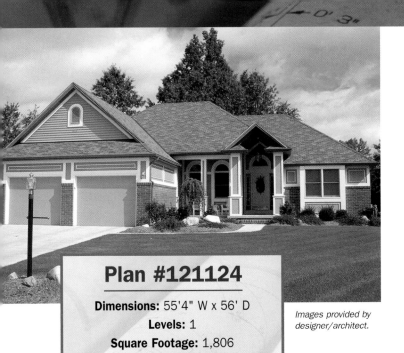

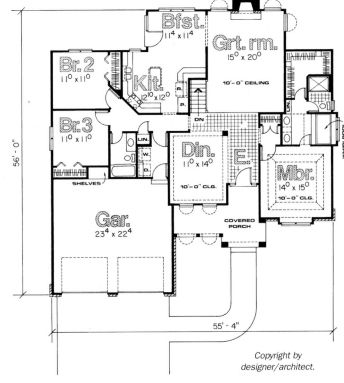

Plan #121124

Dimensions: 55'4" W x 56' D

Levels: 1

Square Footage: 1,806

Bedrooms: 3

Bathrooms: 2

Foundation: Basement;
crawl space for fee

Material List Available: Yes

Price Category: D

Images provided by designer/architect.

Copyright by designer/architect.

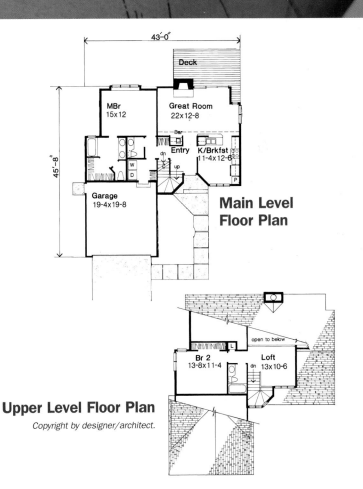

Main Level Floor Plan

Upper Level Floor Plan

Copyright by designer/architect.

Plan #271013

Dimensions: 43' W x 45'8" D

Levels: 2

Square Footage: 1,498

Main Level Sq. Ft.: 1,044

Upper Level Sq. Ft.: 454

Bedrooms: 2

Bathrooms: 2½

Foundation: Basement

Materials List Available: Yes

Price Category: B

Images provided by designer/architect.

Plan #391021

Dimensions: 54' W x 48'4" D
Levels: 1
Square Footage: 1,568
Bedrooms: 3
Bathrooms: 2
Foundation: Crawl space, slab, or basement
Materials List Available: Yes
Price Category: C

Images provided by designer/architect.

• Master Suite: This private retreat is situated far from the public areas. A large walk-in closet with a private bath and double vanity add to the suite's intimate appeal.

• Bedrooms: The two additional bedrooms boast large closets and bright windows. The generous hall bathroom is located conveniently nearby.

A peaked porch roof and luminous Palladian window play up the exterior appeal of this ranch home, while other archectectural components dramatize the interior.

Features:

• Living Room: There is a soaring ceiling in this living room, where a corner fireplace and built-in bookshelves provide cozy comfort.

• Dining Room: Open to the living room, this room features sliders to the wood deck, which makes it conductive to both casual and formal entertaining.

• Kitchen: This well-planned kitchen seems to have it all--a built-in pantry, a double sink, and a breakfast bar that feeds into the dining room. The bar provides additional serving space when needed.

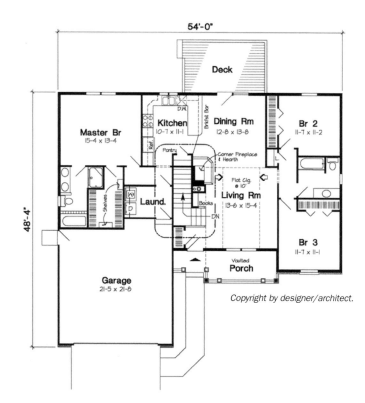

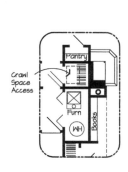

Copyright by designer/architect.

Plan #401023

Dimensions: 76' W x 63'4" D
Levels: 1
Square Footage: 2,806
Bedrooms: 3
Bathrooms: 2½
Foundation: Basement, walkout
Materials List Available: Yes
Price Category: F

Images provided by designer/architect.

The lower level of this magnificent home includes unfinished space that could have a future as a den and a family room with a fireplace. This level could also house extra bedrooms or an in-law suite.

Features:

- **Foyer:** On the main level, this foyer spills into a tray ceiling living room with a fireplace and an arched, floor-to-ceiling window wall.

- **Family Room:** Up from the foyer, a hall introduces this vaulted room with built-in media center and French doors that open to an expansive railed deck.

- **Kitchen:** Featured in this gourmet kitchen are a food-preparation island with a salad sink, double-door pantry, corner-window sink, and breakfast bay.

- **Master Bedroom:** The vaulted master bedroom opens to the deck, and the deluxe bath offers a raised whirlpool spa and a double-bowl vanity under a skylight.

- **Bedroom:** Two family bedrooms share a compartmented bathroom.

Rear Elevation

Copyright by designer/architect.

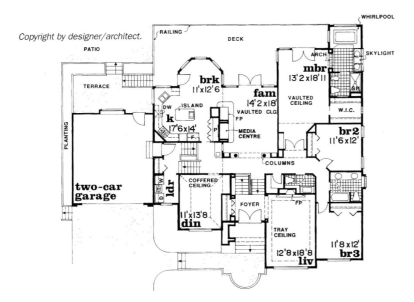

Optional Floor Plan

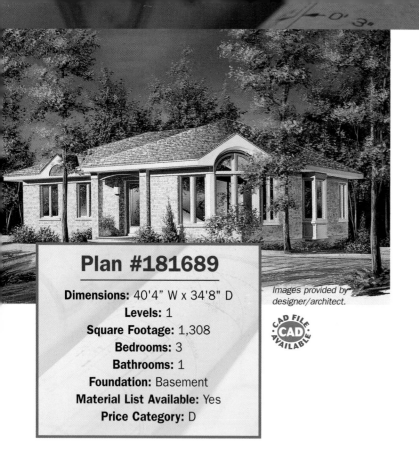

Plan #181689

Dimensions: 40'4" W x 34'8" D
Levels: 1
Square Footage: 1,308
Bedrooms: 3
Bathrooms: 1
Foundation: Basement
Material List Available: Yes
Price Category: D

Images provided by designer/architect.

CAD FILE AVAILABLE

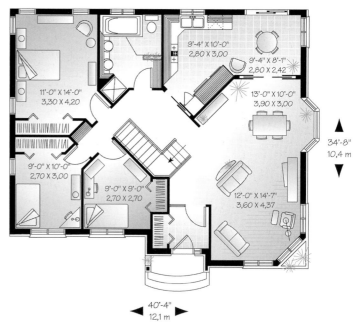

9'-4" X 10'-0"
2,80 X 3,00

9'-4" X 8'-1"
2,80 X 2,42

11'-0" X 14'-0"
3,30 X 4,20

13'-0" X 10'-0"
3,90 X 3,00

9'-0" X 10'-0"
2,70 X 3,00

9'-0" X 9'-0"
2,70 X 2,70

12'-0" X 14'-7"
3,60 X 4,37

34'-8"
10,4 m

40'-4"
12,1 m

Plan #451138

Dimensions: 64'4" W x 73' D
Levels: 1
Square Footage: 4,484
Main Level Sq. Ft.: 2,242
Basement Level Sq. Ft.: 2,242
Bedrooms: 4
Bathrooms: 3
Foundation: Basement – insulated concrete form
Material List Available: No
Price Category: I

Images provided by designer/architect.

CAD FILE AVAILABLE

COV. PORCH
25' X 12'

GREAT ROOM
10' X 16'

MASTER SUITE
14' X 15'

GREAT ROOM
29' X 19'

BDRM. #2
12' X 12'

WIC
10' X 6'

DINING
13' X 11'

BDRM. #3
12' X 12'

UTILITY
10' X 10'

GARAGE
25' X 25'

SEWING
24' X 19'

FAMILY ROOM
22' X 21'

BDRM. #4
12' X 12'

WIC
10' X 10'

MECH.
10' X 10'

STORAGE

OFFICE
12' X 14'

Basement Level Floor Plan

Copyright by designer/architect.

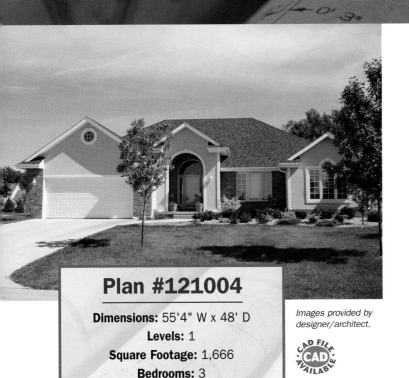

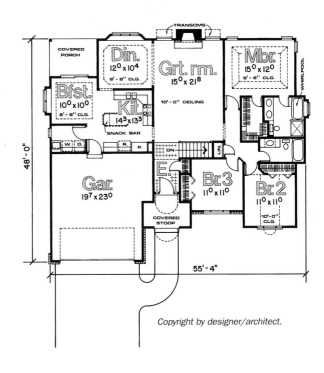

Copyright by designer/architect.

Plan #121004

Dimensions: 55'4" W x 48' D

Levels: 1

Square Footage: 1,666

Bedrooms: 3

Bathrooms: 2

Foundation: Basement

Materials List Available: Yes

Price Category: C

Images provided by designer/architect.

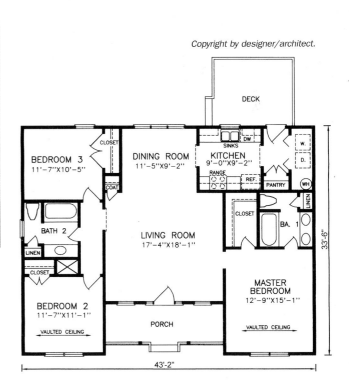

Copyright by designer/architect.

Plan #341012

Dimensions: 43'2" W x 33'6" D

Levels: 1

Square Footage: 1,316

Bedrooms: 3

Bathrooms: 2

Foundation: Crawl space, slab, or basement

Materials List Available: Yes

Price Category: B

Images provided by designer/architect.

Plan #271037

Dimensions: 66' W x 65' D

Levels: 2

Square Footage: 4,220

Main Level Sq. Ft.: 2,768

Upper Level Sq. Ft.: 1,452

Bedrooms: 3

Bathrooms: 4½

Foundation: Basement

Materials List Available: No

Price Category: I

This design allows family members to carry out their work and leisure activities inside the home. The options for leisure and study are almost countless!

Features:

- "Us" Room: The home's sunken "Us" room is the center of attention, with its vaulted ceiling and two-story fireplace. The room is surrounded by the family living areas.

- Master Suite: Relax in this oasis, which offers twin walk-in closets and a lovely bath.

- Upper Floor: Study areas, an office, and an exercise space are just the beginning!

Dining Room / "Us" Room

CAD FILE AVAILABLE

Main Level Floor Plan

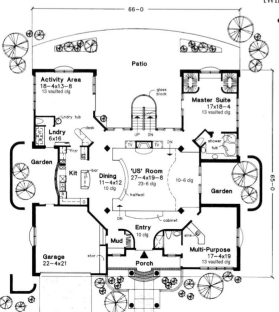

Copyright by designer/architect.

Upper Level Floor Plan

Plan #271033

Dimensions: 40' W x 41'4" D

Levels: 2

Square Footage: 1,516

Main Level Sq. Ft.: 817

Upper Level Sq. Ft.: 699

Bedrooms: 3

Bathrooms: 2½

Foundation: Basement

Materials List Available: Yes

Price Category: C

Images provided by designer/architect.

A pronounced roofline and a pleasing mix of brick and lap siding give a sunny disposition to this charming home.

Features:

• Great Room: Introduced by the sidelighted entry, this large space offers tall corner windows for natural light and a cheery corner fireplace for warmth.

• Dining Room: Joined to the great room only by air, this formal dining room basks in the glow from a broad window.

• Kitchen: Plenty of open space allows this kitchen to include ample counter space and incorporate an eating area into it. From here, a door leads to the backyard.

• Family Room: Flowing directly from the kitchen, this large family room allows passage to a backyard deck via sliding glass doors.

• Master Suite: Secluded to the upper floor, the master bedroom offers a private bath with a walk-in closet beyond.

Main Level Floor Plan

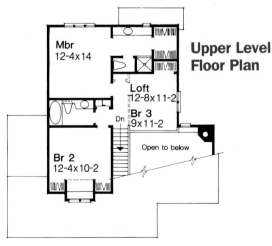

Upper Level Floor Plan

Copyright by designer/architect.

Color

No other decorating component has more power and greater effect at such little cost than color. It can fill a space and make furnishings look fresh and new. Color can also show off fine architectural details or downplay a room's structural flaws. A particular color can make a cold room cozy, while another hue can cool down a sunny cooker. And color comes cheap, giving a tremendous impact for your decorating dollar: elbow grease, supplies, prep work, and paint will all cost pretty much the same if you choose a gorgeous hue over plain white.

But finding the color—the right color—isn't easy. Where do you begin to look? Like the economy, color has leading indicators. You have a market basket full of choices, and there are lots of signposts to direct you where to go.

The Lay of the Land

For the past 200 years, white has been the most popular choice for American home exteriors. And it still is, followed by tan, brown, and beige. You can play it safe and follow the leader. But you should also think about the architecture of your house and where you live when you're considering exterior color. For example, traditional Colonials have a color-combination range of about two that look appropriate: white with black or green shutters and gray with white trim. Mediterranean-style houses typically pick up the colors of terra-cotta and the tile that are indigenous to the regions that developed the architecture—France, Italy, and Spain. A ranch-style house shouldn't be overdone—it is, after all, usually a modest structure. On the other hand, a cottage can be fanciful. Whimsical colors also look charming on Victorian houses in San Francisco, but they would be out of place in conservative Scarsdale, New York, where you must check with the local building board even when you want to change the exterior color of your house.

How's the Weather?

Like exteriors, interiors often take their color cues from their environs and local traditions. In the rainy and often chilly Pacific Northwest, cozy blanket plaids in strong reds and black abound. In the hot-and-arid climate of the West, indigo or brown ticking-stripes and faded denim look appropriately casual and cool. Subtle grays and neutrals, reflecting steel, lime-stone, and concrete, look apropos for sophisticated city life. In extremely warm southern climates, the brilliant sun tends to overpower lighter colors. That explains the popularity of strong hues in tropical, sun-drenched locales.

Natural Light. That's the one you don't pay for. Its direction and intensity greatly affects color. A room with a window that faces trees will look markedly different in summer, when warm white sunlight is filtered through the leaves, than in winter, when the trees are bare and the color of natural light takes on a cool blue cast. Time of day affects color, too. Yellow walls that are pleasant and cheerful in the early morning can be stifling and blinding in the afternoon. That's because afternoon sun is stronger than morning sun.

The yellow-colored wall, above, complements the antique painted dresser.

Warm neutral-color walls, opposite, and touches of red make this bedroom cozy.

When you're choosing a color for an interior, always view it at different times of day, but especially during the hours in which you will inhabit the room.

Artificial Light. Because artificial light affects color rendition as much as natural light, don't judge a color in the typically chilly fluorescence of a hardware store. The very same color chip will look completely different when you bring it home, which is why it's so important to test out a paint color in your own home. Most fluorescent light is bluish and distorts colors. It depresses red and exaggerates green, for example. A romantic faded rose on your dining room walls will just wash out in the kitchen if your use a fluorescent light there. Incandescent light, the type produced by the standard bulbs you probably use in your chandelier and in most of your home's light fixtures, is warm but slightly yellow. Halogen light, which comes from another newer type of incandescent bulb, is white and the closest to natural sunlight. Of all three types of bulbs, halogen is truest in rendering color.

red

RED is powerful, dramatic, motivating. Red is also hospitable, and it stimulates the appetite, which makes it a favorite choice for dining rooms. Some studies have indicated that a red room actually makes people feel warmer.

yellow

YELLOW illuminates the colors it surrounds. It warms rooms that receive northern light but can be too bright in a sunny room. It's best for daytime rooms, not bedrooms. It has a short range, which means as white is added to yellow, it disappears. Yellow highlights and calls attention to features—think of bright taxicabs.

green

GREEN is tranquil, nurturing, rejuvenating. It is a psychological primary, and because it is mixed from yellow and blue, it can appear both warm and cool. Time seems to pass more quickly in green rooms. Perhaps that's why waiting rooms off-stage are called "green rooms."

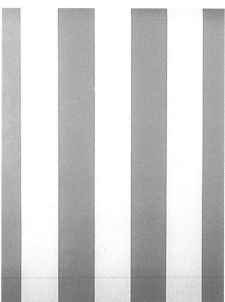

neutrals

GRAY goes with all colors—it is a good neighbor. Various tones of gray range from dark charcoal to pale oyster.

BLACK (technically the absence of color) enhances and brightens other colors, making for livelier decorating schemes when used as an accent.

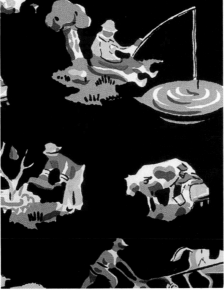

 pink

PINK is perceived as outgoing and active. It's also a color that flatters skin tones. Hot shades are invigorating, while soft, toned-down versions can be relaxed and charming.

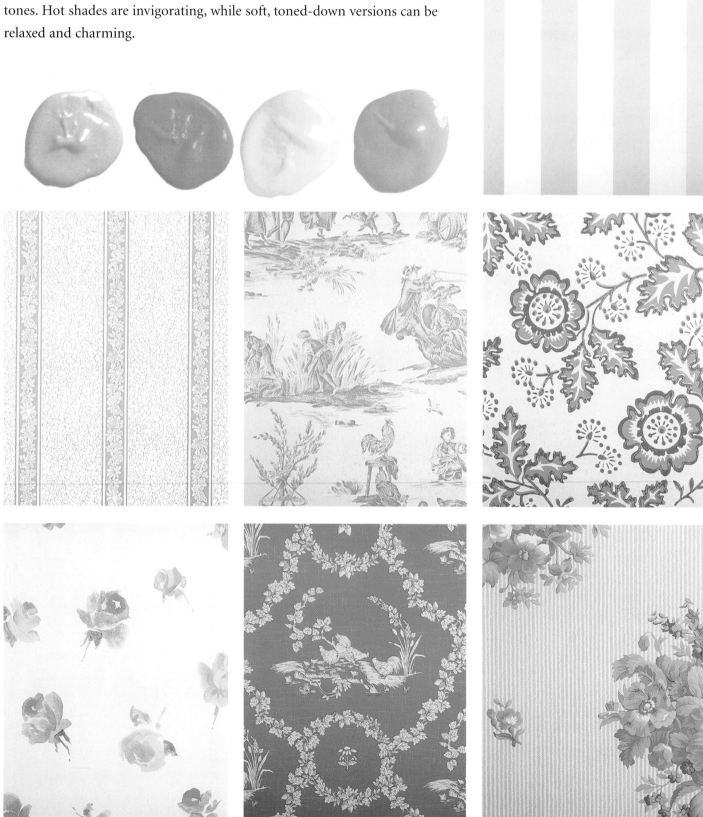

order direct: 1-800-523-6789

blue

BLUE, with its associations of sea and sky, offers serenity, which is why it is a favorite in bedrooms. Studies have shown that people think better in blue rooms. Perhaps that explains the popularity of the navy blue suit. Cooler blues show this color's melancholy side, however.

Plan #111031

Dimensions: 56' W x 53' D
Levels: 1.5
Square Footage: 2,869
Main Level Sq. Ft.: 2,152
Upper Level Sq. Ft.: 717
Bedrooms: 4
Bathrooms: 3
Foundation: Crawl space, slab
Materials List Available: No
Price Category: G

Images provided by designer/architect.

This home is ideal for any family, thanks to its spaciousness, beauty, and versatility.

Features:

- Ceiling Height: 9 ft.

- Front Porch: The middle of the three French doors with circle tops here opens to the foyer.

- Living Room: Archways from the foyer open to both this room and the equally large dining room.

- Family Room: Also open to the foyer, this room features a two-story sloped ceiling and a balcony from the upper level. You'll love the fireplace, with its raised brick hearth and the

two French doors with circle tops, which open to the rear porch.

- Kitchen: A center island, range with microwave, built-in desk, and dining bar that's open to the breakfast room add up to comfort and efficiency.

- Master Suite: A Palladian window and linen closet grace this suite's bedroom, and the bath has an oversized garden tub, standing shower, two walk-in closets, and double vanity.

Copyright by designer/architect.

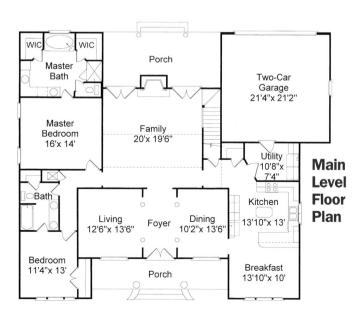

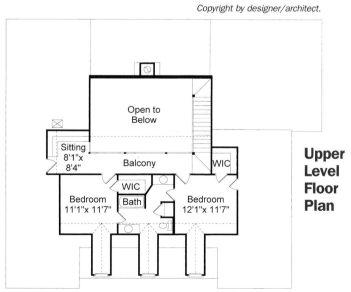

Entry

Kitchen

Living Room

SMARTtip

Preparing to Use a Clay Chiminea

Before getting started, there are a couple of general rules about using a clay chiminea. Make sure the chiminea is completely dry before lighting a fire, or else it will crack. Also, line the bottom of the pot with about 4 inches of sand. Finally, always build the fire slowly, and never use kerosene or charcoal lighter fluid.

To cure a new clay chiminea, follow these simple steps:

- Build a small paper fire inside the pot. For kindling, use strips of newspaper rolled into a few balls. Place one newspaper ball on the sand inside the chiminea. Ignite it with a match. Then add another ball, and another, one at a time, until the outside walls of the chiminea are slightly warm. Allow the fire to burn out; then let the pot cool completely before the next step.

- Once the chiminea feels cool, light another small fire, this time using wood. Again, let the fire burn out naturally, and then allow the unit to completely cool.

- Repeat the process of lighting a wood fire three more times, adding more kindling and building a larger fire with each consecutive attempt. Remember to let the chiminea cool completely between fires.

After the fifth fire, the chiminea should be cured and ready to use anytime you want a cozy fire.

Living Room

Plan #101010

Dimensions: 70' W x 47' D

Levels: 1

Square Footage: 2,187

Bedrooms: 4

Bathrooms: 2½

Foundation: Crawl space, slab, or basement

Materials List Available: Yes

Price Category: D

This stately ranch features a brick-and-stucco exterior, layered trim, and copper roofing returns.

Features:

- Ceiling Height: 11 ft. unless otherwise noted.

- Special Ceilings: Vaulted and raised ceilings adorn the living room, family room, dining room, foyer, kitchen, breakfast room, and master suite.

- Kitchen: This roomy kitchen is brightened by an abundance of windows.

- Breakfast Room: Located off the kitchen, this breakfast room is the perfect spot for informal family meals.

- Master Suite: This truly exceptional master suite features a bath, and a spacious walk in closet.

- Morning Porch: Step out of the master bedroom, and greet the day on this lovely porch.

- Additional Bedrooms: The three additional bedrooms each measure approximately 11 ft. x 12 ft. Two of them have walk-in closets.

Images provided by designer/architect.

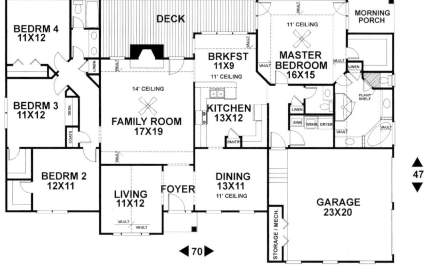

Copyright by designer/architect.

SMARTtip

Using Slipcovers in Your Dining Area

Change the look of your dining room by slipcovering chairs. Short-skirted slipcovers give a more informal appearance; fabrics in graphic patterns, such as checks or floral prints, complement this style of slipcover best. Long-skirted covers are elegant additions to a formal dining room, particularly in solid color or tone-on-tone fabrics. Ties, buttons, or trim can add personality.

Plan #351001

Dimensions: 72'8" W x 51' D
Levels: 1
Square Footage: 1,855
Bedrooms: 3
Bathrooms: 2½
Foundation: Crawl space, slab, or basement
Materials List Available: Yes
Price Category: D

Images provided by designer/architect.

From the lovely arched windows on the front to the front and back covered porches, this home is as comfortable as it is beautiful.

Features:

- **Great Room:** Come into this room with 12-ft. ceilings, and you're sure to admire the corner gas fireplace and three windows overlooking the porch.

- **Dining Room:** Set off from the open design, this room is designed to be used formally or not.

- **Kitchen:** You'll love the practical walk-in pantry, broom closet, and angled snack bar here.

- **Breakfast Room:** Brightly lit and leading to the covered porch, this room will be a favorite spot.

- **Bonus Room:** Develop a playroom or study in this area.

- **Master Suite:** The large bedroom is complemented by the private bath with garden tub, separate shower, double vanity, and spacious walk-in closet.

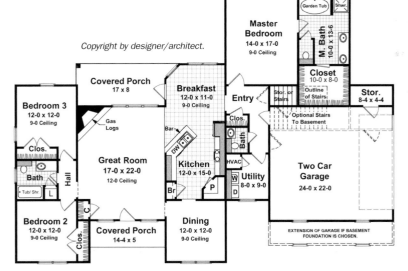

Copyright by designer/architect.

Kitchen

Bonus Area Floor Plan

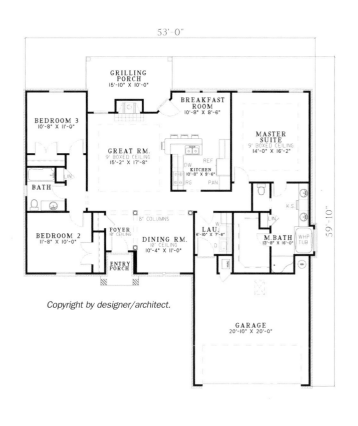

Images provided by designer/architect.

Copyright by designer/architect.

Plan #151043

Dimensions: 53' W x 59'10" D

Levels: 1

Square Footage: 1,636

Bedrooms: 3

Bathrooms: 2

Foundation: Crawl space, slab; basement option for fee

CompleteCost List Available: Yes

Price Category: E

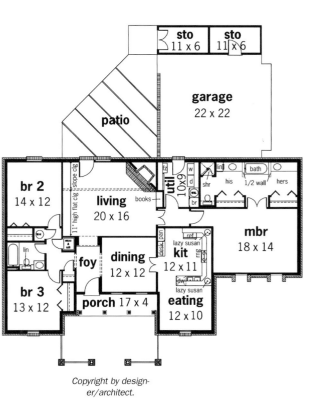

Images provided by designer/architect.

Plan #211039

Dimensions: 62' W x 64' D

Levels: 1

Square Footage: 1,868

Bedrooms: 3

Bathrooms: 2

Foundation: Slab

Materials List Available: Yes

Price Category: D

Copyright by designer/architect.

Images provided by designer/architect.

Copyright by designer/architect.

Optional Basement Floor Plan

Plan #121092

Dimensions: 65'4" W x 52'8" D

Levels: 1

Square Footage: 1,887

Bedrooms: 3

Bathrooms: 2½

Foundation: Basement

Materials List Available: Yes

Price Category: D

Plan #151054

Dimensions: 67' W x 54'10" D

Levels: 1

Square Footage: 1,746

Bedrooms: 3

Bathrooms: 2

Foundation: Crawl space or slab; basement option for fee

CompleteCost List Available: Yes

Price Category: C

Images provided by designer/architect.

CAD FILE CAD AVAILABLE

Copyright by designer/architect.

SMARTtip

Mixing and Matching Windows

Windows, both fixed and operable, are made in various styles and shapes. While mixing styles should be carefully avoided, a variety of interesting window sizes and shapes may nevertheless be combined to achieve symmetry, harmony, and rhythm on the exterior of a home.

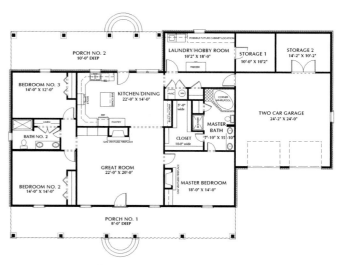

Images provided by designer/architect.

Plan #191032

Dimensions: 80'4" W x 52' D

Levels: 1

Square Footage: 2,091

Bedrooms: 3

Bathrooms: 2

Foundation: Slab

Materials List Available: No

Price Category: D

Copyright by designer/architect.

Plan #151003

Dimensions: 51'6" W x 52'4" D

Levels: 1

Square Footage: 1,680

Bedrooms: 3

Bathrooms: 2

Foundation: Crawl space, slab, or basement

CompleteCost List Available: Yes

Price Category: C

Images provided by designer/architect.

This home, as shown in the photograph, may differ from the actual blueprints. For more detailed information, please check the floor plans carefully.

Copyright by designer/architect.

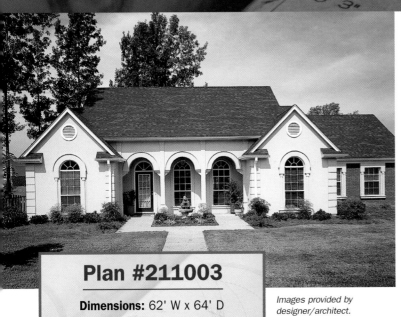

Plan #211003

Dimensions: 62' W x 64' D

Levels: 1

Square Footage: 1,856

Bedrooms: 3

Bathrooms: 2

Foundation: Slab; crawl space for fee

Materials List Available: Yes

Price Category: D

Images provided by designer/architect.

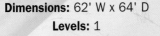

sto 11 x 6

sto 11 x 6

garage 22 x 22

patio

br 3 13 x 12

skylight

util

slope

living 20 x 16

van

bath

skylight

seat
shr

clo

slope

mbr 18 x 14

slope

bath

hall

ref

kit 12 x 12

ov

mng

dining 12 x 12

foy

br 2 13 x 12
slope

porch 20 x 4

pan

dw

eating 12 x 10
slope slope

Copyright by designer/architect.

Plan #211058

Dimensions: 74'6" W x 68' D

Levels: 1

Square Footage: 2,564

Bedrooms: 4

Bathrooms: 4

Foundation: Slab

Materials List Available: No

Price Category: E

Images provided by designer/architect.

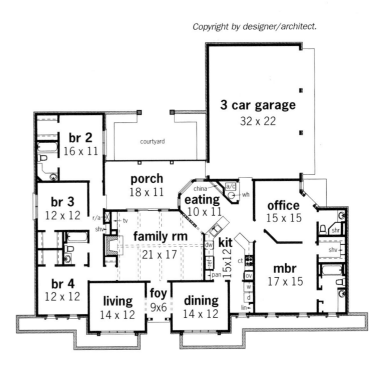

Copyright by designer/architect.

3 car garage 32 x 22

br 2 16 x 11

courtyard

porch 18 x 11

china

a/c

wh

eating 10 x 11

office 15 x 15

br 3 12 x 12

r/a

tv

family rm 21 x 17

kit 15x12

dw

shr

shv

pan

mbr 17 x 15

ref

ct

br 4 12 x 12

living 14 x 12

foy 9x6

dining 14 x 12

ov

w
d

lin

Plan #121003

Dimensions: 76' W x 55'4" D
Levels: 1
Square Footage: 2,498
Bedrooms: 4
Bathrooms: 2½
Foundation: Basement
Materials List Available: Yes
Price Category: E

Images provided by designer/architect.

Repeated arches bring style and distinction to the interior and exterior of this spacious home.

Features:

- Ceiling Height: 8 ft. except as noted.

- Den: A decorative volume ceiling helps make this spacious retreat the perfect place to relax after a long day.

- Formal Living Room: The decorative volume ceiling carries through to the living room that invites large formal gatherings.

- Formal Dining Room: There's plenty of room for all the guests to move into this gracious formal space that also features a decorative volume ceiling.

- Master Suite: Retire to this suite with its glamorous bayed whirlpool, his and her vanities, and a walk-in closet.

- Optional Sitting Room: With the addition of French doors, one of the bedrooms can be converted into a sitting room for the master suite.

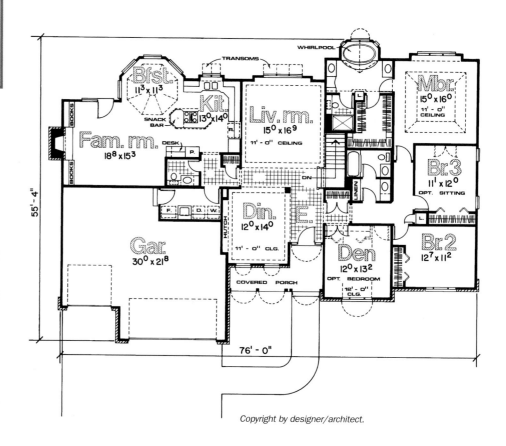

Copyright by designer/architect.

Plan #151002

Dimensions: 67' W x 66' D
Levels: 1
Square Footage: 2,444
Bedrooms: 3
Bathrooms: 2½
Foundation: Crawl space or slab; basement or walkout for fee
CompleteCost List Available: Yes
Price Category: F

This gracious, traditional home is designed for practicality and convenience.

Features:

- Ceiling Height: 9 ft. except as noted below.

- Great Room: This room is ideal for entertaining, thanks to its lovely fireplace and French doors that open to the covered rear porch. Built-in cabinets give convenient storage space.

- Family Room: With access to the kitchen as well as the rear porch, this room will become your family's "headquarters."

- Study: Enjoy the quiet in this room with its 12-ft. ceiling and doorway to a private patio on the side of the house.

- Dining Room: Take advantage of the 8-in. wood columns and 12-ft. ceilings to create a formal dining area.

This home, as shown in the photograph, may differ from the actual blueprints. For more detailed information, please check the floor plans carefully.

Images provided by designer/architect.

- Kitchen: An eat-in bar is a great place to snack, and the handy computer nook allows the kids to do their homework while you cook.

- Breakfast Room: Opening from the kitchen, this area gives added space for the family to gather any time.

- Master Suite: Featuring a 10-ft. boxed ceiling, the master bedroom also has a doorway that opens onto the covered rear porch. The master bathroom has a step-up whirlpool tub, separate shower, and twin vanities with a makeup area.

Copyright by designer/architect.

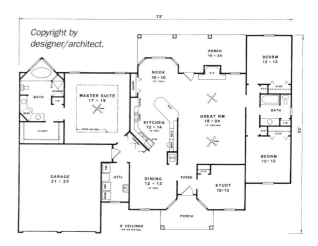

Plan #171004

Dimensions: 72' W x 52' D
Levels: 1
Square Footage: 2,256
Bedrooms: 3
Bathrooms: 2
Foundation: Crawl space, slab
Materials List Available: Yes
Price Category: E

SMARTtip

Windows – Privacy

You can easily stencil a work of art onto a windowpane, perhaps only as a border around the edge. Choose or create a design that gives you as little or as much privacy and light control as you need. Use a ready-made stencil or a piece of openwork fabric such as lace, or mask a design onto the glass using tape and a razor knife. Then apply glass paint or frosted glass spray, referring to the instructions and guidelines that come with the product.

Main Level Floor Plan

Upper Level Floor Plan
Copyright by designer/architect.

Plan #121062

Dimensions: 70' W x 62' D
Levels: 2
Square Footage: 3,448
Main Level Sq. Ft.: 2,375
Upper Level Sq. Ft.: 1,073
Bedrooms: 4
Bathrooms: 3½
Foundation: Basement
Materials List Available: Yes
Price Category: G

Main Level Floor Plan

Images provided by designer/architect.

Upper Level Floor Plan

Copyright by designer/architect.

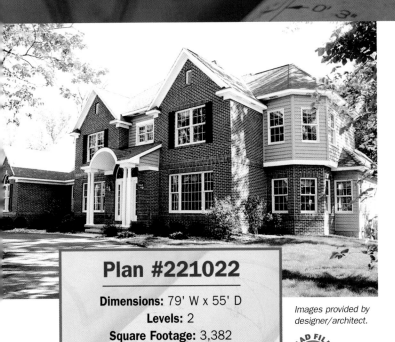

Plan #221022

Dimensions: 79' W x 55' D

Levels: 2

Square Footage: 3,382

Main Level Sq. Ft.: 2,376

Upper Level Sq. Ft.: 1,006

Bedrooms: 4

Bathrooms: 3½

Foundation: Basement

Materials List Available: No

Price Category: G

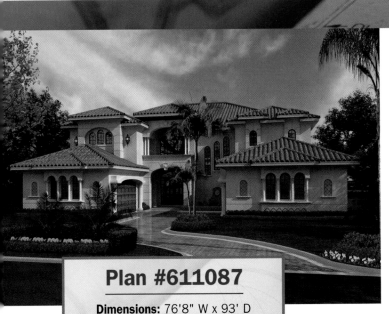

Plan #611087

Dimensions: 76'8" W x 93' D

Levels: 2

Square Footage: 6,175

Main Level Sq. Ft.: 3,251

Upper Level Sq. Ft.: 2,924

Bedrooms: 6

Bathrooms: 6½

Foundation: Slab

Materials List Available: No

Price Category: K

Images provided by designer/architect.

Main Level Floor Plan

Upper Level Floor Plan

Copyright by designer/architect.

Plan #121067

Dimensions: 56' W x 59'4" D

Levels: 2

Square Footage: 2,708

Main Level Sq. Ft.: 1,860

Upper Level Sq. Ft.: 848

Bedrooms: 4

Bathrooms: 3½

Foundation: Basement

Materials List Available: Yes

Price Category: F

Images provided by designer/architect.

You'll love this home because it is such a perfect setting for a family and still has room for guests.

Features:

- Family Room: Expect everyone to gather in this room, near the built-in entertainment centers that flank the lovely fireplace.

- Living Room: The other side of the see-through fireplace looks out into this living room, making it an equally welcoming spot in chilly weather.

- Kitchen: This room has a large center island, a corner pantry, and a built-in desk. It also features a breakfast area where friends and family will congregate all day long.

- Master Suite: Enjoy the oversized walk-in closet and bath with a bayed whirlpool tub, double vanity, and separate shower.

Main Level Floor Plan

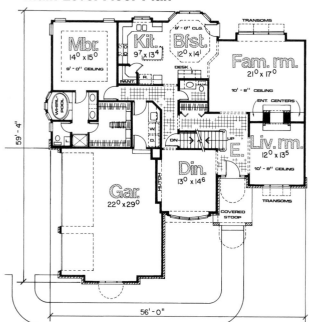

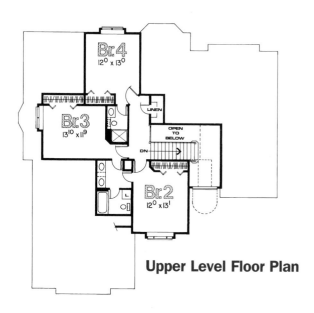

Upper Level Floor Plan

Copyright by designer/architect.

Plan #151004

Dimensions: 64'8" W x 62'1" D
Levels: 1
Square Footage: 2,107
Bedrooms: 4
Bathrooms: 2½
Foundation: Crawl space or slab; basement for fee
CompleteCost List Available: Yes
Price Category: E

This home, as shown in the photograph, may differ from the actual blueprints. For more detailed information, please check the floor plans carefully.

Images provided by designer/architect.

You'll love the spacious feeling in this comfortable home designed for a family.

Features:

- Foyer: A 10-ft. ceiling greets you in this home.

- Great Room: A 10-ft. ceiling complements this large room, with its fireplace, built-in cabinets, and easy access to the rear covered porch.

- Dining Room: The 9-ft. boxed ceiling in this large room helps to create a beautiful formal feeling.

- Kitchen: The island in this kitchen is open to the breakfast room for true convenience.

- Breakfast Room: Morning light will stream through the bay window here.

- Master Suite: A 9-ft. pan ceiling adds a distinctive note to this room with access to the rear porch. In the bath, you'll find a whirlpool tub, separate shower, double vanities, and two walk-in closets.

Copyright by designer/architect.

Plan #161001

Dimensions: 67'2" W x 47' D
Levels: 1
Square Footage: 1,782
Bedrooms: 3
Bathrooms: 2
Foundation: Basement
Materials List Available: Yes
Price Category: C

An all-brick exterior displays the solid strength that characterizes this gracious home.

Features:

- **Great Room:** A feeling of spaciousness permeates the gathering area created by the foyer, great room, and dining room. Multiple windows provide natural light that dances along a sloped ceiling, spilling onto decorative columns and a fireplace.

- **Breakfast Area:** A continuation of the sloped ceiling leads to the breakfast area where French doors open to a screened porch.

- **Kitchen:** An abundance of cabinets and counter space are the hallmarks of this large kitchen with its easy access to a spacious laundry room and storage area.

- **Master Suite:** A tray ceiling and spacious walk-in closet in the master bedroom, along with a whirlpool tub and double-bowl vanity in the bathroom, enable you to pamper yourself.

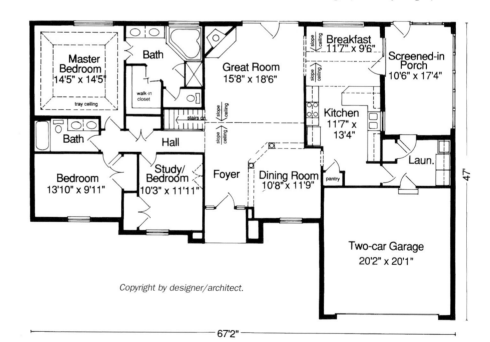

Great Room/Foyer

Rear Elevation

Plan #211011

Dimensions: 84' W x 54' D
Levels: 1
Square Footage: 2,791
Bedrooms: 3 or 4
Bathrooms: 2
Foundation: Slab or crawl space
Materials List Available: Yes
Price Category: F

SMARTtip

Types of Decks

Ground-level decks resemble a low platform and are best for flat locations. They can be the most economical type to build because they don't require stairs.

Raised decks can rise just a few steps up or meet the second story of a house. Lifted high on post supports, they adapt well to uneven or sloped locations.

Multilevel decks feature two or more stories and are connected by stairways or ramps. They can follow the contours of a sloped lot, unifying the deck with the outdoors.

Images provided by designer/architect.

Plenty of room plus an open, flexible floor plan make this a home that will adapt to your needs.

Features:

• Ceiling Height: 8 ft. unless otherwise noted.

• Living Room: This distinctive room features a 12-ft. ceiling and is designed so that it can also serve as a master suite with a sitting room.

• Family Room: The whole family will want to gather in this large, inviting family room.

• Morning Room: The family room blends

into this sunny spot, which is perfect for informal family meals.

• Kitchen: This spacious kitchen offers a smart layout. It is also contiguous to the family room.

• Master Suite: You'll look forward to the end of the day when you can enjoy this master suite. It includes a huge, luxurious master bath with two large walk-in closets and two vanity sinks.

• Optional Bedroom: This optional fourth bedroom is located so that it can easily serve as a library, den, office, or music room.

Copyright by designer/architect.

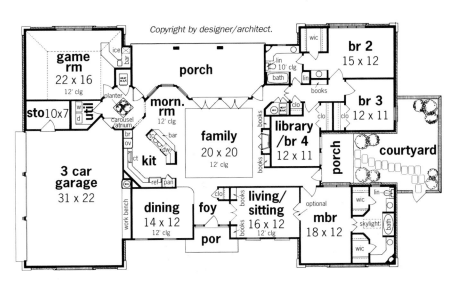

Plan #121050

Dimensions: 64' W x 50' D
Levels: 1
Square Footage: 1,996
Bedrooms: 2
Bathrooms: 2
Foundation: Basement
Materials List Available: Yes
Price Category: D

Images provided by designer/architect.

This compact design includes features usually reserved for larger homes and has styling that is typical of more-exclusive home designs.

Features:

- Entry: As you enter this home, you'll see the formal living and dining rooms—both with special ceiling detailing—on either side.

- Great Room: Located in the rear of the home for convenience, this great room is likely to be your favorite spot. The fireplace is framed by transom-topped windows, so you'll love curling up here, no matter what the weather or time of day.

- Kitchen: Ample counter and cabinet space make this kitchen a dream in which to work.

- Master Suite: A tray ceiling and lovely corner windows create an elegant feeling in the bedroom, and two walk-in closets make it easy to keep this space tidy and organized. The private bath has a skylight, corner whirlpool tub, and two separate vanities.

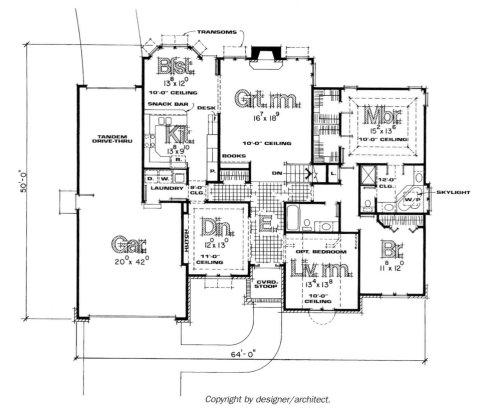

Copyright by designer/architect.

Plan #161028

Dimensions: 84'6" W x 69'4" D
Levels: 1
Square Footage: 3,570
**Optional Finished Basement
Sq. Ft.:** 2,367
Bedrooms: 3
Bathrooms: 3½
Foundation: Basement
Materials List Available: Yes
Price Category: H

From the gabled stone-and-brick exterior to the wide-open view from the foyer, this home will meet your greatest expectations.

Images provided by designer/architect.

Features:

- Great Room/Dining Room: Columns and 13-ft. ceilings add exquisite detailing to the dining room and great room.

- Kitchen: The gourmet-equipped kitchen with an island and a snack bar merges with the cozy breakfast and hearth rooms.

- Master Suite: The luxurious master bed room pampers with a separate sitting room with a fireplace and a dressing room boasting a tub and two vanities.

- Additional: Two bedrooms include a private bath and walk-in closet. The optional finished basement solves all your recreational needs: bar, media room, billiards room, exercise room, game room, as well as an office and fourth bedroom.

Rear Elevation

Main Level Floor Plan

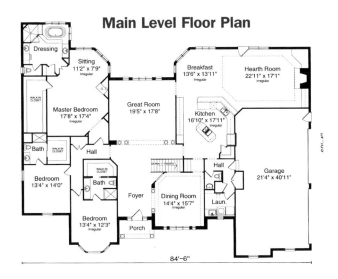

Basement Level Floor Plan

Copyright by designer/architect.

Plan #131036

Dimensions: 72' W x 69'10" D
Levels: 1
Square Footage: 2,585
Bedrooms: 4
Bathrooms: 3
Foundation: Crawl space or slab; basement for fee
Materials List Available: Yes
Price Category: F

Images provided by designer/architect.

This sprawling brick home features living spaces for everyone in the family and makes a lovely setting for any sort of entertaining.

Features:

• Foyer: Pass through this foyer, which leads into either the living room or dining room.

• Living Room: An elegant 11-ft. stepped ceiling here and in the dining room helps to create the formality their lines suggest.

• Great Room: This room, with its 10-ft.-7-in.-high stepped ceiling, fireplace, and many built-ins, leads to the rear covered porch.

• Kitchen: This kitchen features an island, a pantry closet, and a wraparound snack bar that serves the breakfast room and gives a panoramic view of the great room.

• Master Suite: Enjoy a bayed sitting area, walk-in closet, and private bath with garden tub.

• Office: A private entrance and access to a full bath give versatility to this room.

Copyright by designer/architect.

Optional Upper Level Floor Plan

Rear View

Great Room

Plan #121007

Dimensions: 74' W x 67'8" D

Levels: 1

Square Footage: 2,512

Bedrooms: 3

Bathrooms: 2½

Foundation: Basement

Materials List Available: Yes

Price Category: E

CAD FILE AVAILABLE

Images provided by designer/architect.

A series of arches brings grace to this home's interior and exterior.

Features:

- Ceiling Height: 8 ft.

- Formal Dining Room: Tapered columns give this dining room a classical look that lends elegance to any dinner party.

- Great Room: Just beyond the dining room is this light-filled room, with its wall of arched windows and see-through fireplace.

- Hearth Room: On the other side of the fire place you will find this cozy area, with its corner entertainment center.

- Dinette: A gazebo-shaped dinette is the architectural surprise of the house layout.

- Kitchen: This well-conceived working kitchen features a generous center island.

- Garage: With three garage bays you'll never be short of parking space or storage.

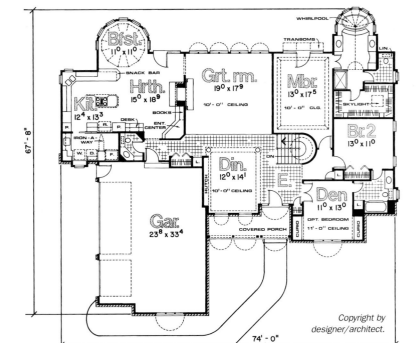

Optional Bedroom

Plan #321037

Dimensions: 78'8" W x 50'6" D

Levels: 1

Square Footage: 2,397

Bedrooms: 3

Bathrooms: 2

Foundation: Basement or walkout

Materials List Available: Yes

Price Category: F

Images provided by designer/architect.

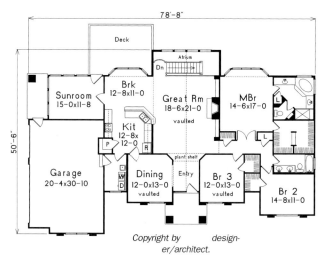

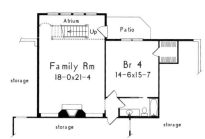

Optional Basement Level Floor Plan

Plan #271079

Dimensions: 104' W x 55' D

Levels: 1

Square Footage: 2,228

Bedrooms: 1-3

Bathrooms: 1½

Foundation: Daylight basement

Materials List Available: No

Price Category: E

Images provided by designer/architect.

CAD FILE AVAILABLE

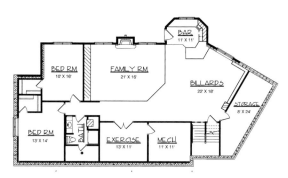

Optional Basement Level Floor Plan

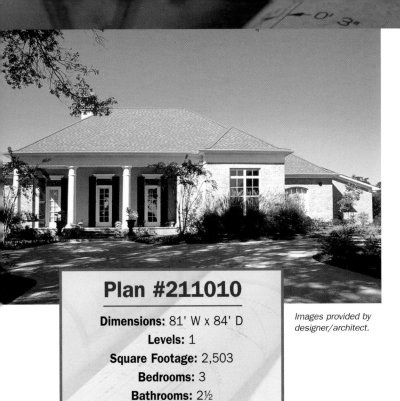

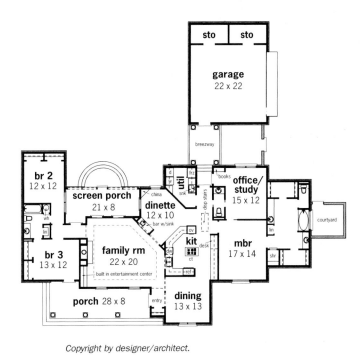

Images provided by designer/architect.

Copyright by designer/architect.

Plan #211010

Dimensions: 81' W x 84' D

Levels: 1

Square Footage: 2,503

Bedrooms: 3

Bathrooms: 2½

Foundation: Slab

Materials List Available: Yes

Price Category: E

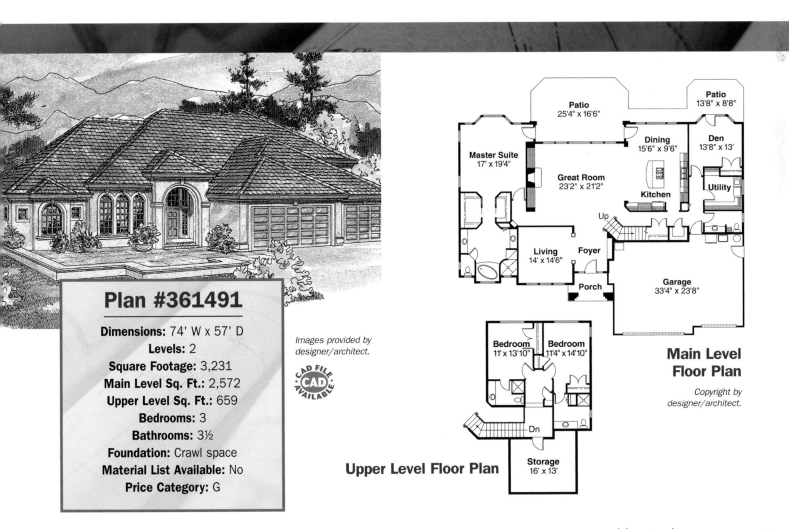

Plan #361491

Dimensions: 74' W x 57' D

Levels: 2

Square Footage: 3,231

Main Level Sq. Ft.: 2,572

Upper Level Sq. Ft.: 659

Bedrooms: 3

Bathrooms: 3½

Foundation: Crawl space

Material List Available: No

Price Category: G

Images provided by designer/architect.

CAD FILE AVAILABLE

Main Level Floor Plan

Copyright by designer/architect.

Upper Level Floor Plan

Plan #121019

Dimensions: 70' W x 60' D
Levels: 2
Square Footage: 3,775
Main Level Sq. Ft.: 1,923
Upper Level Sq. Ft.: 1,852
Bedrooms: 4
Bathrooms: 3
Foundation: Basement
Materials List Available: Yes
Price Category: H

Images provided by designer/architect.

The grand exterior presence is carried inside, beginning with the dramatic curved staircase.

Features:

- Den: French doors lead to this sophisticated den, with its bayed windows and wall of bookcases.

- Living Room: A curved wall and a series of arched windows highlight this large space.

- Formal Dining Room: This room shares the curved wall and arched windows found in the living room.

- Screened Porch: This huge space features skylights and is accessible by another French door from the dining room.

- Family Room: Family and guests alike will be drawn to this room, with its trio of arched windows and fireplace flanked by bookcases.

- Kitchen: An island adds convenience and distinction to this large, functional kitchen.

- Garage: This spacious three-bay garage provides plenty of space for cars and storage.

Main Level Floor Plan

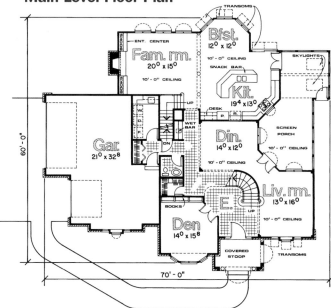

Upper Level Floor Plan

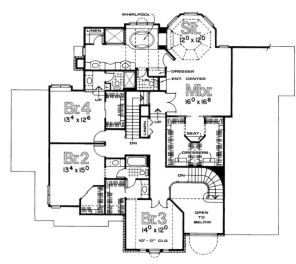

Copyright by designer/architect.

Plan #151007

Dimensions: 54'2" W x 56'2" D

Levels: 1

Square Footage: 1,787

Bedrooms: 3

Bathrooms: 2

Foundation: Crawl space or slab; basement or walkout for fee

CompleteCost List Available: Yes

Price Category: C

This home, as shown in the photograph, may differ from the actual blueprints. For more detailed information, please check the floor plans carefully.

Images provided by designer/architect.

This compact, well-designed home is graced with amenities usually reserved for larger houses.

Features:

- Foyer: A 10-ft. ceiling creates unity between the foyer and the dining room just beyond it.

- Dining Room: 8-in. boxed columns welcome you to this dining room, with its 10-ft. ceilings.

- Great Room: The 9-ft. boxed ceiling suits the spacious design. Enjoy the fireplace in the winter and the rear-grilling porch in the summer.

- Breakfast Room: This bright room is a lovely spot for any time of day.

- Master Suite: Double vanities and a large walk-in closet add practicality to this quiet room with a 9-ft. pan ceiling. The master bath includes whirlpool tub with glass block and a separate shower.

- Bedrooms: Bedroom 2 features a bay window, and both rooms are convenient to the bathroom.

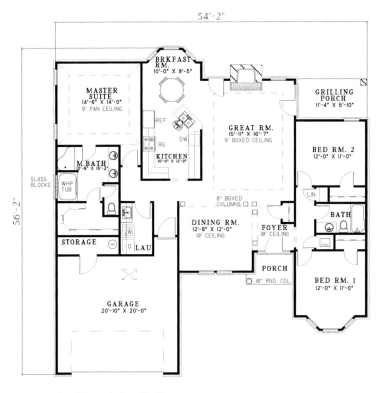

Copyright by designer/architect.

Plan #391034

Dimensions: 72'4" W x 43' D

Levels: 1

Square Footage: 1,737

Bedrooms: 3

Bathrooms: 2

Foundation: Crawl space, slab, or basement

Material List Available: Yes

Price Category: C

Images provided by designer/architect.

This home, as shown in the photograph, may differ from the actual blueprints. For more detailed information, please check the floor plans carefully.

Copyright by designer/architect.

Plan #151033

Dimensions: 81'6" W x 93'2" D

Levels: 2

Square Footage: 5,548

Main Level Sq. Ft.: 3,276

Upper Level Sq. Ft.: 2,272

Bedrooms: 5

Bathrooms: 4½

Foundation: Crawl space or slab; basement option for fee

CompleteCost List Available: Yes

Price Category: I

Images provided by designer/architect.

Main Level Floor Plan

Upper Level Floor Plan

Copyright by designer/architect.

Plan #211004

Dimensions: 64' W x 62' D

Levels: 1

Square Footage: 1,828

Bedrooms: 4

Bathrooms: 2

Foundation: Crawl space, slab, or basement

Materials List Available: Yes

Price Category: D

Images provided by designer/architect.

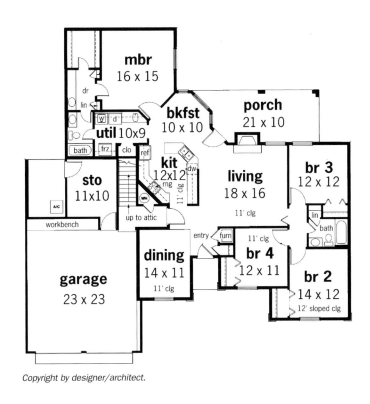

Copyright by designer/architect.

Plan #151057

Dimensions: 73'6" W x 80'6" D

Levels: 1

Square Footage: 2,951

Bedrooms: 4

Bathrooms: 3

Foundation: Crawl space or slab; basement for fee

CompleteCost List Available: Yes

Price Category: G

Images provided by designer/architect.

CAD FILE CAD AVAILABLE

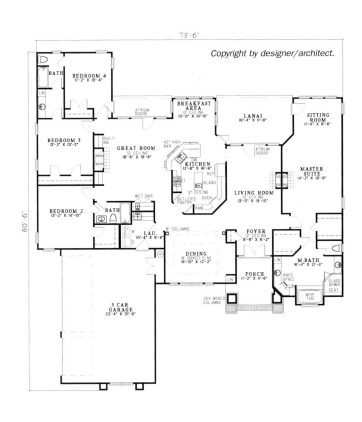

Copyright by designer/architect.

Plan #121065

Dimensions: 62' W x 55'4" D
Levels: 2
Square Footage: 3,407
Main Level Sq. Ft.: 1,719
Upper Level Sq. Ft.: 1,688
Bedrooms: 4
Bathrooms: 2½
Foundation: Basement
Materials List Available: Yes
Price Category: G

Images provided by designer/architect.

If you love contemporary design, the unusual shapes of the rooms in this home will delight you.

Features:

- Entry: You'll see a balcony from the upper level that overlooks this entryway, as well as the lovely curved staircase to this floor.

- Great Room: This room is sunken to set it apart. A fireplace, wet bar, spider-beamed ceiling, and row of arched windows give it character.

- Dining Room: Columns define this lovely octagon room, where you'll love to entertain guests or create lavish family dinners.

- Master Suite: A multi-tiered ceiling adds a note of grace, while the fireplace and private library create a real retreat. The gracious bath features a gazebo ceiling and a skylight.

Main Level Floor Plan

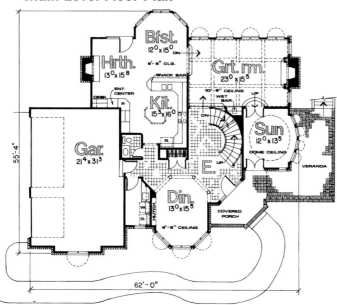

Upper Level Floor Plan

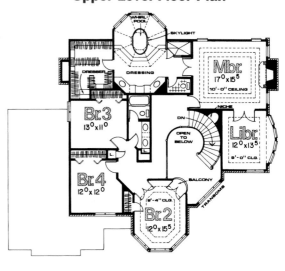

Copyright by designer/architect.

Plan #121073

Dimensions: 70' W x 52' D
Levels: 2
Square Footage: 2,579
Main Level Sq. Ft.: 1,933
Upper Level Sq. Ft.: 646
Bedrooms: 4
Bathrooms: 2½
Foundation: Basement
Materials List Available: Yes
Price Category: E

Images provided by designer/architect.

Luxury will surround you in this home with contemporary styling and up-to-date amenities at every turn.

Features:

• Great Room: This large room shares both a see-through fireplace and a wet bar with the adjacent hearth room. Transom-topped windows add both light and architectural interest to this room.

• Den: Transom-topped windows add visual interest to this private area.

• Kitchen: A center island and corner pantry add convenience to this well-planned kitchen, and a lovely ceiling treatment adds beauty to the bayed breakfast area.

• Master Suite: A built-in bookcase adds to the ambiance of this luxury-filled area, where you're sure to find a retreat at the end of the day.

Main Level Floor Plan

Upper Level Floor Plan

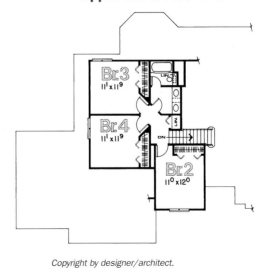

Copyright by designer/architect.

Living Room

Plan #111004

Dimensions: 72' W x 89' D

Levels: 1

Square Footage: 2,968

Bedrooms: 4

Full Bathrooms: 3½

Foundation: Crawl space or slab

Materials List Available: No

Price Category: G

Images provided by designer/architect.

If you've been looking for a home that includes a special master suite, this one could be the answer to your dreams.

Features:

- Living Room: Make a sitting area around the fireplace here so that the whole family can enjoy the warmth on chilly days and winter evenings. A door from this room leads to the rear covered porch, making this room the heart of your home.

- Kitchen: An island with a cooktop makes cooking a pleasure in this well-designed kitchen, and the breakfast bar invites visitors at all times of day.

- Utility Room: A sink and a built-in ironing board make this room totally practical.

- Master Suite: A private fireplace in the corner sets a romantic tone for this bedroom, and the door to the covered porch allows you to sit outside on warm summer nights. The bath has two vanities, a divided walk-in closet, a standing shower, and a deluxe corner bathtub.

Copyright by designer/architect.

Bonus Area

Gameroom 13'5"x17'

Wood Deck

Covered Porch

Master Bedroom 16'9"x21'5"

Master Bath

WIC

Breakfast 14'x12'1"

Living 24'8"x19'3"

Bedroom 12'4"x12'1"

Kitchen 18'4"x14'10"

Dining 13'1"x14'7"

Foyer

Bedroom 13'x12'

Bedroom 12'1"x13'

Utility

Porch

Garage 21'2"x27'2"

Front Elevation

Kitchen

Dining Room

Master Bath

Master Bath

SMARTtip

How to Quit Smoking — Lighting Your Fireplace

Before attempting to light a wood fire, make certain that the damper is open all the way. This allows a good draft (flow of air up the chimney) to prevent smoke from blowing back into the room. To ensure a good draft—particularly if your home is well insulated —open a window a bit when lighting a fire.

The opposite of draft is downdraft, which occurs when cold air flows down the chimney and into the room. If the fireplace is properly designed and maintained, the smoke shelf will prevent backpuffing from downdraft most of the time by redirecting cold air currents back up the chimney. The open damper also helps prevent backpuffing.

Also, build a fire slowly to let the chimney liner heat up, which will create a good draft and minimize the chances of downdraft.

Don't wait until fall to inspect the chimney. Do this job, or call a chimney sweep, when the weather is mild. Because some repairs take a while to make, it's best to have them done when the fireplace is not normally in use. If you do the inspection yourself, wear old clothes, eye goggles, and a mask.

Plan #151010

Dimensions: 38'4" W x 68'6" D
Levels: 1
Square Footage: 1,379
Bedrooms: 3
Bathrooms: 2
Foundation: Crawl space, slab
CompleteCost List Available: Yes
Price Category: C

This French Country home has a spacious great room for friends and family to gather, but you can sneak away to the covered rear porch or patio off the master suite for cozy tête-à-têtes.

Features:

- Entry: Take advantage of the marvelous 10-ft. ceilings to hang groups of potted flowering plants.

- Great Room: This spacious room, with an optional 10-ft. boxed ceiling, is the place to curl up by the gas fireplace on a cold winter night.

- Kitchen: The kitchen includes a bar for casual meals, and is open to the breakfast room.

- Rear Porch: Enjoy leisurely meals on the covered rear porch that you can access from both the master suite and the breakfast room.

- Master Suite: The 10-ft. boxed ceiling in the bedroom and the master bath with a whirlpool tub and separate shower make this suite a luxurious place to end a long day.

Images provided by designer/architect.

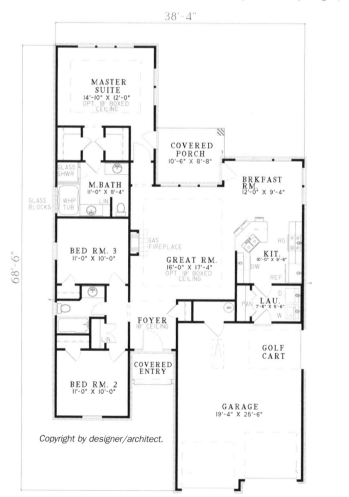

Copyright by designer/architect.

Plan #121023

Dimensions: 85'5" W x 74'8" D

Levels: 2

Square Footage: 3,904

Main Level Sq. Ft.: 2,813

Upper Level Sq. Ft.: 1,091

Bedrooms: 4

Bathrooms: 3½

Foundation: Basement; crawl space, slab, basement or walkout for fee

Materials List Available: Yes

Price Category: H

Spacious and gracious, here are all the amenities you expect in a fine home.

Features:

- Ceiling Height: 8 ft. except as noted.

- Foyer: This magnificent entry features a graceful curved staircase with balcony above.

- Sunken Living Room: This sunken room is filled with light from a row of bowed windows. It's the perfect place for social gatherings both large and small.

- Den: French doors open into this truly distinctive den with its 11-ft. ceiling and built-in bookcases.

- Formal Dining Room: Entertain guests with style and grace in this dining room with corner column.

- Master Suite: Another set of French doors leads to this suite that features two walk-in closets, a tub flanked by vanities, and a private sitting room with built-in bookcases.

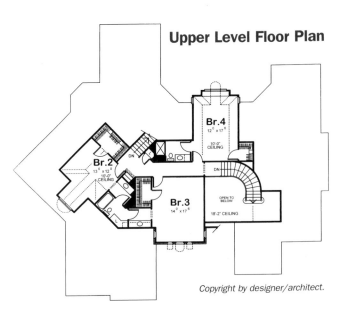

Copyright by designer/architect.

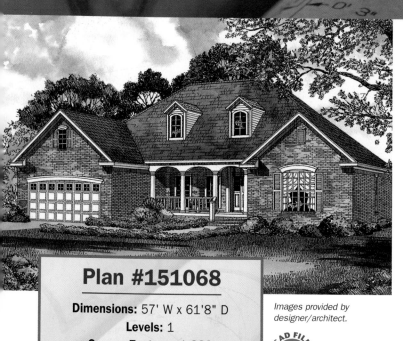

Plan #151068

Dimensions: 57' W x 61'8" D

Levels: 1

Square Footage: 1,880

Bedrooms: 4

Bathrooms: 2

Foundation: Crawl space, slab, basement or walkout

CompleteCost List Available: Yes

Price Category: D

Images provided by designer/architect.

CAD FILE AVAILABLE **CAD**

GRILLING PORCH
27'-0" X 10'-0"

BREAKFAST ROOM
9'-11" X 9'-7"

MASTER SUITE
13'-7" X 15'-0"
10" BOXED CEILING

GREAT ROOM
16'-0" X 17'-8"
10" BOXED CEILING

BEDROOM 2
11'-2" X 10'-6"

KITCHEN
9'-11" X 14'-9"

BEDROOM 3
10'-0" X 10'-4"

M.BATH
13'-7" X 11'-8"

RG
DW
REF
PAN

8" COLUMNS

KNEE SPACE

WHP TUB
W
D
LAU.
DN

DINING ROOM
12'-6" X 12'-4"
10" CEILING

FOYER
8'-0" X 10'-4"
10" CEILING

BATH

BEDROOM 4
13'-6" X 12'-4"

DESK

OPTIONAL SIDE LOAD

GARAGE
19'-4" X 19'-6"

7' COVERED PORCH
10" CEILING

57'-0"

61'-8"

Copyright by designer/architect.

Plan #221005

Dimensions: 72' W x 42' D

Levels: 1

Square Footage: 1,851

Bedrooms: 3

Bathrooms: 2

Foundation: Basement

Materials List Available: No

Price Category: D

Images provided by designer/architect.

MBR.
13'8" X 17'0"

DIN.
11'8" X 14'8"

KIT.
10'8" X 13'0"

STOR.
13'0" X 11'8"

LIN

SOFFIT

LIV.
10'4 7/8" CEILING
20'8" X 17'8"

2 CAR GAR.
24'0" X 26'0"

BR. #2
13'0" X 11'6"

BR. #3
10'4" X 13'8"

E.
VAULTED CEILING

SOFFIT

42'-0"

72'-0"

Rear

Copyright by designer/architect.

Plan #131015

Dimensions: 57'4" W x 56'10" D

Levels: 1

Square Footage: 1,860

Bedrooms: 3

Bathrooms: 2

Foundation: Crawl space or slab; basement for fee

Materials List Available: Yes

Price Category: E

This home, as shown in the photograph, may differ from the actual blueprints. For more detailed information, please check the floor plans carefully.

Copyright by designer/architect.

Rear Elevation

Great Room

Plan #211006

Dimensions: 61' W x 77' D

Levels: 1

Square Footage: 2,177

Bedrooms: 3

Bathrooms: 2

Foundation: Crawl space or slab

Materials List Available: Yes

Price Category: D

SMARTtip

Deck Furniture Style

Mix-and-match tabletops, frames, and legs are stylish. Combine materials such as glass, metal, wood, and mosaic tiles.

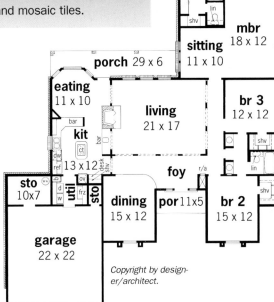

Copyright by designer/architect.

Images provided by designer/architect.

Plan #151011

Dimensions: 59'6" W x 74'4" D
Levels: 2
Square Footage: 3,437
Main Level Sq. Ft.: 2,184
Upper Level Sq. Ft.: 1,253
Bedrooms: 5
Bathrooms: 4
Foundation: Crawl space or slab; basement or daylight basement for fee
CompleteCost List Available: Yes
Price Category: F

Beauty, comfort, and convenience are yours in this luxurious, split-level home.

Features:

• Ceiling Height: 10 ft. unless otherwise noted.

• Master Suite: The 11-ft. pan ceiling sets the tone for this secluded area, with a lovely bay window that opens onto a rear porch, a pass-through fireplace to the great room, and a sitting room.

• Great Room: The pass-through fireplace makes this spacious room a cozy spot,

while the French doors leading to a rear porch make it a perfect spot for entertaining.

• Dining Room: Gracious 8-in. columns set off the entrance to this room.

• Kitchen: An island bar provides an efficient work area that's fitted with a sink.

• Breakfast Room: Open to the kitchen, this room is defined by a bay window and a spiral staircase to the second floor.

• Laundry Room: Large enough to accommodate a folding table, this room can also be fitted with a swinging pet door.

• Play Room: French doors in the children's playroom open onto a balcony where they can continue their games.

• Bedrooms: The 9-ft. ceilings on the second story make the rooms feel bright and airy.

Copyright by designer/architect.

Main Level Floor Plan

Upper Level Floor Plan

Plan #321061

Dimensions: 55' W x 49'4" D

Levels: 2

Square Footage: 3,169

Main Level Sq. Ft.: 1,679

Upper Level Sq. Ft.: 1,490

Bedrooms: 4

Bathrooms: 2½

Foundation: Basement

Materials List Available: Yes

Price Category: G

Images provided by designer/architect.

This spacious home combines a truly elegant appearance with family-oriented, comfortable design elements.

Features:

• Entryway: This large area features a hand crafted stairway to the upper floor, French doors leading to the living room, and an adjacent powder room.

• Living Room: This lovely room is ideal for quiet times or lively entertaining.

• Family Room: You'll enjoy all the amenities in this large room, with its lovely bay window, handsome fireplace, and walk-in wet bar.

• Dining Area: This area is open to the living room but is visually set apart by a gracious tray ceiling.

• Study: Adjacent to the front bedroom on the main floor, this study provides a place for quiet times.

• Master Suite: Located on the second floor for privacy, this area is luxurious in every respect.

CAD FILE AVAILABLE

Main Level Floor Plan

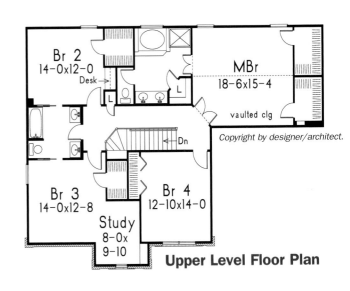

Copyright by designer/architect.

Upper Level Floor Plan

Plan #161016

Dimensions: 59'4" W x 58'8" D

Levels: 1.5

Square Footage: 2,101

Main Level Sq. Ft.: 1,626

Upper Level Sq. Ft.: 475

Bedrooms: 3

Bathrooms: 2½

Foundation: Basement;
crawl space option available for fee

Materials List Available: Yes

Price Category: D

Note: Home in photo reflects a modified garage entrance.

Images provided by designer/architect.

Features:

• **Great Room:** Made for relaxing and entertaining, the great room is sunken to set it off from the rest of the house. A balcony from the second floor looks down into this spacious area, making it easy to keep track of the kids while they are playing.

• **Kitchen:** Convenience marks this well laid-out kitchen where you'll love to cook for guests and for family.

• **Master Suite:** A vaulted ceiling complements the unusual octagonal shape

of the master suite. Located on the first floor, this room allows some privacy from the second floor bedrooms. It is also ideal for anyone who no longer wishes to climb stairs to reach a bedroom.

You'll love the exciting roofline that sets this elegant home apart from its neighbors as well as the embellished, solid look that declares how well-designed it is—from the inside to the exterior.

Rear Elevation

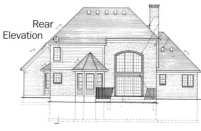

CAD FILE AVAILABLE

Main Level Floor Plan

Copyright by designer/architect.

Upper Level Floor Plan

Plan #121008

Dimensions: 62' W x 56' D
Levels: 1
Square Footage: 1,651
Bedrooms: 2
Bathrooms: 2
Foundation: Basement
Materials List Available: Yes
Price Category: C

CAD FILE AVAILABLE

This elegant home is packed with amenities that belie its compact size.

Features:

- Ceiling Height: 8 ft.

- Dining Room: The foyer opens into a view of the dining room, with its distinctive boxed ceiling.

- Great Room: The whole family will want to gather around the fireplace and enjoy the views and sunlight streaming through the transom-topped window.

- Breakfast Area: Next to the great room and sharing the transom-topped windows, this cozy area invites you to linger over morning coffee.

- Covered Porch: When the weather is nice, take your coffee through the door in the breakfast area and enjoy this large covered porch.

- Master Suite: French doors lead to this comfortable suite featuring a walk-in closet. Enjoy long, luxurious soaks in the corner whirlpool accented with boxed windows.

Images provided by designer/architect.

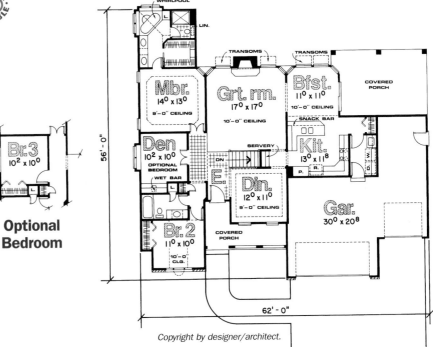

Optional Bedroom

Br.3
10² x 10⁰

WHIRLPOOL
LIN.
Mbr.
14⁰ x 13⁰
9'-0" CEILING
TRANSOMS
TRANSOMS
Grt. rm.
17⁰ x 17⁰
10'-0" CEILING
Bfst.
11⁰ x 11⁰
10'-0" CEILING
COVERED PORCH
SNACK BAR
Den
10² x 10⁰
OPTIONAL BEDROOM
SERVERY
Kit.
13⁰ x 11⁸
WET BAR
56'-0"
ON
Dn.
Dn.
E
Din.
12⁰ x 11⁰
9'-0" CEILING
Gar.
30⁰ x 20⁸
Br. 2
11⁰ x 10⁰
10'-0" CLG.
COVERED PORCH
62'-0"

Copyright by designer/architect.

SMARTtip
Finishing Your Fireplace with Tile

An excellent finishing material for a fireplace is tile. Luckily, there are reproductions of art tiles today. Most showrooms carry examples of Arts and Crafts, Art Nouveau, California, Delft, and other European tiles. Granite, limestone, and marble tiles are affordable alternatives to custom stone slabs.

Plan #271096

Dimensions: 66' W x 90' D
Levels: 2
Square footage: 3,190
Main Level Sq. Ft.: 2,152
Upper Level Sq. Ft.: 1,038
Bedrooms: 4
Bathrooms: 3½
Foundation: Crawl space
Materials List Available: No
Price Category: G

Images provided by designer/architect.

This traditional home contains quite possibly everything you're dreaming of, and even more!

Features:

• Formal Rooms: These living and dining rooms flank the entry foyer, making a large space for special occasions.

• Family Room: A fireplace is the highlight of this spacious area, where the kids will play with their friends and watch TV.

• Kitchen: A central island makes cooking a breeze. The adjoining dinette is a sunny spot for casual meals.

• Master Suite: A large sleeping area is followed by a deluxe private bath with a whirlpool tub and a walk-in closet. Step through a French door to the backyard, which is big enough to host a deck with an inviting hot tub!

• Guest Suite: One bedroom upstairs has its own private bath, making it perfect for guests.

• A future room above the garage awaits your decision on how to use it.

Main Level Floor Plan

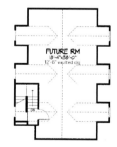

Upper Level Floor Plan

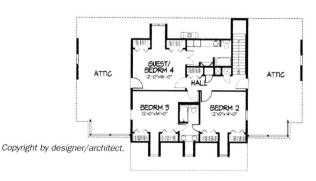

Copyright by designer/architect.

Plan #111015

Dimensions: 64' W x 58' D
Levels: 1
Square Footage: 2,208
Bedrooms: 4
Bathrooms: 2
Foundation: Slab
Materials List Available: No
Price Category: F

Images provided by designer/architect.

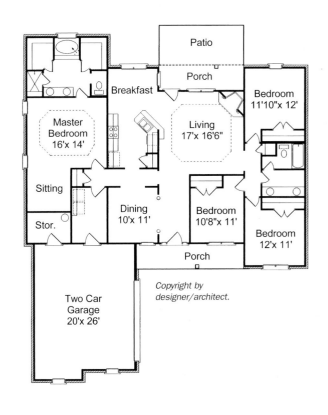

Copyright by designer/architect.

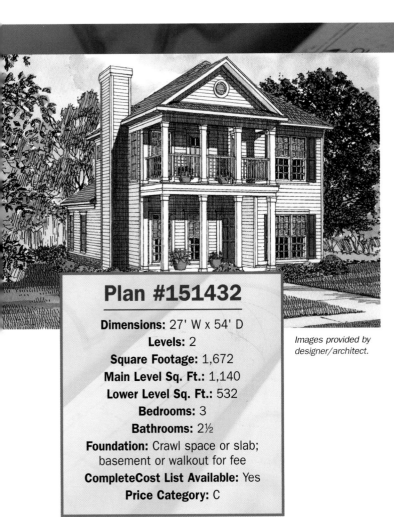

Plan #151432

Dimensions: 27' W x 54' D
Levels: 2
Square Footage: 1,672
Main Level Sq. Ft.: 1,140
Lower Level Sq. Ft.: 532
Bedrooms: 3
Bathrooms: 2½
Foundation: Crawl space or slab; basement or walkout for fee
CompleteCost List Available: Yes
Price Category: C

Images provided by designer/architect.

Main Level Floor Plan

Upper Level Floor Plan

Copyright by designer/architect.

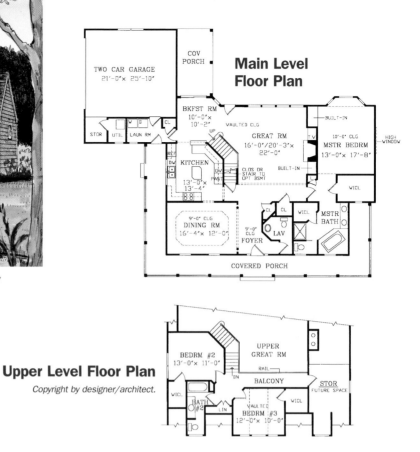

Main Level Floor Plan

TWO CAR GARAGE 21'-0" x 25'-10"

COV PORCH

BKFST RM 10'-0" x 10'-2"

VAULTED CLG

STOR

UTIL

LAUN RM

CL

GREAT RM 16'-0"/20'-3" x 22'-0"

10'-0" CLG MSTR BEDRM 13'-0" x 17'-8"

HIGH WINDOW

BUILT-IN

BUILT-IN

KITCHEN 13'-0" x 13'-4"

CLOS OR STAIR TO OPT BSMT

WICL

DINING RM 16'-4" x 12'-0"

9'-0" CLG

9'-0" CLG FOYER

CL CL WICL

LAV

MSTR BATH

COVERED PORCH

Images provided by designer/architect.

Upper Level Floor Plan

Copyright by designer/architect.

BEDRM #2 13'-0" x 11'-0"

UPPER GREAT RM

RAIL

DN

BALCONY

STOR FUTURE SPACE

WICL

BATH #2

LIN

VAULTED BEDRM #3 12'-0" x 10'-0"

WICL

Plan #131046

Dimensions: 68' W x 57'6" D

Levels: 2

Square Footage: 2,245

Main Level Sq. Ft.: 1,720

Upper Level Sq. Ft.: 525

Bedrooms: 3

Bathrooms: 2½

Foundation: Crawl space or slab; basement for fee

Materials List Available: Yes

Price Category: F

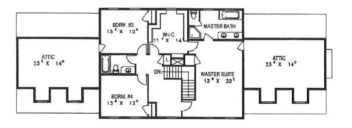

Upper Level Floor Plan

ATTIC 23'-8" x 14'-0"

BDRM #3 13'-8" x 12'-0"

WIC 11'-? x 14'-?

MASTER BATH

DN

MASTER SUITE 13'-8" x 22'-2"

BDRM #4 13'-8" x 12'-0"

ATTIC 23'-8" x 14'-0"

Main Level Floor Plan

90'-0"

UTILITY

EATING AREA 13'-8" x 12'-0"

KITCHEN 14'-? x 16'-?

DINING ROOM 13'-8" x 19'-0"

2 CAR GARAGE 23'-8" x 22'-2"

GATHERING ROOM 23'-8" x 28'-0"

35'-0"

BDRM #2 13'-8" x 12'-0"

ENTRY

MEDIA ROOM 13'-8" x 14'-0"

UP

Copyright by designer/architect.

Plan #451157

Dimensions: 90' W x 35' D

Levels: 2

Square Footage: 3,527

Main Level Sq. Ft.: 2,183

Upper Level Sq. Ft.: 1,344

Bedrooms: 4

Bathrooms: 3

Foundation: Crawl space

Material List Available: No

Price Category: H

Images provided by designer/architect.

CAD FILE AVAILABLE

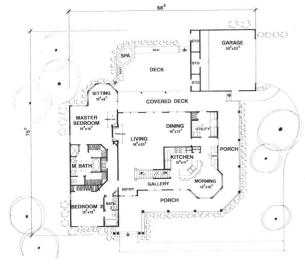

Main Level Floor Plan

Plan #331003

Dimensions: 68'8" W x 75' D

Levels: 2

Square Footage: 2,660

Main Level Sq. Ft.: 2,000

Upper Level Sq. Ft.: 660

Bedrooms: 4

Bathrooms: 3

Foundation: Crawl space, slab or basement

Materials List Available: No

Price Category: F

Images provided by designer/architect.

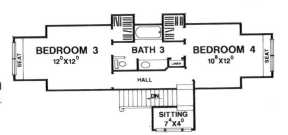

Upper Level Floor Plan

Copyright by designer/architect.

Plan #371065

Dimensions: 92'10" W x 70' D

Levels: 2

Square Footage: 3,266

Main Level Sq. Ft.: 2,313

Upper Level Sq. Ft.: 953

Bedrooms: 4

Bathrooms: 3½

Foundation: Slab

Material List Available: No

Price Category: G

Images provided by designer/architect.

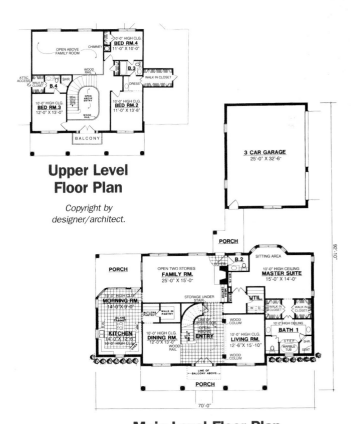

Upper Level Floor Plan

Copyright by designer/architect.

Main Level Floor Plan

Plan #111024

Dimensions: 46'10" W x 68'5" D
Levels: 2
Square Footage: 2,356
Main Level Sq. Ft.: 1,516
Upper Level Sq. Ft.: 840
Bedrooms: 4
Bathrooms: 2½
Foundation: Slab
Materials List Available: No
Price Category: F

Images provided by designer/architect.

A Southern-style home with a front porch and round-top windows, this is a great place to raise a family.

Features:

• **Living Room:** This gathering area features a ceiling that is two stories tall. The cozy fireplace will add warmth to a cool night.

• **Kitchen:** This U-shape kitchen with an abundance of cabinets and counter space would be a welcome addition to any home. The raised bar, which is open to the breakfast room, adds seating space to the area.

• **Master Suite:** Located on the main level for privacy, this oasis boasts a large walk-in closet. The master bath features his and her vanities, a stall shower, and a whirlpool tub.

• **Upper Level:** Three additional bedrooms and a full bathroom occupy this level. The balcony overlooks the living room.

Main Level Floor Plan

Upper Level Floor Plan
Copyright by designer/architect.

Plan #151101

Dimensions: 87'10" W x 54'6" D

Levels: 1

Square Footage: 2,804

Bedrooms: 4

Bathrooms: 2½

Foundation: Slab; basement for fee

CompleteCost List Available: Yes

Price Category: F

This one-story home has everything you would find in a two-story house and more. This home plan is keeping up with the times.

CAD FILE AVAILABLE

Features:

• Porches: The long covered front porch is perfect for sitting out on warm evenings and greeting passersby. The back grilling porch, which opens through French doors from the great room, is great for entertaining guests with summer barbecues.

• Utility: Accessible from outside as well as the three-car garage, this small utility room is a multipurpose space. Through the breakfast area is the unique hobby/laundry area, a room made large enough for both the wash and the family artist.

• Cooking and Eating Areas: In one straight shot, this kitchen flows into both the sunlit breakfast room and the formal dining room,

for simple transitions no matter the meal. The kitchen features tons of work and storage space, as well as a stovetop island with a seated snack bar and a second eating bar between the kitchen and breakfast room.

• Study: For bringing work home with you or simply paying the bills, this quiet study sits off the foyer through French doors.

• Master Suite: A triplet of windows allows the

morning sun to shine in on this spacious, relaxing area. The full master bath features two separate vanities, a glass shower, a whirlpool tub, and a large walk-in closet.

• Secondary Bedrooms: Two of the three bedrooms include computer centers, keeping pace with the technological times, and all three-share access to the second full bathroom, with its dual sinks and whirlpool tub.

Images provided by designer/architect.

Copyright by designer/architect.

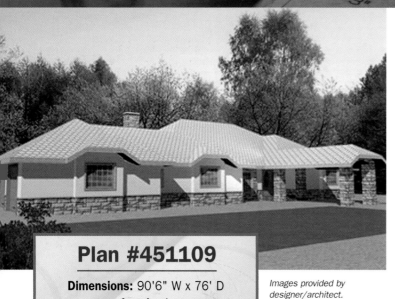

Plan #451109

Dimensions: 90'6" W x 76' D

Levels: 1

Square Footage: 4,475

Main Level Sq. Ft.: 3,235

Basement Level Sq. Ft.: 1,240

Bedrooms: 2

Bathrooms: 2½

Foundation: Crawl space – insulated concrete form

Material List Available: No

Price Category: I

Images provided by designer/architect.

CAD FILE AVAILABLE — CAD

Basement Level Floor Plan

Copyright by designer/architect.

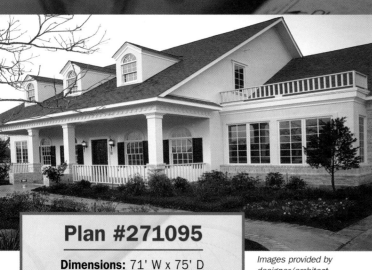

Plan #271095

Dimensions: 71' W x 75' D

Levels: 2

Square Footage: 3,220

Main Level Sq. Ft.: 2,040

Upper Level Sq. Ft.: 1,180

Bedrooms: 3

Bathrooms: 4

Foundation: Crawl space, slab

Material List Available: No

Price Category: G

Images provided by designer/architect.

Main Level Floor Plan

Upper Level Floor Plan

Copyright by designer/architect.

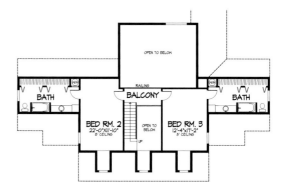

**Main Level
Floor Plan**

GARAGE
23'-6" X 20'-0"

STORAGE

STORAGE

UTIL.

NOOK
10'-0" X 12'-0"

10'-0" HIGH CLG.

B.2

PANT.

RAISED BAR

FAMILY RM.
16'-0" X 18'-0"

PORCH

GLASS SHR.

10'-0" HIGH CLG.

DINING RM.
12'-0" X 13'-0"

10'-0" HIGH CLG.

KITCH.
11'-0" X 14'-0"

10'-0" HIGH CLG.

BATH 1

LIN

10'-0" HIGH CLG.

LIVING RM.
18'-0" X 13'-0"

10'-0" HIGH CLG.

ABOVE

ENTRY

10'-0" HIGH CLG.

MASTER SUITE
18'-0" X 13'-0"

PORCH

**Upper Level
Floor Plan**

*Copyright by
designer/architect.*

OPEN ABOVE FAMILY RM.

BED RM.4
12'-6" X 13'-0"

B.4

LIN

WOOD RAIL

SHR.

B.3

LIN

LOFT

STAIR DOWN

WOOD RAIL

RETURN AIR

BED RM.3
18'-0" X 13'-0"

OPEN ABOVE ENTRY

BED RM.2
18'-6" X 13'-0"

Plan #371064

Dimensions: 63' W x 69'4" D

Levels: 2

Square Footage: 3,140

Main Level Sq. Ft.: 1,965

Upper Level Sq. Ft.: 1,175

Bedrooms: 4

Bathrooms: 3½

Foundation: Slab

Materials List Available: No

Price Category: G

*Images provided by
designer/architect.*

Plan #451098

Dimensions: 86' W x 48' D

Levels: 1

Square Footage: 2,428

Bedrooms: 3

Bathrooms: 2

Foundation: Walkout –
insulated concrete form

Material List Available: No

Price Category: E

*Images provided by
designer/architect.*

CAD FILE AVAILABLE

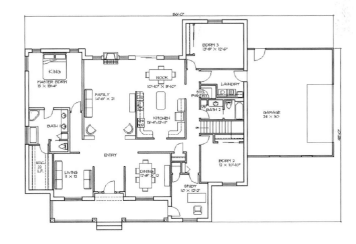

KING

MASTER BDRM
15 X 19'-6"

BDRM 3
13'-6" X 12'-6"

FAMILY
14'-6" X 21

NOOK
10'-10" X 8'-0"

LAUNDRY

STG. PANTRY

BATH 2

GARAGE
24 X 30

BATH 3

KITCHEN
13'-4" X 10'-11"

ENTRY

BDRM 2
12 X 10'-6"

W.I.C.
22 L.F.

LIVING
11 X 13

DINING
17'-6" X 13

STUDY
10' X 12'-2"

Copyright by designer/architect.

Plan #431001

Dimensions: 58'8" W x 62' D

Levels: 1

Square Footage: 1,792

Bedrooms: 3

Bathrooms: 2½

Foundation: Crawl space or basement

Material List Available: Yes

Price Category: C-

Images provided by designer/architect.

Your neighbors will envy this Southern-style home.

Features:

- Great Room: The entry overlooks this room, where a fireplace warms gatherings on chilly evenings. A large window and French doors allow a view of the yard.

- Kitchen: The primary workstation in this kitchen is a peninsula, which faces the fireplace in the great room. The peninsula is equipped with a sink and snack counter.

- Master Suite: This private space is located on the other side of the home from the other bedrooms. It contains expansive his and her walk-in closets, a spa tub, and a double vanity area in the salon.

- Bedrooms: Two additional bedrooms are separated from the master suite. Both bedrooms have large closets and share a hall bathroom.

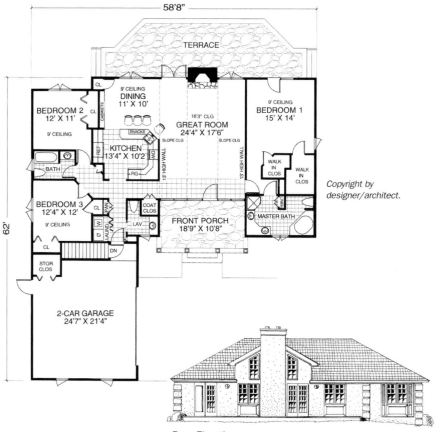

Copyright by designer/architect.

Rear Elevation

Plan #101005

Dimensions: 63' W x 57'2" D
Levels: 1
Square Footage: 1,992
Bedrooms: 3
Bathrooms: 2½
Foundation: Crawl space, slab, or basement
Materials List Available: Yes
Price Category: D

CAD FILE AVAILABLE

Images provided by designer/architect.

This midsized ranch is accented with Palladian windows and inviting front porch.

Features:

- Ceiling Height: 9 ft. unless otherwise noted.

- Special Ceilings: Tray or vaulted ceilings adorn the living room, family room, dining room, and master suite.

- Kitchen: This bright and airy kitchen is designed to be a pleasure in which to work. It shares a big bay window with the contiguous breakfast room.

- Breakfast Room: The light streaming in from the bay window makes this the perfect place to linger with coffee and the Sunday paper.

- Master Suite: This lovely suite is exceptional, with its sitting area and direct access to the deck, as well as a full-featured bath, and spacious walk-in closet.

- Secondary Bedrooms: The other bedrooms each measure about 13 ft. x 11 ft. They have walk-in closets and share a "Jack-and-Jill" bath.

Rear View

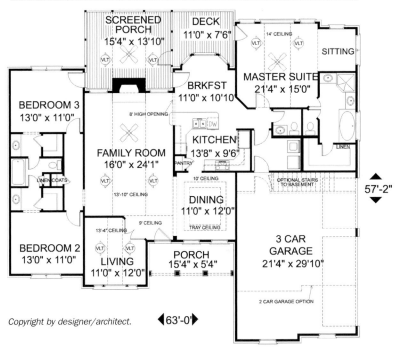

SCREENED PORCH 15'4" x 13'10"
DECK 11'0" x 7'6"
14' CEILING
SITTING
MASTER SUITE 21'4" x 15'0"
BRKFST 11'0" x 10'10"
8' HIGH OPENING
BEDROOM 3 13'0" x 11'0"
KITCHEN 13'8" x 9'6"
FAMILY ROOM 16'0" x 24'1"
PANTRY
10' CEILING
13'-10" CEILING
LINEN COATS
OPTIONAL STAIRS TO BASEMENT
LINEN
DINING 11'0" x 12'0"
TRAY CEILING
9' CEILING
57'-2"
BEDROOM 2 13'0" x 11'0"
13'-4" CEILING
3 CAR GARAGE 21'4" x 29'10"
LIVING 11'0" x 12'0"
PORCH 15'4" x 5'4"
2 CAR GARAGE OPTION

Copyright by designer/architect.

◄63'-0'►

Images provided by designer/architect.

Plan #181652

Dimensions: 29' W x 44' D
Levels: 2
Square Footage: 1,579
Main Level Sq. Ft.: 709
Upper Level Sq. Ft.: 870
Bedrooms: 3
Bathrooms: 1½
Foundation: Basement
Material List Available: Yes
Price Category: E

This is an attractive home with an appealing Mediterranean look.

CAD FILE AVAILABLE

Features:

- Entry: This covered entry welcomes you home. The sidelights on the front door flood the interior with light. A coat closet and a half bath add convenience.

- Family Room: Open to the kitchen for an airy feel, this gathering area will be the place to unwind after a long day.

- Kitchen: The family chef will love this kitchen. The room contains extra seating at the island and a convenient breakfast nook. A three-panel sliding-glass door brings plenty of natural light to the area.

- Upper Level: Three bedrooms, a full bathroom, and the laundry area are located on this level.

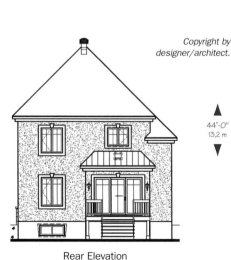

Rear Elevation

Copyright by designer/architect.

Main Level Floor Plan

14'-8" X 19'-0"
4,40 X 5,70

12'-8" X 14'-0"
3,80 X 4,20

44'-0"
13,2 m

12'-0" X 20'-8"
3,60 X 6,20

29'-0"
8,7 m

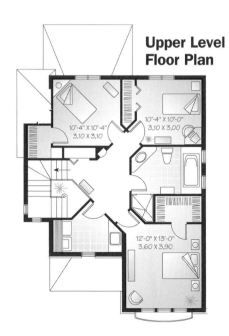

Upper Level Floor Plan

10'-4" X 10'-4"
3,10 X 3,10

10'-4" X 10'-0"
3,10 X 3,00

12'-0" X 13'-0"
3,60 X 3,90

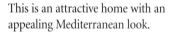

Plan #121063

Dimensions: 84' W x 52' D
Levels: 2
Square Footage: 3,473
Main Level Sq. Ft.: 2,500
Upper Level Sq. Ft.: 973
Bedrooms: 4
Bathrooms: 3½
Foundation: Basement; crawl space for fee
Materials List Available: Yes
Price Category: G

Images provided by designer/architect.

Enjoy the many amenities in this well-designed and gracious home.

Features:

- Entry: A large sparkling window and a tapering split staircase distinguish this lovely entryway.
- Great Room: This spacious great room will be the heart of your new home. It has a 14-ft. spider-beamed ceiling that serves to highlight its built-in bookcase, built-in entertainment center, raised hearth fireplace,

wet bar, and lovely arched windows topped with transoms.

- Kitchen: Anyone who walks into this kitchen will realize that it's designed for both convenience and efficiency.
- Master Suite: The tiered ceiling in the bedroom gives an elegant touch, and the bay window adds to it. The two large walk-in closets and the spacious bath, with columns setting off the whirlpool tub and two vanities, complete this dream of a suite.

Main Level Floor Plan

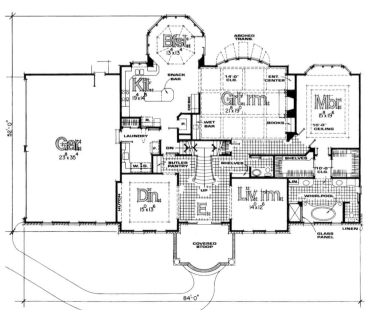

Upper Level Floor Plan

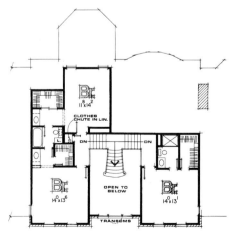

Copyright by designer/architect.

Plan #121070

Dimensions: 50' W x 58' D
Levels: 2
Square Footage: 2,139
Main Level Sq. Ft.: 1,506
Upper Level Sq. Ft.: 633
Bedrooms: 4
Bathrooms: 2½
Foundation: Basement
Materials List Available: Yes
Price Category: D

Images provided by designer/architect.

You'll love this design if you're looking for a bright, airy home where you can easily entertain.

Features:

- Entry: A volume ceiling sets the tone for this home when you first walk in.

- Great Room: With a volume ceiling extending from the entry, this great room has an open feeling. Transom-topped windows contribute

natural light during the day.

- Dining Room: Because it is joined to the great room through a cased opening, this dining room can serve as an extension of the great room.

- Kitchen: An island with a snack bar, desk, and pantry make this kitchen a treat, and a door from the breakfast area leads to a private covered patio where dining will be a pleasure.

Main Level Floor Plan

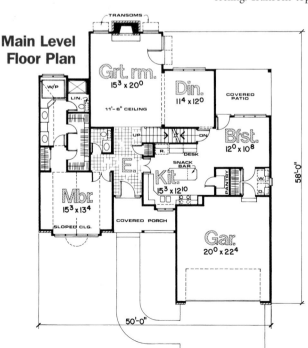

Upper Level Floor Plan

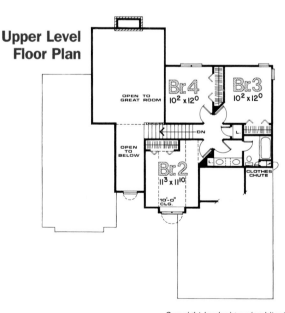

Copyright by designer/architect.

Plan #311003

Dimensions: 70'10" W x 65'4" D
Levels: 2
Square Footage: 2,428
Main Level Sq. Ft.: 2,348
Upper Level Sq. Ft.: 80
Bedrooms: 3
Bathrooms: 2½
Foundation: Crawl space, slab
Materials List Available: Y
Price Category: F

Images provided by designer/architect.

If you admire the gracious colonnaded porch, curved brick steps, and stunning front windows, you'll fall in love with the interior of this home.

Features:

- Great Room: Enjoy the vaulted ceiling, balcony from the upper level, and fireplace with flanking windows that let you look out to the patio.

- Dining Room: Columns define this formal room, which is adjacent to the breakfast room.

- Kitchen: A bayed sink area and extensive curved bar provide visual interest in this well-designed kitchen, which every cook will love.

- Breakfast Room: Huge windows let the sun shine into this room, which is open to the kitchen.

- Master Suite: The sitting area is open to the rear porch for a special touch in this gorgeous suite. Two walk-in closets and a vaulted ceiling and double vanity in the bath will make you feel completely pampered.

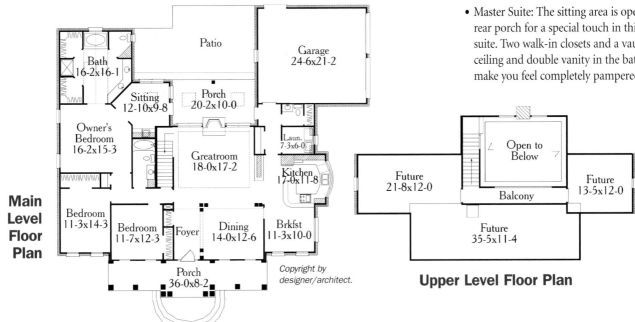

Copyright by designer/architect.

Main Level Floor Plan

Upper Level Floor Plan

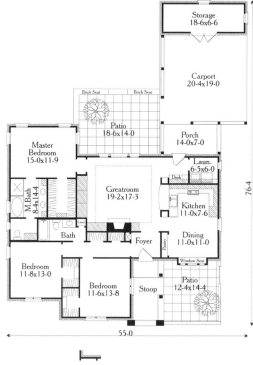

Storage
18-6x6-6

Carport
20-4x19-0

Brick Seat   Brick Seat

Patio
18-6x14-0

Porch
14-0x7-0

Master
Bedroom
15-0x11-9

Laun.
6-5x6-0

Deck

M.Bath
8-4x14-4

Greatroom
19-2x17-3

Kitchen
11-0x7-6

Bath

Foyer

Dining
11-0x11-0

Window Seat

Bedroom
11-8x13-0

Bedroom
11-6x13-8

Stoop

Patio
12-4x14-4

76-4

55-0

Plan #311058

Dimensions: 55' W x 76'4" D

Levels: 1

Square Footage: 1,702

Bedrooms: 3

Bathrooms: 2

Foundation: Crawl space, slab, or basement

Material List Available: Yes

Price Category: D

Images provided by designer/architect.

Basement Stair Location

Greatroom
15-3x17-3

Bath

Copyright by designer/architect.

Upper Level Floor Plan

Copyright by designer/architect.

Deck

Bedroom 2
13⁹ · 12⁹

Loft

Open To Below

Bath

Bedroom 3
13⁹ · 12⁹

Open To Below

Bedroom 4
13⁹ · 12⁹

Plan #661213

Dimensions: 77'8" W x 67' D

Levels: 2

Square Footage: 3,393

Main Level Sq. Ft.: 2,422

Upper Level Sq. Ft.: 971

Bedrooms: 5

Bathrooms: 3½

Foundation: Slab

Material List Available: No

Price Category: G

Images provided by designer/architect.

CAD FILE AVAILABLE

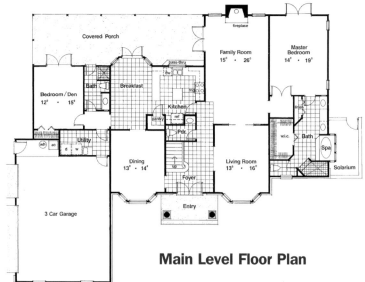

Covered Porch

fireplace

Family Room
15⁹ · 26⁹

Master Bedroom
14⁹ · 19⁹

pass-thru

Bedroom / Den
12⁹ · 15⁹

Bath

Breakfast

Kitchen

Pdr.

w.i.c.

Bath

Spa

Utility

pantry   ref

Dining
13⁹ · 14⁹

Living Room
13⁹ · 16⁹

Solarium

3 Car Garage

Foyer

Entry

Main Level Floor Plan

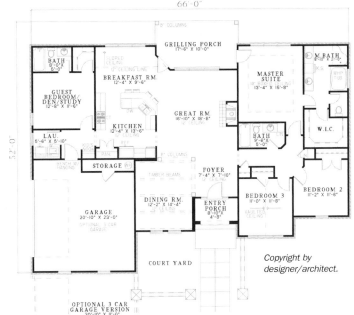

Plan #151850

Dimensions: 66' W x 52' D

Levels: 1

Square Footage: 2,075

Bedrooms: 4

Bathrooms: 3

Foundation: Crawl space or slab; basement or walkout for fee

CompleteCost List Available: Yes

Price Category: D

Images provided by designer/architect.

CAD FILE AVAILABLE

Copyright by designer/architect.

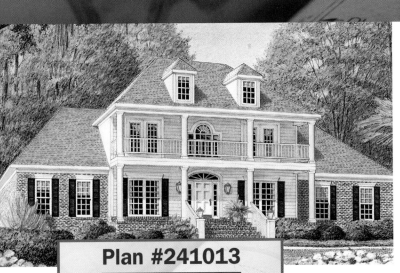

Plan #241013

Dimensions: 68' W x 46' D

Levels: 2

Square Footage: 3,033

Main Level Sq. Ft.: 1,918

Upper Level Sq. Ft.: 1,115

Bedrooms: 4

Bathrooms: 3½

Foundation: Crawl space, slab, or walkout

Materials List Available: No

Price Category: G

Images provided by designer/architect.

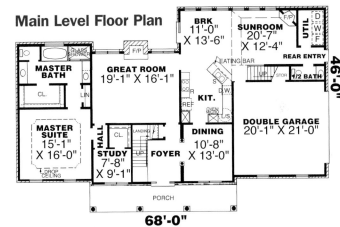

Main Level Floor Plan

Upper Level Floor Plan

Copyright by designer/architect.

Plan #271100

Dimensions: 69'10" W x 66'5" D
Levels: 2
Square Footage: 3,263
Main Level Sq. Ft.: 2,017
Upper Level Sq. Ft.: 1,246
Bedrooms: 4
Bathrooms: 2½
Foundation: Basement
Material List Available: No
Price Category: G

Images provided by designer/architect.

A main level master suite is just the home you have been looking for.

Features:

- **Family Room:** The cathedral ceiling and cozy fireplace strike a balance that creates the perfect gathering place for family and friends. An abundance of space allows you to tailor this room to your needs.

- **Kitchen:** Great for the busy family, this kitchen has all the workspace and storage that the family chef needs, as well as a snack bar that acts as a transition to the large dinette area.

- **Master Bedroom:** Away from the busy areas of the home, this master suite is ideal for shedding your daily cares and relaxing in a romantic atmosphere. It includes a full master bath with his and her sinks, a stall shower, and a whirlpool tub.

- **Second Floor:** Three bedrooms share the second full bathroom. The game room is also located on this level, making it the perfect entertainment area.

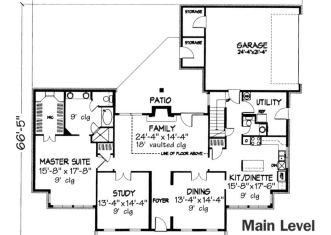

Main Level Floor Plan

Upper Level Floor Plan

Copyright by designer/architect.

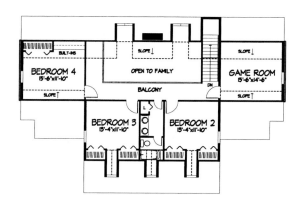

Plan #121047

Dimensions: 67'8" W x 57' D

Levels: 2

Square Footage: 3,072

Main Level Sq. Ft.: 2,116

Upper Level Sq. Ft.: 956

Bedrooms: 4

Bathrooms: 3½

Foundation: Slab; crawl space or basement for fee

Materials List Available: Yes

Price Category: G

Images provided by designer/architect.

CAD FILE AVAILABLE

A long porch and a trio of roof dormers give this gracious home a sophisticated country look.

Features:

- Ceiling Height: 8 ft. unless otherwise noted.
- Balcony: This balcony overlooks the entry and the staircase hall.
- Dining Room: Columns and a cased opening lend elegance, making this the perfect venue for stylish dinner parties.

- Family Room: A cathedral ceiling gives this room a light and airy feel. The handsome fireplace framed by windows is sure to become a favorite family gathering place.
- Master Suite: This architecturally distinctive suite features a bayed sitting area and a tray ceiling.
- Bedrooms: One of the bedrooms enjoys a private bath, making it a perfect guest room. Other bedrooms feature walk-in closets.

Main Level Floor Plan

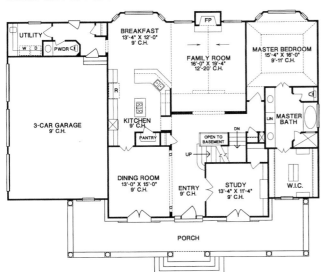

Upper Level Floor Plan

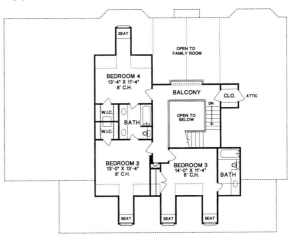

Copyright by designer/architect.

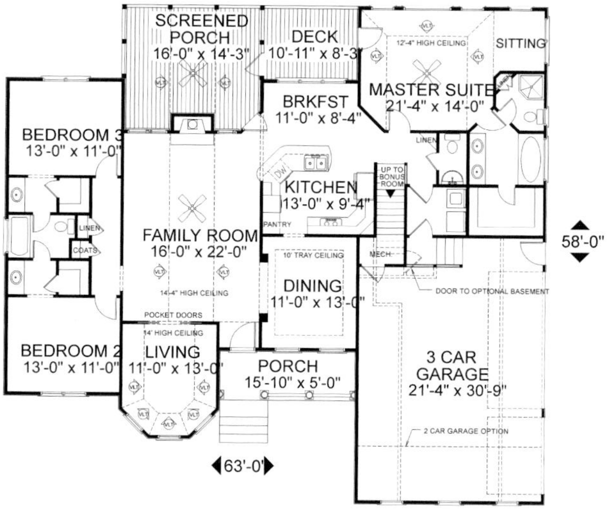

Images provided by designer/architect.

Copyright by designer/architect.

Plan #101006

Dimensions: 63' W x 58' D

Levels: 1

Square Footage: 1,982

Bedrooms: 3

Bathrooms: 2½

Foundation: Crawl space, slab basement, or walkout

Materials List Available: Yes

Price Category: D

CAD FILE AVAILABLE

SMARTtip

Art in Pools

The tiled walls and floor of a pool make great canvases for art, so incorporate a serious or whimsical design. Also, make the stairs wide and shallow to form a wading area for kids.

Floor plan labels:
- SCREENED PORCH 16'-0" x 14'-3"
- DECK 10'-11" x 8'-3"
- SITTING
- 12'-4" HIGH CEILING
- BEDROOM 3 13'-0" x 11'-0"
- BRKFST 11'-0" x 8'-4"
- MASTER SUITE 21'-4" x 14'-0"
- LINEN
- KITCHEN 13'-0" x 9'-4"
- UP TO BONUS ROOM
- FAMILY ROOM 16'-0" x 22'-0"
- PANTRY
- 10' TRAY CEILING
- LINEN
- COATS
- 14'-4" HIGH CEILING
- DINING 11'-0" x 13'-0"
- MECH
- DOOR TO OPTIONAL BASEMENT
- 58'-0"
- BEDROOM 2 13'-0" x 11'-0"
- LIVING 11'-0" x 13'-0"
- POCKET DOORS
- 14' HIGH CEILING
- PORCH 15'-10" x 5'-0"
- 3 CAR GARAGE 21'-4" x 30'-9"
- 2 CAR GARAGE OPTION
- 63'-0"

Copyright by designer/architect.

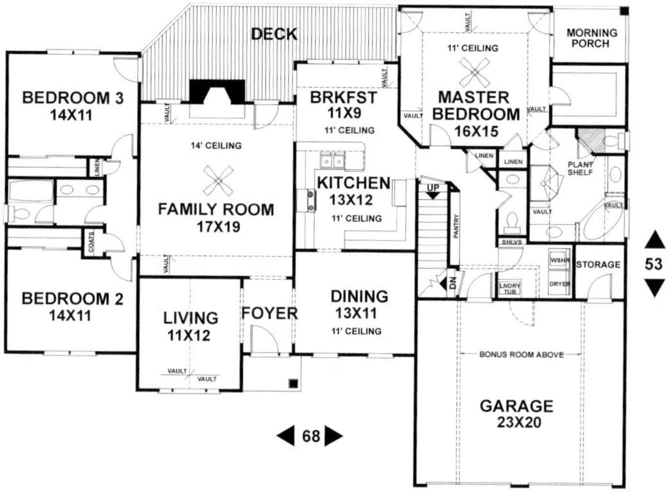

Plan #101008

Dimensions: 68' W x 53' D

Levels: 1

Square Footage: 2,088

Bedrooms: 3

Bathrooms: 2½

Foundation: Crawl space, slab, or basement

Materials List Available: Yes

Price Category: E

Images provided by designer/architect.

CAD FILE AVAILABLE

SMARTtip

Accentuating Your Bathroom with Details

No matter how big or small the room, details will pull the style together. Some of the best details that you can include are the smallest—drawer pulls from an antique store or shells in a glass jar or just left on the countertop. Add period flavor with crown molding, or dress up contemporary fixtures with polished stone fittings.

Floor plan labels:
- DECK
- 11' CEILING
- MORNING PORCH
- BEDROOM 3 14X11
- BRKFST 11X9
- MASTER BEDROOM 16X15
- VAULT
- 11' CEILING
- LINEN
- PLANT SHELF
- 14' CEILING
- KITCHEN 13X12
- UP
- FAMILY ROOM 17X19
- PANTRY
- VAULT
- 53
- BEDROOM 2 14X11
- LIVING 11X12
- FOYER
- DINING 13X11
- 11' CEILING
- DN
- WSHR
- DRYER
- LNDRY TUB
- STORAGE
- BONUS ROOM ABOVE
- GARAGE 23X20
- 68

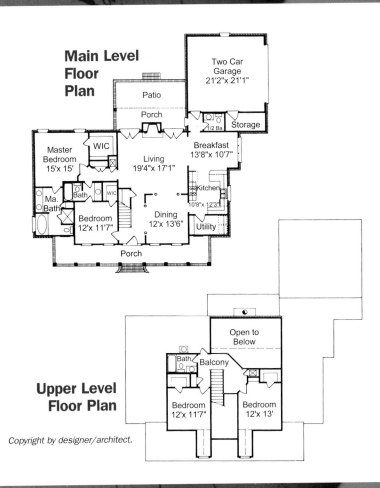

Main Level Floor Plan

Two Car Garage 21'2"x 21'1"

Patio

Porch

Storage

1/2 Ba

Master Bedroom 15'x 15'

WIC

Living 19'4"x 17'1"

Breakfast 13'8"x 10'7"

Ma. Bath

Bath

WIC

Kitchen 10'8"x 12'3"

Bedroom 12'x 11'7"

Dining 12'x 13'6"

Utility

Porch

Images provided by designer/architect.

Plan #111026

Dimensions: 66' W x 65' D
Levels: 2
Square Footage: 2,406
Main Level Sq. Ft.: 1,796
Upper Level Sq. Ft.: 610
Bedrooms: 4
Bathrooms: 3½
Foundation: Crawlspace
Materials List Available: No
Price Category: F

Open to Below

Bath

Balcony

Upper Level Floor Plan

Bedroom 12'x 11'7"

Bedroom 12'x 13'

Bonus Area Floor Plan

STOR.

ATTIC ACCESS

SLOPED CLG.

UNFINISHED BONUS ROOM 18'-8" X 18'-0" (CLEAR) 8'-0" C.H.

SLOPED CLG.

9-0 Clg. Ht.

LIN.

MASTER BATH 17-4 X 9-2

JET TUB

10-0 Clg. Ht.

MASTER BEDROOM 14-6 X 17-6

3-SIDED MIRROR

SHWR.

SEAT

CLOS. 6-8 X 8

CLOS. 10-4 X 8

OPEN STORAGE

Main Level Floor Plan

DESK

BEDROOM 4 14-0 X 11-6 9-0 C.H.

COVERED PORCH 20-8 X 10-10

BREAKFAST 13-8 X 15-2 9-0 C.H.

HALL

HALF BATH

ENTRY 8-2 X 6-4

DESK

THREE CAR GARAGE 23-8 X 35-0

CLOSET

BATH 9-10 X 5-6

BATH 12-2 X 5-8

HALL

TV SPACE

VAULT

GAS LOGS

GREAT ROOM 20-0 X 17-6 (CLEAR)

VAULT

RAISED BAR

DW

KITCHEN 16-0 X 13-2 9-0 C.H.

MUD ROOM

PAN.

CLOSET

TUB/SHWR

CLOSET

BEDROOM 3 12-2 X 11-6 9-0 C.H.

BEDROOM 2 11-6 X 12-0 9-0 C.H.

COAT

FOYER 6-0 X 12-0

DINING OR STUDY 11-6 X 12-0 9-0 C.H.

OVEN

STORAGE 5-10 X 9-2

LAUN. 14-4 X 8-0

BR

SHLV.

COVERED PORCH 35-0 X 6-0

Plan #351104

Dimensions: 84' W x 67'10" D
Levels: 1
Square Footage: 2,755
Bedrooms: 4
Bathrooms: 3½
Foundation: Crawl space or slab
Material List Available: Yes
Price Category: G

Images provided by designer/architect.

CAD FILE AVAILABLE **CAD**

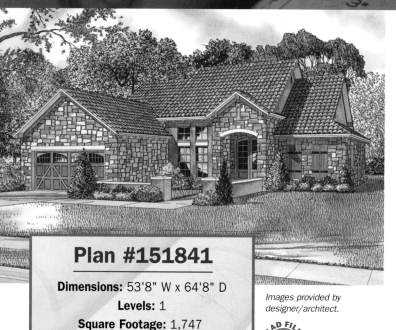

Plan #151841

Dimensions: 53'8" W x 64'8" D

Levels: 1

Square Footage: 1,747

Bedrooms: 3

Bathrooms: 2

Foundation: Crawl space or slab; basement or walkout for fee

CompleteCost List Available: Yes

Price Category: C

Images provided by designer/architect.

CAD FILE AVAILABLE

Copyright by designer/architect.

Plan #101009

Dimensions: 70'2" W x 59' D

Levels: 1

Square Footage: 2,097

Bedrooms: 3

Bathrooms: 3

Foundation: Crawl space, slab, or basement

Materials List Available: Yes

Price Category: E

Images provided by designer/architect.

CAD FILE AVAILABLE

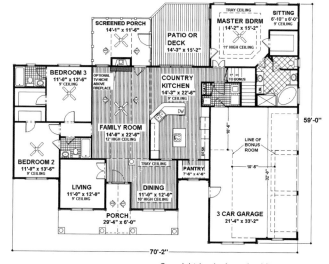

Copyright by designer/architect.

SMARTtip

Single-Level Decks

A single-level deck can use a strong vertical element, such as a pergola or a gazebo, to make it interesting. A simple and less-expensive option is a potted conical shrub or a clematis growing on a trellis.

Plan #131001

Dimensions: 72'4" W x 32'4" D

Levels: 1

Square Footage: 1,615

Bedrooms: 3

Bathrooms: 2

Foundation: Crawl space or slab; basement or walkout for fee

Materials List Available: Yes

Price Category: D

Images provided by designer/architect.

Copyright by designer/architect.

Main Level Floor Plan

Upper Level Floor Plan

Plan #151014

Dimensions: 70'2" W x 51'4" D

Levels: 1.5

Square Footage: 2,698

Main Level Sq. Ft.: 1,813

Upper Level Sq. Ft.: 885

Bedrooms: 5

Bathrooms: 3

Foundation: Crawl space or slab; basement or walkout for fee

CompleteCost List Available: Yes

Price Category: F

Images provided by designer/architect.

CAD FILE AVAILABLE

Copyright by designer/architect.

Images provided by designer/architect.

Plan #211076

Dimensions: 95' W x 90' D
Levels: 2
Square Footage: 4,242
Main Level Sq. Ft.: 3,439
Upper Level Sq. Ft.: 803
Bedrooms: 4
Bathrooms: 4 full, 3 half
Foundation: Raised slab
Materials List Available: Yes
Price Category: I

Build this country manor home on a large lot with a breathtaking view to complement its beauty.

Features:

- Foyer: You'll love the two-story ceiling here.
- Living Room: A sunken floor, two-story ceiling, large fireplace, and generous balcony above combine to create an unusually beautiful room.
- Kitchen: Use the breakfast bar at any time of the day. The layout guarantees ample working space, and the pantry gives room for extra storage.

- Master Suite: A sunken floor, wood-burning fireplace, and 200-sq.-ft. sitting area work in concert to create a restful space.
- Bedrooms: The guest room is on the main floor, and bedrooms 2 and 3, both with built-in desks in special study areas, are on the upper level.
- Outdoor Grilling Area: Fitted with a bar, this area makes it a pleasure to host a large group.

Kitchen

Kitchen

Main Level Floor Plan

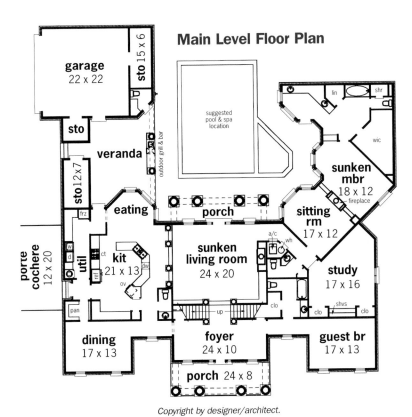

garage
22 x 22

sto 15 x 6

sto

veranda

sto 12x7

frz

eating

porre
cochere
12 x 20

util

w
d
ref

kit
21 x 13

dw
ov

ct

pan

outdoor grill & bar

suggested
pool & spa
location

porch

sunken
living room
24 x 20

a/c
wh

dining
17 x 13

foyer
24 x 10

porch 24 x 8

up

lin

shr

wic

sunken
mbr
18 x 12
fireplace

sitting
rm
17 x 12

study
17 x 16

clo

shvs

clo

clo

guest br
17 x 13

Copyright by designer/architect.

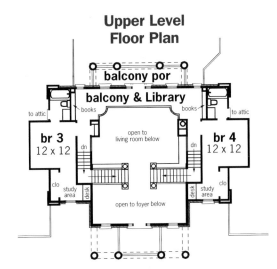

Master Bathroom

Upper Level Floor Plan

balcony por

balcony & Library

to attic

books

books

to attic

br 3
12 x 12

dn

open to
living room below

dn

br 4
12 x 12

clo

study
area

desk

open to foyer below

desk

study
area

clo

Dining Room

Living Room

Rear View

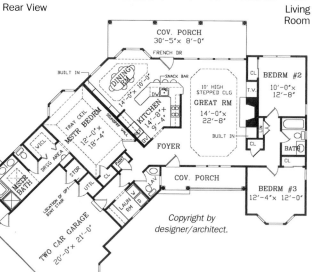
Living Room

Plan #131002

Dimensions: 70'1" W x 60'7" D

Levels: 1

Square Footage: 1,709

Bedrooms: 3

Bathrooms: 2½

Foundation: Crawl space or slab; basement or walkout for fee

Materials List Available: Yes

Price Category: D

Images provided by designer/architect.

CAD FILE AVAILABLE

Copyright by designer/architect.

Plan #151015

Dimensions: 72'4" W x 48'4" D

Levels: 2

Square Footage: 2,789

Main Level Sq. Ft.: 1,977

Upper Level Sq. Ft.: 812

Bedrooms: 4

Bathrooms: 3

Foundation: Crawl space or slab; basement for fee

CompleteCost List Available: Yes

Price Category: F

Images provided by designer/architect.

Main Level Floor Plan

Upper Level Floor Plan

Copyright by designer/architect.

Plan #131017

Dimensions: 69'8" W x 39'4" D

Levels: 1

Square Footage: 1,480

Bedrooms: 3

Bathrooms: 2

Foundation: Crawl space or slab; basement for fee

Materials List Available: Yes

Price Category: C

Images provided by designer/architect.

Alternate Floor Plan

Part Plan with Optional Basement

Copyright by designer/architect.

Rear Elevation

Plan #101022

Dimensions: 66'2" W x 62' D

Levels: 1

Square Footage: 1,992

Bedrooms: 3

Bathrooms: 3

Foundation: Crawl space, slab, or basement

Materials List Available: Yes

Price Category: D

Images provided by designer/architect.

CAD FILE AVAILABLE

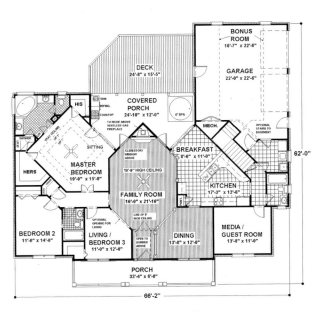

Copyright by designer/architect.

Plan #211127

Dimensions: 94' W x 71' D
Levels: 2
Square Footage: 5,474
Main Level Sq. Ft.: 4,193
Upper Level Sq. Ft.: 1,281
Bedrooms: 4
Bathrooms: 4 full, 2 half
Foundation: Slab; crawl space or walkout for fee
Materials List Available: No
Price Category: I

Images provided by designer/architect.

This is a truly grand southern-style home, with stately columns and eye-pleasing symmetry.

Features:

• Ceiling Height: 12 ft.

• Foyer: A grand home warrants a grand entry, and here it is. The graceful curved staircase will impress your guests as they move from this foyer to the fireplace.

• Family Room: Great for entertaining, this family room features a vaulted

ceiling. A handsome fireplace adds warmth and ambiance.

• Den: Another fireplace enhances this smaller and cozier den. Here the kids can play, supervised by the family chef working in the adjacent kitchen.

• Verandas: As is fitting for a gracious southern home, you'll find verandas at front and rear.

• Master Suite: A romantic third fireplace is found in this sprawling master bedroom. The master bath provides the utmost in privacy and organization.

Main Level Floor Plan

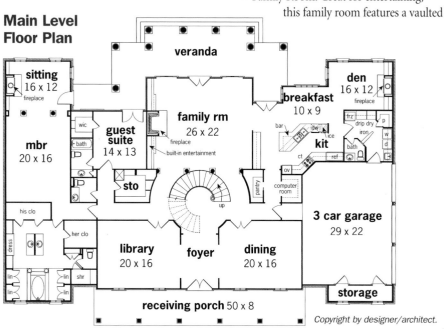

Copyright by designer/architect.

Upper Level Floor Plan

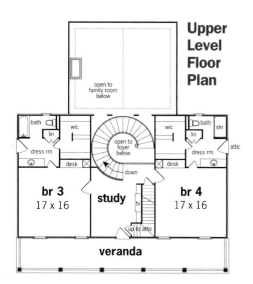

Plan #271030

Dimensions: 55'8" W x 45' D
Levels: 2
Square Footage: 1,926
Main Level Sq. Ft.: 1,490
Upper Level Sq. Ft.: 436
Bedrooms: 3
Bathrooms: 2½
Foundation: Basement or crawl space
Materials List Available: Yes
Price Category: D

This traditional home's main-floor master suite is hard to resist, with its inviting window seat and delightful bath.

Features:

• Master Suite: Just off from the entry foyer, this luxurious oasis is entered through double doors, and offers an airy vaulted ceiling, plus a private bath that includes a separate tub and shower, dual-sink vanity, and walk-in closet.

• Great Room: This space does it all in style, with a breathtaking wall of windows and a charming fireplace.

• Kitchen: A cooktop island makes dinnertime tasks a breeze. You'll also love the roomy pantry. The adjoining breakfast room, with its deck access and built-in desk, is sure to be a popular hangout for the teens.

• Secondary Bedrooms: Two additional bedrooms reside on the upper floor and allow the younger family members a measure of desired—and necessary—privacy.

CAD FILE AVAILABLE

Main Level Floor Plan

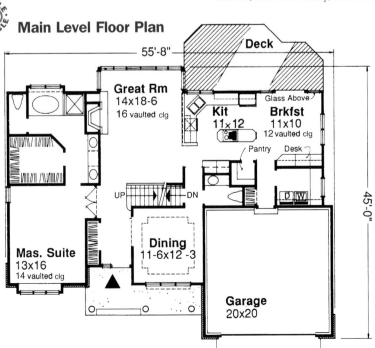

Upper Level Floor Plan

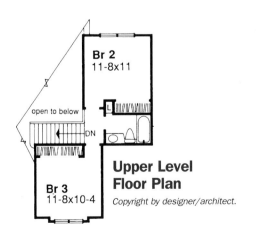

Copyright by designer/architect.

Plan #101004

Dimensions: 55'8" W x 56'6" D

Levels: 1

Square Footage: 1,787

Bedrooms: 3

Bathrooms: 2

Foundation: Crawl space, slab, or basement

Materials List Available: Yes

Price Category: D

Images provided by designer/architect.

This carefully designed ranch provides the feel and features of a much larger home.

Features:

• Ceiling Height: 9 ft. unless otherwise noted.

• Entry: Guests will step up onto the inviting front porch and into this entry, with its impressive 11-ft. ceiling.

• Dining Room: Open to the entry and to its left is this elegant dining room, perfect for entertaining or informal family gatherings.

• Family Room: This family gathering place features an 11-ft. ceiling to enhance its sense of spaciousness.

• Kitchen: This intelligently designed kitchen has an open plan. A breakfast bar and a serving bar are features that add to its convenience.

• Master Suite: This suite is loaded with amenities, including a double-step tray ceiling, direct access to the screened porch, a sitting room, deluxe bath, and his and her walk-in closets.

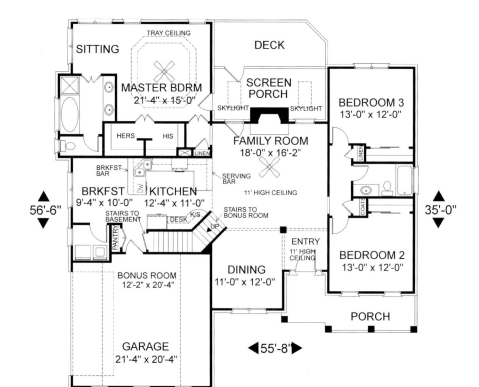

Copyright by designer/architect.

Plan #161101

Dimensions: 136'3" W x 69' D
Levels: 2
Square Footage: 6,209
Main Level Sq. Ft.: 4,011
Upper Level Sq. Ft.: 2,198
Optional Lower Level Sq. Ft.: 2,205
Bedrooms: 4
Bathrooms: 4 full, 2 half
Foundation: Walkout; basement for fee
Material List Available: Yes
Price Category: K

Images provided by designer/architect.

The grandeur of this mansion-style home boasts period stone, two-story columns, an angular turret, a second-floor balcony, and a gated courtyard.

Features:

- Formal Living: Formal areas consist of the charming living room and adjacent music room, which continues to the library, with its sloped ceilings and glass surround. Various ceiling treatments, with 10-ft. ceiling heights, and 8-ft.-tall doors add luxury and artistry to the first floor.

- Hearth Room: This large room, with false wood-beamed ceiling, adds a casual yet rich atmosphere to the family gathering space. Dual French doors on each side of the fireplace create a pleasurable indoor-outdoor relationship.

- Kitchen: This space is an enviable work place for the gourmet cook. Multiple cabinets and expansive counter space create a room that may find you spending a surprisingly enjoyable amount of time on food preparation. The built-in grill on the porch makes outdoor entertaining convenient and fun.

- Master Suite: This suite offers a vaulted ceiling, dual walk-in closets, and his and her vanities. The whirlpool tub is showcased on a platform and surrounded by windows for a relaxing view of the side yard. Private access to the deck is an enchanting surprise.

Rear View

Copyright by designer/architect.

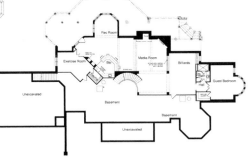

Main Level Floor Plan

Upper Level Floor Plan

Optional Lower Level Floor Plan

Plan #211071

Dimensions: 72' W x 58' D
Levels: 2
Square Footage: 2,888
Main Level Sq. Ft.: 1,768
Upper Level Sq. Ft.: 1,120
Bedrooms: 4
Bathrooms: 3½
Foundation: Crawl space;slab for fee
Materials List Available: Yes
Price Category: F

Images provided by designer/architect.

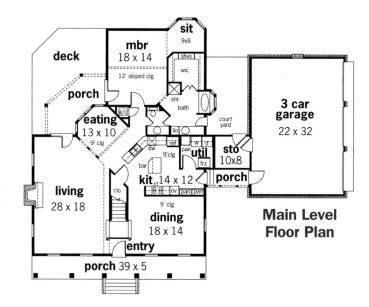

Main Level Floor Plan

Upper Level Floor Plan

Copyright by designer/architect.

Plan #151822

Dimensions: 108'10" W x 73'10" D
Levels: 1
Square Footage: 3,602
Bedrooms: 4
Bathrooms: 3½
Foundation: Crawl space or slab; basement or walkout for fee
CompleteCost List Available: Yes
Price Category: G

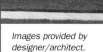

Images provided by designer/architect.

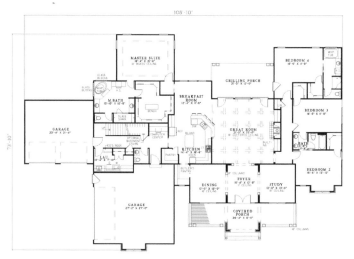

Copyright by designer/architect.

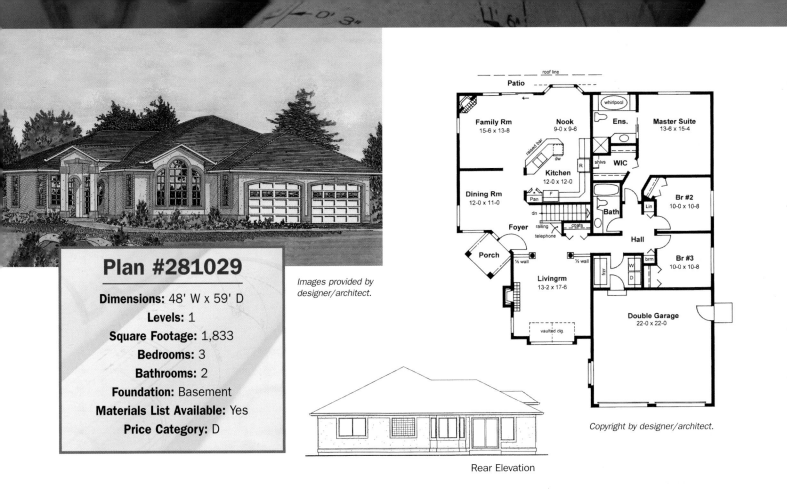

Plan #281029

Dimensions: 48' W x 59' D

Levels: 1

Square Footage: 1,833

Bedrooms: 3

Bathrooms: 2

Foundation: Basement

Materials List Available: Yes

Price Category: D

Images provided by designer/architect.

Copyright by designer/architect.

Rear Elevation

Plan #151056

Dimensions: 56'8" W x 58'4" D

Levels: 1

Square Footage: 1,950

Bedrooms: 3

Bathrooms: 2

Foundation: Crawl space, slab or basement

CompleteCost List Available: Yes

Price Category: D

Images provided by designer/architect.

CAD FILE AVAILABLE

Copyright by designer/architect.

Upper Level Floor Plan

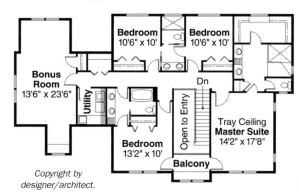

Bonus Room
13'6" x 23'6"

Bedroom
10'6" x 10'

Bedroom
10'6" x 10'

Utility

Bedroom
13'2" x 10'

Open to Entry

Dn

Tray Ceiling
Master Suite
14'2" x 17'8"

Balcony

Copyright by designer/architect.

Kitchen

Nook
11'6" x 14'2"

Family
15'8" x 21'

Garage
23'6" x 33'

Study
13'2" x 12'6"

Up

Living
14' x 15'8"

Entry

Vaulted Porch

Main Level Floor Plan

Plan #361077

Dimensions: 65' W x 44' D

Levels: 2

Square Footage: 2,887

Main Level Sq. Ft.: 1,454

Upper Level Sq. Ft.: 1,433

Bedrooms: 4

Bathrooms: 3½

Foundation: Crawl space

Material List Available: No

Price Category: F

Images provided by designer/architect.

CAD FILE AVAILABLE

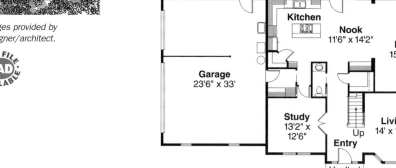

Copyright by designer/architect.

SCREENED PORCH
15'-2" x 11'-6"

PATIO OR DECK
13'-11" x 16'-0"

TRAY CEILING
HIS
HERS

MASTER SUITE
21'-2" x 16'-3"

SITTING

BEDROOM 3
11'-0" x 13'-6"

OPTIONAL TV NICHE ABOVE FIREPLACE

COUNTRY KITCHEN
14'-3" x 22'-6"

TO BONUS

FAMILY ROOM
15'-2" x 22'-6"

BEDROOM 2
11'-0" x 13'-6"

OPT. STAIRS TO BASEMENT

LINE OF BONUS ROOM

BOOKSHELVES

LIVING
11'-0" x 12'-0"

TRAY CEILING

DINING
11'-0" x 12'-0"

PANTRY
7'-6" x 4'-6"

GARAGE
21'-2" x 24'-0"

PORCH
29'-4" x 6'-0"

58'-1"

71'-2"

Plan #101011

Dimensions: 71'2" W x 58'1" D

Levels: 1

Square Footage: 2,184

Bedrooms: 3

Bathrooms: 3

Foundation: Crawl space, slab, basement, or walkout

Materials List Available: Yes

Price Category: E

Images provided by designer/architect.

CAD FILE AVAILABLE

Kitchen

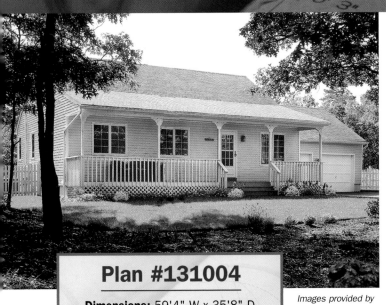

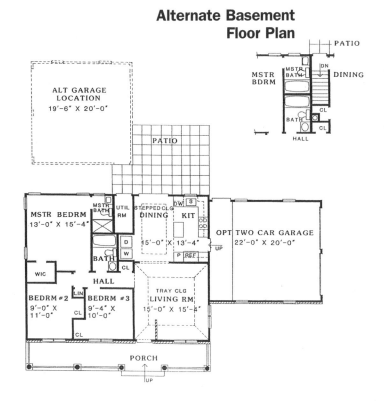

Alternate Basement Floor Plan

Plan #131004

Dimensions: 59'4" W x 35'8" D

Levels: 1

Square Footage: 1,097

Bedrooms: 3

Bathrooms: 2

Foundation: Crawl space or slab; basement or walkout for fee

Materials List Available: Yes

Price Category: B

Images provided by designer/architect.

This home, as shown in the photograph, may differ from the actual blueprints. For more detailed information, please check the floor plans carefully.

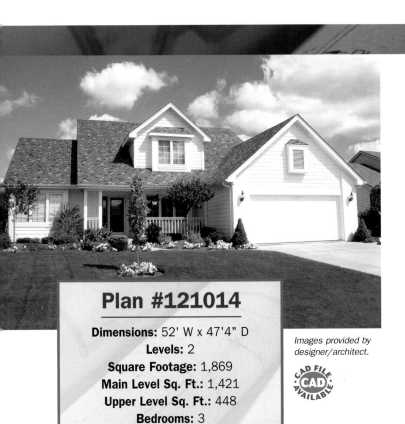

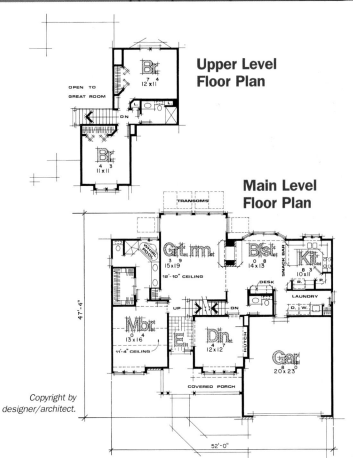

Upper Level Floor Plan

Main Level Floor Plan

Plan #121014

Dimensions: 52' W x 47'4" D

Levels: 2

Square Footage: 1,869

Main Level Sq. Ft.: 1,421

Upper Level Sq. Ft.: 448

Bedrooms: 3

Bathrooms: 2½

Foundation: Basement, crawl space and slab for fee

Materials List Available: Yes

Price Category: D

Images provided by designer/architect.

CAD FILE AVAILABLE

Copyright by designer/architect.

Plan #291016

Dimensions: 69'9" W x 58'3" D
Levels: 2
Square Footage: 2,721
Main Level Sq. Ft.: 1,447
Upper Level Sq. Ft.: 1,274
Bedrooms: 3
Bathrooms: 2½
Foundation: Basement
Materials List Available: No
Price Category: F

Images provided by designer/architect.

This fine example of Greek revival architecture begs to be visited!

Features:

- **Entry:** This area is the central hub of the home, with access to the kitchen, dining room, office, and upper level. There are two coat closets here.

- **Living Room:** This gathering area features a cozy fireplace and has access to the rear sunroom.

- **Kitchen:** Generous in size, this family-oriented kitchen has an informal dining area and a morning room that has access to the rear deck.

- **Upper Level:** Located upstairs are two secondary bedrooms that share the hall bathroom. The master suite, also on this level, features a private bath and a large walk-in closet.

Rear View

Copyright by designer/architect.

Upper Level Floor Plan

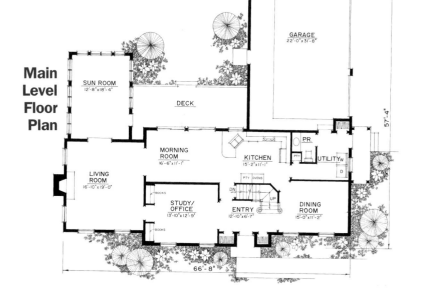

Main Level Floor Plan

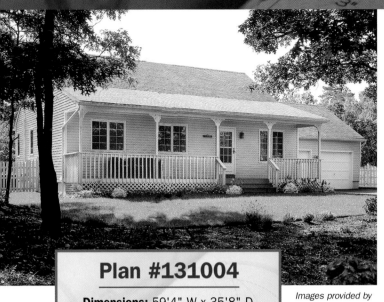

Plan #131004

Dimensions: 59'4" W x 35'8" D
Levels: 1
Square Footage: 1,097
Bedrooms: 3
Bathrooms: 2
Foundation: Crawl space or slab;
basement or walkout for fee
Materials List Available: Yes
Price Category: B

Images provided by designer/architect.

This home, as shown in the photograph, may differ from the actual blueprints. For more detailed information, please check the floor plans carefully.

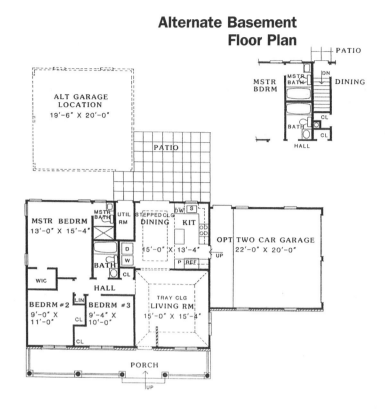

Alternate Basement Floor Plan

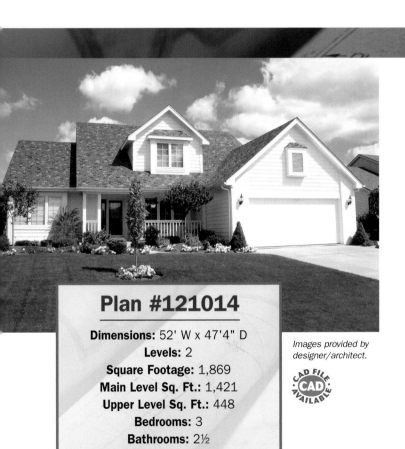

Plan #121014

Dimensions: 52' W x 47'4" D
Levels: 2
Square Footage: 1,869
Main Level Sq. Ft.: 1,421
Upper Level Sq. Ft.: 448
Bedrooms: 3
Bathrooms: 2½
Foundation: Basement, crawl space and slab for fee
Materials List Available: Yes
Price Category: D

Images provided by designer/architect.

CAD FILE AVAILABLE

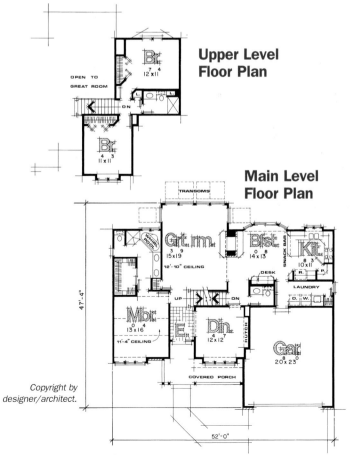

Upper Level Floor Plan

Main Level Floor Plan

Copyright by designer/architect.

Plan #291016

Dimensions: 69'9" W x 58'3" D
Levels: 2
Square Footage: 2,721
Main Level Sq. Ft.: 1,447
Upper Level Sq. Ft.: 1,274
Bedrooms: 3
Bathrooms: 2½
Foundation: Basement
Materials List Available: No
Price Category: F

This fine example of Greek revival architecture begs to be visited!

Features:

- Entry: This area is the central hub of the home, with access to the kitchen, dining room, office, and upper level. There are two coat closets here.

- Living Room: This gathering area features a cozy fireplace and has access to the rear sunroom.

- Kitchen: Generous in size, this family-oriented kitchen has an informal dining area and a morning room that has access to the rear deck.

- Upper Level: Located upstairs are two secondary bedrooms that share the hall bathroom. The master suite, also on this level, features a private bath and a large walk-in closet.

Images provided by designer/architect.

Rear View

Copyright by designer/architect.

Upper Level Floor Plan

Main Level Floor Plan

Plan #121076

Dimensions: 64' W x 60'8" D
Levels: 2
Square Footage: 3,067
Main Level Sq. Ft.: 2,169
Upper Level Sq. Ft.: 898
Bedrooms: 4
Bathrooms: 3½
Foundation: Basement
Materials List Available: Yes
Price Category: G

Images provided by designer/architect.

You'll love the combination of formal features and casual, family-friendly areas in this spacious home with an elegant exterior.

Features:

• Entry: The elegant windows in this two-story area are complemented by the unusual staircase.

• Family Room: This family room features an 11-ft. ceiling, wet bar, fireplace, and trio of windows that look out to the covered porch.

• Living Room: Columns set off both this room and the dining room. Decorate to accentuate their formality, or make them blend into a more casual atmosphere.

• Master Suite: Columns in this suite highlight a bayed sitting room where you'll be happy to relax at the end of the day or on weekend mornings.

• Bedrooms: Bedroom 2 has a private bath, making it an ideal guest room, and you'll find private vanities in bedrooms 3 and 4.

Main Level Floor Plan

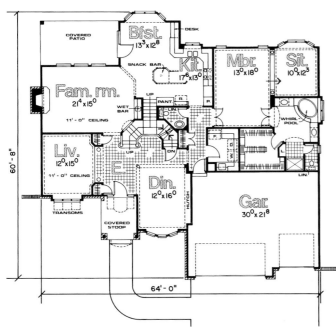

Upper Level Floor Plan

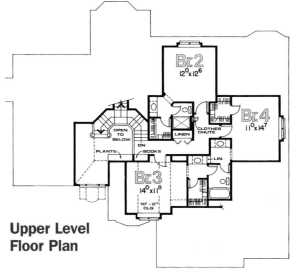

Copyright by designer/architect.

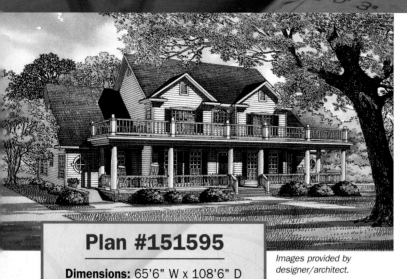

Plan #151595

Dimensions: 65'6" W x 108'6" D
Levels: 2
Square Footage: 3,820
Main Level Sq. Ft.: 2,484
Upper Level Sq. Ft.: 1,336
Bedrooms: 4
Bathrooms: 3½
Foundation: Crawl space, slab
CompleteCost List Available: Yes
Price Category: H

Images provided by designer/architect.

CAD FILE AVAILABLE · CAD

Main Level Floor Plan

Upper Level Floor Plan

Copyright by designer/architect.

Plan #101013

Dimensions: 72' W x 66' D
Levels: 1
Square Footage: 2,564
Bedrooms: 3
Bathrooms: 2½
Foundation: Walkout; crawl space, slab or basement for fee
Materials List Available: Yes
Price Category: F

Images provided by designer/architect.

CAD FILE AVAILABLE · CAD

Master Bedroom

Copyright by designer/architect.

Images provided by designer/architect.

Plan #131016

Dimensions: 75' W x 45' D

Levels: 1

Square Footage: 1,902

Bedrooms: 3

Bathrooms: 2

Foundation: Crawl space or slab; basement for fee

Materials List Available: Yes

Price Category: E

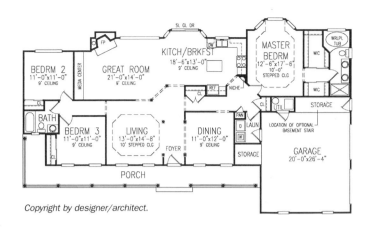

Great Room

Plan #641006

Dimensions: 66' W x 32' D

Levels: 1

Square Footage: 1,232

Bedrooms: 2

Bathrooms: 2

Foundation: Basement; crawl space, slab or walkout for fee

Materials List Available: Yes

Price Category: C

Images provided by designer/architect.

Living Room

Plan #271099

Dimensions: 71' W x 74'2" D
Levels: 2
Square Footage: 2,949
Main Level Sq. Ft.: 2,000
Upper Level Sq. Ft.: 949
Bedrooms: 3
Bathrooms: 2½
Foundation: Crawl space
CompleteCost List Available: No
Price Category: F

Gracious symmetry highlights the lovely facade of this traditional two-story home.

Images provided by designer/architect.

Features:

• Foyer: With a high ceiling and a curved staircase, this foyer gives a warm welcome to arriving guests.

• Family Room: At the center of the home, this room will host gatherings of all kinds. A fireplace adds just the right touch.

• Kitchen: An expansive island with a cooktop anchors this space, which easily serves the adjoining nook and the nearby dining room.

• Master Suite: A cozy sitting room with a fireplace is certainly the highlight here. The private bath is also amazing, with its whirlpool tub, separate shower, dual vanities, and walk-in closet.

• Bonus Room: This generous space above the garage could serve as an art studio or as a place for your teenagers to play their electric guitars.

Main Level Floor Plan

Upper Level Floor Plan

Copyright by designer/architect.

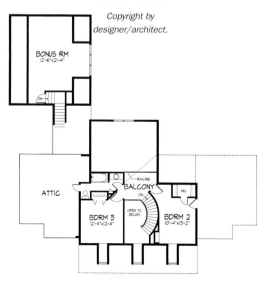

Plan #271047

Dimensions: 68' W x 47' D
Levels: 2
Square Footage: 2,729
Main Level Sq. Ft.: 1,778
Upper Level Sq. Ft.: 951
Bedrooms: 4
Bathrooms: 2½
Foundation: Basement
Materials List Available: No
Price Category: F

Constructed with materials chosen with your health in mind, this two-story home promises to pamper your body and soul.

Features:

• **Great Room:** Not only does this room host a media nook and a two-story ceiling, it also includes a sealed gas fireplace for zero emissions.

• **Kitchen:** Here, cultured-marble countertops replace traditional pressed-wood and laminate.

• **Kitchen: Master Suite:** Here's a lovely retreat. A tray ceiling, cavernous walk-in closet, and private bath are just the beginning.

• **Air Safety:** A radon-detection ystem and exhaust fan in the garage help to eliminate airborne irritants. Tile floors replace carpet in much of the home, too.

CAD FILE AVAILABLE

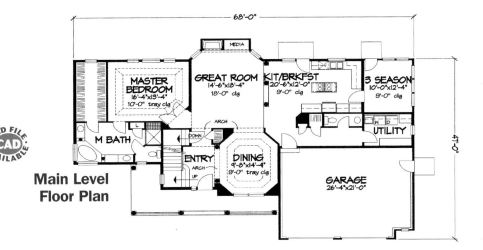

Main Level Floor Plan

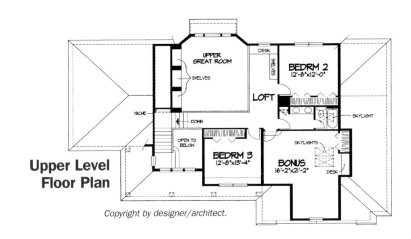

Upper Level Floor Plan

Copyright by designer/architect.

Kitchens: Focus on Style

Most people spend a lot of time in the kitchen relaxing and socializing, perhaps even more than cooking and cleaning up. So take the time to decide how you want the room to look, what colors, fabrics, and textures you're drawn to, and the mood you'd like to create. If you're still weighing the warmth and casual feeling of country decor against the grace and formality of a traditional setting, examine some of the ele- ments that make up different decorating styles. Look at art books, and pay close attention to furniture styles, which are influencing today's cabinet design. Think about favorite decorating themes from other rooms in the house that can be carried into the kitchen. In this article you'll get some style-specific ideas and learn how to create a decorating scheme for your kitchen that suits your taste and your lifestyle.

the smart approach to
kitchen DESIGN

CREATIVE HOMEOWNER

THIRD EDITION revised and expanded

Susan Maney Lovett

The following article was reprinted from *The Smart Approach to Kitchen Design* (Creative Homeowner 2006).

Plain white cabinets
and stainless-steel
appliances, opposite,
put a fresh face on
country style. Blue
backsplash tile adds
subtle color.

Furniture details,
right, and classical
elements, such as
crown moldings and
fluted panels, under-
score the formal look
of this kitchen. The
cabinets have been
finished a warm
antique white.

Ornate brackets,
inset, carved with the
classic acanthus leaf
motif almost appear
to hold up the
island's granite coun-
tertop. Actually, they
are just decorative.

SMARTtip

Traditional Style

You don't have to replace your kitchen cabinetry to
get some of the fine furniture-quality details dis-
cussed above. Custom-made details will be expensive, but you can purchase prefabricated trims at
local lumber mills and home centers. For example,
crown molding, applied to the top of existing cabinetry and stained or painted to match the door style,
may be all you need. Likewise, you can replace old
hardware with reproduction polished-brass door and
drawer knobs or pulls for a finishing touch.

Traditional Style

Today's traditional style incorporates elements of English and
American eighteenth- and early nineteenth-century design.
Marked by symmetry and balance and enhanced by the look of
fine-crafted details, it is dignified, rich, and formal.

Choose wood cabinetry finished with a cherry or mahogany
stain or painted white, with details like fluted panels, bull's-eye corner blocks, and dentil and crown molding. For the door style, a
raised cathedral panel (top slightly arched) is typical. An elegant
marble countertop or a laminate faux version fit well here, as do
hand-painted tiles. Polished brass hardware and fittings add an
Old World touch.

Colors to consider include classic Wedgwood blue or deep
jewel tones. Windows and French doors with true divided lights or
double-hung units with pop-in muntins have great traditional-
style appeal. Dress them with formal curtain panels or swags.
Botanical-inspired patterns, formal stripes, and tapestry or crewel-
work look-alikes can tie the room together.

Furnish this kitchen with an antique or reproduction hutch,
where you can display formal china, and a table and chairs in traditional Windsor or Queen Anne style.

Contemporary Style

What's referred to as "contemporary" style evokes images of clean architectural lines; an absence of decoration and color; and materials such as stainless steel, chrome, glass, and stone. Indeed, its roots are at the turn of the last century, when architects and designers flatly rejected the exaggerated artificial embellishments of the Victorians by turning to natural products and pared-down forms. Various modern movements, evolving over the course of the industrialized twentieth century, gradually incorporated new

man-made materials into their streamlined forms. Hence the high-tech look popularized in the 1970s and 1980s.

Today, contemporary style is taking a softer turn, even in the kitchen, a place where hard edges, cool reflective surfaces, and cutting-edge technology abound. Kitchen designers are taking another look at time-honored forms and giving them a new spin. It's not unusual to see updated versions of traditional fixtures and fittings or new uses for natural materials in a contemporary kitchen, especially as improved finishes make these products more durable and easier to maintain. And although black and white have been the

Geometric shapes always play a part in Modern design, above. Various neutral tones add relief to several banks of cabinetry in this open design.

Contemporary Style

Incorporate elements of Arts and Crafts, Art Deco, or other designs associated with the modern movements of the twentieth century; their clean, geometric lines are quite compatible with this environment. This eclectic approach can result in a sophisticated look. Shop for framed fine art prints, vintage-inspired wallpaper, reproduction hardware, faucets, or light fixtures to underscore your theme.

classic mainstays in a contemporary room, the stark white palette of the last two decades has been replaced with earthy wood hues, bold color (especially on modern European-inspired designs), and warmer shades of white.

When selecting cabinets for your contemporary kitchen, pair a frameless door with a wood finish. Laminate cabinetry is still compatible with this style, but for an updated look, wood is it. Although a contemporary room is often monochromatic or neutral, don't be afraid to use color or to mix several materials or finishes, such as wood and metal. Combinations of wood and various metals—stainless steel, chrome, copper, brass, and pewter on surfaces like cabinet doors, countertops, and floors—make strong statements, as do stone and glass. Creative combinations like these keep the overall appearance of the room sleek but not sterile. For more visual interest, apply a glazed or textured finish to neutral-colored walls. And bring as much of the outdoors into this room as possible. Install casement-style windows, skylights, or roof windows to blend with contemporary architecture. Easy access to adjoining outdoor living spaces, such as decks or open-air kitchens, is highly desirable. For window treatments, Roman shades or vertical blinds offer a crisp, tailored look.

Stay with metals for lighting fixtures and hardware. Chrome, pewter, or nickel would work well. Keep your eye on function, not frills. The contemporary room revels in the pure architecture of the space.

Furnishings for a contemporary kitchen tend to have a sleek architectural look, too. In fact, much of what is considered classic contemporary furniture has been designed by well-known twentieth-century architects. Chair and table legs are typically straight, with no turnings or ornamentation. For a sophisticated look, mix complementary materials; for example, pair a glass table with upholstered chairs or a metal table with wood chairs. Display contemporary pottery on a shelf or inside a glass cabinet.

Contemporary design has taken a warmer turn today, above. These cabinets feature a medium-tone wood that is complemented by the flooring and the tones in the granite counters.

SMARTtip

Country Style

Keep it simple, and avoid cutesy clutter. A touch of whimsy is fine and always looks at home in a country kitchen, especially when it is handcrafted. One way to achieve a country look is with hardware. Pick up an accent color from the tile or wallpaper, and paint unfinished knobs and pulls, which are available at craft stores. Or mix and match standard metal or glass pieces with a few fun ones. Designs you might consider include fruit, vegetable, or animal motifs.

Country Style

Whether you call it American, French, English, Italian, or Scandinavian, this style is always a favorite because of its basic, casual, relaxed feeling. In fact, every country has its own version. "Country" implies a deeper connection to the outdoors and the simple life than other styles and uses an abundance of natural elements. Start off with plain wood cabinetry stained a light maple, or add a distressed, crackled, or pickled finish. This is the perfect kitchen for mixing different finishes because unmatched pieces underpin the informal ambiance of a country room. Cabinet door styles are typically framed, sometimes with a raised panel. Beadboard cabinets are a typical American country choice. Or leave the doors off, allowing colorful dishes and canned and boxed goods to create a fun display. For the countertop, install butcher block or hand-painted or silk-screened tiles. Another option is a colorful or patterned countertop fabricated from inlaid solid-surfacing material. Also, consider concrete or stone. Once thought of as too modern for a country kitchen, these materials can blend in beautifully with an updated country sensibility. A working fireplace will add charm to your country kitchen, but a simple potted herb garden on the windowsill will, too.

Wood floors are a natural choice in this setting, whether they are real, engineered, or laminate. Terra-cotta tiles are also an attractive accent to a European-inspired country setting. Be sure to use throw rugs in front of the sink for added comfort.

For a custom touch, add a stenciled backsplash or wall border. Or try a faux finish like sponging,

A small antique table brings added charm, above, to this updated country kitchen. When meals are not being served, it can be used as a worktable in lieu of a center island.

An oak floor and cabinets, opposite, open storage on cabinet shelves, and reproduction schoolhouse lamps suggest an old-fashioned country store.

Just about anything goes in a cottage kitchen, above, which tends to have a playful look. Here, the owners installed refurbished vintage appliances and light fixtures and put their collections on display.

SMARTtip

Cottage Look

For authenticity, the overall look has to appear slightly worn, but not shabby. You can accomplish this by distressing wood surfaces, such as a table-top, or adding a crackle finish to woodwork. Another idea is to use a natural dye on table linens or cotton fabric window treatments. Compared with synthetics, these dyes seem slightly faded and will lend a comfortable lived-in feeling to your cottage-style kitchen.

ragging, or combing. These techniques are fun and easy, and they add texture to your walls. For a Continental flavor, apply a glaze that imitates a rustic fresco finish. Use extra space to hang herbs for drying.

Install double-hung windows. (Standard casement windows look too contemporary in this setting.) Finish them with full trim, and dress them with simple cotton curtains.

The Cottage Look

This vintage look, inspired by quaint English-country style, is appealing in the kitchen because it's cozy, casual, and warm. Framed wood cabinets with an unfitted or unmatched appearance—especially in a mix of finishes, such as a honey maple paired with a color stain that looks aged or distressed—provide a good starting point for building on this theme. Muntin-glass doors and built-in open plate or pot racks and display shelves should be part of the cabinetry's design. Milk- or clear-glass knobs and pulls will dress the cabinets nicely, or use forged metal hardware for a rustic appearance.

Bead board on the walls always looks at home in this style kitchen, as does brick. Either material would make an attractive backsplash treatment. Paint or stain the bead board to complement the colors used in the room. An English import, the AGA cooker is a great way to bring the old-time European look of a cast-iron stove into the room while providing all the modern-day conveniences. Install an exposed-apron (farmhouse-style) sink with a reproduction chrome and porcelain faucet set to add more charm. On the floor, use wide wood planks or stone with a colorful hand-painted floorcloth on top. Something with a pattern of big, chubby blooms would be attractive. Bring more color into the room with blue-green surfaces accented in varying shades of rose and cream. Introduce vintage linens for added nostalgia.

A double-hung window lends a traditional note, but if you can make the style work with the exterior of your house, a Gothic-inspired architectural design would tie it all together. This style, with Medieval roots, was popular with the Victorians. Accent with lighting fixtures that resemble old-fashioned gas lamps or electrified candle sconces.

For furniture, include a good-size farmhouse table in your plan, as well as a Welsh dresser and plate rack for displaying a pretty collection of Majolica or similar earthenware.

Provencal Style

This French-country style evokes images of the Mediterranean and warm, sunny days. Its origins go back to the one- and two-room farmhouses of southern France built centuries ago, when the kitchen was a large communal room. To re-create its charming ambiance, whitewash walls or apply a subtle glaze finish in an earth tone, such as rose ocher or sienna. Install wood on the ceiling beams with an aged or distressed look.

Original Provençal kitchens had large limestone hearths and, of course, working fireplaces. Your modern-day version may or may not have a working fireplace, but you can introduce limestone by installing it on the floor. Otherwise, use rustic clay tiles, which also have a warm, earthy appeal. For the appearance of a hearth, design a cooking alcove to house the range or cooktop. Accent it with colorful tiles or brick. Create a focal point at the cooking area with a handsome copper range hood. Hang a rack for copper pots and pans. Carry the copper over to the sink; one with a hammered finish will look spectacular. The copper will need a little extra care, so you may want to reserve it for the bar sink and use a more practical porcelain model—preferably a deep one with an exposed apron—for heavy-duty use. Pair that sink with a wall-mounted chrome faucet that has a high-arc spout.

Unfitted cabinetry in the form of a dresser with shelves, a cupboard, or an armoire is quintessential to this style, but you'll probably need storage that is more practical and efficient for contemporary use, too. One way to achieve this is to substitute wall cabinets for open shelves, then use one of the pieces of furniture as an accent and for extra storage. Include wrought-iron hardware in your design, which will coordinate with a wrought-iron chandelier or baker's rack.

Decorate with provincial mini-print fabrics and wallcoverings in mustard yellow, clay red, and the deep blue that is inspired by the lavender that grows all over the region. For authenticity, paint window and door trims blue. Dress windows with lace café curtains and stencil a pretty fleur de lis border around the trim.

Add details, such as flavored oils and vinegars displayed in pretty glass bottles, fresh herbs growing from racks in sunny windows, and blue and white tiles.

Sunflowers, a ceramic rooster, and mustard-color pottery are some of the accessories that can bring French country style to your kitchen (below).

SMARTtip

Provencal Style

No French country kitchen would be complete without a massive harvest table. If you can't find an affordable antique, create your own. Buy a long, unfinished pine table, and stain it a rich walnut color. Because pine is a soft wood, you won't have to add "authentic" distress marks because normal wear and tear will do that for you. Pair the table with an assortment of unmatched chairs to add casual ambiance.

Plan #131027

Dimensions: 62'4" W x 53'6" D
Levels: 1.5
Square Footage: 2,567
Main Level Sq. Ft.: 2,017
Upper Level Sq. Ft.: 550
Bedrooms: 4
Bathrooms: 3
Foundation: Crawl space or slab; basement for fee
Materials List Available: Yes
Price Category: F

This home, as shown in the photograph, may differ from the actual blueprints. For more detailed information, please check the floor plans carefully.

Images provided by designer/architect.

The features of this home are so good that you may have trouble imagining all of them at once.

Features:

- Great Room: Imagine a stepped ceiling, corner fireplace, built-media center, and wall of windows with a glass door to the backyard—in one room.

- Dining Room: A stepped ceiling and server with a sink add to the elegance of this formal room.

- Breakfast Room: Eat at the bar this room shares with the island kitchen, and admire the 12-ft. cathedral ceiling and bayed group of 8- and 9-ft. windows. Or go through the sliding glass door to the covered side porch.

- Master Suite: The bedroom has a tray ceiling and cozy sitting area, and a whirlpool tub, shower, and walk-in closet are in the skylighted bath.

- Optional Study: The private bath in bedroom 2 makes it ideal for a study or home office.

Breakfast Nook

Rear View

Great Room

Main Level Floor Plan

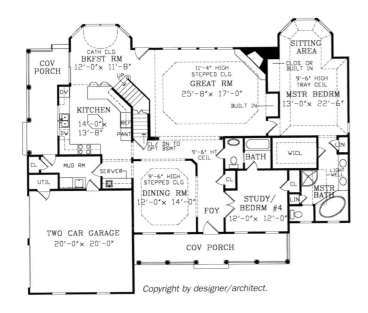

Copyright by designer/architect.

Upper Level Floor Plan

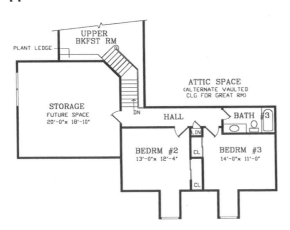

Painting Tips

As with any skill, there is a right and a wrong way to paint. There is a right way to hold a brush, a right way to maneuver a roller, a right way to spray a wall, etc. Follow these basic professional tips:

Brushing vs. Rolling. Some painters insist that only a brush-painted job looks right. However, most painters will "cut in" the edges with a brush, and then finish the main body of a wall or ceiling using a roller. Brushing alone can be time-consuming, and it is typically reserved for architectural woodwork.

Using the Right Brush. Use the largest brush with which you are comfortable. Professional painters seldom pick up anything smaller than a 4-inch brush. Most homeowners will achieve good results using a 4-inch brush for "cutting in" and for large surfaces, and an angled 2½- to 3-inch sash brush for trim around windows and doors. Be sure, also, to use brushes that are appropriate for the type of paint being applied. Oil-based paints require a natural bristle (also called "China bristles"), while water-based paints are applied with a synthetic bristle brush.

Handling a Brush. Many people grip a paintbrush as if they were shaking someone's hand. It is better to grip a brush more like a pencil, with the fingers and thumb wrapped around the metal ferrule. This grip provides the hand and wrist with a wider range of motion and therefore greater speed and precision. If your hand cramps, switch hands or switch temporarily to the handshake grip.

Wiping Rags. Before you begin painting, put a dust rag in your pocket. This is helpful for clearing away cobwebs and dust before painting. It is also handy for wiping off paint drips before they have a chance to dry.

Paint Hooks. When working on a ladder, use a good-quality paint hook to secure the paint bucket to your ladder. Avoid makeshift hooks made with wire or coat hangers. Paint hooks are inexpensive and available at virtually all paint and hardware stores.

Plan #211074

Dimensions: 64' W x 89' D
Levels: 2
Square Footage: 3,486
Main Level Sq. Ft.: 2,575
Upper Level Sq. Ft.: 911
Bedrooms: 4
Bathrooms: 3
Foundation: Crawl space
Materials List Available: Yes
Price Category: G

This plantation-style home may have an old-fashioned charm, but the energy-efficient design and many amenities inside make it thoroughly contemporary.

Features:

- Ceiling Height: 9 ft.
- Porches: This wraparound front porch is fully 10 ft. wide, so you can group rockers, occasional tables, and even a swing here and save the rear porch for grilling and alfresco dining.

- Entry: A two-story ceiling here sets an elegant tone for the rest of the home.

- Living Room: Somewhat isolated, this room is an ideal spot for quiet entertaining. It has built-in bookshelves and a nearby wet bar.

- Kitchen: You'll love the large counter areas and roomy storage space in this lovely kitchen, where both friends and family are sure to congregate.

- Master Suite: It's easy to pamper yourself in this comfortable bedroom and luxurious bath.

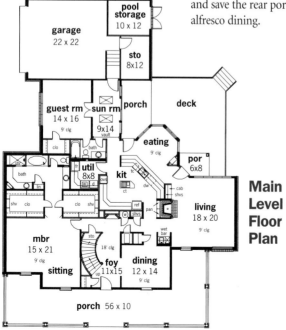

Main Level Floor Plan

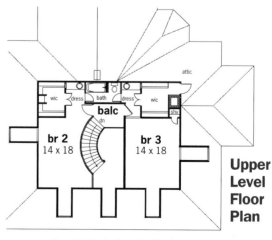

Upper Level Floor Plan

Copyright by designer/architect.

Plan #101020

Dimensions: 55'8" W x 49'2" D

Levels: 2

Square Footage: 2,972

Main Level Sq. Ft.: 1,986

Upper Level Sq. Ft.: 986

Bedrooms: 4

Bathrooms: 3½

Foundation: Crawl space, slab, basement or walkout

Materials List Available: No

Price Category: F

CAD FILE AVAILABLE

This luxurious country home has an open-design main level that maximizes the use of space.

Features:

- Ceiling Height: 9 ft. unless otherwise noted.
- Foyer: Guests will be greeted by this grand two-story entry, with its graceful angled staircase.
- Dining Room: At nearly 12 ft. x 15 ft., this elegant dining room has plenty of room for large parties.
- Family Room: Everyone will be drawn to this 17-ft. x 19-ft. room, with its dramatic two-story ceiling and its handsome fireplace.
- Kitchen: This spacious kitchen is open to the family room and features a breakfast bar and built-in table in the cooktop island.
- Master Suite: This elegant retreat includes a bayed 18-ft.-5-in. x 14-ft.-9-in. bedroom and a beautiful corner his and her bath/closet arrangement.
- Secondary Bedrooms: Upstairs you'll find three spacious bathrooms, one with a private bath and two with access to a shared bath.

Main Level Floor Plan

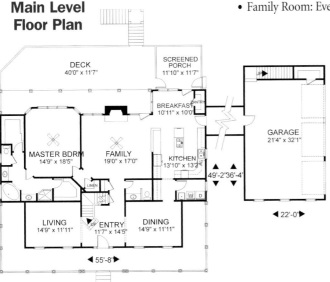

Upper Level Floor Plan

Copyright by designer/architect.

Copyright by designer/architect.

Plan #351088

Dimensions: 66'8" W x 73'2" D

Levels: 1

Square Footage: 2,500

Bedrooms: 4

Bathrooms: 3

Foundation: Crawl space or slab

Material List Available: Yes

Price Category: G

Images provided by designer/architect.

CAD FILE AVAILABLE

Rear Elevation

Bonus Area Floor Plan

Plan #211030

Dimensions: 75' W x 37' D

Levels: 1

Square Footage: 1,600

Bedrooms: 3

Bathrooms: 2

Foundation: Slab

Materials List Available: Yes

Price Category: C

Images provided by designer/architect.

SMARTtip

Brackets in Window Treatments

Although it is rarely noticed, a bracket plays an important role in supporting rods and poles. If a treatment rubs against a window frame, an extension bracket solves the problem. It projects from the wall at an adjustable length, providing enough clearance. A hold-down bracket anchors a cellular shade or a blind to the bottom of a door, preventing the treatment from moving when the door is opened or closed.

Copyright by designer/architect.

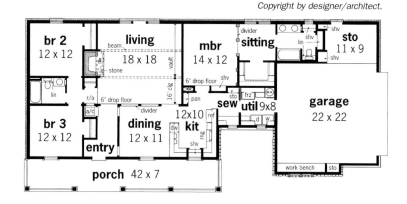

Plan #151016

Dimensions: 60'2" W x 39'10" D

Levels: 2

Square Footage: 1,783;
2,107 with bonus

Main Level Sq. Ft.: 1,124

Upper Level Sq. Ft.: 659

Bonus Room Sq. Ft.: 324

Bedrooms: 3

Bathrooms: 2½

Foundation: Crawl space, slab,
basement or walkout

CompleteCost List Available: Yes

Price Category: C

Images provided by designer/architect.

CAD FILE AVAILABLE

Main Level Floor Plan

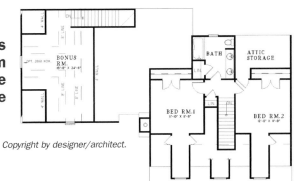

Bonus Room Above Garage

Upper Level Floor Plan

Copyright by designer/architect.

Plan #151089

Dimensions: 84' W x 55'6" D

Levels: 1

Square Footage: 1,921

Bedrooms: 3

Bathrooms: 3

Foundation: Crawl space or slab;
basement or walkout for fee

CompleteCost List Available: Yes

Price Category: E

Images provided by designer/architect.

CAD FILE AVAILABLE

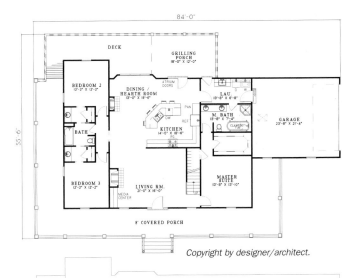

Copyright by designer/architect.

Bonus Area Floor Plan

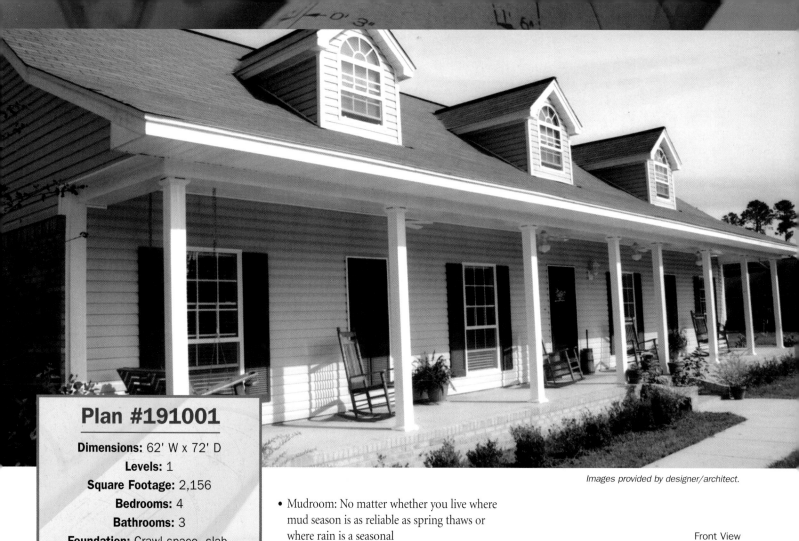

Plan #191001

Dimensions: 62' W x 72' D

Levels: 1

Square Footage: 2,156

Bedrooms: 4

Bathrooms: 3

Foundation: Crawl space, slab, or basement

Materials List Available: No

Price Category: D

This lovely home has the best of old and new — a traditional appearance combined with fabulous comforts and conveniences.

Features:

- **Great Room:** A tray ceiling gives stature to this expansive room, and its many windows let natural light stream into it.

- **Kitchen:** When you're standing at the sink in this gorgeous kitchen, you'll have a good view of the patio. But if you turn around, you'll see the island cooktop, wall oven, walk-in pantry, and snack bar, all of which make this kitchen such a pleasure.

- **Master Suite:** Somewhat isolated for privacy, this area is ideal for an evening or weekend retreat. Relax in the gracious bedroom or luxuriate in the spa-style bath, with its corner whirlpool tub, large shower, two sinks, and access to the walk-in closet, which measures a full 8 ft. x 10 ft.

- **Mudroom:** No matter whether you live where mud season is as reliable as spring thaws or where rain is a seasonal event, you'll love having a spot to confine the muddy mess.

Images provided by designer/architect.

Front View

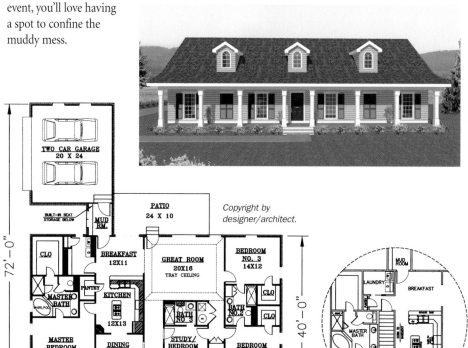

Copyright by designer/architect.

Plan #131022

Dimensions: 54'8" W x 43' D

Levels: 2

Square Footage: 2,092

Main Level Sq. Ft.: 1,152

Upper Level Sq. Ft.: 940

Bedrooms: 4

Bathrooms: 2½

Foundation: Crawl space or slab; basement for fee

Materials List Available: Yes

Price Category: E

This home, as shown in the photograph, may differ from the actual blueprints. For more detailed information, please check the floor plans carefully.

Images provided by designer/architect.

You'll love the way this charming home reminds you of an old-fashioned farmhouse.

Features:

- Ceiling Height: 8 ft.
- Living Room: This large living room can be used as guest quarters when the need arises.
- Dining Room: This bayed, informal room is large enough for all your dining and entertaining needs. It could also double as an office or den.
- Garage: An expandable loft over the garage offers an ideal playroom or fourth bedroom.

Rear Elevation

Main Level Floor Plan

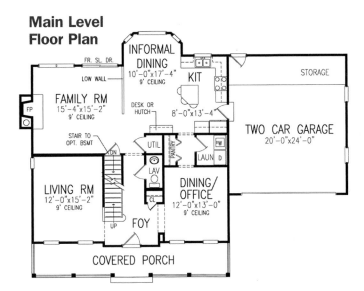

Upper Level Floor Plan

Copyright by designer/architect.

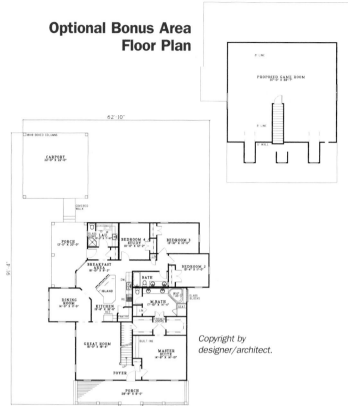

Optional Bonus Area Floor Plan

Plan #151113

Dimensions: 62'10" W x 91'4" D

Levels: 1

Square Footage: 2,186

Bedrooms: 4

Bathrooms: 3

Foundation: Crawl space or slab; basement or walkout for fee

CompleteCost List Available: Yes

Price Category: D

Images provided by designer/architect.

CAD FILE AVAILABLE

Copyright by designer/architect.

Plan #351008

Dimensions: 64'6" W x 61'4" D

Levels: 1

Square Footage: 2,002

Bedrooms: 3

Bathrooms: 2

Foundation: Crawl space or basement

Materials List Available: Yes

Price Category: E

Images provided by designer/architect.

CAD FILE AVAILABLE

Copyright by designer/architect.

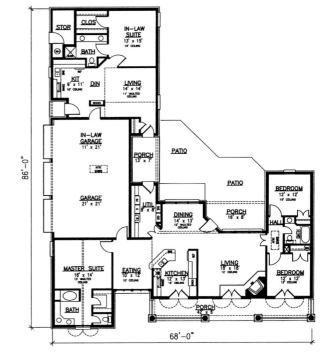

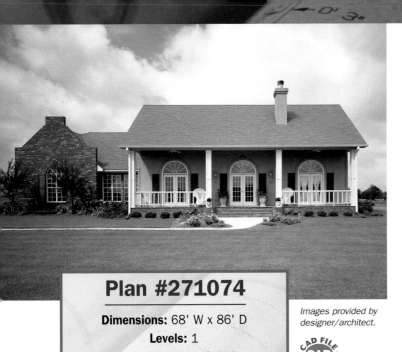

Plan #271074

Dimensions: 68' W x 86' D

Levels: 1

Square Footage: 2,400

Bedrooms: 4

Bathrooms: 3

Foundation: Crawl space or slab

Materials List Available: No

Price Category: E

Images provided by designer/architect.

CAD FILE AVAILABLE

Copyright by designer/architect.

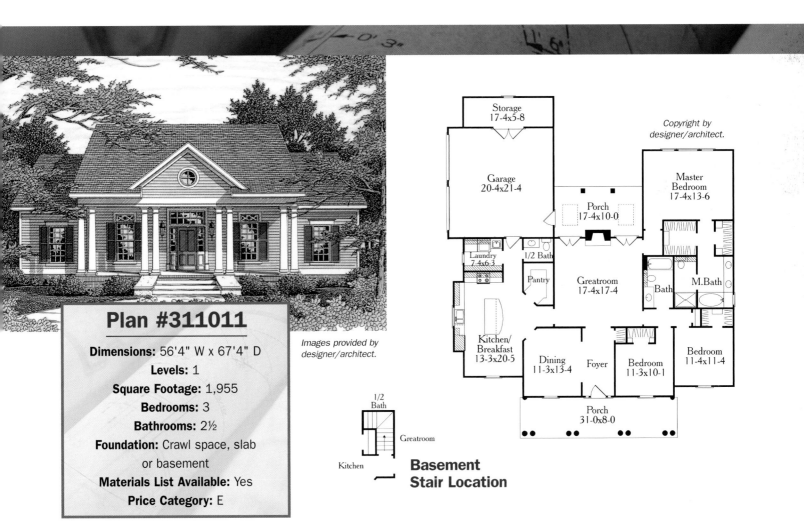

Plan #311011

Dimensions: 56'4" W x 67'4" D

Levels: 1

Square Footage: 1,955

Bedrooms: 3

Bathrooms: 2½

Foundation: Crawl space, slab or basement

Materials List Available: Yes

Price Category: E

Images provided by designer/architect.

Copyright by designer/architect.

Basement Stair Location

Plan #121021

Dimensions: 46' W x 48' D
Levels: 2
Square Footage: 2,270
Main Level Sq. Ft.: 1,150
Upper Level Sq. Ft.: 1,120
Bedrooms: 4
Bathrooms: 2½
Foundation: Basement
Materials List Available: Yes
Price Category: E

This home, as shown in the photograph, may differ from the actual blueprints. For more detailed information, please check the floor plans carefully.

Images provided by designer/architect.

With its wraparound porch, this home evokes the charm of a traditional home.

Features:

• Ceiling Height: 8 ft.

• Foyer: The dramatic two-story entry enjoys views of the formal dining room and great room. A second floor balcony overlooks the entry and a plant shelf.

• Formal Dining Room: This gracious room is perfect for family holiday gatherings and for more formal dinner parties.

• Great Room: All the family will want to gather in this comfortable, informal room which features bay windows, an entertainment center, and a see-through fireplace.

• Breakfast Area: Conveniently located just off the great room, the bayed breakfast area features a built-in desk for household bills and access to the backyard.

• Kitchen: An island is the centerpiece of this kitchen. Its intelligent design makes food preparation a pleasure.

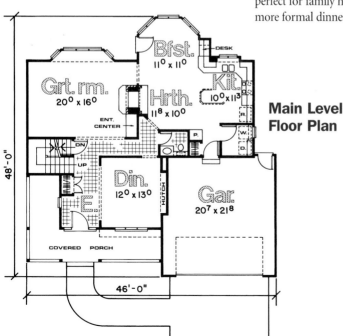

Main Level Floor Plan

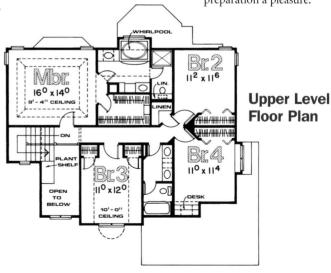

Upper Level Floor Plan

Copyright by designer/architect.

Plan #351020

Dimensions: 54' W x 48' D

Levels: 1

Square Footage: 1,488

Bedrooms: 3

Bathrooms: 2

Foundation: Crawl space, slab, or basement

Materials List Available: Yes

Price Category: C

This is a lot of house for its size and is an excellent example of the popular split bedroom layout.

Features:

- **Great Room:** This large room is open to the dining room.

- **Kitchen:** This fully equipped kitchen has a peninsula counter and is open into the dining room.

- **Master Suite:** This private area, located on the other side of the home from the secondary bedrooms, features large walk-in closets and bath areas.

- **Bedrooms:** The two secondary bedrooms have large closets and share a hall bathroom.

Copyright by designer/architect.

Copyright by designer/architect.

Plan #351004

Dimensions: 78' W x 49'6" D
Levels: 1
Square Footage: 1,852
Bedrooms: 3
Bathrooms: 2½
Foundation: Crawl space, slab, or basement
Materials List Available: Yes
Price Category: D

CAD FILE AVAILABLE — CAD

Images provided by designer/architect.

Rear View

Bonus Room

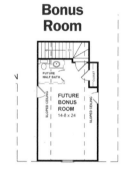

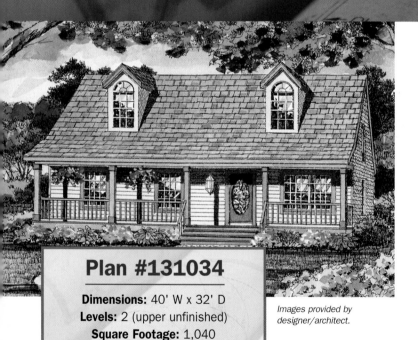

Plan #131034

Dimensions: 40' W x 32' D
Levels: 2 (upper unfinished)
Square Footage: 1,040
Bedrooms: 5 or 4
Bathrooms: 2½
Foundation: Crawl space or slab; basement for fee
Materials List Available: Yes
Price Category: C

Images provided by designer/architect.

Main Level Floor Plan

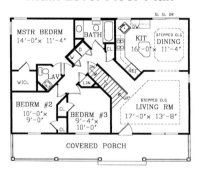

Optional Main Level Floor Plan

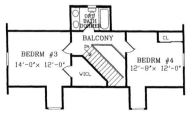

Optional Upper Level Floor Plan

Copyright by designer/architect.

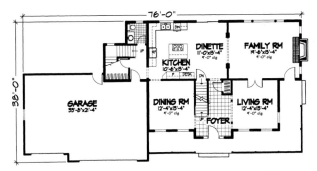

Main Level Floor Plan

Upper Level Floor Plan

Copyright by designer/architect.

Plan #271072

Dimensions: 76' W x 38' D

Levels: 2

Square Footage: 3,081

Main Level Sq. Ft.: 1,358

Upper Level Sq. Ft.: 1,723

Bedrooms: 3

Bathrooms: 2½

Foundation: Crawl space or basement

Materials List Available: No

Price Category: G

Images provided by designer/architect.

CAD FILE AVAILABLE

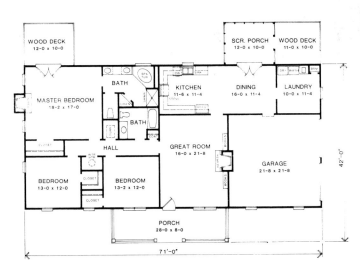

Plan #301005

Dimensions: 71' W x 42' D

Levels: 1

Square Footage: 1,930

Bedrooms: 3

Bathrooms: 2

Foundation: Crawl space, slab

Materials List Available: Yes

Price Category: D

Images provided by designer/architect.

Copyright by designer/architect.

Plan #121083

Dimensions: 72' W x 45'4" D
Levels: 2
Square Footage: 2,695
Main Level Sq. Ft.: 1,881
Upper Level Sq. Ft.: 814
Bedrooms: 4
Bathrooms: 3½
Foundation: Basement
Materials List Available: Yes
Price Category: F

Images provided by designer/architect.

You'll love this home for its soaring entryway ceiling and well-designed layout.

Features:

- **Entry:** A balcony from the upper level looks down into this two-story entry, which features a decorative plant shelf.
- **Great Room:** Comfort is guaranteed in this large room, with its built-in bookcases framing a lovely fireplace and trio of transom-topped windows along one wall.
- **Living Room:** Save both this formal room and the formal dining room, both of which flank the entry, for guests and special occasions.
- **Kitchen:** This convenient work space includes a gazebo-shaped breakfast area where friends and family will gather at any time of day.

Main Level Floor Plan

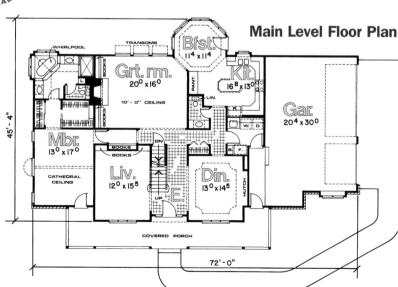

Upper Level Floor Plan

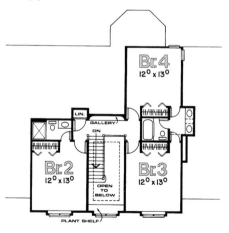

Copyright by designer/architect.

Plan #131047

Dimensions: 69'10" W x 51'8" D
Levels: 1
Square Footage: 1,793
Bedrooms: 3
Bathrooms: 2
Foundation: Crawl space or slab; basement for fee
Materials List Available: Yes
Price Category: D

The country charm of this well-designed home is mixed with the convenience and luxury normally reserved for more contemporary plans.

Images provided by designer/architect.

Features:

- Great Room: The spaciousness of this great room is enhanced by the 11-ft. stepped ceiling. A fireplace makes it cozy on cool evenings or on chilly winter days, and two sets of French sliding glass doors open to the back porch.

- Kitchen: In addition to the convenient layout of this design, you'll also love its bright, airy position. It includes an old-fashioned pantry, a sink under a window, and a sunny breakfast area that opens to the wraparound porch.

- Master Suite: You'll find 11-ft. ceilings in both the master bedroom and the bayed sitting area that the suite includes. In the bath, the circular spa tub is surrounded by a glass-block wall.

- Bonus Space: A permanent staircase leads to an unfinished bonus space on the upper level.

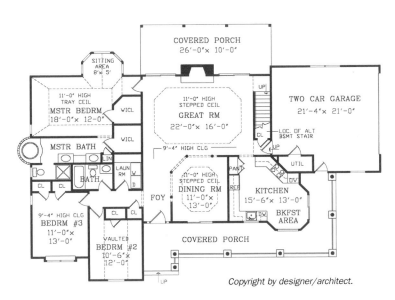

Copyright by designer/architect.

Rear Elevation

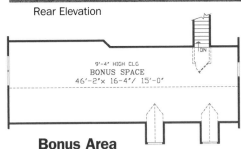

Bonus Area

Images provided by designer/architect.

Plan #301002

Dimensions: 57'2" W x 54'10" D

Levels: 1

Square Footage: 1,845

Bedrooms: 3

Bathrooms: 2½

Foundation: Crawl space, slab

Materials List Available: Yes

Price Category: D

Copyright by designer/architect.

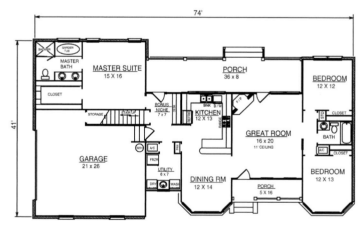

Images provided by designer/architect.

Plan #171023

Dimensions: 74' W x 41' D

Levels: 1

Square Footage: 1,684

Bedrooms: 3

Bathrooms: 2

Foundation: Crawl space or slab

Material List Available: Yes

Price Category: C

Bonus Level Floor Plan

Copyright by designer/architect.

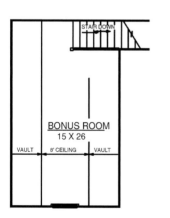

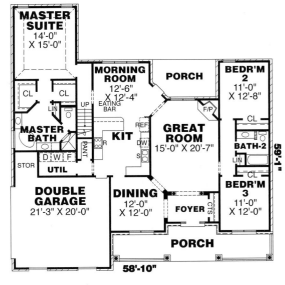

Bonus Area Floor Plan

Copyright by designer/architect.

Images provided by designer/architect.

Plan #241007

Dimensions: 58'10" W x 59'1" D

Levels: 1

Square Footage: 2,036

Bedrooms: 3

Bathrooms: 2

Foundation: Crawl space, slab

Materials List Available: No

Price Category: D

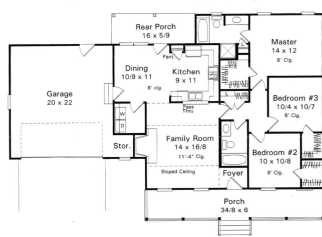

Copyright by designer/architect.

Plan #251001

Dimensions: 61'3" W x 40'6" D

Levels: 1

Square Footage: 1,253

Bedrooms: 3

Bathrooms: 2

Foundation: Crawl space, basement

Materials List Available: No

Price Category: B

Images provided by designer/architect.

Plan #131051

Dimensions: 64'4" W x 53'4" D

Levels: 2

Square Footage: 2,431

Main Level Sq. Ft.: 1,293

Upper Level Sq. Ft.: 1,138

Bedrooms: 4

Bathrooms: 2½

Foundation: Crawl space or slab; basement for fee

Materials List Available: Yes

Price Category: F

Gracious and charming with a wraparound front porch and a backyard terrace, this home also has a ready-to-finish third floor all-purpose room and a full bath.

Features:

- Main Level Ceiling Height: 9 ft.

- Family Room: A comfortable space for the entire family to gather, this delightful room can be warmed by a heat-circulating fireplace.

- Dining Room: A cozy dinette boasts a sliding glass door with access to a gorgeous backyard terrace with an optional calm reflecting pool.

- Kitchen: Adjoining the dining area, the kitchen offers plenty of storage and counter space. The laundry room and half-bath are nearby for convenience.

- Garage: The garage is tucked way back to keep it from intruding into the traditional facade.

Main Level Floor Plan

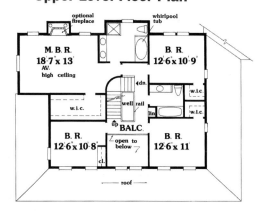

Images provided by designer/architect.

This home, as shown in the photograph, may differ from the actual blueprints. For more detailed information, please check the floor plans carefully.

Rear Elevation

Upper Level Floor Plan

Optional 3rd Level Floor Plan

Copyright by designer/architect.

Plan #151031

Dimensions: 60'2" W x 60'2" D
Levels: 2
Square Footage: 3,130
Main Level Sq. Ft.: 1,600
Upper Level Sq. Ft.: 1,530
Bedrooms: 3
Bathrooms: 3½
Foundation: Crawl space, slab
CompleteCost List Available: Yes
Price Category: F

If you love traditional Southern plantation homes, you'll want this house with its wraparound porches that are graced with boxed columns.

Features:

- **Great Room:** Use the gas fireplace for warmth in this comfortable room, which is open to the kitchen.

- **Living Room:** 8-in. columns add formality as you enter this living and dining room.

- **Kitchen:** You'll love the island bar with a sink. An elevator here can take you to the other floors.

- **Master Suite:** A gas fireplace warms this area, and the bath is luxurious.

- **Bedrooms:** Each has a private bath and built-in bookshelves for easy organizing.

- **Optional Features:** Choose a 2,559-sq.-ft. basement and add a kitchen to it, or finish the 1,744-sq.-ft. bonus room and add a spiral staircase and a bath.

Images provided by designer/architect.

Main Level Floor Plan

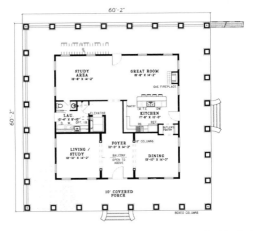

Upper Level Floor Plan

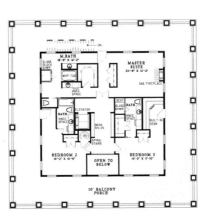

Images provided by designer/architect.

Basement Level Floor Plan

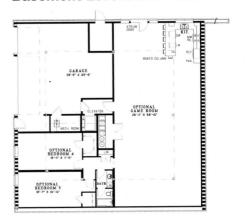

Optional Upper Level Floor Plan

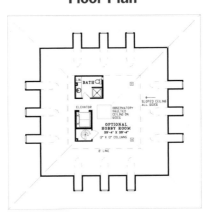

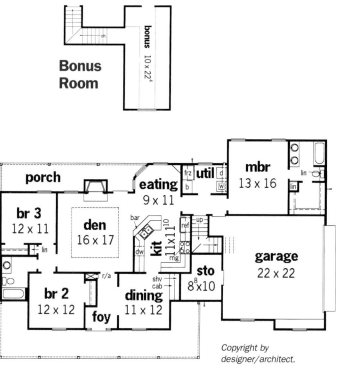

Bonus Room

bonus 10 x 22⁴

porch

br 3
12 x 11

den
16 x 17

eating
9 x 11

util

mbr
13 x 16

kit
11x11

ref

up

garage
22 x 22

br 2
12 x 12

foy

dining
11 x 12

sto
8 x10

Plan #201086

Dimensions: 68'6" W x 46' D

Levels: 1

Square Footage: 1,573

Bedrooms: 3

Bathrooms: 2

Foundation: Crawl space, slab

Materials List Available: Yes

Price Category: C

Images provided by designer/architect.

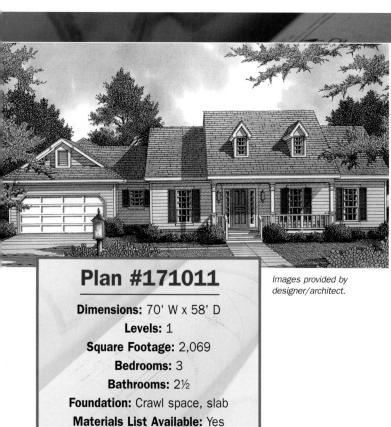

Plan #171011

Dimensions: 70' W x 58' D

Levels: 1

Square Footage: 2,069

Bedrooms: 3

Bathrooms: 2½

Foundation: Crawl space, slab

Materials List Available: Yes

Price Category: D

Images provided by designer/architect.

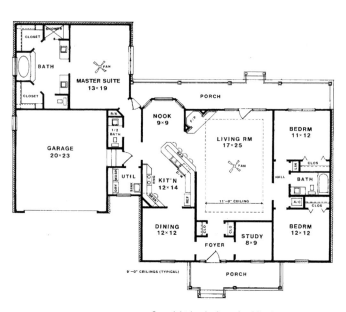

CLOSET

BATH

CLOSET

MASTER SUITE
13×19

PORCH

GARAGE
20×23

1/2
BATH

NOOK
9×9

LIVING RM
17×25

11'-0" CEILING

BEDRM
11×12

HALL

BATH

UTIL

KIT'N
12×14

DINING
12×12

STUDY
8×9

BEDRM
12×12

FOYER

9 -0" CEILINGS (TYPICAL)

PORCH

Copyright by designer/architect.

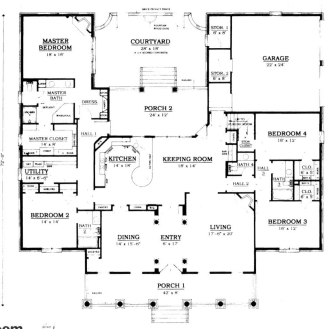

Plan #171013

Dimensions: 74' W x 72' D

Levels: 1

Square Footage: 3,084

Bedrooms: 4

Bathrooms: 3½

Foundation: Crawl space or slab

Materials List Available: Yes

Price Category: G

Images provided by designer/architect.

Bonus Room
Copyright by designer/architect.

Future Rm

Copyright by designer/architect.

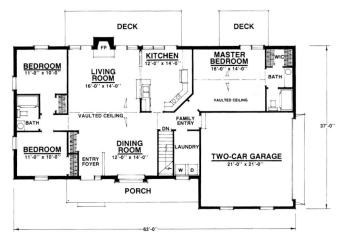

Plan #291002

Dimensions: 63' W x 37' D

Levels: 1

Square Footage: 1,550

Bedrooms: 3

Bathrooms: 2

Foundation: Basement

Materials List Available: No

Price Category: C

Images provided by designer/architect.

Copyright by designer/architect.

Rear View

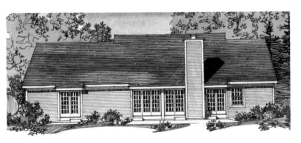

Plan #181151

Dimensions: 50' W x 46' D
Levels: 2
Square Footage: 2,283
Main Level Sq. Ft.: 1,274
Second Level Sq. Ft.: 1,009
Bedrooms: 3
Bathrooms: 2½
Foundation: Basement
Materials List Available: Yes
Price Category: F

Images provided by designer/architect.

- **Kitchen:** This efficient and well-designed kitchen has double sinks and offers a separate eating area for those impromptu family meals.

- **Master Suite:** This master retreat has a walk-in closet and its own sumptuous bath.

- **Home Office:** Whether you work at home or just need a place for the family computer and keeping track of family finances, this home office fills the bill.

Multiple porches, stately columns, and arched multi-paned windows adorn this country home.

Features:

- Ceiling Height: 8 ft. unless otherwise noted.

- Great Room: The second-floor mezzanine overlooks this great room. With its soaring ceiling, this dramatic room is the centerpiece of a spacious and flowing design that is just as suited to entertaining as it is to family life.

- Dining Area: Guests will naturally flow into this dining area when it is time to eat. After dinner they can step directly out onto the porch to enjoy coffee and dessert when the weather is fair.

Front View

Main Level Floor Plan

21'-0" X 20'-8"
6,30 X 6,20

17'-0" X 11'-8"
5,10 X 3,50

9'-8" X 8'-8"
2,90 X 2,60

9'-0" X 10'-0"
2,70 X 3,00

10'-0" X 12'-0"
3,00 X 3,60

9'-8" X 9'-4"
2,90 X 2,80

12'-0" X 20'-8"
3,60 X 6,20

46'-0"
13,8 m

50'-0"
15,0 m

Upper Level Floor Plan

13'-4" X 10'-0"
4,00 X 3,00

17'-0" X 13'-0"
5,10 X 3,90

14'-0" X 10'-0"
4,20 X 3,00

Copyright by designer/architect.

SMARTtip

Coping Chair Rails

If the teeth of your rasp tend to break out thin edges of the cope, try wrapping the rasp with sandpaper to make fine adjustments.

Dining Room

Living Room

Master Bath

Plan #181085

Dimensions: 56'4" W x 44' D
Levels: 2
Square Footage: 2,183
Main Level Sq. Ft.: 1,232
Second Level Sq. Ft.: 951
Bedrooms: 3
Bathrooms: 2½
Foundation: Basement
Materials List Available: Yes
Price Category: G

This country home features an inviting front porch and a layout designed for modern living.

Features:

- Ceiling Height: 8 ft.
- Solarium: Sunlight streams through the windows of this solarium at the front of the house.
- Living Room: Walk through French doors, and you will enter this inviting living room. Family and friends will be drawn to the corner fireplace.
- Formal Dining Room: Usher your guests directly from the living room into this formal dining room. The kitchen is located on the

other side of the dining room for convenient service.

- Kitchen: This generously sized kitchen is a delight, it offers a center island, separate eat-in area, and access to the back deck.
- Bonus Room: This room just off the entry hall can become a family room, a bedroom, or an office.
- Master Suite: Curl up by the corner fireplace in this master retreat, with its walk-in closet and lavish bath with separate shower and tub.

Main Level Floor Plan

Upper Level Floor Plan

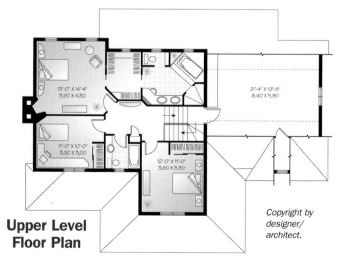

Copyright by designer/architect.

Plan #161024

Dimensions: 54'4" W x 26'8" D
Levels: 2
Square Footage: 1,698
Main Level Sq. Ft.: 868
Upper Level Sq. Ft.: 830
Bonus Space Sq. Ft.: 269
Bedrooms: 3
Bathrooms: 2½
Foundation: Basement
Materials List Available: No
Price Category: C

The covered porch, dormers, and center gable that grace the exterior let you know how comfortable your family will be in this home.

Features:

- **Great Room:** Walk from windows overlooking the front porch to a door into the rear yard in this spacious room, which runs the width of the house.

- **Dining Room:** Adjacent to the great room, the dining area gives your family space to spread out and makes it easy to entertain a large group.

- **Kitchen:** Designed for efficiency, the kitchen area includes a large pantry.

- **Master Suite:** Tucked away on the second floor, the master suite features a walk-in closet in the bedroom and a luxurious attached bathroom.

- **Bonus Room:** Finish the 269-sq.-ft. area over the 2-bay garage as a guest room, study, or getaway for the kids.

This home, as shown in the photograph, may differ from the actual blueprints. For more detailed information, please check the floor plans carefully.   *Images provided by designer/architect.*

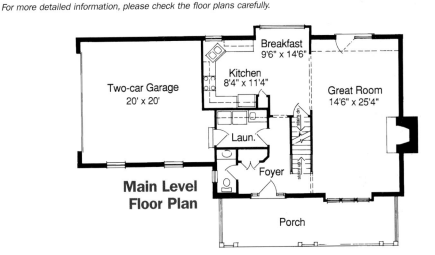

Main Level Floor Plan

Copyright by designer/architect.

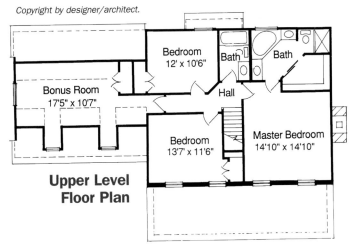

Upper Level Floor Plan

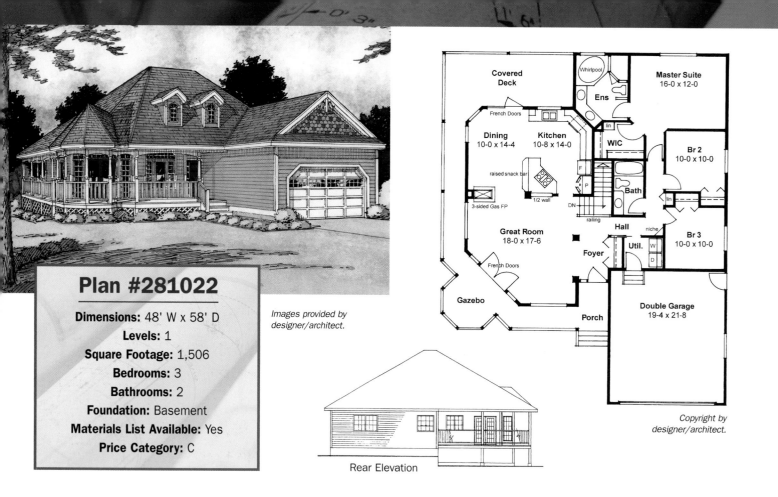

Plan #281022

Dimensions: 48' W x 58' D

Levels: 1

Square Footage: 1,506

Bedrooms: 3

Bathrooms: 2

Foundation: Basement

Materials List Available: Yes

Price Category: C

Images provided by designer/architect.

Rear Elevation

Copyright by designer/architect.

Plan #111043

Dimensions: 42' W x 49' D

Levels: 2

Square Footage: 1,737

Main Level Sq. Ft.: 1,238

Upper Level Sq. Ft.: 499

Bedrooms: 3

Bathrooms: 2½

Foundation: Crawl space

Materials List Available: No

Price Category: C

Images provided by designer/architect.

Copyright by designer/architect.

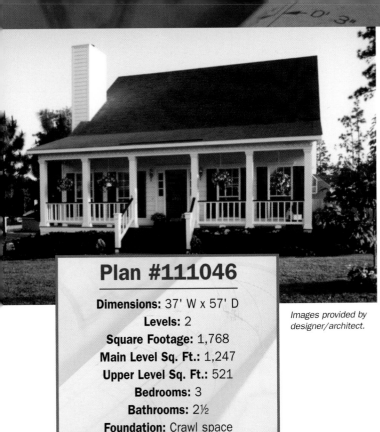

Plan #111046

Dimensions: 37' W x 57' D

Levels: 2

Square Footage: 1,768

Main Level Sq. Ft.: 1,247

Upper Level Sq. Ft.: 521

Bedrooms: 3

Bathrooms: 2½

Foundation: Crawl space

Materials List Available: No

Price Category: D

Images provided by designer/architect.

Main Level Floor Plan

Wood Deck 12'6" x 8'

Covered Porch 12'2" x 10'

Ext. Storage

Master Bath

WIC

Breakfast 11'10" x 9'6'

Utility

Master Bedroom 12'6" x 15'6"

1/2 Ba.

Kitchen 10'x 11'6"

Living 14'4"x 17'6"

Dining 13'x 12'

Porch 32'x 5'

Upper Level Floor Plan

Bedroom 12'6" x 14'

Bedroom 10'6" x 13'2"

Balcony

Bath

Copyright by designer/architect.

Plan #221008

Dimensions: 60'4" W x 46' D

Levels: 1

Square Footage: 1,540

Bedrooms: 3

Bathrooms: 2

Foundation: Basement

Materials List Available: No

Price Category: C

Images provided by designer/architect.

CAD FILE AVAILABLE

MBR. 13'4" x 14'8"

DIRECT VENT GAS FIREPLACE

LIV. VAULTED CEILING 13'8" X 18'0"

DIN. 12'0" X 10'8"

SCREEN PORCH 14'0" X 16'0"

KIT. 12'0" X 12'6"

STORAGE 14'0" X 7'8"

BR. #2 11'6" X 11'8"

BR. #3 11'0" X 11'8"

E. VAULTED CEILING

2 CAR GAR. 22'0" X 22'0"

Copyright by designer/architect.

46'-0"

60'-4"

Rear Elevation

Plan #121010

Dimensions: 50' W x 62' D
Levels: 1
Square Footage: 1,902
Bedrooms: 2
Bathrooms: 2
Foundation: Basement
Materials List Available: Yes
Price Category: D

Images provided by designer/architect.

This home is replete with architectural details that provide a convenient and gracious lifestyle.

Features:

• Ceiling Height: 8 ft.

• Great Room: The entry enjoys a long view into this room. Family and friends will be drawn to the warmth of its handsome fireplace flanked by windows.

• Breakfast Area: You'll pass through cased openings from the great room into the cozy breakfast area that will lure the whole family to linger over informal meals.

• Kitchen: Another cased opening leads from the breakfast area into the well-designed kitchen with its convenient island.

• Master Bedroom: To the right of the great room special ceiling details highlight the master bedroom where a cased opening and columns lead to a private sitting area.

• Den/Library: Whether you are listening to music or relaxing with a book, this special room will always enhance your lifestyle.

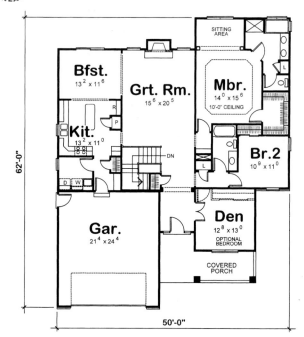

SMARTtip

Accentuating Your Fireplace with Faux Effects

Experiment with faux effects to add an aged look or a specific style to a fireplace mantel and surround. Craft stores sell inexpensive kits with directions for adding the appearance of antiqued or paneled wood or plaster, rusticated stone, marble, terra cotta, and other effects that make any style achievable.

Copyright by designer/architect.

Plan #391051

Dimensions: 63'6" W x 42'8" D
Levels: 2
Square Footage: 1,738
Main Level Sq. Ft.: 1,164
Upper Level Sq. Ft.: 574
Bedrooms: 3
Bathrooms: 2
Foundation: Crawl space, slab, or basement
Material List Available: Yes
Price Category: C

This home, as shown in the photograph, may differ from the actual blueprints. For more detailed information, please check the floor plans carefully.

Images provided by designer/architect.

Simple can be stupendous. The classic lines of this farmhouse-style design make it an instant favorite.

Features:

• **Living Room:** As you arrive home, you enter this spacious living room, which is full of natural light from the two front windows. In the evening, the light from the fireplace fills this room.

• **Solar Room:** An optional solar greenhouse and large triple-glazed windows make the most of the sun's warmth.

• **Master Suite:** Access to a rear private patio is just one amenity of this retreat. It also boasts his and her closets and a sumptuous master bath complete with a large tub.

• **Upper Level:** The upstairs has two ample bedrooms and a full bathroom.

Rear View

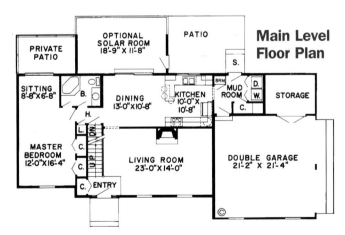

Main Level Floor Plan

Upper Level Floor Plan

Copyright by designer/architect.

Main Level Floor Plan

44'-0"
13,2 m

11'-8" X 16'-4"
3,50 X 4,90

26'-0" X 15'-0"
7,80 X 4,50

20'-4" X 21'-4"
6,10 X 6,40

12'-4" X 14'-0"
3,70 X 4,20

18'-4" X 20'-0"
5,50 X 6,00

60'-0"
18,0 m

Upper Level Floor Plan

Copyright by designer/architect.

11'-0" X 11'-0"
3,30 X 3,30

11'-8" X 16'-4"
3,50 X 4,90

18'-0" X 15'-0"
5,40 X 4,50

12'-0" X 21'-4"
3,60 X 6,40

11'-8" X 9'-8"
3,50 X 2,90

12'-4" X 13'-4"
3,70 X 4,00

12'-4" X 14'-0"
3,70 X 4,20

Plan #181034

Dimensions: 60' W x 44' D
Levels: 2
Square Footage: 2,687
Main Level Sq. Ft.: 1,297
Upper Level Sq. Ft.: 1,390
Bedrooms: 3
Bathrooms: 2½
Foundation: Full basement
Materials List Available: Yes
Price Category: H

Images provided by designer/architect.

Main Level Floor Plan

Copyright by designer/architect.

61'-6"

DECK

BREAKFAST AREA

KITCHEN

MUD ROOM

PWDR

FAMILY ROOM

3 CAR GARAGE

DINING ROOM

FOYER

LIVING ROOM

Images provided by designer/architect.

Plan #641001

Dimensions: 61'6" W x 56' D
Levels: 2
Square Footage: 3,034
Main Level Sq. Ft.: 1,323
Upper Level Sq. Ft.: 1,711
Bedrooms: 4
Bathrooms: 2½
Foundation: Basement
Materials List Available: No
Price Category: G

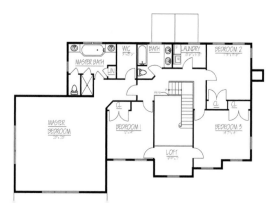

Upper Level Floor Plan

MASTER BATH

WIC

BATH

LAUNDRY

BEDROOM 2

MASTER BEDROOM

BEDROOM 1

BEDROOM 3

LOFT

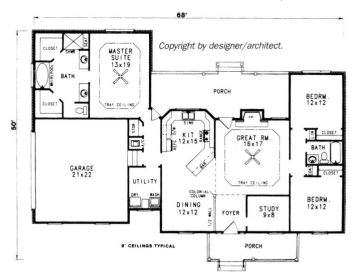

Images provided by designer/architect.

Plan #171009

Dimensions: 68' W x 50' D

Levels: 1

Square Footage: 1,771

Bedrooms: 3

Bathrooms: 2

Foundation: Crawl space, slab

Materials List Available: Yes

Price Category: C

SMARTtip

Deck Awnings

Awnings come in bright colors. As light filters through, it will cast a hue to anything under the deck. Warm colors, such as red or pink, will create a rosy glow; cool colors, such blues or greens, will enhance the shade.

Plan #191003

Dimensions: 56' W x 42' D

Levels: 1

Square Footage: 1,785

Bedrooms: 3

Bathrooms: 3

Foundation: Crawl space, slab, or basement

Materials List Available: No

Price Category: C

Images provided by designer/architect.

56'-0" Width

Plan #181081

Dimensions: 58' W x 33' D

Levels: 2

Square Footage: 2,350

Main Level Sq. Ft.: 1,107

Second Level Sq. Ft.: 1,243

Bedrooms: 3

Bathrooms: 2½

Foundation: Basement

Materials List Available: Yes

Price Category: G

This traditional country home features a wrap-around porch and a second-floor balcony.

Features:

- Ceiling Height: 8 ft. unless otherwise noted.
- Family Room: Double French doors and a fireplace in this inviting front room enhance the beauty and warmth of the home's open floor plan.
- Kitchen: You'll love working in this bright and convenient kitchen. The breakfast bar is the perfect place to gather for informal meals.

- Master Suite: You'll look forward to retiring to this elegant upstairs suite at the end of a busy day. The suite features a private bath with separate shower and tub, as well as dual vanities.
- Secondary Bedrooms: Two family bedrooms share a full bath with a third room that opens onto the balcony.
- Basement: An unfinished full basement provides plenty of storage and the potential to add additional finished living space.

Main Level Floor Plan

Upper Level Floor Plan

Plan #191009

Dimensions: 62' W x 76' D

Levels: 1

Square Footage: 2,172

Bedrooms: 4

Bathrooms: 2

Foundation: Crawl space, slab

Materials List Available: No

Price Category: D

Images provided by designer/architect.

This charming home is equally attractive in a rural or a settled area, thanks to its classic lines.

Features:

- **Porches:** Covered front and back porches emphasize the comfort you'll find in this home.

- **Great Room:** A tray ceiling gives elegance to this spacious room, where everyone is sure to gather. A fireplace makes a nice focal point, and French doors open onto the rear covered porch.

- **Dining Room:** Arched openings give distinction to this room, where it's easy to serve meals for the family or host a large group.

- **Kitchen:** You'll love the cooktop island, walk-in pantry, wall oven, snack bar, and view out of the windows in the adjoining breakfast area.

- **Master Suite:** The large bedroom here gives you space to spread out and relax, and the bath includes a corner whirlpool tub, shower, and dual sinks. An 8-ft. x 10-ft. walk-in closet is off the bath.

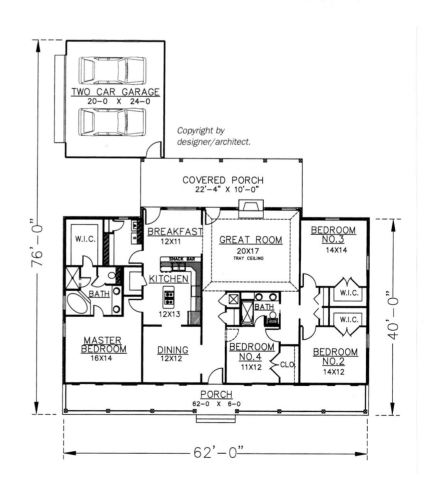

Copyright by designer/architect.

Plan #321054

Dimensions: 70'6" W x 55'6" D
Levels: 2
Square Footage: 2,828
Main Level Sq. Ft.: 2,006
Upper Level Sq. Ft.: 822
Bedrooms: 5
Bathrooms: 3½
Foundation: Basement
Materials List Available: Yes
Price Category: F

Images provided by designer/architect.

The wraparound porch welcomes visitors to this spacious home built for a large family.

Features:

- **Foyer:** Flanked by the study on one side and the dining room on the other, the foyer leads to the staircase, breakfast room, and family room.

- **Family Room:** You'll feel comfortable in this room, with its vaulted ceiling, wet bar, ample window area, and door to the patio.

- **Kitchen:** A center island adds work space to this well-planned room with large corner windows and a convenient door to the outside patio.

- **Master Suite:** Doors to the covered porch flank the fireplace here, and the luxurious bath includes a corner tub, two vanities, and separate shower. A huge walk-in closet is in the hall.

- **Upper Floor:** You'll find four bedrooms, each with a large closet, and two full baths here. Bay windows grace the two front bedrooms.

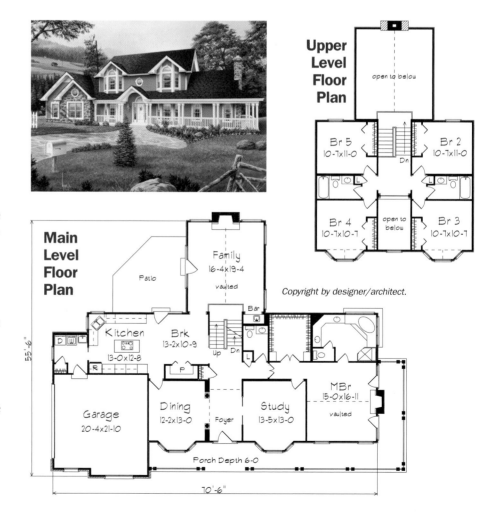

Copyright by designer/architect.

Plan #321041

Dimensions: 64' W x 34' D
Levels: 2
Square Footage: 2,286
Main Level Sq. Ft.: 1,283
Upper Level Sq. Ft.: 1,003
Bedrooms: 4
Bathrooms: 2½
Foundation: Crawl space, slab, or basement
Materials List Available: No
Price Category: E

Images provided by designer/architect.

If you love the way these gorgeous windows look from the outside, you'll be thrilled with the equally gracious interior of this home.

Features:

- **Entryway:** This two-story entryway shows off the fine woodworking on the railing and balustrades.

- **Living Room:** The large front windows form a glamorous background in this spacious room.

- **Family Room:** A handsome fireplace and a sliding glass door to the backyard enhance the open design of this room.

- **Breakfast Room:** Large enough for a crowd, this room makes a perfect dining area.

- **Kitchen:** The angled bar and separate pantry are highlights in this step-saving design.

- **Master Suite:** Enjoy this suite's huge walk-in closet, vaulted ceiling, and private bath, which features a double vanity, tub, and shower stall.

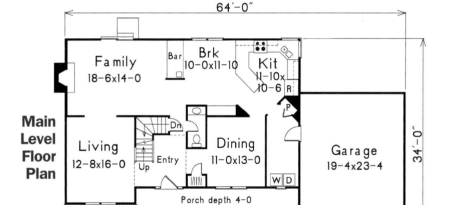

Main Level Floor Plan

Upper Level Floor Plan

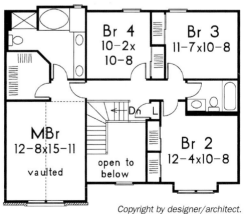

Front View

Copyright by designer/architect.

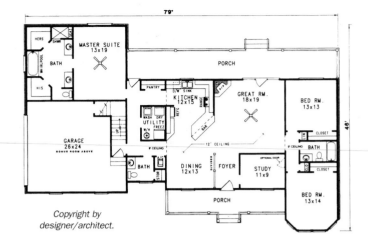

Plan #171015

Dimensions: 79' W x 52' D

Levels: 1

Square Footage: 2,089

Bedrooms: 3

Bathrooms: 2½

Foundation: Crawl space, slab

Materials List Available: Yes

Price Category: D

Images provided by designer/architect.

Copyright by designer/architect.

Bonus Area

Plan #561006

Dimensions: 61'4" W x 72'8" D

Levels: 1

Square Footage: 2,408

Bedrooms: 3

Bathrooms: 2½

Foundation: Basement

Material List Available: Yes

Price Category: D

Images provided by designer/architect.

Copyright by designer/architect.

CAD FILE AVAILABLE

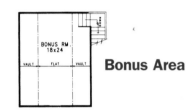

Rear Elevation

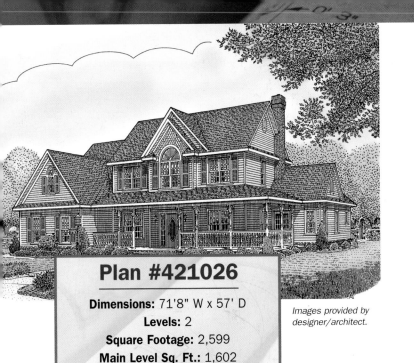

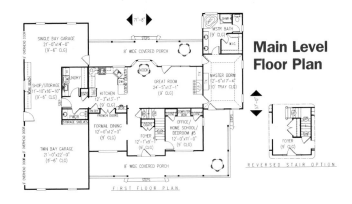

Main Level
Floor Plan

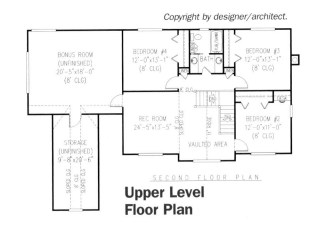

Copyright by designer/architect.

Upper Level
Floor Plan

Plan #421026

Dimensions: 71'8" W x 57' D

Levels: 2

Square Footage: 2,599

Main Level Sq. Ft.: 1,602

Upper Level Sq. Ft.: 997

Bedrooms: 5

Bathrooms: 2½

Foundation: Basement, crawl space, slab

Materials List Available: Yes

Price Category: E

Images provided by designer/architect.

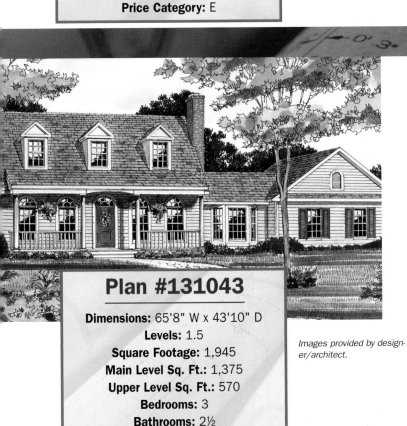

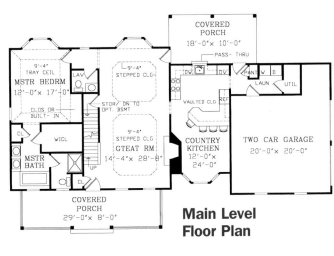

Main Level
Floor Plan

Images provided by designer/architect.

Upper Level
Floor Plan

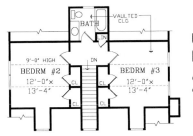

Copyright by designer/architect.

Plan #131043

Dimensions: 65'8" W x 43'10" D

Levels: 1.5

Square Footage: 1,945

Main Level Sq. Ft.: 1,375

Upper Level Sq. Ft.: 570

Bedrooms: 3

Bathrooms: 2½

Foundation: Crawl space or slab; basement for fee

Materials List Available: Yes

Price Category: E

Plan #111013

Dimensions: 33' W x 59' D
Levels: 1
Square Footage: 1,606
Bedrooms: 3
Bathrooms: 2
Foundation: Slab
Materials List Available: No
Price Category: D

Images provided by designer/architect.

This is the home you have been looking for to fit on that narrow building lot.

Features:

- Living Room: Entering this home from the front porch, you arrive in this gathering area. The corner fireplace adds warmth and charm to the area.

- Kitchen: This island kitchen features two built-in pantries and is open to the breakfast room. The oversize laundry room is close by and has room for the large items the kitchen needs to store.

- Master Suite: Located toward the rear of the home to give some extra privacy, this suite boasts a large sleeping area. The master bath has amenities such as his and her walk-in closets, dual vanities, and a whirlpool tub.

- Rear Porch: Just off the breakfast room is this covered rear porch with storage area. On nice days you can sit outside in the shaded area and watch the kids play outside.

Copyright by designer/architect.

Plan #401039

Dimensions: 69'8" W x 46' D

Levels: 2

Square Footage: 2,462

Main Level Sq. Ft.: 1,333

Upper Level Sq. Ft.: 1,129

Bedrooms: 4

Bathrooms: 2½

Foundation: Basement

Materials List Available: Yes

Price Category: E

Images provided by designer/architect.

A large wraparound porch graces the exterior of this home and gives it great outdoor livability.

Features:

• Foyer: This raised foyer spills into a hearth-warmed living room and the bay-windowed dining room beyond; French doors open from the breakfast and dining rooms to the spacious porch.

• Family Room: Built-ins surround a second hearth in this cozy gathering room.

• Study: Located in the front, this room is adorned by a beamed ceiling and, like the family room, features built-ins.

• Bedrooms: You'll find three family bedrooms on the second floor.

• Master Suite: This restful area, located on the second floor, features a walk-in closet and private bath.

• Garage: Don't miss the workshop area in this garage.

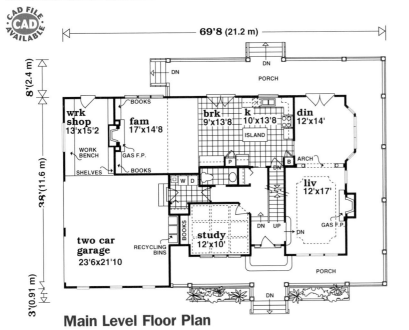

Main Level Floor Plan

Upper Level Floor Plan

Copyright by designer/architect.

Plan #161061

Dimensions: 90' W x 69'10" D
Levels: 2
Square Footage: 3,816
Main Level Sq. Ft.: 2,725
Upper Level Sq. Ft.: 1,091
Bedrooms: 4
Bathrooms: 3½
Foundation: Basement, walkout basement
Materials List Available: No
Price Category: H

Images provided by designer/architect.

Luxurious amenities make living in this spacious home a true pleasure for the whole family.

Features:

• **Great Room:** A fireplace, flanking built-in shelves, a balcony above, and three lovely windows create a luxurious room that's always comfortable.

• **Hearth Room:** Another fireplace with surrounding built-ins and double doors to the outside deck (with its own fireplace) highlight this room.

• **Kitchen:** A butler's pantry, laundry room, and mudroom with a window seat and two walk-in closets complement this large kitchen.

• **Library:** Situated for privacy and quiet, this spacious room with a large window area may be reached from the master bedroom as well as the foyer.

• **Master Suite:** A sloped ceiling and windows on three walls create a lovely bedroom, and the huge walk-in closet, dressing room, and luxurious bath add up to total comfort.

Main Level Floor Plan

Upper Level Floor Plan

Copyright by designer/architect.

Rear Elevation

Right Side Elevation

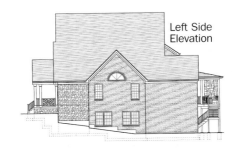

Left Side Elevation

Great Room

Hearth Room

Kitchen

Dining Room   Library

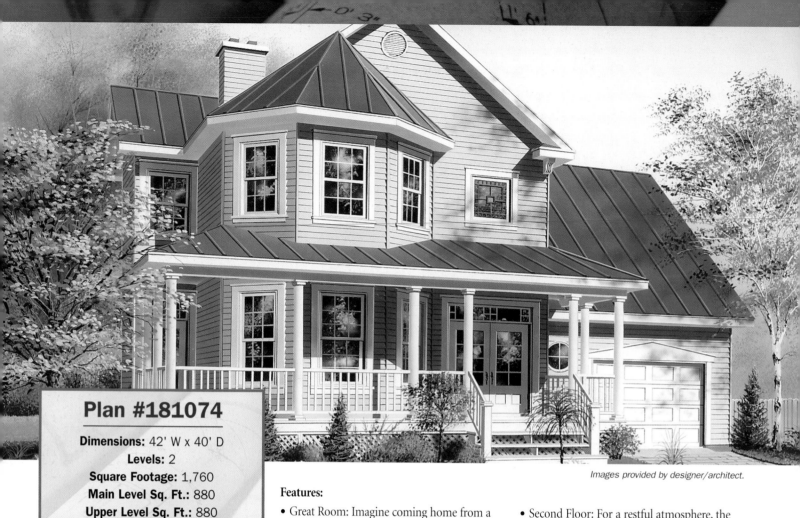

Plan #181074

Dimensions: 42' W x 40' D
Levels: 2
Square Footage: 1,760
Main Level Sq. Ft.: 880
Upper Level Sq. Ft.: 880
Bedrooms: 3
Full Baths: 2½
Foundation: Basement; Crawl space, slab; walkout for fee
Materials List Available: Yes
Price Category: F

-A front porch and a standing-seam metal roof add to the country charm of this home.

Images provided by designer/architect.

Features:

- **Great Room:** Imagine coming home from a hard day of working or chauffeuring the kids and being welcomed by comfy couch and warm fire. This is the perfect room to help you unwind.

- **Kitchen:** From culinary expert to family cook, everyone will find this kitchen's workspaces and storage just what they need to create special meals. A sun-drenched family area shares the space and opens onto the future patio.

- **Second Floor:** For a restful atmosphere, the bedrooms are separated from the hum of daily life. The spacious master bedroom receives light from the bay windows. The area features a walk-in closet and a private bathroom. The two additional bedrooms share access to a Jack-and-Jill bathroom.

- **Garage:** A single-car garage adds convenience to this plan. It can be used as additional storage space.

Main Level Floor Plan

Copyright by designer/architect.

Upper Level Floor Plan

Plan #281018

Dimensions: 50' W x 52'6" D
Levels: 1
Square Footage: 1,565
Bedrooms: 3
Bathrooms: 2
Foundation: Basement
Materials List Available: Yes
Price Category: C

You'll love the arched window that announces the grace of this home to the rest of the world.

Features:

- Living Room: Scissor trusses on the ceiling and a superb window design make this room elegant.

- Dining Room: Open to the living room, this dining room features an expansive window area and contains a convenient, inset china closet.

- Family Room: A gas fireplace in the corner and a doorway to the patio make this room the heart of the house.

- Breakfast Room: The bay window here makes it a lovely spot at any time of day.

- Kitchen: A raised snack bar shared with both the family and breakfast rooms adds a nice touch to this well-planned, attractive kitchen.

- Master Suite: A bay window, walk-in closet, and private bath add up to luxurious comfort in this suite.

Rear Elevation

Left Side Elevation

Right Side Elevation

Plan #121123

Dimensions: 54' W x 52' D
Levels: 1.5
Square Footage: 2,277
Main Level Sq. Ft.: 1,570
Upper Level Sq. Ft.: 707
Bedrooms: 4
Bathrooms: 2½
Foundation: Basement;
crawl space for fee
Material List Available: Yes
Price Category: E

Images provided by designer/architect.

This country-style home, with its classic wraparound porch, is just the plan you have been searching for.

Features:

• Entry: This two-story entry gives an open and airy feeling when you enter the home. A view into the dining room and great room adds to the open feeling.

• Great Room: This grand gathering area with cathedral ceiling is ready for your friends and family to come and visit. The fireplace, flanked by large windows, adds a cozy feeling to the space.

• Kitchen: The chef in the family will love how efficiently this island kitchen was designed. An abundance of cabinets and counter space is always a plus.

• Master Suite: This main level oasis will help you relieve all the stresses from the day. The master bath boasts dual vanities and a large walk-in closet.

• Secondary Bedrooms: Three generously sized bedrooms occupy the upper level. The full bathroom is located for easy access to all three bedrooms.

Main Level Floor Plan

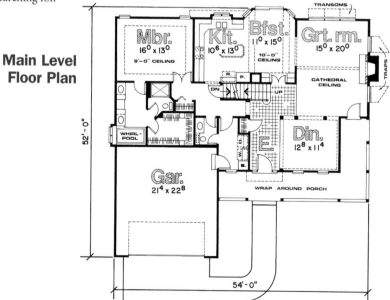

Upper Level Floor Plan

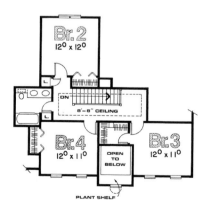

Copyright by designer/architect.

Plan #121167

Dimensions: 84'10" W x 102'3" D

Levels: 1.5

Square Footage: 4,629

Main Level Sq. Ft.: 3,337

Upper Level Sq. Ft.: 1,292

Bedrooms: 4

Bathrooms: 4½

Foundation: Slab; basement for fee

Material List Available: No

Price Category: I

The exquisite exterior of this stunning design offers hints of the stylish features waiting inside.

Images provided by designer/architect.

Features:

- **Family Room:** This large entertaining area features a coffered ceiling and a beautiful fireplace. French doors allow access to the rear yard.

- **Kitchen:** This island workspace has everything the chef in the family could want. The breakfast room merges with the main kitchen, allowing conversation during cleanup.

- **Master Suite:** This ground-level suite features a cathedral ceiling and access to the rear yard. The master bath has a marvelous whirlpool tub, dual vanities, and a separate toilet room.

- **Upper Level:** A large game room, with an overhead view of the family room, and bedrooms 3 and 4 occupy this level. Each bedroom has a private bathroom.

Main Level Floor Plan

Upper Level Floor Plan

Copyright by designer/architect.

Plan #461092

Dimensions: 81' W x 54' D
Levels: 2
Square Footage: 2,844
Main Level Sq. Ft.: 2,128
Upper Level Sq. Ft.: 716
Bedrooms: 4
Bathrooms: 4
Foundation: Slab or basement; crawl space for fee
Material List Available: No
Price Category: F

Enjoy country living at its best in this well-designed home.

Images provided by designer/architect.

Features:

- Dining Room: Located at the entry, this formal dining room features a nook for your hutch. Pocket doors lead into the foyer, adding the ability for the space to work as a home office.

- Guest Suite: This main-level suite offers your guests privacy while staying connected to what is happening in other parts of the house. The accessible full bathroom is a bonus for the area.

- Master Suite: Located on the main level, this retreat boasts two large walk-in closets. The master bath features a whirlpool tub and a stall shower.

- Upper Level: This level is home to the two secondary bedrooms, each with a walk-in closet. Each bedroom has a private bathroom.

Rear View

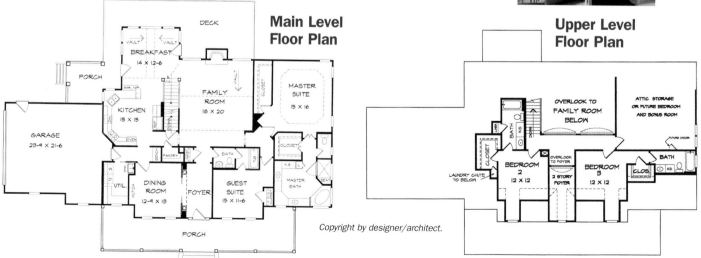

Main Level Floor Plan

Upper Level Floor Plan

Copyright by designer/architect.

Plan #281032

Dimensions: 66' W x 49' D
Levels: 2
Square Footage: 2,904
Main Level Sq. Ft.: 1,494
Upper Level Sq. Ft.: 1,410
Bedrooms: 4
Bathrooms: 2½
Foundation: Basement
Material List Available: Yes
Price Category: F

Images provided by designer/architect.

Country style is alive and well in this attractive home.

Features:

- **Front Porch:** This front porch welcomes guests to your home. It's the perfect spot to sit and sip lemonade while visiting with friends or family.

- **Family Room:** Opening onto the rear porch, which comes in handy for enjoying the outdoors, this family room also features a fireplace for the times you would rather stay inside.

- **Kitchen:** This efficiently designed space features an L-shaped work area, pantry, and island with a raised eating bar. The room opens to the breakfast nook, giving meal times plenty of possibilities.

- **Master Suite:** Imagine a relaxing breakfast in bed in this luxurious master suite. It contains two large walk-in closets and a full master bath.

Rear Elevation

Main Level Floor Plan

Copyright by designer/architect.

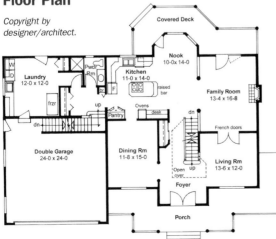

Upper Level Floor Plan

Plan #391056

Dimensions: 73'10" W x 53'4" D
Levels: 2
Square Footage: 2,607
Main Level Sq. Ft.: 1,429
Upper Level Sq. Ft.: 1,178
Bedrooms: 3
Bathrooms: 2½
Foundation: Basement
Materials List Available: No
Price Category: F

Images provided by designer/architect.

The spectacular pavilion front with Palladian window creates a dramatic picture indoors and out.

Features:

- Walk up the steps, onto the porch, and then through the front door with sidelights, this entry opens into a two-story space and feels light and airy. The nearby coat closet is a convenient asset.

- Living Room: This "sunken" room features a cozy fireplace flanked by two doors, allowing access to the wraparound deck. The dining room is open to the area, creating a nice flow between the two spaces.

- Family Room: This casual relaxing area is one step down from the kitchen; it boasts another fireplace and access to the large wraparound deck.

- Kitchen: This island kitchen features plenty of cabinet and counter space and is waiting for the chef in the family to take control. The breakfast area with bay window is the perfect place to start the day.

- Upper Level: This area is dedicated to the master suite with full master bath and two family bedrooms. Enjoy the dramatic view as you look down into the entry.

Main Level Floor Plan

Upper Level Floor Plan

Rear View

Kitchen

Living Room

Master Bath

Master Bedroom

Bedroom

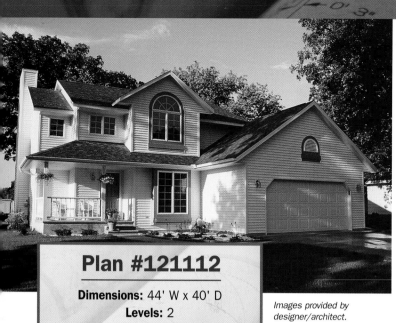

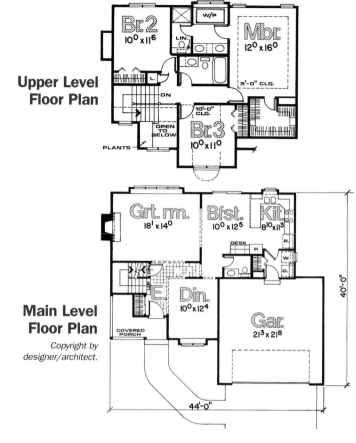

Upper Level Floor Plan

Br.2 10⁰ x 11⁶
w/p
Mbr. 12⁰ x 16⁰
9'-0" CLG.
LIN
L.
DN
10'-0" CLG.
OPEN TO BELOW
Br.3 10⁰ x 11⁰
PLANTS

Main Level Floor Plan

Copyright by designer/architect.

Grt. rm. 18¹ x 14⁰
Bfst. 10⁰ x 12⁵
Kit. 8¹⁰ x 11³
DESK
P.
Din. 10⁰ x 12⁴
Gar. 21³ x 21⁸
COVERED PORCH
44'-0"
40'-0"

Images provided by designer/architect.

Plan #121112

Dimensions: 44' W x 40' D

Levels: 2

Square Footage: 1,650

Main Level Sq. Ft.: 891

Upper Level Sq. Ft.: 759

Bedrooms: 3

Bathrooms: 2½

Foundation: Basement; crawl space for fee

Material List Available: Yes

Price Category: C

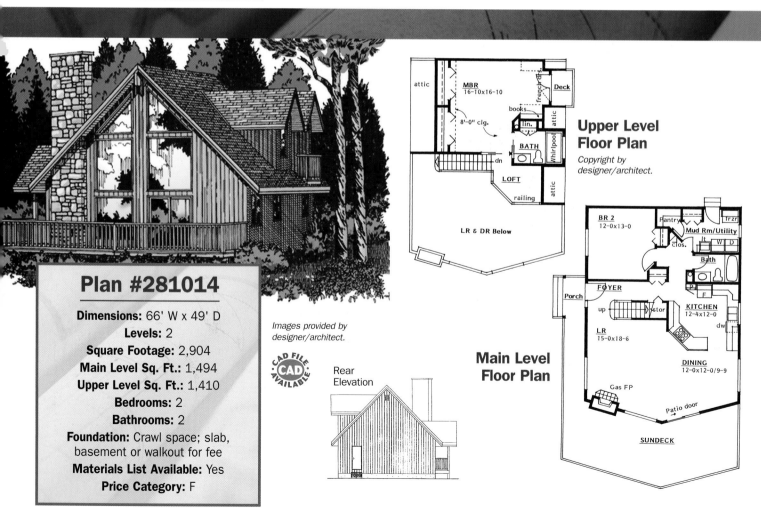

Plan #281014

Dimensions: 66' W x 49' D

Levels: 2

Square Footage: 2,904

Main Level Sq. Ft.: 1,494

Upper Level Sq. Ft.: 1,410

Bedrooms: 2

Bathrooms: 2

Foundation: Crawl space; slab, basement or walkout for fee

Materials List Available: Yes

Price Category: F

Images provided by designer/architect.

CAD FILE AVAILABLE

Rear Elevation

Upper Level Floor Plan

Copyright by designer/architect.

attic
MBR 16-10x16-10
8'-0" clg.
Deck
french drs.
books
attic
lin.
BATH
Whirlpool
LOFT
railing
attic
dn
LR & DR Below

Main Level Floor Plan

BR 2 12-0x13-0
Pantry
frzr
Mud Rm/Utility
Clos.
W D
Bath
FOYER
Porch
KITCHEN 12-4x12-0
up
stor
F
LR 15-0x18-6
dw
DINING 12-0x12-0/9-9
Gas FP
Patio door
SUNDECK

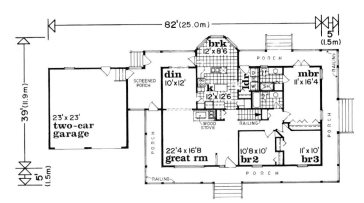

Images provided by
designer/architect.

Copyright by designer/architect.

Plan #401008

Dimensions: 87' W x 44' D

Levels: 1

Square Footage: 1,541

Bedrooms: 3

Bathrooms: 2

Foundation: Basement

Materials List Available: Yes

Price Category: C

Plan #521006

Dimensions: 99'2" W x 47'5" D

Levels: 1.5

Square Footage: 2,818

Main Level Sq. Ft.: 1,787

Upper Level Sq. Ft.: 1,031

Bedrooms: 4

Bathrooms: 3½

Foundation: Crawl space

Material List Available: No

Price Category: F

Images provided by
designer/architect.

CAD FILE AVAILABLE

Copyright by
designer/architect.

Main Level Floor Plan

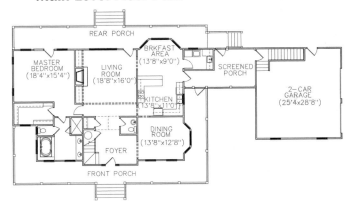

Upper Level Floor Plan

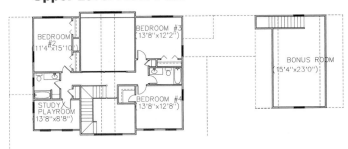

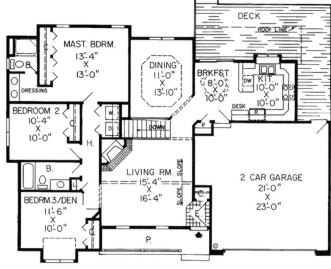

Images provided by designer/architect.

Plan #391211

Dimensions: 58' W x 40' D

Levels: 1

Square Footage: 1,461

Bedrooms: 3

Bathrooms: 2

Foundation: Basement

Material List Available: Yes

Price Category: B

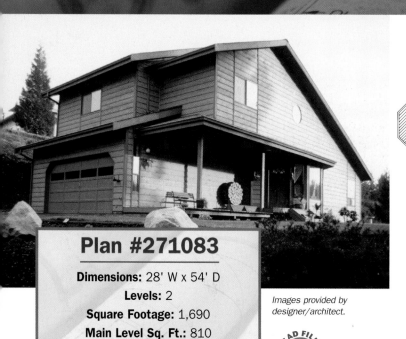

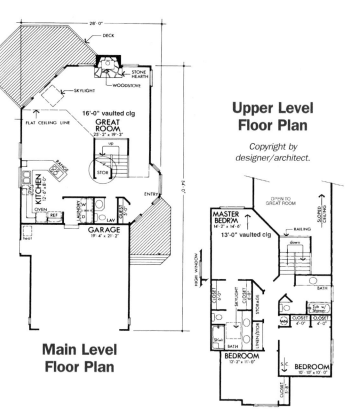

Images provided by designer/architect.

CAD FILE AVAILABLE

Plan #271083

Dimensions: 28' W x 54' D

Levels: 2

Square Footage: 1,690

Main Level Sq. Ft.: 810

Upper Level Sq. Ft.: 880

Bedrooms: 3

Bathrooms: 2½

Foundation: Crawl space

Materials List Available: Yes

Price Category: C

Upper Level Floor Plan

Copyright by designer/architect.

Main Level Floor Plan

Plan #521017

Dimensions: 94'11" W x 94'10" D

Levels: 1

Square Footage: 2,359

Bedrooms: 3

Bathrooms: 3

Foundation: Slab

Material List Available: No

Price Category: E

Images provided by designer/architect.

Copyright by designer/architect.

Rear View

MASTER BEDROOM (15'4"x20'2")

DECK

BREAKFAST AREA (13'4"x11'10")

LIVING ROOM (17'6"x16'0")

KITCHEN (18'0"x8'6")

SCREENED PORCH (16'0"x15'0")

DINING ROOM (10'10"x16'0")

GALLERY

FRONT PORCH

BEDROOM #2 (15'4"x12'8")

BEDROOM #3 (15'8"x14'4")

2-CAR GARAGE (25'4"x23'4")

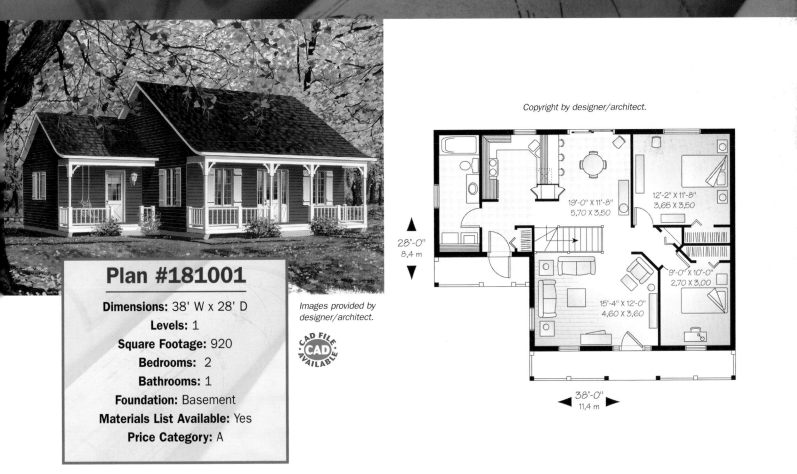

Plan #181001

Dimensions: 38' W x 28' D

Levels: 1

Square Footage: 920

Bedrooms: 2

Bathrooms: 1

Foundation: Basement

Materials List Available: Yes

Price Category: A

Images provided by designer/architect.

Copyright by designer/architect.

28'-0"
8,4 m

19'-0" X 11'-8"
5,70 X 3,50

12'-2" X 11'-8"
3,65 X 3,50

9'-0" X 10'-0"
2,70 X 3,00

15'-4" X 12'-0"
4,60 X 3,60

38'-0"
11,4 m

Plan #151490

Dimensions: 52' W x 69'6" D

Levels: 1

Square Footage: 1,869

Bedrooms: 3

Bathrooms: 2

Foundation: Crawl space or slab

CompleteCost List Available: Yes

Price Category: D

Beautiful brick and wood siding impart warmth to this French Country design.

Features:

- Open Plan: Elegance is achieved in this home by using boxed columns and 10-ft.-high ceilings. The foyer and dining room are lined with columns and adjoin the great room, all with high ceilings.

- Kitchen: This combined kitchen and breakfast room is great for entertaining and has access to the grilling porch.

- Master Suite: The split-bedroom plan features this suite, with its large walk-in closet, whirlpool tub, shower, and private area.

- Bedrooms: The two bedrooms and a large bathroom are located on the other side of the great room, giving privacy to the entire family.

Bonus Area Floor Plan

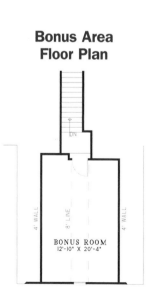

Plan #121147

Dimensions: 40' W x 51' D
Levels: 1.5
Square Footage: 2,051
Main Level Sq. Ft.: 1,497
Upper Level Sq. Ft.: 554
Bedrooms: 3
Bathrooms: 2½
Foundation: Basement;
   crawl space for fee
Material List Available: Yes
Price Category: D

Images provided by designer/architect.

This home, as shown in the photograph, may differ from the actual blueprints. For more detailed information, please check the floor plans carefully.

CAD FILE AVAILABLE

Multiple rooflines add to the charm of this home.

Features:

- Family Room: This room is sure to be your family's headquarters, thanks to the sloped ceiling, central location, and cozy fireplace.

- Kitchen: This island kitchen with double sink includes a snack bar open to the family room. The walk-in pantry provides ample storage space, and the nearby computer niche comes in handy when planning meals.

- Master Suite: For the sake of privacy, this retreat is located on the main floor away from the secondary bedrooms. The large walk-in closet and luxurious private bath are welcome amenities.

- Garage: This front-loading two-car garage can keep your cars warm and dry.

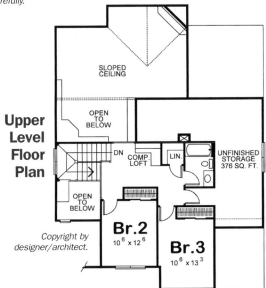

Upper Level Floor Plan

Copyright by designer/architect.

Main Level Floor Plan

Images provided by designer/architect.

Plan #181630

Dimensions: 38' W x 31'4" D
Levels: 2
Square Footage: 2,098
Main Level Sq. Ft.: 1,092
Upper Level Sq. Ft.: 1,006
Bedrooms: 3
Bathrooms: 1½
Foundation: Basement
Material List Available: Yes
Price Category: F

This country-style home would look great in any neighborhood.

Features:

- Entry: This two-story space welcomes you to this home. The center staircase, with a balcony above, gives a spacious feeling to the home.

- Family Room: The glow of natural light from the windows and the fireplace envelops this room. Whether you are relaxing with your family or entertaining guests, this room is ideal for bringing people together.

- Dining Room: This large space has plenty of room to serve formal meals. The room's closeness to the kitchen makes serving a snap.

- Upper Level: Three bedrooms make this level their home; they share a common bathroom. The master bedroom boasts a sitting area.

Main Level Floor Plan

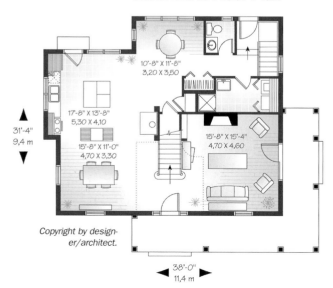

10'-8" X 11'-8"
3,20 X 3,50

17'-8" X 13'-8"
5,30 X 4,10

15'-8" X 11'-0"
4,70 X 3,30

15'-8" X 15'-4"
4,70 X 4,60

31'-4"
9,4 m

38'-0"
11,4 m

Copyright by designer/architect.

Upper Level Floor Plan

13'-8"/11'-8" X 21'-8"
4,10/3,50 X 6,50

11'-8" X 10'-0"
3,50 X 3,00

11'-8" X 12'-0"
3,50 X 3,60

Plan #321002

Dimensions: 72' W x 28' D
Levels: 1
Square Footage: 1,400
Bedrooms: 3
Bathrooms: 2
Foundation: Crawl space, basement
Materials List Available: Yes
Price Category: D

If you're looking for a well-designed compact home with contemporary amenities, this could be the home of your dreams.

Features:

- Porch: Just the right size for some rockers and a swing, this porch could become your outdoor living area when the weather is fine.

- Living Room: A vaulted ceiling adds to the spacious feeling in this room, where friends and family are sure to gather.

- Kitchen: This space-saving design, in combination with the ample counter and cabinet space, makes cooking a pleasure.

- Utility Room: This large room is fitted with cabinets for extra storage space. You'll find storage space in the large garage, too.

- Master Bedroom: This room is somewhat secluded for privacy, making it an ideal place for some quiet time at the end of the day.

Images provided by designer/architect.

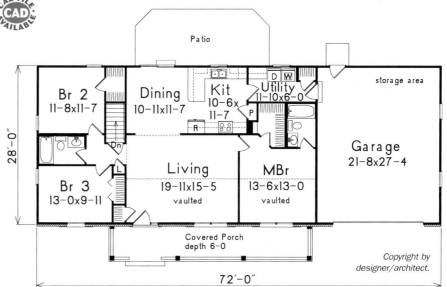

CAD FILE AVAILABLE

Copyright by designer/architect.

SMARTtip

Fabric Draping Ability

Test a fabric's draping ability by looking at a large piece in a fabric store. Gather at least two to three yards of material, holding one end in your hand. Check how it drapes. Does it fall into folds easily? Also look at the pattern when it is gathered. Does the design become lost in the folds? Ask a salesclerk or a friend to hold the fabric, and look at it from a few feet away.

Plan #151035

Dimensions: 37'8" W x 38'4" D
Levels: 1.5
Square Footage: 1,451
Main Level Sq. Ft.: 868
Upper Level Sq. Ft: 583
Bedrooms: 3
Bathrooms: 2
Foundation: Crawl space or slab; basement or walkout for fee
CompleteCost List Available: Yes
Price Category: B

Images provided by designer/architect.

Country living meets the modern day family in this well designed home.

CAD FILE AVAILABLE

Features:

- Den: The large stone fireplace is the focal point in this gathering area. Located just off the entry porch, the area welcomes you home.

- Kitchen: This efficiently designed kitchen has an abundance of cabinets and counter space. The eat-at counter, open to the den, adds extra space for family and friends.

- Grilling Porch: On nice days, overflow your dinner guests onto this rear covered grilling porch. From the relaxing area you can watch the kids play in the backyard.

- Upper Level: Two bedrooms, with large closets, and a full bathroom occupy this level. The dormers in each of the bedrooms add more space to these rooms.

Kitchen/Den

Porch

Kitchen

Master Bedroom

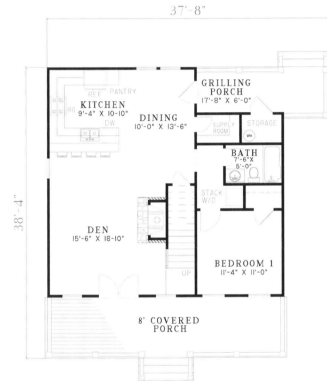

Main Level Floor Plan

KITCHEN 9'-4" X 10-10"

REF | PANTRY

RG | DW

DINING 10'-0" X 13'-6"

GRILLING PORCH 17'-8" X 6'-0"

SUPPLY ROOM | STORAGE | WH

BATH 7'-6" X 5'-0"

DEN 15'-6" X 18-10"

STACK W/D

BEDROOM 1 11'-4" X 11'-0"

UP

8' COVERED PORCH

37'-8"

38'-4"

Upper Level Floor Plan

Images provided by designer/architect.

6'4" WALL | 6'4" WALL

BATH 7'-8" X 7'-0"

LIN | R A | 8' LINE

DN

BEDROOM 2 13'-4" X 14'-6"

BEDROOM 3 11'-4" X 14'-5"

8' LINE | 8' LINE

4' WALL | 4' WALL

Den

Dining Room

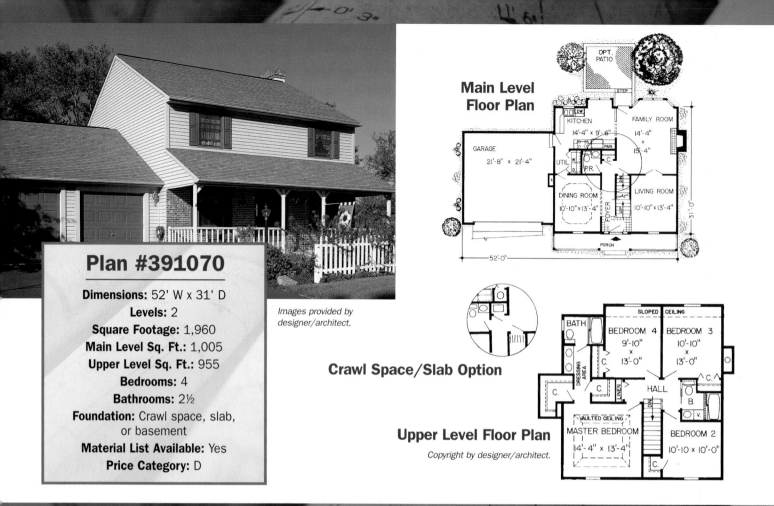

Main Level Floor Plan

Images provided by designer/architect.

Crawl Space/Slab Option

Upper Level Floor Plan

Copyright by designer/architect.

Plan #391070

Dimensions: 52' W x 31' D

Levels: 2

Square Footage: 1,960

Main Level Sq. Ft.: 1,005

Upper Level Sq. Ft.: 955

Bedrooms: 4

Bathrooms: 2½

Foundation: Crawl space, slab, or basement

Material List Available: Yes

Price Category: D

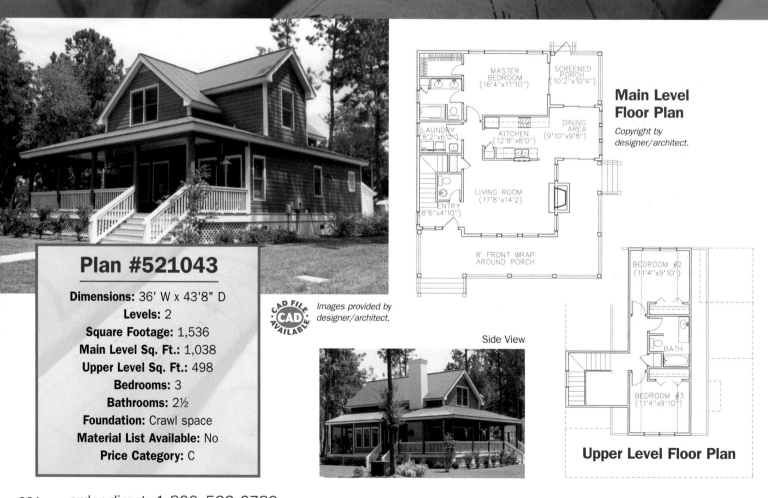

Main Level Floor Plan

Copyright by designer/architect.

Images provided by designer/architect.

Side View

Upper Level Floor Plan

Plan #521043

Dimensions: 36' W x 43'8" D

Levels: 2

Square Footage: 1,536

Main Level Sq. Ft.: 1,038

Upper Level Sq. Ft.: 498

Bedrooms: 3

Bathrooms: 2½

Foundation: Crawl space

Material List Available: No

Price Category: C

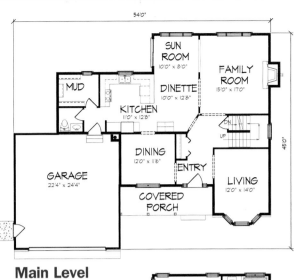

Main Level Floor Plan

Images provided by designer/architect.

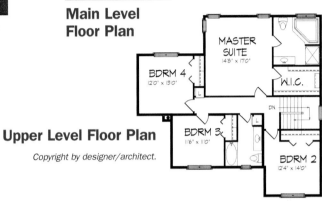

Upper Level Floor Plan

Copyright by designer/architect.

Plan #271062

Dimensions: 54' W x 45' D

Levels: 2

Square Footage: 2,356

Main Level Sq. Ft.: 1,222

Upper Level Sq. Ft.: 1,134

Bedrooms: 4

Bathrooms: 2½

Foundation: Daylight basement

Materials List Available: No

Price Category: E

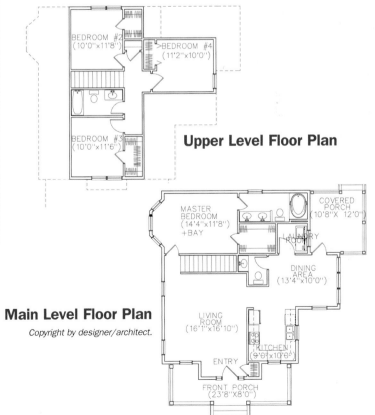

Upper Level Floor Plan

Main Level Floor Plan

Copyright by designer/architect.

Plan #521030

Dimensions: 41'8" W x 41' D

Levels: 2

Square Footage: 1,660

Main Level Sq. Ft.: 1,034

Upper Level Sq. Ft.: 626

Bedrooms: 4

Bathrooms: 2½

Foundation: Crawl space

Material List Available: No

Price Category: C

Images provided by designer/architect.

CAD FILE AVAILABLE

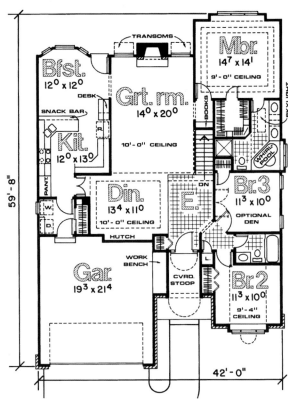

Plan #121118

Dimensions: 42' W x 59'8" D

Levels: 1

Square Footage: 1,636

Bedrooms: 3

Bathrooms: 2

Foundation: Basement; crawl space for fee

Material List Available: Yes

Price Category: C

Images provided by designer/architect.

Copyright by designer/architect.

Floor plan labels: Bfst. 12⁰ x 12⁰; Grt. rm. 14⁰ x 20⁰, 10'-0" CEILING; Mbr. 14⁷ x 14¹, 9'-0" CEILING; TRANSOMS; DESK; SNACK BAR; BOOKS; SKYLIGHT; Kit. 12⁰ x 13⁰; PANT.; WHIRL-POOL; Br.3 11³ x 10⁰, OPTIONAL DEN; Din. 13⁴ x 11⁰, 10'-0" CEILING; HUTCH; DN; E; Gar. 19³ x 21⁴; WORK BENCH; CVRD. STOOP; L; Br.2 11³ x 10⁰, 9'-4" CEILING; 59'-8"; 42'-0"

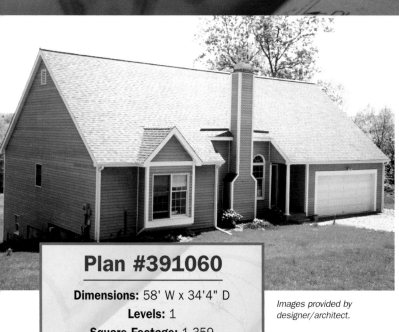

Plan #391060

Dimensions: 58' W x 34'4" D

Levels: 1

Square Footage: 1,359

Bedrooms: 3

Bathrooms: 2

Foundation: Crawl space, slab or basement

Materials List Available: Yes

Price Category: B

Images provided by designer/architect.

Copyright by designer/architect.

Floor plan labels: Deck; Dining 11-0 x 11-2, Decor. Ceiling; Br #2 10-10 x 11-10; Den/Br #3 10-0 x 11-10, Optional Door Location; Kit 10-0 x 11-2; Ldry; Sink; Range; DW; Ref.; Pan.; Railing; DN; Solid Wall w/ Opt. Door Location; Plant Ledge; Living Rm 14-10 x 17-0, 10' clg; MBr #1 11-7 x 13-0, Decor. Ceiling; Seat; Garage 20-4 x 21-8

Rear View

Plan #521040

Dimensions: 42'2" W x 57' D

Levels: 1

Square Footage: 1,555

Bedrooms: 3

Bathrooms: 2½

Foundation: Slab

Material List Available: No

Price Category: C

CAD FILE AVAILABLE CAD

Images provided by designer/architect.

This home, as shown in the photographs, may differ from the actual blueprints. For more detailed information, please check the floor plans carefully.

Front View

Rear View

Plan #321030

Dimensions: 61' W x 51' D

Levels: 1

Square Footage: 2,029

Bedrooms: 4

Bathrooms: 2

Foundation: Crawl space, slab, basement, or walkout

Materials List Available: Yes

Price Category: F

Images provided by designer/architect.

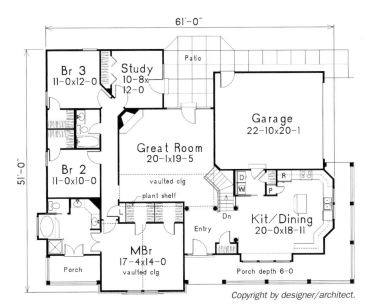

SMARTtip

Measuring Angles

A sure-fire way to accurately measure the wall-frame acute angle is to cut a piece of scrap lumber to emulate the angle, and then measure it.

Plan #181126

Dimensions: 35' W x 30' D
Levels: 2
Square Footage: 1,468
Main Level Sq. Ft.: 958
Upper Level Sq. Ft.: 510
Bedrooms: 3
Bathrooms: 2
Foundation: Basement
Materials List Available: Yes
Price Category: B

CAD FILE AVAILABLE

A multiple-gabled roof and a covered entry give this home a charming appearance.

Features:

- **Entry:** You'll keep heating and cooling costs down with this air-lock entry. There is also a large closet here.

- **Kitchen:** This efficient L-shaped eat-in kitchen has access to the rear deck.

- **Great Room:** This two-story space has a cozy fireplace and is open to the kitchen.

- **Master Bedroom:** Located on the main level, this area has access to the main bathroom, which has an oversized tub and a compartmentalized lavatory.

- **Bedrooms:** The two secondary bedrooms are located on the upper level and share a common bathroom.

Great Room

Main Level Floor Plan

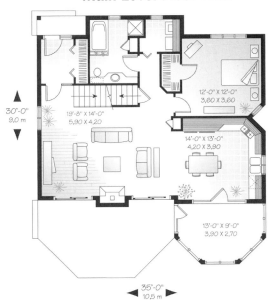

30'-0"
9,0 m

19'-8" X 14'-0"
5,90 X 4,20

12'-0" X 12'-0"
3,60 X 3,60

14'-0" X 13'-0"
4,20 X 3,90

13'-0" X 9'-0"
3,90 X 2,70

35'-0"
10,5 m

Upper Level Floor Plan

Copyright by designer/architect.

10'-0" X 11'-0"
3,00 X 3,30

15'-0" X 11'-0"
4,50 X 3,30

Rear View

Dining Room

Kitchen

Stairs

Plan #211069

Dimensions: 58' W x 42' D
Levels: 1.5
Square Footage: 1,600
Main Level Sq. Ft.: 1,136
Upper Level Sq. Ft.: 464
Bedrooms: 3
Bathrooms: 2
Foundation: Crawl space
Materials List Available: Yes
Price Category: C

Images provided by designer/architect.

Enjoy the large front porch on this traditionally styled home when it's too sunny for the bugs, and use the screened back porch at dusk and dawn.

Features:

• Living Room: Call this the family room if you wish, but no matter what you call it, expect friends and family to gather here, especially when the fireplace gives welcome warmth.

• Kitchen: You'll love the practical layout that pleases everyone from gourmet chefs to beginning cooks.

• Master Suite: Positioned on the main floor to give it privacy, this suite has two entrances for convenience. You'll find a large walk-in closet here as well as a dressing room that includes a separate vanity and mirror makeup counter.

• Storage Space: The 462-sq.-ft. garage is roomy enough to hold two cars and still have space to store tools, out-of-season clothing, or whatever else that needs a dry, protected spot.

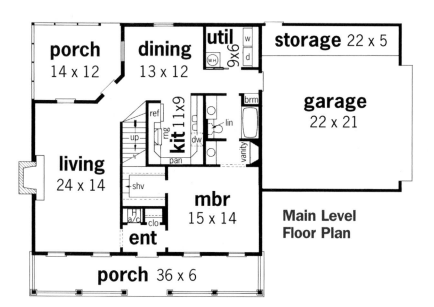

Main Level Floor Plan

Upper Level Floor Plan

Copyright by designer/architect.

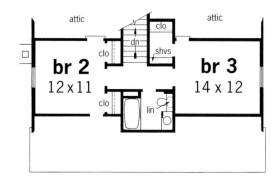

Plan #121212

Dimensions: 54' W x 44' D
Levels: 2
Square Footage: 2,219
Main Level Sq. Ft.: 1,132
Upper Level Sq. Ft.: 1,087
Bedrooms: 4
Bathrooms: 2½
Foundation: Basement;
crawl space for fee
Material List Available: Yes
Price Category: E

Images provided by designer/architect.

Country charm abounds in this lovely home.
Features:

- **Entry:** The central location of this large entry allows access to the dining room or great room. The area features a handy closet.

- **Great Room:** This gathering area features a 10-ft.-high ceiling and large windows, which allow plenty of natural light into the space.

- **Upper Level:** Three bedrooms and the master suite occupy this level. The master suite features a tray ceiling and a well-appointed bath.

- **Garage:** A front-loading two-car garage with additional storage completes the floor plan.

Rear View

Main Level Floor Plan

Copyright by designer/architect.

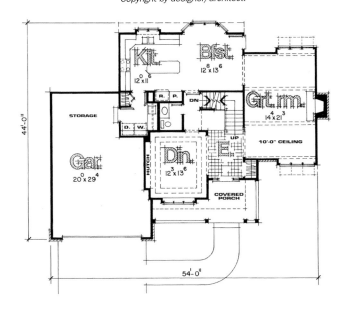

Upper Level Floor Plan

Plan #161037

Dimensions: 46' W x 59'4" D
Levels: 1
Square Footage: 2,469
Main Level Sq. Ft.: 1,462
Basement Level Sq. Ft.: 1,007
Bedrooms: 2
Bathrooms: 2½
Foundation: Walkout; basement for fee
Materials List Available: Yes
Price Category: E

Images provided by designer/architect.

A brick-and-stone facade welcomes you into this lovely home, which is designed to fit into a narrow lot.

Features:

- **Foyer:** This entrance, with vaulted ceiling, introduces the graciousness of this home.

- **Great Room:** A vaulted center ceiling creates the impression that this large great room and dining room are one space, making entertaining a natural in this area.

- **Kitchen:** Designed for efficiency with ample storage and counter space, this kitchen also allows casual dining at the counter.

- **Master Suite:** A tray ceiling sets this room off from the rest of the house, and the lavishly equipped bathroom lets you pamper yourself.

- **Lower Level:** Put extra bedrooms or a library in this finished area, and use the wet bar in a game room or recreation room.

Dining Room

Rear Elevation

Copyright by designer/architect.

Main Level Floor Plan

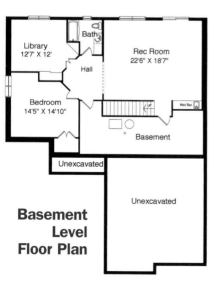

Basement Level Floor Plan

Plan #121144

Dimensions: 40' W x 48'8" D

Levels: 1

Square Footage: 1,195

Bedrooms: 3

Bathrooms: 2

Foundation: Basement; crawl space for fee

Material List Available: Yes

Price Category: B

This is the right design if you want a home that will be easy to expand as your family grows.

Features:

- **Front Porch:** Hang baskets of plants from the roof of this porch, which is just the right size for a couple of comfortable rocking chairs and a side table.

- **Family Room:** This family room welcomes you as you enter the home. A crackling fire enhances the ambiance of the room.

- **Kitchen:** This intelligently designed kitchen has an efficient U-shape layout. A serving bar open to the dining area is a feature that makes entertaining easier.

- **Master Suite:** This is a compact space that is designed to feel large, and it includes a walk-in closet. The master bath is an added bonus.

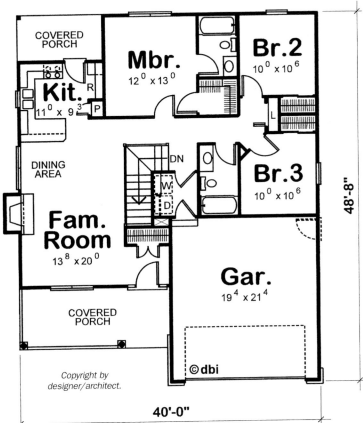

Plan #131029

Dimensions: 56'4" W x 45'10" D
Levels: 2
Square Footage: 2,718
Main Level Sq. Ft.: 1,515
Upper Level Sq. Ft.: 1,203
Bedrooms: 4
Bathrooms: 2½
Foundation: Crawl space or slab;
basement for feet
Materials List Available: Yes
Price Category: G

Images provided by designer/architect.

This home, as shown in the photograph, may differ from the actual blueprints. For more detailed information, please check the floor plans carefully.

This home is ideal if you love the look of a country-style farmhouse.

Features:

• **Foyer:** Walk across the large wraparound porch that defines this home to enter this two-story foyer.

• **Living Room:** French doors from the foyer lead into this living room.

• **Family Room:** The whole family will love this room, with its vaulted ceiling, fireplace, and sliding glass doors that open to the wooden rear deck.

• **Kitchen:** A beautiful sit-down center island opens to the family room. There's also a breakfast nook with a lovely bay window.

• **Master Suite:** Luxury abounds with vaulted ceilings, walk-in closets, private bath with whirlpool tub, separate shower, and dual sinks.

• **Loft:** A special place with vaulted ceiling and view into the family room below.

Main Level Floor Plan

Copyright by designer/architect.

Upper Level Floor Plan

Rear Elevation

Dining Room

Breakfast Area

Kitchen Island

Kitchen

Master Bathroom

Plan #311009

Dimensions: 68' W x 56'6" D
Levels: 1
Square Footage: 1,894
Bedrooms: 3
Bathrooms: 2½
Foundation: Crawl space, slab, or basement
Materials List Available: Yes
Price Category: E

Perfectly at home on a tree-lined street in a quiet neighborhood, this sweet design is a contemporary version of an old-fashioned standard.

Features:

• Great Room: Gather by the glowing fire on cold nights, or expand your entertaining space any other time. This great room is at the center of everything and has plenty of space for friends, family, and anyone else you can think to invite.

• Kitchen: Plenty of workspace, ample storage, a convenient snack bar, and close proximity to both the dining room and breakfast area make this kitchen ideal for chefs and enter-tainers of all kinds. The kitchen layout simplifies hectic mornings, family dinners, and formal parties.

• Master Suite: You'll be close to your family, but in a world of your own in this master suite. The design simplifies your life with dual walk-in closets, his and her sinks, and separate tub and shower.

• Secondary Bedrooms: These bedrooms boast ample closet space and equal distance to a full bathroom. They're also off the beaten path, creating a calmer space for study and sleep.

Images provided by designer/architect.

Rear View

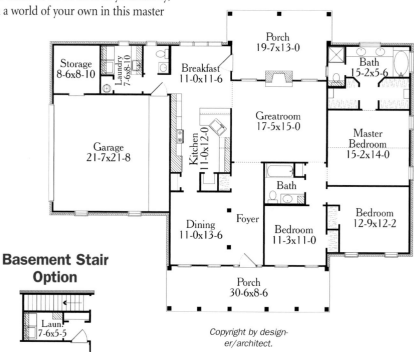

Basement Stair Option

Laun. 7-6x5-5

Copyright by design-er/architect.

Plan #161032

Dimensions: 75'8 W x 70'6" D
Levels: 2
Square Footage: 4,517
Main Level Sq. Footage: 2,562
Lower Level Sq. Footage: 1,955
Bedrooms: 3
Bathrooms: 2 full, 2 half
Foundation: Basement
Material List Available: Yes
Price Category: I

The brick-and-stone exterior, a recessed entry, and a tower containing a large library combine to convey the strength and character of this enchanting house.

Features:

• Hearth Room: Your family or guests will enjoy this large, comfortable hearth room, whcih has a gas fireplace and access to the rear deck, perfect for friendly gatherings.

• Kitchen: This spacious kitchen features a walk-in pantry and a center island.

• Master Suite: Designed for privacy, this master suite includes a sloped ceilng and opens to the rear deck. It also features a deluxe whirlpool bath, walk-in shower, separate his-and-her vanities, and a walk-in closet.

• Lower Level: This lower level includes a separate wine room, exercise room, sauna, two bedrooms, and enough space for a huge recreation room.

SMARTtip

Art Underfoot

Make a simple geometric pattern with your flooring materials. Create a focal point in a courtyard or a small area of a patio by fashioning an intricate mosaic with tile, stone, or colored concrete. By combining elements and colors, a simple garden room floor becomes a wonderful work of art. Whethere you commission a craftsman or do it yourself, you'll have a permanent art installation right in your own backyard.

**Main Level
Floor Plan**

**Lower Level
Floor Plan**

Rear Elevation

Rear Elevation

Plan #121160

Dimensions: 66'4½" W x 49'9½" D
Levels: 1.5
Square Footage: 2,188
Main Level Sq. Ft.: 1,531
Upper Level Sq. Ft.: 657
Bedrooms: 3
Bathrooms: 2½
Foundation: Slab; basement for fee
Materials List Available: Yes
Price Category: D

The standing-seam roof on the wraparound porch gives this home a charming country look.

CAD FILE AVAILABLE

Features:

- **Family Room:** The open design that leads to the adjoining breakfast area makes this space airy and welcoming. The room also features a tray ceiling. The fireplace adds to the comfortable feel of the space.

- **Dining Room / Sunroom:** Featuring three exterior walls with windows, this space can either be your formal dining room or your casual sunroom.

- **Kitchen:** This peninsula kitchen boasts a raised bar open to the breakfast room. The walk-in pantry is always a welcome feature.

- **Master Suite:** Located on the main level, this retreat features a bay window with a view of the backyard. The master bath features a large walk-in closet and dual vanities.

Front View

Main Level Floor Plan

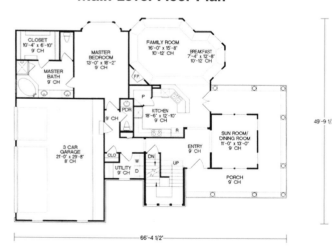

Upper Level Floor Plan

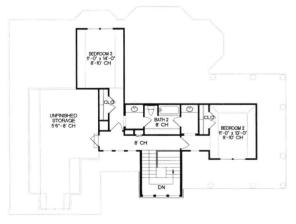

Plan #321033

Dimensions: 38' W x 46' D
Levels: 1
Square Footage: 1,268
Bedrooms: 3
Bathrooms: 2
Foundation: Basement
Materials List Available: Yes
Price Category: B

Clean lines and a layout fit for contemporary living create a graceful and efficient update to a simple cottage design that is perfect for families just starting out.

Features:

- Great Room: At the center of everything, this great room will be the heart of the home. Its unhampered transition into the dining areas and kitchen creates a feeling of openness that will welcome guests into your home.

- Kitchen: This kitchen maximizes space and efficiency with simple transitions and plenty of workspace. The laundry room is adjacent for easy cleanup; the dining room and break-fast area are just steps away; and a snack bar provides the only barrier between the kitchen and great room. Cookouts are also simplified by easy access to the back patio.

- Master Suite: Everyone knows that the master bath makes the master suite, and this home is no different. His and her sinks, a large tub with a view, and a separate standing shower combine to create both a retreat and a remedy for hectic mornings.

- Secondary Bedrooms: Bedroom 2 has plenty of closet space and would be perfect for a nursery or even a converted office. Bedroom 3 also has ample closet space and is opened up by a vaulted ceiling. Both are in a space of their own with a nearby full bathroom.

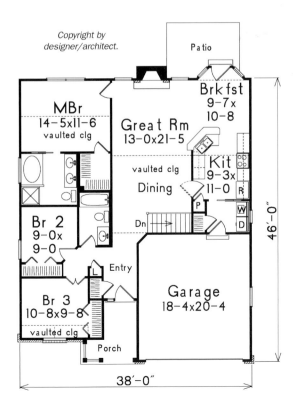

Copyright by designer/architect.

Plan #131030

Dimensions: 51' W x 41'10" D
Levels: 2
Square Footage: 2,470
Main Level Sq. Ft.: 1,290
Upper Level Sq. Ft.: 1,180
Bedrooms: 4
Bathrooms: 2½
Foundation: Crawl space or slab;
basement or walkout for fee
Materials List Available: Yes
Price Category: F

Images provided by designer/architect.

This home, as shown in the photograph, may differ from the actual blueprints. For more detailed information, please check the floor plans carefully.

Master Bedroom

Master Bathroom

Entry

If high ceilings and spacious rooms make you happy, you'll love this gorgeous home.

Features:

- **Family Room:** An 18-ft. vaulted ceiling that's open to the balcony above, a corner fireplace, and a wall of windows make this room feel special.

- **Dining Room:** This formal room, which flows into the living room, also opens to the front porch and optional backyard deck.

- **Kitchen:** A bright breakfast room joins with this kitchen and opens to the backyard deck.

- **Master Suite:** You'll smile when you see the 11-ft. vaulted ceiling, stunning arched window, and two walk-in closets in the bedroom. A skylight lets natural light into the private bath, with its spa tub, separate shower, and dual-sink vanity.

- **Bedrooms:** To reach these three charming bedrooms, you'll admire the view into the family room below as you walk along the balcony hall.

Main Level Floor Plan

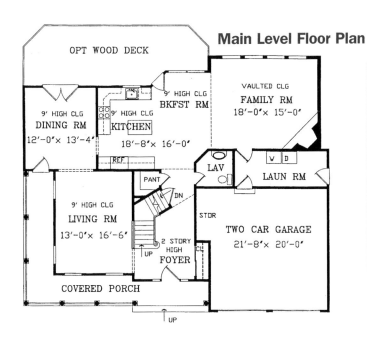

OPT WOOD DECK

BKFST RM
9' HIGH CLG

VAULTED CLG
FAMILY RM
18'-0" x 15'-0"

9' HIGH CLG
DINING RM
12'-0" x 13'-4"

9' HIGH CLG
KITCHEN
18'-8" x 16'-0"

REF

LAV

W D

LAUN RM

PANT

DN

9' HIGH CLG
LIVING RM
13'-0" x 16'-6"

STOR

TWO CAR GARAGE
21'-8" x 20'-0"

UP

2 STORY
HIGH
FOYER

CL

COVERED PORCH

UP

Upper Level Floor Plan

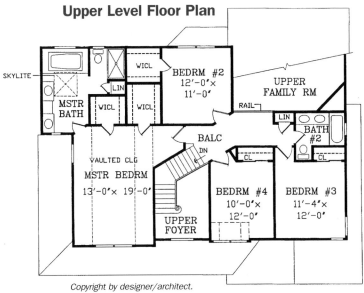

SKYLITE

WICL

BEDRM #2
12'-0" x
11'-0"

UPPER
FAMILY RM

LIN

RAIL

MSTR
BATH

WICL

WICL

LIN

BATH
#2

BALC

DN

CL

CL

VAULTED CLG
MSTR BEDRM
13'-0" x 19'-0"

BEDRM #4
10'-0" x
12'-0"

BEDRM #3
11'-4" x
12'-0"

UPPER
FOYER

Copyright by designer/architect.

Kitchen/Breakfast Area

Dining Room

Living Room

Kitchen/Breakfast Area

Trimwork Basics

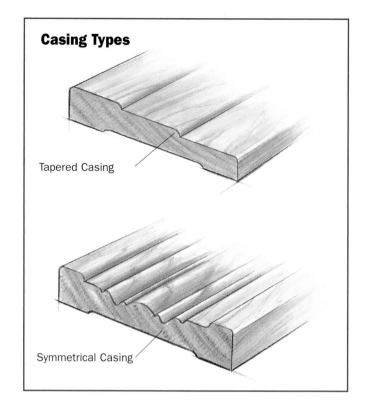

Tapered Casing

Symmetrical Casing

There are two basic types of window casings: tapered and symmetrical. Tapered casing is thinner on the edge closest to the window or door and thicker on the outside edge. Stock Colonial and clamshell casings are tapered casings. When you form corners with tapered casings, you must miter the joints.

Symmetrical casing is the same thickness on both edges and has a uniform pattern across its face. This type of casing rests on top of a plinth block or window stool and joins corner blocks or headers with square-cut butt joints. These casings often look more decorative than stock Colonial-style casings, and they are easier for most do-it-yourselfers to install because you don't have to miter symmetrical casings.

Casing Reveals

The edge of a doorjamb is flush with the surface of the adjoining wall, and there is usually a narrow gap between the jamb and the nearby drywall. Casing has to bridge that gap. Typically, the door side of the casing covers most but not all of the jamb, leaving a narrow edge called a reveal. This helps to add definition to the molding and avoids an unsightly seam where the edge of one board lines up directly over another. When you're working on a new jamb, you have to establish the reveal and stick with it to maintain a uniform appearance. If you're replacing existing trim, you may need to clean up the edge of an old jamb with a sharp scraper and a sander even if you duplicate the old reveal. Although there are several varieties of casing treatments, they all share this detail—a slight setback of at least ⅛ inch from the edge of the jamb. If you install plinths or corner blocks, which are slightly wider than the casing, you may need to experiment with their exact placement to maintain the reveal.

A typical reveal between a doorjamb and casing creates a handsome transition at cased openings.

Door casings can be built up with molding, including an outer strip of backband molding, showing multiple reveals.

Three-Piece Victorian-Style Casing

Although three-piece built-up casing looks large compared with most stock Colonial casing, its scale actually is about halfway between the scale of modern molding and the overwhelming trimwork of the Victorian era. Finished with a clear sealer, it may be a little heavy in modest-size rooms with standard 8-foot ceilings. Finished with paint that complements the wall color, it will add decoration and detail to any room.

The easiest approach is to prepare built-up lengths of this casing on a workbench in three basic steps: sanding, routing, and assembling.

Sanding. Clamp the 1x2 and 1x4 boards to a workbench one at a time, and sand them with a random-orbit sander loaded with 120-grit sandpaper. Sand just the face side of the 1x4s. Sand both sides and the good edge of the 1x2s, but don't tip the sander and round the edge too much. You should ease the edge slightly with a few quick strokes of fine sandpaper.

Detail A

- 1x2 Top Cap
- Base Cap Molding
- 1x4
- Routed Edge

Detail B

- Base Cap Molding
- 1x2 Top Cap
- 1x4
- Horn
- Stool
- Apron

Victorian-Style Mitered Casing

- Head Casing
- A
- Window Casing
- B
- Leg Casing

Routing. Mill a ¾-inch ogee detail onto the bottom edge of the 1x4. You can do this yourself with a router or a router mounted in a specialized worktable, or look around for a small woodworking shop that will perform this work on a shaper with an automatic feed. Working on your own, clamp the stock securely to the bench, and make at least two passes: one to remove about two-thirds of the depth, and a final pass at full depth. Of course, you can rout another shape if you don't happen to have the right-sized ogee bit.

Remember that there is no one correct combination of moldings, as long as you pay attention to basic design principles. You may like the idea of a complex shape built up from different components. Or you may prefer a simpler approach, such as installing a wide casing trimmed on its outside edges with a backband.

Assembly. Start by attaching the 1x2 top cap to the edge of the 1x4. Clamp the 1x4 to the top of the bench with the milled edge down and away from you. (Even two 2x4s spiked together and laid across sawhorses can serve as a bench for this job.) Spread glue along the edge of the 1x4, and nail the top cap to it. Keep the back edges flush. Work from one end to the other, adjusting the free end to keep the surfaces flush.

Release the clamps, and flip the casing over to apply the base cap molding. Apply glue to the back of a length of molding, set it in place, and nail it off, continually pushing it into place as you work from one end to the other.

Installing the Casing

Mark a ⅛-inch reveal line along the edges of all three sides of the window or door frame. Then square off the bottom of the leg casings, and stand one leg casing in place. Make a mark on its inside edge at the point where the inside edge of the leg casing intersects the reveal line on the head casing. Repeat the same process for the other leg casing before mitering at the mark. Then tack the components into place.

Cut and fit the head casing next. If the profiles line up, you can pull the casings off the wall and install them permanently using glue and nails. Use carpenter's glue between the casing and the jamb and in the miters, and dots of panel adhesive between the casing and the wall. When mitering large casings, clamp the casing firmly so that it won't move during the cut. It's difficult to get perfect miter joints with large casings, so you may have to fill some gaps with caulk.

The horns of a window stool typically extend beyond the casing.

Symmetrical Arts & Crafts–Style Casing

A hybrid approach to trimming openings resembles the Arts and Crafts style in some respects but blends with a simplified version of the Neoclassical approach. The leg casings are not fluted, of course, because Arts and Crafts detailing calls for a flat profile and a sometimes almost rugged-looking use of lumber. The idea of this style is to avoid fussy details and use wood more in its natural state with simple joints. In some cases, Arts and Crafts leg casings may be stock boards, with the same-dimension material laid across the top of the opening and overhanging the legs on each side by approximately an inch or so.

You can use the facsimile shown below with or without simple plinth blocks at the base of the leg casings, and make other alterations to suit the style of your house. For example, if you want to stay closer to pure Arts and Crafts style, you may want to dispense with elaborate cornice molding with end returns at the top of the assembly and use something more basic, such as strips of backband molding.

Detail A

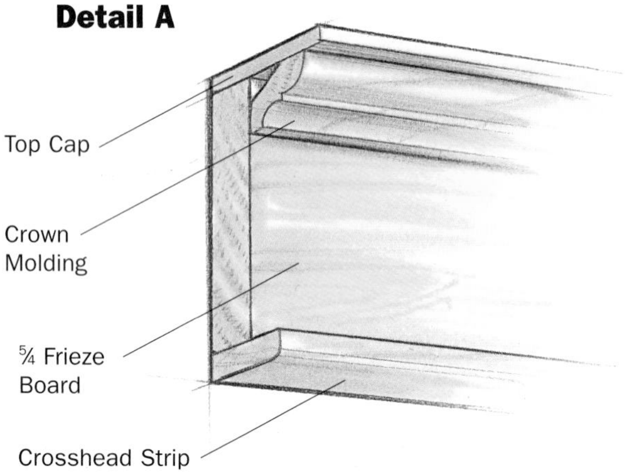

Top Cap

Crown Molding

⁵⁄₄ Frieze Board

Crosshead Strip

Detail B

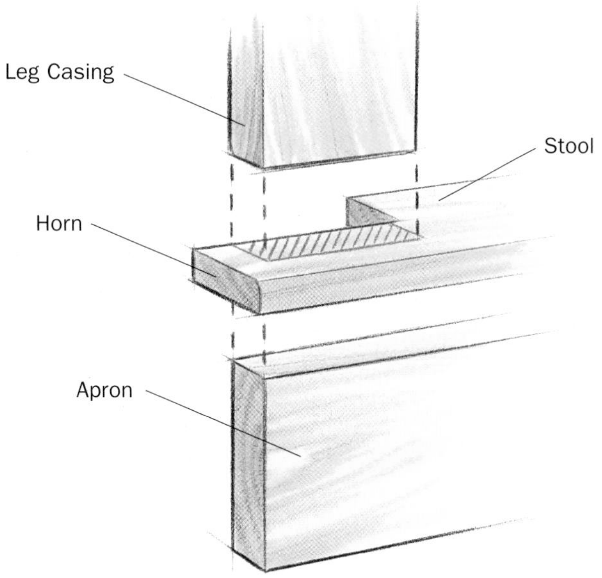

Leg Casing

Horn

Apron

Stool

Arts and Crafts-Style Casing

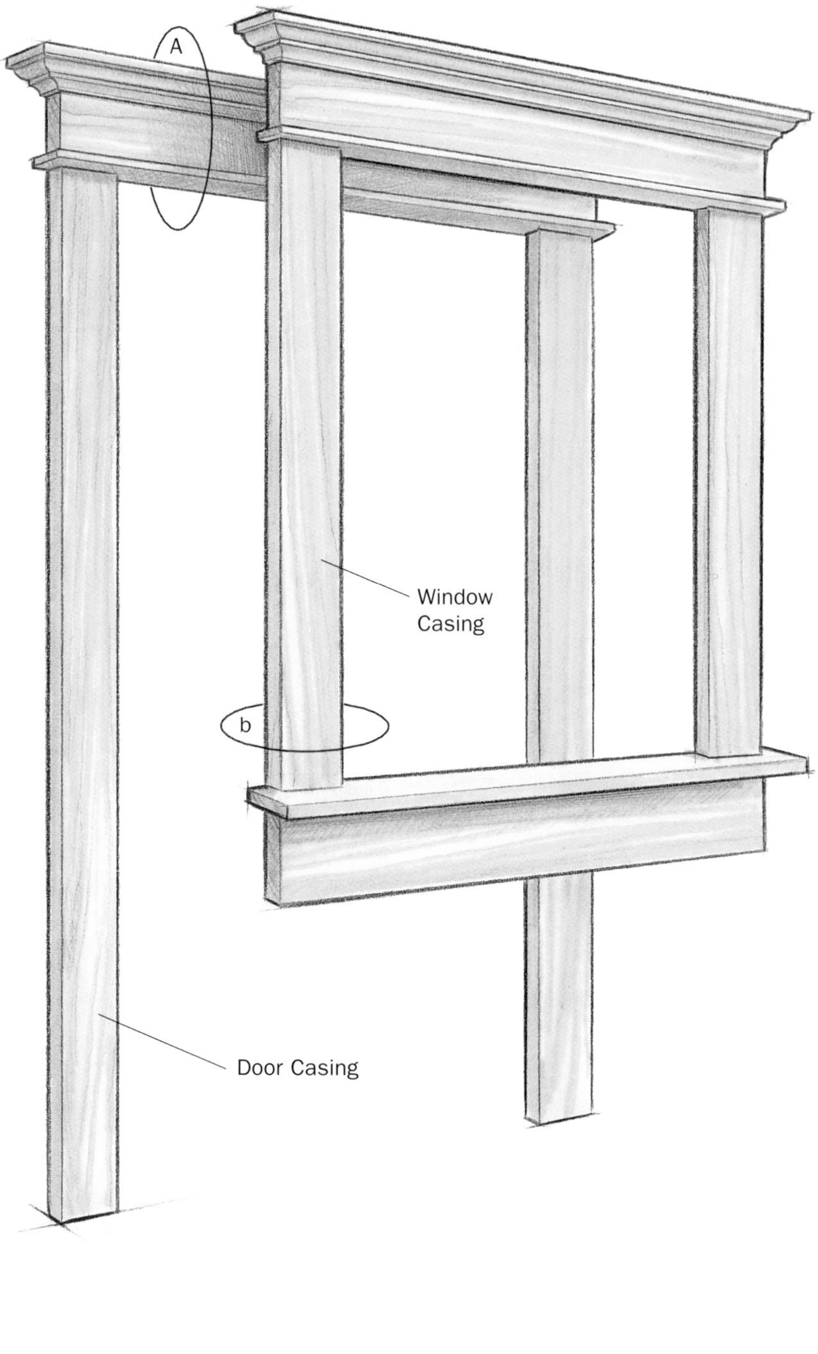

A

b

Window Casing

Door Casing

Building Decorative Crossheads

A crosshead strip is simply a narrow piece of wood that runs horizontally across the top of the opening. It adds depth to the molding treatment and allows you to use basic butt joints on the leg casings.

Depending on the scale of the casings and other moldings you're using, you could select a piece of lattice to use for the crosshead or one-by lumber or even ¾ material. The larger size used below may look better if you're planning a fairly elaborate cap treatment above the opening. (See the illustration opposite.)

Basic Installation

Start by measuring the distance between the outside edges of the leg casings, and cut the ¾ x 6 frieze board to this measurement. Cut a length of 1½-inch-wide bullnose stop molding ¾ inch longer (for a ⅜-inch reveal) as the crosshead strip. Next, cut a strip of crown molding 6 inches longer. Center the length of crown molding on the top edge of the board, with 3 inches hanging off each end. Mark the ends of the crown on its bottom edge. These marks represent the short points of the compound miter cuts that form the outside corners at each end of the crosshead cap. This detail allows the crown molding to return to the wall on both ends of the frieze board.

Making these outside corners is identical to turning outside corners with crown molding on a ceiling. When making the small return pieces, cut the miter onto a piece of molding at least 12 inches long. Remember that to work safely you should never hold small pieces of wood against the fence of a power miter saw.

When you have cut the returns, predrill them to avoid splitting; then glue and nail the molding to the face of the board first, and attach the returns. Now you can make the top cap. If you're using lattice, a typical reveal is ⅜ inch. Measure the distance between the outside edges of the returns, and add ¾ inch. Cut the lattice; then center and fasten it over the crown moldings.

You can build the complete decorative crosshead assembly, above, on a bench. Clamp it in place on the jamb reveal line, right, as you fasten it to the studs.

*"Arts and Crafts detailing calls for a flat profile
and a sometimes almost rugged-looking use of lumber"*

Neoclassical Fluted Casing

Many people can picture flutes as a feature of great stone columns on public buildings. But this design motif, which looks like a series of shallow troughs in the material's surface, is widely used in wood.

You're likely to find that stock fluted casings are too small and special-order casings are too expensive. So you may want to make your own or have a local woodworking shop make them for you.

With this design variation, the troughs become increasingly shallow and finally disappear, leaving several inches of unfluted wood just before the casing joins the top blocks and bottom plinths. This feature takes a lot of planning and some nifty router work. Professional woodworkers have an easier time than amateurs creating boards where the fluted pattern gradually diminishes to nothing near the ends. Do-it-yourselfers will find it much easier to run the flutes through to the ends of the boards.

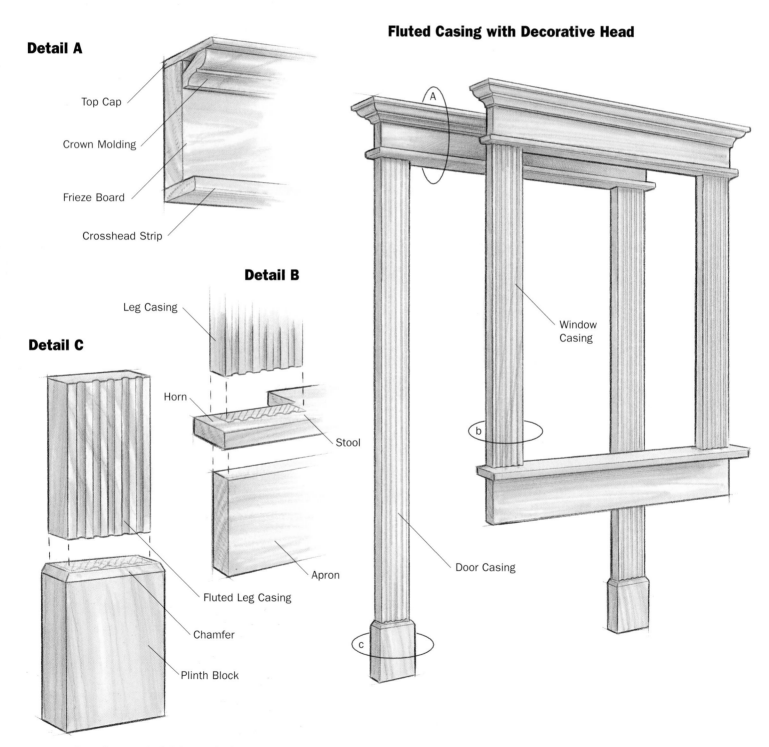

Detail A

Top Cap

Crown Molding

Frieze Board

Crosshead Strip

Detail B

Leg Casing

Detail C

Horn

Stool

Fluted Leg Casing

Apron

Chamfer

Plinth Block

Fluted Casing with Decorative Head

Window Casing

Door Casing

Alternative Window Trim

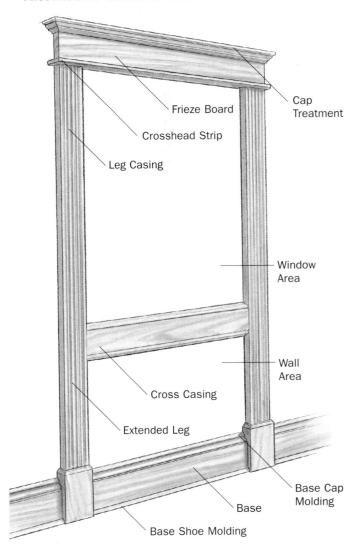

- Frieze Board
- Cap Treatment
- Crosshead Strip
- Leg Casing
- Window Area
- Wall Area
- Cross Casing
- Extended Leg
- Base Cap Molding
- Base
- Base Shoe Molding

Installation

Using a combination square, establish reveal lines along all three sides of the jamb, and install the plinth blocks flush with the inside edges of the leg jambs. This approach calls for some additional planning because you need to accommodate the plinth blocks in your base-trim treatment.

Next, square off the bottoms of the leg casings. Position one of the leg casings on top of one of the plinth blocks, and mark the spot where the reveal line on the head jamb hits the casing. Then square-cut each leg casing to length and install it. Measure from the top outside edge of one leg casing to the top outside edge of the other leg casing, and use this measurement (plus an allowance for a small overhang on each side) to build a decorative crosshead over the opening.

On windows, you have a couple of options. You can stop the leg casings at a window stool or run them down to plinth blocks on the floor. This second approach takes more wood and more time. But it can make short windows, and the room in general, look more expansive. If you run leg casings down to plinth blocks on the floor, you'll need to trim the bottom of the window along the reveal mark on the lower jamb with a piece of cross casing.

A plinth block at the edge of a passageway is chamfered on the side and top edges to provide a transition between the block and the fluted casing above it.

Plan #291015

Dimensions: 88'6" W x 58'3" D
Levels: 1.5
Square Footage: 2,901
Main Level Sq. Ft.: 2,078
Upper Level Sq. Ft.: 823
Bedrooms: 3
Bathrooms: 2½
Foundation: Basement
Materials List Available: No
Price Category: F

Upon entering this home, a cathedral-like timber-framed interior fills the eye.

Features:

- Great Room: This large gathering area's ceiling rises up two stories and is open to the kitchen. The beautiful fireplace is the focal point of this room.

- Kitchen: This island kitchen is open to the great room and the breakfast nook. Warm woods of all species enhance the great room and this space.

- Master Suite: This suite has a sloped ceiling and adjoins a luxurious master bath with twin walk-in closets that open to a sunroom with a private balcony.

- Upper Level: This upper level has an open lounge that leads to two bedrooms with vaulted ceilings and a generous second bath.

Images provided by designer/architect.

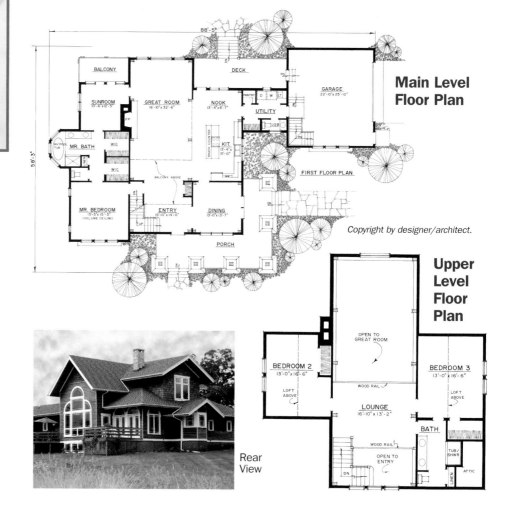

Main Level Floor Plan

Copyright by designer/architect.

Upper Level Floor Plan

Rear View

Kitchen

Master Bath

Rear Porch

Dining Room

Plan #181221

Dimensions: 60' W x 44' D
Levels: 2
Square Footage: 3,411
Main Level Sq. Ft.: 1,488
Upper Level Sq. Ft.: 603
Basement Level Sq. Ft.: 1,321
Bedrooms: 3
Bathrooms: 2½
Foundation: Basement
Materials List Available: Yes
Price Category: I

Images provided by designer/architect.

This stone- and wood-sided home will be a joy to come home to.

Features:

• Living Room: This large entertaining area features a fireplace and large windows.

• Kitchen: Any cook would feel at home in this island kitchen, which has an abundance of cabinets and counter space.

• Master Bedroom: Located on the main level for privacy, this room features a walk-in closet and access to the main-level full bathroom.

• Bedrooms: One bedroom is located on the upper level and the other is located on the main level. Each has a large closet.

Study

Living Room

Dining Room/ Kitchen

Main Level Floor Plan

17'-0" X 14'-2"
5,10 X 4,30

13'-4" X 14'-0"
4,00 X 4,25

16'-4" X 22'-4"
4,90 X 6,80

15'-0" X 15'-0"
4,50 X 4,60

12'-0" X 10'-0"
3,60 X 3,00

44'-0"
13,2 m

60'-0"
18.0 m

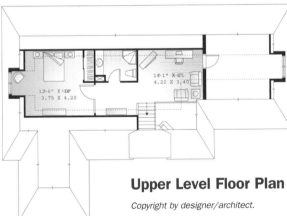

Upper Level Floor Plan

Copyright by designer/architect.

12'-6" X 13'-9"
3,75 X 4,20

14'-1" X 11'-2"
4,22 X 3,40

Basement Level Floor Plan

15'-8" X 28'-0"
4,70 X 8,50

13'-0" X 13'-9"
3,90 X 4,20

11'-8" X 13'-4"
3,50 X 4,00

Foyer

Plan #451356

Dimensions: 52' W x 52'8" D

Levels: 2

Square Footage: 1,834

Main Level Sq. Ft.: 1,444

Basement Level Sq. Ft.: 390

Bedrooms: 3

Bathrooms: 2½

Foundation: Walkout — insulated concrete form

Material List Available: No

Price Category: D

Images provided by designer/architect.

CAD FILE AVAILABLE

Main Level Floor Plan

COVERED ENTRY PORCH

KITCHEN

FOYER

DINING ROOM 12'0" X 12'8"

GREAT ROOM 20'0" X 17'0"

MASTER SUITE 12'0" X 15'0"

DECK AREA

DECK AREA

Upper Level Floor Plan

LOFT AREA 20'0" X 17'0"

ATTIC STORAGE 12'0" X 13'0" UNFINISHED

ATTIC STORAGE 12'0" X 13'0" UNFINISHED

OPEN TO BELOW

Basement Level Floor Plan

FUTURE OFFICE 11'5" X 11'4" UNFINISHED

STORAGE UNFINISHED

MECH 11'5" X 11'4" UNFINISHED

BDRM. #3 11'5" X 14'3"

RECREATION ROOM 20'0" X 17'0"

BDRM. #2 11'5" X 14'3"

Copyright by designer/architect.

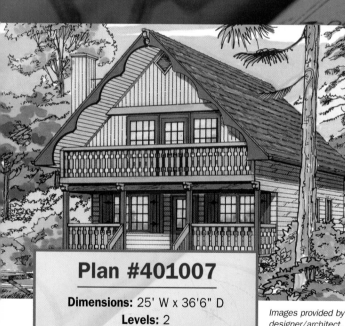

Plan #401007

Dimensions: 25' W x 36'6" D

Levels: 2

Square Footage: 1,286

Main Level Sq. Ft.: 725

Upper Level Sq. Ft.: 561

Bedrooms: 3

Bathrooms: 2

Foundation: Crawl space

Materials List Available: Yes

Price Category: B

Images provided by designer/architect.

CAD FILE AVAILABLE

Main Level Floor Plan

Copyright by designer/architect.

br3 10'3 x 9'

STORAGE

k 9'11 x 8'

liv 13'7 x 15'1

din 10'5 x 10'2

VERANDAH

Rear Elevation

Upper Level Floor Plan

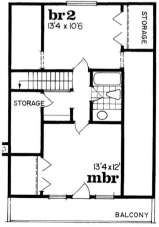

br2 13'4 x 10'6

STORAGE

STORAGE

mbr 13'4 x 12'

BALCONY

Plan #361517

Dimensions: 48' W x 60' D

Levels: 1

Square Footage: 1,321

Bedrooms: 2

Bathrooms: 2

Foundation: Crawl space

Material List Available: No

Price Category: B

Images provided by designer/architect.

CAD FILE AVAILABLE

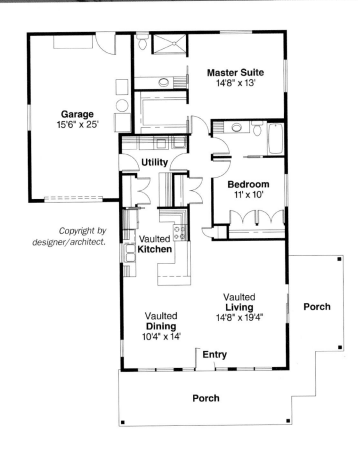

Garage
15'6" x 25'

Master Suite
14'8" x 13'

Utility

Bedroom
11' x 10'

Vaulted Kitchen

Vaulted Living
14'8" x 19'4"

Porch

Vaulted Dining
10'4" x 14'

Entry

Porch

Copyright by designer/architect.

Plan #271085

Dimensions: 51' W x 54' D

Levels: 2

Square Footage: 1,541

Main Level Sq. Ft.: 1,028

Upper Level Sq. Ft.: 513

Bedrooms: 3

Bathrooms: 2

Foundation: Basement

Materials List Available: No

Price Category: C

Images provided by designer/architect.

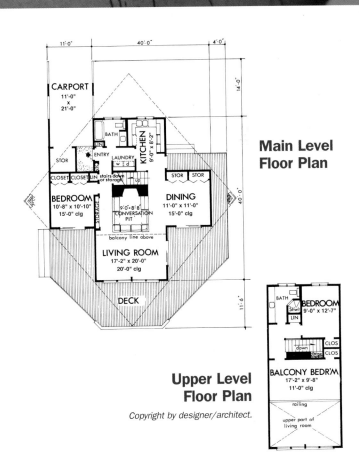

CARPORT
11'-0" x 21'-0"

BATH

KITCHEN
9'-0" x 8'-2"

STOR

ENTRY

LAUNDRY
w d

CLOSET CLOSET LIN

STOR STOR

BEDROOM
10'-8" x 10'-10"
15'-0" clg

STORAGE

stairs down or storage

up

CONVERSATION PIT

DINING
11'-0" x 11'-0"
15'-0" clg

balcony line above

LIVING ROOM
17'-2" x 20'-0"
20'-0" clg

DECK

Main Level Floor Plan

BATH

BEDROOM
9'-0" x 12'-7"

Shwr

LIN

down

CLOS

CLOS

BALCONY BEDR'M
17'-2" x 9'-8"
11'-0" clg

railing

upper part of living room

Upper Level Floor Plan

Copyright by designer/architect.

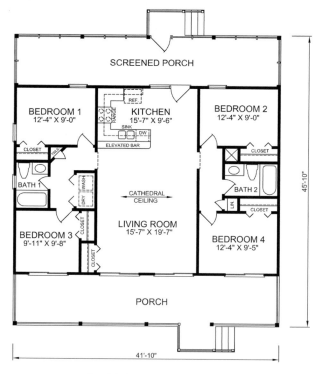

SCREENED PORCH

BEDROOM 1
12'-4" X 9'-0"

KITCHEN
15'-7" X 9'-6"

REF.
RANGE
SINK
DW
ELEVATED BAR

BEDROOM 2
12'-4" X 9'-0"

CLOSET

CLOSET

BATH 1

BATH 2

LIN

DRY DISHWASH

CLOSET

CATHEDRAL
CEILING

45'-10"

BEDROOM 3
9'-11" X 9'-8"

LIVING ROOM
15'-7" X 19'-7"

BEDROOM 4
12'-4" X 9'-5"

CLOSET

PORCH

41'-10"

Plan #341227

Dimensions: 41'10" W x 45'10" D

Levels: 1

Square Footage: 1,248

Bedrooms: 4

Bathrooms: 2

Foundation: Crawl space, slab, basement or walkout

Material List Available: No

Price Category: B

Images provided by designer/architect.

CAD FILE AVAILABLE

Copyright by designer/architect.

Copyright by designer/architect.

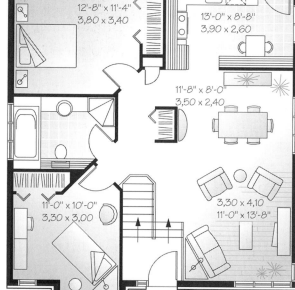

Plan #181399

Dimensions: 29'8" W x 33'4" D

Levels: 1

Square Footage: 960

Bedrooms: 2

Bathrooms: 1

Foundation: Basement

Material List Available: Yes

Price Category: B

Images provided by designer/architect.

CAD FILE AVAILABLE

12'-8" x 11'-4"
3,80 x 3,40

13'-0" x 8'-8"
3,90 x 2,60

11'-8" x 8'-0"
3,50 x 2,40

33'-4"
10,0 m

11'-0" x 10'-0"
3,30 x 3,00

3,30 x 4,10
11'-0" x 13'-8"

29'-8"
8,9 m

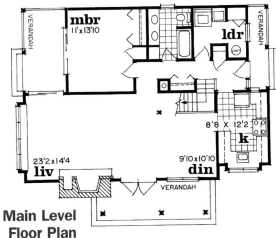

**Main Level
Floor Plan**

*Images provided by
designer/architect.*

Plan #401006

Dimensions: 43' W x 35'4" D

Levels: 1½

Square Footage: 1,670

Main Level Sq.Ft.: 1,094

Upper Level Sq.Ft.: 576

Bedrooms: 3

Bathrooms: 2

Foundation: Crawl space

Materials List Available: Yes

Price Category: C

**Upper Level
Floor Plan**

Copyright by designer/architect.

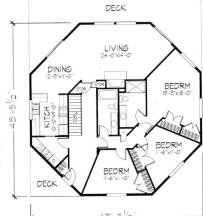

**Main Level
Floor Plan**

*Images provided by
designer/architect.*

Plan #271087

Dimensions: 43'5½" W x 43'5½" D

Levels: 1

Square Footage: 2,734

Main Level Sq. Ft.: 1,564

Lower Level Sq. Ft.: 1,170

Bedrooms: 4

Bathrooms: 3

Foundation: Crawl space or
walkout basement

Material List Available: No

Price Category: F

**Basement Level
Floor Plan**

Copyright by designer/architect.

Plan #181106

Dimensions: 32'4" W x 25'6" D

Levels: 1

Square Footage: 1,648

Main Level Sq. Ft.: 824

Upper Level Sq. Ft.: 824

Bedrooms: 3

Bathrooms: 2

Foundation: Basement or walkout

Material List Available: Yes

Price Category: E

Images provided by designer/architect.

This vacation-styled home makes a perfect year-round residence, giving the feeling of the great outdoors.

Features:

• Porch: This porch occupies the front and one side of the home, providing plenty of room to relax with family and friends.

• Family Room: The cathedral ceiling in this family room extends into the kitchen. The two-story windows allow an abundance of light into this area.

• Kitchen: This L-shaped kitchen features an eating area and a triple sliding glass door onto the front deck. The fireplace, which it shares with the family room, will warm this area on cold mornings.

• Lower Level: Two bedrooms and a den with a wood stove highlight this area. The full bathrooom has room for the washer and dryer.

Lower Level Floor Plan

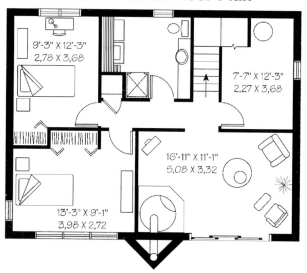

Main Level Floor Plan

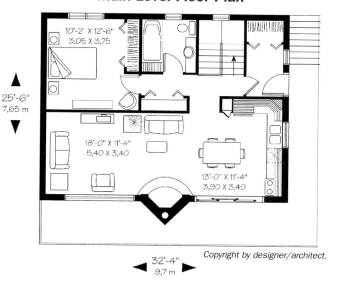

Copyright by designer/architect.

Plan #441009

Dimensions: 94' W x 53' D
Levels: 1
Square Footage: 2,650
Bedrooms: 4
Bathrooms: 2½
Foundation: Crawl space; slab or basement available for fee
Materials List Available: Yes
Price Category: F

You'll love to call this plan home. It's large enough for the whole family and has a façade that will make you the envy of the neighborhood.

Images provided by designer/architect.

Features:

- **Foyer:** The covered porch protects the entry, which has a transom and sidelights to brighten this space.

- **Great Room:** To the left of the foyer, beyond decorative columns, lies this vaulted room, with its fireplace and media center. Additional columns separate the room from the vaulted formal dining room.

- **Kitchen:** A casual nook and this island work center are just around the corner from the great room. The second covered porch can be reached via a door in the nook.

- **Master Suite:** This luxurious space boasts a vaulted salon, a private niche that could be a small study, and a view of the front yard. The master bath features a spa tub, separate shower, compartmented toilet, huge walk-in closet, and access to the laundry room.

- **Bedrooms:** The two additional bedrooms are located at the back of the plan and share the Jack-and-Jill bathroom.

Copyright by designer/architect.

Rear Elevation

Plan #561002

Dimensions: 61' W x 75' D
Levels: 1.5
Square Footage: 3,416
Main Level Sq. Ft.: 2,479
Upper Level Sq. Ft.: 937
Bedrooms: 4
Bathrooms: 3½
Foundation: Basement
Material List Available: Yes
Price Category: G

Images provided by designer/architect.

Traditional Cape Cod styling provides this home with incredible street appeal.

Features:

• **Great Room:** There is plenty of room for your family and friends to gather in this large room. The fireplace will add a feeling of coziness to the expansive space

• **Kitchen:** Open to the great room and a dining area, this island kitchen adds to the open feeling of the home. Additional seating, located at the island, enables guests to mingle with the chef of the family without getting in the way.

• **Lower Level:** This level (finishing is optional) adds a fourth bedroom suite, enough space for a family room or media room, and a wet bar for entertaining.

• **Garage:** Split garages allow the daily drivers their spaces plus a separate garage for that special vehicle or even a golf cart.

Main Level Floor Plan

Upper Level Floor Plan

Copyright by designer/architect.

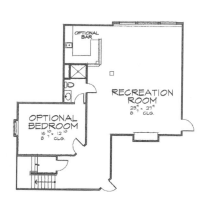

Basement Level Floor Plan

Great Room

Great Room

Kitchen

Office

Master Bedroom

Master Bath

Plan #491003

Dimensions: 46' W x 28' D

Levels: 2

Square Footage: 1,235

Main Level Sq. Ft.: 893

Second Level Sq. Ft.: 342

Bedrooms: 3

Bathrooms: 2

Foundation: Walk out

Materials List Available: Yes

Price Category: B

The rear-oriented view makes this home perfect for lake-front property.

Features:

• Living Room: This gathering area, with its vaulted ceiling and fireplace, has skylights, which flood the space with natural light.

• Kitchen: An island kitchen is always a welcome feature. This one is open to the dining and living rooms and makes the home feel spacious.

• Master Suite: The upper level is dedicated to this private oasis with vaulted ceiling. The secluded sun deck is the perfect place to watch the sun set.

• Secondary Bedrooms: Located on the main level are these two equal-size bedrooms with private closets. Each room also has a view of the backyard.

Main Level Floor Plan

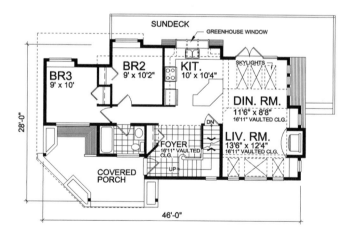

Upper Level Floor Plan

Plan #441026

Dimensions: 60' W x 52' D
Levels: 2
Square Footage: 3,623
Main Level Sq. Ft.: 1,835
Upper Level Sq. Ft.: 1,788
Bedrooms: 4
Bathrooms: 2½
Foundation: Crawl space
Materials List Available: Yes
Price Category: H

Images provided by designer/architect.

CAD FILE AVAILABLE · CAD

Crazy about Craftsman styling? This exquisite plan has it in abundance and doesn't skimp on the floor plan, either. Massive stone bases support the Arts and Crafts columns at the entry porch.

Features:

• **Living Room:** This large gathering area features a cozy fireplace.

• **Dining Room:** This formal room is connected to the island kitchen via a butler's pantry.

• **Master Suite:** Located upstairs, this suite features a walk-in closet and luxury bath.

• **Bedrooms:** The three family bedrooms share a centrally located compartmented bathroom.

Rear Elevation

Main Level Floor Plan

Copyright by designer/architect.

Upper Level Floor Plan

Plan #111049

Dimensions: 60' W x 50' D
Levels: 2
Square Footage: 2,205
Main Level Sq. Ft.: 1,552
Upper Level Sq. Ft.: 653
Bedrooms: 3
Bathrooms: 2
Foundation: Pier
Materials list available: No
Price Code: F

This stately beach home offers many waterfront views.

Images provided by designer/architect.

Features:

- Ceiling Height: 8 ft.

- Entrance: This home features raised stairs, with two wings that lead to the central staircase.

- Front Porch: This area is 110 square feet.

- Living Room: This huge room features a wood-burning fireplace and large windows, and it leads to the rear covered porch and a spacious deck. It is also open to the kitchen and dining area.

- Kitchen: This room has ample counter space and an island that is open to the dining area.

- Master Suite: This upper level room has a large balcony. This balcony is a perfect place to watch the sun set over the beach. This room also a walk-in closet.

- Master Bath: This room has all the modern amenities, with separate vanities, large corner tub and walk-in shower.

- Lower Level Bedrooms: These rooms each have a walk in closet and share a bathroom.

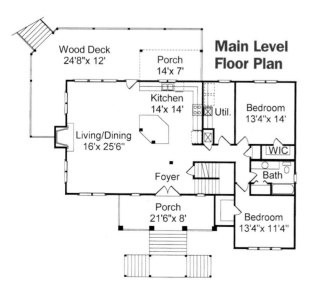

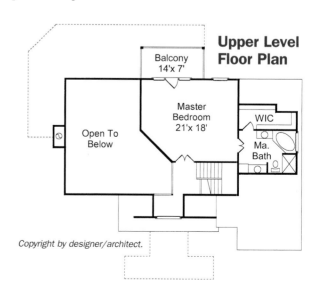

Copyright by designer/architect.

Rear View

Removing Carpet Stains in Kid's Rooms

Kids will be kids, and so accidents will happen. The cardinal rule for removing a stain from carpeting is to always clean up a spot or spill immediately, using white cloths or paper towels. Blot, never rub or scrub, a stain. Work from the outer edge in toward the center of the spot, and then follow up with clean water to remove any residue of the stain. Blot up any moisture remaining from the cleanup by layering white paper towels over the spot and weighing them down with a heavy object.

To remove a water-soluble stain, blot as much of it as possible with white paper towels that have been dampened with cold water. If necessary, mix a solution of 1¼ teaspoon of clear, mild, nonbleach laundry detergent with 32 ounces of water, and then spray it lightly onto the spot. Blot it repeatedly with white paper towels. Rinse it with a spray of clean water; then blot it dry.

To treat soils made by urine or vomit, mix equal parts of white vinegar and water, and blot it onto the spot with white paper towels; then clean with detergent solution.

To remove an oil-based stain, blot as much of it as you can; then apply a nonflammable spot remover made specifically for grease, oil, or tar to a clean, white paper towel. Don't apply the remover directly to the carpet, or you may damage the backing. Blot the stain with the treated towel. Wear rubber gloves to protect your hands. Use this method for stains caused by crayons, cosmetics, ink, paint, and shoe polish.

For spots made by cola, chocolate, or blood, apply a solution of 1 tablespoon of ammonia and 1 cup of water to the stain; then go over it with the detergent solution. Do not use ammonia on a wool carpet. Try an acid stain remover—lemon juice or white vinegar diluted with water.

To remove chewing gum or candle wax, try freezing the spot with ice cubes, and then gently scrape off the gum or wax with a blunt object. Follow this with a vacuuming. If this doesn't work, apply a commercial gum remover to the area, following the manufacturer's directions.

Plan #271048

Dimensions: 60' W x 32'6" D
Levels: 2
Square Footage: 2,143
Main Level Sq. Ft.: 1,200
Upper Level Sq. Ft.: 943
Bedrooms: 4
Bathrooms: 3
Foundation: Crawl space, basement
Materials List Available: No
Price Category: D

Images provided by designer/architect.

With a nod to historical architecture, this authentic Cape Cod home boasts a traditional exterior with an updated floor plan.

Features:

- Living Room: This spacious area is warmed by an optional fireplace and merges with the dining room.

- Kitchen: Efficient and sunny, this walk-through kitchen handles almost any task with aplomb.

- Family Room: The home's second optional fireplace can be found here, along with a smart log-storage bin that can be loaded from the garage. Sliding-glass-door access to a backyard patio is a bonus.

- Guest Bedroom: Private access to a bath and plenty of room to relax make this bedroom a winner.

- Master Suite: Amenities abound in the master bedroom, including two closets, a separated dressing spot, and a dormer as a sitting area.

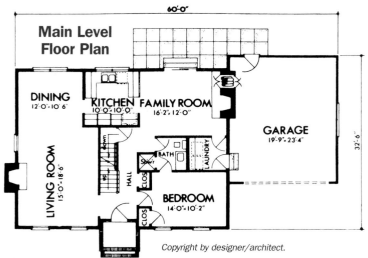

Copyright by designer/architect.

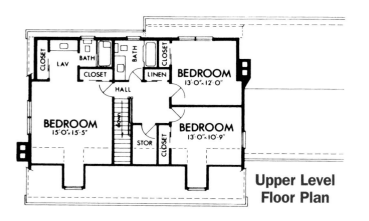

Plan #391001

Dimensions: 32' W x 40' D
Levels: 2
Square Footage: 2,015
Main Level Sq. Ft.: 1,280
Upper Level Sq. Ft.: 735
Bedrooms: 3
Bathrooms: 2½
Foundation: Crawl space
Materials List Available: Yes
Price Category: D

Images provided by designer/architect.

- Kitchen: This L-shaped kitchen features an expansive cooktop/lunch counter.
- Utility Areas: A utility room handles the laundry and storage, and a half bath with linen closet takes care of other necessities.
- Master Suite: This main-floor master suite is just that—sweet! The spa-style bath features

a corner tub nestled against a greenhouse window. Plus, there are double sinks and a separate shower.

- Upstairs: The sun-washed loft overlooks the activity below while embracing two dreamy bedrooms and a sizable bath with double sinks.

Follow your dream to this home surrounded with decking. The A-frame front showcases bold windowing (on two levels), and natural lighting fills the house.

Features:

- Dining Room: This dining room and the family room are completely open to each other, perfect for hanging out in the warmth of the hearth.

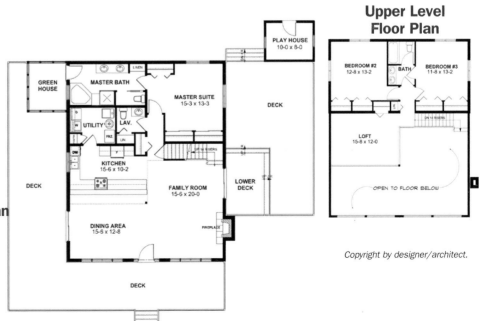

Upper Level Floor Plan

Main Level Floor Plan

Copyright by designer/architect.

Plan #111047

Dimensions: 36' W x 54' D
Levels: 2
Square Footage: 1,863
Main Level Sq. Ft.: 1,056
Upper Level Sq. Ft.: 807
Bedrooms: 4
Bathrooms: 3
Foundation: Pier
Materials List Available: No
Price Category: E

Designed for a coastline, this home is equally appropriate as a year-round residence or a vacation retreat.

Features:

- Orientation: The rear-facing design gives you an ocean view and places the most attractive side of the house where beach-goers can see it.

- Entryway: On the waterside, a large deck with a covered portion leads to the main entrance.

- Carport: This house is raised on piers that let you park underneath it and that protect it from water damage during storms.

- Living Room: A fireplace, French doors, and large windows grace this room, which is open to both the kitchen and the dining area.

- Master Suite: Two sets of French doors open to a balcony on the ocean side, and the suite includes two walk-in closets and a fully equipped bath.

Main Level Floor Plan

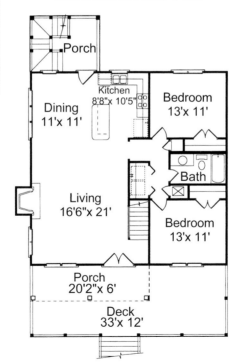

Upper Level Floor Plan

Copyright by designer/architect.

Plan #451360

Dimensions: 59' W x 69'2" D
Levels: 2
Square Footage: 2,600
Main Level Sq. Ft.: 1,523
Upper Level Sq. Ft.: 1,077
Bedrooms: 3
Bathrooms: 2½
Foundation: Walkout –
insulated concrete form
Material List Available: No
Price Category: F

Images provided by designer/architect.

This rustic-looking home would suit the bustle of a busy neighborhood or the quietness of a secluded lake.

Features:

- **Great Room:** This area is the interior highlight of the home. The large, exciting space features a soaring ceiling, massive fireplace, and magnificent window wall to capture the view.
- **Kitchen:** An abundance of cabinets and counter space makes this kitchen functional

as well as attractive. The built-in pantry is large enough to hold supplies and extra treats.

- **Master Suite:** Pamper yourself in this lavish master suite. Enjoy the privacy and convenience of a main-level location. The master bath boasts an oversized stall shower and a whirlpool tub.
- **Secondary Bedrooms:** Located on the upper level are two bedrooms joined by an open loft.

Main Level Floor Plan

Upper Level Floor Plan

Basement Level Floor Plan

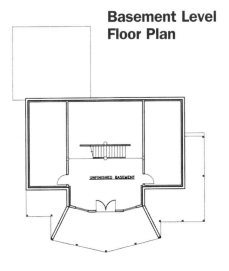

Copyright by designer/architect.

Plan #101015

Dimensions: 26' W x 46' D
Levels: 2
Square Footage: 1,647
Main Level Sq. Ft.: 1,288
Upper Level Sq. Ft.: 359
Bedrooms: 2
Bathrooms: 1
Foundation: Slab
Materials List Available: No
Price Category: D

This comfortable vacation retreat has handsome board-and-batten siding with stone accents.

Features:

- Ceiling Height: 20 ft. unless otherwise noted.

- Front Porch: This delightful front porch is perfect for spending relaxing vacation time in an old-fashioned rocker or porch swing.

- Great Room: From the porch you'll enter this enormous great room, where the whole family will enjoy spending time together under its 20-ft. vaulted ceiling.

- Kitchen: Within the great room is this open kitchen. An island provides plenty of food-preparation space, and there's a breakfast bar for casual vacation meals. The large pantry area provides space for a stacked washer and dryer.

- Bath: Also located downstairs is a compartmented bath with a 2-ft.-8-in. door that allows wheelchair access.

- Loft: Upstairs is an enormous loft with an 11-ft. ceiling. Use it to augment the two downstairs bedrooms or for recreation space.

Images provided by designer/architect.

Main Level Floor Plan

Upper Level Floor Plan

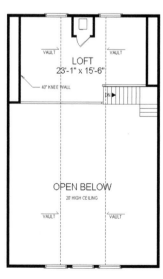

Copyright by designer/architect.

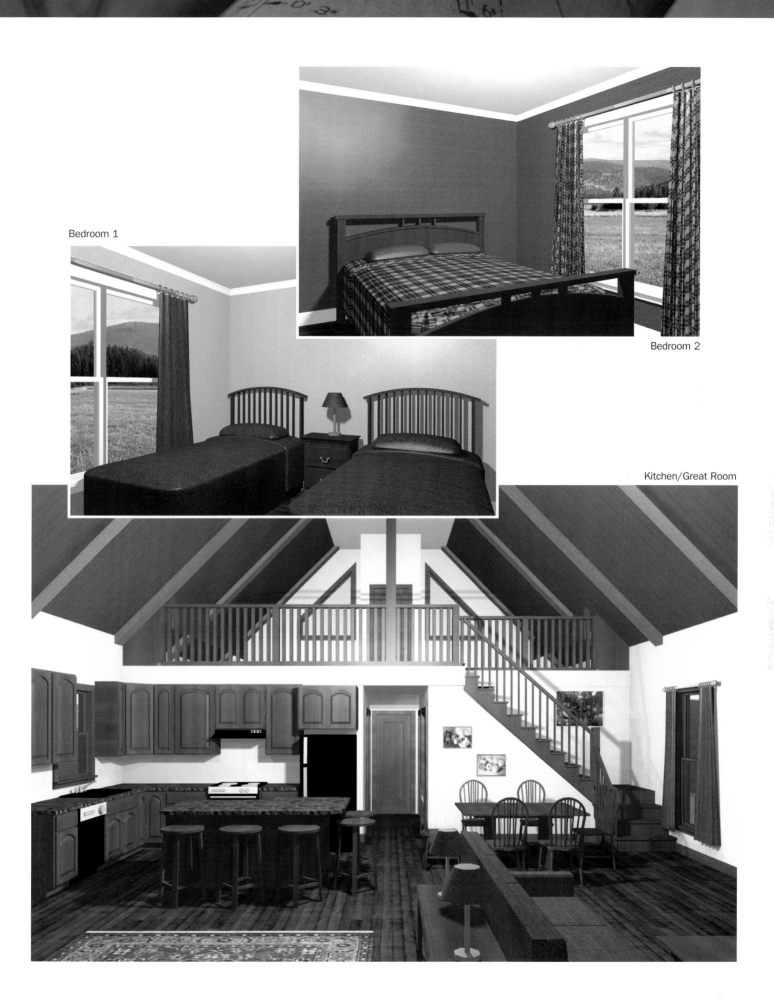

Bedroom 1

Bedroom 2

Kitchen/Great Room

Plan #271053

Dimensions: 70' W x 33'10" D
Levels: 2
Square Footage: 2,458
Main Level Sq. Ft.: 1,067
Upper Level Sq. Ft.: 346
Bedrooms: 3
Bathrooms: 2½
Foundation: Crawl space or daylight basement
Materials List Available: No
Price Category: E

Images provided by designer/architect.

The octagonal shape and window-filled walls of this home create a powerful interior packed with panoramic views.

Features:

- **Great Room:** Straight back from the angled entry, this room is brightened by sunlight through windows and sliding glass doors. Beyond the doors, a huge wraparound deck offers plenty of space for tanning or relaxing. A spiral staircase adds visual interest.

- **Kitchen:** This efficient space includes a convenient pantry.

- **Master Suite:** On the upper level, this romantic master suite overlooks the great room below. Several windows provide scenic outdoor views. A walk-in closet and a private bath round out this secluded haven.

- **Basement:** The optional basement includes a recreation room, as well as an extra bedroom and bath.

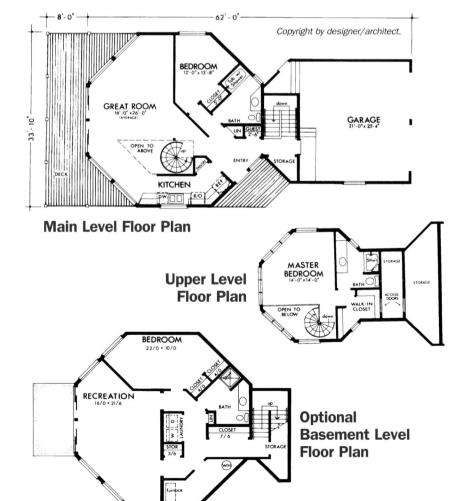

Copyright by designer/architect.

Main Level Floor Plan

Upper Level Floor Plan

Optional Basement Level Floor Plan

Plan #111021

Dimensions: 34' W x 44' D
Levels: 2
Square Footage: 2,221
Main Level Sq. Ft.: 1,307
Upper Level Sq. Ft.: 914
Bedrooms: 4
Bathrooms: 3
Foundation: Pier
Materials List Available: No
Price Category: F

If you've got a view you want to admire, choose this well-designed home, with its comfortable front porch and spacious second-floor balcony.

Features:

- **Porch:** Double doors open to both the living and dining rooms for complete practicality.

- **Living Room:** The spacious living room anchors the open floor plan in this lovely home.

- **Dining Room:** Natural light pours into this room from the large front windows.

- **Kitchen:** An angled snack bar that's shared with the dining room doubles as a large counter.

- **Master Suite:** Double doors lead from the bedroom to the balcony. The bath includes a tub, separate shower, and double vanity.

- **Sitting Area:** This quiet area is nestled into a windowed alcove between the study and the master suite.

Main Level Floor Plan

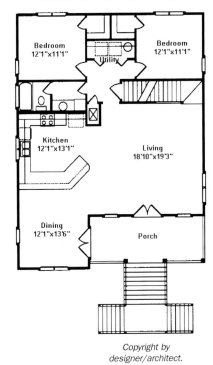

Copyright by designer/architect.

Upper Level Floor Plan

Main Level Floor Plan

PORCH

DINING AREA
9'-5" X 9'-7"

KITCHEN
11'-1" X 9'-7"

STORAGE

W.H.

DOWN

R.

BATH

BEDROOM
10'-7" X 11'-5"

W.

D.

LIVING AREA
11'-5" X 25'-2"

UP

COATS

CLOSET

CLOS.

BEDROOM
11'-5" X 10'-7"

PORCH

42'-0"

Images provided by designer/architect.

Plan #341234

Dimensions: 32' W x 42' D

Levels: 1.5

Square Footage: 1,476

Main Level Sq. Ft.: 1,049

Upper Level Sq. Ft.: 427

Bedrooms: 4

Bathrooms: 2

Foundation: Crawl space, slab, basement or walkout

Material List Available: No

Price Category: B

Upper Level Floor Plan

BEDROOM
11'-5" X 11'-5"

BATH

CLOS.

BEDROOM
11'-5" X 11'-5"

LINEN

CLOSET

CLOSET

DOWN

32'-0"

Copyright by designer/architect.

Plan #181053

Dimensions: 56' W x 53'2" D

Levels: 2

Square Footage: 2,353

Main Level Sq. Ft.: 1,606

Upper Level Sq. Ft.: 747

Bedrooms: 3

Bathrooms: 2½

Foundation: Basement, crawl space

Materials List Available: Yes

Price Category: E

Images provided by designer/architect.

CAD FILE AVAILABLE

Main Level Floor Plan

53'-2"
15.95 m

56'-0"
16.8 m

Upper Level Floor Plan

Copyright by designer/architect.

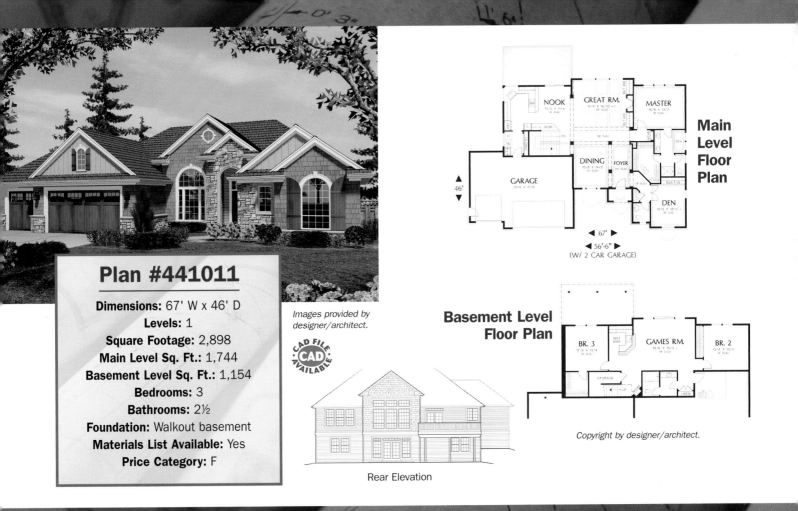

Plan #441011

Dimensions: 67' W x 46' D
Levels: 1
Square Footage: 2,898
Main Level Sq. Ft.: 1,744
Basement Level Sq. Ft.: 1,154
Bedrooms: 3
Bathrooms: 2½
Foundation: Walkout basement
Materials List Available: Yes
Price Category: F

Images provided by designer/architect.

CAD FILE AVAILABLE

Main Level Floor Plan

Basement Level Floor Plan

Copyright by designer/architect.

Rear Elevation

Plan #181120

Dimensions: 32' W x 40' D
Levels: 2
Square Footage: 1,480
Main Level Sq. Ft.: 1,024
Second Level Sq. Ft.: 456
Bedrooms: 2
Bathrooms: 2
Foundation: Basement
Materials List Available: Yes
Price Category: E

Images provided by designer/architect.

CAD FILE AVAILABLE

Copyright by designer/architect.

Main Level Floor Plan

Upper Level Floor Plan

Front Elevation

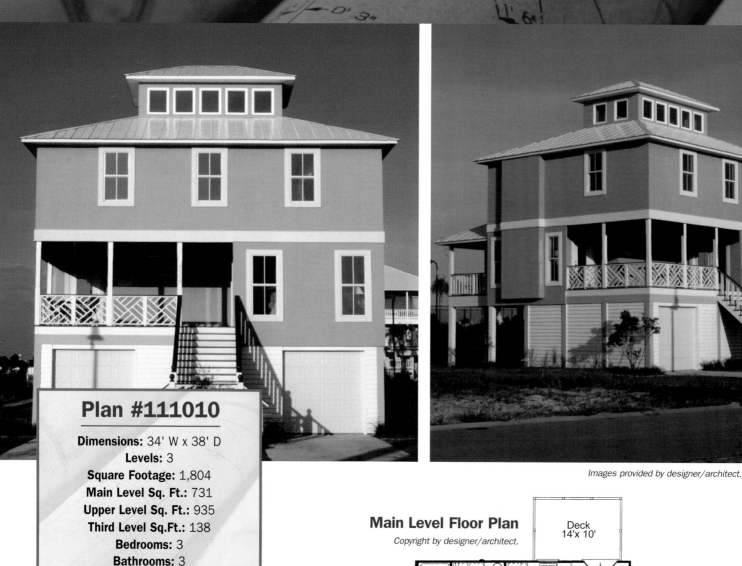

Plan #111010

Dimensions: 34' W x 38' D
Levels: 3
Square Footage: 1,804
Main Level Sq. Ft.: 731
Upper Level Sq. Ft.: 935
Third Level Sq.Ft.: 138
Bedrooms: 3
Bathrooms: 3
Foundation: Piers
Materials List Available: No
Price Category: E

Images provided by designer/architect.

This vacation home is designed for practicality and convenience.

Features:

- **Porch:** This cozy porch opens to the dining room and the living room. Relax on the porch, and invite a passing neighbor to join you for a cup of coffee.

- **Living Room:** French doors connect this brightly lit room to the porch. The corner fireplace adds warmth and elegance to the area.

- **Kitchen:** This island kitchen, with a snack bar, is open to the dining room and living room. A full bathroom and the laundry area are just a few steps away.

- **Master Suite:** This private retreat is located on the upper level close to the secondary bedrooms. Pass his and her closets that lead into the private bath, complete with an oversized tub.

Main Level Floor Plan

Copyright by designer/architect.

Deck 14'x 10'
Kitchen 10'6"x 13'9"
Dining 9'x 13'8"
Living 14'x 19'
Screen Porch 19'6"x 10'

Upper Level Floor Plan

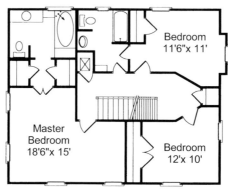

Bedroom 11'6"x 11'
Master Bedroom 18'6"x 15'
Bedroom 12'x 10'

Third Level Floor Plan

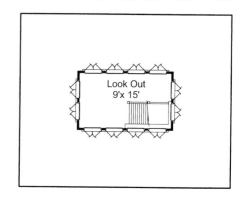

Look Out 9'x 15'

Plan #531040

Dimensions: 42' W x 81' D
Levels: 2
Square Footage: 3,325
Main Level Sq. Ft.: 1,272
Upper Level Sq. Ft.: 2,053
Bedrooms: 3
Bathrooms: 3½
Foundation: Slab
Material List Available: No
Price Category: G

This home is tailor-made for a site with dramatic views.

Features:

- Dining Room: This dining room is located just off the foyer and features a built-in butler's pantry. Large windows will flood this area with natural light.

- Kitchen: This island kitchen is open to the family room and has access to the tower above. The breakfast nook offers great views and additional seating at the bar.

- Master Suite: Also located on the upper level, this oasis has access to the rear lanai. The master bath features a large walk-in closet and a whirlpool tub.

- Lower Level: The third bedroom, with a large walk-in closet, is located on this level. The game room and office make their home here as well.

CAD FILE AVAILABLE

Main Level Floor Plan

Upper Level Floor Plan

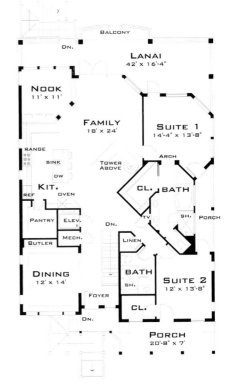

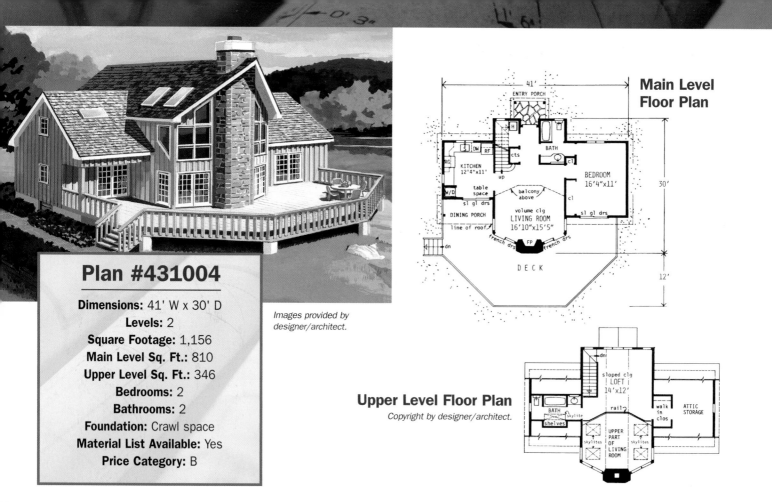

Main Level Floor Plan

Images provided by designer/architect.

Upper Level Floor Plan

Copyright by designer/architect.

Plan #431004

Dimensions: 41' W x 30' D

Levels: 2

Square Footage: 1,156

Main Level Sq. Ft.: 810

Upper Level Sq. Ft.: 346

Bedrooms: 2

Bathrooms: 2

Foundation: Crawl space

Material List Available: Yes

Price Category: B

Copyright by designer/architect.

Plan #321007

Dimensions: 76' W x 55'2" D

Levels: 1

Square Footage: 2,695

Bedrooms: 3

Bathrooms: 2½

Foundation: Basement

Materials List Available: Yes

Price Category: G

Images provided by designer/architect.

CAD FILE AVAILABLE

SMARTtip

Decorative Poles

Drapery poles are supported by the brackets fastened to the window frame or wall. The brackets that are provided with the poles generally coordinate and blend in with the pole finish. Brackets can be simple but also decorative. If you opt for a spectacular, attention-grabbing bracket, consider choosing less showy finials for the ends of the pole.

**Main Level
Floor Plan**

*Images provided by
designer/architect.*

Upper Level Floor Plan

Copyright by designer/architect.

Plan #471019

Dimensions: 31' W x 36' D

Levels: 2

Square Footage: 1,024

Main Level Sq. Ft.: 710

Upper Level Sq. Ft.: 314

Bedrooms: 2

Bathrooms: 2

Foundation: Crawl space or basement

Material List Available: Yes

Price Category: C

Plan #571039

Dimensions: 40' W x 34' D

Levels: 1

Square Footage: 2,144

Main Level Sq. Ft.: 1,072

Lower Level Sq. Ft.: 1,072

Bedrooms: 3

Bathrooms: 2½

Foundation: Basement

Material List Available: Yes

Price Category: D

*Images provided by
designer/architect.*

**Basement Level
Floor Plan**

*Copyright by
designer/architect.*

Plan #611069

Dimensions: 61'8" W x 75' D
Levels: 2
Square Footage: 5,445
Main Level Sq. Ft.: 2,900
Upper Level Sq. Ft.: 2,545
Bedrooms: 6
Bathrooms: 4
Foundation: Slab
Material List Available: No
Price Category: J

Images provided by designer/architect.

Luxury abounds in this six-bedroom home for larger families. You'll find lavish comforts throughout the design.

Features:

• **Living Room:** This open room hosts a bar and wine storage for entertaining family and friends. The two-story space boasts a dramatic fireplace and access to the rear covered porch.

• **Family Room:** An open snack bar faces this room, which will become a favorite for the family to enjoy a movie and popcorn. On nice days or evenings you can step out the double doors and onto the rear covered porch.

• **Master Suite:** This private oasis features a large sleeping area, a sitting area, and an exercise room complete with a sauna and steam room. The large master bath features a spa tub, dual vanities, a separate shower, and a private lavatory area.

• **Bedrooms:** Five additional bedrooms, each with a private full bathroom, complete the floor plan. Two bedrooms are located on the first level, with the remaining three on the upper level with the master suite.

Rear View.

Main Level Floor Plan

Copyright by designer/architect.

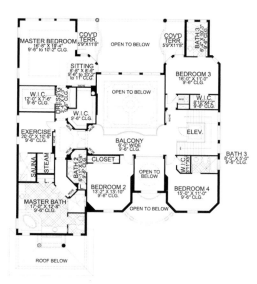

Upper Level Floor Plan

Plan #391052

Dimensions: 68' W x 34'10" D
Levels: 2
Square Footage: 1,778
Main Level Sq. Ft.: 1,306
Upper Level Sq. Ft.: 472
Bedrooms: 3
Bathrooms: 2
Foundation: Crawl space, slab, or basement
Material List Available: Yes
Price Category: C

This home, as shown in the photograph, may differ from the actual blueprints. For more detailed information, please check the floor plans carefully.

Images provided by designer/architect.

The contemporary styling of the angled walls and center tower helps this design stand apart.

Features:

- Entry: This airlock entry will help conserve energy. The two-story entry allows an overview from the master suite above.

- Kitchen: Centrally located, this kitchen has an efficiently designed work area. The raised bar divides the dining room from the kitchen, while maintaining the open floor plan.

- Master Suite: The entire upper level is dedicated to this retreat, which features a sitting area and a view down into the living room and entry. The master bath boasts dual vanities.

- Garage: Although capable of holding two cars, this garage would also make a great workshop.

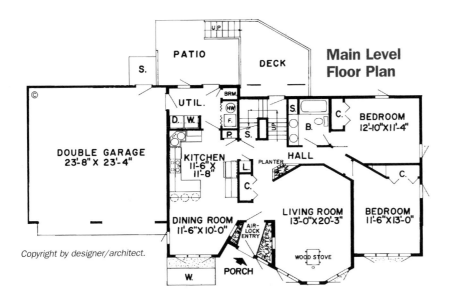

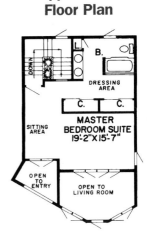

Copyright by designer/architect.

Plan #131056

Dimensions: 40' W x 54' D

Levels: 1.5

Square Footage: 1,396

Main Level Sq. Ft.: 964

Upper Level Sq. Ft.: 432

Bedrooms: 3

Bathrooms: 2

Foundation: Slab; basement for fee

Materials List Available: Yes

Price Category: C

This ruggedly handsome home is a true A-frame. The elegance of the roof virtually meeting the ground and the use of rugged stone veneer and log-cabin siding make it stand out.

Features:

- Living Room: This area is the interior highlight of the home. The large, exciting space features a soaring ceiling, a massive fireplace, and a magnificent window wall to capture a view.

- Side Porch: The secondary entry from this side porch leads to a center hall that provides direct access to the first floor's two bedrooms, bathroom, kitchen, and living room.

- Kitchen: This kitchen is extremely efficient and includes a snack bar and access to the screened porch.

- Loft Area: A spiral stairway leads from the living room to this second-floor loft, which overlooks the living room. The area can also double as an extra sleeping room.

Main Level Floor Plan

Copyright by designer/architect

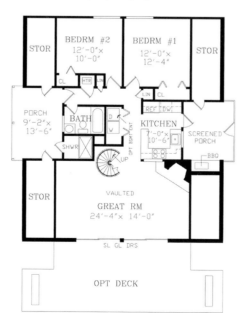

Great Room

Upper Level Floor Plan

Right Side View

Rear View

Kitchen

Dining Room/Great Room

Images provided by designer/architect.

Plan #521005

Dimensions: 62' W x 104'2" D
Levels: 1.5
Square Footage: 2,932
Main Level Sq. Ft.: 2,026
Upper Level Sq. Ft.: 906
Bedrooms: 3
Bathrooms: 3½
Foundation: Slab
Material List Available: No
Price Category: F

This country home contains plenty of room for entertaining.

Features:

- **Front Porch:** This outdoor relaxing area attaches to the side screened porch. The breezeway attaches to the two-car garage.

- **Foyer:** This area welcomes you to the home. Pocket doors allow access to the computer room, which leads to the laundry room.

- **Living Room:** This large, centrally located gathering area features triple French doors, allowing the fun to spill out onto the rear covered deck. The fireplace adds a focal point to the room.

- **Kitchen:** An abundance of cabinets and counter space fill this island kitchen. A bay window creates a bright and warm space.

- **Master Suite:** This main-level oasis features a large walk-in closet. The master bath boasts a whirlpool tub and a separate shower.

CAD FILE AVAILABLE

Main Level Floor Plan

LOWER DECK (21'7"x8'4")
SUNROOM (14'4"x13'8")
COVERED DECK (20'0"x7'0")
MASTER BEDROOM (14'4"x18'8")
DINING AREA (12'8"x11'4") +bay
LIVING ROOM (16'10"x20'6")
KITCHEN (12'8"x12'6")
FOYER 10'8"x6'0"
SCREENED SIDE PORCH (8'0"x11'4")
COMPUTER ROOM LAUNDRY ROOM
FRONT PORCH (57'0"x8'0")
BREEZE WAY (7'0"x11'6")
SERVICE YARD
2 CAR GARAGE (21'4"x26'8")
GOLF CART AREA (8'0"x15'4")

Bonus Area Floor Plan

BONUS ROOM

Upper Level Floor Plan

Copyright by designer/architect.

OPEN TO LIVING ROOM
BEDROOM #2 (14'4"x14'6") +bay
BEDROOM #3 (12'8"x12'8")

RearView

324   order direct: 1-800-523-6789

Plan #391004

Dimensions: 66' W x 52' D
Levels: 1
Square Footage: 1,750
Bedrooms: 2
Bathrooms: 2
Foundation: Crawl space, slab, or basement
Materials List Available: Yes
Price Category: C

This creatively compact ranch is made especially for effortless everyday living.

Features:

• Kitchen: This centralized U-shaped kitchen and look-alike breakfast nook with professional pantry have a wonderful view of the porch.

• Laundry Room: Laundry facilities are cleverly placed within reach while neatly out of the way.

• Great Room: Step into this lavish-looking sunken great room for fireside gatherings, and move easily into the nearby formal dining area where a screened porch allows you to entertain guests after dinner.

• Master Suite: Flanking one side of the house, this master suite is serenely private and amenity-filled. Its features include full bath, a wall of walk-in closets and a dressing area.

This home, as shown in the photograph, may differ from the actual blueprints. Images provided by designer/architect. For more detailed information, please check the floor plans carefully.

• Bedroom: This second spacious bedroom enjoys great closeting (with double-doors), a full bath, and a close-at-hand den (or bedroom #3).

• Garage: This three-car garage goes beyond vehicle protection, providing plenty of storage and work space.

Crawl Space/Slab Option

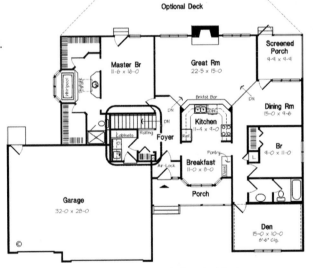

Copyright by designer/architect.

Rear View

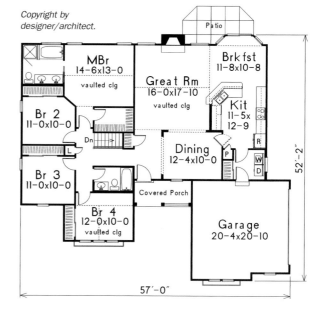

Plan #321008

Dimensions: 57' W x 52'2" D

Levels: 1

Square Footage: 1,761

Bedrooms: 4

Bathrooms: 2

Foundation: Basement

Materials List Available: Yes

Price Category: C

Images provided by designer/architect.

CAD FILE AVAILABLE

SMARTtip

Hanging Wallpaper

Use liner paper to smooth out a damaged wall and to provide uniform support for expensive paper.

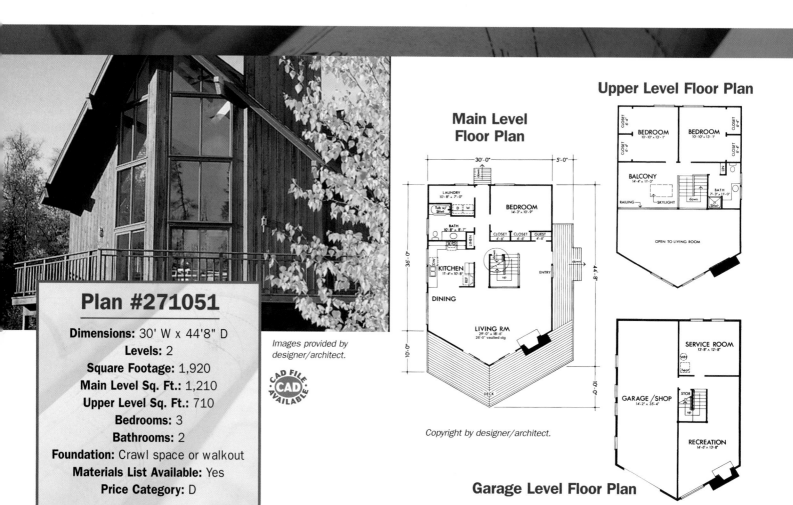

Main Level Floor Plan

Upper Level Floor Plan

Garage Level Floor Plan

Plan #271051

Dimensions: 30' W x 44'8" D

Levels: 2

Square Footage: 1,920

Main Level Sq. Ft.: 1,210

Upper Level Sq. Ft.: 710

Bedrooms: 3

Bathrooms: 2

Foundation: Crawl space or walkout

Materials List Available: Yes

Price Category: D

Images provided by designer/architect.

CAD FILE AVAILABLE

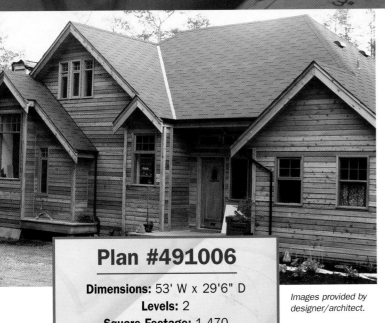

Main Level Floor Plan

SUNDECK

DINING
14' x 12'
16'11" VAULTED CLG.

BR.
11' x 12'4"
10' VAULTED CLG.

LIVING
16' x 15'
16'11" VAULTED CLG.

FOYER

SEAT

SITTING

COVERED PORCH

LDR

UP

10'-0"

29'-6"

53'-0"

4'-0"

Images provided by designer/architect.

Front View

BALCONY

BR.
12'2" x 10'
10' VAULTED CLG.

LOFT
VAULTED

OPEN TO BELOW

RAILING

RAILING

PLANT LEDGE

OPEN

DN

Upper Level Floor Plan

Copyright by designer/architect.

Plan #491006

Dimensions: 53' W x 29'6" D
Levels: 2
Square Footage: 1,470
Main Level Sq. Ft.: 1,130
Upper Level Sq. Ft.: 340
Bedrooms: 2
Bathrooms: 2
Foundation: Crawl space
Material List Available: Yes
Price Category: B

Deck
20'4"x 8'

Deck
14'10"x 8'

Porch
20'4"x 8'

Deck
14'10"x 8'

Bedroom
13' x 15'6"

Living
18'8"x 18'

Master Bedroom
14'8"x 20'

Breakfast
18'8"x 11'2"

Bedroom
11'10"x 12'6"

Kitchen
18'8"x 10'

Deck
13'x 4'

Main Level Floor Plan

Copyright by designer/architect.

Images provided by designer/architect.

Upper Level Floor Plan

Storage
12'7"x 10'4"

Bedroom
11'10"x 16'4"

Foyer
24'9"x 4'6"

Ground Level Floor Plan

Open to Below

Loft
19'8"x 21'

Plan #111032

Dimensions: 50' W x 56' D
Levels: 3
Square Footage: 2,904
Ground Level Sq. Ft.: 449
Main Level Sq. Ft.: 2,000
Upper Level Sq. Ft.: 455
Bedrooms: 4
Bathrooms: 3
Foundation: Pier
Materials List Available: No
Price Category: G

Plan #321004

Dimensions: 91'8" W x 62'4" D
Levels: 1
Square Footage: 2,808
Bedrooms: 3
Bathrooms: 2½
Foundation: Basement
Materials List Available: Yes
Price Category: H

Images provided by designer/architect.

SMARTtip

Ornaments in a Garden

Placement is everything with ornaments in a garden. Some elements are best sitting by themselves. Others are better when they are part of a cohesive whole, perhaps placed in the greenery at a corner or flanking a structure.

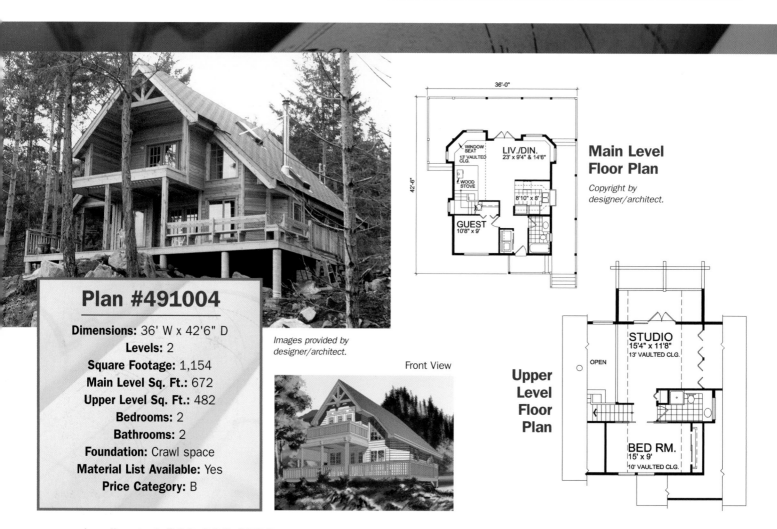

Copyright by designer/architect.

Plan #491004

Dimensions: 36' W x 42'6" D
Levels: 2
Square Footage: 1,154
Main Level Sq. Ft.: 672
Upper Level Sq. Ft.: 482
Bedrooms: 2
Bathrooms: 2
Foundation: Crawl space
Material List Available: Yes
Price Category: B

Images provided by designer/architect.

Front View

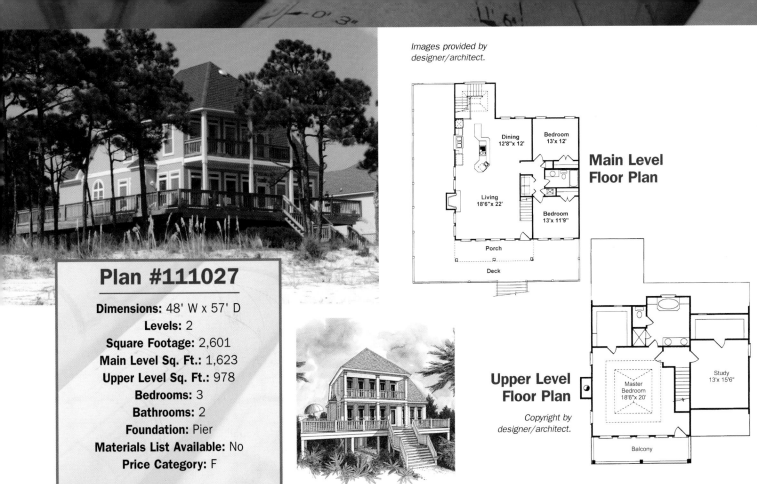

Main Level Floor Plan

Dining 12'8"x 12'

Bedroom 13'x 12'

Living 18'6"x 22'

Bedroom 13'x 11'9"

Porch

Deck

Upper Level Floor Plan

Master Bedroom 18'6"x 20'

Study 13'x 15'6"

Balcony

Copyright by designer/architect.

Plan #111027

Dimensions: 48' W x 57' D

Levels: 2

Square Footage: 2,601

Main Level Sq. Ft.: 1,623

Upper Level Sq. Ft.: 978

Bedrooms: 3

Bathrooms: 2

Foundation: Pier

Materials List Available: No

Price Category: F

Upper Level Floor Plan

10'-0" X 11'-8" 3,00 X 3,50

12'-0" X 11'-8" 3,60 X 3,50

Copyright by designer/architect.

Plan #181128

Dimensions: 36' W x 36' D

Levels: 2

Square Footage: 1,625

Main Level Sq. Ft.: 1,108

Second Level Sq. Ft.: 517

Bedrooms: 3

Bathrooms: 2

Foundation: Basement

Materials List Available: Yes

Price Category: F

Front View

14'-0" X 12'-0" 4,20 X 3,80

20'-0" X 14'-0" 6,00 X 4,20

13'-0" X 17'-0" 3,90 X 5,10

36'-0" 10,8 m

Main Level Floor Plan

Plan #531020

Dimensions: 74' W x 97' D
Levels: 1
Square Footage: 3,371
Bedrooms: 4
Bathrooms: 3½
Foundation: Slab; basement or pier/pole for fee
Material List Available: No
Price Category: G

Beauty meets practicality in this charming home. Lovely architectural details and an interior designed with daily living in mind create an ideal environment for the growing family.

Features:

• Living Room: Open to the foyer and dining room, this gathering area boasts a fireplace flanked by built-in shelves. On nice days, expand living space by opening the doors to the rear lanai.

• Dining Room: This oversize dining room greets your guests, setting the mood for fun. A pair of large windows floods this space with natural light.

• Master Suite: Located on the opposite side of the home from the secondary bedrooms, this private oasis features an oversize sleeping area. His and her walk-in closets open to the private bath, which boasts a separate toilet area.

• Secondary Bedrooms: Three additional bedrooms and two full bathrooms are located toward the rear of the home.

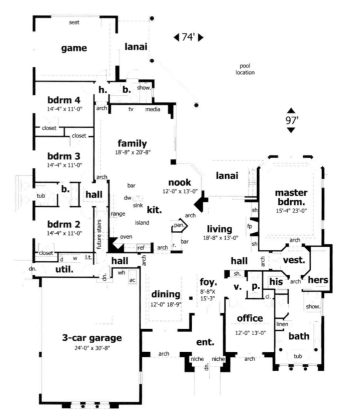

Plan #161026

Dimensions: 67'6" W x 63'6" D
Levels: 1
Square Footage: 2,041
Bedrooms: 3
Bathrooms: 2
Foundation: Basement
Materials List Available: No
Price Category: D

You'll love the special features of this home, which has been designed for efficiency and comfort.

CAD FILE AVAILABLE · CAD

Images provided by designer/architect.

Features:

- Foyer: This raised foyer offers a view through the great room and beyond it to the covered deck.

- Great Room: Elegant windows allow versatility — decorate casually or more formally.

- Kitchen: You'll find ample counter space and cabinets in this spacious room, which adjoins the dining room and opens onto the rear yard.

- Library: Curl up on the window seat that wraps around the tower in this quiet spot.

- Laundry Room: A tub makes this large room practical for crafts as well as laundry.

- Master Suite: A vaulted ceiling gives grace to the sitting area, and the garden bath with a walk-in closet and whirlpool tub adds luxury.

Rear Elevation

Main Level Floor Plan

Basement Level Floor Plan

Copyright by designer/architect.

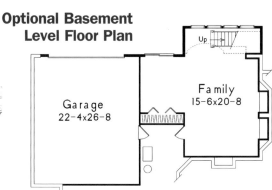

55'-8"

46'-4"

Balcony

MBr
18-4x13-0

Kit
10-2x
11-9

Dining   Dn

Great Rm
16-0x21-4
vaulted

L   W D

Entry

Br 2
12-8x14-0

Br 3
11-4x12-6

Porch depth 6-0

Copyright by
designer/architect.

Plan #321009

Dimensions: 55'8" W x 46'4" D

Levels: 1

Square Footage: 2,295

Bedrooms: 3

Bathrooms: 2

Foundation: Basement

Materials List Available: Yes

Price Category: E

Images provided by
designer/architect.

CAD FILE AVAILABLE · CAD ·

Rear View

Optional Basement Level Floor Plan

Up

Garage
22-4x26-8

Family
15-6x20-8

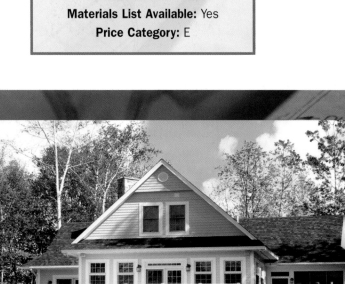

Main Level Floor Plan

40'-0"
12,0 m

15'-0" X 14'-8"
4,50 X 4,40

13'-8" X 11'-4"
4,10 X 3,40

12'-0" X 16'-0"
3,60 X 4,80

15'-8" X 14'-8"
4,10 X 4,40

11'-0" X 16'-0"
3,30 X 4,80

38'-0"
11,4 m

Images provided by
designer/architect.

CAD FILE AVAILABLE · CAD ·

Plan #181133

Dimensions: 38' W x 40' D

Levels: 2

Square Footage: 1,832

Main Level Sq. Ft.: 1,212

Second Level Sq. Ft. 620

Bedrooms: 3

Bathrooms: 2

Foundation: Walkout; crawl space, slab, or basement for fee

Materials List Available: Yes

Price Category: G

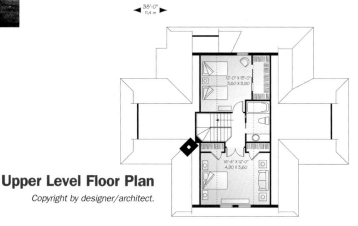

12'-0" X 13'-0"
3,60 X 3,90

16'-4" X 12'-0"
4,90 X 3,60

Upper Level Floor Plan

Copyright by designer/architect.

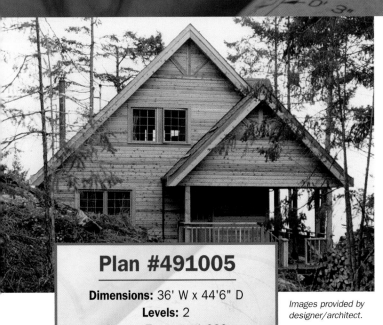

Plan #491005

Dimensions: 36' W x 44'6" D

Levels: 2

Square Footage: 1,333

Main Level Sq. Ft.: 768

Upper Level Sq. Ft.: 565

Bedrooms: 2

Bathrooms: 2

Foundation: Crawl space

Material List Available: Yes

Price Category: B

Images provided by designer/architect.

Main Level Floor Plan

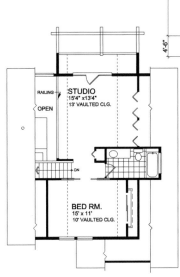

Upper Level Floor Plan

Copyright by designer/architect.

Rear View

Plan #321035

Dimensions: 55'8" W x 46' D

Levels: 1

Square Footage: 1,384

Bedrooms: 2

Bathrooms: 2

Foundation: Walkout

Materials List Available: Yes

Price Category: D

Images provided by designer/architect.

CAD FILE AVAILABLE

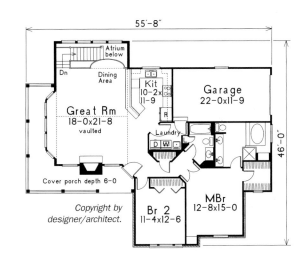

Copyright by designer/architect.

Rear View

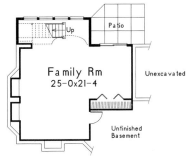

Optional Basement Level Floor Plan

Landscaping Ideas

Landscapes change over the years. As plants grow, the overall look evolves from sparse to lush. Trees cast cool shade where the sun used to shine. Shrubs and hedges grow tall and dense enough to provide privacy. Perennials and ground covers spread to form colorful patches of foliage and flowers. Meanwhile, paths, arbors, fences, and other structures gain the patina of age.

Constant change over the years—sometimes rapid and dramatic, sometimes slow and subtle—is one of the joys of landscaping. It is also one of the challenges. Anticipating how fast plants will grow and how big they will eventually get is difficult, even for professional designers.

To illustrate the kinds of changes to expect in a planting, these pages show a landscape design at three different "ages." Even though a new planting may look sparse at first, it will soon fill in. And because of careful spacing, the planting will look as good in 10 to 15 years as it does after 3 to 5. It will, of course, look different, but that's part of the fun.

At Planting

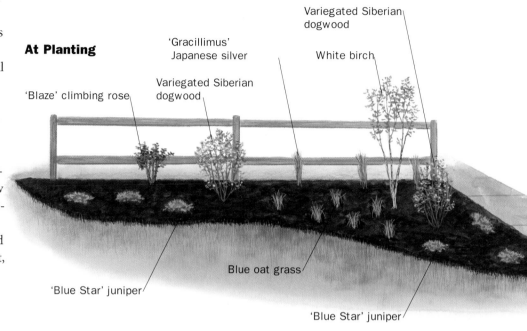

'Blaze' climbing rose

'Gracillimus' Japanese silver

Variegated Siberian dogwood

Variegated Siberian dogwood

White birch

'Blue Star' juniper

Blue oat grass

'Blue Star' juniper

Three to Five Years

At Planting—Here's how the corner might appear in early summer immediately after planting. The white birch tree is only 5 to 6 ft. tall, with trunks no thicker than broomsticks. The variegated Siberian dogwoods each have a few main stems about 3 to 4 ft. tall. The 'Blaze' rose has just short stubs where the nursery cut back the old stems, but it will grow fast and may bloom the first year. The 'Blue Star' junipers are low mounds about 6 to 10 in. wide. The blue oat grass forms small, thin clumps of sparse foliage. The 'Gracillimus' Japanese silver grass may still be dormant, or it may have a short tuft of new foliage. Both grasses will grow vigorously the first year.

Three to Five Years—The birch tree has grown 1 to 2 ft. taller every year but is still quite slender. Near the base, it's starting to show the white bark typical of maturity. The variegated Siberian dogwoods are well established now. If you cut them to the ground every year or two in spring, they grow back 4 to 6 ft. tall by midsummer, with strong, straight stems. The 'Blaze' rose covers the fence, and you need to prune out a few of its older stems every spring. The slow-growing 'Blue Star' junipers make a series of low mounds; you still see them as individuals, not a continuous patch. The grasses have reached maturity and form lush, robust clumps. It would be a good idea to divide and replant them now, to keep them vigorous.

Ten to Fifteen Years—The birch tree is becoming a fine specimen, 20 to 30 ft. tall, with gleaming white bark on its trunks. Prune away the lower limbs up to 6 to 8 ft. above ground to expose its trunks and to keep it from crowding and shading the other plants. The variegated dogwoods and 'Blaze' rose continue to thrive and respond well to regular pruning. The 'Blue Star' junipers have finally merged into a continuous mass of glossy foliage. The blue oat grass and Japanese silver grass will still look good if they have been divided and replanted over the years. If you get tired of the grasses, you could replace them with cinnamon fern and astilbe, as shown here, or other perennials or shrubs.

Ten to Fifteen Years

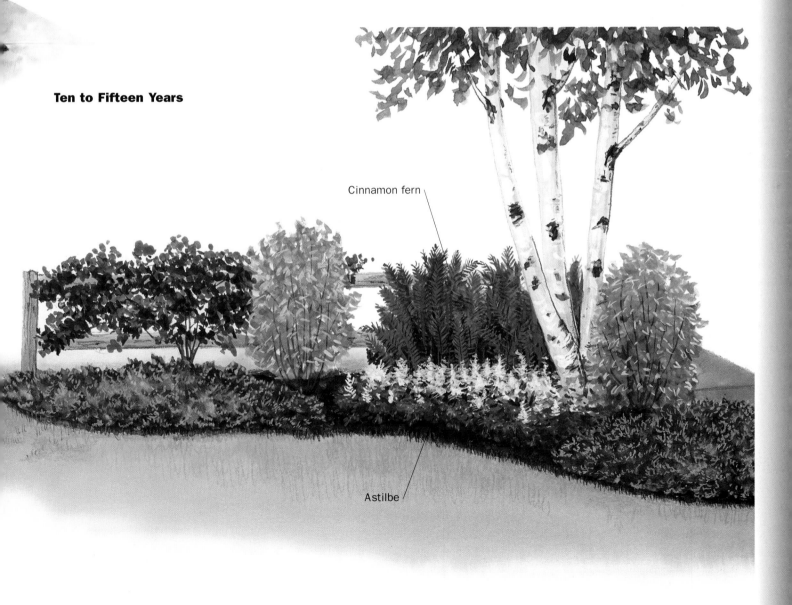

Cinnamon fern

Astilbe

A Warm Welcome

Make a Pleasant Passage to Your Front Door

Why wait until a visitor reaches the front door to extend a cordial greeting? Have your landscape offer a friendly welcome and a helpful "Please come this way." Well-chosen plants and a revamped walkway not only make a visitor's short journey a pleasant one, but they can also enhance your home's most public face.

This simple arrangement of plants and paving produces an elegant entrance that deftly mixes formal and informal elements.

A wide walk of neatly fitted flagstones and a rectangular bed of roses have the feel of a small formal courtyard, complete with a pair of "standard" roses in planters, each displaying a mound of flowers atop a single stem. Clumps of ornamental grass rise from the paving like leafy fountains.

Gently curving beds of low-growing evergreens and shrub roses edge the flagstones, softening the formality and providing a comfortable transition to the lawn.

Morning glories and clematis climb simple trellises to brighten the walls of the house.

Flowers in pink, white, purple, and violet are abundant from early summer until frost. They are set off by the rich green foliage of the junipers and roses and the gray leaves of the catmint edging.

Add a bench, as shown here, so you can linger and enjoy the scene; in later years, the lovely star magnolia behind it will provide comfortable dappled shade.

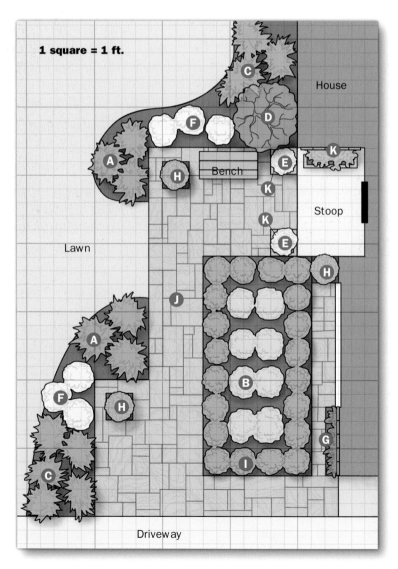

1 square = 1 ft.

Plants and Projects

Once established, these shrubs and perennials require little care beyond deadheading and an annual pruning. Ask the nursery where you buy the standard roses for advice on how to protect the plants in winter.

A **'Blue Star' juniper** *Juniperus squamata* (use 6 plants)
The sparkly blue foliage of this low-growing evergreen shrub neatly edges the opening onto the lawn.

B **'Bonica' rose** *Rosa* (use 8)
This deciduous shrub blooms from June until frost, producing clusters of double, soft pink flowers.

C **Dwarf creeping juniper** *Juniperis procumbens* 'Nana' (use 8)
This low, spreading evergreen with prickly green foliage makes a tough, handsome ground cover.

D **Star magnolia** *Magnolia stellata* (use 1)
This small, multitrunked deciduous tree graces the entry with lightly scented white flowers in early spring.

E **'The Fairy' rose** *Rosa* (use 2)
Clusters of small, double, pale pink roses appear in abundance from early summer to frost. Buy plants

trained as standards at a nursery. Underplant with impatiens.

F **'White Meidiland' rose** *Rosa* (use 6)
A low, spreading shrub, it is covered with clusters of lovely single white flowers all summer.

G **Jackman clematis** *Clematis* × *Jackmanii* (use 2)
Trained to a simple lattice, this deciduous vine produces large, showy, dark purple flowers for weeks in summer.

H **'Gracillimus' Japanese silver grass** *Miscanthus* (use 3)
The arching leaves of this perennial grass are topped by fluffy seed heads from late summer through winter.

I **'Six Hills Giant' catmint** *Nepeta* × *faassenii* (use 20)
A perennial with violet-blue flowers and aromatic gray-green foliage edges the roses.

J **Flagstone paving**
Rectangular flagstones in random sizes.

K **Planters**
Simple wooden boxes contain blue-flowered annual morning glories (on the stoop, trained to a wooden lattice) and standard roses (in front of the stoop).

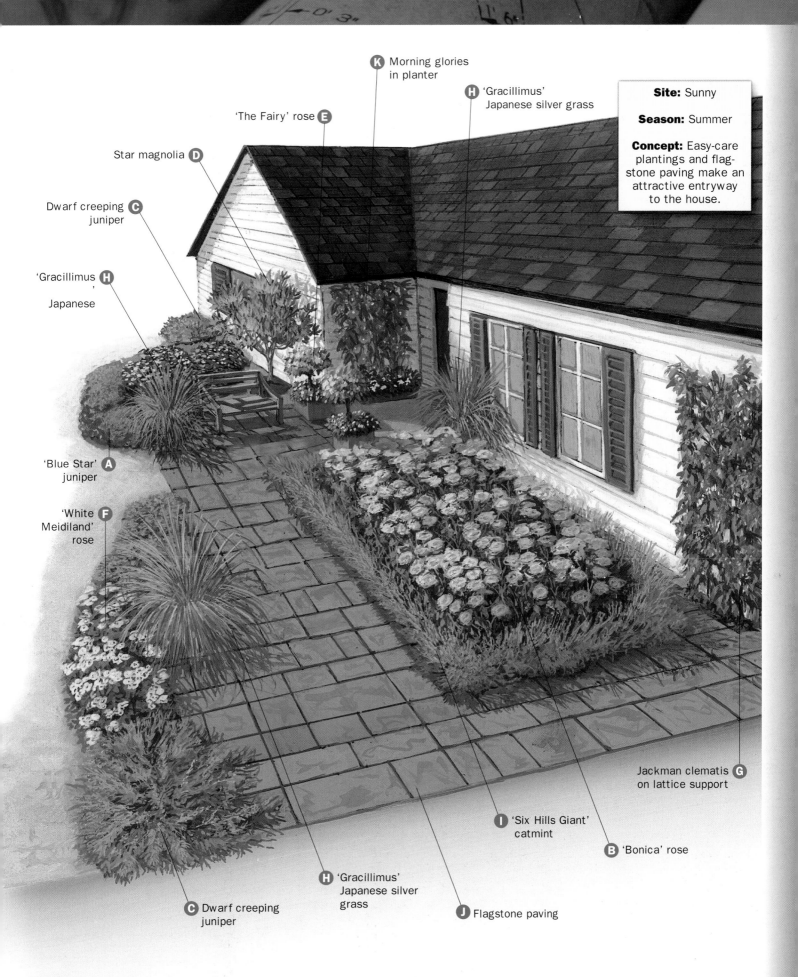

K Morning glories in planter

H 'Gracillimus' Japanese silver grass

'The Fairy' rose E

Star magnolia D

Dwarf creeping juniper C

'Gracillimus' H
Japanese

'Blue Star' A
juniper

'White F
Meidiland'
rose

Site: Sunny

Season: Summer

Concept: Easy-care plantings and flag-stone paving make an attractive entryway to the house.

Jackman clematis G
on lattice support

I 'Six Hills Giant' catmint

B 'Bonica' rose

C Dwarf creeping juniper

H 'Gracillimus' Japanese silver grass

J Flagstone paving

Note: All plants are appropriate for USDA Hardiness Zones 4, 5, and 6.

Up Front and Formal
Greet Visitors with Classic Symmetry

Formal gardens have a special appeal. Their simple geometry can be soothing in a hectic world, and the look is timeless, never going out of style. The front yard of a classical house, like the one shown here, invites a formal makeover. (A house with a symmetrical facade in any style has similar potential.)

In this design, a paved courtyard and a planting of handsome trees, shrubs, and ground covers have transformed a site typically given over to lawn and a cement walkway. The result is a more dramatic entry, but also one where you can happily linger with guests on a fine day.

Tall hedges on the borders of the design and the centrally placed redbud provide a modicum of privacy in this otherwise public space. Lower hedges along the sidewalk and front of the driveway allow a view of the street and make these approaches more welcoming.

A matched pair of viburnums make a lovely setting for the front door. To each side, layered groups of shrubs give depth and interest to the house's facade. From spring through fall, the planting's flowers and foliage make the courtyard a comfortable spot, and there is ample evergreen foliage to keep up appearances in winter. Completing the scene is an ornamental focal point and a bench for enjoying the results of your landscaping labors.

> **Site:** Sunny
>
> **Season:** Early summer
>
> **Concept:** Wide paving, hedges, trees, and shrubs create an appealing entry courtyard.

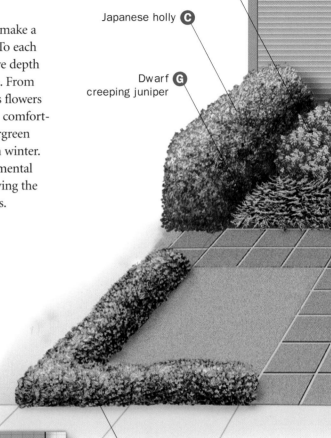

'Janet Blair' **F** rhododendron

Japanese holly **C**

Dwarf **G** creeping juniper

D 'Crimson Pygmy' Japanese barberry

Plants and Projects

Spring is the season for flowers in this planting, with redbud, rhododendron, and candytuft blossoms in shades of pink and white. The colorful leaves and berries of viburnum, redbud, and barberry brighten the fall. While the hedge plants are dependable and problem-free, you'll need to shear them at least once a year to maintain the formal shapes.

A **Redbud** *Cercis canadensis* (use 1 plant)
Small pink flowers line the branches of this deciduous tree in early spring before the foliage appears. The heart-shaped leaves emerge reddish, mature to a lustrous green, and turn gold in fall. Bare branches form an attractive silhouette in winter, especially as the tree ages.

Note: All plants are appropriate for USDA Hardiness Zones 4, 5, and 6.

1 square = 1 ft.

House

Stoop

Lawn

Lawn

Driveway

Sidewalk

E Dwarf double-file
viburnum

H Evergreen
candytuft

C Japanese holly

K Bench

B Pachysandra

D 'Crimson Pygmy'
Japanese barberry

A Redbud

I Pavers

See site plan for J.

B **Pachysandra** *Pachysandra terminalis*
(use 250)
Hardy, adaptable evergreen ground cover
that will spread in the shade of the redbud,
forming an attractive, weed-smothering,
glossy green carpet.

C **Japanese holly** *Euonymus alatus*
'Compactus' (use 19)
Choose an upright cultivar of this evergreen
shrub to form a hedge of dark green leaves.
In Zones 4 and 5 substitute the hardier com-
pact burning bush, *Euonymus alatus*
'Compactus.'

D **'Crimson Pygmy' Japanese barberry**
Berberis thunbergii (use 34)
This rugged deciduous shrub puts on a colorful show, with small maroon leaves that
turn red in fall when they're joined by bright
red berries. A small rounded plant, it can be
sheared, as shown here, or pruned lightly
into an informal low hedge.

E **Dwarf double-file viburnum** *Viburnum*

plicatum var. *tomentosum* (use 2)
A pair of these deciduous shrubs make an
elegant frame for the door. Tiers of horizon-
tal branches are smothered with small clusters of pure white flowers from May through
fall. Large, crinkled leaves are medium green.

F **'Janet Blair' rhododendron**
Rhododendron (use 6)
The wonderful evergreen foliage and light
pink flowers of this compact shrub anchor
the planting at the corners of the house.
Blooms in late spring. 'Mist Maiden' and
'Anna Hall' rhododendrons are good sub-
stitutes.

G **Dwarf creeping juniper** *Juniperus*
procumbens 'Nana' (use 10)
Layered sprays of this evergreen shrub's
prickly bright green foliage lay like thick
rugs on the edge of the lawn. A lovely
contrast to the dark green rhododendrons behind. For extra color in spring,
plant handfuls of crocuses, snowdrops, or

grape hyacinths next to the junipers.

H **Evergreen candytuft** *Iberis sempervirens*
(use 12)
An evergreen perennial ground cover, it
forms a low, sprawling mound of glossy
foliage next to the viburnums. Bears small
white flowers for weeks in the spring.

I **Pavers**
The courtyard is surfaced with 2-ft.-square
precast pavers. Use two complementary
colors to create patterns, if you choose.
Substitute flagstones or bricks if they
would look better with your house.

J **Ornament**
An ornament centered in the courtyard
paving provides a focal point. Choose a
sculpture, sundial, reflecting ball, birdbath,
or large potted plant to suit your taste.

K **Bench**
Enjoy the courtyard garden from a comfortable bench in a style that complements the
garden and the house.

Landscaping a Low Wall

Two-Tier Garden Replaces a Short Slope

Some things may not love a wall, but plants and gardeners do. For plants, walls offer warmth for an early start in spring and good drainage for roots. Gardeners appreciate the rich visual potential of composing a garden on two levels, as well as the practical advantage of working on two relatively flat surfaces instead of a single sloping one. If you have a wall, or have a place to put one, grasp the opportunity for some handsome landscaping.

This design places two complementary perennial borders above and below a wall bounded at one end by a set of stairs. While each bed is narrow enough for easy maintenance, when viewed from the lower level they combine to form a border almost 8 ft. deep, with plants rising to eye level. The planting can be easily extended on both sides of the steps.

Building the wall that makes this impressive sight possible doesn't require the time

or skill it once did. Nor is it necessary to scour the countryside for tons of fieldstone or to hire an expensive contractor. Thanks to precast retaining-wall systems, a knee-high do-it-yourself wall can be installed in as little as a weekend. More experienced or ambitious wall builders may want to tackle a natural stone wall, but anyone with a healthy back (or access to energetic teenagers) can succeed with a prefabricated system.

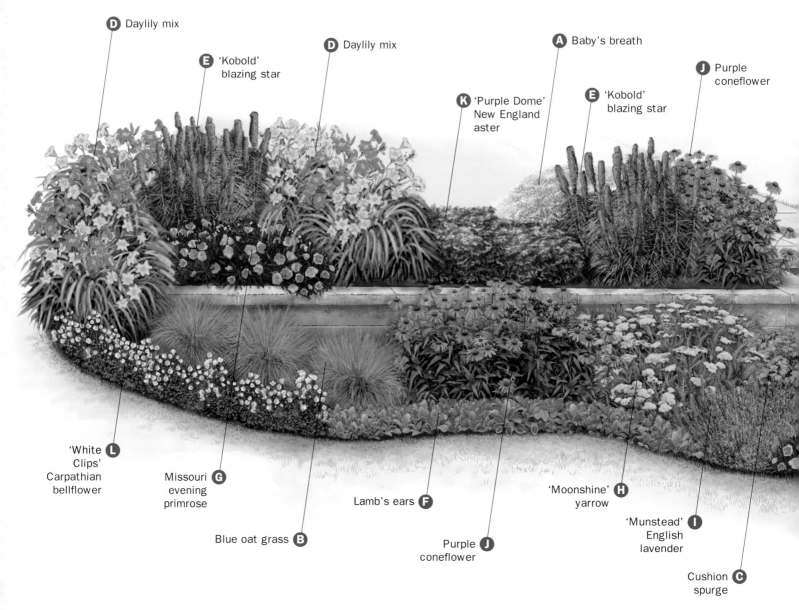

D Daylily mix

E 'Kobold' blazing star

D Daylily mix

A Baby's breath

K 'Purple Dome' New England aster

E 'Kobold' blazing star

J Purple coneflower

'White Clips' Carpathian bellflower L

Missouri evening primrose G

Blue oat grass B

Lamb's ears F

Purple coneflower J

'Moonshine' yarrow H

'Munstead' English lavender I

Cushion spurge C

Plants and Projects

These plants provide color from spring until frost with little care from you. All are perennials or grasses that need minimal maintenance beyond clipping of spent blooms and a fall or spring cleanup. Several offer excellent flowers for cutting or drying.

A Baby's breath *Gypsophila paniculata* (use 3 plants)
This popular perennial produces a cloud of tiny white flowers in June and July that add an airy texture to the garden and are excellent for cutting. A good foil to the stronger colors and textures of the adjacent plants.

B Blue oat grass *Helictotrichon sempervirens* (use 3)
A carefree grass, it forms a neat, dense clump of thin blue leaves that maintain their color through winter.

C Cushion spurge *Euphorbia polychroma* (use 1)
The electric-yellow spring color of this showy perennial is produced by long-lasting flower bracts, not petals, so it serves as a garden focal point for weeks. Its mound of foliage neatly fills

the corner by the steps and turns red in fall.

D Daylily mix *Hemerocallis* (use 6)
For an extended show of lovely lilylike flowers, combine early- and late-blooming cultivars in a selection of your favorite colors. The grassy foliage of this perennial covers the end of the wall.

E 'Kobold' blazing star *Liatris spicata* (use 6)
Magenta flower spikes of this durable perennial rise from a clump of dark green foliage from late July through August. A good mate for its prairie companion, purple coneflower. Flowers are great for cutting and drying, and butterflies love them.

F Lamb's ears *Stachys byzantina* (use 6)
The large soft leaves of this spreading perennial ground cover are a season-long presence; their silvery color is a nice foil to the blues and yellows nearby. Bears small purple flowers in early summer.

G Missouri evening primrose *Oenothera missouriensis* (use 6)
Large, glowing yellow flowers

cover the glossy foliage of this low spreading perennial, which will cascade over the wall. Blooms from late June through August.

H 'Moonshine' yarrow *Achillea* (use 3)
This perennial's flat heads of lemon yellow flowers light up the center of the garden much of the summer. Grayish foliage is fragrant, surprisingly tough despite its lacy looks. Flowers are good for drying.

I 'Munstead' English lavender *Lavandula angustifolia* (use 3)
The gray foliage of this classic bushy herb seems to deepen the greens nearby. Bears a profusion of fragrant pale lavender flower spikes in July, a pretty combination with the yellow yarrow and primroses.

J Purple coneflower *Echinacea purpurea* (use 6)
In July and August, stiff stalks carrying large daisylike pink flowers with dark brown cone-shaped centers rise above this native perennial's basal clump of rich green leaves. Leave some flower stalks standing for winter interest and to provide seeds for songbirds.

K 'Purple Dome' New England aster *Aster novaeangliae* (use 2)
This native perennial makes a

mound of foliage and is covered with purple flowers in the fall, when the garden needs a shot of color.

L 'White Clips' Carpathian bellflower *Campanula carpatica* (use 6)
A hardy little perennial with tufts of glossy green leaves and white cuplike flowers that stand out beside the blue oat grass from July until frost.

M Wall and steps
This wall and steps are built from a readily available prefabricated wall system. It is 15 ft. long and 24 in. high. Select a system to match the colors and style of your home.

N Walkway
This is built from flagstone dressed to random rectangular sizes. Precast concrete pavers or gravel would also go well with a prefabricated wall.

> **Site:** Sunny
>
> **Season:** Summer
>
> **Concept:** Low retaining wall creates easy-to-maintain beds for a distinctive two-level planting.

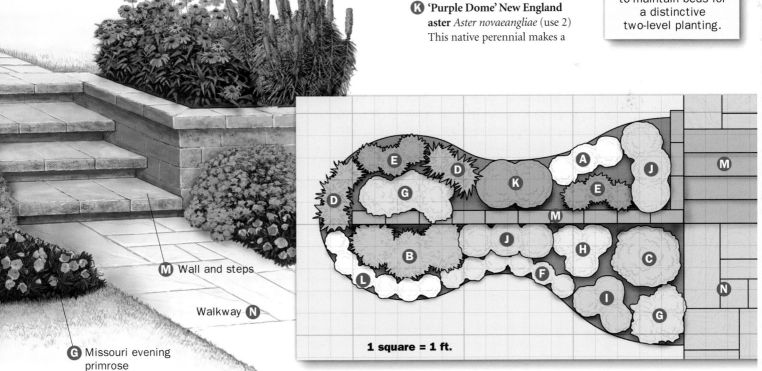

M Wall and steps

Walkway N

G Missouri evening primrose

1 square = 1 ft.

Note: All plants are appropriate for USDA Hardiness Zones 4, 5, and 6.

Plan #121066

Dimensions: 46' W x 41'5" D
Levels: 2
Square Footage: 2,078
Main Level Sq. Ft.: 1,113
Upper Level Sq. Ft.: 965
Bedrooms: 4
Bathrooms: 2½
Foundation: Basement
Materials List Available: Yes
Price Category: D

Images provided by designer/architect.

This lovely home has an unusual dignity, perhaps because its rooms are so well-proportioned and thoughtfully laid out.

Features:

- Gathering Room: This room is sunken, giving it an unusually cozy, comfortable feeling. Its abundance of windows let natural light stream in during the day, and the fireplace warms it when the weather's chilly.

- Dining Room: This dining room links to the parlor beyond through a cased opening.

- Parlor: A tall, angled ceiling highlights a large, arched window that's the focal point of this room.

- Breakfast Area: A wooden rail visually links this bayed breakfast area to the family room.

- Master Suite: A roomy walk-in closet adds a practical touch to this luxurious suite. The bath features a skylight, whirlpool tub, and separate shower.

Main Level Floor Plan

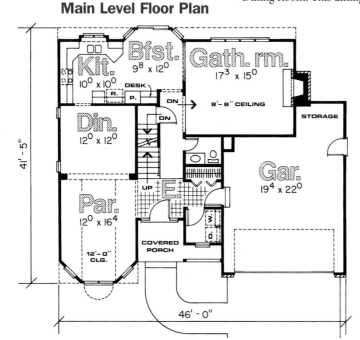

Upper Level Floor Plan

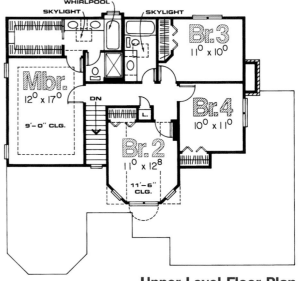

Copyright by designer/architect.

Plan #441031

Dimensions: 78'2" W x 68' D
Levels: 2
Square Footage: 4,150
Main Level Sq. Ft.: 2,572
Upper Level Sq. Ft.: 1,578
Bedrooms: 4
Bathrooms: 4½
Foundation: Crawl space;
slab or basement available for fee
Materials List Available: Yes
Price Category: I

Images provided by designer/architect.

Features:

- **Great Room:** The main level offers this commodious room, with its beamed ceiling, alcove, fireplace, and built-ins.
- **Kitchen:** Go up a few steps to the dining nook and this kitchen, and you'll find a baking center, walk-in pantry, and access to a covered side porch.

- **Formal Dining Room:** This formal room lies a few steps up from the foyer and sports a bay window and hutch space.
- **Guest Suite:** This suite, which is located at the end of the hall, features a private bathroom and walk-in closet.
- **Master Suite:** A fireplace flanked by built-ins warms this suite. Its bath contains a spa tub, compartmented toilet, and huge shower.

Graceful and gracious, this superb shingle design delights with handsome exterior elements. A whimsical turret, covered entry, upper-level balcony, and bay window all bring their charm to the facade.

CAD FILE AVAILABLE

Main Level Floor Plan

Upper Level Floor Plan

Copyright by designer/architect.

Plan #161102

Dimensions: 99'6" W x 84'2" D
Levels: 1
Square Footage: 6,659
Main Level Sq. Ft.: 3,990
Lower Level Sq. Ft: 2,669
Bedrooms: 4
Bathrooms: 4 full, 2 half
Foundation: Walkout; basement for fee
Material List Available: Yes
Price Category: K

A brick-and-stone exterior with lime-stone trim and arches decorates the exterior, while the interior explodes with design elements and large spaces to dazzle all who enter.

Features:

- Great Room: The 14-ft. ceiling height in this room is defined with columns and a fireplace wall. Triple French doors with an arched transom create the rear wall, and built-in shelving adds the perfect spot to house your big-screen TV.

- Kitchen: This spacious gourmet kitchen opens generously to the great room and allows everyone to enjoy the daily activities. A two-level island with cooktop provides casual seating and additional storage.

- Breakfast Room: This room is surrounded by windows, creating a bright and cheery place to start your day. Sliding glass doors to the covered porch in the rear add a rich look for outdoor entertaining, and the built-in fire place provides a cozy, warm atmosphere.

- Master Suite: This master bedroom suite is fit for royalty, with its stepped ceiling treatment, spacious dressing room, and private exercise room.

- Lower Level: This lower level is dedicated to fun and entertaining. A large media area, billiards room, and wet bar are central to sharing this spectacular home with your friends.

Images provided by designer/architect.

Rear Elevation

Front View

Right Side Elevation

Left Side Elevation

Copyright by designer/architect.

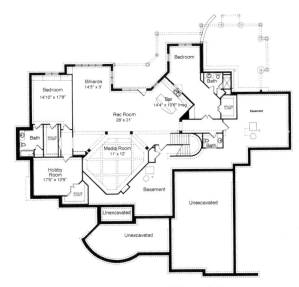

Basement Level Floor Plan

Foyer/Dining Room

Kitchen

Great Room

Porch

Plan #151032

Dimensions: 84'8" W x 48'4" D
Levels: 2
Square Footage: 2,824
Main Level Sq. Ft.: 2,279
Upper Level Sq. Ft.: 545
Bedrooms: 4
Bathrooms: 3
Foundation: Crawl space, slab;
basement option for fee
CompleteCost List Available: Yes
Price Category: F

Images provided by designer/architect.

This luxurious two-story home combines a stately exterior with a large, functional floor plan.

Features:

- **Great Room:** The spacious foyer leads directly into this room, which opens to the rear yard, providing natural light and views of the outdoors.

- **Kitchen:** This fully equipped kitchen is located to provide the utmost convenience in serving both the formal dining room and the informal breakfast area. The combination of breakfast room, hearth room, and kitchen creatively forms a comfortable family gathering place.

- **Master Suite:** Located on the main level for privacy, this private retreat has a boxed ceiling in the sleeping area. The master bath boasts a large tub, dual vanities, and a walk-in closet.

- **Upper Level:** This level is where you'll find the two secondary bedrooms. Each has ample space, and they share the full bathroom.

Upper Level Floor Plan

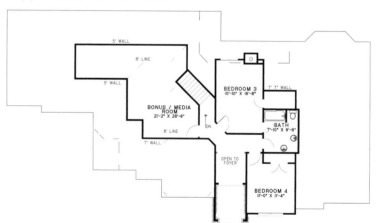

Main Level Floor Plan

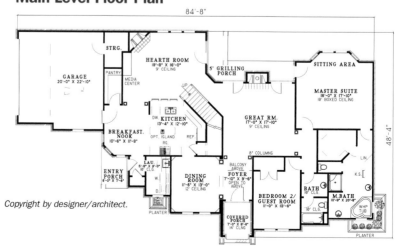

Copyright by designer/architect.

Plan #271093

Dimensions: 74' W x 52' D
Levels: 2
Square Footage: 2,813
Main Level Sq. Ft.: 1,828
Upper Level Sq. Ft.: 985
Bedrooms: 3
Bathrooms: 3
Foundation: Basement
Materials List Available: No
Price Category: F

This Craftsman-style home will be the envy of your neighbors.

Images provided by designer/architect.

Features:

- Entry: Enter the home through the covered porch and into this entry with a view into the great room.

- Great Room: This large gathering area, with two-sided fireplace, has window looking out to the backyard.

- Kitchen: This peninsula kitchen has plenty of cabinets and counter space. The garage is just a few steps away though the laundry room.

- Hearth Room: Just off the kitchen this hearth room shares the fireplace with the great room and is open into the dining room.

- Master Suite: Located upstairs, with a secondary bedroom, this suite has a sitting area, large closet, and master bath.

Great Room

Kitchen

Main Level Floor Plan

Copyright by designer/architect.

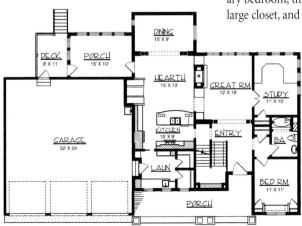

Upper Level Floor Plan

Plan #161033

Dimensions: 78'2" W x 74'6" D
Levels: 2
Square Footage: 3,809
Main Level Sq. Ft.: 2,782
Upper Level Sq. Ft.: 1,027
Optional Lower Level Sq. Ft.: 1,316
Bedrooms: 4
Bathrooms: 3½
Foundation: Basement
Materials List Available: Yes
Price Category: H

Images provided by designer/architect.

The dramatic design of this home, combined with its comfort and luxuries, suit those with discriminating tastes.

Features:

• Great Room: Let the fireplace and 14-ft. ceilings in this room set the stage for all sorts of gatherings, from casual to formal.

• Dining Room: Adjacent to the great room and kitchen fit for a gourmet, the dining room allows you to entertain with ease.

• Music Rom: Give your music the space it

desreves in this specially-designed room.

• Library: Use this room as an office, or reserve it for quiet reading and studying.

• Master Suite: You'll love the separate dressing area and walk-in closet in the bedroom.

• Lower Level: A bar and recreational area give even more space for entertaining.

Rear view

Main Level Floor Plan

Upper Level Floor Plan

Copyright by designer/architect.

Optional Lower Level Floor Plan

Plan #271069

Dimensions: 63'5" W x 51'8" D
Levels: 2
Square Footage: 2,376
Main Level Sq. Ft.: 1,248
Upper Level Sq. Ft.: 1,128
Bedrooms: 4
Bathrooms: 2½
Foundation: Crawl space, basement
Materials List Available: No
Price Category: E

Images provided by designer/architect.

This home's Federal-style facade has a simple elegance that is still popular among today's homeowners.

Features:

- Living Room: This formal space is perfect for serious conversation or thoughtful reflection. Optional double doors would open directly into the family room beyond.

- Dining Room: You won't find a more elegant room than this for hosting holiday feasts.

- Kitchen: This room has everything the cook could hope for—a central island, a handy pantry, and a menu desk. Sliding glass doors in the dinette let you step outside for some fresh air with your cup of coffee.

- Family Room: Here's the spot to spend a cold winter evening. Have hot chocolate in front of a crackling fire!

- Master Suite: With an optional vaulted ceiling, the sleeping chamber is bright and spacious. The private bath showcases a splashy whirlpool tub.

Main Level Floor Plan

Upper Level Floor Plan

Copyright by designer/architect.

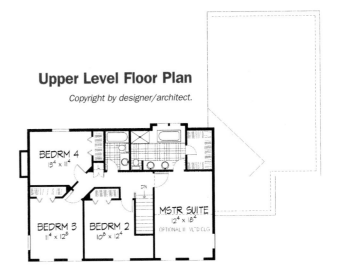

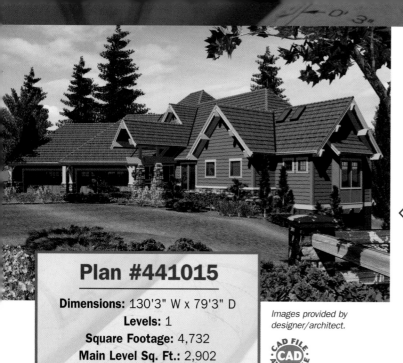

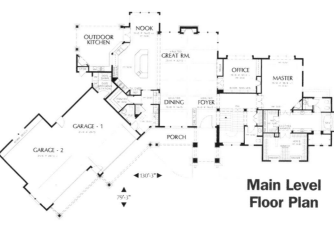

Main Level Floor Plan

Plan #441015

Dimensions: 130'3" W x 79'3" D

Levels: 1

Square Footage: 4,732

Main Level Sq. Ft.: 2,902

Lower Level Sq. Ft.: 1,830

Bedrooms: 4

Bathrooms: 3 full, 2 half

Foundation: Walkout basement

Materials List Available: Yes

Price Category: I

Images provided by designer/architect.

CAD FILE AVAILABLE

Basement Level Floor Plan

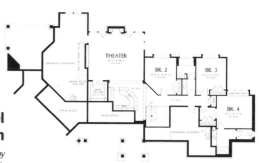

Copyright by designer/architect.

Plan #441003

Dimensions: 50' W x 48' D

Levels: 1

Square Footage: 1,580

Bedrooms: 3

Bathrooms: 2½

Foundation: Crawl space; slab or basement available for fee

Materials List Available: Yes

Price Category: C

Images provided by designer/architect.

CAD FILE AVAILABLE

Copyright by designer/architect.

Rear Elevation

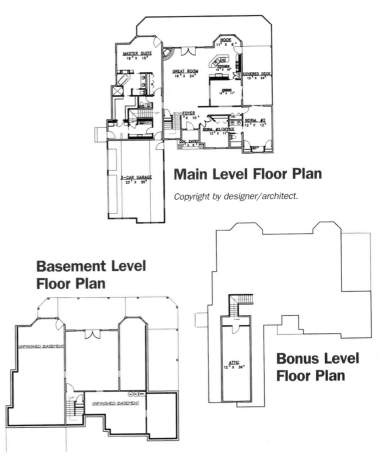

Main Level Floor Plan

Copyright by designer/architect.

Images provided by designer/architect.

CAD FILE AVAILABLE

Plan #451359

Dimensions: 70' W x 86'8" D
Levels: 2
Square Footage: 3,039
Main Level Sq. Ft.: 2,558
Upper Level Sq. Ft.: 481
Bedrooms: 3
Bathrooms: 2½
Foundation: Basement – insulated concrete form
Material List Available: No
Price Category: G

Basement Level Floor Plan

Bonus Level Floor Plan

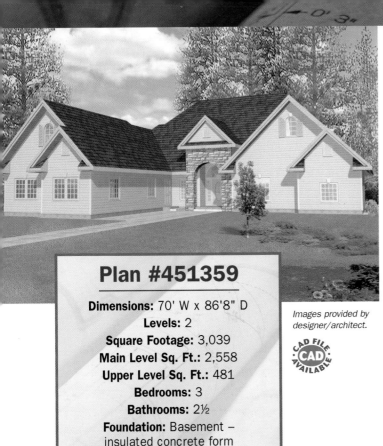

Main Level Floor Plan

Images provided by designer/architect.

CAD FILE AVAILABLE

Plan #151731

Dimensions: 55' W x 58'6" D
Levels: 1.5
Square Footage: 2,099
Bedrooms: 3
Bathrooms: 2
Foundation: Crawl space, slab
CompleteCost List Available: Yes
Price Category: D

Upper Level Floor Plan

Copyright by designer/architect

Plan #271021

Dimensions: 38'4" W x 58' D

Levels: 2

Square Footage: 1,551

Main Level Sq. Ft.: 1,099

Upper Level Sq. Ft.: 452

Bedrooms: 3

Bathrooms: 2½

Foundation: Basement

Materials List Available: Yes

Price Category: C

Images provided by designer/architect.

The exterior of this cozy country-style home boasts a charming combination of woodwork and stone that lends an air of England to the facade.

Features:

• Living Room: An arched entryway leads into the living room, with its vaulted ceiling, tall windows, and fireplace.

• Dining Room: This space also features a vaulted ceiling, plus a view of the patio.

• Master Suite: Find a vaulted ceiling here, too, as well as a walk-in closet, and private bath.

Living Room

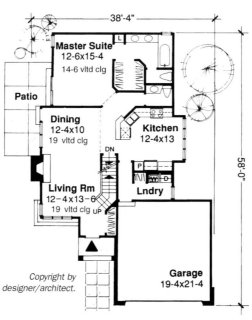

Main Level Floor Plan

Copyright by designer/architect.

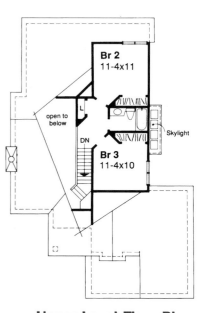

Upper Level Floor Plan

Images provided by designer/architect.

Plan #361004

Dimensions: 77' W x 81' D

Levels: 1

Square Footage: 2,191

Bedrooms: 3

Bathrooms: 2

Foundation: Crawl space or basement

Materials List Available: No

Price Category: D

If your family loves contemporary designs, this home with an open plan and unusually shaped rooms could be their dream house.

Features:

- **Great Room:** This area occupies the majority of the central hexagon.

- **Deck:** Doors from every living area, including the bedrooms, open to this wraparound deck, which surrounds the back of this home.

- **Living Room:** This area has a fireplace and sliding glass doors leading to the deck.

- **Dining Room:** Sliding glass doors and proximity to the kitchen define this dining area.

- **Kitchen:** The angled bar defines this room, where a walk-in pantry provides good storage space.

- **Master Suite:** This master wing includes a sitting room, door to the deck, window extension, walk-in closet, and luxury bath.

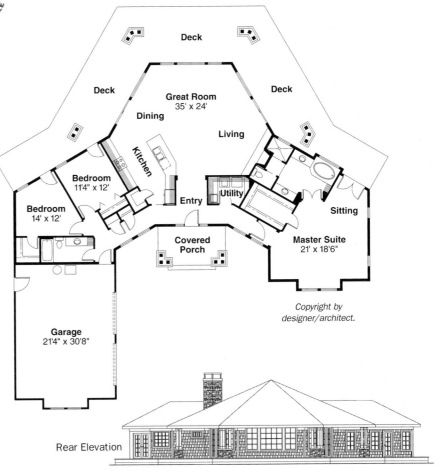

Copyright by designer/architect.

Plan #441014

Dimensions: 119'6" W x 87'6" D
Levels: 1
Square Footage: 3,940
Bedrooms: 3
Bathrooms: 3 full, 2 half
Foundation: Crawl space; slab or basement available for fee
Materials List Available: No
Price Category: H

CAD FILE AVAILABLE

Though this is but a single-story home, it satisfies and delights on many levels. The exterior has visual appeal, with varied rooflines, a mixture of materials, and graceful traditional lines.

Features:

• **Great Room:** This huge room boasts a sloped, vaulted ceiling, a fireplace, and built-ins. There is also a media room with double-door access.

• **Kitchen:** This kitchen has an island, two sink prep areas, a butler's pantry connecting it to the formal dining room, and a walk-in pantry.

• **Bedrooms:** Family bedrooms sit at the front of the plan and are joined by a Jack-and-Jill bathroom.

• **Master Suite:** This master suite is on the far right side. Its grand salon has an 11-ft.-high ceiling, a fireplace, built-ins, a walk-in closet, and a superb bathroom.

• **Garage:** If you need extra space, there's a bonus room on an upper level above the three-car garage.

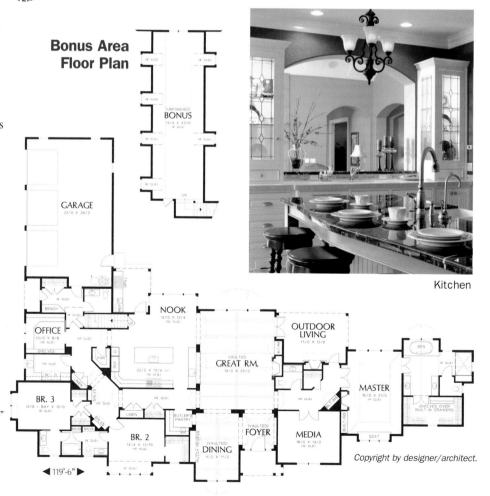

Bonus Area Floor Plan

Kitchen

Plan #151536

Dimensions: 37' W x 74'4" D
Levels: 1
Square Footage: 1,933
Bedrooms: 3
Bathrooms: 2
Foundation: Crawl space or slab
CompleteCost List Available: Yes
Price Category: D

CAD FILE AVAILABLE

The design of this home reflects the attention to detail of the Craftsman style.

Features:

• Foyer: The covered porch leads to this foyer, which separates the secondary bedrooms from the rest of the home.

• Great Room: This gathering room has eight-inch-diameter columns that add to the drama of the design. Additional amenities include a media center, a cozy fireplace, and a hidden computer center for study time or to serve as a small office.

• Kitchen: This spacious kitchen, with snack bar seating, has a wall of windows for plenty of natural light. Conveniently located just off the kitchen is a kids' play nook that helps keep the work area clutter free.

• Master Suite: A 10-ft.-high boxed ceiling, a large walk-in closet, whirlpool tub, and a separate shower, with built-in seat, make this master suite the ultimate in privacy and relaxation.

Plan #211008

Dimensions: 56' W x 93' D

Levels: 1

Square Footage: 2,259

Bedrooms: 3

Bathrooms: 2½

Foundation: Slab

Materials List Available: Yes

Price Category: E

Images provided by designer/architect.

If you're looking for a design that suits a narrow building lot, you'll love this home, with its exterior that resembles an old European cottage.

Features:

• Ceiling Height: 10-ft. except as noted.

• Courtyards: Use formal gardens full of easy-care plants to make the most of the lovely courtyards.

• Living Room: The massive glass wall in this room with 16-ft. ceilings looks out to the entry courtyard. In cool weather you'll love the fireplace, which is flanked by lovely built-ins that can hold everything from books to collectables.

• Kitchen: With a contemporary layout and up-to-date conveniences, this kitchen is as convenient as it is attractive.

• Master Suite: Relax beside the bedroom fireplace, or luxuriate in the bath, with its two walk-in closets, soaking tub, shower, two vanities, linen closet, and private room for toilet and bidet.

Copyright by designer/architect.

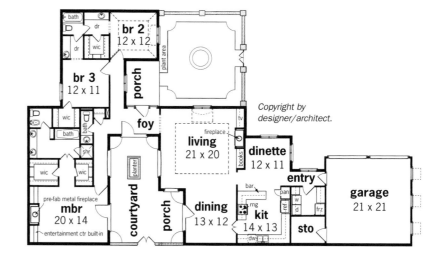

Plan #151529

Dimensions: 43' W x 66'6" D
Levels: 1
Square Footage: 1,474
Bedrooms: 2
Bathrooms: 2
Foundation: Crawl space or slab
CompleteCost List Available: Yes
Price Category: B

CAD FILE AVAILABLE

Images provided by designer/architect.

This elegant design is reflective of the Arts and Crafts era. Copper roofing and carriage style garage doors warmly welcome guests into this split-bedroom plan.

Features:

- **Great Room:** With access to the grilling porch as a bonus, this large gathering area features a 10-ft.-high ceiling and a beautiful fireplace.

- **Kitchen:** This fully equipped island kitchen has a raised bar and a built-in pantry. The area is open to the great room and dining room, giving an open and airy feeling to the home.

- **Master Suite:** Located on the opposite side of the home from the secondary bedroom, this retreat offers a large sleeping area and two large closets. The master bath features a spa tub, a separate shower, and dual vanities.

- **Bedroom:** This secondary bedroom has a large closet and access to the full bathroom in the hallway.

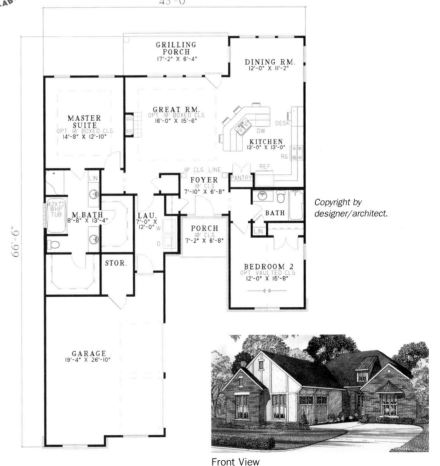

Copyright by designer/architect.

Front View

Plan #441002

Dimensions: 70' W x 51' D

Levels: 1

Square Footage: 1,873

Bedrooms: 3

Bathrooms: 2

Foundation: Crawl space

Materials List Available: Yes

Price Category: D

Images provided by designer/architect.

CAD FILE AVAILABLE

Rear Elevation

Copyright by designer/architect.

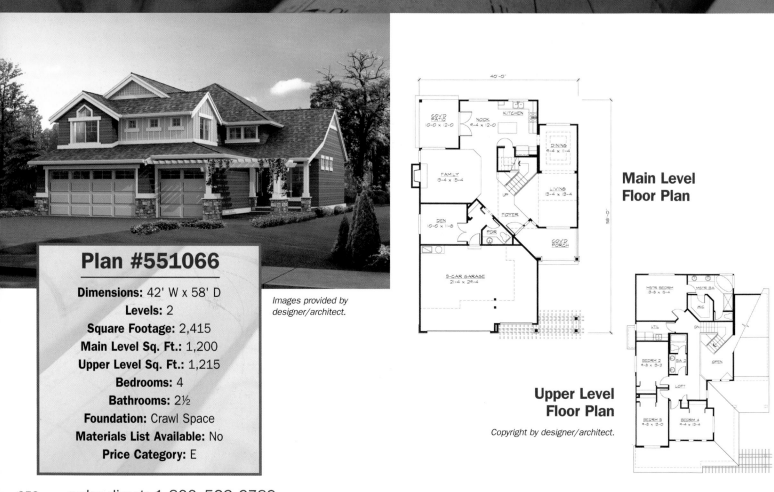

Plan #551066

Dimensions: 42' W x 58' D

Levels: 2

Square Footage: 2,415

Main Level Sq. Ft.: 1,200

Upper Level Sq. Ft.: 1,215

Bedrooms: 4

Bathrooms: 2½

Foundation: Crawl Space

Materials List Available: No

Price Category: E

Images provided by designer/architect.

Main Level Floor Plan

Upper Level Floor Plan

Copyright by designer/architect.

Plan #441005

Dimensions: 50' W x 59' D

Levels: 1

Square Footage: 1,800

Bedrooms: 3

Bathrooms: 2

Foundation: Crawl space; slab or basement for fee

Materials List Available: Yes

Price Category: D

Images provided by designer/architect.

CAD FILE AVAILABLE

Rear Elevation

Plan #121203

Dimensions: 67' W x 56' D

Levels: 1.5

Square Footage: 2,690

Main Level Sq. Ft.: 1,792

Upper Level Sq. Ft.: 898

Bedrooms: 4

Bathrooms: 2½

Foundation: Basement; crawl space or slab for fee

Materials List Available: Yes

Price Category: F

Images provided by designer/architect.

Main Level Floor Plan

Vaulted Living 15'6" x 20'4"

Owners' Suite 14' x 13'6"

Utility

Garage 23' x 21'

Up

Covered Deck 16' x 14'8"

Dining 11'8" x 15'

Kitchen

Porch

Dn

Covered Breezeway

Upper Level Floor Plan

Copyright by designer/architect.

Open to Living Below

Bedroom 13'10" x 11'4"

Dn

Recreation Room 18'4" x 15'

Dn

Bedroom 13' x 11'

Plan #361556

Dimensions: 36' W x 48' D

Levels: 2

Square Footage: 1,855

Main Level Sq. Ft.: 1,311

Upper Level Sq. Ft.: 544

Bedrooms: 3

Bathrooms: 3½

Foundation: Crawl space

Material List Available: No

Price Category: D

Images provided by designer/architect.

CAD FILE AVAILABLE CAD

Plan #641005

Dimensions: 50' W x 38' D

Levels: 2

Square Footage: 2,669

Main Level Sq. Ft.: 1,017

Upper Level Sq. Ft.: 1,652

Bedrooms: 3

Bathrooms: 2½

Foundation: Crawl space; Slab, basement or walkout for fee

Materials List Available: No

Price Category: F

Images provided by designer/architect.

CAD FILE AVAILABLE CAD

Main Level Floor Plan

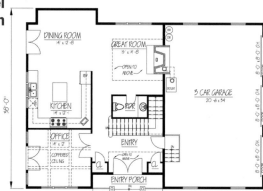

DINING ROOM 14' x 12'-8"

GREAT ROOM 15' x 14'-8"

OPEN TO ABOVE

3 CAR GARAGE 20'-6 x 34'

KITCHEN 14' x 12'

PWDR

OFFICE 14' x 12'

COFFERED CEILING

ENTRY

ENTRY PORCH

Upper Level Floor Plan

Copyright by designer/architect.

DECK

ROOF BELOW

DECK

SITTING AREA 15' x 7'-6"

MASTER BATH

OPEN TO BELOW

RAILING

BEDROOM 2 20'-6 x 13'-9"

WIC

LAUNDRY

BATH

DECK

MASTER SUITE 15' x 11'-8"

OPEN TO BELOW

PLANT SHELF BELOW

BEDROOM 3 20'-6 x 13'-9"

UPPER DECK

Plan #161224

Dimensions: 87'4" W x 57'4" D

Levels: 1

Square Footage: 2,796

Bedrooms: 2

Bathrooms: 2 1/2

Foundation: Walkout

Materials List Available: Yes

Price Category: F

Images provided by designer/architect.

Plan #441006

Dimensions: 48' W x 64' D

Levels: 1

Square Footage: 1,891

Bedrooms: 3

Bathrooms: 2

Foundation: Crawl space; slab or basement for fee

Materials List Available: Yes

Price Category: D

Images provided by designer/architect.

Rear Elevation

CAD FILE AVAILABLE

Plan #121125

Dimensions: 54' W x 58'8" D
Levels: 1
Square Footage: 1,978
Bedrooms: 3
Bathrooms: 2½
Foundation: Basement;
crawl space or slab for fee
Material List Available: Yes
Price Category: D

You'll love this plan if you are looking for a home with fantastic curb appeal outside and comfortable amenities inside.

Features:

- **Living Room:** Family and friends will love to gather in this large area, which features a 10-ft.-high ceiling.

- **Dining Room:** This formal dining area is open to the entry foyer and features a stepped ceiling. The triple-window unit, with the transom above, floods the space with natural light.

- **Kitchen:** Convenience marks this well-laid-out kitchen, where you'll love to cook for family and friends. Open to both the family room and the breakfast room, the space has an airy feeling.

- **Master Suite:** The 10-ft.-high boxed ceiling in the sleeping area makes this space feel airy. The master bath features dual vanities and a whirlpool tub.

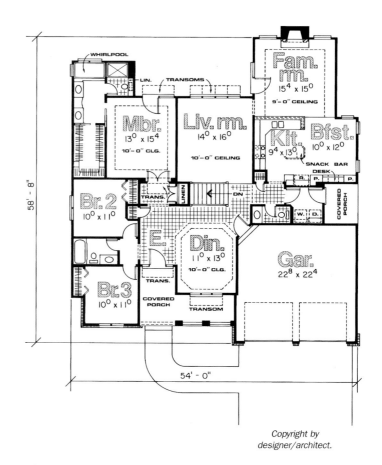

Plan #361553

Dimensions: 59' W x 44' D
Levels: 2
Square Footage: 1,990
Main Level Sq. Ft.: 734
Upper Level Sq. Ft.: 1,256
Bedrooms: 3
Bathrooms: 2½
Foundation: Crawl space
Material List Available: No
Price Category: D

Images provided by designer/architect.

This craftsman-style home blends traditional and country architecture with an interior designed for contemporary living.

Features:

- **Living Room:** Welcome guests from the shady covered porch into the foyer, hanging their coats in the hall closet and ushering them into this spacious living area. Create a quiet conversation area or a fully featured entertainment area.

- **Kitchen:** This is a kitchen in which you can get completely wrapped up. The house chef will be nearly surrounded by workspace and storage. The formal dining area is located just steps away. It is bathed in light from the numerous windows.

- **Master Suite:** Out of reach of the boisterous living area downstairs and down a small hallway of its own is this comfortable master suite. His and her sinks and a large walk-in closet simplify the morning rush.

- **Secondary Bedrooms:** Both secondary bedrooms have ample closet space and are similarly sized to quell any sibling rivalry on the subject. A large recreation room sits over the garage, ready to fulfill any need you have. Create a quiet study space or a decked-out entertainment area. There's even space for both to suit changing moods.

Copyright by designer/architect.

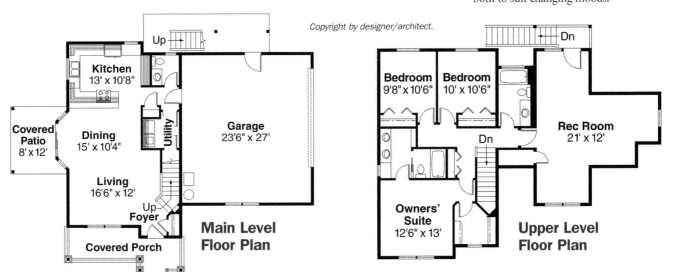

Plan #121121

Dimensions: 47'4" W x 45'8"D
Levels: 1
Square Footage: 1,341
Bedrooms: 3
Bathrooms: 2
Foundation: Basement;
crawl space for fee
Material List Available: Yes
Price Category: C

Images provided by designer/architect.

This traditional home is charming and bound to make your life simpler with all its amenities.

Features:

• Great Room: Already equipped with an entertainment center, bookcase and a fireplace by which you can enjoy those books, this room has endless possibilities. This is a room that will bring the whole family together.

• Kitchen: This design includes everything you need and everything you want: a pantry waiting to be filled with your favorite foods, plenty of workspace, and a snack bar that acts as a useful transition between kitchen and breakfast room.

• Breakfast Room: An extension of the kitchen, this room will fill with the aroma of coffee and a simmering breakfast, so you'll be immersed in your relaxing morning. With peaceful daylight streaming in through a window-lined wall, this will easily become the best part of your day.

• Master Suite: Plenty of breathing room for both of you, there will be no fighting for sink or closet space in this bedroom. The full master bath includes dual sinks, and the walk-in closet will hold everything you both need. Another perk of this bathroom is the whirlpool bathtub.

• Garage: This two-car garage opens directly into the home, so there is no reason to get out of your warm, dry car and into unpleasant weather.

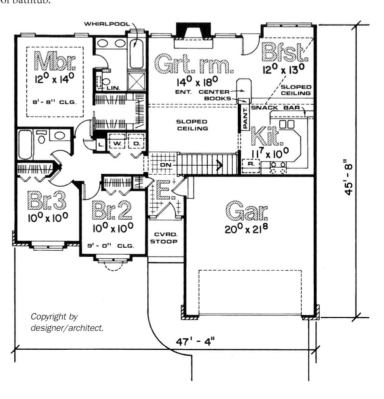

Copyright by designer/architect.

Plan #441008

Dimensions: 60' W x 50' D
Levels: 1
Square Footage: 2,001
Bedrooms: 3
Bathrooms: 2
Foundation: Crawl space;
slab or basement available for fee
Materials List Available: Yes
Price Category: D

Images provided by designer/architect.

A fine design for a country setting, this one-story plan offers a quaint covered porch at the entry, cedar shingles in the gables, and stonework at the foundation line.

Features:

- Entry: The pretty package on the outside is prelude to the fine floor plan on the inside. It begins at this entry foyer, which opens on the right to a den with a 9-ft.-high ceiling and space for a desk or closet.

- Great Room: This entertaining area is vaulted and contains a fireplace and optional media center. The rear windows allow a view onto the rear deck.

- Kitchen: Open to the dining room and great room to form one large space, this kitchen boasts a raised bar and a built-in desk.

- Master Suite: The vaulted ceiling in this master suite adds an elegant touch. The master bath features a dual vanities and a spa tub.

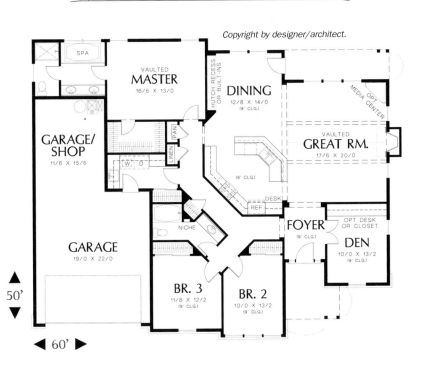

Rear Elevation

Copyright by designer/architect.

Plan #121032

Dimensions: 54' W x 45'4" D
Levels: 2
Square Footage: 2,339
Main Level Sq. Ft.: 1,665
Upper Level Sq. Ft.: 674
Bedrooms: 4
Bathrooms: 2½
Foundation: Basement
Materials List Available: Yes
Price Category: E

This home is designed for gracious living and is distinguished by many architectural details.

Features:

- Ceiling Height: 8 ft. unless otherwise noted.
- Foyer: This is truly a grand foyer with a dramatic ceiling that soars to 18 ft.
- Great Room: The foyer's 18-ft. ceiling extends into the great room where an open staircase adds architectural windows. Warm yourself by the fireplace that is framed by windows.
- Kitchen: An island is the centerpiece of this handsome and efficient kitchen that features a breakfast area for informal family meals. The room also includes a handy desk.
- Private Wing: The master suite and study are in a private wing of the house.
- Room to Expand: In addition to the three bedrooms, the second level has an unfinished storage space that can become another bedroom or office.

Main Level Floor Plan

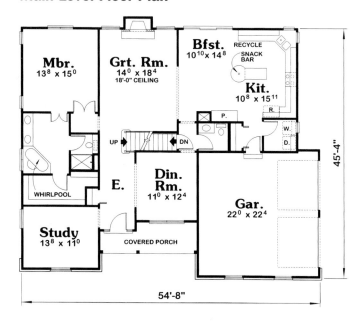

Upper Level Floor Plan

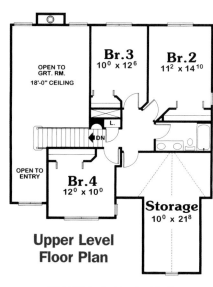

Plan #441049

Dimensions: 50' W x 47'6" D
Levels: 2
Square Footage: 2,124
Main Level Sq. Ft.: 1,157
Upper Level Sq. Ft.: 967
Bedrooms: 3
Bathrooms: 2½
Foundation: Crawl space; slab or basement for fee
Materials List Available: Yes
Price Category: D

Images provided by designer/architect.

Take a quaint cottage design, and expand naturally with a second-floor addition over the garage-the result is a comfortable home with all the charm of bungalow style.

Features:

• Foyer: Enter the home through the covered entry porch, with Arts and Crafts columns, into this foyer brightened by sidelights and a transom at the front door. The half-bathroom and coat closet make the entry area convenient.

• Great Room: This gathering area features a vaulted ceiling and a fireplace. Tall windows allow the room to be flooded with natural light, giving a warm and airy feeling.

• Kitchen: This island kitchen boasts long counters lined with cabinetry, making it a gourmet's delight to prepare meals in the area. The raised bar is open to the great room and dining room.

• Upper Level: This upper level is devoted to sleeping space. There is the vaulted master salon with private master bath and walk-in closet, plus the two family bedrooms, which that share the other full bathroom. Note the large linen closet in the upper-level hall.

Rear Elevation

Main Level Floor Plan

Upper Level Floor Plan

Copyright by designer/architect.

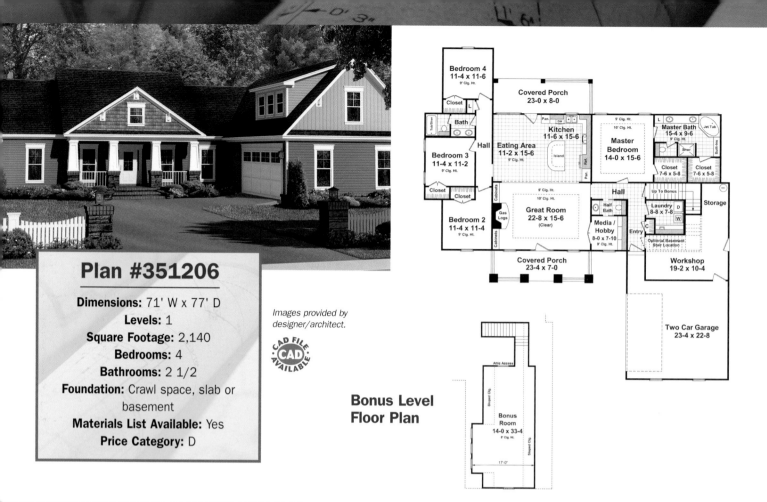

Plan #351206

Dimensions: 71' W x 77' D

Levels: 1

Square Footage: 2,140

Bedrooms: 4

Bathrooms: 2 1/2

Foundation: Crawl space, slab or basement

Materials List Available: Yes

Price Category: D

Images provided by designer/architect.

CAD FILE AVAILABLE

Bonus Level Floor Plan

Plan #461074

Dimensions: 40'6" W x 72'6" D

Levels: 2

Square Footage: 2,187

Main Level Sq. Ft.: 1,479

Upper Level Sq. Ft: 708

Bedrooms: 3

Bathrooms: 2½

Foundation: Slab; crawl space or basement for fee

Materials List Available: No

Price Category: D

Images provided by designer/architect.

Copyright by designer/architect.

Upper Level Floor Plan

Main Level Floor Plan

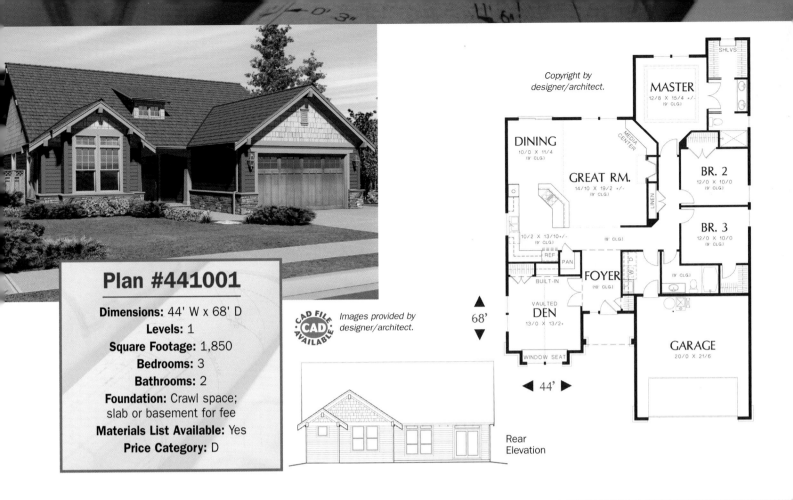

Plan #441001

Dimensions: 44' W x 68' D

Levels: 1

Square Footage: 1,850

Bedrooms: 3

Bathrooms: 2

Foundation: Crawl space; slab or basement for fee

Materials List Available: Yes

Price Category: D

Images provided by designer/architect.

CAD FILE AVAILABLE

Copyright by designer/architect.

Rear Elevation

MASTER 12/8 X 15/4 +/- (9' CLG.)

SHLVS

DINING 10/0 X 11/4 (9' CLG.)

MEDIA CENTER

GREAT RM. 14/10 X 19/2 +/- (9' CLG.)

LINEN

BR. 2 12/0 X 10/0 (9' CLG.)

BR. 3 12/0 X 10/0 (9' CLG.)

10/2 X 13/10 +/- (9' CLG.)

(9' CLG.)

REF PAN

BUILT-IN

FOYER (10' CLG.)

W D

(9' CLG.)

VAULTED DEN 13/0 X 13/2+/-

WINDOW SEAT

GARAGE 20/0 X 21/6

68'

44'

Plan #151530

Dimensions: 38'10" W x 70'4" D

Levels: 2

Square Footage: 2,146

Main Level Sq. Ft.: 1,654

Upper Level Sq. Ft.: 492

Bedrooms: 3

Bathrooms: 2½

Foundation: Crawl space or slab

CompleteCost List Available: Yes

Price Category: D

Images provided by designer/architect.

CAD FILE AVAILABLE

38' 10"

GARAGE 21'-0" X 22'-0"

M.BATH 16'-0" X 12'-0"

W.I.C.

LAU

MASTER SUITE 16'-0" X 12'-2"

BREAKFAST ROOM 12'-4" X 12'-0"

GRILLING PORCH 8'-0" X 20'-0"

COURT YARD PATIO

KITCHEN 11'-3" X 12'-0"

DINING 11'-8" X 14'-0"

FOYER 7'-6" X 12'-3"

GREAT ROOM 17'-0" X 18'-0"

COVERED PORCH 22'-0" X 8'-0"

70' 4"

Main Level Floor Plan

Upper Level Floor Plan

Copyright by designer/architect.

FUTURE BONUS SPACE

BEDROOM 2 12'-0" X 14'-4"

BEDROOM 3 11'-3" X 12'-0"

BATH

Front View

Custom Flooring

Floors are rarely the focal point of a room. However, this need not be the case. Flooring can steal the show. One way is to design your own custom floor. Many flooring materials lend themselves to customization. Another approach is to enhance an otherwise plain floor with decorative accents, such as medallions and borders. You can design your own or buy them ready-made. Painted designs on floor cloths, carpet, or wood can also grab attention. Even concrete and stone flooring can be etched or sandblasted with the textures, patterns, or images you desire.

design ideas for CREATIVE HOMEOWNER®

Flooring

| products | | inspiration | | materials |

Joseph R. Provey

The following article was reprinted from *Design Ideas for Flooring* (Creative Homeowner 2006).

This painted compass, opposite, looks like an inlay of marble, wood, and metal. The artist muted the wood grain and coloring of the surrounding floor to heighten the contrast.

This detail shows an elaborate border, right, based upon a classic pattern popular in the Victorian era. Composed of pieces of veneer glued to solid tongue-and-groove planks, it is available by the foot.

For a more contemporary feeling, a border (bottom left) is fashioned by alternating light and dark segments of solid-wood planking.

Ready-made borders, bottom middle, are available for vinyl flooring that's made to look like wood.

Borders, bottom right, can also be very simple. In this sunroom, two tones of wood plank are used to create a

Borders

Borders are another way to bring attention to your floors. They work in much the same way as a frame around a picture. Use them with just about any kind of flooring, including wood, stone, ceramic, vinyl, cork, and linoleum. Opt for ready-made patterns that range from floral to geometric designs, or compose your own. Border modules include straight sections and 90-degree turns for corners. Wood borders are available prefinished or unfinished, so you can match the stain and finish to your site-finished floor. When selecting borders, keep scale in mind. A wide, elaborate border may overpower a small room. If you are going to fill the room with furniture, you may be wise to skip the borders because you won't see much of them and they are costly—$10 to $70 per lineal foot (before installation), depending on design complexity. Save them for a large space or entry.

Medallions and Accents

Medallions make dramatic focal points, best suited to large floor areas where they can be seen. They are typically round or oval, but they're also available in octagonals, stars, and squares. They are created from exotic woods, marble, granite, limestone, onyx, and ceramics. Brass or aluminum inlay can be used to set off the shapes. Sizes usually range from 2 to 6 feet in diameter.

Wood medallions can be set into either solid or engineered wood floors. Computerized cutting machines make a wide variety of designs possible. Even small wood medallions can cost over $1,000. Check with the manufacturer about how the medallion finish will wear in traffic before you install one in your foyer.

Stone medallions are best suited to stone and ceramic floors. They typically come preassembled on mesh backings, allowing the joints to be grouted on site. Water jet technology, where water and an abrasive are shot through small nozzles at high pressure to create the desired cuts, have made such works of art more economically feasible—but they are still expensive. A 30-inch-diameter marble-and-granite medallion, for example, can easily cost $2,000. Labor to install it will add to the cost. Medallions can be created with other materials as well, including ceramic and glass tile or linoleum.

Decorative accents are a more subtle way to bring attention to your floors. They are smaller, often only a few inches square, and usually used in repetitive patterns. Otherwise, they are made using the same methods as medallions.

Most stone medallions are custom-made—not stock items—so home-owners can select materials that coordinate with their floor, left.

Variations, left, on compass and rose motifs are popular for medallions in both stone and wood.

This wood medallion, bottom left, was site-finished to match the finish on the rest of the room's flooring.

Decorative wood accents, below top, are available in stock patterns, including this rose motif.

Decorative accents, below center, such as this one, are fabricated using water-jet technology.

Etched slate tiles, bottom right, are available in a variety of patterns and sizes. Custom designs are also an option.

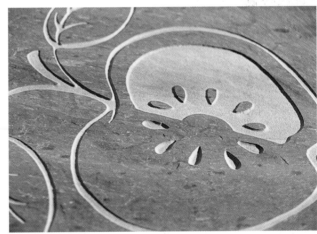

Mosaics

Mosaic floors are composed of small pieces of colored stone, glass, tile, and other materials. They may be used to create interesting textures, patterns, or pictures. An ancient craft first popularized by the Greeks using pebbles and later by Romans using small tiles, mosaic floors often have a classical look. They can, however, be used in traditional, eclectic, and contemporary decorating schemes as well. Mosaics can be used to create borders, inlay strips (between larger field tiles), inserts (to replace larger tiles), and medallions. Pictorial subjects may include historical reproductions and a vast array of floral, animal, and celestial motifs. Mosaic tiles are sold individually or in preassembled motifs; set them with either mortar or adhesive. Some manufacturers allow you to design your own pattern, tile by tile. Then they ship it to you preassembled on a mesh backing or held together with a paper top sheet.

Versatile ceramic mosaics, left, can be used to create free-form patterns, as in this contemporary bath.

Patterns, inset, can be generated with computer design software and then pre-assembled in sections for easier installation.

The mosaics in this shower, opposite, have a baked-on finish that makes them resistant to lime deposits, dirt, and mold.

Pictorial mosaics, opposite, make interesting decorative accents in floors, especially when they are placed along a border.

Translucent glass mosaics sparkle against the opaque matte-finished field tiles in this foyer floor, left.

Traditional white hexagonal mosaics, with borders and accents, above, evoke the turn of the last century in this kitchen.

Inexpensive accents in stone and ceramic, below, transform a plain tile floor.

Plan #161060

Dimensions: 113'10" W x 60'6" D
Levels: 2
Square Footage: 5,143
Main Level Sq. Ft.: 3,323
Upper Level Sq. Ft.: 1,820
Bedrooms: 4
Bathrooms: 3½
Foundation: Basement,
walkout basement
Materials List Available: No
Price Category: J

Luxury, comfort, beauty, spaciousness—
this home has everything you've been wanting,
including space for every possible activity.

Features:

• Courtyard: Enjoy the privacy here before
entering this spacious home.

• Great Room: Open to the foyer, dining area,
and kitchen, this great room has a fireplace
flanked by windows and leads to the open
rear deck.

• Dining Room: Situated between the foyer
and the kitchen, this room is ideal for formal
dining.

• Library: Located just off the foyer, this
library offers a calm retreat from activities in
the great room.

• Utility Area: The mudroom, pantry, half-bath
and laundry room add up to household
convenience.

• Master Suite: You'll love the huge walk-in
closet, extensive window feature, and bath
with a dressing room and two vanities.

Left Side Elevation

Stairs

Rear Elevation

Right Side Elevation

Dining Room

Media Room

Main Level Floor Plan

Master Bedroom
17'8" X 17'

Dressing

Hakk

Library
14' X 16'4"

Great Room
17'9" x 29'4"

Deck

Kitchen
16'9" x 19'6"

Dining

Laun.

Pantry

Three Car Garage
23'6" x 37'2"

Mud Room

Bath

Foyer
17'9" x 11'4"

Dining Room
14' x 16'4"

Court Yard

CUSTOM CABINETS

DRAWER BASE

Great Room

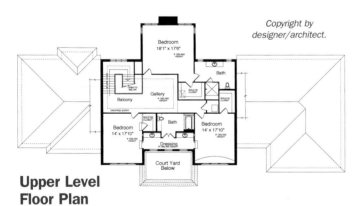

Copyright by designer/architect.

Upper Level Floor Plan

Bedroom
18'1" x 17'6"

Bath

Balcony

Gallery

Walk-in Closet

Bedroom
14' x 17'10"

Bath

Bedroom
14' x 17'10"

Dressing

Court Yard Below

OPEN TO BELOW

DROPPED SOFFIT

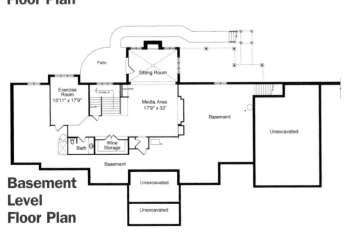

Kitchen

Basement Level Floor Plan

Patio

Sitting Room

Exercise Room
13'11" x 17'9"

Media Area
17'9" x 32'

Basement

STAIRS UP

COUNTER

Bath

Wine Storage

Basement

Unexcavated

Unexcavated

Unexcavated

Plan #121064

Dimensions: 44' W x 40' D
Levels: 2
Square Footage: 1,846
Main Level Sq. Ft.: 919
Upper Level Sq. Ft.: 927
Bedrooms: 4
Bathrooms: 2½
Foundation: Basement
Materials List Available: Yes
Price Category: D

You'll love the features and design in this compact but amenity-filled home.

Features:

- **Entry:** A balcony overlooks this two-story entry, where a plant shelf tops the coat closet.
- **Great Room:** A trio of tall windows points up the large dimensions of this room, which is sure to be the hub of your home. Arrange the furniture to create a cozy space around the fireplace, or leave it open to the room.
- **Kitchen:** You'll love to work in this well-designed kitchen area.
- **Master Suite:** On the second floor, this master suite features a tiered ceiling and two walk-in closets. In the bath, you'll find a double vanity, whirlpool tub, and separate shower.

Main Level Floor Plan

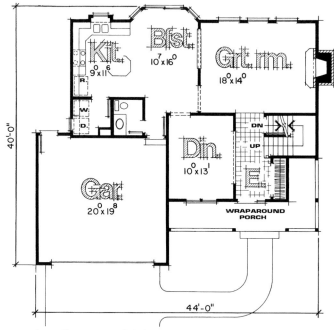

Upper Level Floor Plan

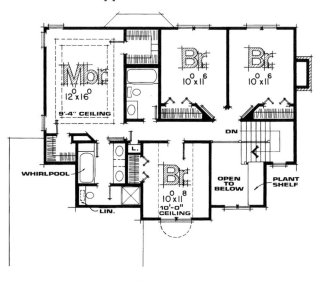

Plan #351002

Dimensions: 64' W x 45'10" D
Levels: 1
Square Footage: 1,751
Bedrooms: 3
Bathrooms: 2
Foundation: Crawl space, slab, or basement
Materials List Available: Yes
Price Category: D

Images provided by designer/architect.

This is a beautiful classic traditional home with a European touch.

Features:

- **Great Room:** This gathering area has a gas log fireplace that is flanked by two built-in cabinets. The area has a 10-ft.-tall tray ceiling.

- **Kitchen:** This L-shaped island kitchen has a raised bar and is open to the eating area and great room. The three open spaces work together as one large room.

- **Master Suite:** Located on the opposite side of the home from the secondary bedrooms, this suite has a vaulted ceiling. The master bath has dual vanities and a garden tub.

- **Bedrooms:** The two secondary bedrooms share a hall bathroom and have ample closet space.

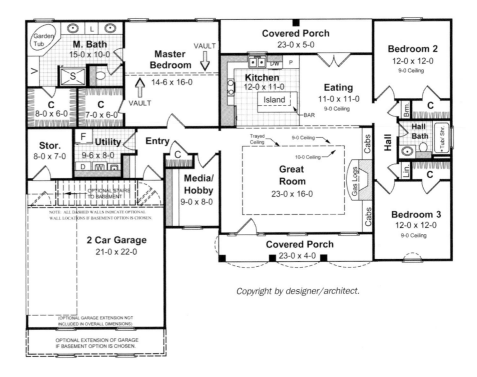

Copyright by designer/architect.

Plan #131003

Dimensions: 60' W x 39'10" D
Levels: 1
Square Footage: 1,466
Bedrooms: 3
Bathrooms: 2
Foundation: Crawl space or slab; basement for fee
Materials List Available: Yes
Price Category: C

Victorian styling adds elegance to this compact and easy-to-maintain ranch design.

This home, as shown in the photograph, may differ from the actual blueprints. For more detailed information, please check the floor plans carefully.

Images provided by designer/archite

Features:

- Ceiling Height: 8 ft.

- Foyer: Bridging between the front door and the great room, this foyer is a surprise feature.

- Great Room: A 10-ft. ceiling adds to the spacious feeling of this room, while the corner fireplace gives it an intimate feeling. Sliding glass doors at the rear of the room open to the backyard.

- Dining Room: This formal room adjoins the great room, allowing guests and family to flow between the rooms.

- Breakfast Room: Turrets add a Victorian feeling to this room that's just off the kitchen and overlooks the front porch.

- Master Suite: Privacy is assured in this suite, which is separated from the main part of the house. A separate toilet room and large walk-in closet add convenience to its beauty.

Copyright by designer/architect.

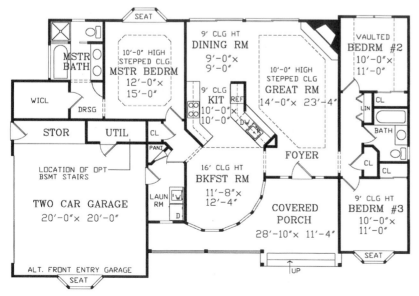

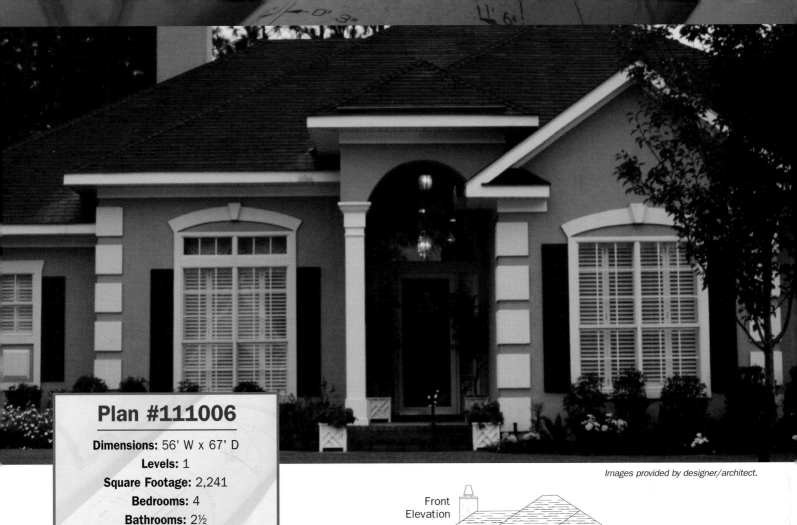

Plan #111006

Dimensions: 56' W x 67' D
Levels: 1
Square Footage: 2,241
Bedrooms: 4
Bathrooms: 2½
Foundation: Slab
Materials List Available: No
Price Category: F

You'll love this plan if you're looking for a home with fantastic curb appeal on the outside and comfortable amenities on the inside.

Features:

- **Foyer:** This lovely foyer opens to both the living and dining rooms.

- **Dining Room:** Three columns in this room accentuate both its large dimensions and its slightly formal air.

- **Living Room:** This room gives an airy feeling, and the fireplace here makes it especially inviting when the weather's cool.

- **Kitchen:** This G-shaped kitchen is designed to save steps while you're working, and the ample counter area adds even more to its convenience. The breakfast bar is a great gathering area.

- **Master Suite:** Two walk-in closets provide storage space, and the bath includes separate vanities, a standing shower, and a deluxe corner bathtub.

Front Elevation

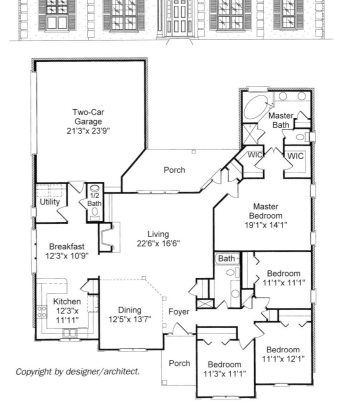

Copyright by designer/architect.

Plan #161041

Dimensions: 63'4" W x 48' D
Levels: 2
Square Footage: 2,738
Main Level Sq. Ft.: 1,915
Upper Level Sq. Ft.: 823
Bedrooms: 4
Bathrooms: 3½
Foundation: Basement
Materials List Available: Yes
Price Category: F

Images provided by designer/architect.

This two-level European country home is perfect for a large family, and makes entertaining a pleasure.

Features:

- **Great Room:** From the foyer, view the dramatic great room with its high windows and fireplace. Open stairs with rich wood trim lead to the second floor. The balcony on the second floor draws the eye up to the vaulted ceiling and also gives an exciting bird's eye view for those looking down. You can enter the formal dining room from either the great room or the kitchen.

- **Breakfast Room/Hearth Room:** Appreciate these rooms as two cozy nooks or as one large space for entertaining.

- **Master Bedroom:** The master bedroom encourages pampering in its private sitting room with an 11-ft. ceiling and garden bath.

- **Additional bedrooms:** You'll find a bedroom with a private bath, and two others that share a bath on the second floor.

- **Basement and Garage:** A full basement and two-car garage add extra storage capabilities to this family-friendly home.

Rear Elevation

Upper Level Floor Plan

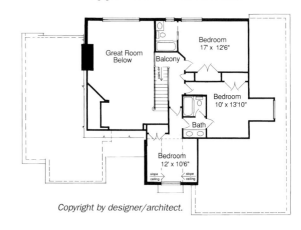

Main Level Floor Plan

Copyright by designer/architect.

Plan #121018

Dimensions: 95'9" W x 70'2" D
Levels: 2
Square Footage: 3,950
Main Level Sq. Ft: 2,839
Upper Level Sq. Ft. : 1,111
Bedrooms: 4
Bathrooms: 2 full, 2 half
Foundation: Basement
Material List Available: Yes
Price Category: H

Images provided by designer/architect.

A spectacular two-story entry with a floating curved staircase welcomes you home.

Features:

• Ceiling Height: 8 ft. except as noted.

• Den: To the left of the entry, French doors lead to a spacious and stylish den featuring a spider-beamed ceiling.

• Living Room: The volume ceiling, transom windows, and large fireplace evoke a gracious traditional style.

• Gathering Rooms: There is plenty of space for large-group entertaining in the gathering rooms that also feature fireplaces and transom windows.

• Master Suite: Here is the height of luxurious living. The suite features an oversized walk-in closet, tiered ceilings, and a sitting room with fireplace. THe pampering bath has a corner whirlpool and shower.

Garage: An angle minimizes the appearance of the four-car garage.

Main Level Floor Plan

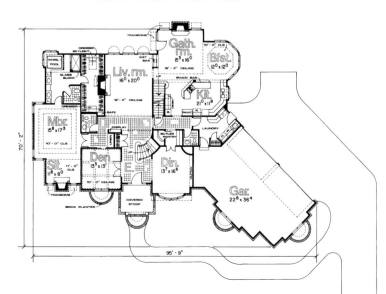

Upper Level Floor Plan

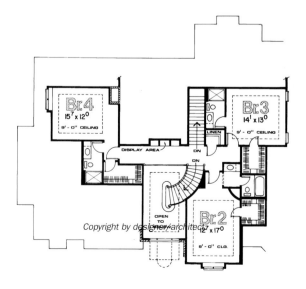

Images provided by designer/architect.

Plan #291014

Dimensions: 102' W x 54' D
Levels: 2
Square Footage: 4,372
Main Level Sq. Ft.: 3,182
Upper Level Sq. Ft.: 1,190
Bedrooms: 3
Bathrooms: 3 full, 2 half
Foundation: Basement
Materials List Available: No
Price Category: I

Cottage-like architectural details and an abundance of windows add warmth and personality to this generously designed home.

Features:

- **Entry:** Welcome family and friends from a shaded porch into this grand foyer. A curving stairway ahead and a vaulted library to the left make an elegant impression.

- **Kitchen:** The heart of any home, this kitchen will be the center of all your entertaining. Plenty of workspace, a nearby pantry, and an island complete with cooktop will appease chefs of any skill level. The kitchen's proximity to the dining room, the living room, and the sunlit morning room, as well as to a small back porch, creates a simple transition for any kind of dining.

- **Master Suite:** This area is a sybaritic retreat where you can shut out the frenzied world and simply relax. The attached master bath includes dual walk-in closets, his and her sinks, a standing shower, and a separate tub-perfect for busy mornings and romantic evenings.

- **Second Floor:** Great for guests or growing siblings, both secondary bedrooms have ample closet space and private bathrooms. A bonus room over the three-car garage and laundry area can fulfill whatever need you have. Create a quiet study environment or a fully featured entertainment area.

Main Level Floor Plan

Copyright by designer/architect.

Upper Level Floor Plan

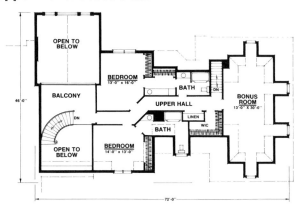

Plan #221054

Dimensions: 63'8" W x 75'4" D
Levels: 2
Square Footage: 3,206
Main Level Sq. Ft.: 2,064
Upper Level Sq. Ft.: 1,142
Bedrooms: 4
Bathrooms: 3½
Foundation: Basement
Materials List Available: No
Price Category: G

The large turret of this European beauty is sure to capture your attention as you enter the two-story home.

Features:

- **Great Room:** This room features a two-story ceiling, a wall of windows, and a see-through fireplace to the master suite.

- **Kitchen:** This kitchen, with its eat-in island overlooking the dining room and hearth room, works together with those two rooms to create a comfortable living area.

- **Master Suite:** You'll be impressed by the large walk-in closet of this suite, which opens directly to a main floor laundry room, as well as the spacious master bath.

- **Bedrooms:** Upstairs you can look over the railing into the great room below as you proceed to one of the three additional bedrooms. Bedroom 4 has its own full bathroom, while the remaining two share a Jack and Jill bathroom.

CAD FILE AVAILABLE

Images provided by designer/architect.

Upper Level Floor Plan

Copyright by designer/architect.

BR. #2
9'-1 1/8" CEILING
14'4"x13'4"

OPEN TO BELOW

BR. #3
9'-1 1/8" CEILING
14'8"x15'0"

OPEN TO BELOW

BR. #4
9'-1 1/8" CEILING
12'8"x13'0"

SEAT

Rear Elevation

Main Level Floor Plan

CVRD. PORCH
13'0"x14'0"

DIN.
10'-1 1/8" CEILING
13'2"x11'4"

GRT. RM.
2 STORY CEILING
16'8"x15'6"

MBR.
10'-1 1/8" CEILING
16'0"x15'8"

SEE THROUGH FIREPLACE

HRTH. RM.
10'-1 1/8" CEILING
10'4"x15'2"

KIT.
10'-1 1/8" CEILING
12'6"x12'0"

E.
2 STORY CEILING

PAN.

3 CAR GARAGE
23'4"x37'4"

63'-8"

75'-4"

Plan #161029

Dimensions: 87' W x 82' D

Levels: 2

Square Footage: 4,470

Main Level Sq. Ft.: 3,300

Upper Level Sq. Ft.: 1,170

Bedrooms: 4

Bathrooms: 3 full, 2 half

Foundation: Basement

Materials List Available: Yes

Price Category: I

Images provided by designer/architect.

This gracious home is so impressive — inside and out — that it suits the most discriminating tastes.

Features:

- **Foyer:** A balcony overlooks this gracious area decorated by tall columns.

- **Hearth Room:** Visually open to the kitchen and the breakfast area, this room is ideal for any sort of gathering.

- **Great Room:** Colonial columns also form the entry here, and a magnificent window treatment that includes French doors leads to the terrace.

- **Library:** Built-in shelving adds practicality to this quiet retreat.

- **Kitchen:** Spread out on the oversized island with a cooktop and seating.

- **Additional Bedrooms:** Walk-in closets and private access to a bath define each bedroom.

Main Level Floor Plan

Upper Level Floor Plan

Copyright by designer/architect.

Rear View

Living Room

Living Room/Kitchen

Ideas for Entertaining

Whether an everyday family meal or a big party for 50, make it memorable and fun. With a world of options, it's easier than you think. Be imaginative with food and decoration. Although it is true that great hamburgers and hot dogs will taste good even if served on plain white paper plates, make the meal more fun by following a theme of some sort — color, occasion, or seasonal activity, for example. Be inventive with the basic elements as well as the extraneous touches, such as flowers and lighting. Here are some examples to get you started.

- For an all-American barbecue, set a picnic table with a patchwork quilt having red, white, and blue in it. Use similar colors for the napkins, and perhaps even bandannas. Include a star-studded centerpiece.

- Make a children-size dining set using an old door propped up on crates, and surround it with appropriate-size benches or chairs. Cover the table with brightly colored, easy-to-clean waxed or vinyl-covered fabric.

- If you're planning an elegant dinner party, move your dining room table outside and set it with your best linens, china, silver, and crystal. Add romantic lighting with candles in fabulous candelabras, and set a beautiful but small floral arrangement at each place setting.

- Design a centerpiece showcasing the flowers from your garden. Begin the arrangement with a base of purchased flowers, and fill in with some of your homegrown blooms. That way your flower beds will still be full of blossoms when the guests arrive.

- Base your party theme on the vegetables growing in your yard, and let them be the inspiration for the menu. When your zucchini plants are flowering, wow your family or guests by serving steamed squash blossoms. Or if the vegetables are starting to develop, lightly grill them with other young veggies — they have a much more delicate flavor than mature vegetables do.

- During berry season, host an elegant berry brunch. Serve mixed-berry crepes on your prettiest plates.

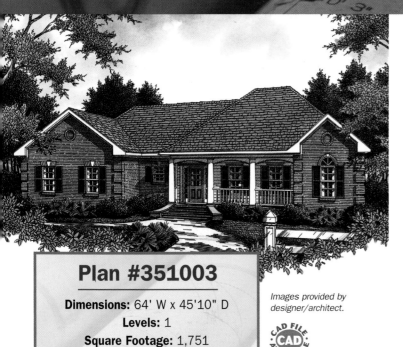

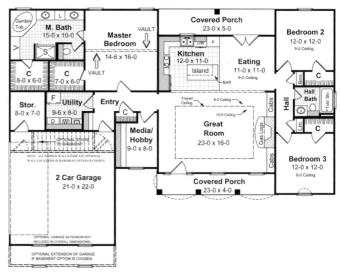

Images provided by
designer/architect.

*Copyright by
designer/architect.*

Plan #351003

Dimensions: 64' W x 45'10" D

Levels: 1

Square Footage: 1,751

Bedrooms: 3

Bathrooms: 2

Foundation: Crawl space, slab,
or basement

Materials List Available: Yes

Price Category: D

CAD FILE AVAILABLE • CAD

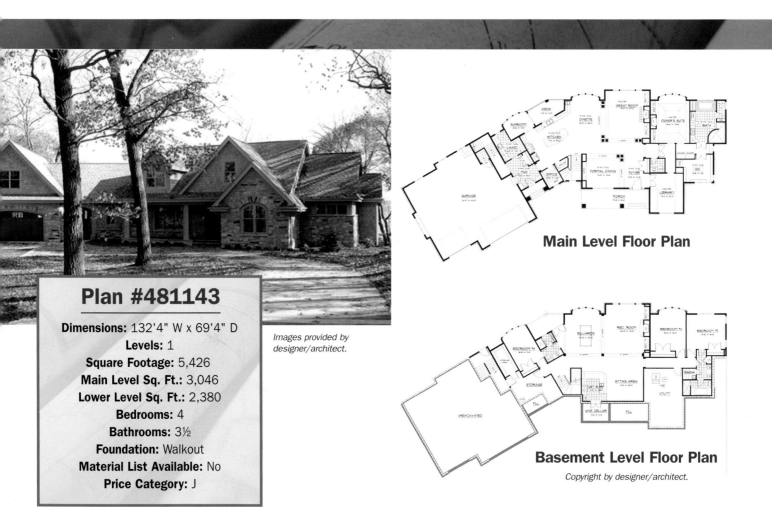

Main Level Floor Plan

Basement Level Floor Plan

Copyright by designer/architect.

Plan #481143

Dimensions: 132'4" W x 69'4" D

Levels: 1

Square Footage: 5,426

Main Level Sq. Ft.: 3,046

Lower Level Sq. Ft.: 2,380

Bedrooms: 4

Bathrooms: 3½

Foundation: Walkout

Material List Available: No

Price Category: J

Images provided by
designer/architect.

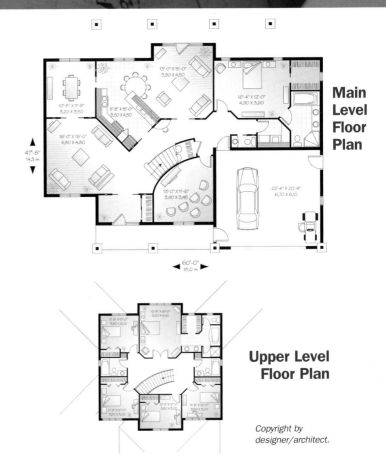

Main Level Floor Plan

Plan #181079

Dimensions: 60' W x 47'8" D

Levels: 2

Square Footage: 3,016

Main Level Sq. Ft.: 1,716

Upper Level Sq. Ft.: 1,300

Bedrooms: 6

Bathrooms: 4½

Foundation: Crawl space

Material List Available: Yes

Price Category: G

Images provided by designer/architect.

CAD FILE AVAILABLE

Upper Level Floor Plan

Copyright by designer/architect.

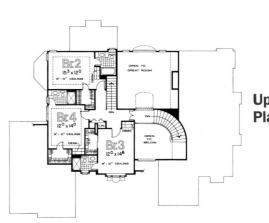

Upper Level Floor Plan

Lower Level Floor Plan

Copyright by designer/architect.

Plan #121081

Dimensions: 76'8" W x 68' D

Levels: 1.5

Square Footage: 3,623

Main Level Sq. Ft.: 2,603

Upper Level Sq. Ft.: 1,020

Bedrooms: 4

Bathrooms: 4 full, 1 half

Foundation: Basement

Material List Available: Yes

Price Category: G

Images provided by designer/architect.

Plan #181224

Dimensions: 36' W x 39'8" D

Levels: 2

Square Footage: 1,727

Main Level Sq. Ft.: 837

Upper Level Sq. Ft.: 890

Bedrooms: 3

Bathrooms: 2

Foundation: Basement

Material List Available: Yes

Price Category: E

CAD FILE AVAILABLE

This elegant home occupies a small footprint.

Images provided by designer/architect.

Features:

- Living Room: This two-story gathering place features a cozy fireplace and tall windows, which flood the room with natural light.

- Kitchen: This island kitchen has plenty of cabinet and counter space. It is open to the breakfast room.

- Upper Level: On this level you will find a balcony that overlooks the living room. Also, there are three bedrooms and a large bathroom.

- Garage: This one-car garage has room for a car plus some storage area.

Kitchen

Main Level Floor Plan

Copyright by designer/architect.

Upper Level Floor Plan

Plan #351086

Dimensions: 82'6" W x 65' D
Levels: 1
Square Footage: 2,201
Bedrooms: 3
Bathrooms: 2½
Foundation: Crawl space or slab
Material List Available: Yes
Price Category: E

Images provided by designer/architect.

This stunning European country home is designed with the contemporary family in mind.

CAD FILE AVAILABLE

Features:

- **Porches:** Beautiful brick arches welcome guests into your covered front porch, indicating the warmth and hospitality within the home. A screened back porch, accessible from the dining area, is ideal for enjoying meals in the fresh air.

- **Great Room:** Three entrances from the covered porch, elegant archways into the kitchen and dining area, raised ceilings, a fireplace, and built-in cabinets combine to make this an ideal space for entertaining.

- **Kitchen:** The efficient L-shaped design of this work area includes an island with a vegetable sink and raised bar. The kitchen is open to the dining area and great room to provide a feeling of openness and informality.

- **Master Suite:** This suite features vaulted ceilings and a walk-in closet. But the compartmentalized master bath, with its second walk-in closet, his and her sinks and linen cabinets, standing shower, vanity, and jetted tub, really makes the suite special.

- **Secondary Bedrooms:** The secondary bedrooms have a wing of their own, and both include computer desks, large closets, and shared access to a bathtub through their individual half-baths.

- **Garages:** Two separate garages house up to three cars, or use the one-car bay for storage or hobby needs.

Rear Elevation

Copyright by designer/architect.

Plan #211049

Dimensions: 73' W x 66' D
Levels: 1
Square Footage: 2,023
Bedrooms: 3
Bathrooms: 2
Foundation: Slab
Materials List Available: Yes
Price Category: D

Images provided by designer/architect.

This European-style home features an open floor plan that maximizes use and flexibility of space.

Features:

• Ceiling Height: 8 ft. unless otherwise noted.

• Living/Dining Area: This combined living-and-dining area features high ceilings, which make the large area seem even more spacious. Corner windows will fill the room with light. The wet bar and cozy fireplace make this the perfect place for entertaining.

• Backyard Porch: This huge covered backyard

porch is accessible from the living/dining area, so the entire party can step outdoors on a warm summer night.

• Kitchen: More than just efficient, this modern kitchen is actually an exciting place to cook. It features a dramatic high ceiling and plenty of work space.

• Utility Area: Located off the kitchen, this area has extra freezer space, a walk-in pantry, and access to the garage.

• Eating Nook: Informal family meals will be a true delight in this nook that adjoins the kitchen and faces a lovely private courtyard.

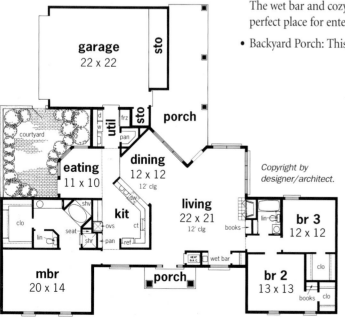

Copyright by designer/architect.

SMARTtip
Outdoor Lighting Safety

Lighting is necessary for walkways, paths, stairways, and transition areas (from the deck to the yard, hot tub, or pool) to prevent accidents. Choose from low-voltage rail, path, and post lighting for these areas. The corners of planters or built-in seating should also be delineated with lighting. Consider installing floodlights near doorways or large open spaces for security reasons.

Plan #161105

Dimensions: 90'2" W x 104'5" D

Levels: 2

Square Footage: 6,806

Main Level Sq. Ft.: 4,511

Upper Level Sq. Ft.: 2,295

Bedrooms: 4

Bathrooms: 4 full, 2 half

Foundation: Walkout basement

Material List Available: No

Price Category: K

The opulence and drama of this European-inspired home features a solid brick exterior with limestone detail, arched dormers, and a parapet.

Images provided by designer/architect.

Features:

- Foyer: A large octagonal skylight tops a water fountain feature displayed in this exquisite entryway. The formal dining room and library flank the entry and enjoy a 10-ft. ceiling height.

- Family Living Area: The gourmet kitchen, breakfast area, and cozy hearth room comprise this family activity center of the home. Wonderful amenities such as a magnificent counter with seating, a celestial ceiling over the dining table, an alcove for an entertainment center, a stone-faced wood-burning fireplace, and access to the rear porch enhance the informal area.

- Master Suite: This luxurious suite enjoys a raised ceiling, a seating area with bay window, and access to the terrace. The dressing room pampers the homeowner with a whirlpool tub, a ceramic tile shower enclosure, two vanities, and a spacious walk-in closet.

- Upper Level: Elegant stairs lead to the second-floor study loft and two additional bedrooms, each with a private bathroom and large walk-in closet. On the same level, and located for privacy, the third bedroom serves as a guest suite, showcasing a cozy sitting area and private bathroom.

Copyright by designer/architect.

Upper Level Floor Plan

Main Level Floor Plan

Optional Basement Level Floor Plan

Plan #401050

Dimensions: 81' W x 61' D
Levels: 2
Square Footage: 6,841
Main Level Sq. Ft.: 2,596
Upper Level Sq. Ft.: 2,233
Finished Basement Sq. Ft.: 2,012
Bedrooms: 4
Bathrooms: 3 full, 2 half
Foundation: Basement
Materials List Available: Yes
Price Category: I

Images provided by designer/architect.

- Kitchen: A butler's pantry joins the dining room to this gourmet kitchen, which holds a separate wok kitchen, an island work center, and a breakfast room with double doors that lead to the rear patio.

- Family Room: Located near the kitchen, this room enjoys a built-in aquarium, media center, and fireplace.

- Den: This room with a tray ceiling, window seat, and built-in computer center is tucked in a corner for privacy.

- Master Suite: The second floor features this spectacular space, which has a separate sitting room, an oversized closet, and a bath with a spa tub.

This grand two-story European home is adorned with a facade of stucco and brick, meticulously appointed with details for gracious living.

Features:

- Foyer: Guests enter through a portico to find this stately two-story foyer.

- Living Room: This formal area features a tray ceiling and a fireplace and is joined by a charming dining room with a large bay window.

Right Side Elevation

Kitchen

Rear Elevation

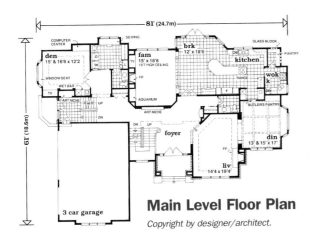

Main Level Floor Plan

Copyright by designer/architect.

Upper Level Floor Plan

Basement Level Floor Plan

Master Bedroom

Great Room

Master Bathroom

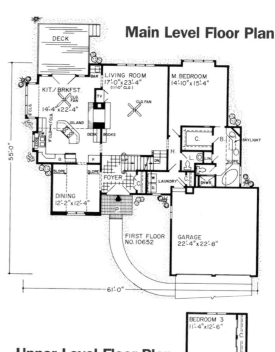

Main Level Floor Plan

DECK

KIT./BRKFST.
14'-4"x22'-4"

LIVING ROOM
17'-0"x23'-4"
(11'-0" CLG.)

M. BEDROOM
14'-10"x15'-4"

SKYLIGHT

FOYER

DINING
12'-2"x12'-4"

LAUNDRY

FIRST FLOOR
NO. 10652

GARAGE
22'-4"x22'-8"

55'-0"

61'-0"

Images provided by designer/architect.

Upper Level Floor Plan

Copyright by designer/architect.

BEDROOM 3
11'-4"x12'-6"

BEDROOM 2
11'-4"x11'-10"
10'CLG.

CEDAR CLOSET

Plan #391173

Dimensions: 61' W x 55' D

Levels: 2

Square Footage: 2,357

Main Level Sq. Ft.: 1,789

Upper Level Sq. Ft.: 568

Bedrooms: 3

Bathrooms: 2½

Foundation: Basement

Material List Available: Yes

Price Category: E

Plan #561003

Dimensions: 58'8" W x 67'4" D

Levels: 1.5

Square Footage: 3,164

Main Level Sq. Ft.: 2,085

Upper Level Sq. Ft.: 1,079

Bedrooms: 4

Bathrooms: 3½

Foundation: Basement

Material List Available: Yes

Price Category: G

Images provided by designer/architect.

CAD FILE AVAILABLE

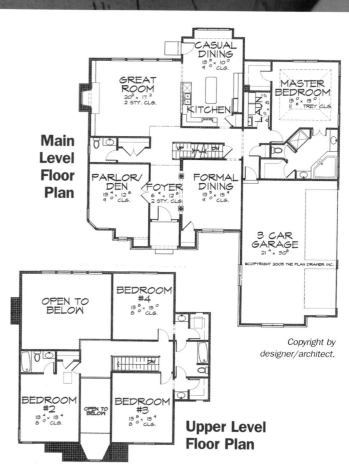

Main Level Floor Plan

CASUAL DINING
9'-0" x 10'-0"
9'-4" CLG.

GREAT ROOM
20'-0" x 17'-2"
2 STY. CLG.

KITCHEN

MASTER BEDROOM
15'-0" x 15'-0"
11'-6" TREY CLG.

PARLOR/DEN
15'-4" x 12'-8"
9'-4" CLG.

FOYER
6'-4" x 12'-0"
2 STY. CLG.

FORMAL DINING
13'-4" x 15'-4"
9'-4" CLG.

3 CAR GARAGE
21'-4" x 30'-0"

©COPYRIGHT 2005 THE PLAN DRAWER INC.

Upper Level Floor Plan

OPEN TO BELOW

BEDROOM #4
13'-8" x 15'-0"
8'-0" CLG.

BEDROOM #2
13'-4" x 13'-4"
8'-0" CLG.

OPEN TO BELOW

BEDROOM #3
13'-8" x 15'-0"
8'-0" CLG.

Copyright by designer/architect.

Plan #461033

Dimensions: 67'6" W x 50'9"D

Levels: 1

Square Footage: 1,802

Bedrooms: 3

Bathrooms: 2

Foundation: Slab; crawl space, or basement for fee

Material List Available: No

Price Category: D

Images provided by designer/architect.

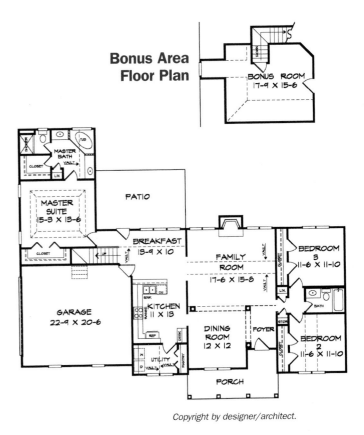

Bonus Area Floor Plan

BONUS ROOM 17-9 X 15-6

Copyright by designer/architect.

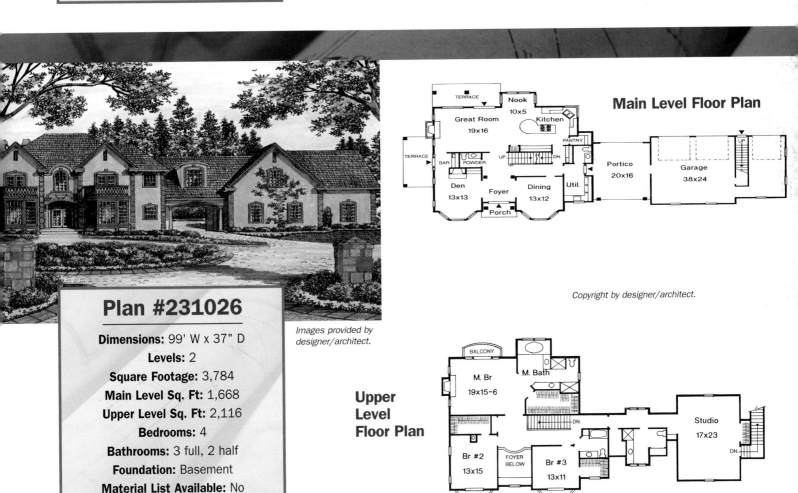

Plan #231026

Dimensions: 99' W x 37" D

Levels: 2

Square Footage: 3,784

Main Level Sq. Ft: 1,668

Upper Level Sq. Ft: 2,116

Bedrooms: 4

Bathrooms: 3 full, 2 half

Foundation: Basement

Material List Available: No

Price Category: H

Images provided by designer/architect.

Main Level Floor Plan

Copyright by designer/architect.

Upper Level Floor Plan

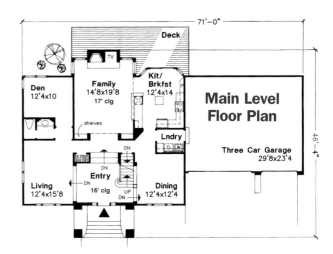

Main Level Floor Plan

Deck

Den
12'4x10

Family
14'8x19'8
17' clg

TV

Kit/
Brkfst
12'4x14

shelves

Lndry

Three Car Garage
29'8x23'4

71'-0"

46'-4"

Living
12'4x15'8

Entry
16' clg

DN

Dining
12'4x12'4

Plan #271041

Dimensions: 71' W x 47' D
Levels: 2
Square Footage: 2,416
Main Level Sq. Ft.: 1,416
Upper Level Sq. Ft.: 1,000
Bedrooms: 4
Bathrooms: 2½
Foundation: Basement
Materials List Available: No
Price Category: E

Images provided by designer/architect.

CAD FILE AVAILABLE

Upper Level Floor Plan

Copyright by designer/architect.

M. Suite
12'4x18
9'6 tray clg

open to below

Br 2
12'4x10

low shelves

roof wdws

Bonus
17'4x14

9'6 tray clg

open to below

Br 3
12'4x10

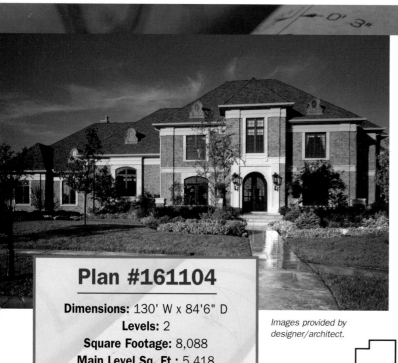

Plan #161104

Dimensions: 130' W x 84'6" D
Levels: 2
Square Footage: 8,088
Main Level Sq. Ft.: 5,418
Upper Level Sq. Ft.: 2,670
Bedrooms: 4
Bathrooms: 4 full, 2 half
Foundation: Basement
Material List Available: No
Price Category: L

Images provided by designer/architect.

Main Level Floor Plan

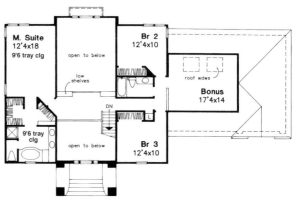

Upper Level Floor Plan

Basement Level Floor Plan

Copyright by designer/architect.

Main Level Floor Plan

Images provided by designer/architect.

Plan #151025

Dimensions: 71' W x 55' D

Levels: 2

Square Footage: 3,914

Main Level Sq. Ft.: 2,291

Upper Level Sq. Ft.: 1,623

Bedrooms: 3

Bathrooms: 3

Foundation: Crawl space, slab; full basement or walkout for fee

CompleteCost List Available: Yes

Price Category: H

Upper Level Floor Plan

Copyright by designer/architect

Main Level Floor Plan

Copyright by designer/architect.

Plan #221077

Dimensions: 57'8" W x 44' D

Levels: 2

Square Footage: 2,440

Main Level Sq. Ft.: 1,206

Upper Level Sq. Ft.: 1,234

Bedrooms: 4

Bathrooms: 2½

Foundation: Basement; crawl space or slab for fee

Material List Available: No

Price Category: E

Images provided by designer/architect.

Rear Elevation

Upper Level Floor Plan

Main Level
Floor Plan

Upper Level
Floor Plan

Plan #161103

Dimensions: 89'10" W x 89'4" D

Levels: 2

Square Footage: 5,633

Main Level Sq. Ft.: 3,850

Upper Level Sq. Ft.: 1,783

Bedrooms: 4

Bathrooms: 3½

Foundation: Walkout; basement for fee

Material List Available: No

Price Category: J

Images provided by designer/architect.

Optional
Basement Level
Floor Plan

Copyright by designer/architect.

Main Level
Floor Plan

40'-4"
12,1 m

32'-4"
9,7 m

Plan #181710

Dimensions: 32'4" W x 40'4" D

Levels: 2

Square Footage: 1,767

Main Level Sq. Ft.: 857

Upper Level Sq. Ft.: 910

Bedrooms: 3

Bathrooms: 2½

Foundation: Basement

Materials List Available: Yes

Price Category: E

Images provided by designer/architect.

CAD FILE AVAILABLE

Upper Level Floor Plan

Copyright by designer/architect.

Plan #181617

Dimensions: 33' W x 35' D

Levels: 2

Square Footage: 1,745

Main Level Sq. Ft.: 805

Upper Level Sq. Ft.: 940

Bedrooms: 3

Bathrooms: 2½

Foundation: Basement

Materials List Available: Yes

Price Category: E

Main Level Floor Plan

Copyright by designer/architect.

Upper Level Floor Plan

Rear Elevation

Images provided by designer/architect.

CAD FILE AVAILABLE — CAD

Plan #561005

Dimensions: 58'4" W x 71' D

Levels: 1

Square Footage: 2,358

Bedrooms: 3

Bathrooms: 2

Foundation: Basement

Material List Available: Yes

Price Category: E

Images provided by designer/architect.

CAD FILE AVAILABLE — CAD

Copyright by designer/architect.

Rear Elevation

PROPOSED DECK

CASUAL DINING

GREAT ROOM

MASTER BEDROOM

KITCHEN

BDRM. #3

FOYER

FORMAL DINING

BDRM. #2

GARAGE

**Main Level
Floor Plan**

Upper Level Floor Plan

Copyright by designer/architect.

*Images provided by
designer/architect.*

Plan #181643

Dimensions: 42' W x 34' D

Levels: 2

Square Footage: 1,929

Main Level Sq. Ft.: 938

Upper Level Sq. Ft.: 991

Bedrooms: 4

Bathrooms: 2½

Foundation: Basement

Materials List Available: Yes

Price Category: F

Plan #161114

Dimensions: 50' W x 36'8" D

Levels: 2

Square Footage: 2,246

Main Level Sq. Ft.: 1,072

Upper Level Sq. Ft.: 1,174

Bedrooms: 4

Bathrooms: 2½

Foundation: Basement;
crawl space for fee

Material List Available: Yes

Price Category: E

*Images provided by
designer/architect.*

**Upper
Level
Floor
Plan**

**Main
Level
Floor
Plan**

Rear Elevation

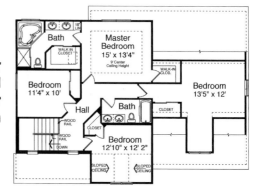

Copyright by designer/architect.

Main Level Floor Plan

Plan #561001

Dimensions: 63'4" W x 64' D

Levels: 2

Square Footage: 5,079

Main Level Sq. Ft.: 3,301

Upper Level Sq. Ft.: 1,778

Bedrooms: 3

Bathrooms: 2½

Foundation: Basement

Material List Available: Yes

Price Category: J

Images provided by designer/architect.

Upper Level Floor Plan

Copyright by designer/architect.

Plan #151851

Dimensions: 73'4" W x 86'8" D

Levels: 1.5

Square Footage: 2,846

Main Level Sq. Ft.: 2,560

Upper Level Sq. Ft.: 286

Bedrooms: 4

Bathrooms: 3½

Foundation: Crawl space or slab; basement or walkout for fee

CompleteCost List Available: Yes

Price Category: F

Images provided by designer/architect.

Main Level Floor Plan

Upper Level Floor Plan

Copyright by designer/architect.

Main Level Floor Plan

40'-0"
12,0 m

Upper Level Floor Plan

Images provided by designer/architect.

Copyright by designer/architect.

CAD FILE AVAILABLE

Rear Elevation

Plan #181615

Dimensions: 36' W x 40' D
Levels: 2
Square Footage: 1,613
Main Level Sq. Ft.: 845
Upper Level Sq. Ft.: 768
Bedrooms: 3
Bathrooms: 1½
Foundation: Basement
Materials List Available: Yes
Price Category: E

Main Level Floor Plan

Upper Level Floor Plan

Images provided by designer/architect.

Copyright by designer/architect.

CAD FILE AVAILABLE

Plan #151849

Dimensions: 54'6" W x 59' D
Levels: 2
Square Footage: 2,095
Main Level Sq. Ft.: 1,839
Upper Level Sq. Ft.: 256
Bedrooms: 3
Bathrooms: 2
Foundation: Crawl space or slab; basement or walkout for fee
CompleteCost List Available: Yes
Price Category: D

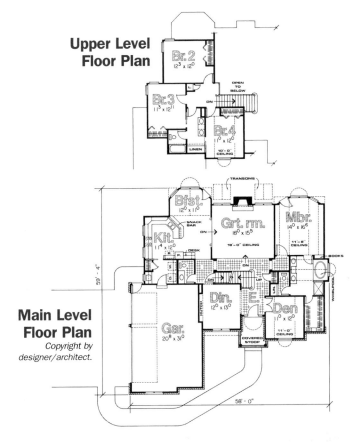

Upper Level Floor Plan

Br. 2
12³ x 12⁰

Br. 3
11⁵ x 12¹¹

OPEN TO BELOW

Br. 4
11⁰ x 12⁰

LINEN

10'-0" CEILING

TRANSOMS

Bfst
11² x 11⁰

SNACK BAR

Grt. rm.
18⁰ x 15⁵

16'-0" CEILING

Mbr.
14⁰ x 16⁶

11'-8" CEILING

Kit.
11⁴ x 12⁰

DESK

BOOKS

Din.
12⁰ x 13⁰

Den
11⁰ x 12⁰

11'-0" CEILING

Gar.
20⁸ x 31⁰

COVERED STOOP

Main Level Floor Plan

Copyright by designer/architect.

59' - 4"

58' - 0"

Plan #121127

Dimensions: 58' W x 59'4" D

Levels: 1.5

Square Footage: 2,496

Main Level Sq. Ft.: 1,777

Upper Level Sq. Ft.: 719

Bedrooms: 4

Bathrooms: 2½

Foundation: Basement; crawl space for fee

Material List Available: Yes

Price Category: E

Images provided by designer/architect.

CAD FILE AVAILABLE

10' COVERED DECK

NOOK
10⁵ x 10⁰

GREAT ROOM
22⁴ x 15⁵

DEN
10⁴ x 12⁴

DINING

Main Level Floor Plan

COV. ENTRY PORCH
18⁸ x 6⁰

PARLOR
12⁵ x 23⁵

GARAGE / STORAGE
35⁵ x 23⁵

OPEN DECK

10' SITTING

BDRM. #3
10⁵ x 12⁵

MASTER SUITE
12⁴ x 17⁰

Upper Level Floor Plan

BDRM. #2
10⁵ x 14⁵

OPEN TO BELOW

WIC
12⁵ x 6⁵

Copyright by designer/architect.

Plan #451308

Dimensions: 71'1" W x 68'5" D

Levels: 2

Square Footage: 2,430

Main Level Sq. Ft.: 1,422

Upper Level Sq. Ft.: 1,008

Bedrooms: 3

Bathrooms: 2½

Foundation: Walkout

Material List Available: No

Price Category: E

Images provided by designer/architect.

CAD FILE AVAILABLE

Plan #181253

Dimensions: 68' W x 50' D

Levels: 2

Square Footage: 3,614

Main Level Sq. Ft.: 1,909

Upper Level Sq. Ft.: 1,705

Bedrooms: 3

Bathrooms: 3½

Foundation: Basement

Material List Available: Yes

Price Category: J

Images provided by designer/architect.

CAD FILE AVAILABLE / CAD

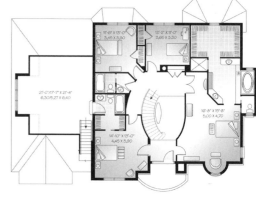

Main Level Floor Plan

Upper Level Floor Plan

Plan #121094

Dimensions: 40'8" W x 46' D

Levels: 2

Square Footage: 1,768

Main Level Sq. Ft.: 905

Upper Level Sq. Ft.: 863

Bedrooms: 3

Bathrooms: 2½

Foundation: Basement

Materials List Available: Yes

Price Category: C

Images provided by designer/architect.

Main Level Floor Plan

Upper Level Floor Plan

Copyright by designer/architect.

Plan #311005

Dimensions: 87' W x 57'3" D

Levels: 1

Square Footage: 2,497

Bedrooms: 3

Bathrooms: 3½

Foundation: Crawl space, slab, or basement

Materials List Available: Yes

Price Category: F

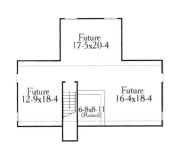

Copyright by designer/architect.

Images provided by designer/architect.

Bonus Area Floor Plan

Plan #131069

Dimensions: 52' W x 38' D

Levels: 2

Square Footage: 3,169

Main Level Sq. Ft.: 1,535

Upper Level Sq. Ft.: 1,634

Bedrooms: 5

Bathrooms: 3½

Foundation: Crawl space; basement for fee

Material List Available: Yes

Price Category: H

Images provided by designer/architect.

Main Level Floor Plan

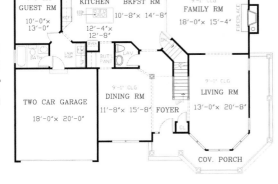

Upper Level Floor Plan

Copyright by designer/architect.

Plan #161036

Dimensions: 74'10" W x 65' D
Levels: 2
Square Footage: 3,664
Main Level Sq. Ft.: 2,497
Upper Level Sq. Ft.: 1,167
Bedrooms: 4
Bathrooms: 2½
Foundation: Basement
Materials List Available: No
Price Category: H

Images provided by designer/architect.

The traditional European brick-and-stone facade on the exterior of this comfortable home will thrill you and make your guests feel welcome.

Features:

• **Pub:** The beamed ceiling lends a casual feeling to this pub and informal dining area between the kitchen and the great room.

• **Dining Room:** Columns set off this formal dining room, from which you can see the fireplace in the expansive great room.

• **Library:** Close to the master suite, this room lends itself to quiet reading or work.

• **Master Suite:** The ceiling treatment makes the bedroom luxurious, while the tub, double-bowl vanity, and large walk-in closet make the bath a pleasure.

• **Upper Level:** Each of the three bedrooms features a large closet and easy access to a convenient bathroom.

Main Level Floor Plan

Upper Level Floor Plan

Copyright by designer/architect.

Rear Elevation

Left Elevation

Right Elevation

Living Room

Kitchen

Dining Room

Living Room

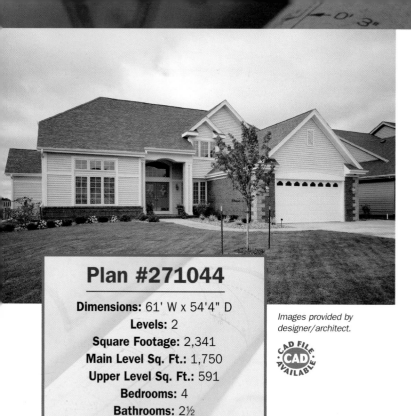

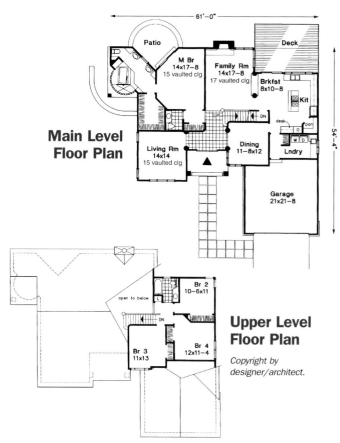

**Main Level
Floor Plan**

*Images provided by
designer/architect.*

Plan #271044

Dimensions: 61' W x 54'4" D
Levels: 2
Square Footage: 2,341
Main Level Sq. Ft.: 1,750
Upper Level Sq. Ft.: 591
Bedrooms: 4
Bathrooms: 2½
Foundation: Basement
Materials List Available: No
Price Category: E

**Upper Level
Floor Plan**

*Copyright by
designer/architect.*

Plan #391003

Dimensions: 47' W x 39' D
Levels: 2
Square Footage: 1,907
Main Street Sq. Ft.: 1,269
Upper Street Sq. Ft.: 638
Bedrooms: 3
Bathrooms: 2½
Foundation: Crawl space, slab,
or basement
Materials List Available: Yes
Price Category: D

*Images provided by
designer/architect.*

**Upper Level
Floor Plan**

**Slab/Crawl
Space Option**

**Main Level
Floor Plan**

*Copyright by
designer/architect.*

Main Level Floor Plan

Plan #441012

Dimensions: 65' W x 55' D
Levels: 1
Square Footage: 3,682
Main Level Sq. Ft.: 2,192
Basement Level Sq. Ft.: 1,490
Bedrooms: 4
Bathrooms: 4
Foundation: Walk out
Materials List Available: Yes
Price Category: H

Images provided by designer/architect.

CAD FILE AVAILABLE

Rear Elevation

Basement Level Floor Plan

Copyright by designer/architect.

Plan #151029

Dimensions: 59'4" W x 74'2" D
Levels: 1½
Square Footage: 2,777
Main Level Sq. Ft.: 2,082
Upper Level Sq. Ft.: 695
Bedrooms: 4
Bathrooms: 2½
Foundation: Crawl space, slab; basement for fee
CompleteCost List Available: Yes
Price Category: F

Images provided by designer/architect.

CAD FILE AVAILABLE

Main Level Floor Plan

Upper Level Floor Plan

Copyright by designer/architect.

Plan #271043

Dimensions: 57'8" W x 36'4" D
Levels: 2
Square Footage: 2,396
Main Level Sq. Ft.: 1,238
Upper Level Sq. Ft.: 1,158
Bedrooms: 4
Bathrooms: 2½
Foundation: Basement
Materials List Available: Yes
Price Category: E

Images provided by designer/architect.

CAD FILE AVAILABLE

Main Level Floor Plan

Upper Level Floor Plan

Copyright by designer/architect.

Plan #351085

Dimensions: 70'6" W x 65' D
Levels: 1
Square Footage: 2,200
Bedrooms: 3
Bathrooms: 2½
Foundation: Crawl space or slab
Material List Available: Yes
Price Category: E

Images provided by designer/architect.

CAD FILE AVAILABLE

Copyright by designer/architect.

Rear Elevation

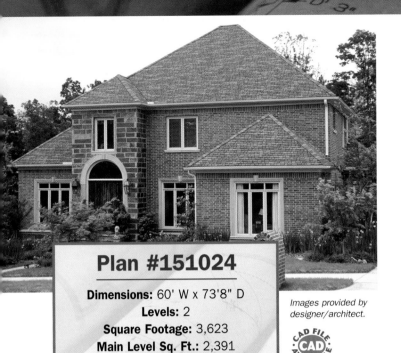

Plan #151024

Dimensions: 60' W x 73'8" D

Levels: 2

Square Footage: 3,623

Main Level Sq. Ft.: 2,391

Upper Level Sq. Ft.: 1,232

Bedrooms: 3

Bathrooms: 3½

Foundation: Crawl space, slab;
full basement for fee

CompleteCost List Available: Yes

Price Category: H

Images provided by designer/architect.

CAD FILE AVAILABLE

**Main Level
Floor Plan**

**Upper Level
Floor Plan**

Copyright by designer/architect.

Plan #341285

Dimensions: 74'6" W x 37'5" D

Levels: 1

Square Footage: 1,481

Bedrooms: 3

Bathrooms: 2

Foundation: Crawl space, slab,
basement, or walkout

Material List Available: Yes

Price Category: B.

Images provided by designer/architect.

CAD FILE AVAILABLE

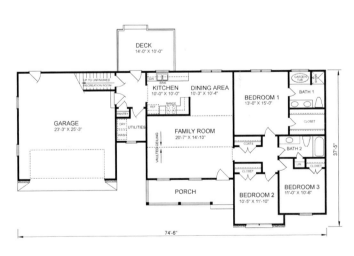

Copyright by designer/architect.

Main Level Floor Plan

Plan #181252

Dimensions: 92' W x 50' D

Levels: 2

Square Footage: 3,631

Main Level Sq. Ft.: 2,153

Upper Level Sq. Ft.: 1,478

Bedrooms: 3

Bathrooms: 3½

Foundation: Basement

Materials List Available: Yes

Price Category: J

Images provided by designer/architect.

Upper Level Floor Plan

Copyright by designer/architect.

Main Level Floor Plan

Plan #441047

Dimensions: 50' W x 42' D

Levels: 2

Square Footage: 2,605

Main Level Sq. Ft.: 1,142

Upper Level Sq. Ft.: 1,463

Bedrooms: 3

Bathrooms: 2½

Foundation: Crawl space; slab or basement available for fee

Material List Available: Yes

Price Category: F

Images provided by designer/architect.

Copyright by designer/architect.

Upper Level Floor Plan

Rear Elevation

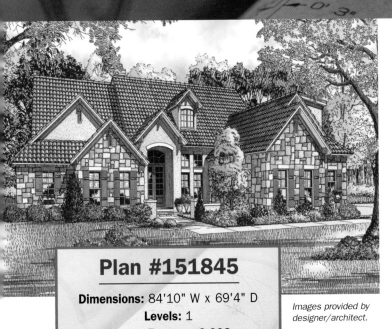

Plan #151845

Dimensions: 84'10" W x 69'4" D
Levels: 1
Square Footage: 3,003
Bedrooms: 5
Bathrooms: 4
Foundation: Crawl space, slab
CompleteCost List Available: Yes
Price Category: G

Images provided by designer/architect.

CAD FILE AVAILABLE CAD

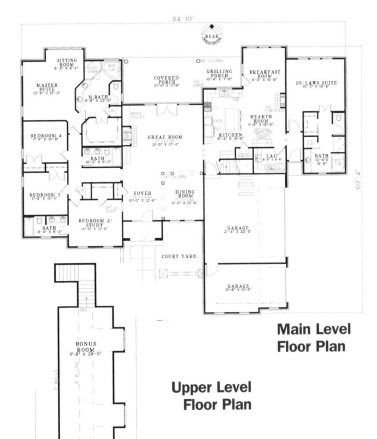

Main Level Floor Plan

Upper Level Floor Plan

Plan #161034

Dimensions: 56' W x 53' D
Levels: 2
Square Footage: 2,156
Main Level Sq. Ft.: 1,605
Upper Level Sq. Ft.: 551
Bedrooms: 3
Bathrooms: 2½
Foundation: Basement
Materials List Available: No
Price Category: D

Images provided by designer/architect.

Main Level Floor Plan

Copyright by designer/architect.

Upper Level Floor Plan

Rear View

Plan #481024

Dimensions: 87'2" W x 59'8" D
Levels: 1
Square Footage: 3,458
Main Level Sq. Ft.: 2,016
Lower Level Sq. Ft.: 1,442
Bedrooms: 4
Bathrooms: 3
Foundation: Walkout basement
Material List Available: No
Price Category: G

Images provided by designer/architect.

Basement Level Floor Plan

Copyright by designer/architect.

Plan #441028

Dimensions: 53'6" W x 73' D
Levels: 2
Square Footage: 3,165
Main Level Sq. Ft.: 1,268
Upper Level Sq. Ft.: 931
Lower Level Sq. Ft.: 966
Bedrooms: 4
Bathrooms: 3½
Foundation: Slab
Materials List Available: Yes
Price Category: G

Images provided by designer/architect.

CAD FILE AVAILABLE

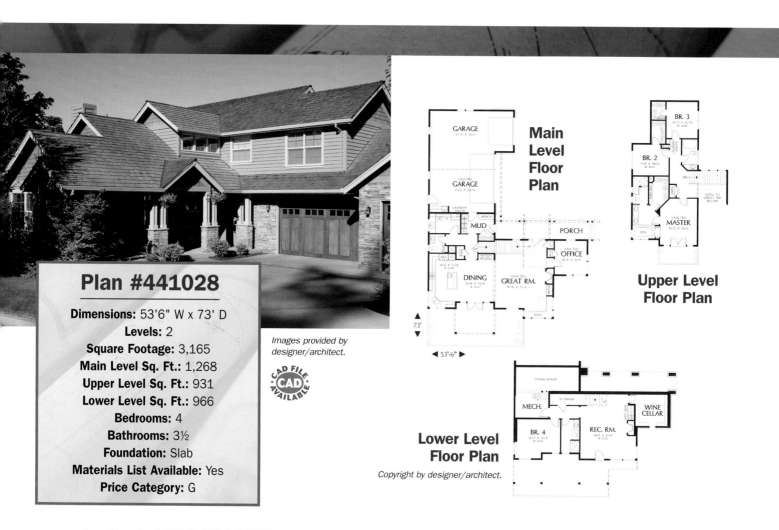

Main Level Floor Plan

Upper Level Floor Plan

Lower Level Floor Plan

Copyright by designer/architect.

Plan #161093

Dimensions: 70'8" W x 64' D

Levels: 1

Square Footage: 4,328

Main Level Sq. Ft.: 2,582

Lower Level Sq. Ft.: 1,746

Bedrooms: 3

Bathrooms: 3½

Foundation: Walkout

Materials List Available: Yes

Price Category: I

Main Level Floor Plan

Images provided by designer/architect.

Lower Level Floor Plan

Copyright by designer/architect.

Plan #441004

Dimensions: 55' W x 48' D

Levels: 1

Square Footage: 1,728

Bedrooms: 2

Bathrooms: 2

Foundation: Crawl space; slab or basement available for fee

Materials List Available: Yes

Price Category: C

CAD FILE AVAILABLE

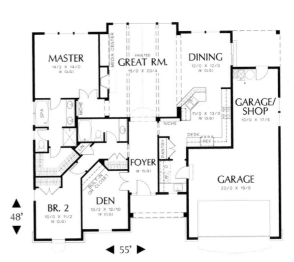

Copyright by designer/architect.

Rear Elevation

Plan #151524

Dimensions: 79'10" W x 60'6" D

Levels: 2

Square Footage: 4,461

Main Level Sq. Ft.: 2,861

Upper Level Sq. Ft.: 1,600

Bedrooms: 5

Bathrooms: 4½

Foundation: Crawl space or slab; basement or walkout available for fee

CompleteCost List Available: Yes

Price Category: H

This home is the culmination of classic French design and ambiance.

Images provided by designer/architect.

Features:

- Great Room: This gathering area features a vaulted ceiling and a built-in media center. Step through the French doors to the rear porch.

- Kitchen: An island kitchen is the most desirable layout in today's home. The raised bar in this kitchen is open to the breakfast room.

- Master Suite: The tray ceiling in this room adds a unique look to the sleeping area. The master bath features a large walk-in closet, vaulted ceiling, and whirlpool tub.

- Secondary Bedrooms: Four bedrooms and three bathrooms are located on the upper level.

Upper Level Floor Plan

Copyright by designer/architect.

Main Level Floor Plan

Plan #221025

Dimensions: 69'8" W x 72' D

Levels: 2

Square Footage: 3,009

Main Level Sq. Ft.: 2,039

Upper Level Sq. Ft.: 970

Bedrooms: 4

Bathrooms: 2½

Foundation: Basement; crawl space for fee

Materials List Available: No

Price Category: G

Images provided by designer/architect.

Designed to resemble a country home in France, this two-story beauty will delight you with its good looks and luxurious amenities.

CAD FILE AVAILABLE

Features:

• **Great Room:** You'll look into this great room as soon as you enter the two-story foyer. A fireplace flanked by built-in bookcases and large windows looking out to the deck highlight this room.

• **Dining Room:** This formal room is located just off the entry for the convenience of your guests.

• **Kitchen:** A huge central island and large pantry make this kitchen a delight for any cook. The large nook looks onto the deck and opens to the lovely three-season porch.

• **Master Suite:** You'll love this suite, with its charming bay shape, great windows, walk-in closet, luxurious bath, and door to the deck.

• **Upper Level:** Everyone will love the two bedrooms, large bath, and huge game.

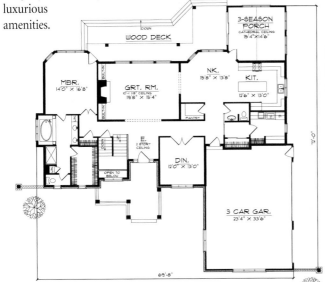

Main Level Floor Plan

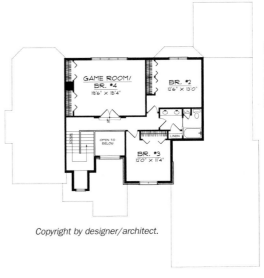

Upper Level Floor Plan

Copyright by designer/architect.

Plan #451180

Dimensions: 74' W x 60' D
Levels: 2
Square Footage: 4,272
Main Level Sq. Ft.: 2,213
Upper Level Sq. Ft.: 1,822
Lower Lever Sq. Ft.: 237
Bedrooms: 3
Bathrooms: 3½
Foundation: Walkout
Material List Available: No
Price Category: I

Images provided by designer/architect.

Classic style shines through in this spectacular two-story home.

Features:

- **Foyer:** This large, open foyer welcomes you home and features a convenient coat closet. The angled stairs add drama to the space.

- **Mud Room:** This family entrance is perfect for coats, hats, book bags, sporting equipment, and the like. There is even a handy sink.

- **Great Room:** This large gathering area features a cozy fireplace and French doors that lead to the rear deck. The two-story ceiling imparts an open and airy feeling to the space.

- **Lower Level:** In addition to a four-car garage, there is a utility room, which holds the washer and dryer.

CAD FILE AVAILABLE

Copyright by designer/architect.

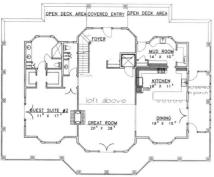

Main Level Floor Plan

Upper Level Floor Plan

Basement Level Floor Plan

Plan #441038

Dimensions: 59' W x 51'6" D
Levels: 2
Square Footage: 2,518
Main Level Sq. Ft.: 1,464
Upper Level Sq. Ft.: 1,054
Bedrooms: 4
Bathrooms: 3
Foundation: Crawl space;
slab or basement available for fee
Materials List Available: Yes
Price Category: E

Images provided by designer/architect.

Features:

- Kitchen: This kitchen contains gourmet appointments with an island countertop, a large pantry, and a work desk built in.
- Dining Room: This formal room connects directly to the kitchen for convenience.
- Master Suite: This suite features a fine bath with a spa tub and separate shower.

- Bedrooms: A bedroom (or make it a home office) is tucked away behind the two-car garage and has the use of a full bathroom across the hall. Three additional bedrooms are found on the upper level, along with a large bonus space that could be developed later into bedroom 5.

Victorians are such a cherished style; it's impossible not to admire them. This one begins with all the classic details and adds a most up-to-date floor plan.

CAD FILE AVAILABLE

Main Level Floor Plan

Upper Level Floor Plan

Copyright by designer/architect.

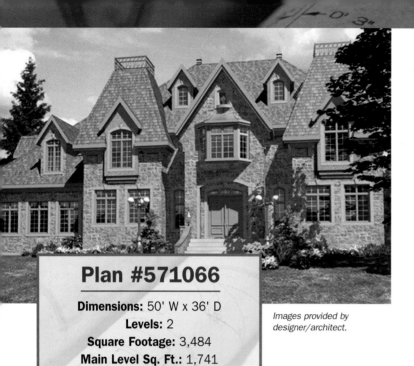

Main Level Floor Plan

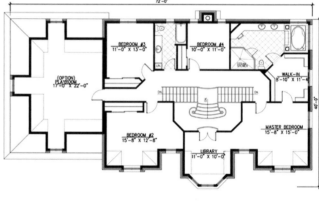

Plan #571066

Dimensions: 50' W x 36' D
Levels: 2
Square Footage: 3,484
Main Level Sq. Ft.: 1,741
Upper Level Sq. Ft.: 1,743
Bedrooms: 3
Bathrooms: 2½
Foundation: Basement
Material List Available: Yes
Price Category: D

Images provided by designer/architect.

Upper Level Floor Plan

Copyright by designer/architect.

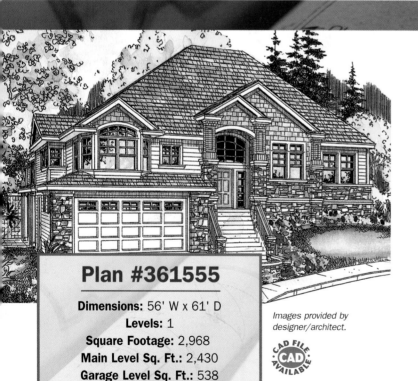

Plan #361555

Dimensions: 56' W x 61' D
Levels: 1
Square Footage: 2,968
Main Level Sq. Ft.: 2,430
Garage Level Sq. Ft.: 538
Bedrooms: 4
Bathrooms: 2
Foundation: Basement
Material List Available: No
Price Category: E

Images provided by designer/architect.

CAD FILE AVAILABLE

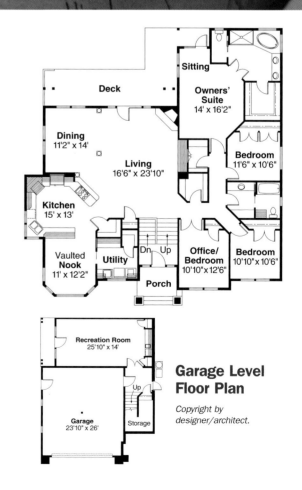

Garage Level Floor Plan

Copyright by designer/architect.

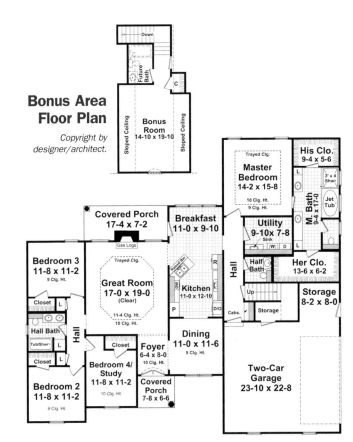

Bonus Area Floor Plan

Copyright by designer/architect.

Future Bath

Bonus Room
14-10 x 19-10

Sloped Ceiling

Sloped Ceiling

Down

C

Plan #351106

Dimensions: 65'2" W x 61' D

Levels: 1

Square Footage: 2,202

Bedrooms: 4

Bathrooms: 2½

Foundation: Crawl space or slab

Material List Available: Yes

Price Category: E

Images provided by designer/architect.

CAD FILE AVAILABLE

His Clo.
9-4 x 5-6

3' x 4 Shwr

Master Bedroom
14-2 x 15-8
10 Clg. Ht.
9 Clg. Ht.

Trayed Clg.

M. Bath
9-4 x 17-0

Jet Tub

Covered Porch
17-4 x 7-2

Gas Logs

Breakfast
11-0 x 9-10

Utility
9-10x 7-8
Sink
W   D

Bedroom 3
11-8 x 11-2
9 Clg. Ht.

Closet

Trayed Clg.

Great Room
17-0 x 19-0
(Clear)
11-4 Clg. Ht.
10 Clg. Ht.

Kitchen
11-0 x 12-10

DW

R

P

D/O

Half Bath

Her Clo.
13-6 x 6-2

Hall

Up

Cabs.

Storage

Storage
8-2 x 8-0

Hall Bath

Tub/Shwr

Hall

Closet

Closet

Bedroom 4/Study
11-8 x 11-2
10 Clg. Ht.

Foyer
6-4 x 8-0
10 Clg. Ht.

Dining
11-0 x 11-6
9 Clg. Ht.

Two-Car Garage
23-10 x 22-8

Bedroom 2
11-8 x 11-2
9 Clg. Ht.

Covered Porch
7-8 x 6-6

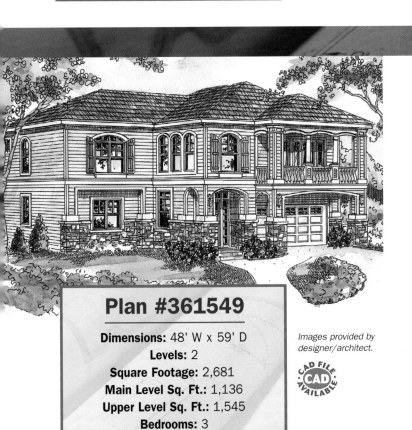

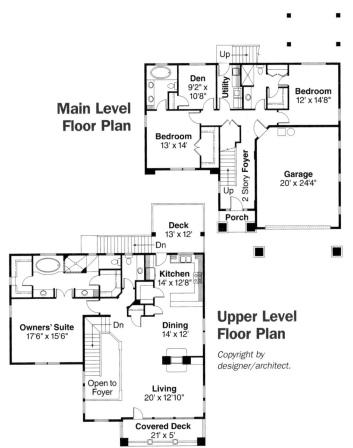

Plan #361549

Dimensions: 48' W x 59' D

Levels: 2

Square Footage: 2,681

Main Level Sq. Ft.: 1,136

Upper Level Sq. Ft.: 1,545

Bedrooms: 3

Bathrooms: 3½

Foundation: Crawl space

Material List Available: No

Price Category: F

Images provided by designer/architect.

CAD FILE AVAILABLE

Main Level Floor Plan

Up

Den
9'2" x 10'8"

Utility

Bedroom
12' x 14'8"

Bedroom
13' x 14'

2 Story Foyer

Garage
20' x 24'4"

Up

Porch

Deck
13' x 12'

Dn

Kitchen
14' x 12'8"

Upper Level Floor Plan

Copyright by designer/architect.

Owners' Suite
17'6" x 15'6"

Dn

Dining
14' x 12'

Open to Foyer

Living
20' x 12'10"

Covered Deck
21' x 5'

Plan #481034

Dimensions: 84'8" W x 77'8" D
Levels: 2
Square Footage: 2,830
Main Level Sq. Ft.: 1,673
Upper Level Sq. Ft.: 1,157
Bedrooms: 3
Bathrooms: 2½
Foundation: Walkout
Materials List Available: No
Price Category: F

This European-influenced two-story home has stone accents and wide board siding.

Images provided by designer/architect.

Features:

- **Great Room:** The fireplace, flanked by built-in cabinets, is the focal point of this gathering area. Because the area is located just off the foyer, your guests can easily enter this area.

- **Dining Room:** This formal dining area features a built-in cabinet and a 9-ft,-high ceiling. The triple window has a view of the front yard.

- **Kitchen:** This large island kitchen is a bonus in any home. Open to the dinette and the great room, the area has a light and open feeling. The built-in pantry is ready to store all of your supplies.

- **Master Suite:** Occupying most of the upper level, this retreat boasts a vaulted ceiling in the sleeping area and a large walk-in closet. The master bath features his and her vanities and a large stall shower.

Rear View

Main Level Floor Plan

Upper Level Floor Plan

Copyright by designer/architect.

Plan #401017

Dimensions: 79' W x 44' D

Levels: 2

Square Footage: 2,632

Main Level Sq. Ft.: 1,362

Upper Level Sq. Ft.: 1,270

Bedrooms: 4

Bathrooms: 2½

Foundation: Crawl space or basement

Material List Available: Yes

Price Category: F

Rich in Victorian details-scalloped shingles, wraparound porch, and turrets-this beautiful facade conceals a modern floor plan.

Features:

- **Living Room:** Archways announce this distinctive living room, which features a lovely tray ceiling.

- **Den:** This octagonal den, located across the foyer from the living room, is the perfect private spot for reading or studying.

- **Kitchen:** This U-shaped island kitchen holds an octagonal breakfast bay and a pass-through breakfast bar that connects to the family room.

- **Master Suite:** This master suite is complete with a sitting room and a bay window. A well-appointed master bath is located in one of the turrets.

- **Secondary Bedrooms:** Three family bedrooms share a bathroom. One of the bedrooms is located within a turret.

Images provided by designer/architect.

Rear Elevation

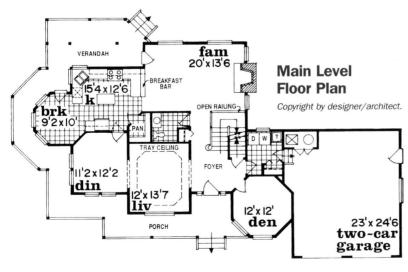

Main Level Floor Plan

Copyright by designer/architect.

Upper Level Floor Plan

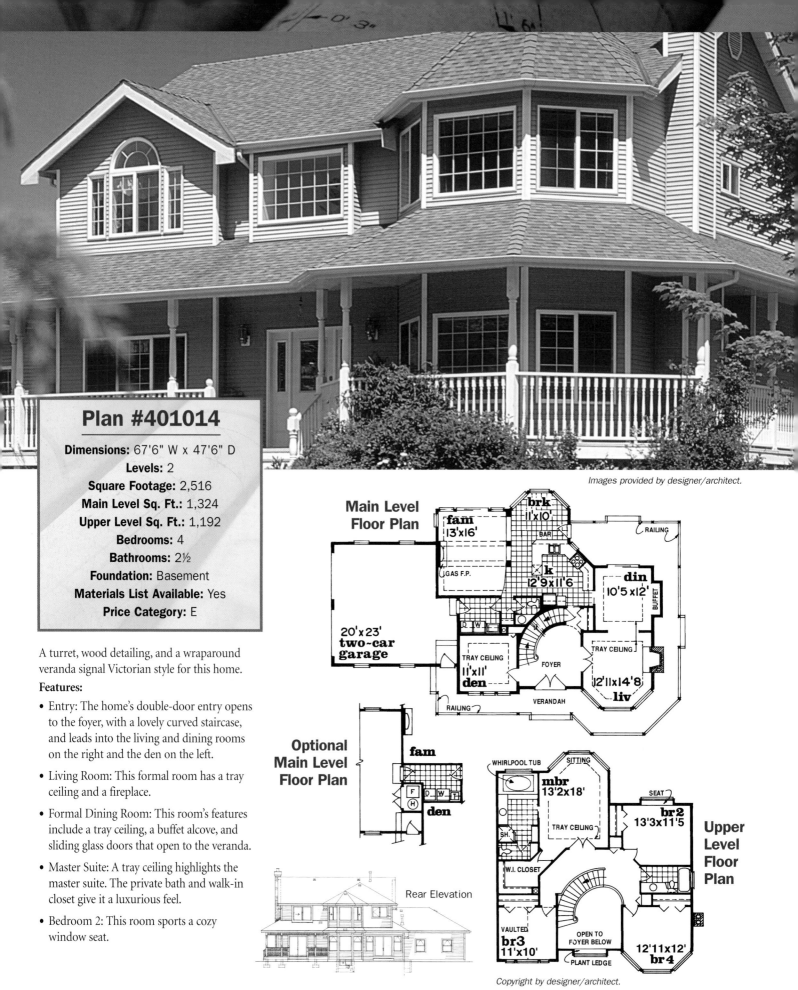

Plan #401014

Dimensions: 67'6" W x 47'6" D
Levels: 2
Square Footage: 2,516
Main Level Sq. Ft.: 1,324
Upper Level Sq. Ft.: 1,192
Bedrooms: 4
Bathrooms: 2½
Foundation: Basement
Materials List Available: Yes
Price Category: E

A turret, wood detailing, and a wraparound veranda signal Victorian style for this home.

Features:

• Entry: The home's double-door entry opens to the foyer, with a lovely curved staircase, and leads into the living and dining rooms on the right and the den on the left.

• Living Room: This formal room has a tray ceiling and a fireplace.

• Formal Dining Room: This room's features include a tray ceiling, a buffet alcove, and sliding glass doors that open to the veranda.

• Master Suite: A tray ceiling highlights the master suite. The private bath and walk-in closet give it a luxurious feel.

• Bedroom 2: This room sports a cozy window seat.

Images provided by designer/architect.

Main Level Floor Plan

brk 11'x10'
fam 13'x16'
BAR
GAS F.P.
k 12'9x11'6
din 10'5x12'
BUFFET
RAILING
TRAY CEILING
11'x11' den
FOYER
TRAY CEILING
12'11x14'8 liv
VERANDAH
RAILING
20'x23' two-car garage
D W

Optional Main Level Floor Plan

fam
den
F H D W

Upper Level Floor Plan

WHIRLPOOL TUB
SITTING
mbr 13'2x18'
SEAT
br2 13'3x11'5
TRAY CEILING
SH.
W.I. CLOSET
VAULTED
br3 11'x10'
OPEN TO FOYER BELOW
PLANT LEDGE
12'11x12' br4

Rear Elevation

Copyright by designer/architect.

Plan #391002

Dimensions: 76'4" W x 45'10" D
Levels: 2
Square Footage: 2,281
Main Level Sq. Ft.: 1,260
Upper Level Sq. Ft.: 1,021
Bedrooms: 3
Bathrooms: 2½
Foundation: Crawl space, slab, or basement
Materials List Available: Yes
Price Category: E

The luxurious amenities in this compact, well designed home are sure to delight everyone in the family.

Features:

- Ceiling Height: 9-ft. ceilings add to the spacious feeling created by the open design.

- Family Room: A vaulted ceiling and large window area add elegance to this comfortable room, which will be the heart of this home.

- Dining Area: Adjoining the kitchen, this room features a large bayed area as well as French doors that open onto the back deck.

- Kitchen: This step-saving design will make cooking a joy for everyone in the family.

- Utility Room: Near the kitchen, this room includes cabinets and shelves for extra storage space.

- Master Suite: A triple window, tray ceiling, walk-in closet, and luxurious bath make this area a treat.

Images provided by designer/architect.

Main Level Floor Plan

Copyright by designer/architect.

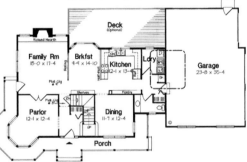

Alternate Crawl Space/Slab

Upper Level Floor Plan

SMARTtip

Creating Depth with Wall Frames

Wall frames create an illusion of depth and density because 1) they are three-dimensional and 2) they divide the wall area into smaller, denser segments. The three-dimensional quality of wall frames is fundamentally different from that of the alternative treatment: raised panels. Despite the name, raised panels actually produce a concave-like, or receding, effect whereas wall frames are more convex, protruding outward. In terms of sculpture, concave units create negative space while convex units create positive space. Raised panels, therefore, deliver a uniform sense of volume, mass, and density, while wall frames create a higher level of tension and dramatic interest.

Plan #361106

Dimensions: 128'5" W x 77' D
Levels: 2
Square Footage: 6,043
Main Level Sq. Ft.: 2,613
Upper Level Sq. Ft.: 3,430
Bedrooms: 5
Bathrooms: 4½
Foundation: Basement
Material List Available: No
Price Category: K

This magnificent Victorian, with wraparound porches, balconies, and rooms to spare, is more than just a home.

CAD FILE AVAILABLE

Features:

• **Entry:** Welcome guests from the encircling veranda into the two-story foyer. From there, sit down for quiet conversation in the library or gather around the fireplace in the living room while younger guests head off to the family or game room. The porch forms an attractive pathway between both formal and informal entertainment areas.

• **Master Suite:** This master suite will certainly make you feel like the master of your home. Off by itself, the master bedroom has a fireplace and entrances to a balcony on one side and an upper-level deck on the other. A few steps separate the bedroom from a comfortable sitting room. Add to this a spacious walk-in closet, separate his and her vanities, a large corner tub, and a standing shower, and you have the very definition of luxury.

• **Secondary Bedrooms:** Three additional bedrooms offer ample closet space and proximity to a full bathroom, complete with dual sinks, a tub, and a separate standing shower. One of the bedrooms, located under a spire, offers an inspiring view from flanking windows.

• **Caretaker's Quarters:** Whether you have a full-time staff member or a live-in family member, this attached apartment is complete with everything an individual needs. Almost a miniature home, the space includes a large bedroom, a walk-in closet, a full bathroom, a full kitchen, and ample extra living space.

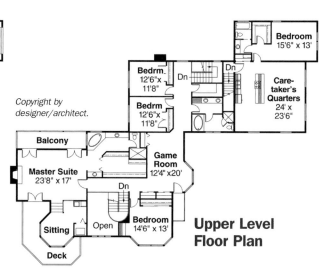

Copyright by designer/architect.

Main Level Floor Plan

- Garage 28' x 13'
- Garage 24' x 23'6"
- Family 21'2" x 23'6"
- Util
- To Gazebo
- Porch
- Kitchen
- Nook 9'8" x 10'
- Carport
- Living 23'6" x 17'
- Library 11' x 11'
- Foyer
- Dining 14'6"x17'8"
- Veranda

Upper Level Floor Plan

- Bedroom 15'6" x 13'
- Bedrm 12'6"x 11'8"
- Bedrm 12'6"x 11'8"
- Care-taker's Quarters 24' x 23'6"
- Balcony
- Master Suite 23'8" x 17'
- Game Room 12'4" x 20'
- Sitting
- Open
- Bedroom 14'6" x 13'
- Deck

Plan #481035

Dimensions: 99' W x 64' D
Levels: 2
Square Footage: 3,204
Main Level Sq. Ft.: 1,701
Upper Level Sq. Ft.: 1,503
Bedrooms: 3
Bathrooms: 2½
Foundation: Walkout
Material List Available: No
Price Category: G

Images provided by designer/architect.

Distinctive design details set this home apart from others in the neighborhood.

Features:

- **Foyer:** This large foyer welcomes you home and provides a view through the home and into the family room. The adjoining study can double as a home office.

- **Family Room:** This two-story gathering space features a fireplace flanked by built-in cabinets. The full-height windows on the rear wall allow natural light to flood the space.

- **Kitchen:** This island kitchen flows into the nearby family room, allowing mingling between both spaces when friends or family are visiting. The adjacent dinette is available for daily meals.

- **Master Suite:** This private retreat waits for you to arrive home. The tray ceiling in the sleeping area adds elegant style to the area.

Rear Elevation

Main Level Floor Plan

Copyright by designer/architect.

Upper Level Floor Plan

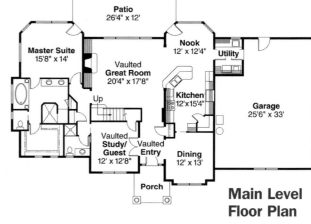

Plan #361481

Dimensions: 78' W x 46' D

Levels: 2

Square Footage: 2,471

Main Level Sq. Ft.: 1,903

Upper Level Sq. Ft.: 568

Bedrooms: 4

Bathrooms: 3

Foundation: Crawl space

Materials List Available: No

Price Category: E

Images provided by designer/architect.

CAD FILE AVAILABLE

Main Level Floor Plan

Patio 26'4" x 12'

Master Suite 15'8" x 14'

Nook 12' x 12'4"

Utility

Vaulted Great Room 20'4" x 17'8"

Kitchen 12'x15'4"

Garage 25'6" x 33'

Up

Vaulted Study/Guest 12' x 12'8"

Vaulted Entry

Dining 12' x 13'

Porch

Upper Level Floor Plan

Bedroom 12' x 12'4"

Open to Great Room Below

Bonus Room 17'8" x 13'

Dn

Open to Entry

Vaulted Bedroom 12' x 12'

Copyright by designer/architect.

Plan #351105

Dimensions: 69' W x 59'10" D

Levels: 1

Square Footage: 2,000

Bedrooms: 3

Bathrooms: 2½

Foundation: Crawl space or slab

Material List Available: Yes

Price Category: E

Images provided by designer/architect.

CAD FILE AVAILABLE

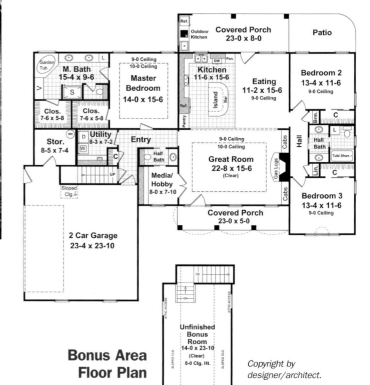

Covered Porch 23-0 x 8-0

Outdoor Kitchen

Patio

Garden Tub

M. Bath 15-4 x 9-6

9-0 Ceiling
10-0 Ceiling

Master Bedroom 14-0 x 15-6

Kitchen 11-6 x 15-6

Island

Eating 11-2 x 15-6
9-0 Ceiling

Bedroom 2 13-4 x 11-6
9-0 Ceiling

Clos. 7-6 x 5-8

Clos. 7-6 x 5-8

Pantry

Hall Bath

Stor. 8-5 x 7-4

Utility 8-3 x 7-2

Entry

9-0 Ceiling
10-0 Ceiling

Great Room 22-8 x 15-6 (Clear)

Gas Logs

Cabs

Hall

Sloped Clg.

Half Bath

Media/Hobby 8-0 x 7-10

Cabs

Bedroom 3 13-4 x 11-6
9-0 Ceiling

2 Car Garage 23-4 x 23-10

Covered Porch 23-0 x 5-0

Bonus Area Floor Plan

Unfinished Bonus Room 14-0 x 23-10 (Clear)
8-0 Clg. Ht.

Copyright by designer/architect.

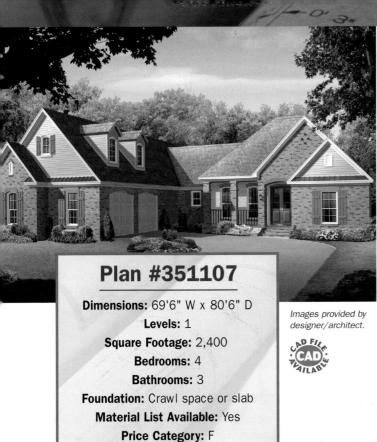

Plan #351107

Dimensions: 69'6" W x 80'6" D

Levels: 1

Square Footage: 2,400

Bedrooms: 4

Bathrooms: 3

Foundation: Crawl space or slab

Material List Available: Yes

Price Category: F

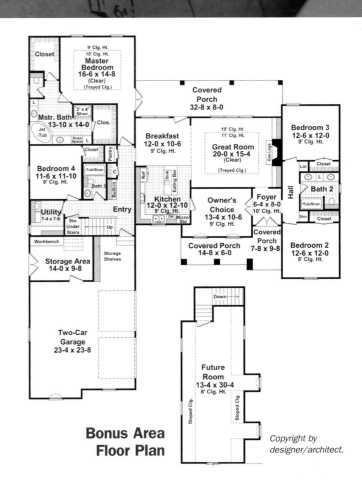

Images provided by designer/architect.

CAD FILE AVAILABLE

Bonus Area Floor Plan

Copyright by designer/architect.

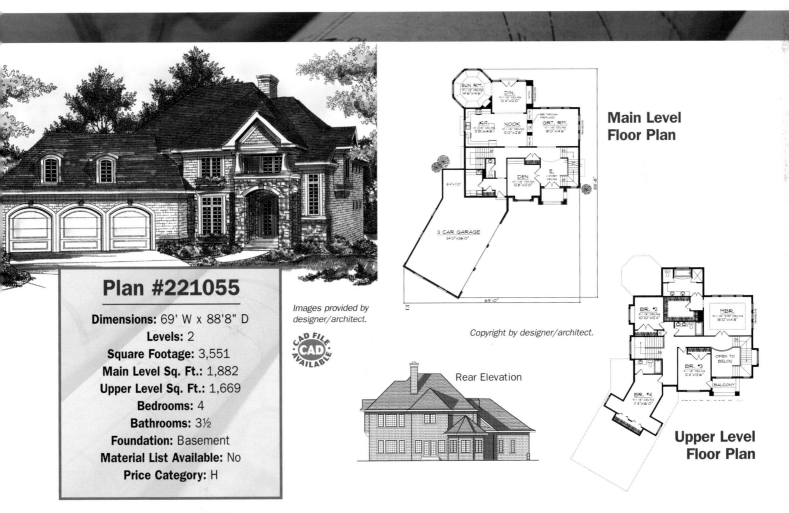

Plan #221055

Dimensions: 69' W x 88'8" D

Levels: 2

Square Footage: 3,551

Main Level Sq. Ft.: 1,882

Upper Level Sq. Ft.: 1,669

Bedrooms: 4

Bathrooms: 3½

Foundation: Basement

Material List Available: No

Price Category: H

Images provided by designer/architect.

CAD FILE AVAILABLE

Main Level Floor Plan

Copyright by designer/architect.

Rear Elevation

Upper Level Floor Plan

Plan #161100

Dimensions: 89' W x 59'2" D

Levels: 1

Square Footage: 5,377

Main Level Sq. Ft.: 2,961

Basement Level Sq. Ft.: 2,416

Bedrooms: 3

Bathrooms: 2 full, 2 half

Foundation: Walkout; basement for fee

Material List Available: No

Price Category: J

This luxury home is perfect for you and your family.

Images provided by designer/architect.

Features:

- Foyer: This beautiful foyer showcases the two-sided fireplace, which warms its space, as well as that of the great room.

- Gathering Areas: The kitchen, breakfast area, and hearth room will quickly become a favorite gathering area, what with the warmth of the fireplace and easy access to a covered porch. Expansive windows with transoms create a light and airy atmosphere.

- Master Suite: This suite makes the most of its circular sitting area and deluxe dressing room with platform whirlpool tub, dual vanities, commode room with closet, and two-person shower.

- Lower Level: This lower level is finished with additional bedrooms and areas dedicated to entertaining, such as the wet bar, billiards area, media room, and exercise room

Rear View

Main Level Floor Plan

Basement Level Floor Plan

Copyright by designer/architect.

Plan #281015

Dimensions: 32' W x 48' D
Levels: 2
Square Footage: 1,660
Main Level Sq. Ft.: 964
Upper Level Sq. Ft.: 696
Bedrooms: 4
Bathrooms: 2½
Foundation: Basement
Materials List Available: Yes
Price Category: C

You'll love the gracious features and amenities in this charming home, which is meant for a narrow lot.

Features:

- **Foyer:** This two-story foyer opens into the spacious living room.

- **Living Room:** The large bay window in this room makes a perfect setting for quiet times alone or entertaining guests.

- **Dining Room:** The open flow between this room and the living room adds to the airy feeling.

- **Family Room:** With a handsome fireplace and a door to the rear patio, this room will be the heart of your home.

- **Kitchen:** The U-shaped layout, pantry, and greenhouse window make this room a joy.

- **Master Suite:** The bay window, large walk-in closet, and private bath make this second-floor room a true retreat.

Images provided by designer/architect.

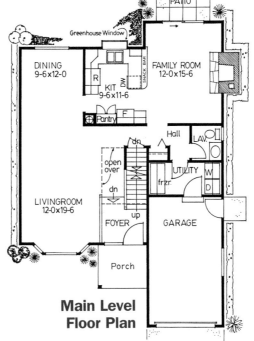

Main Level Floor Plan

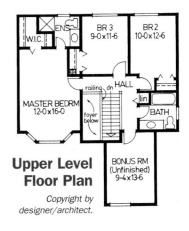

Upper Level Floor Plan

Copyright by designer/architect.

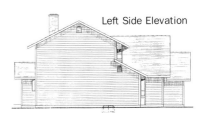

Left Side Elevation

Rear Elevation

Right Side Elevation

Plan #481036

Dimensions: 84'8" W x 82'4" D
Levels: 1
Square Footage: 4,258
Main Level Sq. Ft.: 2,440
Basement Level Sq. Ft.: 1,818
Bedrooms: 4
Bathrooms: 3½
Foundation: Walkout
Material List Available: No
Price Category: I

Images provided by designer/architect.

Old-world style with a modern floor plan makes this home perfect for you.

Rear Elevation

Features:

- Great Room: With a 12-ft.-high ceiling and a glowing fireplace, this room welcomes you home. Relax with your family, or entertain your friends.

- Study: Located off the foyer, this room would make a perfect home office; clients can come and go without disturbing the family.

- Master Suite: Unwind in this private space, and enjoy its many conveniences. The full master bath includes a standing shower, his and her sinks, a large tub, and a spacious walk-in closet.

- Garage: This large storage space has room for three full-size cars and includes a convenient sink. The stairs to the storage area in the basement will help keep things organized.

Front View

Main Level
Floor Plan

Basement Level
Floor Plan

Copyright by designer/architect.

Breakfast Room/Kitchen

Master Bath

Study

Great Room

Plan #441024

Dimensions: 90'6" W x 84' D
Levels: 2
Square Footage: 3,517
Main Level Sq. Ft.: 2,698
Upper Level Sq. Ft.: 819
Bedrooms: 3
Bathrooms: 3½
Foundation: Crawl space;
slab or basement available for fee
Materials List Available: Yes
Price Category: H

You'll feel like royalty every time you pull into the driveway of this European-styled manor house.

Images provided by designer/architect.

Features:

- Kitchen: This gourmet chef's center hosts an island with a vegetable sink. The arched opening above the primary sink provides a view of the fireplace and entertainment center in the great room. A walk-in food pantry and a butler's pantry are situated between this space and the dining room.

- Master Suite: Located on the main level, this private retreat boasts a large sleeping area and a sitting area. The grand master bath features a large walk-in closet, dual vanities, a large tub, and a shower.

- Bedrooms: Two secondary bedrooms are located on the upper level, and each has its own bathroom.

- Laundry Room: This utility room houses cabinets, a folding counter, and an ironing board.

- Garage: This large three-car garage has room for storage. Family members entering the home from this area will find a coat closet and a place to stash briefcases and backpacks.

Main Level Floor Plan

Upper Level Floor Plan

Copyright by designer/architect.

Plan #391050

Dimensions: 67' W x 51' D
Levels: 2
Square Footage: 2,674
Main Level Sq. Ft.: 1,511
Upper Level Sq. Ft.: 1,163
Bedrooms: 3
Bathrooms: 2½
Foundation: Crawl space, slab, or basement
Materials List Available: Yes
Price Category: F

This home, as shown in the photograph, may differ from the actual blueprints. For more detailed information, please check the floor plans carefully.

Images provided by designer/architect.

This home truly transforms tutor styling for today. Charming Old World half-timbering dramatizes exterior dormers and the deeply recessed pillared porch, while New World surprises fill the interior.

Features:

• Kitchen: Beyond the living room and study and past the double-entry stairway, this elaborately open-ended kitchen feeds into other important spaces, including the breakfast room, which is bathed in natural light on three sides as it looks out on the patio and three-season porch.

• Family Room: This open family room is also a big draw, with its fireplace, two-story cathedral ceilings, and porch access.

• Master Suite: The second level, enjoying the spacious aura of the vaulted ceiling, high lights this master suite, with its generous windowing, spectacular closeting, and bathroom with tub situated in a wide windowed corner.

• Bedrooms: Two additional bedrooms feature plentiful closeting and pretty front-view windows (one with window seat) and share a second full bath.

Main Level Floor Plan

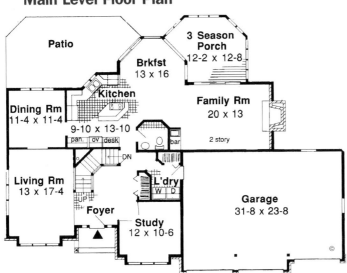

Upper Level Floor Plan

Copyright by designer/architect.

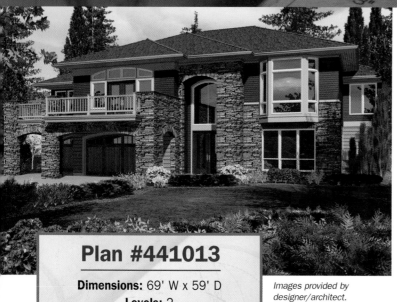

**Main Level
Floor Plan**

Lower Level Floor Plan

Plan #441013

Dimensions: 69' W x 59' D

Levels: 2

Square Footage: 3,317

Main Level Sq. Ft.: 2,657

Lower Level Sq. Ft.: 660

Bedrooms: 4

Bathrooms: 3½

Foundation: Slab

Materials List Available: Yes

Price Category: G

Images provided by designer/architect.

CAD FILE AVAILABLE

**Main Level
Floor Plan**

Upper Level Floor Plan

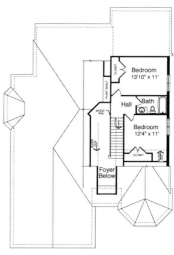

Rear Elevation

Plan #161119

Dimensions: 44'9" W x 67'10" D

Levels: 2

Square Footage: 2,334

Main Level Sq. Ft.: 1,858

Upper Level Sq. Ft.: 476

Bedrooms: 4

Bathrooms: 3

Foundation: Basement

Material List Available: Yes

Price Category: E

Images provided by designer/architect.

Images provided by designer/architect.

CAD FILE AVAILABLE · CAD ·

Plan #151178

Dimensions: 52'6" W x 58'10" D

Levels: 1

Square Footage: 1,600

Bedrooms: 3

Bathrooms: 2

Foundation: Crawl space, slab

CompleteCost List Available: Yes

Price Category: C

Copyright by designer/architect.

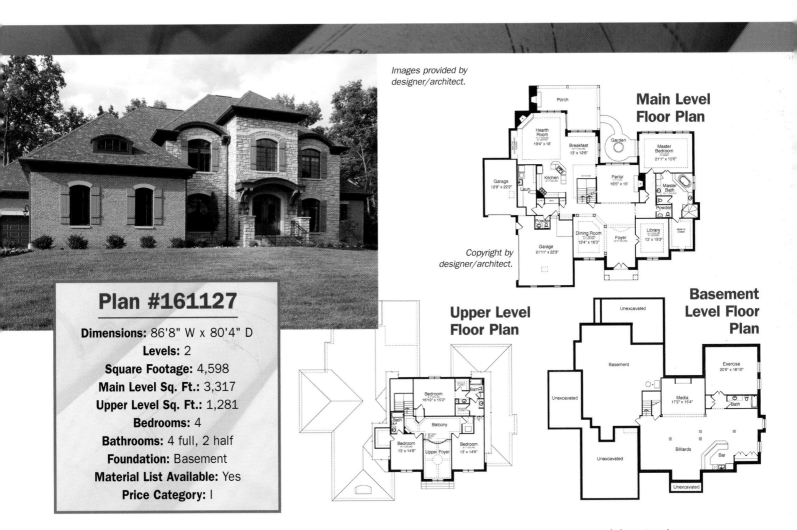

Images provided by designer/architect.

Copyright by designer/architect.

Plan #161127

Dimensions: 86'8" W x 80'4" D

Levels: 2

Square Footage: 4,598

Main Level Sq. Ft.: 3,317

Upper Level Sq. Ft.: 1,281

Bedrooms: 4

Bathrooms: 4 full, 2 half

Foundation: Basement

Material List Available: Yes

Price Category: I

Plan #401012

Dimensions: 48' W x 52'6" D
Levels: 2
Square Footage: 2,301
Main Level Sq. Ft.: 1,180
Upper Level Sq. Ft.: 1,121
Bedrooms: 3-4
Bathrooms: 2½
Foundation: Basement
Materials List Available: Yes
Price Category: E

A turret roof, prominent bay window, and wraparound veranda designate this four bedroom design as classic Victorian. The plans include two second-level layouts – one with four bedrooms or one with three bedrooms and a vaulted ceiling over the family room.

Features:

- **Living Room:** This formal room has windows that overlook the veranda.

- **Family Room:** This gathering space includes a fireplace for atmosphere.

- **Kitchen:** This U-shaped kitchen has a sunny breakfast bay; you'll find a half-bath and a laundry room in the service area that leads to the two-car garage.

- **Master Suite:** This lavish area has an octagonal tray ceiling in the sitting room, a walk-in closet, and a private bath with a colonnaded whirlpool spa and separate shower.

Images provided by designer/architect.

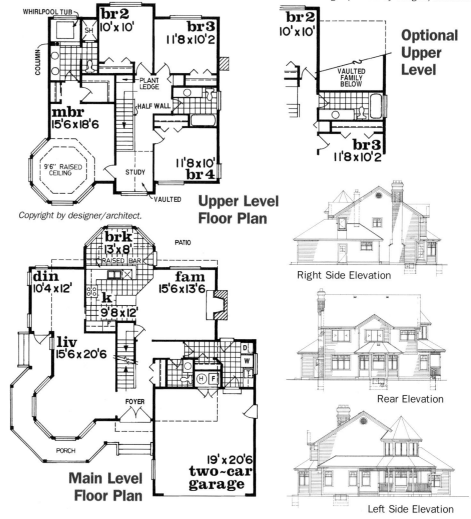

WHIRLPOOL TUB
COLUMN
br 2 10' x 10'
br 3 11'8 x 10'2
PLANT LEDGE
HALF WALL
mbr 15'6 x 18'6
9'6" RAISED CEILING
STUDY
br 4 11'8 x 10'
VAULTED
Upper Level Floor Plan
Copyright by designer/architect.

br 2 10' x 10'
Optional Upper Level
VAULTED FAMILY BELOW
br 3 11'8 x 10'2

brk 13' x 8'
RAISED BAR
PATIO
din 10'4 x 12'
k 9'8 x 12'
fam 15'6 x 13'6
liv 15'6 x 20'6
FOYER
PORCH
19' x 20'6 **two-car garage**
Main Level Floor Plan

Right Side Elevation

Rear Elevation

Left Side Elevation

Plan #281016

Dimensions: 46' W x 44' D
Levels: 2
Square Footage: 1,945
Main Level Sq. Ft.: 1,211
Upper Level Sq. Ft.: 734
Bedrooms: 3
Bathrooms: 3
Foundation: Combination basement/slab
Materials List Available: Yes
Price Category: D

The fabulous window shapes on this Tudor-style home give just a hint of the beautiful interior design.

Features:

- **Living Room:** A vaulted ceiling in this raised room adds to its spectacular good looks.

- **Dining Room:** Between the lovely bay window and the convenient door to the covered sundeck, this room is an entertainer's delight.

- **Family Room:** A sunken floor, cozy fireplace, and door to the patio make this room special.

- **Study:** Just off the family room, this quiet spot can be a true retreat away from the crowd.

- **Kitchen:** The family cooks will be delighted by the ample counter and storage space here.

- **Master Suite:** A large walk-in closet, huge picture window, and private bath add luxurious touches to this second-floor retreat.

Images provided by designer/architect.

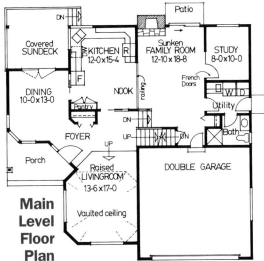

Main Level Floor Plan

Upper Level Floor Plan

Copyright by designer/architect.

Rear Elevation

Left Side Elevation

Right Side Elevation

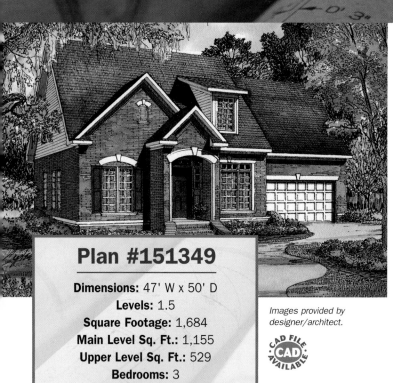

Copyright by designer/architect.

Plan #151349

Dimensions: 47' W x 50' D

Levels: 1.5

Square Footage: 1,684

Main Level Sq. Ft.: 1,155

Upper Level Sq. Ft.: 529

Bedrooms: 3

Bathrooms: 2½

Foundation: Crawl space or slab; basement or walkout for fee

CompleteCost List Available: Yes

Price Category: C

Images provided by designer/architect.

Bonus Area Floor Plan

Main Level Floor Plan

Copyright by designer/architect.

Upper Level Floor Plan

Plan #161228

Dimensions: 64'4" W x 66'8" D

Levels: 2

Square Footage: 2,873

Main Level Sq. Ft.: 2,050

Upper Level Sq. Ft.: 823

Bedrooms: 4

Bathrooms: 2½

Foundation: Walkout

Material List Available: Yes

Price Category: F

Images provided by designer/architect.

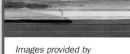

Rear Elevation

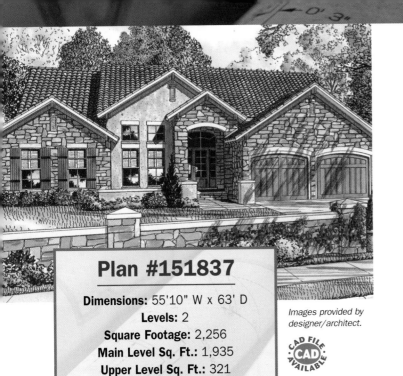

Plan #151837

Dimensions: 55'10" W x 63' D

Levels: 2

Square Footage: 2,256

Main Level Sq. Ft.: 1,935

Upper Level Sq. Ft.: 321

Bedrooms: 3

Bathrooms: 2

Foundation: Crawl space or slab; basement or walkout for fee

CompleteCost List Available: Yes

Price Category: E

Images provided by designer/architect.

CAD FILE AVAILABLE

Main Level Floor Plan

Upper Level Floor Plan

Copyright by designer/architect.

Plan #571014

Dimensions: 36' W x 39' D

Levels: 2

Square Footage: 2,134

Main Level Sq. Ft.: 1,065

Upper Level Sq. Ft.: 1,069

Bedrooms: 3

Bathrooms: 2½

Foundation: Basement

Material List Available: Yes

Price Category: D

Images provided by designer/architect.

Upper Level Floor Plan

Main Level Floor Plan

Copyright by designer/architect.

Plan #391017

Dimensions: 77' W x 41'6" D
Levels: 2
Square Footage: 2,176
Main Level Sq. Ft.: 1,671
Upper Level Sq. Ft.: 505
Bedrooms: 3
Bathrooms: 2½
Foundation: Crawl space, slab, or basement
Materials List Available: Yes
Price Category: D

Quaint, complex pitched rooflines and long, light-filled windows make this house a proper Tudor-style home befitting today's lifestyles.

Features:

- **Entry:** This formal entry, with its double doors, opens on a sophisticated library on one side and a formal dining room on the other.

- **Living Room:** This living room is central to the layout, inviting folks to gather at the fireplace, hang out on the screened porch, join the hustle bustle in the kitchen, or take meals to the outdoor patio.

- **Master Suite:** This master suite, with its special ceiling and dreamy full bath (tub tucked beneath a corner of windows, plus a separate shower) enjoys main-floor access to the library and a front yard view.

- **Bedrooms:** Upstairs, a lavishly long hallway delivers two dramatic-looking bedrooms, built around a spacious bathroom. One bedroom with picture window also features an expansive closet (cedar treatment optional). Another bedroom with wall-length closet enjoys a backyard view.

Main Level Floor Plan

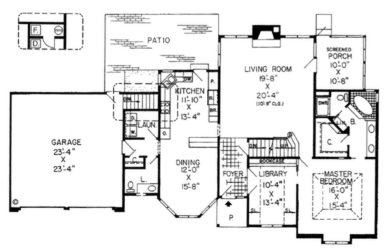

Upper Level Floor Plan

Copyright by designer/architect.

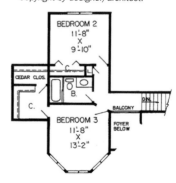

Plan #121090

Dimensions: 60' W x 58' D
Levels: 1.5
Square Footage: 2,645
Main Level Sq. Ft.: 1,972
Upper Level Sq. Ft.: 673
Bedrooms: 4
Bathrooms: 2½
Foundation: Basement
Materials List Available: Yes
Price Category: F

Images provided by designer/architect.

You'll be amazed at the amenities that have been designed into this lovely home.

Features:

• Den: French doors just off the entry lead to this lovely home, with its bowed window and spider-beamed ceiling.

• Great Room: A trio of graceful arched windows highlights the vlume ceiling in this room. You might want to curl up to read next to the see-through fireplace into the hearth room.

• Kitchen: Enjoy the good design in this room.

• Hearth Room: The shared fireplace with the great room makes this a cozy spot in cool weather.

• Master Suite: French doors lead to this well-lit area, with its roomy walk-in closet, sunlit whirlpool tubs, separate shower, and two vanities.

Main Level Floor Plan

Upper Level Floor Plan

Copyright by designer/architect.

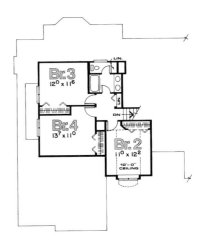

Images provided by designer/architect.

Plan #151846

Dimensions: 69'8" W x 79'6" D
Levels: 2
Square Footage: 2,609
Main Level Sq. Ft.: 2,280
Upper Level Sq. Ft.: 329
Bedrooms: 4
Bathrooms: 3
Foundation: Crawl space or slab; basement, or walkout for fee
CompleteCost List Available: Yes
Price Category: F

CAD FILE AVAILABLE

With all the tantalizing elements of a cottage and the comfortable space of a family-sized home, this European-style two-story design is the best of both worlds.

Features:

• Foyer: The vaulted ceiling soars up to the second level giving this foyer a dramatic feel. A view into the atrium brings the outdoors inside.

• Great Room: This large gathering area features a beautiful fireplace and a sloped ceiling. On nice days, exit through the glass door and relax on the porch.

• Kitchen: The raised snack bar in this efficient kitchen provides additional seating for informal meals. The family will enjoy lazy weekend mornings in the adjoining breakfast nook, which affords a view into the atrium.

• Master Suite: You'll spend many luxurious hours in this beautiful suite, which contains a 10-ft.-high boxed ceiling. The master bath boasts a large walk-in closet, glass shower, whirlpool tub, and double vanity.

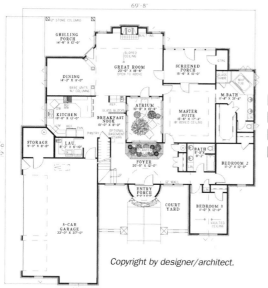

Main Level Floor Plan

Copyright by designer/architect.

Upper Level Floor Plan

Plan #371046

Dimensions: 50'2" W x 70' D
Levels: 2
Square Footage: 2,440
Main Level Sq. Ft.: 1,809
Upper Level Sq. Ft.: 631
Bedrooms: 4
Bathrooms: 2½
Foundation: Slab
Materials List Available: No
Price Category: E

Ornate windows accent the exterior of this two-story home. Beautiful brick and cast stone give it added charm.

CAD FILE AVAILABLE

Features:

- **Living Room:** This spacious formal room has a cathedral ceiling.

- **Family Room:** Large windows flood this open and airy room with natural light; the cozy fireplace makes it comfortable.

- **Dining Room:** This formal room opens into the large entry.

- **Kitchen:** This kitchen has a pantry, raised bar, and breakfast nook that opens to the family room and is great for entertaining.

- **Master Suite:** This secluded area, located downstairs, has a luxurious master bathroom with two walk-in closets.

- **Bedrooms:** Upstairs are three additional bedrooms with walk-in closets that share a convenient hall bathroom with a dressing room.

Upper Level Floor Plan

Copyright by designer/architect.

Main Level Floor Plan

Images provided by designer/architect.

Plan #361230

Dimensions: 60'4" W x 39'8" D
Levels: 2
Square Footage: 2,091
Main Level Sq. Ft.: 1,546
Upper Level Sq. Ft.: 545
Bedrooms: 3
Bathrooms: 2½
Foundation: Crawl space
Material List Available: No
Price Category: D

The mix of stone and wood siding, along with a column-supported porch, creates eye-catching appeal for this lovely home.

CAD FILE AVAILABLE

Features:

• **Living Room:** The high ceilings and large windows, which provide a great view of the backyard, make this room a favorite gathering area. The cozy fireplace creates a relaxing atmosphere.

• **Kitchen:** This island kitchen boasts an abundance of cabinet and counter space. The adjoining breakfast nook's large windows flood the space with natural light.

• **Master Suite:** This private oasis boasts an oversize sleeping area and large windows. The master bath features dual vanities, a large shower, and separate toilet area.

• **Upper Level:** Two secondary bedrooms share a full bathroom on this level. A bonus room can be finished to your liking as a game room, a home theater, or an additional bedroom.

Upper Level Floor Plan

Main Level Floor Plan

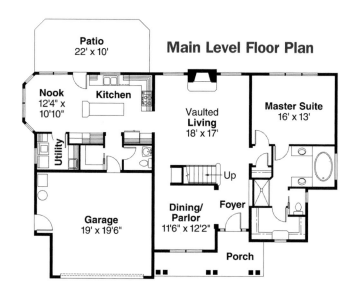

Copyright by designer/architect.

Plan #131032

Dimensions: 69'2" W x 46' D
Levels: 2
Square Footage: 2,455
Main Level Sq. Ft.: 1,499
Upper Level Sq. Ft.: 956
Bedrooms: 4
Bathrooms: 3
Foundation: Crawl space or slab;
basement for fee
Materials List Available: Yes
Price Category: F

If you love Victorian styling, you'll be charmed by the ornate, rounded front porch and the two-story bay that distinguish this home.

Images provided by designer/architect.

Features:

• Living Room: You'll love the 13-ft. ceiling in this room, as well as the panoramic view it gives of the front porch and yard.

• Kitchen: Sunlight streams into this room, where an angled island with a cooktop eases both prepping and cooking.

• Breakfast Room: This room shares an eating bar with the kitchen, making it easy for the family to congregate while the family chef is cooking.

• Guest Room: Use this lovely room on the first level as a home office or study if you wish.

• Master Suite: The dramatic bayed sitting area with a high ceiling has an octagonal shape that you'll adore, and the amenities in the private bath will soothe you at the end of a busy day.

Rear View

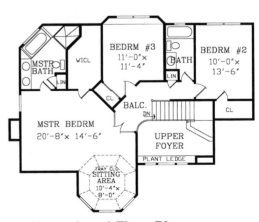

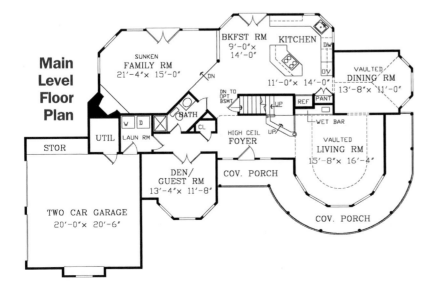

Main Level Floor Plan

Upper Level Floor Plan

Copyright by designer/architect.

Plan #361130

Dimensions: 100'8" W x 74'5" D

Levels: 2

Square Footage: 4,147

Main Level Sq. Ft.: 2,751

Upper Level Sq. Ft.: 1,396

Bedrooms: 4

Bathrooms: 3½

Foundation: Crawl space or basement

Material List Available: No

Price Category: I

This house is a vacation retreat and year-round home rolled into one. Beautiful architecture and an elegant, contemporary design combine to create a graceful paradise.

CAD FILE AVAILABLE

Features:

• Kitchen: This stylishly designed kitchen is surrounded by workspace and storage. Whether you're a professional chef or just like to imagine yourself as one, this area has everything you need, including an attached utility area for easy cleanup.

• Master Suite: Sweet indeed, this impressive area includes an adjacent sunlit study, access to the deck, a walk-in closet, his and her vanities, a stall shower, and a window-lined tub surround.

• Guest Suite: Whether you think it's good or bad, family and friends will love to visit you and stay in this spacious retreat. Secluded by the vaulted ceilings of the first floor, this area provides privacy with elegant amenities.

• Secondary Bedrooms: Two additional bedrooms have large closets and share a library and a full bathroom. A bonus room at the end of the hall can become a quiet study area or a fully featured entertainment area for guests and family alike.

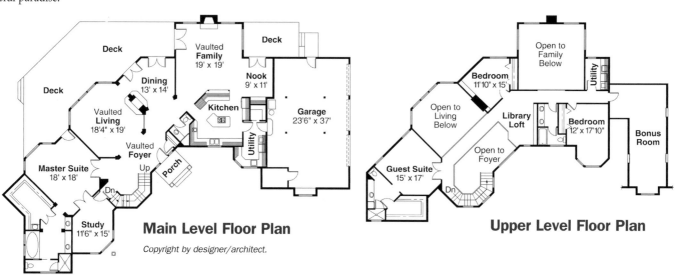

Main Level Floor Plan

Copyright by designer/architect.

Upper Level Floor Plan

Plan #241058

Dimensions: 93' W x 57'2" D
Levels: 2
Square Footage: 4,216
Main Level Sq. Ft.: 2,384
Upper Level Sq. Ft.: 1,832
Bedrooms: 4
Bathrooms: 3½
Foundation: Slab
Material List Available: No
Price Category: I

Images provided by designer/architect.

A brick-and-stone exterior provides a rich solid look to this beautiful two-story home.

Features:

• Entry: This covered entry opens into the two-story foyer. The dining room is located to the right through an entry of floor-to-ceiling columns.

• Great Room: This sunken gathering area boast a fireplace flanked by windows.

• Master Suite: Located on the main level, this retreat boasts a sitting area. The master bath features a large walk-in closet and whirlpool tub.

• Bedrooms: Three secondary bedrooms are located on the upper level. A nearby play-room could serve as a spare bedroom. Two bedrooms share a Jack-and-Jill bathroom.

Main Level Floor Plan

Copyright by designer/architect.

Upper Level Floor Plan

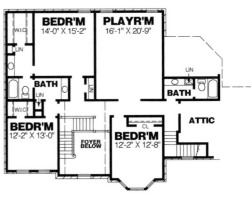

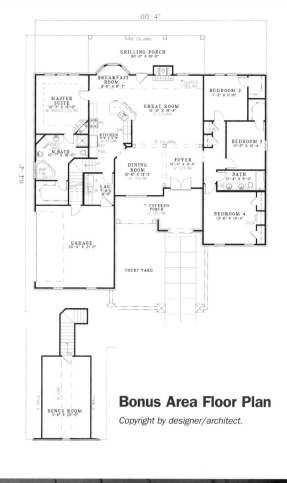

Bonus Area Floor Plan

Copyright by designer/architect.

Plan #151842

Dimensions: 60'4" W x 64'4" D

Levels: 1

Square Footage: 2,135

Bedrooms: 4

Bathrooms: 2

Foundation: Crawl space or slab; basement or walkout for fee

CompleteCost List Available: Yes

Price Category: D

Images provided by designer/architect.

Main Level Floor Plan

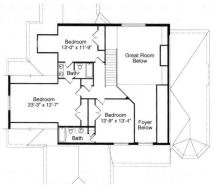

Upper Level Floor Plan

Copyright by designer/architect.

Plan #161187

Dimensions: 65'8" W x 76' D

Levels: 1.5

Square Footage: 3,431

Main Level Sq. Ft.: 2,341

Upper Level Sq. Ft.: 1,090

Bedrooms: 4

Bathrooms: 3½

Foundation: Basement

Materials List Available: Yes

Price Category: G

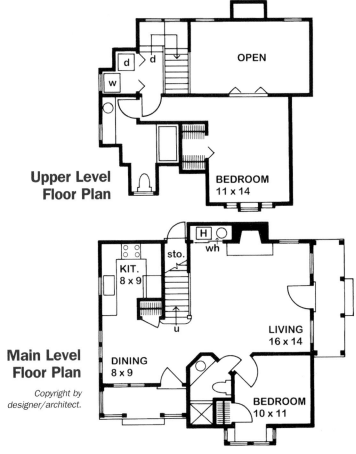

Plan #381062

Dimensions: 28' W x 29' D
Levels: 2
Square Footage: 1,180
Main Level Sq. Ft.: 770
Upper Level Sq. Ft.: 410
Bedrooms: 2
Bathrooms: 2
Foundation: Crawl space
Material List Available: Yes
Price Category: B

Images provided by designer/architect.

Upper Level Floor Plan

OPEN

BEDROOM
11 x 14

d   d
w

Main Level Floor Plan

Copyright by designer/architect.

KIT.
8 x 9

sto.

H
wh

LIVING
16 x 14

DINING
8 x 9

BEDROOM
10 x 11

u

Plan #381058

Dimensions: 68'5" W x 33' D
Levels: 2
Square Footage: 1,895
Main Level Sq. Ft.: 1,180
Upper Level Sq. Ft.: 715
Bedrooms: 4
Bathrooms: 2½
Foundation: Basement
Material List Available: No
Price Category: D

Images provided by designer/architect.

Upper Level Floor Plan

Copyright by designer/architect.

stor.

BEDROOM
12 x 10

BEDROOM
13 x 14

d   attic

stor.

BEDROOM
13 x 13

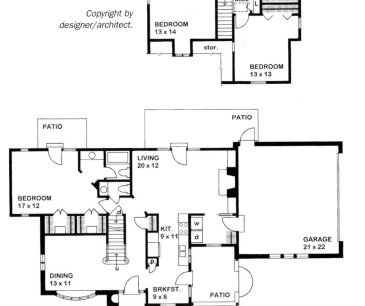

PATIO

PATIO

LIVING
20 x 12

BEDROOM
17 x 12

KIT.
9 x 11

w
d

GARAGE
21 x 22

DINING
13 x 11

u

BRKFST.
9 x 8

PATIO

Main Level Floor Plan

Types of Bathrooms

Master bath, kids' bath, powder room, guest bath—how many bathrooms does one household need? Remember when the typical family shared just a single small bathroom? Times have changed. And although the average family size has decreased, according to the National Association of Home Builders more than 70 percent of the new homes built in the United States in 2004 contained at least two baths; 24 percent contained more than three baths. In this story, you'll discover how to make any bathroom functional and practical, starting with making a list of needs and wants, followed by an analysis of the actual space. Once you've done this, you'll be ready to try out different floor plans on paper. Finally, you'll find suggestions for the specific type of bath you want—full-size, luxury, at-home spa, or modest powder room.

the smart approach to
CREATIVE HOMEOWNER
bath
THIRD EDITION
revised and expanded
DESIGN

Susan Maney Lovett

The following article was reprinted from *The Smart Approach to Bath Design* (Creative Homeowner 2006).

Many of today's larger, luxurious bathrooms, opposite, include spa-like features, such as an oversize shower and and a deep tub.

It's the sophisticated mix, right, of the subtle wall color and elegant materials that supplies the drama in this powder room. Wood floors in a medium tone complement the dark furniture-like wood vanity and black toilet. (Tip: Water and wood don't generally mix, so confine the use of wood floors to powder rooms only.) Note that the decorative hardware, mirror, lighting fixtures, and faucet all feature a similar metallic finish for a cohesive overall appearance.

Bathroom Types

The most-common-size American bathroom measures 60 × 84 inches or 60 × 96 inches. The most common complaint about it is the lack of space. The arrangement may have suited families 50 years ago, but times and habits have changed. If it's the only bathroom in the house, making it work better becomes even more important.

When planning the layout, try angling a sink or shower unit in a corner to free up some floor space. Also, consider installing a pocket door. Instead of a traditional door that takes up wall space when it is open, a pocket door slides into the wall. Another smart way to add function to a small bathroom is to install a pocket door into a wall between the toilet and the sink. That way two people can use the room comfortably at the same time.

You can also make a small bathroom feel roomier by bringing in natural light with a skylight or roof window or by replacing one small standard window with several small casement units that can be installed high on the wall to maintain privacy.

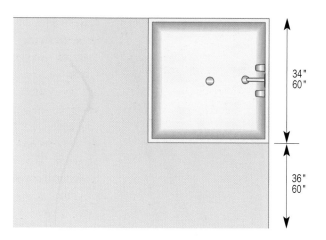

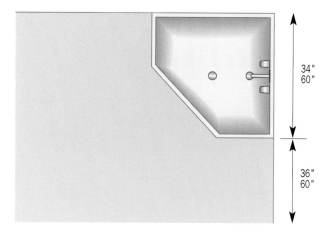

Shower dimensions vary widely from the minimum usable size to the most generous, above left and right. When space is tight, consider a corner unit. Don't forget to plan for clearance; the smaller dimension is the minimum clearance needed.

The Powder Room

The guest bath. The half bath. It has a lot of names, and it may be the most efficient room in the house, providing just what you need often in tight quarters. A powder room normally includes nothing more than a lavatory and a toilet. You can find small-scale fixtures specifically designed for it, from the tiniest lavs to unusually narrow toilets. In general, however, maintain a clearance that meets code on each side of the toilet and include comfortable reaching room for the toilet-paper dispenser. Most powder rooms measure at least 36 inches wide by 54 to 60 inches long, depending on the layout of the space. Keep a small powder room as light and open as possible. Make sure the door swings out against a wall, or use a pocket door for easy access. If it must be accessible for someone in a wheelchair, include a minimum 5-foot-diameter circle of space in the center of the room, which is just large enough for turning around.

Because the powder room is often for guests and is normally located on the ground floor near the living area, take extra care to ensure privacy. The best location is in a hallway away from the living room, kitchen, and dining areas.

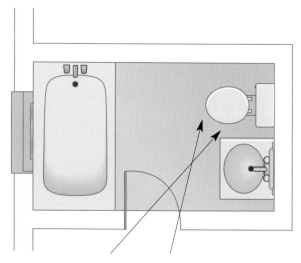

Unfortunately, this bathroom allows full view of the toilet from outside of the room, above.

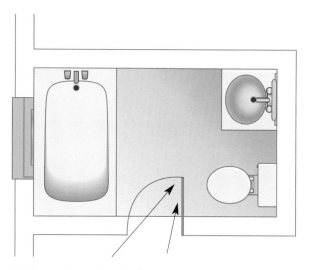

Better privacy is obtained, above, by flopping the toilet and the sink and reversing the door swing.

Crisp white ceramic tiles, opposite, are highlighted simpy and effectively with a border of sharply contrasting red. The oval window and a scattering of decorative lighthouse-motif tiles add a touch of whimsy that works well in either a family or a child's bathroom.

Smart features, left, for any family bath include a slip-resistant floor, towel hooks located within easy reach of the shower, and plenty of accessible storage.

A Children's Bath

What should be included in a children's bath plan depends on the ages and number of children using it. If the bath will be for only one child, the design is easy. You can tailor it to him or her, taking care to plan for growing and changing needs. Anticipate the storage and lighting requirements of an older child's self-grooming habits, for example. However, if more than one child will use this bathroom, consider their genders and whether more than two will be using the bath at the same time. How many lavatories do you really need? The answer is at least two, if not more. The best designs for growing children include compartmentalized spaces—one for the toilet, one for the bath, and one for the lavatories. If this isn't feasible given the existing space, at least try to set the toilet apart. That way the children can take turns going to the bathroom and brushing their teeth

When in doubt, stick to the classics, below, top right, and bottom right. White cabinetry and chrome faucets and hardware—combined with beadboard and decorative moldings—add traditional appeal to a bathroom. If you choose white tiles, install them on the diagonal for texture and interest.

for speedier bedtimes. Two special considerations in a kid's bath are territorial issues and safety. Children are famous for protecting their space. Rather than fight this natural tendency, plan a cabinet drawer or wall shelf for each child. For safety, you may want to install countertops and sinks lower than standard height, build a step into the vanity cabinet's toekick area, or keep a slip-resistant footstool handy. Lastly, remember what it was like to be a child. Get down to a kid's level, and design for a youngster's height and capabilities. Consult your children about decisions regarding the room's decoration.

The Family Bath

Compartmentalizing is the best way to start planning the family bath. But remember, when you separate the bathroom into smaller,

Stick to a monochromatic palette for materials if you aim to create a space that is serene but still great looking, opposite.

distinct areas, you run the risk of making the room feel cramped. Try to alleviate this with extra natural light, good artificial lighting, and translucent partitions made of glass blocks or etched glass. Anything that divides with privacy while also allowing light to enter will help ease the closed-in feeling.

If separating the fixtures is not possible, include a sink in the dressing area within the master bedroom to provide a second place for grooming. Investigate building a back-to-back bath in lieu of one large shared room. Another popular option is to locate both the tub and the shower in the center of the room; install the bidet, toilet, and sink or sinks on either side in their own separate areas. To make the arrangement work, keep each side of the room accessible to the door.

The Master Bath

The concept of the master bath has come of age. It is one of the most popular rooms to remodel and gives one of the highest returns on investment upon resale. It's where you can create that sought-after getaway—the home version of a European spa.

Some popular amenities to include in your plan are a sauna, greenhouse, exercise studio, fireplace, audio and video systems, faucets and sprayers with full massaging options, steam room, whirlpool tub, and dressing table. You are only limited by size and imagination—and some local codes.

Extras can be tempting but may require special planning. For example, you may need additional support in the floor, as well as supplemental heating and ventilation. You wouldn't want to slip in a

tub and have it fall two floors to the middle of the living room. Unfortunately, this really does happen when the weight of an over-

Though not large by today's standards, opposite bottom left, this bath offers many luxury amenities, including a spacious walk-in shower with both a fixed and a handheld showerhead and a convenient built-in toiletry niche.

This deep tub, below, is within easy reach of a warm, dry towel. Both the tub and the windows above it blend elements of modern and classic design.

A double-bowl vanity, right, outfitted with handsome hardware, features plenty of storage for two in drawers and behind doors.

sized contemporary tub is installed on top of a 50-year-old floor. Older houses simply weren't built to accommodate the volume of water some people now use when bathing.

Some of the best floor plans for the modern adult bath also include a separate room for the toilet and bidet, a detached tub and shower, and dual sinks on opposite sides of the room with adjacent dressing rooms and walk-in closets. Modern couples want to share a master bed and bath, but they also want to have privacy and the ease of getting ready in the morning without tripping over their mates. The only way to do this harmoniously is to mingle the parts of the room that invite sharing and separate those elements that are always private.

Plan #161002

Dimensions: 64'2" W x 44'2" D
Levels: 1
Square Footage: 1,860
Bedrooms: 3
Bathrooms: 2
Foundation: Basement
Materials List Available: Yes
Price Category: D

CAD FILE AVAILABLE · CAD ·

Images provided by designer/architect.

The brick, stone, and cedar shake facade provides color and texture to the exterior, while the unique nooks and angles inside this delightful one-level home give it character.

Features:

- Great Room/Dining Room: This spacious great room is furnished with a wood-burning fireplace, a high ceiling, and French doors. Wide entrances to the breakfast room and dining room expand its space to comfortably hold large gatherings.

- Kitchen: The breakfast bar offers additional seating. The covered porch lets you enjoy a view of the landscape and is conveniently located for outdoor meals off this kitchen and breakfast area.

- Master Suite: The master suite is a private retreat. An alcove creates a comfortable sitting area, and an angled entry leads to the bath with whirlpool and a double-bowl vanity.

Great Room/Foyer

Rear Elevation

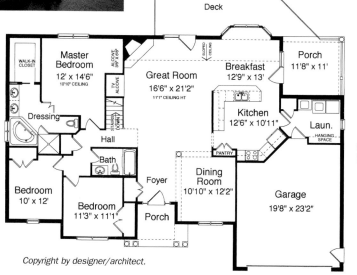

Copyright by designer/architect.

Plan #311024

Dimensions: 56' W x 45' D
Levels: 1
Square Footage: 1,492
Bedrooms: 3
Bathrooms: 2
Foundation: Crawl space, slab, or basement
Materials List Available: Yes
Price Category: C

With its uncomplicated layout, this charming, traditional house is a perfect starter or retirement home.

Features:

- **Porches:** Front and back covered porches allow you to enjoy the outdoors without leaving home. Sit out on warm summer evenings, enjoying the breeze and greeting passersby.

- **Kitchen:** This efficient layout includes a snack bar, which can act as a transition or buffet for the adjacent formal dining room.

- **Master Suite:** Enjoy a private entry to the porch, a walk-in closet, and a large master bath with his and her vanities, a large whirlpool tub, and a separate shower.

- **Secondary Bedrooms:** Two additional bedrooms have ample closet space and access to a shared bathroom, all tucked away from the main area of the home.

Images provided by designer/architect.

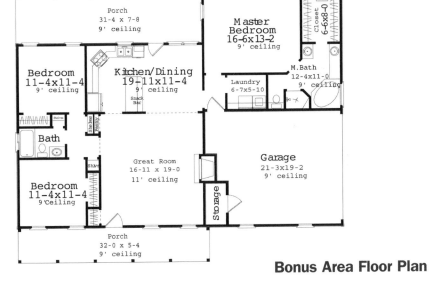

Rear View

Bonus Area Floor Plan

Copyright by designer/architect.

Plan #131021

Dimensions: 60' W x 52'4" D
Levels: 2
Square Footage: 3,110
Main Level Sq. Ft.: 1,818
Upper Level Sq. Ft.: 1,292
Bedrooms: 5
Bathrooms: 2½
Foundation: Crawl space or slab; basement for fee
Materials List Available: Yes
Price Category: H

This home, as shown in the photograph, may differ from the actual blueprints. For more detailed information, please check the floor plans carefully.

Images provided by designer/architect.

Amenities abound in this luxurious two-story beauty with a cozy gazebo on one corner of the spectacular wraparound front porch. Comfort, functionality, and spaciousness characterize this home.

Features:

• Ceiling Height: 8 ft.

• Foyer: This two-story high foyer is breathtaking.

• Family Room: Roomy with open views of the kitchen, the family room has a vaulted ceiling and boasts a functional fireplace and a built-in entertainment center.

• Dining Room: Formal yet comfortable, this spacious dining room is perfect for entertaining family and friends.

• Kitchen: Perfectly located with access to a breakfast room and the family room, this U-shaped kitchen with large center island is charming as well as efficient.

• Master Suite: Enjoy this sizable room with a vaulted ceiling, two large walk-in closets, and a lovely compartmented bath.

Copyright by designer/architect.

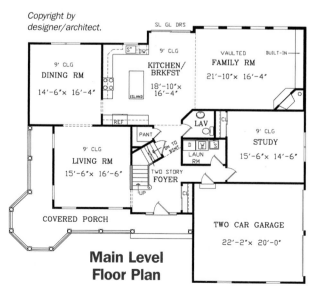

Main Level Floor Plan

Upper Level Floor Plan

Illustration provided by designer/architect.

Plan #101018

Dimensions: 56' W x 67' D
Levels: 2
Square Footage: 2,546
Main Level Sq. Ft.: 1,818
Upper Level Sq. Ft.: 728
Bedrooms: 4
Bathrooms: 3½
Foundation: Basement
Materials List Available: No
Price Category: E

CAD FILE AVAILABLE

The brick exterior of this home is accented with multilevel stucco trim and copper roof details.

Features:

- Ceiling Height: 9 ft. unless otherwise noted.

- Foyer: From the front porch you'll enter this dramatic two-story foyer highlighted by a corner niche.

- Dining Room: To one side of the foyer you will find this elegant dining room.

At 13 ft. x 12 ft., there's plenty of room for large dinner parties.

- Family Room: This dramatic room seems enormous, due to its two-story glass bay. It's open to the kitchen and the breakfast room.

- Master Suite: Just off the breakfast room is this luxurious master retreat. An enormous walk-in closet, a bath highlighted by a 5-ft. x 6-ft. whirlpool tub framed by decorative columns, and a vaulted ceiling with fixed glass above make this the most impressive area of the house.

- Secondary Bedrooms: Two of the upstairs bedrooms have direct access to their bath. All of the upper-level rooms have 8-ft. ceilings.

Main Level Floor Plan

MASTER BR 15x16

DECK

BRKFST 12x10

FAMILY ROOM 21x18

KITCHEN 15x13

3 CAR GARAGE 20x32

DINING 13x12

LIVING 13x12

Upper Level Floor Plan

BEDROOM 2 13x11

OPEN TO FAMILY ROOM

BONUS ROOM 20x36

BEDROOM 3 13x12

BEDROOM 4 13x12

Copyright by designer/architect.

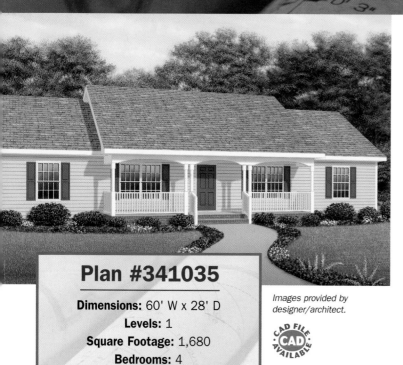

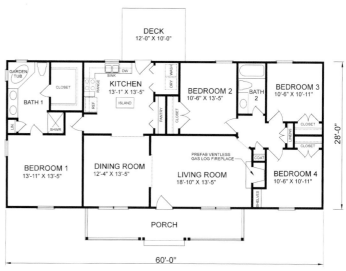

DECK
12'-0" X 10'-0"

GARDEN TUB

BATH 1

CLOSET

KITCHEN
13'-1" X 13'-5"

ISLAND

REF

RANGE

SINK

DW

DRY

WASH

BEDROOM 2
10'-6" X 13'-5"

BATH 2

BEDROOM 3
10'-6" X 11'-11"

PANTRY

CLOSET

CLOSET

LINENS

CLOSET

LIN

SHWR

BEDROOM 1
13'-11" X 13'-5"

DINING ROOM
12'-4" X 13'-5"

PREFAB VENTLESS GAS LOG FIREPLACE

LIVING ROOM
18'-10" X 13'-5"

COAT

BEDROOM 4
10'-6" X 11'-11"

SHELVES

PORCH

28'-0"

60'-0"

Plan #341035

Dimensions: 60' W x 28' D

Levels: 1

Square Footage: 1,680

Bedrooms: 4

Bathrooms: 2

Foundation: Crawl space, slab; basement option for fee

Materials List Available: Yes

Price Category: C

Images provided by designer/architect.

CAD FILE AVAILABLE

Copyright by designer/architect.

Copyright by designer/architect.

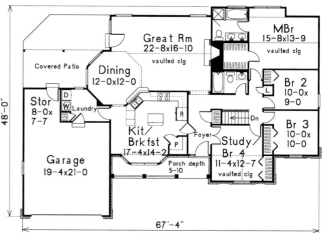

Great Rm
22-8x16-10
vaulted clg

MBr
15-8x13-9
vaulted clg

Covered Patio

Dining
12-0x12-0

Br 2
10-0x
9-0

Stor
8-0x
7-7

D W

Laundry

Kit/
Brkfst
17-4x14-2

Foyer

Dn

Study
Br 4
11-4x12-7
vaulted clg

Br 3
10-0x
10-0

Garage
19-4x21-0

Porch depth
5-10

48'-0"

67'-4"

Plan #321003

Dimensions: 67'4" W x 48' D

Levels: 1

Square Footage: 1,791

Bedrooms: 4

Bathrooms: 2

Foundation: Basement

Materials List Available: Yes

Price Category: E

Images provided by designer/architect.

CAD FILE AVAILABLE

Plan #131028

Dimensions: 69'2" W x 50'2" D
Levels: 2
Square Footage: 2,696
Main Level Sq. Ft.: 1,960
Upper Level Sq. Ft.: 736
Bedrooms: 4
Bathrooms: 3
Foundation: Crawl space or slab; basement for fee
Materials List Available: Yes
Price Category: F

Images provided by designer/architect.

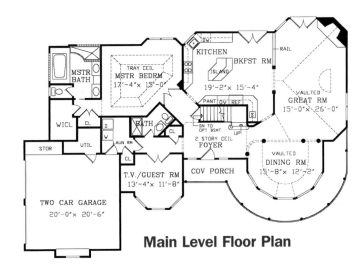

Main Level Floor Plan

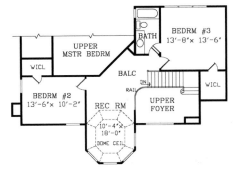

Upper Level Floor Plan

Copyright by designer/architect.

Plan #261001

Dimensions: 77'8" W x 49' D
Levels: 2
Square Footage: 3,746
Main Level Sq. Ft.: 1,965
Upper Level Sq. Ft.: 1,781
Bedrooms: 4
Bathrooms: 3½
Foundation: Basement
Materials List Available: No
Price Category: H

Images provided by designer/architect.

Main Level Floor Plan

Upper Level Floor Plan

Copyright by designer/architect.

Main Level Floor Plan

veranda

sitting 16 x 13

den 16 x 12

bkfst 10 x 9

family room 26 x 22

sloped clg

fireplace

entertainment ctr built-in

guest suite 14 x 13

mbr 21 x 16

bath

wic

util

kit

22 x 12

3 car garage 29 x 22

library 20 x 16

foy 13 x 9

dining 20 x 16

porch

sto 16 x 4

Images provided by designer/architect.

Upper Level Floor Plan

Copyright by designer/architect.

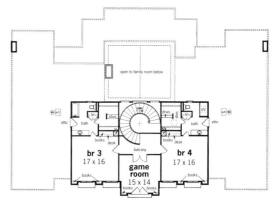

open to family room below

attic

bath

bath

attic

br 3 17 x 16

balcony

br 4 17 x 16

game room 15 x 14

Plan #211077

Dimensions: 94' W x 68' D

Levels: 2

Square Footage: 5,560

Main Level Sq. Ft.: 4,208

Upper Level Sq. Ft.: 1,352

Bedrooms: 4

Bathrooms: 4 full, 2 half

Foundation: Slab; crawl space for fee

Materials List Available: Yes

Price Category: J

DECK 19'-8" x 15'-0"

DINING 15'10" x 11'-0"

VAULTS TO 13'-5" PEAK

HEARTH ROOM 16'-7" x 13'-0"

12" HIGH CEILING TV NICHE

12' HIGH TRAY CEILING UP 1'

14' HIGH

MASTER BDRM 16'-0" x 15'-0"

14' HIGH CEILING

FAMILY ROOM 16'-0" x 19'-0"

KITCHEN 16'-0" x 13'-0"

BRKFST 10'-0" x 10'-6"

HERS

HIS

STAIRS TO BONUS ROOM

PANTRY

LINEN

BEDROOM 2 11'-0" x 14'-0"

BEDROOM 3 11'-0" x 14'-0"

13' HIGH CEILING

ENTRY 12' HIGH CEILING

UP

DN

STAIRS TO BASEMENT

62'-9"

PORCH 12' HIGH CEILING

GARAGE 21'-0" x 23'-0"

BONUS ROOM ABOVE

◄ 69'-4' ►

Images provided by designer/architect.

Copyright by designer/architect.

Plan #101012

Dimensions: 69'4" W x 62'9" D

Levels: 1

Square Footage: 2,288

Bedrooms: 3

Bathrooms: 2½

Foundation: Crawl space, slab, basement, or walkout

Materials List Available: No

Price Category: E

Living Room

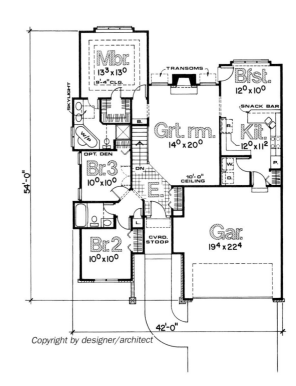

Plan #121002

Dimensions: 42' W x 54' D

Levels: 1

Square Footage: 1,347

Bedrooms: 3

Bathrooms: 2

Foundation: Basement

Materials List Available: Yes

Price Category: B

Images provided by designer/architect.

CAD FILE AVAILABLE

Copyright by designer/architect

Plan #181541

Dimensions: 42' W x 50' D

Levels: 2

Square Footage: 2,017

Main Level Sq. Ft.: 1,026

Upper Level Sq. Ft.: 991

Bedrooms: 3

Bathrooms: 1½

Foundation: Basement

Material List Available: Yes

Price Category: F

Images provided by designer/architect.

CAD FILE AVAILABLE

Main Level Floor Plan

Upper Level Floor Plan

Copyright by designer/architect.

Plan #181080

Dimensions: 44'8" W x 36' D
Levels: 2
Square Footage: 2,042
Main Level Sq. Ft.: 934
Upper Level Sq. Ft.: 1,108
Bedrooms: 3
Bathrooms: 2½
Foundation: Full basement
Materials List Available: Yes
Price Category: G

Images provided by designer/architect.

The second-floor balcony and angled tower are only two of the many design elements you'll love in this beautiful home.

Features:

- **Family Room:** Corner windows and sliding glass doors to the backyard let natural light pour into this spacious, open area.
- **Living Room:** Decorate around the deep bay to separate it from the adjacent dining area.

- **Dining Room:** Large windows and French doors to the kitchen are highlights here.
- **Kitchen:** The U-shaped counter aids efficiency, as does the handy lunch counter.
- **Master Suite:** From the sitting area in the bay to the walk-in closet and bath with tub and shower, this suite will pamper you.
- **Balcony:** Set a row of potted plants and a table and chairs on this perch above the street.

Main Level Floor Plan

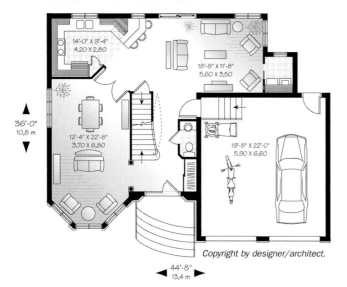

Copyright by designer/architect.

Upper Level Floor Plan

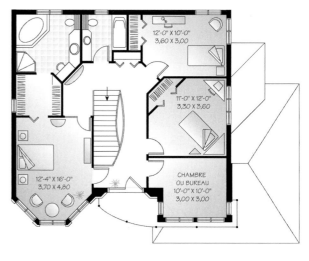

Plan #161095

Dimensions: 59' W x 49'8" D
Levels: 1
Square Footage: 3,620
Main Level Sq. Ft.: 2,068
Basement Level Sq. Ft.: 1,552
Bedrooms: 3
Bathrooms: 3
Foundation: Walkout basement
Material List Available: No
Price Category: H

This elegant ranch design has everything your family could want in a home.

Features:

- **Dining Room:** This column-accented formal area has a sloped ceiling and is open to the great room.

- **Great Room:** Featuring a cozy fireplace, this large gathering area offers a view of the backyard.

- **Kitchen:** This fully equipped island kitchen has everything the chef in the family could want.

- **Master Suite:** Located on the main level for privacy, this suite has a sloped ceiling in the sleeping area. The master bath boasts a whirlpool tub, a walk-in closet, and dual vanities.

Images provided by designer/architect.

This home, as shown in the photograph, may differ from the actual blueprints. For more detailed information, please check the floor plans carefully.

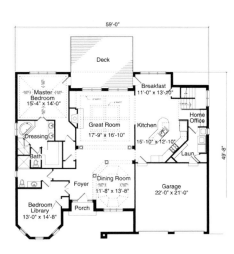

Main Level Floor Plan

Rear View

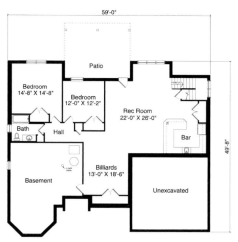

Lower Level Floor Plan

Copyright by designer/architect.

Plan #131026

Dimensions: 55'10" W x 41' D
Levels: 2
Square Footage: 2,796
Main Level Sq. Ft.: 1,481
Upper level Sq. Ft.: 1,315
Bedrooms: 4
Bathrooms: 2½
Foundation: Crawl space or slab; basement for fee
Materials List Available: Yes
Price Category: G

Images provided by designer/architect.

Handsome half rounds add to curb appeal.

Features:

• Ceiling Height: 8 ft.

• Library: This room features a 10-ft. ceiling with a bright bay window.

• Family Room: A 10-ft. ceiling adds to the spacious feeling of this room, while the fireplace gives it an intimate feeling. Sliding glass doors at the rear of the room open to the backyard.

• Dining Room: This formal room adjoins the living room, allowing guests and family to flow between the rooms, and it opens to the backyard through sliding glass doors.

• Breakfast Room: Turrets add a Victorian feeling to this room, which is just off the kitchen and overlooks the front porch.

• Master Suite: Privacy is assured in this suite, which is separated from the main part of the house. A separate toilet room and large walk-in closet add convenience to its beauty.

Master Bathroom

Family Room

Rear
Elevation

Upper Level Floor Plan

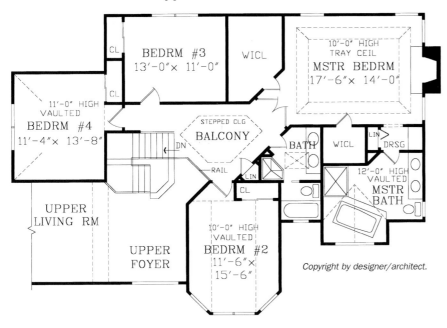

CL

BEDRM #3
13'-0" x 11'-0"

WICL

10'-0" HIGH
TRAY CEIL
MSTR BEDRM
17'-6" x 14'-0"

CL

11'-0" HIGH
VAULTED
BEDRM #4
11'-4" x 13'-8"

STEPPED CLG
BALCONY

DN

BATH

WICL

LIN

DRSG

RAIL

LIN

12'-0" HIGH
VAULTED
MSTR
BATH

CL

UPPER
LIVING RM

UPPER
FOYER

10'-0" HIGH
VAULTED
BEDRM #2
11'-6" x
15'-6"

Copyright by designer/architect.

Main Level Floor Plan

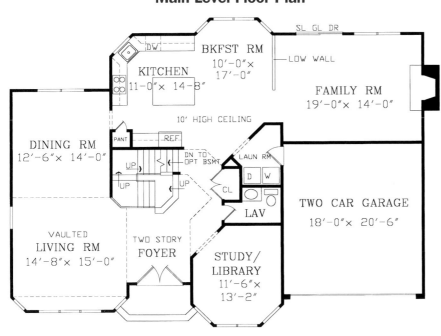

DW

SL GL DR

BKFST RM
10'-0" x
17'-0"

LOW WALL

KITCHEN
11'-0" x 14'-8"

FAMILY RM
19'-0" x 14'-0"

10' HIGH CEILING

PANT

REF.

DINING RM
12'-6" x 14'-0"

DN TO
OPT BSMT

LAUN RM

UP

D W

UP

UP

CL

LAV

TWO CAR GARAGE
18'-0" x 20'-6"

VAULTED
LIVING RM
14'-8" x 15'-0"

TWO STORY
FOYER

STUDY/
LIBRARY
11'-6" x
13'-2"

SMARTtip
Paint Basics

Most interior paints are either alkyd-resin (oil-based) products or latex (water-based) varieties. Oil and water don't mix, and generally neither do the paints based on them. For multi-layered effects, stick to one type or the other.

Alkyd paints are somewhat lustrous, translucent, and hard-wearing. But alkyds, and the solvents needed for cleaning up, are toxic and combustible, requiring good work-site ventilation and special disposal methods. Professional decorative painters often prefer slower-drying alkyds, which allow more time to achieve complex special effects. Alkyd paints are better suited to techniques such as combing and ragging, where glaze is brushed on in sections and then manipulated.

Latex paints, which now approach alkyd's durability and textural range, are nontoxic and quick-drying, and they clean up easily with soap and water. Most nonprofessionals find latex paint easier to deal with and capable of creating many popular decorative finishes. In general, latex paints are best suited to effects that are dabbed on over the base coat, as in sponging or stenciling. The short drying time can be an advantage, because mistakes can be painted over and redone.

Latex paint is usually the best choice for covering an entire wall, too, because the job can be completed from start to finish in just a few hours.

Plan #121024

Dimensions: 60' W x 58' D

Levels: 2

Square Footage: 3,057

Main Level Sq. Ft.: 1,631

Second Level Sq. Ft.: 1,426

Bedrooms: 4

Bathrooms: 2½

Foundation: Basement

Materials List Available: Yes

Price Category: G

Images provided by designer/architect.

This distinctive home offers plenty of space and is designed for gracious and convenient living.

Features:

• Ceiling Height: 8 ft. unless otherwise noted.

• Foyer: A curved staricase in this elegant entry will greet your guests.

• Living Room: This room invites you with a volume ceiling flanked by transom-topped windows that flood the room with sunlight.

• Screened Veranda: On warm summer nights, throw open the French doors in the living room and enjoy a breeze on the huge screened veranda.

• Dining Room: This distinctive room is overlooked by the veranda.

• Family Room: At the back of the home is this comfortable family retreat with its soaring cathedral ceiling and handsome fireplace flanked by bookcases.

• Master Suite: This bayed bedroom features a 10-ft. vaullted ceiling.

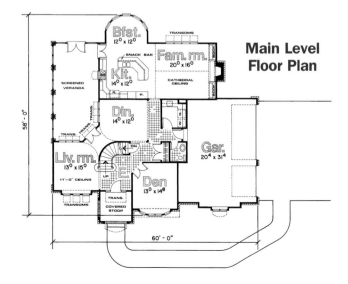

Main Level Floor Plan

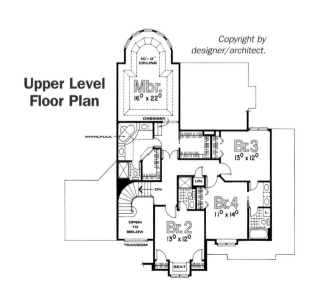

Copyright by designer/architect.

Upper Level Floor Plan

Plan #401015

Dimensions: 56' W x 50'4" D
Levels: 2
Square Footage: 2,618
Main Level Sq. Ft.: 1,464
Upper Level Sq. Ft.: 1,154
Bedrooms: 3
Bathrooms: 3
Foundation: Basement
Materials List Available: Yes
Price Category: F

Images provided by designer/architect.

High vaulted ceilings and floor-to-ceiling windows enhance the spaciousness of this home. Decorative columns separate the living room from the tray-ceiling dining room.

Features:

- Kitchen: This gourmet kitchen offers a center food-preparation island, a pantry, and a pass-through to the family room and breakfast bay.

- Family Room: This spacious room boasts a fireplace and vaulted ceiling open to the second-level hallway.

- Den: This room has a wall closet and private access to a full bath. It can be used as extra guest space if needed.

- Master Suite: Located on the second floor, this area holds a bay-windowed sitting area, a walk-in closet, and a bath with a whirlpool tub and separate shower.

- Bedrooms: Family bedrooms are at the other end of the hall upstairs and share a full bath.

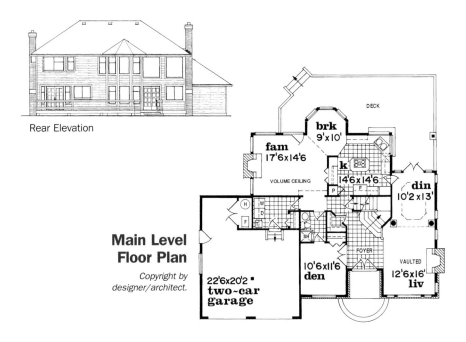

Rear Elevation

Main Level Floor Plan

Copyright by designer/architect.

Upper Level Floor Plan

Plan #161018

Dimensions: 74'4" W x 69'11" D

Levels: 2

Square Footage: 2,816
+ 325 Sq. Ft. bonus room

Main Level Sq. Ft.: 2,231

Upper Level Sq. Ft.: 624

Bedrooms: 3

Bathrooms: 2 full, 2 half

Foundation: Basement

Materials List Available: No

Price Category: F

Images provided by designer/architect.

If you love classic European designs, look closely at this home with its multiple gables and countless conveniences and luxuries.

Features:

• **Foyer:** Open to the great room, the 2-story foyer offers a view all the way to the rear windows.

• **Great Room:** A fireplace makes this room cozy in any kind of weather.

• **Kitchen:** This large room features an island with a sink, and an angled wall with French doors to the back yard.

• **Dining Room:** The furniture alcove and raised ceiling make this room both formal and practical.

• **Master Suite:** You'll love the quiet in the bedroom and the luxuries—a tub, separate shower, and double vanities—in the bath.

• **Basement:** The door from the basement to the side yard adds convenience to outdoor work.

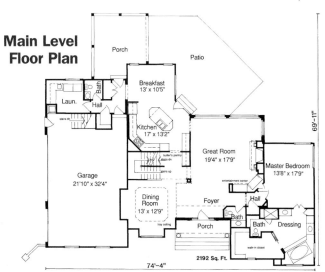

Main Level Floor Plan

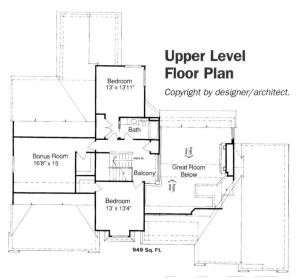

Upper Level Floor Plan

Copyright by designer/architect.

Rear View

Rear Elevation

Foyer/Dining Room

Living Room

Plan #121093

Dimensions: 62' W x 60'8" D
Levels: 2
Square Footage: 2,603
Main Level Sq. Ft.: 1,800
Upper Level Sq. Ft.: 803
Bedrooms: 4
Bathrooms: 3½
Foundation: Basement
Materials List Available: Yes
Price Category: F

If you love family life but also treasure your privacy, you'll appreciate the layout of this home.

Features:

- Entry: This two-story, open area features plant shelves to display a group of lovely specimens.
- Dining Room: Open to the entry, this room features 12-ft. ceilings and corner hutches.
- Den: French doors lead to this quiet room, with its bowed window and spider-beamed ceiling.
- Gathering Room: A three-sided fireplace, shared with both the kitchen and the breakfast area, is the highlight of this room.
- Master Suite: Secluded for privacy, this suite also has a private covered deck where you can sit and recharge at any time of day. A walk-in closet is practical, and a whirlpool tub is pure comfort.

Main Level Floor Plan

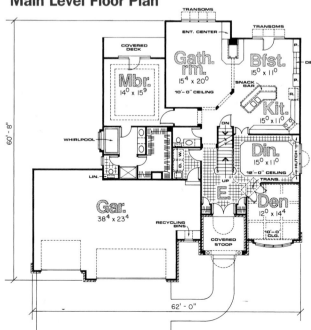

Upper Level Floor Plan

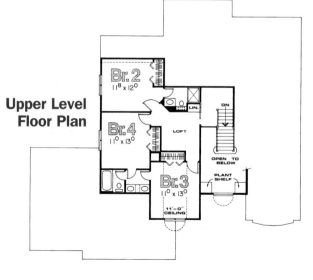

Plan #161094

Dimensions: 68'8" W x 56'8" D
Levels: 2
Square Footage: 3,366
Main Level Sq. Ft.: 1,759
Upper Level Sq. Ft.: 1,607
Bedrooms: 5
Bathrooms: 4
Foundation: Walkout basement
Material List Available: No
Price Category: G

This home, as shown in the photograph, may differ from the actual blueprints. For more detailed information, please check the floor plans carefully.

Images provided by designer/architect.

This luxurious two-story home combines a stately exterior style with a large, functional floor plan.

Features:

- **Great Room:** The volume ceiling in this room is decorated with wood beams and reaches a two-story height, while 9-ft. ceiling heights prevail throughout the rest of the first floor.

- **Bright and Open:** Split stairs lead to the second-floor balcony, which offers a dramatic view of the great room. Light radiates through the multiple rear windows

to flood the great room, breakfast area, and kitchen with natural daylight.

- **Master Suite:** Built-in bookshelves flank the entrance to this lavish retreat, with its large sitting area, which is surrounded by windows, and deluxe master bath, which sports spacious closets, dual vanities, and an oversized whirlpool tub.

- **Bedrooms:** Three more bedrooms, each with large closets and private access to the bathroom, complete this family-friendly home.

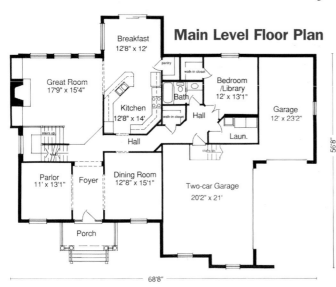

Main Level Floor Plan

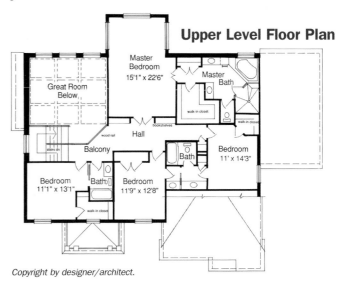

Upper Level Floor Plan

Copyright by designer/architect.

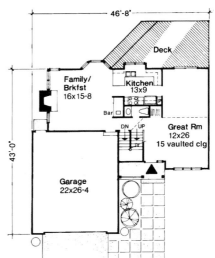

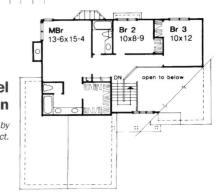

**Main Level
Floor Plan**

*Images provided by
designer/architect.*

Plan #271010

Dimensions: 46'8" W x 43' D

Levels: 2

Square Footage: 1,724

Main Level Sq. Ft.: 922

Upper Level Sq. Ft.: 802

Bedrooms: 3

Bathrooms: 2½

Foundation: Basement

Materials List Available: Yes

Price Category: C

**Upper Level
Floor Plan**

*Copyright by
designer/architect.*

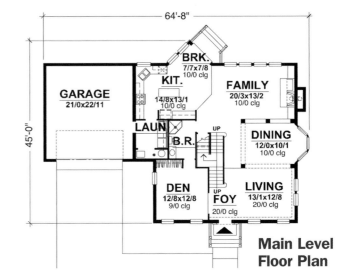

**Main Level
Floor Plan**

*Images provided by
designer/architect.*

Plan #271305

Dimensions: 64'8" W x 45' D

Levels: 2

Square Footage: 2,526

Main Level Sq. Ft.: 1,555

Upper Level Sq. Ft.: 971

Bedrooms: 3

Bathrooms: 3

Foundation: Slab

Material List Available: No

Price Category: E

Upper Level Floor Plan

Copyright by designer/architect.

Plan #181101

Dimensions: 58' W x 43' D

Levels: 2

Square Footage: 1,936

Main Level Sq. Ft.: 1,044

Second Level Sq. Ft.: 892

Bedrooms: 3

Bathrooms: 2½

Foundation: Basement

Materials List Available: Yes

Price Category: F

Images provided by designer/architect.

Upper Level Floor Plan

Main Level Floor Plan

Copyright by designer/architect.

Plan #131014

Dimensions: 48' W x 43'4" D

Levels: 1

Square Footage: 1,380

Bedrooms: 3

Bathrooms: 2

Foundation: Crawl space or slab; basement or walkout for fee

Materials List Available: Yes

Price Category: C

Images provided by designer/architect.

Copyright by designer/architect.

Bonus Room

Rear Elevation

Copyright by designer/architect.

Plan #151117

Dimensions: 66' W x 55' D

Levels: 1

Square Footage: 1,957

Bedrooms: 3

Bathrooms: 3

Foundation: Crawl space or slab; basement for fee

CompleteCost List Available: Yes

Price Category: D

Images provided by designer/architect.

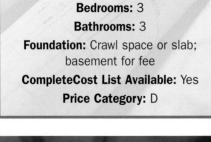

CAD FILE AVAILABLE

Bonus Area

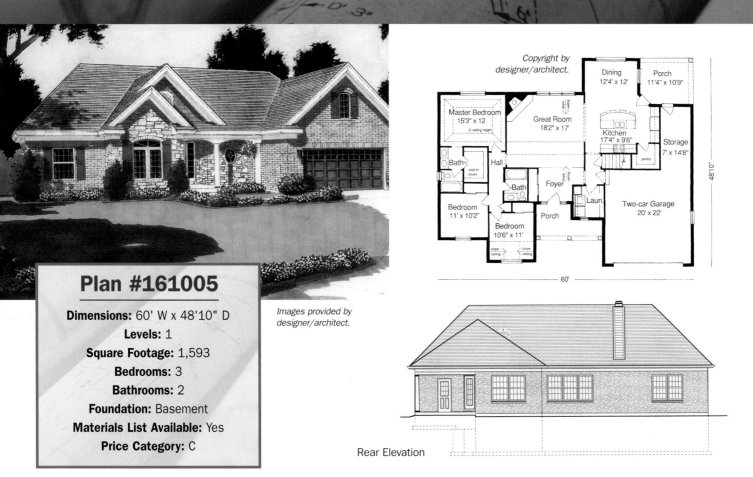

Copyright by designer/architect.

Plan #161005

Dimensions: 60' W x 48'10" D

Levels: 1

Square Footage: 1,593

Bedrooms: 3

Bathrooms: 2

Foundation: Basement

Materials List Available: Yes

Price Category: C

Images provided by designer/architect.

Rear Elevation

Plan #151168

Dimensions: 66' W x 65'2" D

Levels: 1

Square Footage: 2,261

Bedrooms: 4

Bathrooms: 2½

Foundation: Crawl space, slab, basement, or daylight basement

CompleteCost List Available: Yes

Price Category: E

Bonus Room

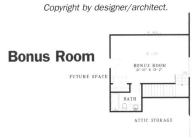

Main Level Floor Plan

Plan #151853

Dimensions: 73'2" W x 86'8" D

Levels: 1.5

Square Footage: 2,885

Main Level Sq. Ft.: 2,599

Upper Level Sq. Ft.: 286

Bedrooms: 4

Bathrooms: 3½

Foundation: Crawl space, slab

Material List Available: No

Price Category: F

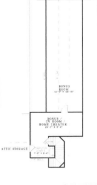

Upper Level Floor Plan

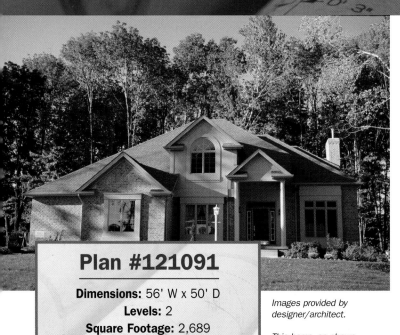

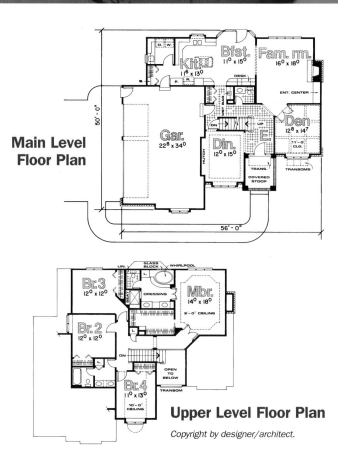

Main Level Floor Plan

Plan #121091

Dimensions: 56' W x 50' D

Levels: 2

Square Footage: 2,689

Main Level Sq. Ft.: 1,415

Upper Level Sq. Ft.: 1,274

Bedrooms: 4

Bathrooms: 2½

Foundation: Basement

Materials List Available: Yes

Price Category: F

Images provided by designer/architect.

This home, as shown in the photograph, may differ from the actual blueprints. For more detailed information, please check the floor plans carefully.

Upper Level Floor Plan

Copyright by designer/architect.

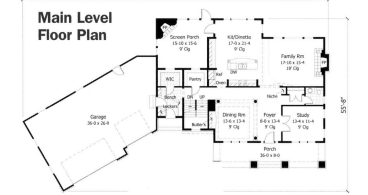

Main Level Floor Plan

Plan #481021

Dimensions: 98'4" W x 55'8" D

Levels: 2

Square Footage: 3,289

Main Level Sq. Ft.: 1,680

Upper Level Sq. Ft.: 1,609

Bedrooms: 3

Bathrooms: 2½

Foundation: Walkout

Material List Available: No

Price Category: G

Images provided by designer/architect.

Upper Level Floor Plan

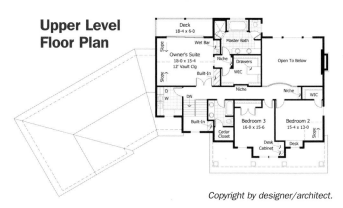

Copyright by designer/architect.

Plan #161025

Dimensions: 63'4" W x 48' D

Levels: 2

Square Footage: 2,738

Main Level Sq. Ft.: 1,915

Upper Level Sq. Ft.: 823

Bedrooms: 4

Bathrooms: 3½

Foundation: Basement

Materials List Available: No

Price Category: F

Images provided by designer/architect.

This home, as shown in the photograph, may differ from the actual blueprints. For more detailed information, please check the floor plans carefully.

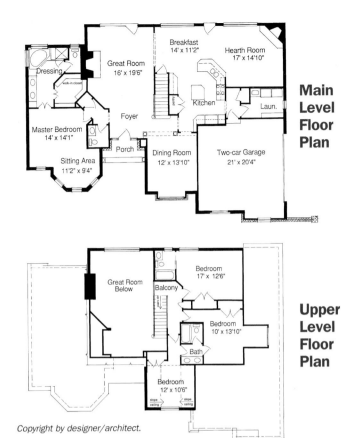

Main Level Floor Plan

- Dressing
- walk-in closet
- Great Room 16' x 19'6"
- Breakfast 14' x 11'2"
- Hearth Room 17' x 14'10"
- Kitchen
- Laun.
- Foyer
- Master Bedroom 14' x 14'1"
- Porch
- Dining Room 12' x 13'10"
- Two-car Garage 21' x 20'4"
- Sitting Area 11'2" x 9'4"

Upper Level Floor Plan

- Great Room Below
- Balcony
- Bedroom 17' x 12'6"
- Bedroom 10' x 13'10"
- Bath
- Bedroom 12' x 10'6"
- slope ceiling / slope ceiling

Copyright by designer/architect.

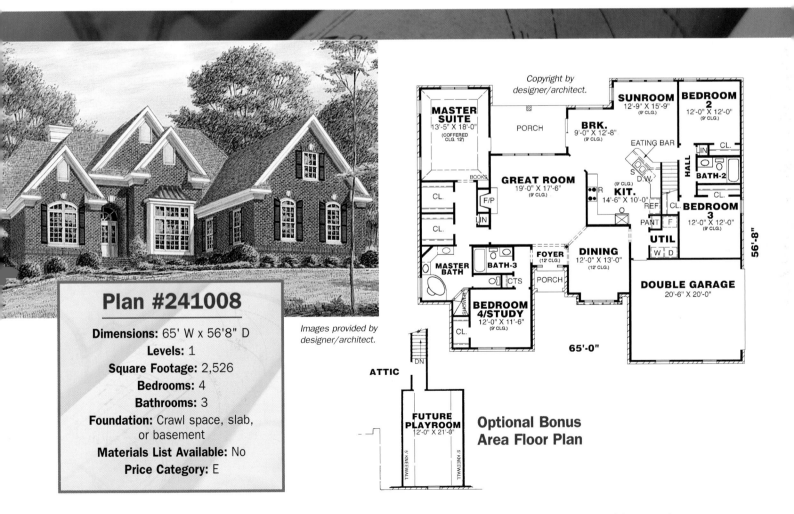

Plan #241008

Dimensions: 65' W x 56'8" D

Levels: 1

Square Footage: 2,526

Bedrooms: 4

Bathrooms: 3

Foundation: Crawl space, slab, or basement

Materials List Available: No

Price Category: E

Images provided by designer/architect.

Copyright by designer/architect.

- MASTER SUITE 13'-5" X 18'-0" (COFFERED CLG. 12)
- PORCH
- BRK. 9'-0" X 12'-8" (9' CLG.)
- SUNROOM 12'-9" X 15'-9" (9' CLG.)
- BEDROOM 2 12'-0" X 12'-0" (9' CLG.)
- EATING BAR
- BOOKS
- GREAT ROOM 19'-0" X 17'-6" (9' CLG.)
- KIT. 14'-6" X 10'-0" (9' CLG.)
- HALL
- BATH-2
- CL.
- F/P
- LIN
- REF
- CL.
- BEDROOM 3 12'-0" X 12'-0" (9' CLG.)
- PANT
- UTIL
- W D
- MASTER BATH
- BATH-3
- CTS
- FOYER (12' CLG.)
- DINING 12'-0" X 13'-0" (12' CLG.)
- PORCH
- DOUBLE GARAGE 20'-6" X 20'-0"
- BEDROOM 4/STUDY 12'-0" X 11'-6" (9' CLG.)
- CL.
- 56'-8"
- 65'-0"

Optional Bonus Area Floor Plan

- ATTIC
- DN
- FUTURE PLAYROOM 12'-0" X 21'-0"
- 5' KNEEWALL

Plan #121114

Dimensions: 64' W x 52' D
Levels: 1.5
Square Footage: 2,115
Main Level Sq. Ft.: 1,505
Upper Level Sq. Ft.: 610
Bedrooms: 4
Bathrooms: 2½
Foundation: Basement;
crawl space for fee
Materials List Available: Yes
Price Category: D

Images provided by designer/architect.

This contemporary home is not only beautifully designed on the outside; it has everything you need on the inside. It will be the envy of the neighborhood.

CAD FILE AVAILABLE

Features:

- Great Room: The cathedral ceiling and cozy fireplace strike a balance that creates the perfect gathering place for family and friends. An abundance of space allows you to tailor this room to your needs.

- Kitchen/Breakfast Room: This combined area features a flood of natural light, workspace to spare, an island with a snack bar, and a door that opens to the backyard, creating an ideal space for outdoor meals and gatherings.

- Dining Room: A triplet of windows projecting onto the covered front porch creates a warm atmosphere for formal dining.

- Master Bedroom: Away from the busy areas of the home, this master suite is ideal for shedding your daily cares and relaxing in a romantic atmosphere. It includes a full master bath with skylight, his and her sinks, a stall shower, a whirlpool tub, and a walk-in closet.

- Second Floor: Three more bedrooms and the second full bathroom upstairs give you plenty of room for a large family. Or if you only need two extra rooms, use the fourth bedroom as a study or entertainment area for the kids.

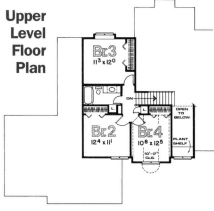

Copyright by designer/architect.

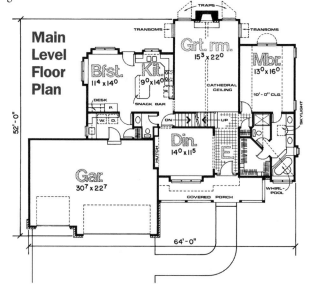

Plan #121086

Dimensions: 55'4" W x 37'8" D

Levels: 2

Square Footage: 1,998

Main Level Sq. Ft.: 1,093

Upper Level Sq. Ft.: 905

Bedrooms: 3

Bathrooms: 2½

Foundation: Basement

Materials List Available: Yes

Price Category: D

Images provided by designer/architect.

You'll love the open design of this comfortable home if sunny, bright rooms make you happy.

Features:

- Entry: Walk into this two-story entry, and you're sure to admire the open staircase and balcony from the upper level.
- Dining Room: To the left of the entry, you'll see this dining room, with its special ceiling detail and built-in display cabinet.

- Living Room: Located immediately to the right, this living room features a charming bay window.
- Family Room: French doors from the living room open into this sunny space, where a handsome fireplace takes center stage.
- Kitchen: Combined with the breakfast area, this kitchen features an island cooktop, a large pantry, and a built-in desk.

Upper Level Floor Plan

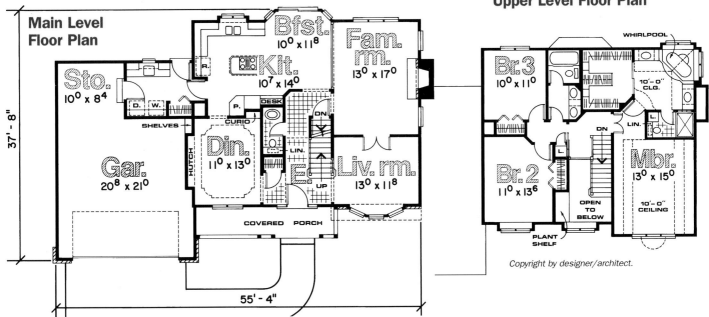

Copyright by designer/architect.

Plan #131007

Dimensions: 59'10" W x 47'8" D

Levels: 1

Square Footage: 1,595

Bedrooms: 3

Bathrooms: 2

Foundation: Crawl space or slab; basement or walkout for fee

Materials List Available: Yes

Price Category: D

Imagine living in this home, with its traditional country comfort and individual brand of charm.

Features:

- Exterior elements: The mixture of a front porch with a cameo front door, decorative posts, bay windows, and dormers will delight you.

- Great Room: A tray ceiling gives distinction to this large room, and a wet bar eases entertaining.

- Screened Porch: At dusk and dawn, this porch is sure to be your favorite outdoor spot.

- Kitchen: Eat any meal in this large kitchen for a touch of homey charm.

- Dining Room: Perfect for hosting a formal dinner, this bayed dining room can increase your enjoyment of simple family meals.

- Master Bedroom: For the sake of privacy, this room is somewhat secluded. Decorate to emphasize the elegant tray ceiling.

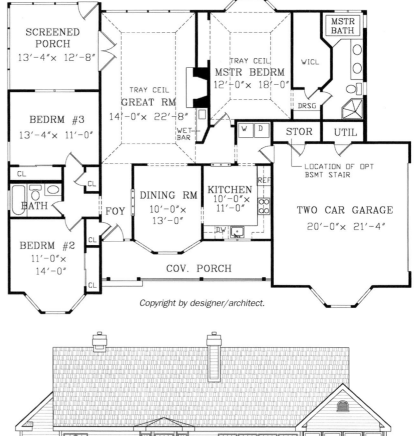

Copyright by designer/architect.

Rear Elevation

Alternate Front View

Foyer / Dining Room

Great Room

Add the Extras

Simple or plain, it's the little conveniences and miscellaneous touches that push the dining experience to perfection. Here are some extra things to think about.

- You can never have too many serving trays when you entertain outside. For carrying food or drinks from the kitchen or the grill, trays are indispensable.

- A serving cart on wheels makes a perfect movable outdoor bar and provides an additional serving surface. Look for one at yard sales or buy one new.

- Chances are you won't have a sideboard, but a few small tables to hold excess items are great substitutes for one. They're also easier to position in the different places where you need them.

- For cooler weather or even a summer's evening with a bit of nip in the air, nothing beats an outdoor fireplace for comfort. You could build one into the house, but various types of stand-alone units are sold in home centers. To add a Southwest ambiance, consider a chiminea, a clay fireplace. Try burning some piñon pine, and you'll feel as if you're in Santa Fe. Be sure to follow manufacturers' instructions when using these fireplaces. You might also have to store them during the winter.

- Pots of fragrant plants—lavender, scented geraniums, flowering tobacco, or jasmine—provide a sensual aroma. Flowers such as roses climbing up an arbor or trellis are beautiful, evoke a romantic feeling, and lend a delicate scent to the atmosphere as well.

Nothing adds romance and intrigue to an evening soiree as candlelight does. Include just a few candles for an intimate dinner. Use more for a larger gathering, placing one or more on each table. Scatter luminaries around the yard. As the beautiful evening dusk begins, light candles, a few at a time, so your eyes can adjust to the dimming light. Not only do the candles illuminate the night in a magical way but they can also keep bugs at bay.

Plan #151118

Dimensions: 54'2" W x 73'6" D
Levels: 2
Square Footage: 2,784
Main Level Sq. Ft.: 1,895
Upper Level Sq. Ft.: 889
Bedrooms: 4
Bathrooms: 2½
Foundation: Crawl space, slab, or basement
CompleteCost List Available: Yes
Price Category: F

Images provided by designer/architect.

CAD FILE AVAILABLE

Upper Level Floor Plan

Main Level Floor Plan

Copyright by designer/architect.

Plan #311002

Dimensions: 56'6" W x 82' D
Levels: 1
Square Footage: 2,402
Bedrooms: 4
Bathrooms: 2½
Foundation: Crawl space, slab
Materials List Available: Yes
Price Category: F

Images provided by designer/architect.

Bonus Area

Main Level Floor Plan

Copyright by designer/architect.

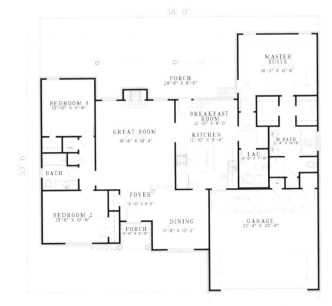

Images provided by designer/architect.

Plan #151173

Dimensions: 58' W x 53'6" D
Levels: 1
Square Footage: 1,739
Bedrooms: 3
Bathrooms: 2
Foundation: Crawl space, slab, basement, or walkout
CompleteCost List Available: Yes
Price Category: C

Copyright by designer/architect.

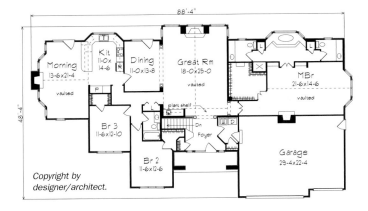

Copyright by designer/architect.

Plan #321018

Dimensions: 88'4" W x 48'4" D
Levels: 1
Square Footage: 2,523
Bedrooms: 3
Bathrooms: 2
Foundation: Basement
Materials List Available: Yes
Price Category: E

Images provided by designer/architect.

SMARTtip

Tiebacks

You don't have to limit yourself to tiebacks made from matching or contrasting fabric. Achieve creative custom looks by making tiebacks from unexpected items. Some materials to consider are old cotton bandannas or silk scarves, strings of beads, lengths of leather, or old belts and chains.

Plan #131023

Dimensions: 78'8" W x 36'2" D
Levels: 2
Square Footage: 2,460
Main Level Sq. Ft.: 1,377
Upper Level Sq. Ft.: 1,083
Bedrooms: 4
Bathrooms: 3½
Foundation: Crawl space or slab;
basement for fee
Materials List Available: Yes
Price Category: F

Images provided by designer/architect.

You'll love the modern floor plan inside this traditional two-story home, with its attractive facade.

Features:

- Ceiling Height: 8 ft.

- Living Room: The windows on three sides of this room make it bright and sunny. Choose the optional fireplace for cozy winter days and the wet bar for elegant entertaining.

- Family Room: Overlooking the rear deck, this spacious family room features a fireplace and a skylight.

- Dining Room: The convenient placement of this large room lets guests flow into it from the living room and allows easy to access from the kitchen.

- Kitchen: The island cooktop and built-in desk make this space both modern and practical.

Rear Elevation

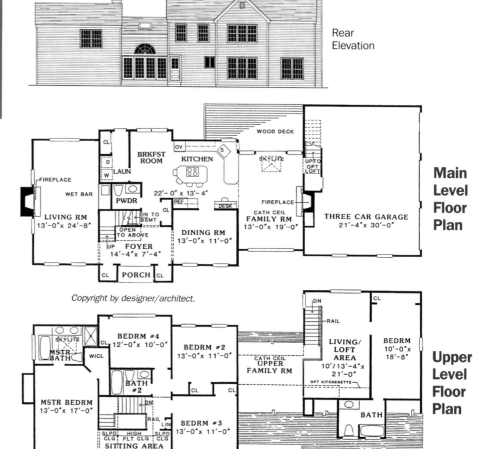

Main Level Floor Plan

Copyright by designer/architect.

Upper Level Floor Plan

Plan #271001

Dimensions: 52'8" W x 35'4" D
Levels: 1
Square Footage: 1,400
Bedrooms: 3
Bathrooms: 2
Foundation: Basement
Materials List Available: Yes
Price Category: B

This contemporary design builds on the basics, creating a comfortable home that offers possibilities for entertaining or quiet downtime.

Features:

• Great room: The heart of the home, this massive gathering room features a handsome fireplace and a handy wet bar, and flows into the dining space. Sliding glass doors between the two spaces lead to a deck.

• Kitchen/Breakfast: This combination space uses available space efficiently and comfortably.

• Master Suite: The inviting master bedroom includes a private bath.

Images provided by designer/architect.

Copyright by designer/architect.

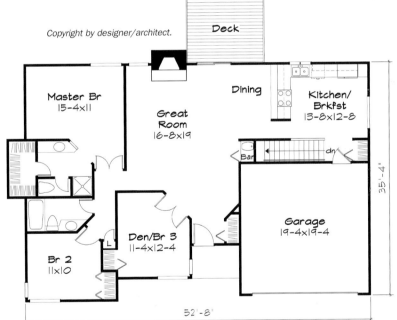

SMARTtip

Candid Camera for Your Landscaping

To see your home and yard as others see them, take some camera shots. Seeing your house and landscaping on film will create an opportunity for objectivity. Problems will become more obvious, and you will then be better able to prioritize your home improvements, as well as your landscaping plan.

Plan #321001

Dimensions: 83' W x 42' D

Levels: 1

Square Footage: 1,721

Bedrooms: 3

Bathrooms: 2

Foundation: Crawl space, slab, or basement

Materials List Available: Yes

Price Category: E

Images provided by designer/architect.

Rear View

You'll love the atrium which creates a warm, naturally lit space inside this gracious home, as well as the roof dormers that give the house wonderful curb appeal from the outside.

Features:

- **Great Room:** Bathed in light from the atrium window wall, this room, with its vaulted ceiling, will be the hub of your family life.

- **Dining Room:** This room also has a vaulted ceiling and is lit by the atrium, but you can draw drapes at night to create a cozy, warm feeling.

- **Kitchen:** Designed for functionality, this step-saving kitchen is easy to organize and makes cooking a pleasure.

- **Breakfast Room:** For convenience, this room is located between the kitchen and the rear covered porch.

- **Master Suite:** Retire with pleasure to this lovely retreat, with its luxurious bath.

Copyright by designer/architect.

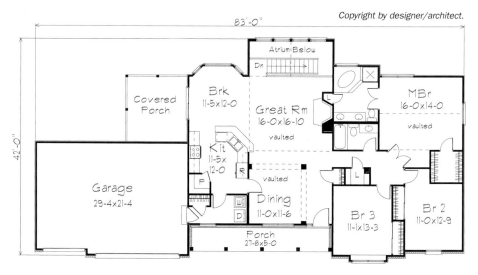

Plan #121072

Dimensions: 64' W x 53'4"D
Levels: 2
Square Footage: 3,031
Main Level Sq. Ft.: 1,640
Upper Level Sq. Ft.: 1,391
Bedrooms: 4
Bathrooms: 2½
Foundation: Basement; slab for fee
Materials List Available: Yes
Price Category: G

Images provided by designer/architect.

If you're looking for a home with well-designed rooms and interesting architectural innovations, this could be your heart's desire.

Features:

- **Foyer:** This foyer has an impressive two-story ceiling and is lit by the arched transom and sidelights at the entryway.

- **Living Room:** Just off the foyer, this room has a 12-ft. angled ceiling. Decorate to emphasize the arched window here.

- **Den:** French doors open to the den, where a spider-beamed ceiling sets an elegant tone.

- **Kitchen:** This well-designed kitchen is sure to be the delight of every cook in the family.

- **Master Suite:** French doors open into this suite, with built-in dressers tucked into a huge closet and a bath with a whirlpool tub and two vanities.

Main Level Floor Plan

Upper Level Floor Plan

Copyright by designer/architect.

57'-6" OVERALL
(77'-10" W/ OPT. GARAGE)

ALT. LOCATION OF GAR. DRS.

OPTIONAL
TWO CAR GARAGE
20'-0" x 20'-0"

ALT. LOCATION OF GAR. DRS.

SL GL DRS

WICL
MSTR BATH
WICL

FIREPLACE
10' CLG
GREAT RM
18'-2" 16'-10"x 19'-8"

OPTIONAL BUILT-IN

10'-5" HIGH TRAY CEIL
MSTR BEDRM
13'-0"x 17'-0"
+ BAY

SEAT

10' CLG
BKFST RM
10'-6" x 9'-6"

DV
KIT
11'-10" x 13'-0"

DN TO OPT. BSMT

10' CLG
OFFICE/ PARLOR/ BEDRM #4
11'-6"x 11'-0"

FOY

BATH
LAUN RM

REF.

BEDRM #3
11'-0"x 11'-0"

10' CLG
DINING RM
11'-6"x 13'-4"

BEDRM #2
12'-2" 11'-0"
+ BAY

SEAT

COVERED PORCH

42'-4" OVERALL
(54'-0" W/ OPT. GARAGE)

Images provided by designer/architect.

Plan #131044

Dimensions: 65'4" W x 45'10" D

Levels: 1

Square Footage: 1,892

Bedrooms: 3

Bathrooms: 2½

Foundation: Crawl space or slab; basement for fee

Materials List Available: Yes

Price Category: E

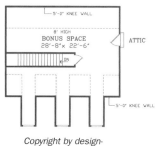

Rear Elevation

Bonus Area

5'-0" KNEE WALL

8' HIGH
BONUS SPACE
28'-8" x 22'-6"

ATTIC

DN

5'-0" KNEE WALL

Copyright by designer/architect.

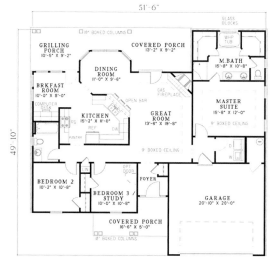

51'-6"

GLASS BLOCKS

GRILLING PORCH
10'-5" x 9'-2"

10" BOXED COLUMNS

COVERED PORCH
13'-2" x 9'-2"

WHP TUB

M. BATH
15'-4" x 10'-8"

BRKFAST ROOM
10'-8" X 8'-0"

DINING ROOM
11'-0" X 9'-6"

GAS FIREPLACE

MASTER SUITE
15'-8" X 12'-0"

COMPUTER DESK

OPEN BAR

9' BOXED CEILING

KITCHEN
15'-2" X 11'-0"

REF

PANTRY

GREAT ROOM
13'-6" X 19'-8"

9' BOXED CEILING

49'-10"

BEDROOM 2
10'-2" X 10'-8"

OPT. DOOR

BEDROOM 3 / STUDY
10'-0" X 10'-8"

FOYER

GARAGE
20'-10" X 20'-0"

COVERED PORCH
16'-6" X 5'-0"

10" BOXED COLUMNS

Copyright by designer/architect.

Plan #151169

Dimensions: 51'6" W x 49'10" D

Levels: 1

Square Footage: 1,525

Bedrooms: 3

Bathrooms: 2

Foundation: Crawl space of slab; basement or walkout for fee

CompleteCost List Available: Yes

Price Category: C

Images provided by designer/architect.

CAD FILE AVAILABLE

Rear Elevation

Plan #151528

Dimensions: 41'4" W x 84'2" D

Levels: 1

Square Footage: 1,747

Bedrooms: 2

Bathrooms: 2

Foundation: Crawl space or slab

CompleteCost List Available: Yes

Price Category: C

Images provided by designer/architect.

Front View

Plan #461168

Dimensions: 58' W x 35'6" D

Levels: 2

Square Footage: 1,756

Main Level Sq. Ft.: 874

Upper Level Sq. Ft.: 882

Bedrooms: 3

Bathrooms: 2½

Foundation: Crawl space, slab

Material List Available: No

Price Category: C

Images provided by designer/architect.

Main Level Floor Plan

Upper Level Floor Plan

Copyright by designer/architect.

Plan #121163

Dimensions: 65'10" W x 75'6" D
Levels: 1
Square Footage: 2,679
Bedrooms: 4
Bathrooms: 3
Foundation: Slab; basement for fee
Material List Available: Yes
Price Category: F

Images provided by designer/architect.

Large rooms give this home a spacious feel in a modest footprint.

Features:

- **Family Room:** This area is the central gathering place in the home. The windows to the rear fill the area with natural light. The fireplace take the chill off on cool winter nights.

- **Kitchen:** This peninsula kitchen with raised bar is open into the family room and the breakfast area. The built-in pantry is a welcomed storage area for today's family.

- **Master Suite:** This secluded area features large windows with a view of the backyard. The master bath boasts a large walk-in closet, his and her vanities and a compartmentalized lavatory area.

- **Secondary Bedrooms:** Bedroom 2 has its own access to the main bathroom, while bedrooms 3 and 4 share a Jack-and-Jill bathroom. All bedrooms feature walk-in closets.

Copyright by designer/architect.

Plan #321005

Dimensions: 69' W x 53'8" D
Levels: 1
Square Footage: 2,483
Bedrooms: 3
Bathrooms: 2
Foundation: Basement
Materials List Available: Yes
Price Category: F

Images provided by designer/architect.

Copyright by designer/architect.

CAD FILE AVAILABLE

You'll love the grand feeling of this home, which combines with the very practical features that make living in it a pleasure.

Features:

- **Porch:** The open brick arches and Palladian door set the tone for this magnificent home.

- **Great Room:** An alcove for the entertainment center and vaulted ceiling show the care that went into designing this room.

- **Dining Room:** A tray ceiling sets off the formality of this large room.

- **Kitchen:** The layout in this room is designed to make your work patterns more efficient and to save you steps and time.

- **Study:** This quiet room can be a wonderful refuge, or you can use it for a fourth bedroom if you wish.

- **Master Suite:** Made for relaxing at the end of the day, this suite will pamper you with luxuries.

Floor plan labels:

- Patio
- MBr 16-7x16-0 vaulted clg
- Brkfst 14-9x13-0 vaulted clg
- Great Rm 19-6x23-10 vaulted clg
- Kitchen 14-4x12-11 vaulted clg
- Br 2 12-0x11-0
- Dn
- Menu Desk
- Laundry
- Br 3 12-0x11-5
- Entry
- Dining 12-0x15-0 tray clg
- Garage 22-4x20-4
- Study 14-4x11-0 vaulted clg
- Porch
- 53'-8"
- 69'-0"

SMARTtip

Art in Pools

The tiled walls and floor of a pool make great canvases for art, so incorporate a serious or whimsical design. Also, make the stairs wide and shallow to form a wading area for kids.

Plan #151232

Dimensions: 79'6" W x 71'4" D
Levels: 1.5
Square Footage: 3,901
Main Level Sq. Ft.: 3,185
Upper Level Sq. Ft.: 716
Bedrooms: 3
Bathrooms: 4
Foundation: Crawl space or slab
CompleteCost List Available: Yes
Price Category: H

Images provided by designer/architect.

This elegant brick home has something for everyone

CAD FILE AVAILABLE

Features:

- Great Room: This large gathering area has a fireplace and access to the rear grilling porch.

- Hearth Room: Relaxing and casual, this cozy area has a fireplace and is open to the kitchen.

- Kitchen: This large island kitchen has a built-in pantry and is open to the breakfast nook.

- Master Suite: A private bathroom with a corner whirlpool tub and a large walk-in closet turn this area into a spacious retreat.

- Bonus Room: This large space located upstairs near the two secondary bedrooms can be turned into a media room.

Main Level Floor Plan

Copyright by designer/architect.

Upper Level Floor Plan

Foyer

Great Room

Living Room

Great Room

Kitchen

Kitchen

Master Bedroom

Master Bath

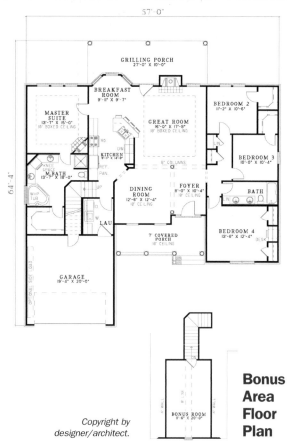

Plan #151170

Dimensions: 57' W x 64'4" D

Levels: 1

Square Footage: 1,965

Bedrooms: 4

Bathrooms: 2

Foundation: Crawl space, slab; basement or daylight basement for fee

CompleteCost List Available: Yes

Price Category: E

Images provided by designer/architect.

CAD FILE AVAILABLE

Copyright by designer/architect.

Bonus Area Floor Plan

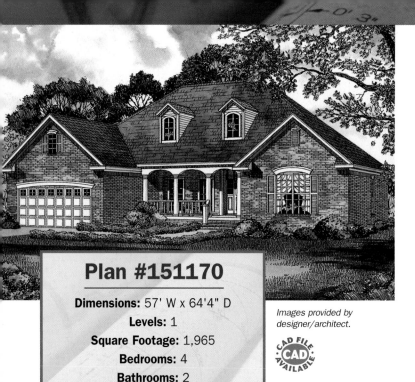

Plan #311001

Dimensions: 65'11" W x 67'9" D

Levels: 1

Square Footage: 2,085

Bedrooms: 3

Bathrooms: 2½

Foundation: Crawl space, slab, or basement

Materials List Available: No

Price Category: E

Images provided by designer/architect.

Copyright by designer/architect.

Rear View

Optional Bonus Area

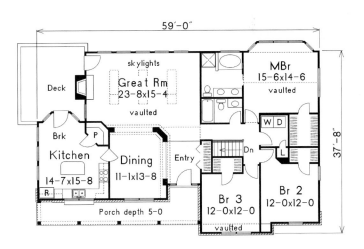

Plan #271003

Dimensions: 64'8" W x 40'4" D

Levels: 1

Square footage: 1,452

Bedrooms: 3

Bathrooms: 2

Foundation: Full basement

Materials List Available: Yes

Price Category: B

Images provided by designer/architect.

Copyright by designer/architect.

Plan #321010

Dimensions: 59' W x 37'8" D

Levels: 1

Square Footage: 1,787

Bedrooms: 3

Bathrooms: 2

Foundation: Basement or walkout

Materials List Available: Yes

Price Category: C

Images provided by designer/architect.

Copyright by designer/architect.

Plan #391049

Dimensions: 78' W x 52'4" D
Levels: 1
Square Footage: 4,064
Main Level Sq. Ft.: 2,466
Lower Level Sq. Ft.: 1,598
Bedrooms: 4
Bathrooms: 3
Foundation: Basement
Materials List Available: Yes
Price Category: I

Images provided by designer/architect.

This home proves that elegance can be comfortable. No need to sacrifice one for the other. Here, a peaked roofline creates a well-mannered covered front porch and classical columns announce the beauty of the dining room.

Features:

• Living Areas: High windows and a fireplace light up the living room, while an open hearth room shares the glow of a three-sided fireplace with the breakfast area and kitchen.

• Kitchen: To please the cook there's a built-in

kitchen desk, cooking island, food-preparation island, double sinks, and pantries.

• Master Suite: To soothe the busy executive, this first-floor master suite includes a lavish bath and a nearby study.

• Recreation: The lower level entertains some big plans for entertaining--a home theater, wet bar, and large recreation room with a double-sided fireplace.

• Bedrooms: Two additional bedrooms with excellent closet spaace and a shared full bath keep family or guests in stylish comfort.

Living Room

Main Level Floor Plan

Main Level

Lower Level Floor Plan

Copyright by designer/architect.

Plan #221018

Dimensions: 67' W x 53' D

Levels: 1

Square Footage: 2,007

Bedrooms: 3

Bathrooms: 2

Foundation: Basement

Materials List Available: No

Price Category: D

Images provided by designer/architect.

You'll love this ranch design, with its traditional stucco facade and interesting roofline.

Features:

• Ceiling Height: 9 ft.

• Great Room: A cathedral ceiling points up the large dimensions of this room, and the handsome fireplace with tall flanking windows lets you decorate for a formal or a casual feeling.

• Dining Room: A tray ceiling imparts elegance to this room, and a butler's pantry just across from the kitchen area lets you serve in style.

• Kitchen: You'll love the extensive counter space in this well-designed kitchen. The adjoining nook is large enough for a full-size dining set and features a door to the outside deck, where you can set up a third dining area.

• Master Suite: Located away from the other bedrooms for privacy, this suite includes a huge walk-in closet, windows overlooking the backyard, and a large bath with a whirlpool tub, standing shower, and dual-sink vanity.

Rear Elevation

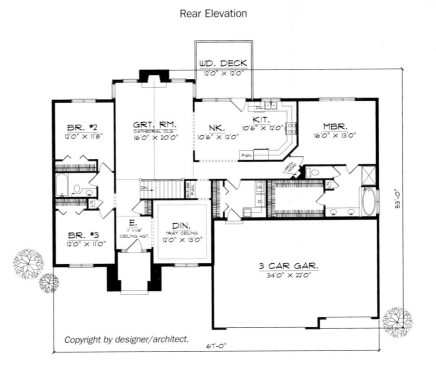

Copyright by designer/architect.

Upper Level
Floor Plan

Copyright by designer/architect.

37'-0"

92'-8"

CARPORT
22'-6" X 21'-8"

STRG

PATIO

GREAT RM.
16'-0" X 24'-8"

COVERED
PORCH
16'-4" X 5'-4"

BUILT
IN

BRKFST
RM.
10'-0" X 9'-0"

MASTER BEDROOM
13'-8" X 16'-6"

LAU.

W

D

BUILT-IN

RG.
DW

M.BATH
12'-3" X 15'-4"

SEAT

GLASS
SHWR.

LIN

WHP
TUB

M.C.

KITCHEN
16'-0" X 13'-0"

REF.

UP

8" COLUMNS

9' CEILING LINE

ATTIC STORAGE

LIN

LIN

BEDROOM 1
12'-8" X 14'-0"

9' CEILING LINE

BEDROOM 2
12'-8" X 14'-0"

9' CEILING LINE

BATH

LIVING RM.
11'-0" X 13'-6"

FOYER
9'-0" X 13'-6"

DINING RM.
11'-4" X 16'-6"

PORCH

*Images provided by
designer/architect.*

CAD FILE AVAILABLE

Plan #151013

Dimensions: 37' W x 92'8" D

Levels: 2

Square Footage: 2,618

Main Level Sq. Ft.: 1,865

Upper Level Sq. Ft.: 753

Bedrooms: 3

Bathrooms: 2½

Foundation: Crawl space or slab;
basement available for fee

CompleteCost List Available: Yes

Price Category: F

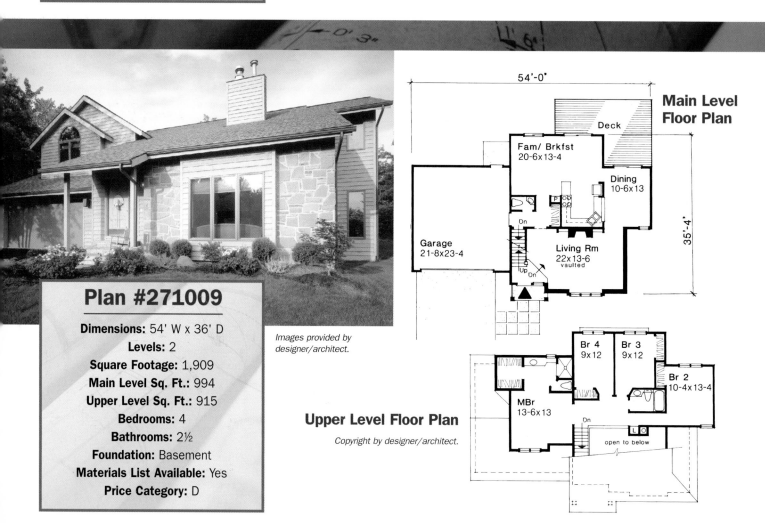

54'-0"

35'-4"

Deck

**Main Level
Floor Plan**

Fam/ Brkfst
20-6x13-4

Dining
10-6x13

Garage
21-8x23-4

Dn

Up
Dn

P
O

Living Rm
22x13-6
vaulted

▲

Plan #271009

Dimensions: 54' W x 36' D

Levels: 2

Square Footage: 1,909

Main Level Sq. Ft.: 994

Upper Level Sq. Ft.: 915

Bedrooms: 4

Bathrooms: 2½

Foundation: Basement

Materials List Available: Yes

Price Category: D

*Images provided by
designer/architect.*

Br 4
9x12

Br 3
9x12

Br 2
10-4x13-4

MBr
13-6x13

Dn

open to below

Upper Level Floor Plan

Copyright by designer/architect.

Rear Elevation

Copyright by designer/architect.

Plan #221015

Dimensions: 69'8" W x 46' D

Levels: 1

Square Footage: 1,926

Bedrooms: 3

Bathrooms: 2½

Foundation: Basement; walkout basement for fee

Materials List Available: No

Price Category: D

Images provided by designer/architect.

Plan #151179

Dimensions: 66'4" W x 67'2" D

Levels: 1.5

Square Footage: 2,405

Opt. Bonus Level Sq. Ft.: 358

Bedrooms: 4

Bathrooms: 3

Foundation: Crawl space, slab; basement or walkout for fee

CompleteCost List Available: Yes

Price Category: E

Images provided by designer/architect.

Copyright by designer/architect.

Bonus Area Floor Plan

Plan #161017

Dimensions: 61' W x 37'6" D

Levels: 2

Square Footage: 2,653

Main Level Sq. Ft.: 1,365

Upper Level Sq. Ft.: 1,288

Bedrooms: 4

Bathrooms: 2½

Foundation: Basement

Materials List Available: Yes

Price Category: F

If a traditional look makes you feel comfortable, you'll love this spacious, family-friendly home.

Features:

- **Family Room:** Accessorize with cozy cushions to make the most of this sunken room. Windows flank the fireplace, adding warm, natural light. Doors leading to the rear deck make this room a family "headquarters."

- **Living and Dining Rooms:** These formal rooms open to each other, so you'll love hosting gatherings in this home.

- **Kitchen:** A handy pantry fits well with the traditional feeling of this home, and an island adds contemporary convenience.

- **Master Suite:** Relax in the whirlpool tub in your bath and enjoy the storage space in the two walk-in closets in the bedroom.

Images provided by designer/architect.

Main Level Floor Plan

Deck

Sunken Family Room 18 x 15-4

Breakfast 9-10 x 13-3

Kitchen 8-10 x 11-11

stairs up

stairs dn

Laun.

Two-car Garage 22-4 x 22

Bath

Hall

Living Room 14-8 x 12-7

Foyer

Dining Room 14-8 x 12-7

Porch

Copyright by designer/architect.

Upper Level Floor Plan

Bath

Bedroom 12-5 x 10-11

Bedroom 10-10 x 10-11

shelves

walk-in closet

walk-in closet

stairs dn

Bath

sky-light

Balcony

laun. chute

Master Bedroom 14-8 x 16-2

Foyer Below

Bedroom 12-3 x 12-7

plant shelf

Plan #121028

Dimensions: 54'8" W x 42' D
Levels: 2
Square Footage: 2,644
Main Level Sq. Ft.: 1,366
Upper Level Sq. Ft.: 1,278
Bedrooms: 4
Bathrooms: 2½
Foundation: Basement
Materials List Available: Yes
Price Category: F

Images provided by designer/architect.

This home is filled with special touches and amenities that add up to gracious living.

Features:

- Ceiling Height: 8 ft.
- Formal Living Room: This large, inviting room is the perfect place to entertain guests.
- Family Room: This cozy, comfortable room is accessed through elegant French doors in the living room. It is sure to be the favorite family gathering place with its bay window, see-through fireplace, and bay window.
- Breakfast Area: This area is large enough for the whole family to enjoy a casual meal as they are warmed by the other side of the see-through fireplace. The area features a bay window and built-in bookcase.
- Master Bedroom: Upstairs, enjoy the gracious and practical master bedroom with its boxed ceiling and two walk-in closets.
- Master Bath: Luxuriate in the whirlpool bath as you gaze through the skylight framed by ceiling accents.

Main Level Floor Plan

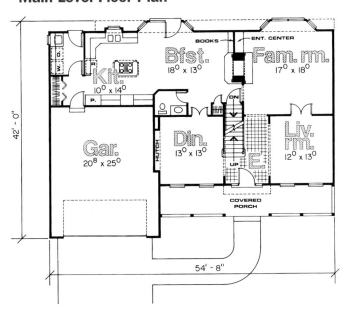

Upper Level Floor Plan

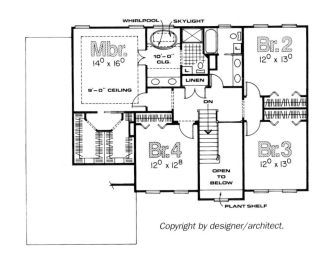

Copyright by designer/architect.

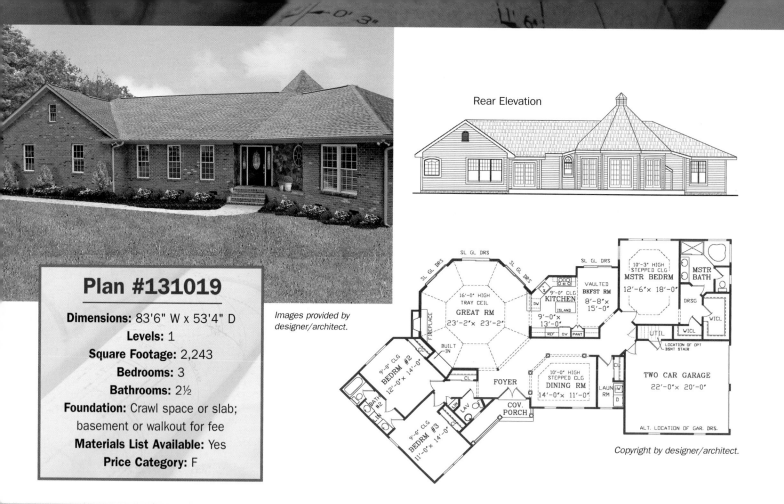

Rear Elevation

Images provided by designer/architect.

Copyright by designer/architect.

Plan #131019

Dimensions: 83'6" W x 53'4" D

Levels: 1

Square Footage: 2,243

Bedrooms: 3

Bathrooms: 2½

Foundation: Crawl space or slab; basement or walkout for fee

Materials List Available: Yes

Price Category: F

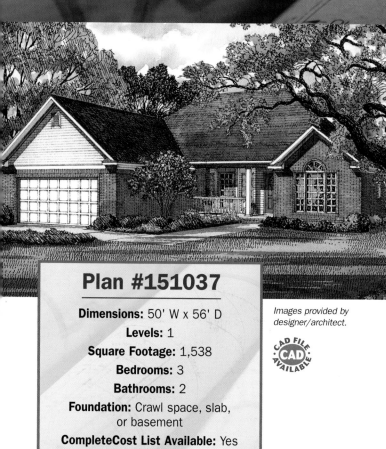

Images provided by designer/architect.

CAD FILE AVAILABLE

Copyright by designer/architect.

Plan #151037

Dimensions: 50' W x 56' D

Levels: 1

Square Footage: 1,538

Bedrooms: 3

Bathrooms: 2

Foundation: Crawl space, slab, or basement

CompleteCost List Available: Yes

Price Category: C

Plan #391131

Dimensions: 63'4" W x 47'10" D

Levels: 2

Square Footage: 2,183

Main Level Sq. Ft.: 1,584

Upper Level Sq. Ft.: 599

Bedrooms: 3

Bathrooms: 2

Foundation: Basement

Material List Available: Yes

Price Category: D

Main Level Floor Plan

Images provided by designer/architect.

Upper Level Floor Plan

Copyright by designer/architect.

Plan #271012

Dimensions: 48' W x 29'10" D

Levels: 2

Square Footage: 1,359

Main Level Sq. Ft.: 668

Upper Level Sq. Ft.: 691

Bedrooms: 3

Bathrooms: 2½

Foundation: Basement

Materials List Available: Yes

Price Category: B

Images provided by designer/architect.

This home, as shown in the photograph, may differ from the actual blueprints. For more detailed information, please check the floor plans carefully.

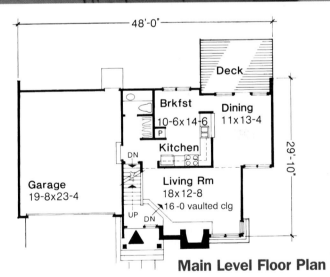

Main Level Floor Plan

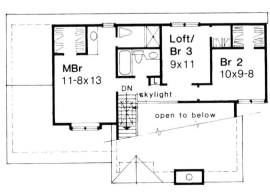

Upper Level Floor Plan

Copyright by designer/architect.

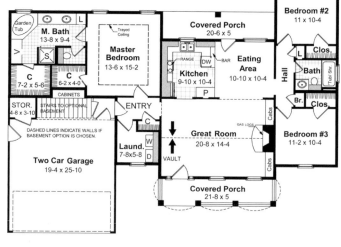

Plan #351005

Dimensions: 61' W x 47'4" D

Levels: 1

Square Footage: 1,501

Bedrooms: 3

Bathrooms: 2

Foundation: Crawl space, slab, or basement

Materials List Available: Yes

Price Category: C

Images provided by designer/architect.

Copyright by designer/architect.

Plan #481023

Dimensions: 67' W x 60' D

Levels: 2

Square Footage: 3,253

Main Level Sq. Ft.: 1,797

Upper Level Sq. Ft.: 1,456

Bedrooms: 3

Bathrooms: 2½

Foundation: Walkout

Material List Available: No

Price Category: G

Images provided by designer/architect.

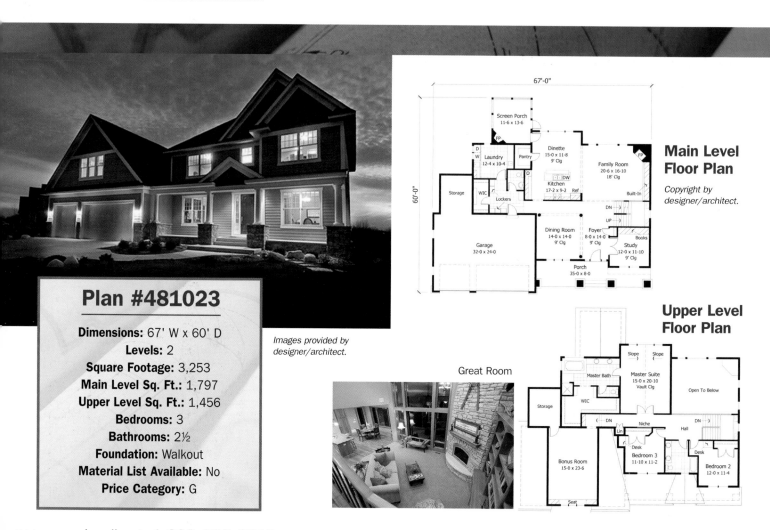

Main Level Floor Plan

Copyright by designer/architect.

Upper Level Floor Plan

Great Room

Copyright by designer/architect.

Plan #151050

Dimensions: 69'2" W x 74'10" D

Levels: 1

Square Footage: 2,096

Bedrooms: 3

Bathrooms: 2½

Foundation: Crawl space, slab, or basement

CompleteCost List Available: Yes

Price Category: F

Images provided by designer/architect.

CAD FILE AVAILABLE

Optional Front View

Upper Level Floor Plan

Plan #481017

Dimensions: 80' W x 49'8" D

Levels: 2

Square Footage: 2,982

Main Level Sq. Ft.: 1,563

Upper Level Sq. Ft.: 1,419

Bedrooms: 4

Bathrooms: 2½

Foundation: Basement

Material List Available: No

Price Category: F

Images provided by designer/architect.

Main Level Floor Plan

Copyright by designer/architect.

Plan #161009

Dimensions: 60'9" W x 49' D

Levels: 1

Square Footage: 1,651

Bedrooms: 3

Bathrooms: 2

Foundation: Basement

Materials List Available: No

Price Category: C

The warm, textured exterior combines with the elegance of double-entry doors to preview both the casual lifestyle and formal entertaining capabilities of this versatile home.

Features:

• Great Room: Experience the openness provided by the sloped ceiling topping both this great room and the formal dining area. Enjoy the warmth and light supplied by the gas fireplace and dual sliding doors.

• Kitchen: This kitchen, convenient to the living space, is designed for easy work patterns and features an open bar that separates the work area from the more richly decorated gathering rooms.

• Master Bedroom: Separated for privacy, this master bedroom includes a tray ceiling and lavishly equipped bath.

• Basement: This full basement allows you to expand your living space to meet your needs.

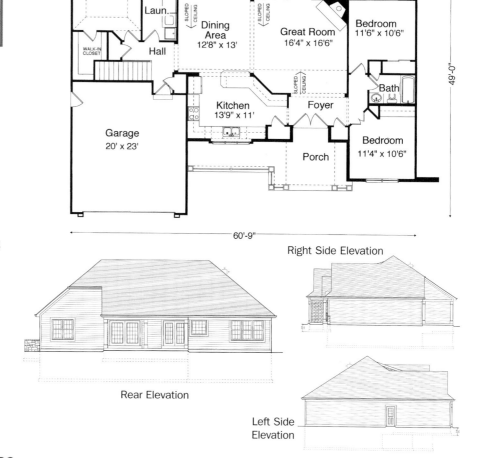

Images provided by designer/architect.

Copyright by designer/architect.

Right Side Elevation

Rear Elevation

Left Side Elevation

Plan #351007

Dimensions: 73'8"W x 53'2" D

Levels: 1

Square Footage: 2,251

Bedrooms: 3

Bathrooms: 2½

Foundation: Crawl space, slab, or basement

Materials List Available: Yes

Price Category: E

CAD FILE AVAILABLE

Images provided by designer/architect.

This three-bedroom brick home with arched window offers traditional styling that features an open floor plan.

Features:

- **Great Room:** This room has a 12-ft.-high ceiling and a corner fireplace.

- **Kitchen:** This kitchen boasts a built-in pantry and a raised bar open to the breakfast area.

- **Dining Room:** This area features a vaulted ceiling and a view of the front yard.

- **Master Bedroom:** This private room has an office and access to the rear porch.

- **Master Bath:** This bathroom has a double vanity, large walk-in closet, and soaking tub.

Bonus Room

Copyright by designer/architect.

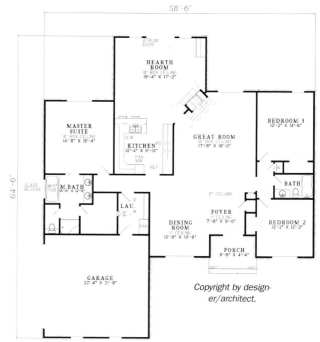

58'-6"

64'-6"

HEARTH ROOM
10' BOX CEILING
19'-4" X 17'-2"

MASTER SUITE
10' BOX CEILING
14'-8" X 15'-4"

KITCHEN
12'-4" X 11'-10"

GREAT ROOM
10' BOX CEILING
17'-8" X 18'-0"

BEDROOM 3
12'-2" X 14'-6"

M. BATH
16'-6" X 12'-4"

LAU.

DINING ROOM
10' CEILING
12'-8" X 13'-8"

FOYER
11' CEILING
7'-8" X 9'-0"

BATH

BEDROOM 2
12'-2" X 12'-2"

PORCH
9'-8" X 4'-4"

GARAGE
22'-4" X 21'-8"

Plan #151034

Dimensions: 58'6" W x 64'6" D

Levels: 1

Square Footage: 2,133

Bedrooms: 3

Bathrooms: 2

Foundation: Crawl space or slab; basement or walkout for fee

CompleteCost List Available: Yes

Price Category: D

Images provided by designer/architect.

This home, as shown in the photograph, may differ from the actual blueprints. For more detailed information, please check the floor plans carefully.

Copyright by designer/architect.

COVERED PORCH
35'-4"x9'-4"

BRKFST AREA

KITCHEN
14'-0"x17'-2"

MASTER BEDRM
12'-0"x17'-4"
10'-4" HIGH STEPPED CLG

GREAT ROOM
22'-4"x16'-0"
10'-8" HIGH STEPPED CEILING

BATH

BDRM 2
11'-0"x10'-0"

OFFICE/ BR4
10'-0"x12'-0"

FOY

DINING
10'-0"x12'-0"
STEPPED CEILING

HALL

BDRM 3
10'-0"x13'-0"

MASTER BATH
VAULTED CLG

WHIRLPOOL TUB

LDRY ROOM

UTILITY

STOR

LOCATION OF OPTIONAL BASEMENT STAIR

TWO CAR GARAGE
21'-0"x22'-8"

COVERED PORCH

STORAGE

Plan #131011

Dimensions: 75'2" W x 60'9" D

Levels: 1

Square Footage: 1,897

Bedrooms: 4

Bathrooms: 2

Foundation: Crawl space or slab; basement for fee

Materials List Available: Yes

Price Category: E

Images provided by designer/architect.

Copyright by designer/architect.

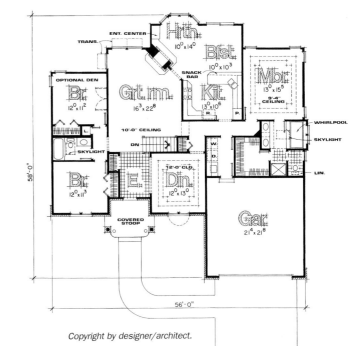

Images provided by designer/architect.

Copyright by designer/architect.

Plan #121001

Dimensions: 56' W x 58' D

Levels: 1

Square Footage: 1,911

Bedrooms: 3

Bathrooms: 2

Foundation: Basement

Materials List Available: Yes

Price Category: D

CAD FILE AVAILABLE

Images provided by designer/architect.

Copyright by designer/architect.

Plan #161008

Dimensions: 64'2" W x 46'6" D

Levels: 1

Square Footage: 1,860

Bedrooms: 3

Bathrooms: 2

Foundation: Slab

Materials List Available: No

Price Category: D

CAD FILE AVAILABLE

SMARTtip

Espaliered Fruit Trees

Try a technique used by the royal gardeners at Versailles—espalier. They trained the fruit trees to grow flat against the walls, creating patterns. It's not difficult, especially if you go to a reputable nursery and purchase an apple or pear tree that has already been espaliered. Plant it against a flat surface that's in a sunny spot.

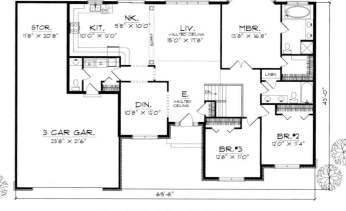

Images provided by designer/architect.

Copyright by designer/architect.

Plan #221020

Dimensions: 69'8" W x 43' D

Levels: 1

Square Footage: 1,859

Bedrooms: 3

Bathrooms: 2½

Foundation: Basement

Materials List Available: No

Price Category: D

Rear Elevation

Images provided by designer/architect.

Plan #111001

Dimensions: 66'8" W x 76'11" D

Levels: 1

Square Footage: 2,832

Bedrooms: 4

Bathrooms: 2½

Foundation: Crawl space or slab

Materials List Available: No

Price Category: F

Copyright by designer/architect.

Images provided by designer/architect.

Copyright by designer/architect.

Basement Level Floor Plan

Plan #481031

Dimensions: 98' W x 72' D

Levels: 1

Square Footage: 4,707

Main Level Sq. Ft.: 2,518

Basement Level Sq. Ft.: 2,189

Bedrooms: 4

Bathrooms: 3½

Foundation: Walkout basement

Material List Available: No

Price Category: I

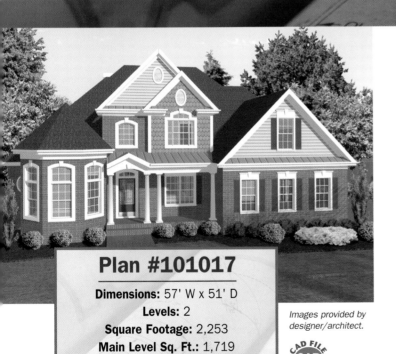

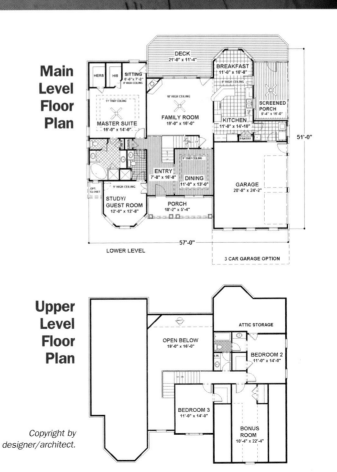

Main Level Floor Plan

Upper Level Floor Plan

Images provided by designer/architect.

CAD FILE AVAILABLE
CAD

Copyright by designer/architect.

Plan #101017

Dimensions: 57' W x 51' D

Levels: 2

Square Footage: 2,253

Main Level Sq. Ft.: 1,719

Upper Level Sq. Ft.: 534

Opt. Upper Level Bonus Sq. Ft.: 247

Bedrooms: 4

Bathrooms: 3

Foundation: Basement

Materials List Available: No

Price Category: E

Images provided by designer/architect.

Plan #161045

Dimensions: 57' W x 49'8" D

Levels: 2

Square Footage: 2,077

Main Level Sq. Ft.: 1,532

Upper Level Sq. Ft.: 545

Bedrooms: 3

Bathrooms: 2½

Foundation: Basement; crawl space or slab for fee

Materials List Available: No

Price Category: D

Multiple gables, arched windows, and the stone accents that adorn the exterior of this lovely two-story home create a dramatic first impression.

Features:

- **Great Room:** With multiple windows to light your way, grand openings, varied ceiling treatments, and angled walls let you flow from room to room. Enjoy the warmth of the gas fireplace in both this great room and the dining area.

- **Master Suite:** Experience the luxurious atmosphere of this master suite, with its coffered ceiling and deluxe bath.

- **Additional Bedrooms:** Angled stairs lead to a balcony with writing desk and to two additional bedrooms.

- **Porch:** Exit two sets of French doors to the rear yard and a covered porch, perfect for relaxing in comfortable weather.

Copyright by designer/architect.

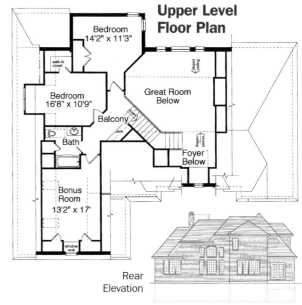

Plan #481028

Dimensions: 86'8" W x 53' D
Levels: 1
Square Footage: 3,980
Main Level Sq. Ft.: 2,290
Lower Level Sq. Ft.: 1,690
Bedrooms: 3
Bathrooms: 2½
Foundation: Walkout basement
Material List Available: No
Price Category: H

Images provided by designer/architect.

- Lower Level: For fun times, this lower level is finished to provide a wet bar and a recreation room. Two bedrooms, which share a full bathroom, are also on this level. Future expansion can include an additional bedroom.

Rear View

This home, with its Southwestern flair, invites friends and family in for some down-home hospitality.

Features:

- Foyer: A 12-ft-high ceiling extends an open welcome to all. With a view through the great room, the open floor plan makes the home feel large and open.

- Kitchen: This spacious gourmet kitchen opens generously to the hearth room, which features an angled fireplace. A two-level island, which contains a two-bowl sink, provides casual seating and additional storage.

- Master Suite: This romantic space features a 10-ft.-high stepped ceiling and a compartmentalized full bath that includes his and her sinks and a whirlpool tub.

Copyright by designer/architect.

Basement Level Floor Plan

Main Level Floor Plan

Copyright by designer/architect.

THREE CAR CARRIAGE HOUSE

FAMILY ENTRY

WRAP AROUND PORCH

MORNING ROOM
14'-0" x 13'-0"

FAMILY ROOM
22'-0" x 14'-2"

OPT BOOKCASE

KITCHEN
13'-0" x 13'-0"

W.I. PANTRY

DINING ROOM
14'-0" x 12'-0"

LIVING ROOM
14'-0" x 16'-0"

STUDY LIBRARY
14'-0" x 12'-0"

OPT LIBRARY CABINETS

ENTRY FOYER

72'-0"

Upper Level Floor Plan

FUTURE LIVING AREA
16'-0" x 31'-0"
Adds 516 square feet

REAR HALL

MASTER BEDROOM
26'-5" x 13'-0"

MASTER BATH

WHIRL POOL TUB

HER WIC

HIS WIC

OPT BOOKCASE

PETIT DEJEUNER

BEDROOM
12'-0" x 14'-2"

DRESSING BATH

BEDROOM
12'-0" x 12'-0"

BEDROOM
12'-0" x 12'-0"

UPPER HALL

65'-0"

Images provided by designer/architect.

Plan #291013

Dimensions: 72' W x 75' D

Levels: 2

Square Footage: 3,553

Main Level Sq. Ft.: 1,830

Upper Level Sq. Ft.: 1,723

Bedrooms: 4

Bathrooms: 2½

Foundation: Basement

Materials List Available: No

Price Category: H

Copyright by designer/architect.

Screened Porch
19' x 12'

Dining
13' x 11'6"

Great Room
16' x 17'2"

Master Bedroom
11'9" x 15'
10' center ceiling height

walk-in closet

Kitchen
11' x 15'6"

Two-Car Garage
20'8" x 21'

Dressing

Laun.

Foyer
10' ceiling height

Bath

Porch

Bedroom
10'8" x 11'6"

Bedroom
10'6" x 10'6"

66'-4"

43'-10"

Images provided by designer/architect.

CAD FILE AVAILABLE

Plan #161007

Dimensions: 66'4" W x 43'10" D

Levels: 1

Square Footage: 1,611

Bedrooms: 3

Bathrooms: 2

Foundation: Basement; crawl space option for fee

Materials List Available: Yes

Price Category: C

Rear Elevation

Main Level Floor Plan

Images provided by designer/architect.

Plan #131050

Dimensions: 72'8" W x 47' D

Levels: 2

Square Footage: 2,874

Main Level Sq. Ft.: 2,146

Upper Level Sq. Ft.: 728

Bedrooms: 4

Bathrooms: 3

Foundation: Crawl space or slab; basement for fee

Materials List Available: Yes

Price Category: G

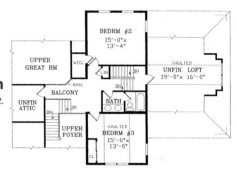

Upper Level Floor Plan

Copyright by designer/architect.

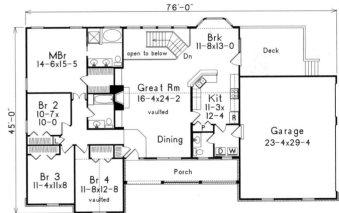

Images provided by designer/architect.

Plan #321006

Dimensions: 76' W x 45' D

Levels: 1, optional lower

Square Footage: 1,977

Optional Basement Level Sq. Ft.: 1,416

Bedrooms: 4

Bathrooms: 2½

Foundation: Basement

Materials List Available: Yes

Price Category: E

Optional Basement Level Floor Plan

Copyright by designer/architect.

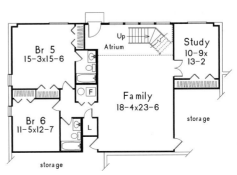

Plan #161006

Dimensions: 78'6" W x 47'7" D

Levels: 1

Square Footage: 1,755

Bedrooms: 3

Bathrooms: 2

Foundation: Basement

Materials List Available: No

Price Category: C

Images provided by designer/architect.

Copyright by designer/architect.

Rear Elevation

Plan #151009

Dimensions: 44' W x 86'2" D

Levels: 1

Square Footage: 1,601

Bedrooms: 3

Bathrooms: 2

Foundation: Crawl space or slab

CompleteCost List Available: Yes

Price Category: C

Images provided by designer/architect.

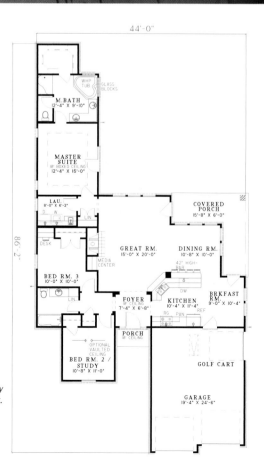

Copyright by designer/architect.

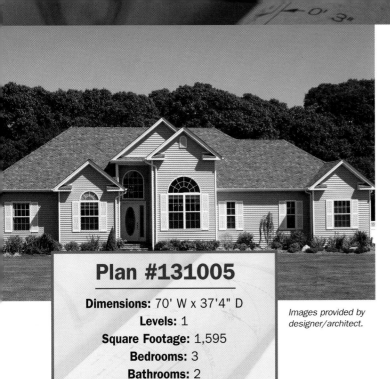

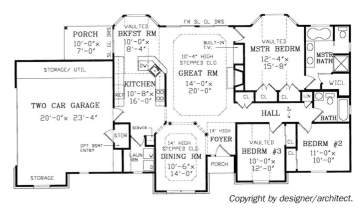

Plan #131005

Dimensions: 70' W x 37'4" D
Levels: 1
Square Footage: 1,595
Bedrooms: 3
Bathrooms: 2
Foundation: Crawl space or slab; basement for fee
Materials List Available: Yes
Price Category: C

Images provided by designer/architect.

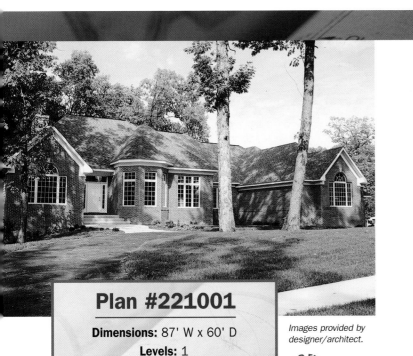

Plan #221001

Dimensions: 87' W x 60' D
Levels: 1
Square Footage: 2,600
Bedrooms: 3
Bathrooms: 2½
Foundation: Basement
Materials List Available: No
Price Category: F

Images provided by designer/architect.

CAD FILE AVAILABLE

Rear Elevation

Kitchen

Plan #661124

Dimensions: 45' W x 68'10 D
Levels: 1
Square Footage: 2,392
Bedrooms: 3
Bathrooms: 2 full, 1 half
Foundation: Slab
Materials List Available: No
Price Category: E

Images provided by designer/architect.

Main Level Floor Plan

Upper Level Floor Plan

Copyright by designer/architect.

Plan #221023

Dimensions: 90'3" W x 65'8" D
Levels: 2
Square Footage: 3,511
Main Level Sq. Ft.: 1,931
Upper Level Sq. Ft.: 1,580
Bedrooms: 4
Bathrooms: 3
Foundation: Basement
Materials List Available: No
Price Category: H

Images provided by designer/architect.

Main Level Floor Plan

Upper Level Floor Plan

Copyright by designer/architect.

Plan #211007

Dimensions: 72' W x 60' D

Levels: 1

Square Footage: 2,252

Bedrooms: 4

Bathrooms: 2

Foundation: Slab

Materials List Available: Yes

Price Category: E

Images provided by designer/architect.

Copyright by designer/architect.

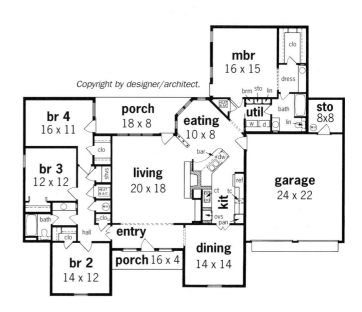

- mbr 16 x 15
- clo
- dress
- br 4 16 x 11
- porch 18 x 8
- eating 10 x 8
- util
- bath
- sto 8x8
- br 3 12 x 12
- living 20 x 18
- bar
- dw
- kit
- ref
- garage 24 x 22
- bath
- entry
- ovs pan
- br 2 14 x 12
- porch 16 x 4
- dining 14 x 14

Front View

Plan #271024

Dimensions: 75' W x 44' D

Levels: 2

Square Footage: 3,107

Main Level Sq. Ft.: 1,639

Upper Level Sq. Ft.: 1,468

Bedrooms: 4

Bathrooms: 2½

Foundation: Basement

Materials List Available: Yes

Price Category: G

Images provided by designer/architect.

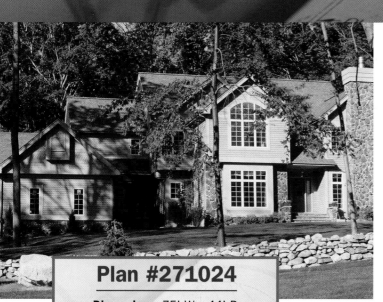

Main Level Floor Plan

- DECK
- BRKFST 11'-0"x12'-0" 9' CEILING
- FAMILY 24'-0"x16'-0" 11' CEILING
- MUD LNDRY
- KITCHEN
- GARAGE 24'-0"x36'-0"
- DINING 14'-6"x12'-0" 9' CEILING
- LIVING 14'-0"x16'-0" 9' CEILING

Upper Level Floor Plan

Copyright by designer/architect.

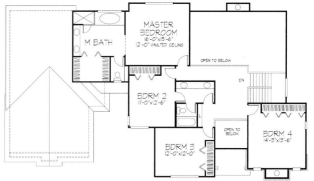

- M BATH
- MASTER BEDROOM 16'-0"x15'-6" 12'-0" VAULTED CEILING
- OPEN TO BELOW
- BDRM 2 11'-0"x12'-6"
- BDRM 4 14'-3"x13'-6"
- OPEN TO BELOW
- BDRM 3 12'-0"x12'-0"

Plan #161056

Dimensions: 86'2" W x 63'8" D
Levels: 1
Square Footage: 3,171
Bedrooms: 3
Bathrooms: 2½
Foundation: Basement or walkout, crawl space for fee
Material List Available: Yes
Price Category: G

Images provided by designer/architect.

CAD FILE AVAILABLE

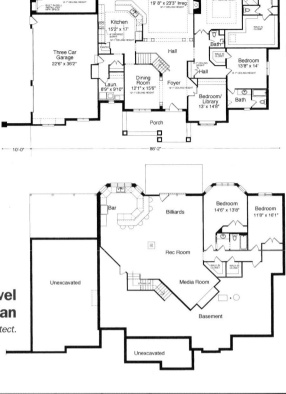

Main Level Floor Plan

Basement Level Floor Plan

Copyright by designer/architect.

Plan #151534

Dimensions: 37'8" W x 71'6" D
Levels: 2
Square Footage: 2,237
Main Level Sq. Ft.: 1,708
Upper Level Sq. Ft.: 529
Bedrooms: 3
Bathrooms: 2½
Foundation: Crawl space or slab
CompleteCost List Available: Yes
Price Category: E

Images provided by designer/architect.

CAD FILE AVAILABLE

Main Level Floor Plan

Upper Level Floor Plan

Copyright by designer/architect.

Front View

Plan #401004

Dimensions: 54' W x 64'4" D

Levels: 2

Square Footage: 2,684

Main Level Sq. Ft.: 1,620

Upper Level Sq. Ft.: 1,064

Bedrooms: 3

Bathrooms: 2 full, 2 half

Foundation: Basement

Materials List Available: Yes

Price Category: F

Images provided by designer/architect.

This home, as shown in the photograph, may differ from the actual blueprints. For more detailed information, please check the floor plans carefully.

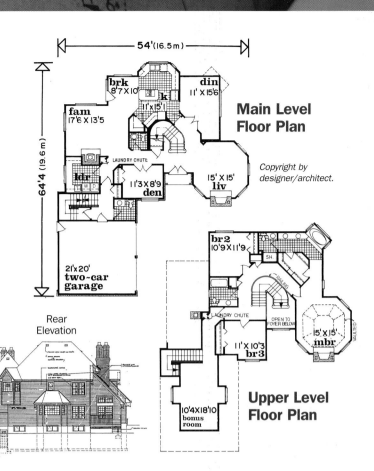

Main Level Floor Plan

Copyright by designer/architect.

Rear Elevation

Upper Level Floor Plan

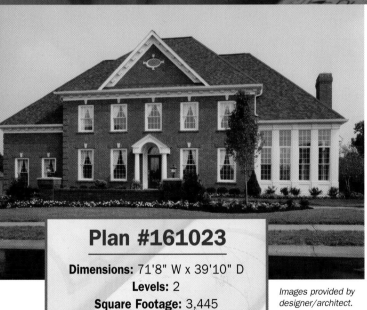

Plan #161023

Dimensions: 71'8" W x 39'10" D

Levels: 2

Square Footage: 3,445

Main Level Sq. Ft.: 1,666

Mid Level Sq. Ft.: 743

Upper Level Sq. Ft.: 1,036

Bedrooms: 4

Bathrooms: 3½

Foundation: Basement

Materials List Available: No

Price Category: G

Images provided by designer/architect.

CAD FILE AVAILABLE

Main Level Floor Plan

Copyright by designer/architect.

Upper Level Floor Plan

Plan #151484

Dimensions: 53'6" W x 76'10" D
Levels: 1.5
Square Footage: 2,211
Bedrooms: 3
Bathrooms: 2
Foundation: Crawl space or slab
CompleteCost List Available: Yes
Price Category: E

Images provided by designer/architect.

This traditional design, perfect for narrow lot, incorporates 10-ft.-tall boxed ceilings and 8-in. round columns.

CAD FILE AVAILABLE

Features:

- **Dining Room:** This room is centrally located and looks through to the great room, which allows access to the rear grilling porch.

- **Master Suite:** The split-bedroom plan gives the ultimate in privacy to this suite, complete with a large walk-in closet and a bath with amenities galore.

- **Kitchen:** At the other end of the house from the master suite is this kitchen and breakfast room combo with island seating, a built-in bench seat, and a walk-in pantry.

- **Den:** Down the hall from the kitchen is this den or extra bedroom. Private access to the full bathroom makes it great for guests.

Front View

Bonus Area Floor Plan
Copyright by designer/architect.

Plan #121011

Dimensions: 50' W x 50' D

Levels: 1

Square Footage: 1,724

Bedrooms: 3

Bathrooms: 2

Foundation: Slab, basement

Materials List Available: Yes

Price Category: C

Images provided by designer/architect.

This home, as shown in the photograph, may differ from the actual blueprints. For more detailed information, please check the floor plans carefully.

This one-level home is perfect for retirement or for convenient living for the growing family.

Features:

• Ceiling Height: 8 ft.

• Master Suite: For privacy and quiet, the master suite is segregated from the other bedrooms.

• Family Room: Sit by the fire and read as light streams through the windows flanking the fireplace. Or enjoy the built-in entertainment center.

• Breakfast Area: Located just off the family room, the sunny breakfast areaa will lure you to linger over impromptu family meals. Here you will find a built-in desk for compiling shopping lists and menus.

• Private Porch: Step out of the breakfast area to enjoy a breeze on this porch.

• Kitchen: Efficient and attractive, this kitchen offers an angled pantry and an island that doubles as a snack bar.

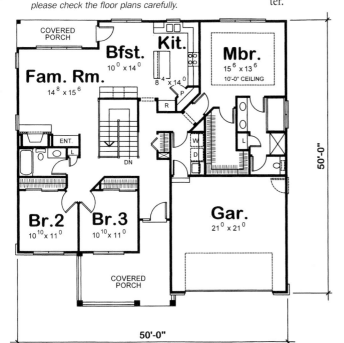

SMARTtip

Measuring for Kitchen Countertops

Custom cabinetmakers will sometimes come to your house to measure for a countertop, but home centers and kitchen stores may require that you come to them with the dimensions already in hand. Be sure to double-check measurements carefully. Being off by only ½ in. can be quite upsetting.

To ensure accuracy, sketch out the countertop on a sheet of graph paper. Include all the essential dimensions. To be on the safe side, have some one else double-check your numbers.

Plan #161022

Dimensions: 52'10" W x 38'2" D

Levels: 2

Square Footage: 1,898

Main Level Sq. Ft.: 1,065

Upper Level Sq. Ft.: 833

Bedrooms: 3

Bathrooms: 2½

Foundation: Basement

Materials List Available: No

Price Category: D

Images provided by designer/architect.

CAD FILE AVAILABLE

Rear Elevation

Main Level Floor Plan

entertainment center

Sunken Great Room 18' x 15'8"

Breakfast 11'6" x 11'3"

slope ceiling

Bath

Laun.

Storage

Kitchen 11'6" x 10'8"

pass thru

pantry

stairs dn

stairs up

Two-car Garage 20' x 32'6"

38'2"

Foyer

DiningRoom 11'4" x 11'11"

Porch

52'10

Copyright by designer/architect.

Upper Level Floor Plan

Bath

walk-in closet

Master Bedroom 18' x 12'

slope ceiling

slope ceiling

Bedroom 11'6" x 10'8"

Bonus Room 20' x 12'

Hall

Bath

linen

stairs dn

wood rail

computer space

Bedroom 11'6"x 10'10"

Plan #661021

Dimensions: 24'4" W x 43'8" D

Levels: 1

Square Footage: 966

Bedrooms: 3

Bathrooms: 1

Foundation: Slab

Materials List Available: No

Price Category: A

Images provided by designer/architect.

CAD FILE AVAILABLE

ac

Bedroom 3 12⁰ · 9⁰

closet

Bedroom 2 9⁰ · 12⁸

ac

Bath

closet

closet

D

W

wh

linen

Bedroom 1 11⁴ · 10⁸

Kitchen

Ref

Family 15⁰ · 12⁴

Dining 8⁴ · 11²

Entry

Copyright by designer/architect.

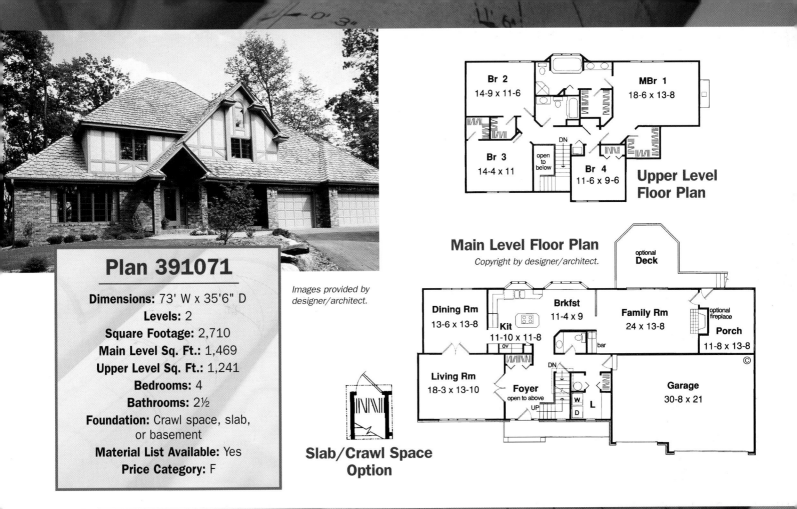

Plan 391071

Dimensions: 73' W x 35'6" D

Levels: 2

Square Footage: 2,710

Main Level Sq. Ft.: 1,469

Upper Level Sq. Ft.: 1,241

Bedrooms: 4

Bathrooms: 2½

Foundation: Crawl space, slab, or basement

Material List Available: Yes

Price Category: F

Images provided by designer/architect.

Upper Level Floor Plan

Br 2
14-9 x 11-6

MBr 1
18-6 x 13-8

Br 3
14-4 x 11

open to below

Br 4
11-6 x 9-6

DN

Main Level Floor Plan
Copyright by designer/architect.

optional Deck

Dining Rm
13-6 x 13-8

Kit
11-10 x 11-8

Brkfst
11-4 x 9

Family Rm
24 x 13-8

optional fireplace

Porch
11-8 x 13-8

Living Rm
18-3 x 13-10

Foyer
open to above

DN

UP

W
D

L

Garage
30-8 x 21

Slab/Crawl Space Option

Plan #271097

Dimensions: 60' W x 42' D

Levels: 2

Square Footage: 1,645

Main Level Sq. Ft.: 1,136

Upper Level Sq. Ft.: 509

Bedrooms: 3

Bathrooms: 2

Foundation: Basement

Materials List Available: No

Price Category: C

Images provided by designer/architect.

60'-0"

42'-0"

PORCH

DINING
10'-0"x10'-4"

KITCH
11'-0"x12'-8"

GARAGE
21'-8"x25'-4"

BATH

D W

WIC

LIVING
13'-4"x23'-0"
8'-6" CLG

BEDROOM I
14'-4"x13'-4"

FOYER

L

PORCH

UP

Main Level Floor Plan

UP

BEDRM 3
9'-4"x11'-10"

HALL

BEDRM 2
10'-10"x14'-6"

WIC

DN

WIC

OPEN TO BELOW

Upper Level Floor Plan
Copyright by designer/architect.

Plan #481005

Dimensions: 67'4" W x 53' D

Levels: 2

Square Footage: 2,825

Main Level Sq. Ft.: 1,412

Upper Level Sq. Ft.: 1,413

Bedrooms: 4

Bathrooms: 2½

Foundation: Walkout basement

Material List Available: No

Price Category: F

Images provided by designer/architect.

Upper Level Floor Plan

Copyright by designer/architect.

Main Level Floor Plan

Plan #461174

Dimensions: 70'4" W x 67' D

Levels: 2

Square Footage: 3,753

Main Level Sq. Ft.: 2,519

Upper Level Sq. Ft.: 1,234

Bedrooms: 4

Bathrooms: 3½

Foundation: Basement, crawl space, slab

Material List Available: No

Price Category: H

Images provided by designer/architect.

Main Level Floor Plan

Copyright by designer/architect.

Upper Level Floor Plan

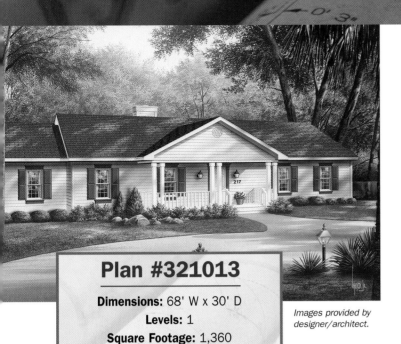

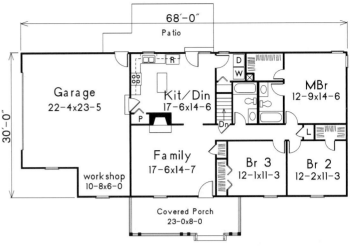

Plan #321013

Dimensions: 68' W x 30' D

Levels: 1

Square Footage: 1,360

Bedrooms: 3

Bathrooms: 2

Foundation: Basement

Materials List Available: Yes

Price Category: B

Images provided by designer/architect.

Copyright by designer/architect.

Plan #151684

Dimensions: 65'2" W x 63' D

Levels: 1

Square Footage: 1,994

Bedrooms: 3

Bathrooms: 2

Foundation: Crawl space, slab, basement, or walkout

CompleteCost List Available: Yes

Price Category: D

Images provided by designer/architect.

Copyright by designer/architect.

Plan #391069

Dimensions: 56' W x 48' D

Levels: 1

Square Footage: 1,492

Bedrooms: 3

Bathrooms: 2

Foundation: Crawl space, slab, or basement

Materials List Available: Yes

Price Category: B

Images provided by designer/architect.

This design opens wide from the living room to the kitchen and dining room. All on one level, even the bedrooms are easy to reach.

Features:

- Living Room: This special room features a fireplace and entry to the deck.

- Dining Room: This formal room shows off special ceiling effects.

- Bedrooms: Bedroom 3 is inspired by a decorative ceiling, and bedroom 2 has double closet doors. There's a nearby bath for convenience.

- Master Suite: This private area features a roomy walk-in closet and private bath.

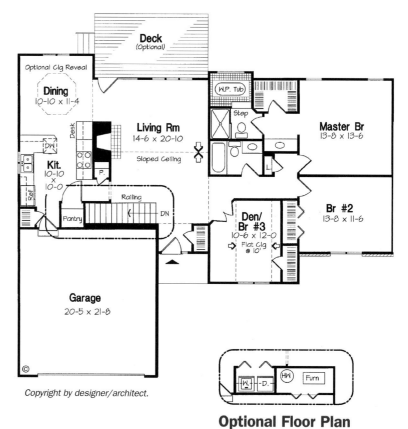

Copyright by designer/architect.

Optional Floor Plan

Plan #271027

Dimensions: 61' W x 44' D

Levels: 2

Square Footage: 2,463

Main Level Sq. Ft.: 1,380

Upper Level Sq. Ft.: 1,083

Bedrooms: 4

Bathrooms: 2½

Foundation: Basement

Materials List Available: Yes

Price Category: D

Images provided by designer/architect.

This post-modern design uses half-round transom windows and a barrel-vaulted porch to lend elegance to its facade.

Features:

- **Living Room:** A vaulted ceiling and a striking fireplace enhance this formal gathering space.

- **Dining Room:** Introduced from the living room by square columns, this formal dining room is just steps from the kitchen.

- **Kitchen:** Thoroughly modern in its design, this walk-through kitchen includes an island cooktop and a large pantry. Nearby, a sunny, bayed breakfast area offers sliding-glass-door access to an angled backyard deck.

- **Family Room:** Columns provide an elegant preface to this fun gathering spot, which sports a vaulted ceiling and easy access to the deck.

- **Master suite:** A vaulted ceiling crowns this luxurious space, which includes a private bath and bright windows.

Main Level Floor Plan

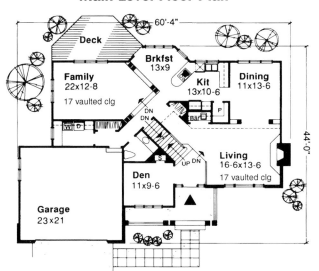

Upper Level Floor Plan

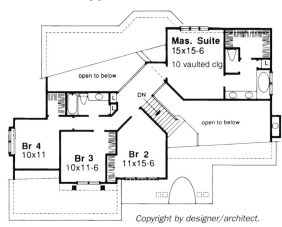

Copyright by designer/architect.

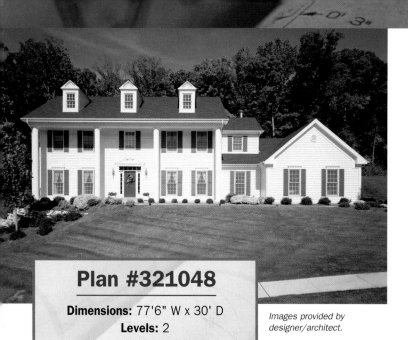

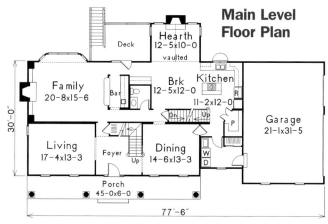

Main Level Floor Plan

Deck

Hearth
12-5x10-0
vaulted

Family
20-8x15-6

Bar

Brk
12-5x12-0

Kitchen

Garage
21-1x31-5

Living
17-4x13-3

Foyer
Up

Dining
14-6x13-3

Porch
45-0x6-0

30-0"

77-6"

Images provided by designer/architect.

Plan #321048

Dimensions: 77'6" W x 30' D

Levels: 2

Square Footage: 3,216

Main Level Sq. Ft.: 1,834

Upper Level Sq. Ft.: 1,382

Bedrooms: 4

Bathrooms: 4½

Foundation: Basement

Materials List Available: Yes

Price Category: G

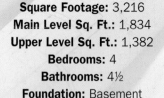

Br 4
12-0x12-0

Br 3
12-0x12-0

MBr
17-4x14-1

open to foyer

Br 2
14-6x13-6

Dn

Copyright by designer/architect.

Upper Level Floor Plan

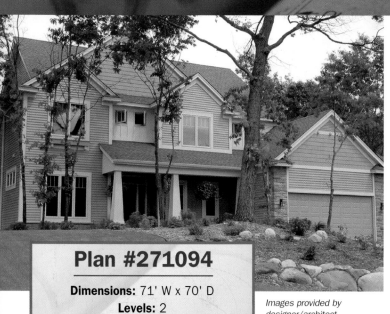

GREAT RM
21' X 18'

DINING
21' X 10'

KITCHEN
15' X 14'

Main Level Floor Plan

STUDY
11' X 13'

MUD RM

PORCH

GARAGE
40' X 24'

BED RM
10' X 14'

BED RM
10' X 14'

OWNER'S SUITE
14' X 18'

LAUN

BED RM
11' X 13'

BED RM
11' X 13'

WIC

BATH

Plan #271094

Dimensions: 71' W x 70' D

Levels: 2

Square Footage: 3,242

Main Level Sq. Ft.: 1,552

Upper Level Sq. Ft.: 1,690

Bedrooms: 5

Bathrooms: 2½

Foundation: Full basement

Materials List Available: No

Price Category: G

Images provided by designer/architect.

Upper Level Floor Plan

Copyright by designer/architect.

Plan #121150

Dimensions: 68'7" W x 57'4" D

Levels: 1.5

Square Footage: 2,639

Main Level Sq. Ft.: 2,087

Upper Level Sq. Ft.: 552

Bedrooms: 4

Bathrooms: 3½

Foundation: Slab; crawl space or basement for fee

Material List Available: Yes

Price Category: F

Images provided by designer/architect.

Main Level Floor Plan

68'-7"

57'-4"

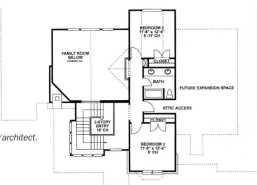

Upper Level Floor Plan

Copyright by designer/architect.

Plan #211130

Dimensions: 68' W x 70' D

Levels: 1

Square Footage: 2,280

Bedrooms: 3

Bathrooms: 2

Foundation: Slab

Materials List Available: Yes

Price Category: E

Images provided by designer/architect.

Front View

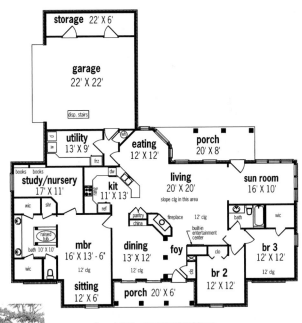

Copyright by designer/architect.

Plan #281033

Dimensions: 40' W x 40' D
Levels: 2
Square Footage: 2,391
Main Level Sq. Ft.: 1,358
Garage Level Sq. Ft.: 1,033
Bedrooms: 4
Bathrooms: 3
Foundation: Basement
Material List Available: Yes
Price Category: E

This home, as shown in the photograph, may differ from the actual blueprints. For more detailed information, please check the floor plans carefully.

The interesting floor plan and gorgeous exterior are sure to make this home a hit with your family.

Features:

• Living Room: The bay window brings natural light into this gathering area, while the fireplace adds a glow of its own. Because it is open to the dining room, guests flow easily between the two areas.

• Kitchen: This U-shaped kitchen, with its breakfast nook, is located next to the dining room to make serving guests easy.

• Bedrooms: A master and two secondary bedrooms are located on the upper level. The master bedroom boasts a private bathroom.

• Garage: A two-car front-loading garage has room for cars or for storage.

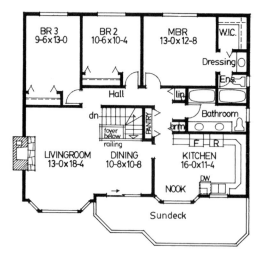

Main Level Floor Plan

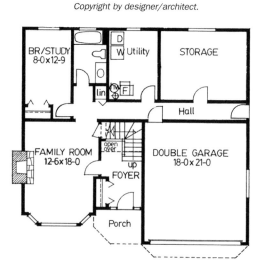

Garage Level Floor Plan

Plan #151242

Dimensions: 74'4" W x 77' D
Levels: 2
Square Footage: 2,710
Main Level Sq. Ft.: 1,819
Upper Level Sq. Ft.: 891
Bedrooms: 4
Bathrooms: 2½
Foundation: Crawl space or slab; basement or walkout for fee
CompleteCost List Available: Yes
Price Category: F

Images provided by designer/architect.

- **Dining Room:** The 8-inch-diameter round columns at the entry add elegance to this formal eating area. The kitchen is close by, making serving guests convenient.

- **Kitchen:** This efficient kitchen features a raised bar to handle the overflow from the breakfast room. The pantry cabinet is always a welcome bonus.

- **Master Suite:** Located on the lower level for privacy, this retreat boasts a large sleeping area allowing for many different furniture layouts. Pamper yourself in the elegant master bath, complete with glass shower, whirlpool tub, and dual vanities.

Multiple rooflines give this home an elegant and unique look.

Features:

- **Great Room:** This large entertaining area features a gas fireplace flanked by built-in cabinets. The atrium doors, which lead to the rear covered porch, will allow plenty of natural light to fill this room.

Upper Level Floor Plan

Copyright by designer/architect.

Main Floor

Plan #191055

Dimensions: 60' W x 76' D

Levels: 1

Square Footage: 2,123

Bedrooms: 3

Bathrooms: 2½

Foundation: Crawl space or slab

Material List Available: No

Price Category: D

Images provided by designer/architect.

60'-0" WIDE
76'-0" DEEP

M. BATH

CLOSET
8'-5" X 10'-0"

MASTER BEDROOM
19'-0" X 18'-0"

PORCH 2
7' DEEP

BEDROOM 3
12'-0" X 11'-8"

PORCH 2
11' DEEP

LAUNDRY
7'-0" X 10'-2"

PANTRY
8'-0" X 7'-2"

GREAT ROOM
22'-4" X 16'-0"

KITCHEN
13'-10" X 11'-10"

BEDROOM 2
11'-10" X 12'-10"

SITTING
7'-8" X 8'-0"

FOYER

1/2 B.

DINING AREA
13'-10" X 12'-0"

PORCH 1
6' DEEP

Copyright by designer/architect.

Plan #151005

Dimensions: 58' W x 54'10" D

Levels: 1

Square Footage: 1,940

Bedrooms: 4

Bathrooms: 2

Foundation: Crawl space, slab, or basement

CompleteCost List Available: Yes

Price Category: D

Images provided by designer/architect.

CAD FILE AVAILABLE

58'-0"

54'-10"

BREAKFAST ROOM
9'-4" X 10'-11"

COVERED PORCH
18'-5" X 4'-0"

MASTER SUITE
15'-0" X 15'-0"
9' PAN CEILING

GREAT ROOM
15'-0" X 19'-6"
9' BOX CEILING

BEDROOM 4
13'-6" X 14'-6"

KITCHEN
9'-11" X 12'-7"

BUILT-INS

BATH

KNEE SPACE

M. BATH
15'-0" X 11'-8"

BEDROOM 3
10'-0" X 10'-4"

GLASS BLOCKS

WHP TUB

DINING ROOM
11'-6" X 9'-8"

FOYER
7'-0" X 7'-0"

LIN

STORAGE

LAU.

BEDROOM 2
12'-4" X 10'-6"

10" RND. COL. W/ BASE

4' PORCH

GARAGE
20'-10" X 20'-0"

Copyright by designer/architect.

Plan #321046

Dimensions: 66' W x 40' D
Levels: 2
Square Footage: 2,411
Main Level Sq. Ft.: 1,293
Upper Level Sq. Ft.: 1,118
Bedrooms: 3
Bathrooms: 2½
Foundation: Basement
Materials List Available: Yes
Price Category: E

Images provided by designer/architect.

This home, as shown in the photograph, may differ from the actual blueprints. For more detailed information, please check the floor plans carefully.

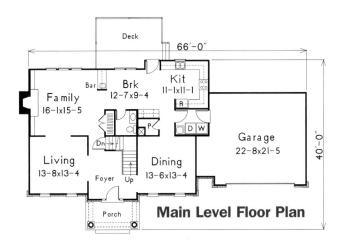

Main Level Floor Plan

Upper Level Floor Plan

Copyright by designer/architect.

Plan #161020

Dimensions: 60' W" x 50'4" D
Levels: 2
Square Footage: 2,082; 2,349 with bonus space
Main Level Sq. Ft.: 1,524
Upper Level Sq. Ft.: 558
Bedrooms: 3
Bathrooms: 2½
Foundation: Basement
Materials List Available: Yes
Price Category: D

Images provided by designer/architect.

Upper Level Floor Plan

Main Level Floor Plan

Copyright by designer/architect.

Plan #391019

Dimensions: 56' W x 32' D

Levels: 1

Square Footage: 1,792

Bedrooms: 3

Bathrooms: 2

Foundation: Basement

Materials List Available: Yes

Price Category: C

Images provided by designer/architect.

Copyright by designer/architect.

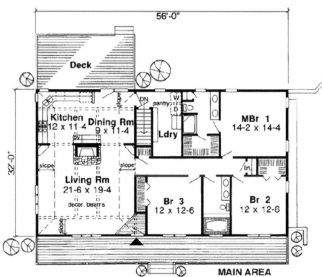

MAIN AREA

Plan #641004

Dimensions: 56' W x 52' D

Levels: 2

Square Footage: 3,030

Main Level Sq. Ft.: 1,778

Upper Level Sq. Ft.: 1,252

Bedrooms: 3

Bathrooms: 3½

Foundation: Crawl space, slab, or basement

Material List Available: No

Price Category: G

Images provided by designer/architect.

CAD FILE AVAILABLE

Main Level Floor Plan

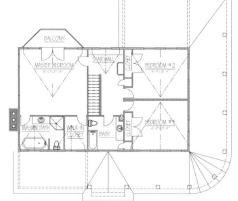

Upper Level Floor Plan

Copyright by designer/architect.

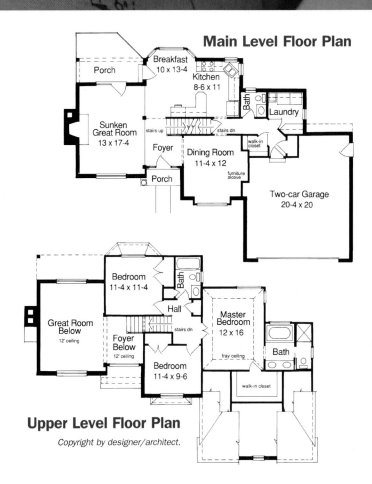

Main Level Floor Plan

Porch

Breakfast
10 x 13-4

Kitchen
8-6 x 11

Bath

Laundry

Sunken
Great Room
13 x 17-4

stairs up   stairs dn

walk-in
closet

Foyer

Dining Room
11-4 x 12

furniture
alcove

Two-car Garage
20-4 x 20

Porch

Images provided by designer/architect.

Bedroom
11-4 x 11-4

Bath

Great Room
Below
12' ceiling

Hall

stairs dn

Master
Bedroom
12 x 16

Foyer
Below
12' ceiling

tray ceiling

Bath

Bedroom
11-4 x 9-6

walk-in closet

Upper Level Floor Plan

Copyright by designer/architect.

Plan #161015

Dimensions: 55'4" W x 40'4" D

Levels: 2

Square Footage: 1,768

Main Level Sq. Ft.: 960

Upper Level Sq. Ft.: 808

Bedrooms: 3

Bathrooms: 2½

Foundation: Walkout

Materials List Available: Yes

Price Category: C

Plan #391066

Dimensions: 78' W x 60' D

Levels: 2

Square Footage: 3,526

Main Level Sq. Ft.: 2,054

Upper Level Sq. Ft.: 1,472

Bedrooms: 4

Bathrooms: 3½

Foundation: Crawl space, slab, or basement

Material List Available: No

Price Category: H

Images provided by designer/architect.

pantry

Furn./W/H

crawl access

D   W

Alternate Foundation Option

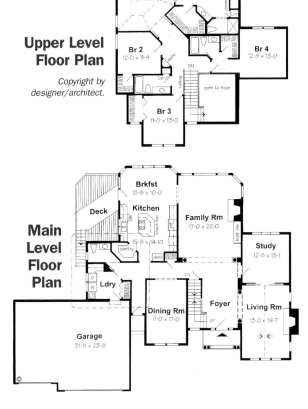

Upper Level Floor Plan

Copyright by designer/architect.

Master Suite
15-8 x 18-6
pan vaults

whirlpool

Br 2
12-0 x 11-4

niche

Br 4
12-8 x 13-0

Lin

DN

open to foyer

railing

Br 3
11-0 x 13-0

Main Level Floor Plan

Brkfst
15-8 x 10-0

Deck

Kitchen
15-8 x 14-10

snack bar

Family Rm
17-0 x 22-0

built-ins

pantry

desk

Study
12-8 x 13-1

D   W
Ldry

DN

Dining Rm
11-0 x 17-0

Foyer

UP

Living Rm
13-0 x 19-7

Garage
31-8 x 23-8

Plan #351033

Dimensions: 64' W x 39' D

Levels: 1

Heated Square Footage: 1,654

Bedrooms: 3

Bathrooms: 2

Foundation: Crawl space, slab, or basement

Materials List Available: Yes

Price Category: C

This gorgeous three-bedroom brick home would be the perfect place to raise your family.

Features:

- Great Room: This terrific room has a gas fireplace with built-in cabinets on either side.

- Kitchen: This island kitchen with breakfast area is open to the great room.

- Master Suite: This private room features a vaulted ceiling and a large walk-in closet. The bath area has a walk-in closet, jetted tub, and double vanities.

- Bedrooms: The two additional bedrooms share a bathroom located in the hall.

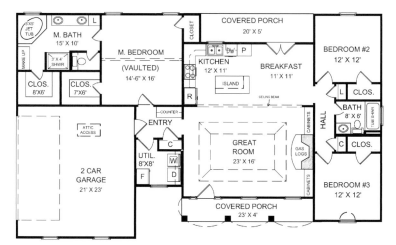

Plan #131025

Dimensions: 62'4" W x 65'10" D
Levels: 1½
Square Footage: 3,204
Main Level Sq. Ft.: 2,196
Upper Level Sq. Ft.: 1,008
Bedrooms: 4
Bathrooms: 4
Foundation: Crawl space or slab; basement for fee
Materials List Available: Yes
Price Category: H

Images provided by designer/architect.

You'll appreciate the flowing layout that's designed for entertaining but also suits an active family.

Features:

- Ceiling Height: 8 ft.

- Great Room: Decorative columns serve as the entryway to the great room that's made for entertaining. A fireplace makes it warm in winter; built-in shelves give a classic appearance; and the serving counter it shares with the kitchen is both practical and attractive.

- Kitchen: A door into the backyard makes outdoor entertaining easy, and the full bathroom near the door adds convenience.

- Master Suite: Enjoy the sunny sitting area that's a feature of this suite. A tray ceiling adds character to the room, and a huge walk-in closet is easy to organize. The bathroom features a corner spa tub.

- Bedrooms: Each of the additional 3 bedrooms is bright and cheery.

Main Level Floor Plan

Upper Level Floor Plan

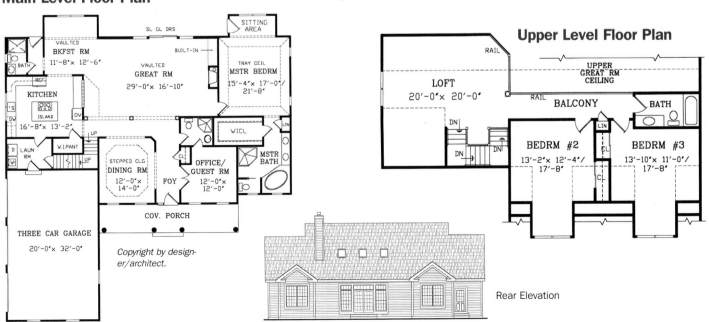

Copyright by designer/architect.

Rear Elevation

Optional Basement Level Floor Plan

Kitchen
8-6 x 8-3

Copyright by designer/architect.

Plan #391064

Dimensions: 54' W x 28' D

Levels: 1

Square Footage: 988

Bedrooms: 3

Bathrooms: 2

Foundation: Crawl space, basement

Materials List Available: Yes

Price Category: A

Images provided by designer/architect.

Mstr. Br.
13-7 x 11-6

Kitchen
8-6 x 8-3

Dining
8-10 x 11-6

Covered Patio

Br 2
9-8 x 11-8

Br 3
11-0 x 10-2

Living Rm
15-8 x 11-7

Garage
13-9 x 19-5

Optional 2-Car Garage

Linen

Crawl Access

Furn

Plant Box

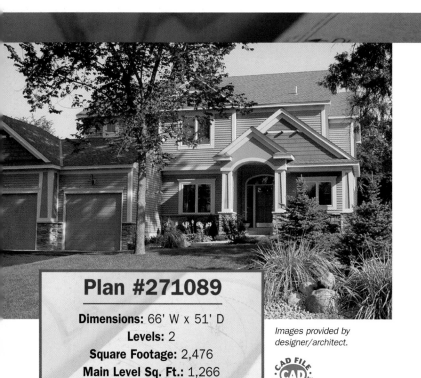

Plan #271089

Dimensions: 66' W x 51' D

Levels: 2

Square Footage: 2,476

Main Level Sq. Ft.: 1,266

Upper Level Sq. Ft.: 1,210

Bedrooms: 3

Bathrooms: 2½

Foundation: Daylight basement

Materials List Available: No

Price Category: E

Images provided by designer/architect.

CAD FILE AVAILABLE

Main Level Floor Plan

DINING RM
12' X 14'

GREAT RM
17' X 14'

KITCHEN
20' X 14'

STUDY
11' X 11'

ENTRY

MUD RM

GARAGE
32' X 24'

Upper Level Floor Plan

BATH

OWNER'S SUITE
15' X 14'

BED RM
11' X 13'

W.I.C.

HALL

BATH

BED RM
11' X 13'

Copyright by designer/architect.

Main Level Floor Plan

Upper Level Floor Plan

Images provided by designer/architect.

CAD FILE AVAILABLE
CAD

Copyright by designer/architect.

Plan #181084

Dimensions: 69'8" W x 73'8" D

Levels: 2

Square Footage: 4,084

Main Level Sq. Ft.: 2,579

Upper Level Sq. Ft.: 1,469

Bedrooms: 4

Bathrooms: 3½

Foundation: Basement

Material List Available: Yes

Price Category: K

Plan #211108

Dimensions: 66' W x 66' D

Levels: 2

Square Footage: 2,954

Main Level Sq. Ft.: 1,984

Upper Level Sq. Ft.: 970

Bedrooms: 4

Bathrooms: 3½

Foundation: Crawl space, slab, or basement

Materials List Available: Yes

Price Category: F

Images provided by designer/architect.

Main Level Floor Plan

Upper Level Floor Plan

Copyright by designer/architect.

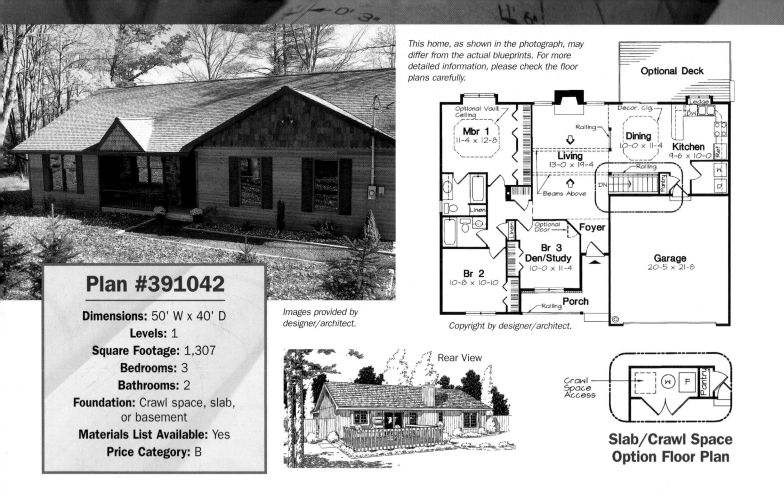

Plan #391042

Dimensions: 50' W x 40' D

Levels: 1

Square Footage: 1,307

Bedrooms: 3

Bathrooms: 2

Foundation: Crawl space, slab, or basement

Materials List Available: Yes

Price Category: B

This home, as shown in the photograph, may differ from the actual blueprints. For more detailed information, please check the floor plans carefully.

Images provided by designer/architect.

Copyright by designer/architect.

Rear View

Slab/Crawl Space Option Floor Plan

Plan #151171

Dimensions: 63'10" W x 72'2" D

Levels: 1

Square Footage: 2,131

Bedrooms: 3

Bathrooms: 2½

Foundation: Crawl space or slab; basement or walkout for fee

CompleteCost List Available: Yes

Price Category: D

Images provided by designer/architect.

Copyright by designer/architect.

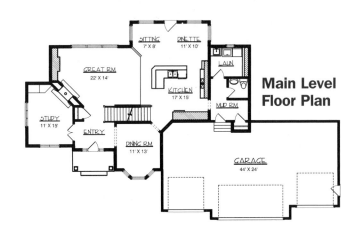

Main Level Floor Plan

Upper Level Floor Plan

Copyright by designer/architect.

Images provided by designer/architect.

Plan #271090

Dimensions: 78' W x 49' D

Levels: 2

Square Footage: 2,708

Main Level Sq. Ft.: 1,430

Upper Level Sq. Ft.: 1,278

Bedrooms: 3

Bathrooms: 2½

Foundation: Daylight basement

Materials List Available: No

Price Category: F

Plan #271007

Dimensions: 52' W x 41' D

Levels: 1

Square Footage: 1,283

Bedrooms: 3

Bathrooms: 2

Foundation: Basement

Materials List Available: Yes

Price Category: B

Images provided by designer/architect.

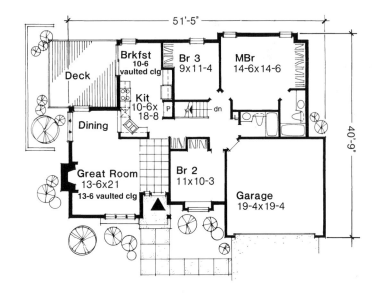

Copyright by designer/architect.

Plan #121216

Dimensions: 40' W x 47'8" D

Levels: 1

Square Footage: 1,205

Bedrooms: 2

Bathrooms: 2

Foundation: Basement; crawl space or slab for fee

Material List Available: Yes

Price Category: B

Images provided by designer/architect.

This home boasts a beautiful arched entry.

Features:

- Great Room: Enter this large gathering area from the foyer; the warmth of the fireplace welcomes you home. The 10-ft.-high ceiling gives the area an open feeling.

- Kitchen: Family and friends will enjoy gathering in this cozy kitchen, with its attached breakfast room. The area provides access to a future rear patio. The garage and laundry area are just a few steps away.

- Master Suite: This private area features a stepped ceiling in the sleeping area and a large window for backyard views. The master bath boasts a whirlpool bathtub, a separate shower, and dual vanities.

- Secondary Bedroom: A large front window brings light into this comfortable bedroom. A full bathroom is located nearby.

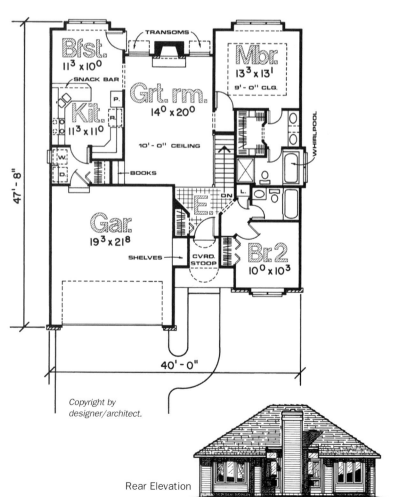

Copyright by designer/architect.

Rear Elevation

Plan #151026

Dimensions: 34' W x 66'8" D
Levels: 2
Square Footage: 1,574
Main Level Sq. Ft.: 1,131
Upper Level Sq. Ft.: 443
Bedrooms: 3
Bathrooms: 2½
Foundation: Crawl space, slab, full basement for fee
Complete Cost Available: Yes
Price Category: C

Images provided by designer/architect.

This French Country home gives space for entertaining and offers privacy.

Features:

• Great Room: Move through the gracious foyer framed by wooden columns into the great room with its lofty 10-ft. ceilings and gas fireplace.

• Dining Room: Set off by 8-in. columns, the dining room opens to the kitchen, both with 9-ft. ceilings.

• Master Suite: Enjoy relaxing in the bedroom with its 10-ft. boxed ceiling and well-placed windows. Atrium doors open to the backyard, where you can mmake a secluded garden. A glass-bricked corner whirlpool tub, corner shower, and double vanity make the master bath luxurious.

• Bedrooms: Upstairs, two large bedrooms with a walk-throuugh bath provide plenty of room as well as privacy for kids and guests.

Main Level Floor Plan

Copyright by designer/architect.

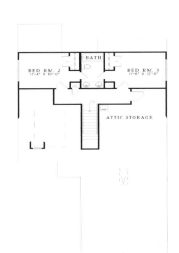

Upper Level Floor Plan

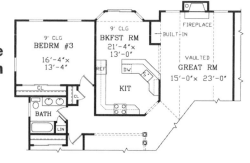

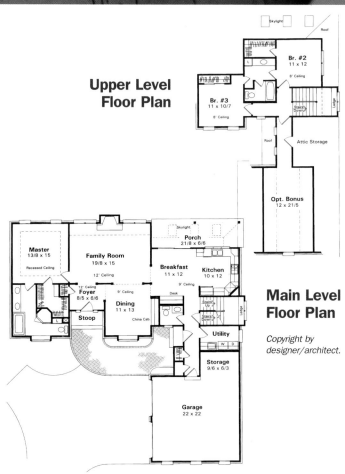

Plan #131006

Dimensions: 61' W x 53'6" D

Levels: 1

Square Footage: 2,193

Bedrooms: 3

Bathrooms: 2

Foundation: Crawl space or slab; basement for fee

Materials List Available: Yes

Price Category: E

Images provided by designer/architect.

Copyright by designer/architect.

Alternate Floor Plan

Plan #251012

Dimensions: 57'9" W x 62'10" D

Levels: 2

Square Footage: 2,009

Main Level Sq. Ft.: 1,520

Upper Level Sq. Ft.: 489

Bedrooms: 3

Bathrooms: 2½

Foundation: Basement

Material List Available: Yes

Price Category: G

Images provided by designer/architect.

T

Upper Level Floor Plan

Main Level Floor Plan

Copyright by designer/architect.

Main Level Floor Plan

29'-0"
8,70 m

12'-0" X 15'-0"
3,60 X 4,50

17'-0" X 15'-0"
5,10 X 4,50

12'-4" X 24'-4"
3,70 X 7,30

14'-0" X 12'-4"
4,20 X 3,70

45'-6"
13,65 m

Images provided by designer/architect.

Plan #181157

Dimensions: 45' 6" W x 29' D

Levels: 2

Square Footage: 1,795

Main Level Sq. Ft.: 890

Upper Level Sq. Ft.: 905

Bedrooms: 3

Bathrooms: 2½

Foundation: Full basement

Materials List Available: Yes

Price Category: E

Upper Level Floor Plan

10'-8" X 12'-0"
3,20 X 3,60

10'-8" X 12'-0"
3,20 X 3,60

12'-4" X 24'-0"
3,70 X 7,20

15'-0" X 15'-0"
4,50 X 4,50

Copyright by designer/architect.

Main Level Floor Plan

KITCHEN

FAMILY ROOM

STORAGE

LAUNDRY

PANTRY

REF.

2 CAR GARAGE

DINING

ENTRY

LIVING

Images provided by designer/architect.

Plan #641009

Dimensions: 61' W x 37'6" D

Levels: 2

Square Footage: 2,648

Main Level Sq. Ft.: 1,373

Upper Level Sq. Ft.: 1,275

Bedrooms: 4

Bathrooms: 2½

Foundation: Basement; crawl space, slab or walkout for fee

Materials List Available: No

Price Category: F

Upper Level Floor Plan

BEDROOM 3

BEDROOM 4

MASTER BEDROOM

UNFINISHED BONUS ROOM

HALL

BATH

BEDROOM 2

WC

WC

MASTER BATH

Copyright by designer/architect.

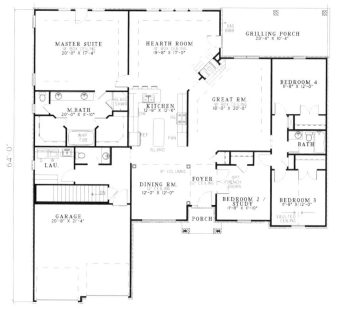

Images provided by designer/architect.

Plan #151063

Dimensions: 64' W x 60'2" D

Levels: 1

Square Footage: 2,554

Bedrooms: 4

Bathrooms: 2½

Foundation: Crawl space or slab; basement or walkout for fee

CompleteCost List Available: Yes

Price Category: D

CAD FILE AVAILABLE

Copyright by designer/architect.

Images provided by designer/architect.

Main Level Floor Plan

Upper Level Floor Plan
Copyright by designer/architect.

Plan #331002

Dimensions: 62'2" W x 66'8" D

Levels: 2

Square Footage: 2,299

Main Level Sq. Ft.: 1,517

Upper Level Sq. Ft.: 782

Bedrooms: 3

Bathrooms: 2½

Foundation: Crawl space, slab, or basement

Materials List Available: No

Price Category: E

Plan #181270

Dimensions: 36' W x 34' D

Levels: 1

Square Footage: 1,127

Bedrooms: 2

Bathrooms: 1

Foundation: Basement

Materials List Available: Yes

Price Category: D

Images provided by designer/architect.

CAD FILE AVAILABLE

34'-0"
10,2 m

10'-4" X 12'-8"
3,10 X 3,80

10'-8" X 13'-8"
3,20 X 4,10

11'-0" X 10'-0"
3,30 X 3,00

12'-0" X 16'-0"
3,60 X 4,80

11'-0" X 12'-0"
3,30 X 3,60

36'-0"
10,8 m

Copyright by designer/architect.

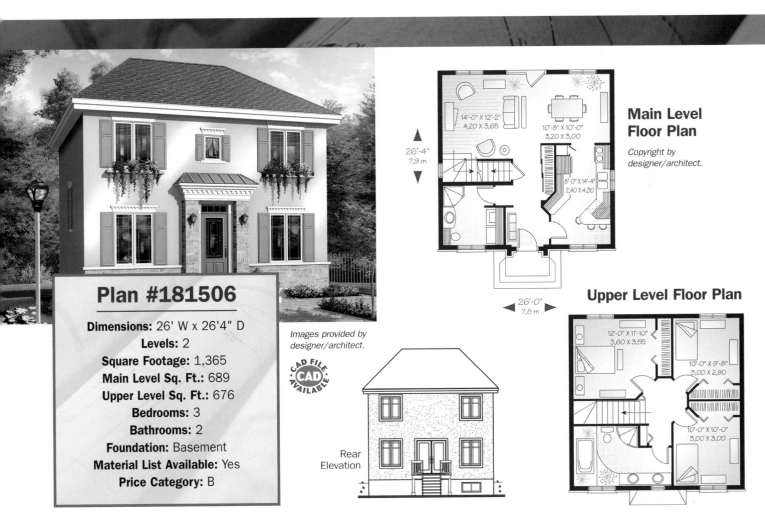

Plan #181506

Dimensions: 26' W x 26'4" D

Levels: 2

Square Footage: 1,365

Main Level Sq. Ft.: 689

Upper Level Sq. Ft.: 676

Bedrooms: 3

Bathrooms: 2

Foundation: Basement

Material List Available: Yes

Price Category: B

Images provided by designer/architect.

CAD FILE AVAILABLE

Main Level Floor Plan

Copyright by designer/architect.

26'-4"
7,9 m

14'-0" X 12'-2"
4,20 X 3,65

10'-8" X 10'-0"
3,20 X 3,00

8'-0" X 14'-4"
2,40 X 4,30

26'-0"
7,8 m

Rear Elevation

Upper Level Floor Plan

12'-0" X 11'-10"
3,60 X 3,55

10'-0" X 9'-8"
3,00 X 2,90

10'-0" X 10'-0"
3,00 X 3,00

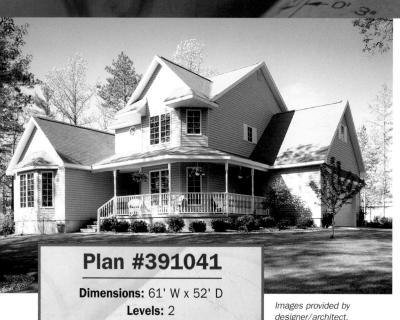

Plan #391041

Dimensions: 61' W x 52' D

Levels: 2

Square Footage: 2,563

Main Level Sq. Ft.: 1,737

Upper Level Sq. Ft.: 826

Bedrooms: 4

Bathrooms: 3½

Foundation: Basement

Materials List Available: No

Price Category: E

Images provided by designer/architect.

Main Level Floor Plan

Deck

Hearth Rm
13-4 x 14-8

Kit
11-4 x 12

slope

W D

Living Rm
13-8 x 22
17'-0" ceiling height

Ldry

FZR

Garage
21-8 x 21-4

UP DN

Balcony above

plant shelf

Foyer

Dining Rm
13 x 13-6

MBr 1
14-4 x 15-4
ceiling vaulted

Upper Level Floor Plan

Copyright by designer/architect.

slope

plant shelf

Guest Br 4
11-4 x 11-8

Br 3
12-2 x 13-4

open to below

DN

Balcony

open to below

Br 2
13 x 11-2

slope

plant shelf

Upper Level Floor Plan

Copyright by designer/architect.

MASTER BEDROOM

OPEN BELOW

BEDROOM #2

BATH

BONUS ROOM

WIC

BALCONY

MASTER BATH

LIN

OPEN BELOW

BEDROOM #3

WIC WIC

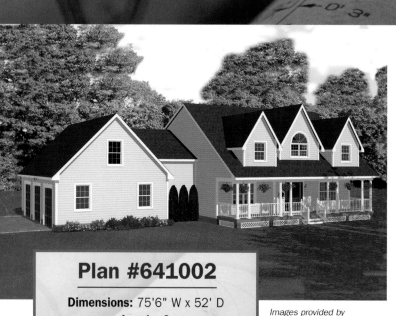

Plan #641002

Dimensions: 75'6" W x 52' D

Levels: 2

Square Footage: 2,655

Main Level Sq. Ft.: 1,512

Upper Level Sq. Ft.: 1,143

Bedrooms: 3

Bathrooms: 3

Foundation: Basement; crawl space, slab or walkout for fee

Material List Available: Yes

Price Category: F

Images provided by designer/architect.

CAD FILE AVAILABLE

Main Level Floor Plan

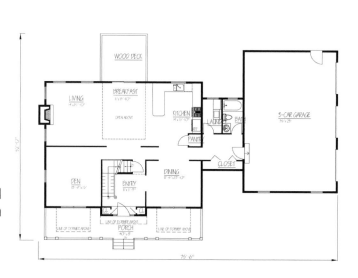

WOOD DECK

LIVING

BREAKFAST

KITCHEN

OPEN ABOVE

3-CAR GARAGE

LAUNDRY BATH

PANTRY

DEN

ENTRY

DINING

CLOSET

PORCH

Upper Level Floor Plan

Copyright by designer/architect.

Plan #181064

Dimensions: 91'4" W x 40'8" D

Levels: 2

Square Footage: 2,802

Main Level Sq. Ft.: 2,219

Upper Level Sq. Ft.: 583

Bedrooms: 4

Bathrooms: 2½

Foundation: Crawl space; slab or basement for fee

Materials List Available: Yes

Price Category: F

Images provided by designer/architect.

Main Level Floor Plan

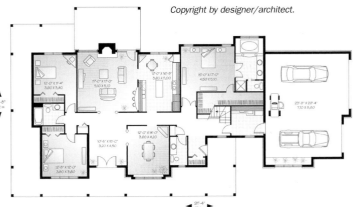

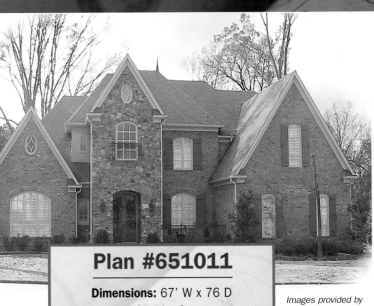

Main Level Floor Plan

Plan #651011

Dimensions: 67' W x 76 D

Levels: 2

Square Footage: 4,169

Main Level Sq. Ft.: 2,939

Upper Level Sq. Ft.: 1,230

Bedrooms: 4

Bathrooms: 3 full, 2 half

Foundation: Slab

Materials List Available: No

Price Category: I

Images provided by designer/architect.

Upper Level Floor Plan

Copyright by designer/architect.

Plan #121170

Dimensions: 68'4" W x 68' D
Levels: 1.5
Square Footage: 3,459
Main Level Sq. Ft.: 2,348
Upper Level Sq. Ft.: 1,111
Bedrooms: 4
Bathrooms: 3½
Foundation: Basement;
crawl space for fee
Material List Available: Yes
Price Category: G

This home, as shown in the photograph, may differ from the actual blueprints. For more detailed information, please check the floor plans carefully.

CAD FILE AVAILABLE

Images provided by designer/architect.

Large rooms make this home very attractive.

Features:

• **Dining Room:** When you enter this home, your eyes are drawn to this elegant formal eating area. The stepped ceiling adds to the feeling of grandeur.

• **Den:** Featuring French door access to the front porch, this den could function as a home office. The fireplace adds a focal point to the room.

• **Master Suite:** This main-level master suite boasts a 10-ft.-high ceiling. The master bath features a stall shower and dual vanities.

• **Upper Level:** Three secondary bedrooms are located on this level. Bedroom 2 boasts a private bathroom.

Front View

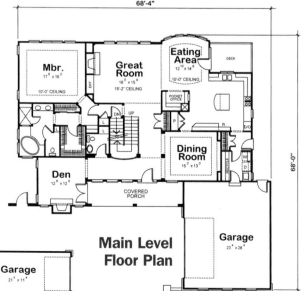

Main Level Floor Plan

Upper Level Floor Plan

Copyright by designer/architect.

Plan #321042

Dimensions: 71' W x 54'7" D
Levels: 2
Square Footage: 3,368
Main Level Sq. Ft.: 2,150
Upper Level Sq. Ft.: 1,218
Bedrooms: 4
Bathrooms: 3 full, 2 half
Foundation: Basement
Materials List Available: Yes
Price Category: G

Images provided by designer/architect.

Inside this traditional exterior lies a home filled with contemporary amenities and design features that are sure to charm the whole family.

Features:

• Great Room: Relax in this sunken room with a cathedral ceiling, wooden beams, skylights, and a masonry fireplace.

• Breakfast Room: Octagon-shaped with a domed ceiling, this room leads to the outdoor patio.

• Library: Situated for privacy and quiet, this room opens up from the master bedroom and the foyer.

• Kitchen: The central island here adds to the ample work and storage space.

• Dining Room: Just off the foyer, this room is ideal for formal dinners and quiet times.

• Master Suite: Enoy the large edroom and bath with a luxurious corner tub, separate shower, two vanities, walk-in closet, and dressing area.

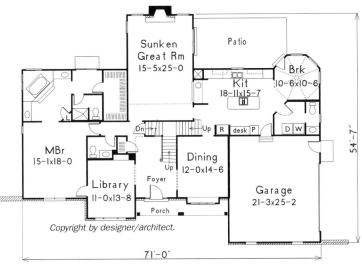

Main Level Floor Plan

Upper Level Floor Plan

Main Level Floor Plan

Plan #151087

Dimensions: 55'4" W x 53'10" D

Levels: 2

Square Footage: 2,942

Main Level Sq. Ft.: 1,547

Upper Level Sq. Ft.: 1,395

Bedrooms: 5

Bathrooms: 4

Foundation: Crawl space or slab; basement or walkout for fee

CompleteCost List Available: Yes

Price Category: F

Images provided by designer/architect.

Upper Level Floor Plan

Copyright by designer/architect.

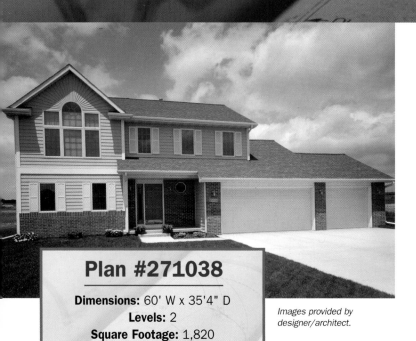

Plan #271038

Dimensions: 60' W x 35'4" D

Levels: 2

Square Footage: 1,820

Main Level Sq. Ft.: 987

Upper Level Sq. Ft.: 833

Bedrooms: 4

Bathrooms: 2½

Foundation: Basement

Materials List Available: No

Price Category: D

Images provided by designer/architect.

Main Level Floor Plan

Copyright by designer/architect.

Upper Level Floor Plan

High Glass above

Plan #111008

Dimensions: 43' W x 69' D

Levels: 2

Square Footage: 2,011

Main Level Sq. Ft.: 1,331

Upper Level Sq. Ft.: 680

Bedrooms: 3

Bathrooms: 2½

Foundation: Slab or basement

Materials List Available: No

Price Category: E

Images provided by designer/architect.

Main Level Floor Plan

Extra Storage 19'4" x 3'4"

Two-Car Carport 20'0" x 24'0"

Patio 20'0" x 8'0"

Great Room 22'8" x 14'0"

Utility

Master Bath

WIC

Breakfast 10'0" x 10'0"

Kitchen 11'4" x 10'10"

Master Bedroom 13'6" x 13'0"

Porch 11'0" x 5'0"

Dining Room 11'4" x 12'0"

Upper Level Floor Plan

Copyright by designer/architect.

Open to Below

Bedroom 10'4" x 10'6"

Bedroom 11'4" x 15'0"

Study 11'10" x 9'2"

Plan #321044

Dimensions: 61' W x 49'4" D

Levels: 2

Square Footage: 2,618

Main Level Sq. Ft.: 1,804

Upper Level Sq. Ft.: 814

Bedrooms: 4

Bathrooms: 2½

Foundation: Basement

Materials List Available: Yes

Price Category: F

Images provided by designer/architect.

CAD FILE AVAILABLE

Main Level Floor Plan

61'-0"

49'-4"

skylts

Deck

Great Rm 22-1x18-2 vaulted

Brk 10-8x15-1 vaulted

Kit 9-10x12-2

Bar

Dn

Dining 12-3x12-5

MBr 17-0x16-0

Up

Entry

Porch depth 4-0

Garage 20-8x20-1

W D

P

Upper Level Floor Plan

open to below

Br 4 14-8x11-1

Br 3 17-0x11-0

Dn

skylt

Br 2 12-3x12-8

Copyright by designer/architect.

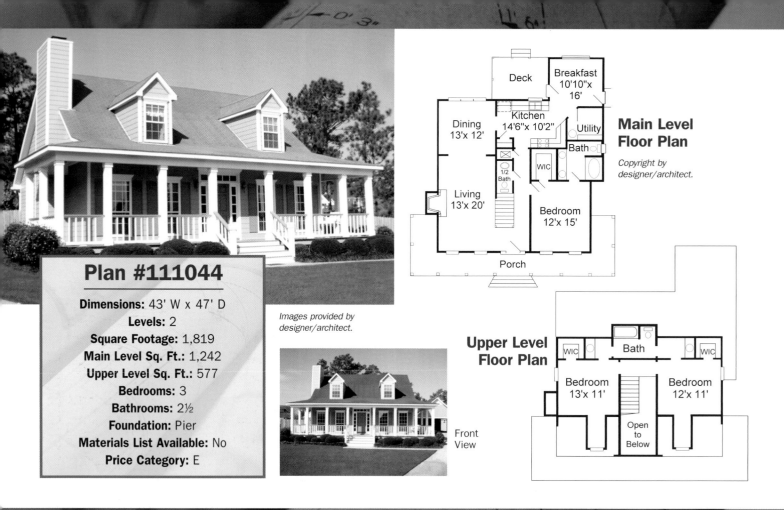

Main Level Floor Plan

Copyright by designer/architect.

Deck

Breakfast 10'10"x 16'

Dining 13'x 12'

Kitchen 14'6"x 10'2"

Utility

Bath

WIC

1/2 Bath

Living 13'x 20'

Bedroom 12'x 15'

Porch

Images provided by designer/architect.

Front View

Upper Level Floor Plan

WIC

Bath

WIC

Bedroom 13'x 11'

Bedroom 12'x 11'

Open to Below

Plan #111044

Dimensions: 43' W x 47' D

Levels: 2

Square Footage: 1,819

Main Level Sq. Ft.: 1,242

Upper Level Sq. Ft.: 577

Bedrooms: 3

Bathrooms: 2½

Foundation: Pier

Materials List Available: No

Price Category: E

Plan #661030

Dimensions: 30' W x 60' D

Levels: 1

Square Footage: 1,396

Bedrooms: 3

Bathrooms: 2

Foundation: Slab

Materials List Available: No

Price Category: B

Images provided by designer/architect.

CAD FILE AVAILABLE

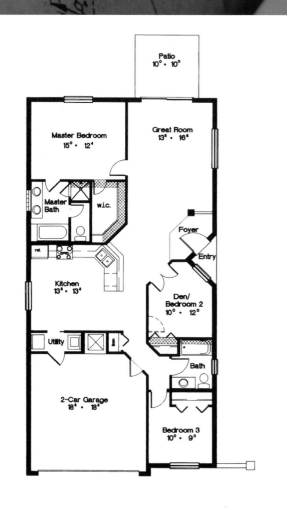

Patio 10⁰ · 10⁰

Master Bedroom 15⁰ · 12⁴

Great Room 13⁸ · 16⁸

Master Bath

w.i.c.

Foyer

Entry

Kitchen 13⁸ · 13⁸

Den/ Bedroom 2 10⁰ · 12⁰

Utility

Bath

2-Car Garage 18⁸ · 18⁸

Bedroom 3 10⁰ · 9⁰

Plan #121148

Dimensions: 36' W x 50' D
Levels: 2
Square Footage: 2,076
Main Level Sq. Ft.: 1,117
Upper Level Sq. Ft.: 959
Bedrooms: 3 or 4
Bathrooms: 2½
Foundation: Basement; crawl space or slab for fee
Material List Available: Yes
Price Category: D

Images provided by designer/architect.

CAD FILE AVAILABLE

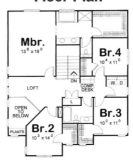

Main Level Floor Plan

Copyright by designer/architect.

Bfst. 10⁰ x 9⁸
Kit. 11⁰ x 11⁰
Fam. Room 14⁰ x 17⁰
Din. 13⁸ x 11⁰
Den 10³ x 12⁰
Gar. 19⁴ x 22⁰
COVERED PORCH
50'-0"
36'-0"

Upper Level Floor Plan

Mbr. 13⁸ x 19⁰
Br.4 10⁴ x 11⁰
Br.3 10⁰ x 11⁰
Br.2 10³ x 14⁰

Optional Upper Level Floor Plan

Mbr. 13⁸ x 11⁰
Br.3 10⁰ x 11⁰
Br.2 10³ x 14⁰

Plan #181066

Dimensions: 25'6" W x 35'6" D
Levels: 2
Square Footage: 1,584
Main Level Sq. Ft.: 805
Upper Level Sq. Ft.: 779
Bedrooms: 3
Bathrooms: 1½
Foundation: Basement
Material List Available: Yes
Price Category: E

Images provided by designer/architect.

CAD FILE AVAILABLE

Main Level Floor Plan

9'-8" X 9'-0" 2,90 X 2,70
11'-0" X 9'-0" 3,30 2,70
13'-0" X 9'-0" 3,90 X 2,70
11'-8" X 16'-0" 3,50 X 4,80
35'-6" 10,65 m
25'-6" 7,65 m

Upper Level Floor Plan

Copyright by designer/architect.

11'-4" X 9'-0" 3,40 X 2,70
11'-8" X 11'-0" 3,50 X 3,30
11'-8" X 15'-0" 3,50 X 4,50

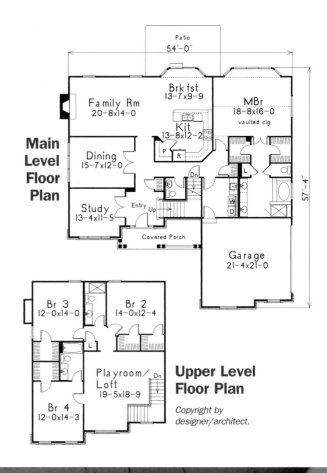

Plan #321062

Dimensions: 54' W x 57'4" D
Levels: 2
Square Footage: 3,138
Main Level Sq. Ft.: 1,958
Upper Level Sq. Ft.: 1,180
Bedrooms: 4
Bathrooms: 3½
Foundation: Basement
Materials List Available: Yes
Price Category: G

Images provided by designer/architect.

This home, as shown in the photograph, may differ from the actual blueprints. For more detailed information, please check the floor plans carefully.

CAD FILE AVAILABLE

Main Level Floor Plan

Upper Level Floor Plan

Copyright by designer/architect.

Plan #351011

Dimensions: 73'8" W x 53'2" D
Levels: 1
Square Footage: 2,251
Bedrooms: 3
Bathrooms: 2½
Foundation: Crawl space, slab, or basement
Materials List Available: Yes
Price Category: F

Images provided by designer/architect.

CAD FILE AVAILABLE

Main Level Floor Plan

Upper Level Floor Plan

Copyright by designer/architect.

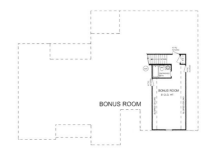

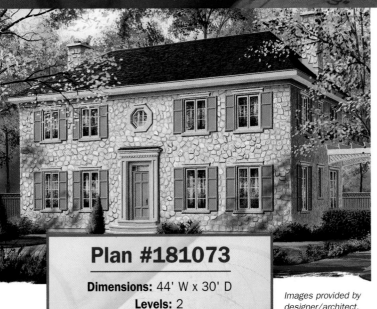

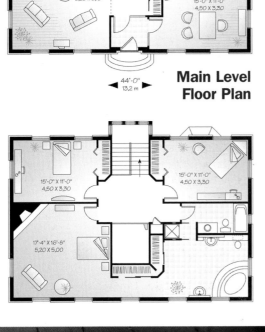

**Main Level
Floor Plan**

Plan #181073

Dimensions: 44' W x 30' D

Levels: 2

Square Footage: 2,663

Main Level Sq. Ft.: 1,343

Upper Level Sq. Ft.: 1,320

Bedrooms: 3

Bathrooms: 2½

Foundation: Basement

Material List Available: Yes

Price Category: H

Images provided by designer/architect.

**Upper Level
Floor Plan**

Copyright by designer/architect.

Plan #391055

Dimensions: 76'6" W x 55' D

Levels: 2

Square Footage: 4,217

Main Level Sq. Ft.: 2,108

Upper Level Sq. Ft.: 2,109

Bedrooms: 4

Bathrooms: 2½

Foundation: Basement

Material List Available: Yes

Price Category: I

Images provided by designer/architect.

This home, as shown in the photograph, may differ from the actual blueprints. For more detailed information, please check the floor plans carefully.

**Main Level
Floor Plan**

**Upper Level
Floor Plan**

Copyright by designer/architect.

Plan #121155

Dimensions: 65'6" W x 56'10" D
Levels: 1.5
Square Footage: 2,638
Main Level Sq. Ft.: 1,844
Upper Level Sq. Ft.: 794
Bedrooms: 4
Bathrooms: 3½
Foundation: Slab; basement for fee
Material List Available: Yes
Price Category: F

This home, as shown in the photograph, may differ from the actual blueprints. For more detailed information, please check the floor plans carefully.

CAD FILE AVAILABLE

Images provided by designer/architect.

This traditional home is so attractive that passersby will want to stop and visit.

Features:

- **Study:** Situated in close proximity to the entry, this study would function well as a home office. The triple-window unit adds light to the area.
- **Kitchen:** This gourmet peninsula kitchen offers a handy pantry. The attached breakfast room offers easy access to the veranda.

- **Master Suite:** This master suite boasts a vaulted ceiling and two walk-in closets. The private bath shows off a whirlpool tub and dual vanities.
- **Secondary Bedrooms:** Residing on the upper level are three family bedrooms. Bedroom 4 boasts its own private bath, while bedrooms 2 and 3 share a Jack-and-Jill bathroom.

Upper Level Floor Plan

Copyright by designer/architect.

Main Level Floor Plan

Plan #121020

Dimensions: 64' W x 46' D
Levels: 2
Square Footage: 2,480
Main Level Sq. Ft.: 1,369
Upper Level Sq. Ft.: 1,111
Bedrooms: 4
Bathrooms: 2½
Foundation: Basement
Materials List Available: Yes
Price Category: E

Images provided by designer/architect.

Tapered columns and an angled stairway give this home a classical style.

Features:

• Ceiling Height 8 ft.

• Living Room: Just off the dramatic two-story entry is this distinctive living room, with its apered columns, transom-topped windows, and boxed ceiling.

• Formal Dining Room: The tapered columns, transom-topped windows, and boxed ceiling

found in the living room continue into this gracious dining space.

• Family Room: Located on the opposite side of the house from the living room and dining room, the family room features a beamed ceiling and fireplace framed by windows.

• Kitchen: An island is the centerpiece of this convenient kitchen.

• Master Suite: Upstairs, a tiered ceiling and corner windows enhance the master bedroom, which is served by a pampering bath.

Main Level Floor Plan

Upper Level Floor Plan

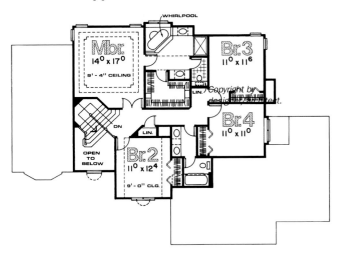

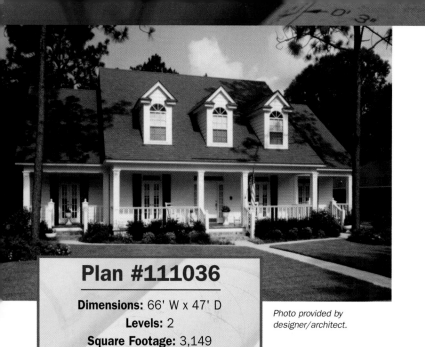

Plan #111036

Dimensions: 66' W x 47' D

Levels: 2

Square Footage: 3,149

Main Level Sq. Ft.: 2,033

Upper Level Sq. Ft.: 1,116

Bedrooms: 4

Bathrooms: 3½

Foundation: Pier

Materials List Available: No

Price Category: H

Photo provided by designer/architect.

Main Level Floor Plan

Upper Level Floor Plan

Copyright by designer/architect.

Plan #181505

Dimensions: 30' W x 28' D

Levels: 2

Square Footage: 1,650

Main Level Sq. Ft.: 825

Upper Level Sq. Ft.: 825

Bedrooms: 3

Bathrooms: 2

Foundation: Basement

Material List Available: Yes

Price Category: E

Images provided by designer/architect.

Main Level Floor Plan

Copyright by designer/architect.

28'-0"
8,4 m

30'-0"
9,0 m

Upper Level Floor Plan

Rear Elevation

CAD FILE AVAILABLE

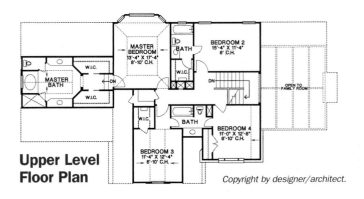

Main Level Floor Plan

Images provided by designer/architect.

Plan #121149

Dimensions: 75'1 1/2" W x 38' D

Levels: 2

Square Footage: 2,715

Main Level Sq. Ft.: 1,400

Upper Level Sq. Ft.: 1,315

Bedrooms: 4

Bathrooms: 3½

Foundation: Slab; basement for fee

Material List Available: Yes

Price Category: F

Upper Level Floor Plan

Copyright by designer/architect.

Main Level Floor Plan

Images provided by designer/architect.

Plan #281001

Dimensions: 54' W x 47' D

Levels: 2

Square Footage: 2,423

Main Level Sq. Ft.: 1,388

Second Level Sq. Ft.: 1,035

Bedrooms: 3

Bathrooms: 2½

Foundation: Basement

Materials List Available: Yes

Price Category: E

Upper Level Floor Plan

Copyright by designer/architect.

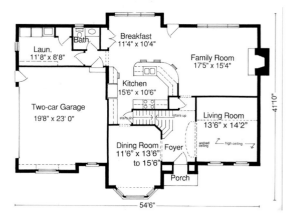

Plan #161019

Dimensions: 54'6" D x 41'10" W

Levels: 2

Square Footage: 2,428

Main Level Sq. Ft.: 1,309

Upper Level Sq. Ft.: 1,119

Bedrooms: 4

Bathrooms: 2½

Foundation: Basement

Materials List Available: No

Price Category: E

Images provided by designer/architect.

Main Level Floor Plan

Copyright by designer/architect.

Upper Level Floor Plan

Plan #391054

Dimensions: 111' W x 72'6" D

Levels: 2

Square Footage: 5,254

Main Level Sq. Ft.: 4,075

Upper Level Sq. Ft.: 1,179

Bedrooms: 5

Bathrooms: 5

Foundation: Slab

Material List Available: Yes

Price Category: J

Images provided by designer/architect.

Rear View

Main Level Floor Plan

Upper Level Floor Plan

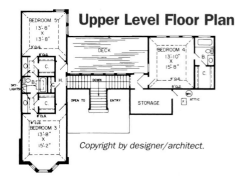

Copyright by designer/architect.

Images provided by designer/architect.

CAD FILE AVAILABLE

Copyright by designer/architect.

Plan #151140

Dimensions: 67'2" W x 55'10" D

Levels: 1

Square Footage: 2,525

Bedrooms: 4

Bathrooms: 3

Foundation: Crawl space, slab

Materials List Available: No

Price Category: E

Upper Level Floor Plan

Main Level Floor Plan

Copyright by designer/architect.

Plan #211070

Dimensions: 46' W x 68' D

Levels: 2

Square Footage: 1,700

Main Level Sq. Ft.: 1,160

Upper Level Sq. Ft.: 540

Bedrooms: 3

Bathrooms: 2½

Foundation: Crawl space or slab; basement option for fee

Materials List Available: Yes

Price Category: C

Images provided by designer/architect.

Plan #391053

Dimensions: 76' W x 63' D

Levels: 2

Square Footage: 3,128

Main Level Sq. Ft.: 2,277

Upper Level Sq. Ft.: 851

Bedrooms: 4

Bathrooms: 3½

Foundation: Crawl space, slab, or basement

Material List Available: Yes

Price Category: G

Images provided by designer/architect.

Main Level Floor Plan

Copyright by designer/architect.

Upper Level Floor Plan

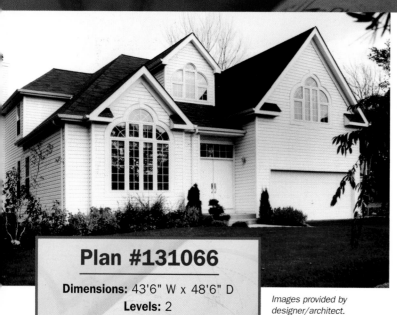

Plan #131066

Dimensions: 43'6" W x 48'6" D

Levels: 2

Square Footage: 2,760

Main Level Sq. Ft.: 1,483

Upper Level Sq. Ft.: 1,277

Bedrooms: 4

Bathrooms: 2½

Foundation: Crawl space or basement

Material List Available: Yes

Price Category: G

Images provided by designer/architect.

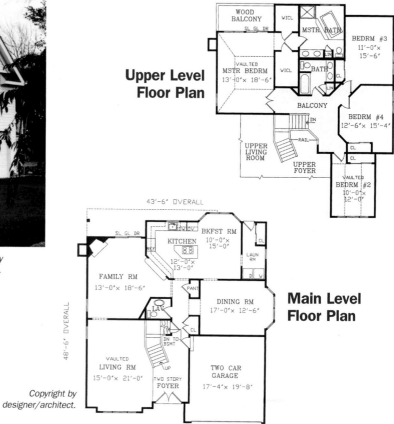

Upper Level Floor Plan

Main Level Floor Plan

Copyright by designer/architect.

Main Level Floor Plan

Plan #131074

Dimensions: 56' W x 41' D

Levels: 2

Square Footage: 2,085

Main Level Sq. Ft.: 1,240

Upper Level Sq. Ft.: 845

Bedrooms: 4

Bathrooms: 2½

Foundation: Slab or basement

Material List Available: Yes

Price Category: E

Images provided by designer/architect.

This home, as shown in the photograph, may differ from the actual blueprints. For more detailed information, please check the floor plans carefully.

Optional Bonus Area Floor Plan

Upper Level Floor Plan

Copyright by designer/architect.

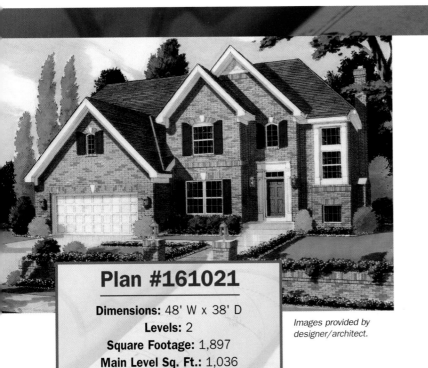

Plan #161021

Dimensions: 48' W x 38' D

Levels: 2

Square Footage: 1,897

Main Level Sq. Ft.: 1,036

Upper Level Sq. Ft.: 861

Bedrooms: 3

Bathrooms: 2½

Foundation: Basement

Materials List Available: No

Price Category: D

Images provided by designer/architect.

Main Level Floor Plan

Rear Elevation

Upper Level Floor Plan

Copyright by designer/architect.

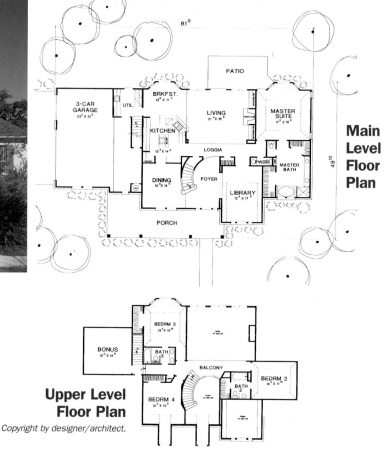

Main Level Floor Plan

Plan #331004

Dimensions: 81' W x 49'10" D

Levels: 2

Square Footage: 3,146

Main Level Sq. Ft.: 2,150

Upper Level Sq. Ft.: 996

Bedrooms: 4

Bathrooms: 3½

Foundation: Crawl space, slab, or basement

Materials List Available: No

Price Category: G

Images provided by designer/architect.

This home, as shown in the photograph, may differ from the actual blueprints. For more detailed information, please check the floor plans carefully.

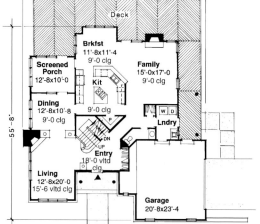

Upper Level Floor Plan

Copyright by designer/architect.

Upper Level Floor Plan

Plan #271029

Dimensions: 53' W x 55'8" D

Levels: 2

Square Footage: 3,039

Main Level Sq. Ft.: 1,612

Upper Level Sq. Ft.: 1,427

Bedrooms: 4

Bathrooms: 2½

Foundation: Basement

Materials List Available: Yes

Price Category: G

Images provided by designer/architect.

Main Level Floor Plan

Copyright by designer/architect.

Plan #391040

Dimensions: 69' W x 55'6" D

Levels: 2

Square Footage: 3,276

Main Level Sq. Ft.: 1,786

Upper Level Sq. Ft.: 1,490

Bedrooms: 4

Bathrooms: 2½

Foundation: Basement

Materials List Available: Yes

Price Category: G

Images provided by designer/architect.

Main Level Floor Plan

Copyright by designer/architect.

DINING RM. 14'-8"x14'-0"

KITCHEN 12'-6"x14'-6"

DINETTE 10'-6"x13'-0"

FAMILY ROOM 18'-0" x 22'-0"

SCREENED PORCH VAULTED CEILING

LIVING RM. 14'-6"x16'-0"

FOYER OPEN TO ABOVE

DEN/STUDY 11'-0"x12'-4"

LAUNDRY/ SEWING 11'-2"x11'-2"

GARAGE 23'-8" x 25'-7"

DRIVEWAY

Upper Level Floor Plan

M. BEDROOM 18'-0"x17'-8" VAULTED CEILING

BEDROOM 2 11'-0"x14'-4"

BEDROOM 3 11'-4"x12'-4"

BEDROOM 4 11'-4"x15'-4"

OPEN TO FOYER

Plan #271035

Dimensions: 43'4" W x 46' D

Levels: 2

Square Footage: 1,891

Main Level Sq. Ft.: 1,075

Upper Level Sq. Ft.: 816

Bedrooms: 3

Bathrooms: 2½

Foundation: Basement

Materials List Available: Yes

Price Category: D

Images provided by designer/architect.

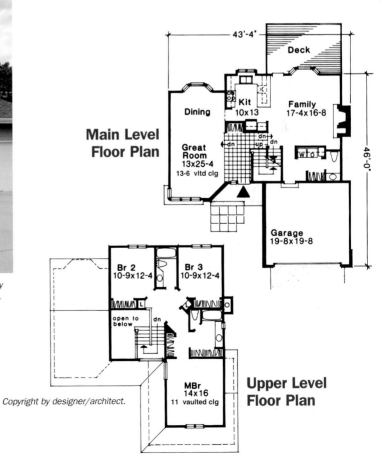

Main Level Floor Plan

43'-4"

Deck

Dining

Kit 10x13

Family 17-4x16-8

Great Room 13x25-4 13-6 vltd clg

Garage 19-8x19-8

46'-0"

Upper Level Floor Plan

Br 2 10-9x12-4

Br 3 10-9x12-4

open to below

MBr 14x16 11 vaulted clg

Copyright by designer/architect.

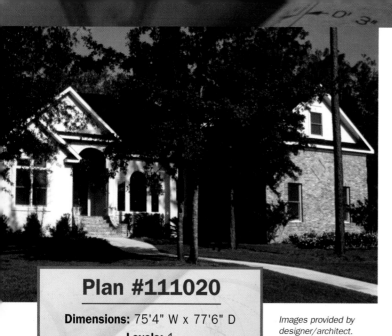

Plan #111020

Dimensions: 75'4" W x 77'6" D

Levels: 1

Square Footage: 2,987

Bedrooms: 4

Bathrooms: 3

Foundation: Slab

Materials List Available: No

Price Category: G

Images provided by designer/architect.

Copyright by designer/architect.

Bonus Area

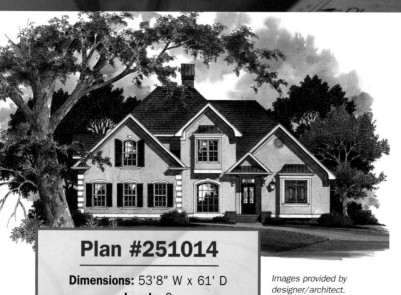

Plan #251014

Dimensions: 53'8" W x 61' D

Levels: 2

Square Footage: 2,210

Main Level Sq. Ft.: 1,670

Upper Level Sq. Ft.: 540

Bedrooms: 3

Bathrooms: 2 1/2

Foundation: Crawl space or basement

Materials List Available: No

Price Category: E

Images provided by designer/architect.

Main Level Floor Plan

Copyright by designer/architect.

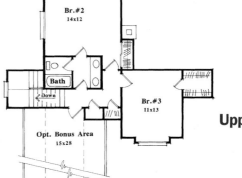

Upper Level Floor Plan

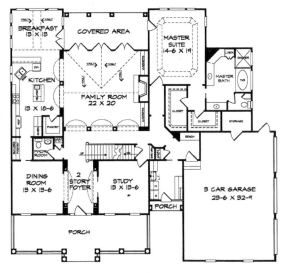

Main Level Floor Plan

BREAKFAST 13 X 13
COVERED AREA
MASTER SUITE 14-6 X 19
MASTER BATH
KITCHEN 13 X 18-6
FAMILY ROOM 22 X 20
PANTRY
POWDER ROOM
DINING ROOM 13 X 13-6
2 STORY FOYER
STUDY 13 X 13-6
3 CAR GARAGE 23-6 X 32-9
PORCH
PORCH

Images provided by designer/architect.

Copyright by designer/architect.

Plan #461028

Dimensions: 69' W x 65' D
Levels: 2
Square Footage: 3,663
Main Level Sq. Ft.: 2,516
Upper Level Sq. Ft.: 1,147
Bedrooms: 4
Bathrooms: 4½
Foundation: Basement, slab
Material List Available: No
Price Category: H

OVERLOOK TO FAMILY ROOM BELOW
ATTIC STORAGE
BEDROOM 4 13 X 13
BATH
BEDROOM 2 14 X 13-6
2 STORY FOYER
BEDROOM 3 20-6 X 12-6
BONUS ROOM 13-4 X 14-6

Upper Level Floor Plan

Rear Elevation

Patio
Porch
Bedroom 15'9"x 13'1"
Breakfast 13'5"x 11'7"
Master Bedroom 14'5"x 18'7"
Bath
Kitchen 13'9"x14'
Living 20'x 19'3"
WIC
Bedroom 12'1"x 13'1"
DRESS
WIC
Utility
Dining 12'7"x 16'1"
Foyer
Master Bath
Storage 12'1"x 6'3"
Bedroom 14'7"x 13'1"
Porch
Two-Car Garage 21'3"x 22'3"

Plan #111018

Dimensions: 67' W x 79' D
Levels: 1
Square Footage: 2,745
Bedrooms: 4
Bathrooms: 3½
Foundation: Slab or walkout
Materials List Available: No
Price Category: G

Images provided by designer/architect.

Copyright by designer/architect.

Main Level Floor Plan

Images provided by designer/architect.

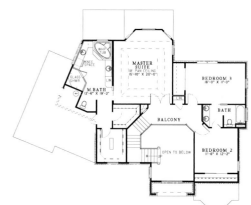

Upper Level Floor Plan

Copyright by designer/architect.

Plan #151019

Dimensions: 63'4" W x 53'10" D

Levels: 2

Square Footage: 2,653

Main Level Sq. Ft.: 1,407

Upper Level Sq. Ft.: 1,246

Bedrooms: 3

Bathrooms: 2½

Foundation: Crawl space, slab; optional full basement plan available for extra fee

CompleteCost List Available: Yes

Price Category: F

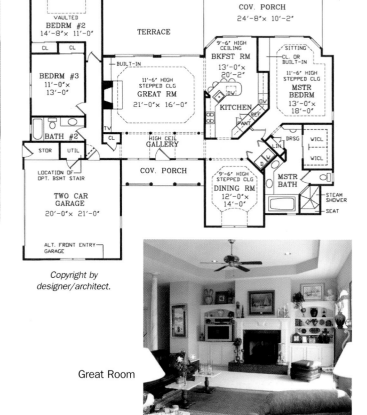

Images provided by designer/architect.

Copyright by designer/architect.

Great Room

Plan #131009

Dimensions: 64'10" W x 57'8" D

Levels: 1

Square Footage: 2,018

Bedrooms: 3

Bathrooms: 2

Foundation: Crawl space or slab; basement or walkout for fee

Materials List Available: Yes

Price Category: E

Plan #271098

Dimensions: 68'10" W x 81'5" D

Levels: 2

Square Footage: 3,382

Main Level Sq. Ft.: 2,136

Upper Level Sq. Ft.: 1,246

Bedrooms: 4

Bathrooms: 3½

Foundation: Slab

Materials List Available: No

Price Category: G

Main Level Floor Plan

Images provided by designer/architect.

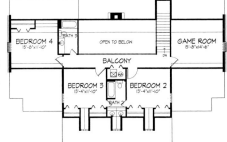

Upper Level Floor Plan

Copyright by designer/architect.

Plan #151022

Dimensions: 79' W x 77'8" D

Levels: 2

Square Footage: 3,059

Main Level Sq. Ft.: 2,650

Upper Level Sq. Ft.: 409

Bedrooms: 4

Bathrooms: 4

Foundation: Crawl space, slab, or basement

CompleteCost List Available: Yes

Price Category: G

Images provided by designer/architect.

Main Level Floor Plan

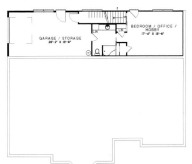

Upper Level Floor Plan

Copyright by designer/architect.

Plan #131010

Dimensions: 70' W x 34'4" D
Levels: 1
Square Footage: 1,667
Bedrooms: 3
Bathrooms: 2
Foundation: Crawl space or slab; basement for fee
Materials List Available: Yes
Price Category: D

Images provided by designer/architect.

Copyright by designer/architect.

Family Room / Kitchen Living Room

Optional Laundry Room with Basement Floor Plan

Plan #121165

Dimensions: 46' W x 55' D
Levels: 1
Square Footage: 1,678
Bedrooms: 3
Bathrooms: 2
Foundation: Basement; crawl space for fee
Material List Available: Yes
Price Category: C

Images provided by designer/architect.

This home, as shown in the photograph, may differ from the actual blueprints. For more detailed information, please check the floor plans carefully.

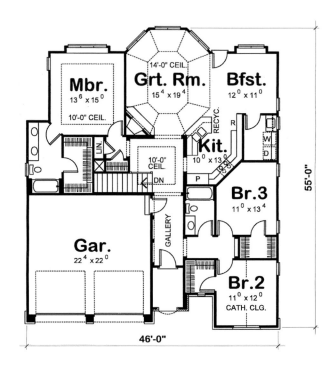

Copyright by designer/architect.

Main Level Floor Plan

Porch

Brkfst. 10-0 x 9-6

Kitchen 10-11 x 13-8

Dining Rm 11-0 x 15-5

Family Rm 13-5 x 19-5

Garage 21-5 x 27-4

OPEN TO ABOVE

Living Rm 13-6 x 16-0

Images provided by designer/architect.

Upper Level Floor Plan

Br 3 13-2 x 11-8

Den/ Br 4 10-0 x 11-7

LEDGE

Mstr. Suite 13-4 x 15-4

SKYLIGHTS

Commons 12-10 x 11-5

Util.

Bonus 21-5 x 15-5

Br 2 13-1 x 11-2

OPEN TO BELOW

RAILING

LEDGE

W.P. TUB

Copyright by designer/architect.

Plan #391067

Dimensions: 69'8" W x 42' D

Levels: 2

Square Footage: 2,897

Main Level Sq. Ft.: 1,435

Upper Level Sq. Ft.: 1,462

Bedrooms: 4

Bathrooms: 2½

Foundation: Crawl space, slab, or basement

Material List Available: No

Price Category: F

Main Level Floor Plan

Extra Storage 21'2"x 6'4"

Two-Car Garage 21'2"x 24'

Utility

Patio

Porch

Kitchen 13'8"x 15'8"

WIC

Master Bath

WIC

Family 22'9"x 17'

Master Bedroom 13'8"x 21'

Breakfast 13'8"x 12'

Living 11'10"x 14'

Dining 11'10"x 14'

Unfinished Gameroom 14'4"x 15'4"

Porch

Upper Level Floor Plan

Copyright by designer/architect.

Bath

Bath

Bedroom 13'6"x 12'2"

WIC

WIC

WIC

WIC

Balcony

Bedroom 11'10"x 17'6"

Open to Below

Bedroom 11'10"x 17'6"

Shelf

Images provided by designer/architect.

Plan #111037

Dimensions: 66' W x 84' D

Levels: 2

Square Footage: 3,176

Main Level Sq. Ft.: 2,183

Upper Level Sq. Ft.: 993

Bedrooms: 4

Bathrooms: 3½

Foundation: Slab

Materials List Available: No

Price Category: H

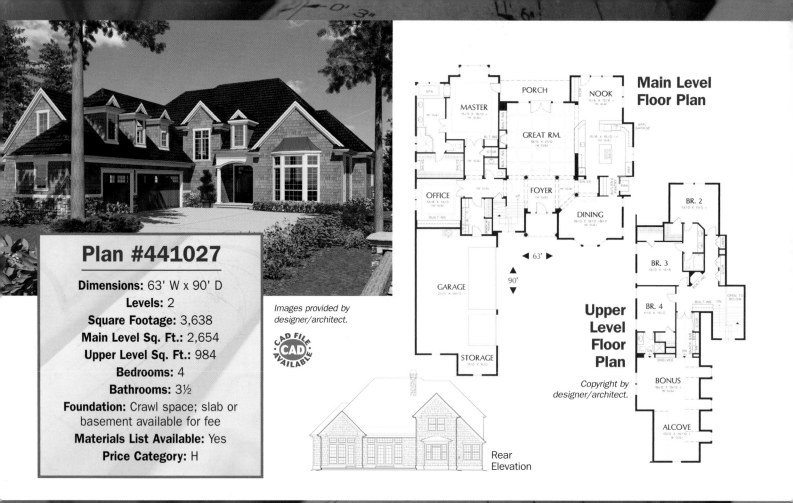

Plan #441027

Dimensions: 63' W x 90' D

Levels: 2

Square Footage: 3,638

Main Level Sq. Ft.: 2,654

Upper Level Sq. Ft.: 984

Bedrooms: 4

Bathrooms: 3½

Foundation: Crawl space; slab or basement available for fee

Materials List Available: Yes

Price Category: H

Images provided by designer/architect.

CAD FILE AVAILABLE

Main Level Floor Plan

Upper Level Floor Plan

Copyright by designer/architect.

Rear Elevation

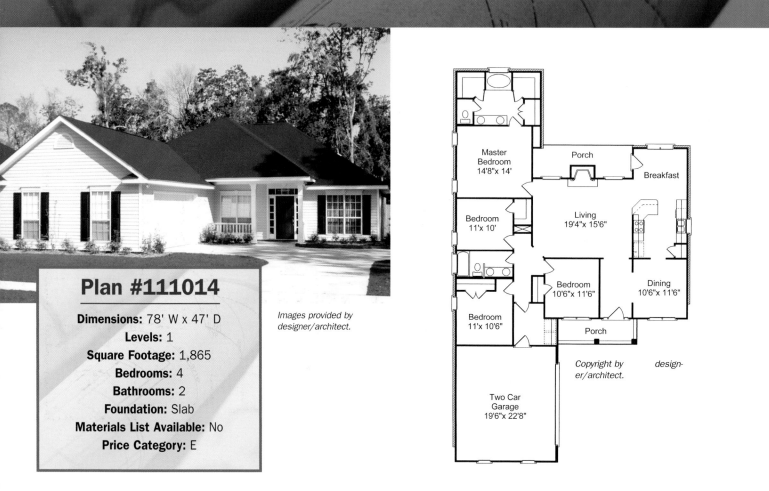

Plan #111014

Dimensions: 78' W x 47' D

Levels: 1

Square Footage: 1,865

Bedrooms: 4

Bathrooms: 2

Foundation: Slab

Materials List Available: No

Price Category: E

Images provided by designer/architect.

Copyright by designer/architect.

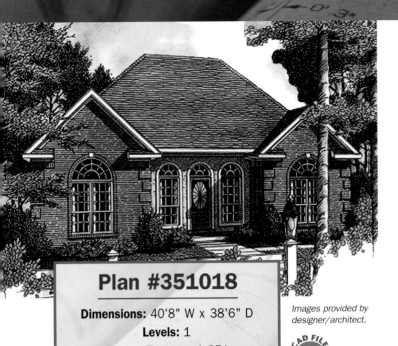

Plan #351018

Dimensions: 40'8" W x 38'6" D

Levels: 1

Square Footage: 1,251

Bedrooms: 3

Bathrooms: 2

Foundation: Crawl space or slab

Materials List Available: Yes

Price Category: B

Images provided by designer/architect.

Bedroom #3
12-0 x 13-8
9' CLG.

Covered Porch
17-0 x 7-0

Dining Room
12-0 x 10-0
9' CLG.

Future Storage/
Shop
14-0 x 6-0

Clos.

Gas Logs

Great Room
17-0 x 22-0
12' CLG.

Kitchen
12-0 x 13-0

Future Garage
22-0 x 24-0

**GARAGE PLANS
ARE INCLUDED**

Hall

Tub/Shr

Bath

Foyer
12' CLG. HT.

Clos.

Bath

Bedroom #2
12-0 x 12-0

Covered Porch
14-4 x 5-0

Bedroom #1
12-0 x 10-6

VAULT

Copyright by designer/architect.

Plan #341024

Dimensions: 49'6" W x 39'8" D

Levels: 1

Square Footage: 1,310

Bedrooms: 3

Bathroom: 2

Foundation: Crawl space

Materials List Available: Yes

Price Category: B

Images provided by designer/architect.

49'-6"

PORCH

KITCHEN/DINING
14'-1" X 16'-0"

BATH 1

GARDEN TUB & SHWR

GARAGE
11'-7" X 21'-3"

REF

RANGE

SINK

DW

PAN

DRY   WASH

WH

BATH 2

BEDROOM 1
12'-9" X 15'-4"

39'-8"

FAMILY ROOM
14'-1" X 15'-7"

COATS

LINENS

CLOSET

CLOSET

CLOSET

BEDROOM 3
10'-1" X 10'-1"

BEDROOM 2
11'-9" X 9'-8"

PORCH

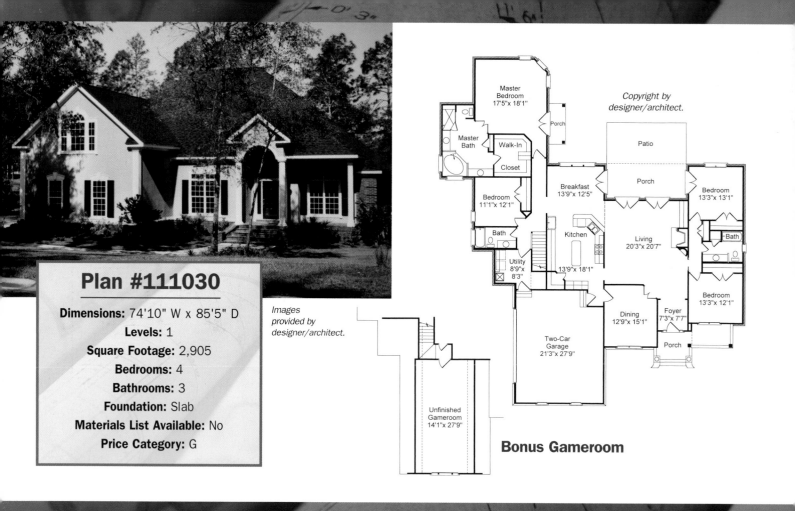

Plan #111030

Dimensions: 74'10" W x 85'5" D
Levels: 1
Square Footage: 2,905
Bedrooms: 4
Bathrooms: 3
Foundation: Slab
Materials List Available: No
Price Category: G

Images provided by designer/architect.

Master Bedroom 17'5"x 18'1"

Copyright by designer/architect.

Porch

Master Bath

Walk-In Closet

Patio

Porch

Breakfast 13'9"x 12'5"

Bedroom 13'3"x 13'1"

Bedroom 11'1"x 12'1"

Bath

Kitchen

Living 20'3"x 20'7"

Bath

Utility 8'9"x 8'3"

13'9"x 18'1"

Bedroom 13'3"x 12'1"

Two-Car Garage 21'3"x 27'9"

Dining 12'9"x 15'1"

Foyer 7'3"x 7'7"

Porch

Unfinished Gameroom 14'1"x 27'9"

Bonus Gameroom

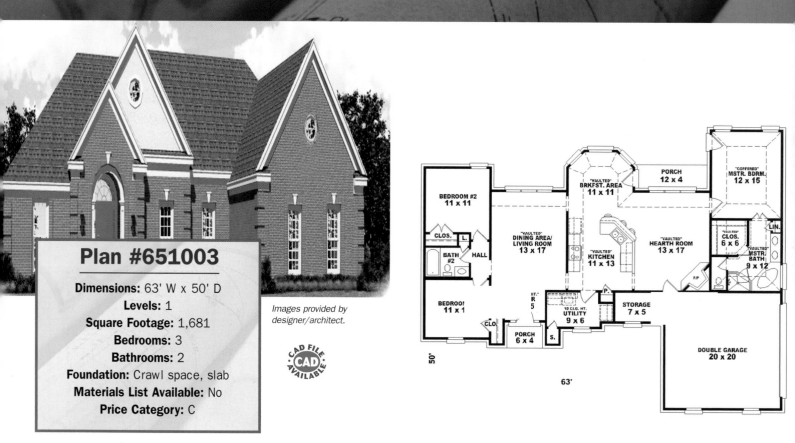

Plan #651003

Dimensions: 63' W x 50' D
Levels: 1
Square Footage: 1,681
Bedrooms: 3
Bathrooms: 2
Foundation: Crawl space, slab
Materials List Available: No
Price Category: C

Images provided by designer/architect.

CAD FILE CAD AVAILABLE

BEDROOM #2 11 x 11

"VAULTED" BRKFST. AREA 11 x 11

PORCH 12 x 4

"COFFERED" MSTR. BDRM. 12 x 15

CLOS.

L.

"VAULTED" DINING AREA/ LIVING ROOM 13 x 17

"VAULTED" KITCHEN 11 x 13

"VAULTED" HEARTH ROOM 13 x 17

"VAULTED" CLOS. 6 x 6

LIN.

BATH #2

HALL

"VAULTED" MSTR. BATH 9 x 12

BEDROOM 11 x 1

HT. R 5

UTILITY 9 x 6

P.

STORAGE 7 x 5

CLO.

PORCH 6 x 4

S.

DOUBLE GARAGE 20 x 20

50'

63'

Plan #151277

Dimensions: 67'8" W x 58' D

Levels: 1

Square Footage: 2,216

Bedrooms: 3

Bathrooms: 2 1/2

Foundation: Crawl space or slab

CompleteCost List Available: Yes

Price Category: E

Images provided by designer/architect.

CAD FILE AVAILABLE

Main Floor

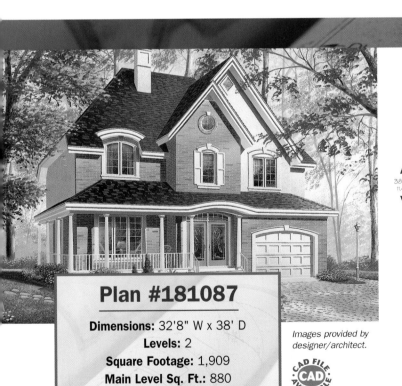

Plan #181087

Dimensions: 32'8" W x 38' D

Levels: 2

Square Footage: 1,909

Main Level Sq. Ft.: 880

Upper Level Sq. Ft.: 1,029

Bedrooms: 4

Bathrooms: 2½

Foundation: Basement

Material List Available: Yes

Price Category: F

Images provided by designer/architect.

CAD FILE AVAILABLE

Main Level Floor Plan

Upper Level Floor Plan

Copyright by designer/architect.

Plan #161135

Dimensions: 42' W x 75' D
Levels: 2
Square Footage: 2,495
Main Level Sq. Ft.: 1,847
Upper Level Sq. Ft.: 648
Bedrooms: 3
Bathrooms: 3
Foundation: Slab or basement; crawl space for fee
Material List Available: Yes
Price Category: E

Images provided by designer/architect.

This charming cottage-style home is both practical and beautiful-the perfect place to raise a family and welcome friends.

Features:

- Foyer: Enter the home through the covered porch into this foyer. The sidelights around the front door brighten the area. The bathroom and walk-in closet add to the convenience of the entry area.

- Great Room: The main gathering area of this home is this two-story great room. A corner fireplace adds a focal point to the room.

- Master Suite: This retreat features a large sleeping area and access to the patio. The master bath boasts dual vanities, a separate shower, a spa tub, and a very large walk-in closet.

- Upper Level: This optional area can be finished to include a loft with a view down into the great room. There is also room for a guest suite.

Main Level Floor Plan

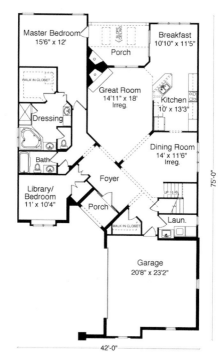

Upper Level Floor Plan

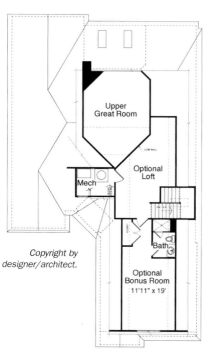

Copyright by designer/architect.

Rear Elevation

Plan #271091

Dimensions: 68' W x 43' D
Levels: 2
Square Footage: 2,854
Main Level Sq. Ft.: 1,219
Upper Level Sq. Ft.: 1,635
Bedrooms: 3
Bathrooms: 2½
Foundation: Daylight basement
Materials List Available: No
Price Category: F

This Craftsman-style home has a unique design to accommodate the needs of a growing family.

Features:

- **Porch:** A long covered porch shelters guests from the elements or gives you outdoor living space where you can sit and greet the neighbors.

- **Great Room:** This large gathering room, with a two-sided fireplace it shares with the study, draws you in to share good times. Open to the dining room and kitchen, it allows friends and family to flow among all three spaces.

- **Master Suite:** Located on the upper level with the secondary bedrooms, this retreat offers privacy. The master bath boasts a double-bowl vanity and whirlpool tub to offer luxury and comfort.

- **Garage:** A large front-load three-car garage can hold cars or other items you need to store.

Images provided by designer/architect.

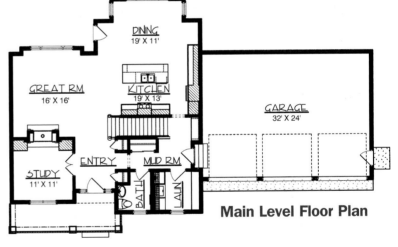

Main Level Floor Plan

Copyright by designer/architect.

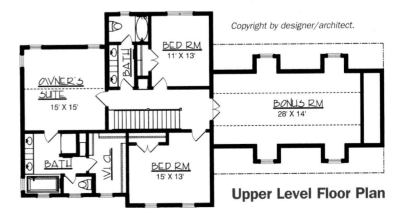

Upper Level Floor Plan

Plan #161133

Dimensions: 42' W x 70'8" D
Levels: 2
Square Footage: 2,412
Main Level Sq. Ft.: 1,820
Upper Level Sq. Ft.: 552
Bedrooms: 3
Bathrooms: 3
Foundation: Slab or basement; crawl space or walkout for fee
Material List Available: Yes
Price Category: F

Images provided by designer/architect.

Dramatic design coupled with elegant architectural detailing contributes to the lovely façade of this home.

Features:

- Great Room: With its cathedral ceiling and glowing fireplace, this room welcomes you home. Relax with your family or entertain your friends.

- Kitchen: Release the chef inside of you with this gourmet kitchen, complete with seating at the peninsula and access to the breakfast area. Step through the glass door to enjoy the fresh air on the rear porch.

- Master Suite: Located on the main level for convenience and privacy, this retreat offers a large sleeping area. The master bath boasts dual vanities and a stall shower.

- Upper Level: A loft, with a view down to the great room, is located on this level. A bonus room with a full bathroom can be finished as a guest suite.

Main Level Floor Plan

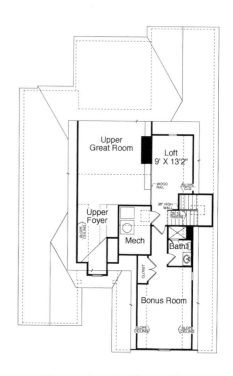

Upper Level Floor Plan

Copyright by designer/architect.

Rear Elevation

Plan #161134

Dimensions: 50' W x 75' D
Levels: 2
Square Footage: 2,605
Main Level Sq. Ft.: 1,953
Upper Level Sq. Ft.: 652
Bedrooms: 3
Bathrooms: 3
Foundation: Slab or basement; crawl space or walkout for fee
Material List Available: Yes
Price Category: F

This home would be great for a new family or an empty nester couple.

Images provided by designer/architect.

Features:

- Great Room: Angled walls and a sloped ceiling add drama to this gathering area. The fireplace will add cozy warmth when your friends visit.
- Library: A bay window adds style to this library located just off the foyer. A large walk-in closet creates the option to make this room an additional bedroom.
- Dining Room: The unique shape of this area adds elegance to this formal eating area. The kitchen is close by, making serving guests convenient.
- Kitchen: This peninsula kitchen boasts long counters lined with cabinetry, making it a gourmet's delight to prepare meals in the area. The raised snack bar is open to the great room and breakfast room.

Main Level Floor Plan

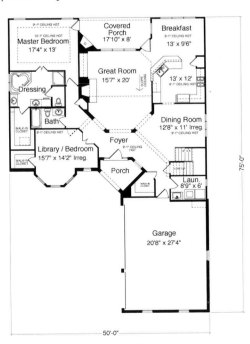

Upper Level Floor Plan

Copyright by designer/architect.

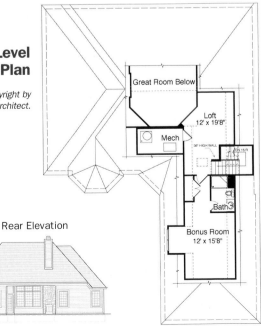

Rear Elevation

Plan #151106

Dimensions: 70' W x 81' D
Levels: 1.5
Square Footage: 3,568
Main Level Sq. Ft.: 3,051
Upper Level Sq. Ft.: 517
Bedrooms: 3
Bathrooms: 3 full, 2 half
Foundation: Crawl space or slab;
basement or walkout for fee
CompleteCost List Available: Yes
Price Category: F

Images provided by designer/architect.

Satisfy your personal needs with this home.

Features:

• **Great Room:** This large gathering space has a cozy fireplace and built-ins for casual get-togethers. French doors lead to a future rear patio.

• **Kitchen:** This efficient U-shaped kitchen has a raised snack bar that looks into the adjoining breakfast room. The laundry room is located just off this space.

• **Master Suite:** This suite, with its sitting area, is the perfect place for an escape after a busy day. The master bath has two walk-in closets, dual vanities, a shower, and a large tub.

• **Secondary Bedrooms:** Bedroom 2 and 3 share a Jack-and-Jill bathroom and are located near the master suite.

Main Level Floor Plan

Upper Level Floor Plan

Copyright by designer/architect.

Plan #131078

Dimensions: 72'8" W x 47' D
Levels: 2
Square Footage: 3,278
Main Level Sq. Ft.: 2,146
Upper Level Sq. Ft.: 1,132
Bedrooms: 3
Bathrooms: 3
Foundation: Foundation: Crawl space or slab; basement for fee
Material List Available: Yes
Price Category: H

This attractive home is a delight when viewed from the outside and features a great floor plan inside.

Images provided by designer/architect.

Features:

- Great Room: This spacious room, with a vaulted ceiling and skylights, is the place to curl up by the fireplace on a cold winter night. Sliding glass doors lead out to the backyard.

- Kitchen: A center island adds convenience to this well-planned kitchen. The bayed breakfast area adds extra room for a table.

- Master Suite: The 10-ft.-high stepped ceiling sets the tone for this secluded area, which features a large walk-in closet. The master bath boasts a whirlpool tub and dual vanities.

- Bonus Room: Located above the garage, this space can be finished as a fourth bedroom or home office.

Rear View

Main Level Floor Plan

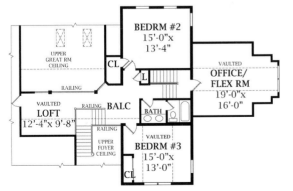

Upper Level Floor Plan

Copyright by designer/architect.

Plan #161138

Dimensions: 42' W x 70'8" D

Levels: 2

Square Footage: 2,112

Main Level Sq. Ft.: 1,616

Upper Level Sq. Ft.: 496

Bedrooms: 3

Bathrooms: 3

Foundation: Slab or basement; crawl space for fee

Material List Available: Yes

Price Category: D

Indoor and outdoor enjoyment is featured in this narrow-lot patio home.

Features:

• Great Room: This elegant area, with a gas fireplace and high ceiling, enjoys a view of the backyard. The open floor plan allows the kitchen and dining area to become an extension of the great room, creating a roomy gathering space.

• Kitchen: Located off the great room, your family will enjoy meals together in this expansive kitchen. It features a raised eating bar and is open into the dining room.

• Master Suite: Luxury enhances your lifestyle in this romantic master suite. A spacious bedroom leads into a full bath, which contains his and her sinks, a separate shower, and a whirlpool tub.

• Bonus Room: A bonus space is available on the second floor. A loft overlooks the great room, and an optional bedroom and bath offer privacy to overnight visitors.

Images provided by designer/architect.

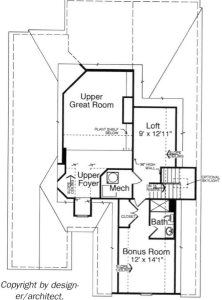

Copyright by designer/architect.

Main Level Floor Plan

Upper Level Floor Plan

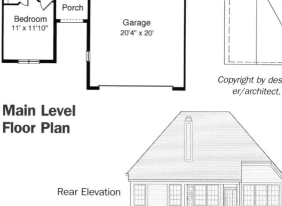

Rear Elevation

Let Us Help You
Plan Your Dream Home

Whether you've always dreamed of building your own home or you can't find the right house from among the dozens you've toured, our collection of affordable plans can help you achieve the home of your dreams. You could have an architect create a one-of-a-kind home for you, but the design services alone could end up costing up to 15 percent of the cost of construction—a hefty premium for any building project. Isn't it a better idea to select from among the hundreds of unique designs shown in our collection for a fraction of the cost?

What does Creative Homeowner Offer?

In this book, Creative Homeowner provides hundreds of home plans from the country's best architects and designers. Our designs are among the most popular available. Whether your taste runs from traditional to contemporary, Victorian to early American, you are sure to find the best house design for you and your family. Our plans packages include detailed drawings to help you or your builder construct your dream house. **(See page 598.)**

Can I Make Changes to the Plans?

Creative Homeowner offers three ways to help you achieve a truly unique home design. Our customizing service allows for extensive changes to our designs. **(See page 599.)** We also provide reverse images of our plans, or we can give you and your builder the tools for making minor changes on your own. **(See page 602.)**

Can You Help Me Manage My Costs?

To help you stay within your budget, Creative Homeowner has teamed up with the leading estimating company to provide one of the most accurate, complete, and reliable building material take-offs in the industry. **(See page 600.)** If that is too much detail for you, we can provide you with general construction costs based on your zip code. **(See page 602.)** Also, many of our plans come with the option of buying detailed materials lists to help you price out construction costs.

How Can I Begin the Building Process?

To get started building your dream home, fill out the order form on page 603, call our order department at 1-800-523-6789, or visit ultimateplans.com. If you plan on doing all or part of the work yourself, or want to keep tabs on your builder, we offer best-selling building and design books available at www.creativehomeowner.com

Our Plans Packages Offer:

"Square footage" refers to the total "heated square feet" of this plan. This number does not include the garage, porches, or unfinished areas. All of our home plans are the result of many hours of work by leading architects and professional designers. Most of our home plans include each of the following:

Frontal Sheet

This artist's rendering of the front of the house gives you an idea of how the house will look once it is completed and the property landscaped.

Detailed Floor Plans

These plans show the size and layout of the rooms. They also provide the locations of doors, windows, fireplaces, closets, stairs, and electrical outlets and switches.

Foundation Plan

A foundation plan gives the dimensions of basements, walk-out basements, crawl spaces, pier foundations, and slab construction. Each house design lists the type of foundation included. If the plan you choose does not have the foundation type you require, our customer service department can help you customize the plan to meet your needs.

Roof Plan

In addition to providing the pitch of the roof, these plans also show the locations of dormers, skylights, and other elements.

Exterior Elevations

These drawings show the front, rear, and sides of the house as if you were looking at it head on. Elevations also provide information about architectural features and finish materials.

Interior Elevations and Details

Interior elevations show specific details of such elements as fireplaces, kitchen and bathroom cabinets, built-ins, and other unique features of the design.

Cross Sections

This shows the structure as if it were sliced to reveal construction requirements, such as insulation, flooring, and roofing details.

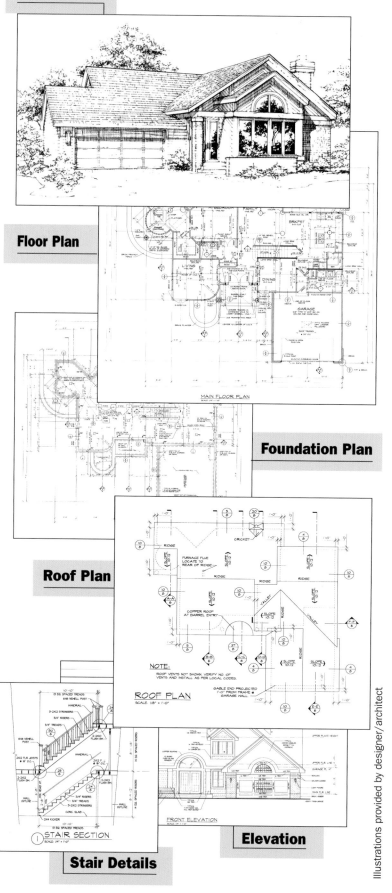

Frontal Sheet

Floor Plan

Foundation Plan

Roof Plan

Stair Details

Elevation

Illustrations provided by designer/architect

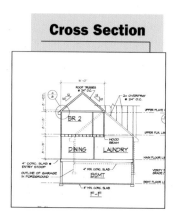

Cross Section

Customize Your Plans in 4 Easy Steps

1 **Select the home plan** that most closely meets your needs. Purchase of a reproducible master, PDF files or CAD files is necessary in order to make changes to a plan.

2 **Call 1-800-523-6789 to place your order.** Tell our sales representative you are interested in customizing your plan, and provide your contact information. Within a day or two you will be contacted (via phone or email) to provide a list or sketch of the changes requested to one of our plans. There is no consultation fee for this service.

3 **Within three business days** of receipt of your request, a detailed cost estimate will be provided to you.

4 **Once you approve the estimate,** you will purchase either the reproducible master, PDF files, or CAD files, and customization work will begin. During all phases of the project, you will receive progress prints by fax or email. On average, the project will be completed in two or three weeks. After completion of the work, modified plans will be shipped. You will receive one set of blueprints in addition to a reproducible master or CAD files, depending on which package you purchased.

Modification Pricing Guide

Categories	Average Cost For Modification
Add or remove living space	Quote required
Bathroom layout redesign	Starting at $150
Kitchen layout redesign	Starting at $120
Garage: add or remove	Starting at $600
Garage: front entry to side load or vice versa	Starting at $300
Foundation changes	Starting at $220
Exterior building materials change	Starting at $200
Exterior openings: add, move, or remove	$75 per opening
Roof line changes	Starting at $600
Ceiling height adjustments	Starting at $280
Fireplace: add or remove	Starting at $90
Screened porch: add	Starting at $300
Wall framing change from 2x4 to 2x6	Starting at $250
Bearing and/or exterior walls changes	Quote required
Non-bearing wall or room changes	$65 per room
Metric conversion of home plan	Starting at $495
Adjust plan for handicapped accessibility	Quote required
Adapt plans for local building code requirements	Quote required
Engineering stamping only	Quote required
Any other engineering services	Quote required
Interactive illustrations (choices of exterior materials)	Quote required

Note: *Any home plan can be customized to accommodate your desired changes. The average prices above are provided only as examples of the most commonly requested changes, and are subject to change without notice. Prices for changes will vary according to the number of modifications requested, plan size, style, and method of design used by the original designer. To obtain a detailed cost estimate, please contact us.*

Before Customization

After

Turn your dream home into reality with

a **Material Take-off** and  LOWE'S **FOR PROS**

When purchasing a home plan with Creative Homeowner, we recommend
you order one of the most complete materials lists in the industry.

1 What comes with a Material Take-off?

Quote

- Basis of the entire estimate.

- Detailed list of all the framing materials needed to build your project, listed from the bottom up, in the order that each one will actually be used.

Comments

- Details pertinent information beyond the cost of materials.

- Includes any notes from our estimates.

Express List

- A combined version of the Quote with SKUs listed for purchasing the items at your local Lowe's.

- Your Lowe's Commercial Sales Specialist can then price out the materials list.

Construction-Ready Framing Diagrams

- Your "map" to exact roof and floor framing.

Millwork Report

- A complete count of the windows, doors, molding, and trim.

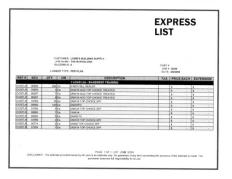

Man-Hour Report

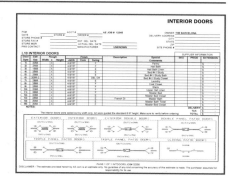

- Calculates labor on a line-by-line basis for all items quoted and presented in man-hours.

2 Why a Material Take-off?

Accurate. Professional estimators break down each individual item from the blueprints using advanced software, techniques, and equipment.

Timely. You will be able to start your home-building project quickly—knowing the exact framing materials you need and how to get them with Lowe's.

Detailed. Work with your Lowe's associate to select the remaining products needed for your new home and get a final, accurate quote.

3 So how much does it cost?

Pricing is determined by the total square feet of the home plan—including living area, garages, decks, porches, finished basements, and finished attics.

Square Feet Range	MT Tier*	Price
Up to 5,000 total square feet	XB	$345.00
5,001 to 10,000 total square feet	XC	$545.00

*Please see the Plan Index to determine your plan's Material Take-off Tier (MT Tier).
Note: All prices subject to change.

Call our toll-free number (800-523-6789), or visit ultimateplans.com to order your Material Take-off (also called Ultimate Estimate online).

4 What else do I need to know?

When you purchase your products from Lowe's you may receive a gift card for the amount of your **Material Take-off.** Please go to **UltimatePlans.com** and select **Ultimate Estimate** located under "Quick Links" for complete details of the program.

The Lowe's Advantage:

What's more is you can save an **additional 10%** (up to $500.00) on your first building material purchase.* You will receive details on this program with your order.

Turn your dream home into reality.

*Good for a single purchase of any in-stock or Special Order merchandise only up to $5,000 (maximum discount $500). Not valid on previous sales, service or installation fees, the purchase of gift cards, or any products by Fisher & Paykel, Electrolux, John Deere, or Weber.

Decide What Type of Plan Package You Need

How many Plans Should You Order?

Standard 8-Set Package. We've found that our 8-set package is the best value for someone who is ready to start building. The 8-set package provides plans for you, your builder, the subcontractors, mortgage lender, and the building department.

Minimum 5-Set Package. If you are in the bidding process, you may want to order only five sets for the bidding round and reorder additional sets as needed.

1-Set Study Package. The 1-set package allows you to review your home plan in detail. The plan will be marked as a study print, and it is illegal to build a house from a study print alone. It is a violation of copyright law to reproduce a blueprint without permission.

Buying Additional Sets. If you require additional copies of blueprints for your home construction, you can order additional sets within 60 days of the original order date at a reduced price. The cost is $50.00 for each additional set. For more information, contact customer service.

Reproducible Masters

If you plan to make minor changes to one of our home plans, you can purchase reproducible masters. These plans are printed on bond or vellum paper that is easy to alter. They clearly indicate your right to modify, copy, or reproduce the plans. Reproducible masters allow an architect, designer, or builder to alter our plans to give you a customized home design. This package allows you to print as many copies of the modified plans as you need for the construction of one home.

PDF Files

PDF files are a complete set of home plans in electronic file format sent to you via email. These files cannot be altered electronically, once printed changes can be hand drawn. A PDF file gives you the license to modify the plans to fit your needs and build one home. Not available for all plans. Please contact our order department or visit our Web site to check the availability of PDF files for your plan.

CAD (Computer-Aided Design) Files

CAD files are the complete set of home plans in an electronic file format. Choose this option if there are multiple changes you wish made to the home plans and you have a local design professional able to make the changes. Not available for all plans. Please contact our order department or visit our Web site to check the availability of CAD files for your plan.

Mirror-Reverse Sets/Right-Reading Reverse

Plans can be printed in mirror-reverse—we can "flip" plans to create a mirror image of the design. This is useful when the house would fit your site or personal preferences if all the rooms were on the opposite side than shown. As the image is reversed, the lettering and dimensions will also be reversed, meaning they will read backwards. Therefore, when ordering mirror-reverse drawings, you must order at least one set of the original plan unreversed. A $50.00 fee per plan order will be charged for mirror-reverse (regardless of the number of mirror-reverse sets ordered). Some plans are available in right-reading reverse; this feature will show the plan in reverse, but the writing on the plan will be readable. A $150.00 fee per plan order will be charged for right-reading reverse (regardless of the number of right-reading reverse sets ordered). Please contact our order department or visit our Web site to check the availibility of this feature for your chosen plan.

EZ Quote® : Home Cost Estimator

EZ Quote® is our response to a frequently asked question we hear from customers: "How much will the house cost me to build?" EZ Quote®: Home Cost Estimator will enable you to obtain a calculated building cost to construct your home, based on labor rates and building material costs within your zip code area. This summary is useful for those who want to get an idea of the total construction costs before purchasing sets of home plans. It will also provide a level of comfort when you begin soliciting bids. The cost is $29.95 for the first EZ Quote and $19.95 for each additional one in the same order. Available only in the U.S. and Canada.

Materials List

Available for most of our plans, the Materials List provides you an invaluable resource in planning and estimating the cost of your home. Each Materials List outlines the quantity, dimensions, and type of materials needed to build your home (with the exception of mechanical systems). You will get faster, more-accurate bids from your contractors and building suppliers. A Materials List may only be ordered with the purchase of at least five sets of home plans.

CompleteCost Estimator

CompleteCost Estimator is a valuable tool for use in planning and constructing your new home. It provides more detail than a materials list and will act as a checklist for all items you will need to select or coordinate during your building process. CompleteCost Estimator is only available for certain plans (please see Plan Index) and may only be ordered with the purchase of at least five sets of home plans. The cost is $125.00 for CompleteCost Estimator

Lowe's Material Take-off (See page 600.)

Material Take-off may take 2 to 3 weeks for delivery.

Before You Order

Our Exchange Policy

Blueprints are nonrefundable. However, should you find that the plan you have purchased does not fit your needs, you may exchange that plan for another plan in our collection within 60 days from the date of your original order. The entire content of your original order must be returned before an exchange will be processed. You will be charged a processing fee of 20% of the amount of the original order, the cost difference between the new plan set and the original plan set (if applicable), and all related shipping costs for the new plans. Contact our order department for more information. Please note: reproducible masters may only be exchanged if the package is unopened. PDF files and CAD files cannot be exchanged and are nonrefundable.

Building Codes and Requirements

All plans offered for sale in this book and on our Web site (www.ultimateplans.com) are continually updated to meet the latest International Residential Code (IRC). Because building codes vary from area to area, some drawing modifications and/or the assistance of a professional designer or architect may be necessary to comply with your local codes or to accommodate specific building site conditions. We strongly advise you to consult with your local building official for information regarding codes governing your area.

Multiple Plan Discount

Purchase **3** different home plans in the **same order** and receive **5% off** the plan price.

Purchase **5** or more different home plans in the **same order** and receive **10% off** the plan price.
(Please Note: Study sets do not apply.)

Blueprint Price Schedule

Price Code	1 Set	5 Sets	8 Sets	Reproducible Masters or PDF Files	CAD	Materials List
A	$431	$494	$572	$693	$1,181	$89
B	$488	$567	$646	$777	$1,376	$89
C	$551	$651	$730	$861	$1,549	$89
D	$604	$704	$782	$914	$1,654	$100
E	$656	$767	$845	$971	$1,759	$100
F	$725	$830	$908	$1,040	$1,890	$100
G	$756	$861	$940	$1,071	$1,937	$100
H	$767	$872	$950	$1,097	$1,995	$100
I	$1,045	$1,150	$1,229	$1,355	$2,216	$110
J	$1,250	$1,355	$1,433	$1,565	$2,415	$110
K	$1,255	$1,360	$1,439	$1,570	$2,415	$110
L	$1,302	$1,402	$1,481	$1,612	$2,520	$110

Note: All prices subject to change

Lowe's Material Take-off (MT Tier)

MT Tier*	Price
XB	$345
XC	$545

* Please see the Plan Index to determine your plan's Lowe's Material Take-off (MT Tier).

Shipping & Handling

	1–4 Sets	5–7 Sets	8+ Sets or Reproducibles	CAD
US Regular (7–10 business days)	$18	$20	$25	$25
US Priority (3–5 business days)	$35	$40	$45	$45
US Express (1–2 business days)	$45	$60	$80	$50
Canada Express (3–4 business days)	$100	$100	$100	$100
Worldwide Express (3–5 business days)	** Quote Required **			

Note: All delivery times are from date the blueprint package is shipped (typically within 1-2 days of placing order).

Order Form
Please send me the following:

Plan Number: _____ **Price Code:** _____ (See Plan Index.)

Indicate Foundation Type: (Select ONE. See plan page for availability.)

❑ Slab   ❑ Crawl space   ❑ Basement   ❑ Walk-out basement

❑ Optional Foundation for Fee _____ $ _____
(Please enter foundation here)

*Please call all our order department or visit our website for optional foundation fee

Basic Blueprint Package   Cost

❑ CAD Files $ _____
❑ PDF Files $ _____
❑ Reproducible Masters $ _____
❑ 8-Set Plan Package $ _____
❑ 5-Set Plan Package $ _____
❑ 1-Set Study Package $ _____
❑ Additional plan sets:
   __ sets at $50.00 per set $ _____
❑ Print in mirror-reverse: $50.00 per order $ _____
   **Please call all our order department
   or visit our website for availibility*
❑ Print in right-reading reverse: $150.00 per order $ _____
   **Please call all our order department
   or visit our website for availibility*

Important Extras

❑ Lowe's Material Take-off (See Price Tier above.) $ _____
❑ Materials List $ _____
❑ CompleteCost Materials Report at $125.00 $ _____
   Zip Code of Home/Building Site _____
❑ EZ Quote® for Plan # _____ at $29.95 $ _____
❑ Additional EZ Quotes for Plan #s _____ $ _____
   at $19.95 each
Shipping (see chart above) $ _____
SUBTOTAL $ _____
Sales Tax (NJ residents only, add 7%) $ _____
TOTAL $ _____

Order Toll Free: 1-800-523-6789   By Fax: 201-760-2431
Creative Homeowner (Home Plans Order Dept.)
24 Park Way
Upper Saddle River, NJ 07458

Name _____
(Please print or type)

Street _____
(Please do not use a P.O. Box)

City _____ State _____

Country _____ Zip _____

Daytime telephone (____) _____

Fax (____) _____
(Required for reproducible orders)

E-Mail _____

Payment   ❑ Bank check/money order. No personal checks.
Make checks payable to Creative Homeowner

❑ VISA   ❑ MasterCard   ❑ American Express Cards   ❑ Discover

Credit card number _____

Expiration date (mm/yy) _____

Signature _____

Please check the appropriate box:
❑ Building home for myself   ❑ Building home for someone else

SOURCE CODE **LH301**

Copyright Notice

All home plans sold through this publication are protected by copyright. Reproduction of these home plans, either in whole or in part, including any form and/or preparation of derivative works thereof, for any reason without prior written permission is strictly prohibited. The purchase of a set of home plans in no way transfers any copyright or other ownership interest in it to the buyer except for a limited license to use that set of home plans for the construction of one, and only one, dwelling unit. The purchase of additional sets of the home plans at a reduced price from the original set or as a part of a multiple-set package does not convey to the buyer a license to construct more than one dwelling.

Similarly, the purchase of reproducible home plans (sepias, mylars) carries the same copyright protection as mentioned above. It is gener-ally allowed to make up to a maximum of 10 copies for the construction of a single dwelling only. To use any plans more than once, and to avoid any copyright license infringement, it is necessary to contact the plan designer to receive a release and license for any extended use. Whereas a purchaser of reproducible plans is granted a license to make copies, it should be noted that because blueprints are copy-righted, making photocopies from them is illegal.

Copyright and licensing of home plans for construction exist to protect all parties. Copyright respects and supports the intellectual property of the original architect or designer. Copyright law has been reinforced over the past few years. Willful infringement could cause settlements for statutory damages to $150,000.00 plus attorney fees, damages, and loss of profits.

CREATIVE
HOMEOWNER®

ultimateplans.com

Order online by visiting our Web site.

Open 24 hours a day, 7 days a week.

Still haven't found your perfect home?
With thousands of plans online at ultimateplans.com, there are plenty more to choose from. Using our automated search tools, we make the process even easier. Just enter your ideal home criteria, and let our search tools find the plans for you!

Other great benefits for many plans at ultimateplans.com include:

- **More photos of both the exterior and interior of many of our most popular homes**
- **More side and rear elevations**
- **More data and information about each particular plan**

In addition, you will find more information about the building process and even free step-by-step DIY projects you can do!

Index

For pricing, see page 603.

Plan #	Price Code	Page	Total Finished Sq. Ft.	Materials List	CompleteCost	MT Tier
101004	D	184	1,787	Y	N	XB
101005	D	165	1,992	Y	N	XB
101006	D	174	1,982	Y	N	XB
101008	E	174	2,088	Y	N	XB
101009	E	176	2,097	Y	N	XB
101010	E	120	2,187	Y	N	XB
101011	E	188	2,184	Y	N	XB
101012	E	470	2,288	N	N	XB
101013	F	192	2,564	Y	N	XB
101015	D	310	1,647	N	N	XB
101015	C	311	1,647	N	N	XB
101017	E	521	2,253	N	N	XB
101018	E	467	2,546	N	N	XB
101019	F	91	2,954	N	N	XB
101020	F	17	2,972	N	N	XB
101022	D	181	1,992	Y	N	XB
111001	G	520	2,832	N	N	XB
111004	G	146	2,968	N	N	XB
111004	G	147	2,968	N	N	XB
111006	F	383	2,241	N	N	XB
111008	E	565	2,011	N	N	XB
111010	E	316	1,804	N	N	XB
111013	C	242	1,606	N	N	XB
111014	E	586	1,865	Y	N	XB
111015	F	157	2,208	N	N	XB
111018	G	581	2,745	N	N	XB
111020	G	580	2,987	N	N	XB
111021	F	313	2,221	N	N	XB
111024	F	160	2,356	N	N	XB
111026	F	175	2,406	N	N	XB
111027	F	329	2,601	N	N	XB
111030	G	588	2,905	N	N	XB
111031	G	118	2,869	N	N	XB
111031	G	119	2,869	N	N	XB
111032	G	327	2,904	N	N	XB
111036	H	572	3,149	N	N	XB
111037	H	585	3,176	N	N	XB
111043	C	230	1,737	N	N	XB
111044	E	566	1,819	N	N	XB
111046	D	231	1,768	N	N	XB
111047	E	308	1,863	N	N	XB
111049	F	304	2,205	N	N	XB
111049	F	305	2,205	N	N	XB
121001	D	519	1,911	Y	N	XB
121002	B	471	1,347	Y	N	XB
121003	E	126	2,498	Y	N	XC
121004	C	107	1,666	Y	N	XB
121007	E	137	2,512	Y	N	XC
121008	C	155	1,651	Y	N	XB
121009	B	21	1,422	Y	N	XB
121010	D	232	1,902	Y	N	XB
121011	C	533	1,724	Y	N	XB
121014	D	189	1,869	Y	N	XB
121015	D	32	1,999	Y	N	XB
121017	E	27	2,353	Y	N	XB
121018	H	385	3,950	Y	N	XB
121019	H	140	3,775	Y	N	XC
121020	E	571	2,480	Y	N	XC
121021	E	214	2,270	Y	N	XB
121023	H	149	3,904	Y	N	XC
121024	G	476	3,057	Y	N	XB
121025	E	28	2,562	Y	N	XC
121026	H	96	3,926	Y	N	XB
121028	F	511	2,644	Y	N	XB
121029	E	29	2,576	Y	N	XB
121031	C	30	1,772	Y	N	XB
121032	E	366	2,339	Y	N	XB
121047	G	173	3,072	Y	N	XC
121049	G	71	3,335	Y	N	XB
121050	D	134	1,996	Y	N	XB
121059	C	47	1,782	Y	N	XB
121061	G	83	3,025	Y	N	XC
121062	G	128	3,448	Y	N	XC
121063	G	167	3,473	Y	N	XC
121064	D	380	1,846	Y	N	XB
121065	G	144	3,407	Y	N	XC
121066	D	342	2,078	Y	N	XC
121067	F	130	2,708	Y	N	XC
121070	D	168	2,139	Y	N	XB
121072	G	497	6,853	Y	N	XC
121073	F	145	2,579	Y	N	XC
121076	G	191	3,067	Y	N	XC
121081	G	391	3,623	Y	N	XC
121083	F	218	2,695	Y	N	XC
121086	D	489	1,998	Y	N	XC

Plan #	Price Code	Page	Total Finished Sq. Ft.	Materials List	CompleteCost	MT Tier
121091	F	486	2,689	Y	N	XB
121092	D	123	3,225	Y	N	XB
121093	F	480	2,603	Y	N	XC
121094	C	408	1,768	Y	N	XB
121111	C	55	1,685	Y	N	XB
121112	C	254	1,650	Y	N	XB
121114	D	488	2,115	Y	N	XB
121117	D	76	2,172	Y	N	XB
121118	C	266	1,636	Y	N	XB
121121	C	364	1,341	Y	N	XB
121123	E	248	2,277	Y	N	XB
121124	D	103	1,806	Y	N	XB
121125	D	362	1,978	Y	N	XB
121127	E	407	2,496	Y	N	XB
121144	B	273	1,195	Y	N	XB
121147	D	259	2,051	Y	N	XB
121148	D	567	2,076	N	N	XB
121149	F	573	2,715	Y	N	XB
121150	F	541	2,639	Y	N	XB
121155	F	570	2,638	Y	N	XB
121160	D	278	2,188	Y	N	XB
121163	F	500	2,679	Y	N	XB
121165	C	584	1,678	Y	N	XB
121167	I	249	4,629	N	N	XC
121170	G	562	3,459	Y	N	XB
121196	F	564	2,512	Y	N	XB
121203	F	359	2,690	Y	N	XB
121212	E	271	2,219	Y	N	XB
121216	B	554	1,205	Y	N	XB
131001	D	177	1,615	Y	N	XB
131002	D	180	1,709	Y	N	XB
131003	C	382	1,466	Y	N	XB
131004	B	189	1,097	Y	N	XB
131005	C	527	1,595	Y	N	XB
131006	E	556	2,193	Y	N	XB
131007	D	490	1,595	Y	N	XB
131007	D	491	1,595	Y	N	XB
131009	E	582	2,018	Y	N	XB
131010	D	584	1,667	Y	N	XB
131011	E	518	1,897	Y	N	XB
131014	C	483	1,380	Y	N	XB
131015	E	151	1,860	Y	N	XB
131016	E	193	1,902	Y	N	XB
131017	C	181	1,480	Y	N	XB
131019	F	512	2,243	Y	N	XB
131021	H	466	3,110	Y	N	XC
131022	E	211	2,092	Y	N	XB
131023	F	494	2,460	Y	N	XB
131025	H	549	3,204	Y	N	XB
131026	G	474	2,796	Y	N	XB
131026	G	475	2,796	Y	N	XB
131027	F	204	2,567	Y	N	XC
131027	F	205	2,567	Y	N	XC
131028	G	469	2,696	Y	N	XB
131029	G	274	2,718	Y	N	XB
131029	G	275	2,718	Y	N	XB
131030	F	280	2,470	Y	N	XB
131030	F	281	2,470	Y	N	XB
131031	I	101	4,027	Y	N	XB
131032	F	451	2,455	Y	N	XB
131033	G	8	2,813	Y	N	XC
131033	G	9	2,813	Y	N	XC
131034	B	216	1,040	Y	N	XB
131036	F	136	2,585	Y	N	XB
131040	C	87	1,630	Y	N	XB
131043	E	241	1,945	Y	N	XB
131044	E	498	1,994	Y	N	XB
131045	E	22	2,347	Y	N	XB
131046	F	158	2,245	Y	N	XB
131047	D	219	1,793	Y	N	XB
131050	F	525	2,874	Y	N	XC
131051	F	222	2,431	Y	N	XB
131054	G	65	2,753	Y	N	XB
131056	C	322	1,396	Y	N	XB
131056	C	323	1,396	Y	N	XB
131066	G	576	2,760	Y	N	XB
131067	E	69	1,909	Y	N	XB
131069	F	409	3,169	Y	N	XB
131074	E	577	2,085	Y	N	XB
131078	H	595	3,278	Y	N	XB
151001	D	20	3,124	N	Y	XB
151002	F	127	2,444	N	Y	XB
151003	C	124	1,680	N	Y	XB
151004	E	131	2,107	N	Y	XB
151005	D	544	1,940	N	Y	XB

Plan #	Price Code	Page	Total Finished Sq. Ft.	Materials List	CompleteCost	MT Tier
151007	C	141	1,787	N	Y	XB
151009	C	526	1,601	N	Y	XB
151010	C	148	1,379	N	Y	XB
151011	F	152	3,437	N	Y	XB
151013	F	508	2,618	N	Y	XB
151014	F	177	2,698	N	Y	XB
151015	F	180	2,798	N	Y	XB
151016	C	209	1,783	N	Y	XB
151019	F	582	2,653	N	Y	XB
151020	I	72	4,532	N	Y	XB
151021	F	36	3,385	N	Y	XB
151022	G	583	3,059	N	Y	XB
151024	H	415	3,623	N	Y	XB
151025	H	401	3,914	N	Y	XC
151026	C	555	1,574	N	Y	XB
151029	F	413	2,777	N	Y	XB
151030	F	102	2,949	N	Y	XB
151031	F	223	3,130	N	Y	XB
151032	F	346	2,824	N	Y	XB
151033	I	142	5,548	N	Y	XC
151034	D	518	2,133	N	Y	XB
151035	B	262	1,451	N	Y	XB
151035	B	263	1,451	N	Y	XB
151037	C	512	1,538	N	Y	XB
151043	E	122	1,636	N	Y	XB
151050	F	515	2,096	N	Y	XB
151054	C	123	1,746	N	Y	XB
151055	E	94	3,183	N	Y	XB
151056	D	187	1,950	N	Y	XB
151057	G	143	2,951	N	Y	XB
151063	E	558	3,285	N	Y	XB
151068	D	150	1,880	N	Y	XB
151087	F	564	4,228	N	Y	XB
151089	E	209	1,921	N	Y	XB
151101	F	161	2,804	N	Y	XB
151106	F	594	3,568	N	Y	XB
151113	D	212	1,957	N	Y	XB
151117	D	484	1,957	N	Y	XB
151118	F	492	2,784	N	Y	XB
151121	G	71	3,108	N	Y	XB
151140	E	575	2,525	N	Y	XB
151168	E	485	2,261	N	Y	XB
151169	C	498	1,525	N	Y	XB
151170	E	504	1,965	N	Y	XB
151171	D	552	2,131	N	Y	XB
151173	C	493	1,739	N	Y	XB
151178	C	441	1,600	N	Y	XB
151179	E	509	2,405	N	Y	XB
151203	B	62	1,214	N	Y	XB
151232	H	502	3,901	N	Y	XB
151232	H	503	3,901	N	Y	XB
151240	E	57	2,007	N	Y	XB
151242	F	543	2,710	N	Y	XB
151253	I	320	4,882	N	Y	XC
151277	E	589	2,216	N	Y	XB
151349	F	444	1,684	N	Y	XB
151383	G	54	2,534	N	Y	XB
151384	F	46	2,742	N	Y	XB
151432	C	157	1,672	N	Y	XB
151484	E	532	2,211	N	Y	XB
151490	D	258	1,869	N	Y	XB
151495	D	17	2,121	N	Y	XB
151524	H	420	4,461	N	Y	XC
151528	C	499	1,747	N	Y	XB
151529	B	357	1,474	N	Y	XB
151530	D	369	2,146	N	Y	XB
151534	E	530	2,237	N	Y	XB
151536	D	355	1,933	N	Y	XB
151595	H	192	3,820	N	Y	XC
151596	H	45	3,823	N	Y	XB
151684	D	537	1,994	N	Y	XB
151711	E	59	2,554	N	Y	XB
151723	C	102	2,164	N	Y	XB
151731	D	351	2,099	N	Y	XB
151822	G	186	3,602	N	Y	XC
151837	E	445	2,256	N	Y	XB
151841	C	176	1,747	N	Y	XB
151842	C	454	2,135	N	Y	XB
151845	G	417	3,003	N	Y	XB
151846	F	448	2,609	N	Y	XB
151849	D	406	2,095	N	Y	XB
151850	D	171	2,075	N	Y	XB
151851	F	405	2,846	N	Y	XB
151853	C	485	2,885	N	Y	XC
161001	C	132	1,782	N	N	XB

Index

For pricing, see page 603.

Plan #	Price Code	Page	Total Finished Sq. Ft.	Materials List	CompleteCost	MT Tier
161002	D	464	1,860	N	N	XB
161005	C	484	1,593	N	N	XB
161006	C	526	1,755	N	N	XB
161007	C	524	1,611	N	N	XB
161008	D	519	1,860	N	N	XB
161009	C	516	1,651	N	N	XB
161015	C	547	1,768	Y	N	XB
161016	D	154	2,101	N	N	XB
161017	F	510	2,653	N	N	XB
161018	F	478	2,816	N	N	XB
161018	F	479	2,816	N	N	XB
161019	E	574	2,428	N	N	XB
161020	D	545	2,082	Y	N	XB
161021	D	577	1,897	Y	N	XB
161022	D	534	1,898	Y	N	XB
161023	G	531	3,445	Y	N	XB
161024	C	229	1,698	N	N	XB
161025	F	487	2,738	N	N	XB
161026	D	331	2,041	N	N	XB
161027	E	16	2,388	N	N	XB
161028	H	135	3,570	N	N	XC
161029	I	388	4,470	N	N	XB
161029	I	389	4,470	Y	N	XB
161031	F	12	2,776	Y	N	XC
161031	F	13	2,776	Y	N	XC
161032	I	277	4,517	Y	N	XB
161033	H	348	3,809	Y	N	XC
161034	D	417	2,156	N	N	XB
161035	H	83	3,688	N	N	XC
161036	H	410	3,664	N	N	XB
161036	H	411	3,664	N	N	XB
161037	E	272	2,469	N	N	XB
161041	F	384	2,738	Y	N	XB
161045	D	522	2,077	N	N	XB
161056	G	530	3,171	Y	N	XC
161060	J	378	5,143	N	N	XC
161060	J	379	5,143	N	N	XC
161061	H	244	3,816	N	N	XC
161061	H	245	3,816	N	N	XC
161093	I	419	4,328	Y	N	XB
161094	G	481	3,366	N	N	XC
161095	H	473	3,620	N	N	XB
161096	G	50	3,435	N	N	XC
161096	G	51	3,435	N	N	XB
161097	G	34	3,144	N	N	XC
161100	J	434	5,377	N	N	XC
161101	K	185	6,209	Y	N	XC
161102	K	344	6,659	Y	N	XC
161102	K	345	6,659	Y	N	XC
161103	J	402	5,633	N	N	XC
161104	L	400	8,088	N	N	XC
161105	K	395	6,806	N	N	XC
161113	I	37	4,365	N	N	XC
161114	E	404	2,246	Y	N	XB
161119	E	440	2,334	Y	N	XB
161127	I	441	4,598	Y	N	XB
161133	F	592	2,412	Y	N	XB
161134	F	593	2,605	Y	N	XC
161135	E	590	2,495	Y	N	XC
161138	D	596	2,102	Y	N	XB
161187	G	454	6,740	Y	N	XC
161224	F	361	6,555	Y	N	XC
161228	F	444	5,855	Y	N	XC
171004	E	128	2,256	Y	N	XB
171009	C	235	1,771	Y	N	XB
171011	D	224	2,069	Y	N	XB
171013	G	225	3,084	Y	N	XC
171015	D	240	2,089	Y	N	XB
171023	C	220	3,059	Y	N	XB
181001	A	257	920	Y	N	XB
181034	F	234	2,687	N	N	XB
181053	E	314	2,353	Y	N	XB
181061	D	15	2,111	Y	N	XB
181063	D	78	2,037	Y	N	XB
181064	F	561	2,802	Y	N	XB
181066	C	567	1,584	Y	N	XB
181073	F	569	2,663	Y	N	XB
181074	D	246	1,760	N	N	XB
181079	G	391	3,016	Y	N	XC
181080	E	472	2,042	Y	N	XB
181081	F	236	2,350	Y	N	XB
181084	I	551	4,048	Y	N	XB
181085	E	228	2,183	Y	N	XB
181087	D	589	1,909	Y	N	XB
181100	I	98	4,200	N	N	XB
181101	D	483	1,936	Y	N	XB
181106	C	298	1,648	Y	N	XB
181120	C	315	1,480	Y	N	XB
181126	B	268	1,468	Y	N	XB
181126	B	269	1,468	Y	N	XB
181128	D	329	1,634	Y	N	XB
181133	E	332	1,832	Y	N	XB
181151	E	226	2,283	Y	N	XB
181151	F	227	2,283	Y	N	XB
181157	C	557	1,795	Y	N	XB
181162	D	35	1,867	Y	N	XB
181221	G	292	3,411	Y	N	XB
181221	G	293	3,411	Y	N	XB
181224	C	392	1,727	Y	N	XB
181228	E	84	2,393	Y	N	XB
181228	E	85	2,393	Y	N	XB
181239	D	56	2,181	Y	N	XB
181252	H	416	3,631	Y	N	XB
181253	H	408	3,614	Y	N	XC
181270	B	559	1,127	Y	N	XB
181329	B	81	1,116	Y	N	XB
181399	A	296	960	Y	N	XB
181412	A	49	947	Y	N	XB
181505	C	572	1,650	Y	N	XB
181506	B	559	1,365	Y	N	XB
181541	D	471	2,017	Y	N	XB
181611	D	444	1,890	Y	N	XB
181615	C	406	1,613	Y	N	XB
181617	C	403	1,745	Y	N	XB
181630	D	260	2,098	Y	N	XB
181643	D	404	1,929	Y	N	XB
181652	C	166	1,579	Y	N	XB
181689	B	106	1,308	Y	N	XB
181710	C	402	1,767	Y	N	XB
191001	D	210	2,156	N	N	XB
191003	C	235	1,785	N	N	XB
191009	D	237	2,172	N	N	XB
191032	D	124	2,091	N	N	XB
191055	D	544	2,123	N	N	XB
201086	F	224	1,573	Y	N	XB
211003	D	125	1,865	Y	N	XB
211004	D	143	1,828	Y	N	XB
211006	D	151	2,177	Y	N	XB
211007	E	529	2,252	Y	N	XB
211008	E	356	2,259	Y	N	XB
211009	E	18	2,396	Y	N	XB
211010	E	139	2,503	Y	N	XB
211011	F	133	2,791	Y	N	XB
211030	C	208	1,600	Y	N	XB
211039	D	122	1,868	Y	N	XB
211049	D	394	2,023	Y	N	XB
211058	E	125	2,564	N	N	XB
211069	C	270	1,600	Y	N	XB
211070	C	575	1,700	Y	N	XB
211071	F	186	2,954	Y	N	XB
211074	G	206	3,486	Y	N	XB
211076	I	178	4,242	Y	N	XC
211076	I	179	4,242	Y	N	XC
211077	J	470	5,560	Y	N	XC
211108	F	551	2,888	Y	N	XB
211125	I	82	4,440	Y	N	XC
211127	J	182	5,474	N	N	XC
211130	E	541	2,280	Y	N	XB
221001	F	527	2,600	N	N	XB
221005	D	150	4,475	N	N	XB
221008	C	231	1,540	N	N	XB
221015	E	509	1,926	N	N	XB
221018	D	507	2,007	N	N	XB
221020	D	520	1,859	N	N	XB
221022	G	129	3,291	N	N	XC
221023	H	528	3,511	N	N	XC
221025	G	421	3,009	N	N	XC
221054	G	387	3,206	N	N	XB
221055	H	433	3,551	N	N	XB
231020	D	14	2,166	N	N	XB
231023	G	56	3,215	N	N	XB
231026	H	399	3,784	N	N	XB
241007	D	221	2,036	N	N	XB
241008	E	487	2,526	N	N	XB
241013	G	171	3,033	N	N	XB
241046	D	49	1,919	N	N	XB
241058	I	453	4,216	N	N	XC
251001	B	221	1,253	Y	N	XB
251012	D	556	4,573	Y	N	XB
251014	E	580	2,210	Y	N	XB
261001	H	469	3,746	N	N	XB
271001	B	495	1,400	Y	N	XC
271002	B	73	1,252	Y	N	XB
271003	B	505	1,452	Y	N	XB
271005	B	79	1,368	Y	N	XB
271007	B	553	1,283	Y	N	XB
271009	D	508	1,909	Y	N	XB
271010	C	482	1,724	Y	N	XB
271011	B	68	1,296	Y	N	XB
271012	B	513	1,359	Y	N	XB
271013	B	103	1,498	Y	N	XB
271015	B	61	1,359	Y	N	XB
271016	D	10	2,170	Y	N	XB
271018	E	95	2,445	Y	N	XB
271019	C	58	1,556	Y	N	XB
271021	C	352	1,551	Y	N	XB
271024	G	529	3,107	Y	N	XB
271025	E	19	2,223	Y	N	XB
271027	E	539	2,463	Y	N	XB
271028	E	67	3,502	Y	N	XB
271029	G	578	3,039	Y	N	XB
271030	D	183	1,926	Y	N	XB
271031	G	100	3,062	Y	N	XB
271032	G	95	3,195	N	N	XB
271033	C	109	1,516	Y	N	XB
271034	C	39	1,531	Y	N	XB
271035	D	579	1,891	Y	N	XB
271036	C	42	1,602	N	N	XB
271037	I	108	4,220	N	N	XB
271038	D	564	1,820	N	N	XB
271041	E	400	2,416	N	N	XB
271042	G	75	3,469	Y	N	XB
271043	E	414	2,396	Y	N	XB
271044	E	412	2,341	N	N	XB
271047	F	195	2,729	N	N	XB
271048	D	306	2,143	N	N	XB
271051	D	326	1,920	Y	N	XB
271052	C	98	1,779	Y	N	XB
271053	E	312	2,458	N	N	XB
271061	C	38	1,750	N	N	XB
271062	E	265	2,356	N	N	XB
271069	E	349	2,376	N	N	XB
271072	G	217	3,081	N	N	XB
271074	E	213	2,400	N	N	XB
271078	H	70	3,620	N	N	XB
271079	B	138	1,088	Y	N	XB
271083	C	256	1,690	Y	N	XB
271084	C	66	1,602	Y	N	XB
271085	C	295	1,541	N	N	XB
271086	D	26	1,910	Y	N	XB
271087	F	297	2,734	N	N	XB
271089	E	550	2,476	N	N	XB
271090	F	553	2,708	N	N	XB
271091	F	591	2,854	N	N	XB
271093	F	347	2,813	N	N	XB
271094	G	540	3,242	N	N	XB
271095	G	162	3,220	N	N	XB
271096	G	156	3,190	N	N	XB
271097	C	535	1,645	N	N	XB
271098	G	583	3,382	N	N	XB
271100	G	172	3,263	N	N	XB
271305	E	482	2,526	N	N	XB
281001	E	573	2,423	Y	N	XB
281014	C	254	1,677	Y	N	XB
281015	C	435	1,660	Y	N	XB
281016	D	443	1,945	Y	N	XB
281018	C	247	1,565	Y	N	XB
281022	C	230	1,506	Y	N	XB
281029	D	187	1,833	Y	N	XB
281030	E	80	2,517	Y	N	XB
281032	F	251	2,904	Y	N	XC
281033	E	542	2,391	Y	N	XB
291013	H	524	3,553	N	N	XC
291014	I	386	4,372	N	N	XC
291015	F	290	2,901	N	N	XC
291015	F	291	2,901	N	N	XC
291016	F	190	2,721	N	N	XC
301001	F	44	2,720	Y	N	XC
301002	D	220	1,845	Y	N	XB
301005	D	217	1,930	Y	N	XB
311001	E	504	2,085	N	N	XB
311002	F	492	2,402	Y	N	XB
311003	F	169	2,428	Y	N	XB
311005	F	409	2,497	Y	N	XB
311009	E	276	1,894	Y	N	XB

Index

For pricing, see page 603.

Plan #	Price Code	Page	Total Finished Sq. Ft.	Materials List	CompleteCost	MT Tier
311011	E	213	2,085	N	N	XB
311024	C	465	2,984	Y	N	XB
311058	D	170	1,702	Y	N	XB
321001	E	496	1,721	Y	N	XB
321002	D	261	1,400	Y	N	XB
321003	E	468	1,791	Y	N	XB
321004	H	328	2,808	N	N	XC
321005	F	501	2,483	Y	N	XB
321006	E	525	1,977	Y	N	XB
321007	G	318	2,695	Y	N	XC
321008	C	326	1,761	Y	N	XB
321009	E	332	2,295	Y	N	XB
321010	C	505	4,013	Y	N	XB
321013	B	537	3,240	Y	N	XB
321018	E	493	2,523	Y	N	XC
321019	E	24	2,452	Y	N	XB
321030	F	267	2,029	Y	N	XB
321033	B	279	1,268	Y	N	XB
321034	H	74	3,508	Y	N	XC
321035	D	333	1,384	Y	N	XB
321036	F	14	2,900	Y	N	XC
321037	F	138	2,397	Y	N	XB
321041	E	239	2,286	Y	N	XB
321042	G	563	3,368	Y	N	XB
321044	F	565	2,618	Y	N	XB
321046	E	545	2,411	Y	N	XB
321048	G	540	3,216	Y	N	XB
321051	F	93	2,624	Y	N	XB
321054	F	238	2,828	Y	N	XB
321057	C	48	1,524	Y	N	XB
321058	C	43	1,700	Y	N	XB
321060	C	45	1,575	Y	N	XB
321062	G	568	3,138	Y	N	XB
331002	E	558	2,299	N	N	XB
331003	F	159	2,660	N	N	XB
331004	G	578	3,125	N	N	XB
331005	H	99	3,585	N	N	XB
341012	B	107	1,316	Y	N	XB
341024	B	587	1,310	Y	N	XB
341035	C	468	1,680	Y	N	XB
341227	B	296	1,248	N	N	XB
341234	B	314	1,476	N	N	XB
341285	B	415	1,481	Y	N	XB
351001	D	121	1,855	Y	N	XB
351002	D	381	1,751	Y	N	XB
351003	D	390	1,751	Y	N	XB
351004	D	175	1,852	Y	N	XB
351005	D	514	1,501	Y	N	XB
351007	E	517	2,251	Y	N	XB
351008	E	212	2,002	Y	N	XB
351011	E	568	2,251	Y	N	XB
351018	C	587	1,251	Y	N	XB
351020	D	215	3,540	Y	N	XB
351033	E	548	3,973	Y	N	XB
351085	E	414	2,200	Y	N	XB
351086	E	393	2,201	Y	N	XB
351088	G	208	3,629	Y	N	XB
351104	D	175	2,755	Y	N	XB
351105	E	432	2,000	Y	N	XB
351106	E	425	2,202	Y	N	XB
351107	F	433	2,400	Y	N	XB
351206	D	368	3,980	Y	N	XB
361004	D	353	2,191	N	N	XB
361073	F	66	2,093	N	N	XB
361077	F	188	2,887	N	N	XB
361096	F	52	2,950	N	N	XB
361106	K	430	6,043	N	N	XC
361130	I	452	4,147	N	N	XC
361230	D	450	2,091	N	N	XB
361231	G	48	3,026	N	N	XB
361382	C	153	1,750	N	N	XB
361435	E	41	2,507	N	N	XB
361440	C	76	1,528	N	N	XB
361441	E	432	2,471	N	N	XB
361486	I	44	4,513	N	N	XC
361491	G	139	3,231	N	N	XB
361493	E	41	2,350	N	N	XB
361517	B	295	1,321	N	N	XB
361549	F	425	2,681	N	N	XB
361553	D	363	1,990	N	N	XB
361555	E	424	2,430	N	N	XB
361556	D	360	1,855	N	N	XB
371046	E	449	2,440	N	N	XB
371064	G	163	3,140	N	N	XC
371065	G	159	3,266	N	N	XB

Plan #	Price Code	Page	Total Finished Sq. Ft.	Materials List	CompleteCost	MT Tier
371092	H	90	3,836	N	N	XC
381058	D	455	1,895	Y	N	XB
381062	B	455	1,180	Y	N	XB
391001	D	307	2,015	Y	N	XB
391002	E	429	2,281	Y	N	XB
391003	D	412	1,907	Y	N	XB
391004	C	325	1,750	Y	N	XB
391009	G	97	3,440	Y	N	XC
391013	D	23	1,894	Y	N	XB
391017	D	446	2,176	Y	N	XB
391019	C	546	1,792	Y	N	XB
391021	C	104	1,568	Y	N	XB
391030	F	77	3,903	Y	N	XB
391034	C	142	1,737	Y	N	XB
391036	C	60	1,710	Y	N	XB
391040	G	579	3,276	Y	N	XC
391041	E	560	2,563	N	N	XB
391042	B	552	1,307	Y	N	XB
391050	F	439	2,674	Y	N	XB
391051	C	233	1,738	Y	N	XB
391052	C	321	1,778	Y	N	XB
391053	G	576	3,128	Y	N	XB
391054	I	574	5,254	Y	N	XC
391055	I	569	4,217	Y	N	XC
391056	F	252	2,607	N	N	XB
391056	F	253	2,607	N	N	XB
391057	F	70	2,851	Y	N	XC
391060	B	266	1,359	Y	N	XB
391064	A	550	988	Y	N	XB
391066	H	547	3,526	N	N	XC
391067	F	585	2,897	N	N	XB
391069	B	538	1,492	Y	N	XB
391070	D	264	1,960	Y	N	XB
391071	F	535	2,710	Y	N	XB
391131	D	513	2,183	Y	N	XB
391168	E	63	2,352	Y	N	XB
391173	E	398	2,357	Y	N	XB
391211	B	256	1,461	Y	N	XB
391212	C	67	1,701	Y	N	XB
401001	D	24	2,071	Y	N	XB
401004	F	531	2,684	Y	N	XB
401006	C	297	1,670	Y	N	XB
401007	B	294	1,286	Y	N	XB
401008	C	255	4,538	Y	N	XB
401012	E	442	2,301	Y	N	XB
401014	E	428	2,516	Y	N	XB
401015	F	477	2,618	Y	N	XB
401016	E	62	2,539	Y	N	XB
401017	F	427	2,632	Y	N	XB
401023	F	105	2,806	Y	N	XB
401029	D	471	2,163	Y	N	XB
401039	E	243	2,462	Y	N	XB
401048	J	528	5,159	Y	N	XC
401049	I	25	4,087	Y	N	XB
401050	K	396	6,841	Y	N	XC
401050	K	397	6,841	Y	N	XC
421026	E	241	2,599	Y	N	XB
431001	C	164	4,109	Y	N	XB
431004	B	318	1,156	Y	N	XB
441001	D	369	1,850	Y	N	XB
441002	D	358	1,873	Y	N	XB
441003	C	350	1,580	Y	N	XB
441004	C	419	1,728	Y	N	XB
441005	D	359	1,800	Y	N	XB
441006	D	361	1,891	Y	N	XB
441007	D	86	2,197	Y	N	XB
441008	D	365	2,001	Y	N	XB
441009	F	299	2,650	Y	N	XB
441011	F	315	2,898	Y	N	XB
441012	H	413	3,682	Y	N	XC
441013	G	440	3,317	Y	N	XB
441014	H	354	3,940	N	N	XB
441015	I	350	4,732	Y	N	XC
441024	H	438	3,517	Y	N	XB
441026	H	303	3,623	Y	N	XB
441027	H	586	3,638	Y	N	XB
441028	G	418	3,165	Y	N	XB
441029	G	11	3,217	Y	N	XB
441031	I	343	4,150	Y	N	XB
441038	E	423	2,518	Y	N	XB
441047	F	416	2,605	Y	N	XB
441049	E	367	1,886	Y	N	XB
451092	E	40	2,752	N	N	XB
451098	E	163	2,428	N	N	XB
451109	I	162	4,475	N	N	XC

Plan #	Price Code	Page	Total Finished Sq. Ft.	Materials List	CompleteCost	MT Tier
451138	I	106	4,484	N	N	XC
451157	H	158	3,527	N	N	XB
451165	D	454	1,933	N	N	XB
451180	I	422	4,272	N	N	XC
451194	F	52	2,618	N	N	XB
451237	D	40	1,898	N	N	XB
451259	H	57	3,798	N	N	XC
451269	H	34	3,952	N	N	XB
451308	E	407	2,430	N	N	XB
451356	D	294	1,834	N	N	XB
451359	G	351	3,039	N	N	XB
451360	F	309	2,600	N	N	XB
451448	F	99	2,717	N	N	XB
451453	I	92	4,868	N	N	XB
461028	H	581	3,663	N	N	XB
461033	D	399	1,802	N	N	XB
461074	D	368	2,187	N	N	XB
461092	F	250	2,844	N	N	XB
461168	C	499	1,756	N	N	XB
461174	H	536	3,753	N	N	XB
461202	E	89	2,215	N	N	XB
471019	C	319	1,662	Y	N	XB
481005	F	536	2,825	N	N	XB
481017	F	515	2,982	N	N	XC
481021	G	486	3,289	N	N	XC
481023	G	514	3,253	N	N	XC
481024	G	418	2,458	N	N	XB
481028	H	523	3,980	N	N	XC
481031	I	521	4,707	N	N	XC
481034	F	426	2,830	N	N	XC
481035	G	431	3,204	N	N	XC
481036	I	436	4,258	N	N	XC
481036	I	437	4,258	N	N	XC
481143	J	390	5,426	N	N	XC
491003	D	302	1,235	Y	N	XB
491004	B	328	1,154	Y	N	XB
491005	B	333	1,333	Y	N	XB
491006	B	327	1,470	Y	N	XB
521005	F	324	2,932	N	N	XB
521006	F	255	2,818	N	N	XC
521017	E	257	2,359	N	N	XB
521030	C	265	1,660	N	N	XB
521040	C	267	1,555	N	N	XB
521043	C	264	1,536	N	N	XB
531020	G	330	3,371	N	N	XB
531040	G	317	3,325	N	N	XC
541038	I	89	4,823	N	N	XC
551066	E	358	2,415	N	N	XB
561001	J	405	5,079	Y	N	XC
561002	G	300	3,416	Y	N	XC
561002	G	301	3,416	Y	N	XC
561003	G	398	3,164	Y	N	XC
561005	E	403	2,358	Y	N	XC
561006	E	240	2,408	Y	N	XB
571014	D	445	2,134	Y	N	XB
571036	K	391	6,175	Y	N	XC
571037	K	92	6,440	Y	N	XC
571039	D	319	2,144	Y	N	XB
571066	H	424	3,968	Y	N	XB
571074	C	88	1,632	Y	N	XB
571088	B	82	1,202	Y	N	XB
611087	K	129	6,175	N	N	XC
611069	J	320	5,445	N	N	XC
641001	G	234	3,034	N	N	XC
641002	F	560	5,347	N	N	XC
641004	G	546	5,579	N	N	XC
641005	F	360	4,549	N	N	XB
641006	B	193	1,780	N	N	XB
641007	H	53	4,588	N	N	XB
641009	F	557	5,070	N	N	XC
651003	C	588	1,681	N	N	XB
651011	I	561	4,169	N	N	XB
661021	A	534	996	N	N	XB
661030	B	566	1,396	N	N	XB
661033	D	35	1,433	N	N	XB
661055	D	88	1,872	N	N	XB
661057	D	47	1,887	N	N	XB
661102	E	75	2,278	N	N	XB
661109	E	53	2,321	N	N	XB
661124	E	528	2,392	N	N	XB
661191	F	64	2,998	N	N	XB
661203	G	74	3,182	N	N	XB
661213	G	170	3,393	N	N	XC

Material Take-off

The fastest way to get started building your dream home

One of the most complete materials lists in the industry

Work with your Lowe's associate to get all the products you need

To learn more go to page 600 or visit

LOWE'S FOR PROS

online at LowesforPros.com